PAGE 34

ON THE ROAD

YOUR COMPLETE DESTINATION GUIDE
In-depth reviews, detailed listings
and insider tips

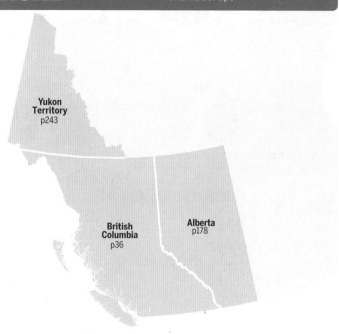

Yukon Territory p243

British Columbia p36

Alberta p178

PAGE 311

SURVIVAL GUIDE

VITAL PRACTICAL INFORMATION TO
HELP YOU HAVE A SMOOTH TRIP

Directory A-Z

THIS EDITION WRITTEN AND RESEARCHED BY

John Lee

Brendan Sainsbury, Ryan Ver Berkmoes

welcome to BC & the Canadian Rockies

Jaw-Dropping Nature

Sighing is the usual reflex when encountering this region's dense diorama of sawtooth peaks, ethereally colored lakes and crenulated coastlines battered by dramatic ocean waves. But it's the vast scale of this seemingly infinite wilderness that strikes most, triggering a humbled, heart-calming response in the face of nature's grand scheme. There has never been a more persuasive argument for tree-hugging, although when it comes to the area's astonishing wildlife, from whales and grizzlies to wolves and moose, it's best to keep the hugging to a minimum.

Active Pursuits

It's not just about the aesthetics here either. Locals with calves-of-steel have been discovering ways to interact with nature for decades and there are hundreds of operators that can help you do the same. From skiing and snowboarding on Whistler's Olympic slopes, to hiking the alpine meadows in Banff National Park or surfing with the West Coast beach bums in Tofino, there are more ways to work up a sweat here than you can swing a paddle at. Which reminds us: these are prime kayaking waters, with tree-lined lakes and rough-and-tumble ocean routes awaiting.

Soul-stirring mountains, mist-shrouded coastal forests and epic tooth-and-claw wildlife – this is Canada's outdoor wonderland. And it comes with adrenalin-pumping activities and a full menu of lively local scenes.

(left) Moraine Lake, Banff National Park, Alberta (p223).
(below) Punnets of Canadian berries.

Eat, Drink & be Merry

Currently noshing its way into a slow-food golden age, British Colombia has amazing farmers markets, juicy seafood, lush Okanagan fruit, velvet-soft ranchland steaks and crunchy veggies flavored by the region that they're grown in. Restaurants fall over themselves to showcase the region's finest food, but it's Vancouver, arguably Canada's top dining city, that leads the way. And alongside the grape-tastic Okanagan and its wine-producing satellite regions, there's been a surge in local beer-making. A tasty round of microbreweries has popped up, making this a thirst-slaking paradise for traveling beer nuts.

Festival Central

Timing is everything if you want to party with the locals at some of the region's annual events. From ice wine-quaffing at January's Winter Okanagan Wine Festival to waving a maple-leaf flag (and donning a face tattoo) at regional Canada Day celebrations on July 1, you'll never be far from a happening. Vancouver lures with its street parades, Chinese New Year, Pride Week and the Santa Claus Parade among them, while excellent arts events include Edmonton's Fringe Theatre Festival, and the Banff Mountain Film and Book Festival. Food and drink are also a big focus: Vancouver Craft Beer Week and Whistler's Cornucopia will have you feasting like a naughty bacchanalian.

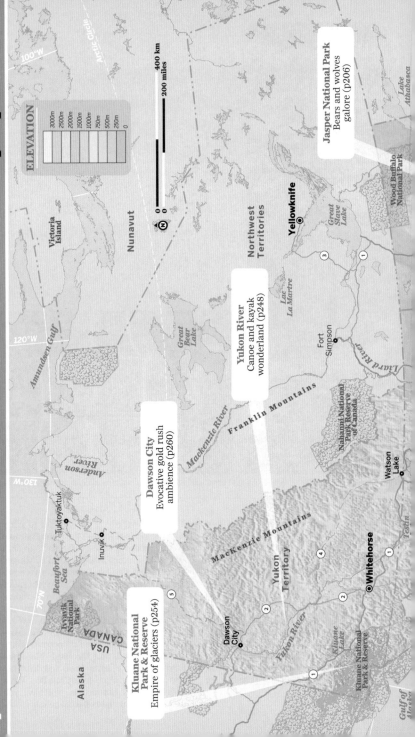

〉British Columbia & the Canadian Rockies Top Experiences 〉

Jasper National Park
Bears and wolves galore (p206)

Yukon River
Canoe and kayak wonderland (p248)

Dawson City
Evocative gold rush ambience (p260)

Kluane National Park & Reserve
Empire of glaciers (p254)

ELEVATION

3000m
2500m
2000m
1500m
1000m
750m
500m
250m
0

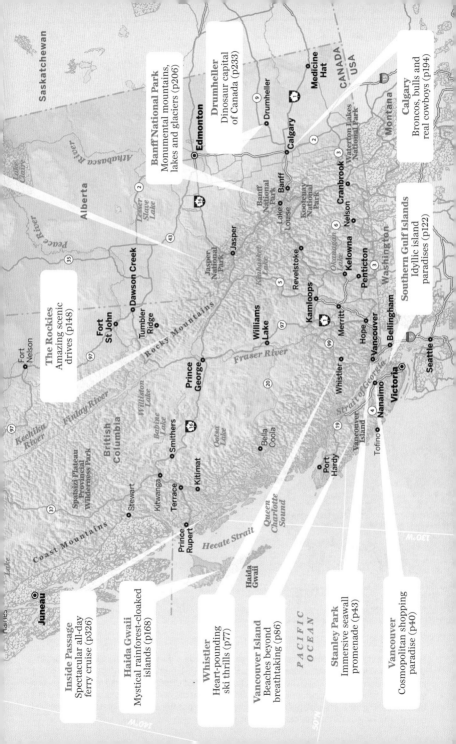

15 TOP EXPERIENCES

Wildlife Watching in Jasper

1 Elk strut defiantly around the town's edge, nervous deer dart among the trees, and giant bald eagles swoop overhead. Jasper National Park's (p206) dramatic mountain setting is enough to keep most camera-wielding visitors happy, but the surfeit of wandering wildlife makes you feel like you're part of a nature documentary. If you're lucky, you might even spot the show's stars: grizzly bears snuffling for berries alongside the highway or, across the other side of a river, a lone wolf silently tracking its next fresh-catch ungulate. Bighorn sheep, Jasper National Park

MIKE GRANDMAISON/ALAMY

Vista Viewing in Banff

3 The colossal, snaggletoothed crags are like natural skyscrapers, while Banff's legendary magazine-cover lakes are so ethereally colored you begin to wonder if Mother Nature has Photoshop. Banff National Park (p206) is so rich in jaw-droppingly wondrous visuals that visitors can't help sighing almost everywhere they turn. And it's not just about the tour-group-luring top attractions; getting off the beaten path you'll stumble on hidden waterfalls, alpine meadows studded with flowers and wildlife-packed valleys. You'll find it all under dome-like blue skies where the surrounding peaks peer down on you.

EMILY RIDDELL/LONELY PLANET IMAGES ©

Sailing the Inside Passage

2 You're on the sun-warmed outer deck on a BC Ferries' day-long service (p323) to Prince Rupert, a breathtaking nautical odyssey guaranteed to slow your heart rate to hibernation levels. With a gentle breeze licking your face, you let the Inside Passage diorama roll past: sharp peaks, tree-covered islands, pristine sandy bays, red-capped lighthouses and tiny settlements with exotic names such as Namu and Dryad Point. Then the captain wakes you from your visual spa treatment with an announcement: you grab your camera just in time as a pod of orcas spout nearby. Daisies along the Inside Passage, Prince Rupert, BC

Skiing at Whistler

4 This picture-postcard village (p77) is frosted with icicles and teeming with chatty visitors during the winter season; but it's the slopes that are the main attraction. Whistler was the host mountain for the 2010 Olympic Winter Games and you can emulate your Lycra-clad heroes on some of North America's most popular downhills. Then it's back to the village to compare your bruises, brag about your black-diamond abilities and imbibe a few hot chocolates. As the fireplace blazes nearby, watch the skiers outside and plan your next assault.

RANDY LINCKS/PHOTOLIBRARY

Beachcombing on Vancouver Island

5 The largest populated landmass off North America's west coast, Vancouver Island (p86) has some fantastic beaches. There's the surf-whipped golden expanses around Tofino and the wide, family-friendly bays around Parksville. But it's the remote north coast that wins our vote. Pushing though the dense, ferny undergrowth of Cape Scott (p122), you'll suddenly emerge blinking in the sunlight on an empty, white-sand beach studded with tide pools and rocky outcrops. The waves lap gently and marine birds swoop around as if they own the place.

Driving through the Rockies

6 Canada's most scenic driving route, the winding Icefields Parkway (p210), is handily located between Banff and Jasper. In an ideal world you'd have a designated driver so you could keep your eyes off the road: colossal peaks rise alongside you, while the promise of spotting wildlife – especially bears and bighorn sheep – keeps things lively. There's even a celebrated attraction to lure you from your car: take a guided tramp on the Athabasca Glacier for an appreciation of how this mountainous region was cut and shaped.

Calgary Stampede

7 You'll be greeted by belt buckles the size of saucers and Stetsons that could house a small animal when you arrive at North America's best rodeo (p199). But you'll soon be won over by this immersive introduction to cowboy culture; don your own hat and dive right in. Don't miss the zinging midway fairground, rootin'-tootin' live country music and the heart-stopping chuck-wagon races. When it comes to food, start with the barbecued steaks and then, if you're feeling adventurous, nibble on a prairie oyster or two.

Shopping in Vancouver

8 While souvenir hunting in Vancouver (p40) previously meant maple syrup cookies or vacuum-packed salmon, the city is currently enjoying a golden age of great shopping districts. Granville Island is perfect for art and craft lovers; Commercial Dr is all about bohemian eclecticism; and Kitsilano's W 4th Ave is a strolling smorgasbord of contemporary west coast cool. But when it comes to hipster clothing and accessories, head to the shops on Main St and the new stores emerging around old-school Gastown. You'll never need to buy a fridge magnet gift again.

Paddling the Yukon River

10 Relive the days of the craggy-faced frontiersfolk by canoeing (or kayaking) from Whitehorse to Dawson City. Not for the faint-of-heart and certainly not for the uninitiated, the 16-day Yukon River paddle (p248) will glide you past rough and tumble rocky landscapes lined with critter-packed forests. Keep your eyes on the water; you might feel like panning for gold if you spot something glittery. For a less-intense taster, take a trip from Dawson City to Eagle City, Alaska: it's just three days (p263).

Dawson City

9 You're bouncing around for hours on some rickety old bus on the Klondike Hwy in the height of summer, not knowing whether it's three o'clock in the morning or afternoon, and suddenly you arrive in Dawson City (p260). Frilly-skirted ladies, straight out of a gambling hall, chat on wooden sidewalks, and a buzz of stories about gold can be heard everywhere – it's like stumbling into another world. True adventurers will try the infamous Sourtoe cocktail, and all who encounter Dawson City will brag about their experience forevermore.
Diamond Tooth Gertie's Gambling Hall (p265), Dawson City

Aboriginal Culture in Haida Gwaii

11 Taking the choppy five-hour ferry crossing from Prince Rupert to this dagger-shaped archipelago (p168) makes you feel like you've traveled to another country: perfect preparation for a place like no other in British Colombia. Visit the Haida Heritage Centre and immerse yourself in the rich, artistic culture of the resident Aboriginals who've called this area home for thousands of years. You'll find intricately carved art works plus current practitioners illustrating the resurgence of Haida culture. Then visit the magical Gwaii Haanas National Park Reserve with its ghostly reminders of ancient communities.

Digging the Dinosaurs in Drumheller

12 If your kids are in that wide-eyed dinosaur phase, there's no better place to take them than this dust-blown Alberta town (p233). You'll find arguably the planet's best dino museum to indulge your kids' insatiable need for facts (and artifacts, including the chance to do their own fossil dig) plus a photo op with the world's biggest T. rex – a 26m fiberglass fella who looms over the town like Godzilla. You're also in the heart of the Badlands region here, an eerie, evocative landscape where it's easy to imagine giant roaming reptiles.

Hopping the Southern Gulf Islands

13 The islands (p122) off BC's mainland wink at you whenever you get close to the shoreline. But it's only when you dive in (not literally) and visit them on short-hop ferry trips that you realize how different life is here. Your body clock will readjust to island time and you'll feel unexpectedly tranquil. If you have time, visit more than one. Start with the Saturday Market on Salt Spring Island, then consider a tipple trip to Saturna Island Winery, a kayak excursion around Mayne Island or a cycling weave on Galiano. Winter Cove, Saturna Island

JOSH MCCULLOCH/LONELY PLANET IMAGES ©

Stanley Park's Seawall Promenade

14 It's likely the finest urban park (p43) in North America but some Vancouverites take it for granted; they may have grown up thinking that everyone has a 404-hectare temperate rainforest lined with hiking and biking trails on their doorstep. It's only when they meet visitors that they realize how lucky they are. Stroll the 8.8km wave-licked forest-backed seawall and you'll be depleting your camera battery in no time. But save some juice for the beady-eyed birdlife (especially blue herons) around Lost Lagoon and for a spectacular panoramic sunset from Third Beach.

Kluane National Park & Reserve

15 From the Alaska Hwy you get just a glimpse of the awesome beauty within the vast 22,015 sq km Kluane National Park (p254). Hike for a day to the interior – or hop on a helicopter – and you'll witness an almost overwhelming, other-worldly beauty that has, not surprisingly, garnered Unesco World Heritage site recognition. Huge icebergs break off glaciers and the water at the shoreline freezes – this is nature in all its grand, terrifying beauty and one of the largest protected wilderness areas in the world.

need to know

Currency
» Canadian dollars ($)

Language
» English

When to Go

Dry climate
Warm to hot summers, mild winters
Warm to hot summers, cold winters
Mild summers, cold winters
Cold climate

Dawson City
GO Jul-Aug

Banff
GO Jul-Sep

Whistler
GO Dec-Mar (skiing)
or Jun-Aug (hiking)

Tofino
GO Jul-Sep

Vancouver
GO Jun-Aug

High Season
(Jun–Aug)
» Sunshine and warm weather prevail through the region
» Accommodation prices reach a peak

Shoulder
(Apr & May, Sep & Oct)
» Temperatures are cool but comfortable; rain is typical
» Crowds and accommodation prices reduced
» Attraction hours outside cities are cut

Low Season
(Nov–Mar)
» Snow and cold (below freezing) temperatures
» The year's best hotel rates, except in ski resorts
» Outside resorts and cities, attractions may be closed

Your Daily Budget

Budget less than
$100
» Dorm bed: $25-45
» Campsite: $20-35
» Markets and supermarkets for self-caterers

Midrange
$100-200
» Motel or small hotel room: $80-125
» Meal in midrange local restaurant: $15-20 (drinks extra)
» Attraction admission: $10-20
» Drink in local pub: $5-7

Top end more than
$200
» Boutique hotel or fancy B&B: $150
» Three-course meal in good restaurant: $50 (drinks extra)
» Car hire: up to $65 per day
» Ski day-pass: $80-100

Money

» ATMs widely available. Credit cards accepted in most restaurants and almost all hotels.

Visas

» For many nationalities, not required for stays of up to 180 days; other nationalities will need a visa.

Cell Phones

» Local SIM cards can be used in European and Australian phones. Other phones must be set to roaming.

Driving

» Drive on the right; steering wheel is on the left side of the car.

Websites

» **Tourism British Columbia** (www. hellobc.com) Official visitor site.

» **Tourism Alberta** (www.travelalberta. com) Official visitor site.

» **Tourism Yukon** (www.travelyukon.com) Official visitor site.

» **Banff-Lake Louise Tourism** (www. banfflakelouise.com) Official visitor site.

» **Tourism Vancouver** (www. tourismvancouver.com) Official visitor site.

» **Lonely Planet** (www. lonelyplanet.com/ british-columbia) Great for pre-planning and forums.

Exchange Rates

Australia	A$1	$1.03
Euro zone	€1	$1.37
Japan	¥100	$1.19
New Zealand	NZ$1	$0.78
UK	UK£1	$1.57
US	US$1	$0.98

For current exchange rates see www.xe.com.

Important Numbers

Country code	☑1
International access code	☑011
Emergency	☑911
Local directory assistance	☑411

Arriving in British Columbia & the Rockies

» **Vancouver International Airport**
SkyTrain Canada Line – every eight to 20 minutes, 5.10am to 12.57am
Taxis – $30 to $40, 30-minute journey

» **Calgary International Airport**
Sundog Tours – every 30 minutes from 8.30am to 9.45pm
Taxis – $35, 30-minute journey

» **Edmonton International Airport**
Sky Shuttle bus – every 30 to 45 minutes
Taxis – $50, 40-minute journey

Pacing Your Trip

Keep in mind that Vancouver is not right next door to Banff so you'll be traveling some large distances if you want to catch all the top sights. But rather than spending your entire trip on the road and visiting a Unesco World Heritage site just long enough to take a photo of it, try to add some extra days to your trip. You'll get much more out your visit if you're able to stop and breathe in the immense grandeur of this region. And as for those vast distances – it's an 859km drive from Vancouver to Banff, by the way – make the journey part of the experience. This could mean a spectacular train ride through the Rockies or a heart-rate-dropping day-long ferry cruise along BC's Inside Passage. You'll likely never have felt so relaxed in your entire adult life.

if you like...

Fantastic Food

Pack those pants with the elasticized waist: British Columbia and the Rockies region offers a stomach-stuffing cornucopia of great grub. Ethnic and local food movements are fresher than a newly ripened heirloom tomato in BC, while Alberta is Canada's carnivore-hugging steak capital.

Vancouver restaurants One of Canada's top dining scenes is also its most diverse – for the best sushi, Asian fusion, seafood and beyond check listings on p58

TacoFino Food carts are finally taking off in this part of Canada but this pioneering Mexican-fusion truck in Tofino is the still best in the west (p114)

Farmers markets Dozens have sprouted here in recent years, with their tempting local fruits – from peaches to cherries – a must-have. Among the best is Edmonton's Old Strathcona Farmers' Market (p192)

Cowichan Bay Artisan cheese and bread makers and restaurants serving locally sourced dishes and regional wines abound in Canada's favorite slow-food community (p102)

Historic Sites

From rich aboriginal heritage to colorful reminders of the pioneer past, this is a perfect pilgrimage spot for history buffs. Many sites have excellent interpretive programs, which might mean panning for gold (good luck!) or chatting to 1850s fur trappers.

North Pacific Historic Fishing Museum You can feel the ghosts of canning workers past at this hulking, wood-built former plant near Prince Rupert (p167)

Fort Langley National Historic Site The colonial outpost where BC was signed into existence offers a kid-friendly smorgasbord of activities and costumed 'residents' (p167)

Head-Smashed-In Buffalo Jump With the region's most eye-popping name, this fascinating aboriginal interpretive center in Alberta recalls the local heritage (p236)

Klondike National Historic Sites The gritty gold-rush days are on every street corner in Dawson City, where frontier buildings stud the area like shiny nuggets (p261)

Barkerville Historic Town Stroll the streets of a pioneer town that once housed thousands of grubby frontiersmen, plus the occasional woman (p163)

Adrenalin Rushes

Welcome to Canada's muscle-straining capital. The locals have moved way beyond just staring at the beautiful peaks and deep waters here –now they jump, climb, ski and dive right in. You don't need calves of steel and tight Lycra-covered buns, but it helps.

Whistler Canada's favorite ski resort is also packed with summer activities, from ziplining to white-water rafting (p78)

Mount Washington Vancouver Island's ski resort transforms into a muscle-popping mountain-biking magnet in summer (p101)

Tofino Idyllic beaches and a spectacular wave-whipped waterfront make this Canada's top surfing spot (p113)

Canmore Perfect for Rockies-region rock fans, the climbing here – including winter waterfall climbs – is spectacular (p113)

Sun Peaks Whistler draws the crowds but this locals-favorite Kamloops-area resort has even bigger downhills (p131)

Athabasca Glacier Avoid the too-easy bus tour and take a breathtaking guided hike on the icy surface, crampons included (p211)

STUART WESTMORLAND/CORBIS

PLAN YOUR TRIP IF YOU LIKE...

» An orca, also known as a killer whale (p308).

Arts & Culture

The locals are not entirely preoccupied with crashing around the outdoors. In fact, they're a cultured bunch, too. Check out these nationally renowned artsy attractions and take home some cool souvenirs from the gifts shops – beats vacuum-packed salmon.

Vancouver Art Gallery This top museum with a keen eye for photoconceptualism stages blockbuster visiting shows in summer (p43)

Whyte Museum of the Canadian Rockies Displays some fascinating pioneer-inspired artwork alongside its history exhibits (p213)

Museum of Anthropology Its spectacular array of northwest coast aboriginal arts has recently broadened to represent other cultures (p49)

Chemainus A former Vancouver Island logging town that's reinvented itself with dozens of large outdoor murals (p103)

Art Gallery of Greater Victoria BC's best collection of Emily Carr paintings, with forest and aboriginal themes from colonial times (p87)

Art Gallery of Alberta Edmonton's fancy new gallery is almost as striking as its mostly Canadian artworks (p182)

Beer & Wine

Mirroring the area's discovery of the wonders of local food, drinkers here also enjoy a full round of regionally made booze. Its wine – from the Okanagan Valley to Vancouver Island – has been renowned for decades, while its microbrewed beer scene has suddenly caught up in the past few years. Either way, you won't go thirsty.

Okanagan Valley This vine-striped, lakeside region is home to dozens of sample-happy wineries (p140)

Cowichan Valley A Vancouver Island alternative to the Okanagan with boutique wineries and a great cidery (p102)

Alibi Room Rather than traveling to BC's far-flung microbreweries, just hit this friendly Vancouver bar and its dozens of tempting taps (p63)

Granville Island Brewing One of Canada's first microbreweries still has a small-batch operation in Vancouver offering tours and tastings (p45)

Jasper Brewing Co A brewpub in a national park? Oh yes. Go for a sampler or dive into the signature Rockhopper IPA (p232)

Wildlife Watching

A main lure for visitors is the possibility of catching sight of a wild animal of the jaw-droppingly large variety. Bears and whales top the must-see list, closely followed by wolves, moose and elk. No one seems to fly in for a porcupine sighting but that's their loss.

Khutzeymateen Grizzly Bear Sanctuary Near Prince Rupert, around 50 of the salmon-snaffling furballs call this area home (p167)

Jasper Often wandering across highways and stopping the traffic, the local elk – plus abundant deer, eagles and bears – make it perfectly clear who's in charge here (p226)

Telegraph Cove Whale-watching operators line Victoria, the Lower Mainland and beyond but this Vancouver Island departure point is an evocative favorite (p119)

Northern Lights Wolf Centre A Yoho National Park refuge for the lupine critters, this is a great spot to learn all about them (p154)

month by month

January

It's peak ski season in resorts, with winter-wonderland views and temperatures well below freezing in Alberta, the Yukon and much of British Columbia; warmer on the south coast with rain more likely.

Winter Okanagan Wine Festival

BC's gable-roofed Sun Peaks Resort warms up with a taste-tripping tipple event (www.thewinefestivals.com) where ice wine is the major draw. Saturday night's progressive tasting weaves around the village and there are additional belt-busting dinners and tempting classes aplenty.

Ice Magic Festival

The spectacular Lake Louise shoreline in Banff National Park is the snow-swathed backdrop for this annual ice-carving event (www.banfflakelouise.com/events-and-festivals). Wrap up warmly, take lots of pictures, then nip inside the nearby Fairmont Chateau Lake Louise for a hot toddy.

February

Spring may be in the air in southern coastal BC – some Victoria residents will be sporting shorts – but winter dominates much of the region. Dressing for rain on the coast is a good idea with thick coats (and hip flasks) advisable elsewhere.

Yukon Quest

This legendary 1600km dog sled race (www.yukonquest.com) zips from Whitehorse to Fairbanks, Alaska through darkness and –50°C temperatures. It's a celebration of the tough north and a test of the relationship between musher and husky.

Chinese New Year

Depending on the calendar, this giant Vancouver celebration (www.vancouverchinatown.com) can take place in January or February but it always includes plenty of color, great food and one of the region's biggest parades.

March

The ski season starts to see the light at the end of a long tunnel across much of the region, although there are still plenty of great slopes to barrel down. Southern coastal cities and Vancouver Island are rainy.

CelticFest Vancouver

Growing larger every year, Vancouver's fiesta-like celebration of St Patrick's Day (www.celticfestvancouver.com) has spread like a puddle of spilled Guinness to include a huge parade, live music and party events across four days.

April

Spring is budding across the region, but it's a good time to bag accommodation and snow gear deals in ski resorts, now milking the last days of snow and entering their shoulder period before summer's hiking and biking visitors.

World Ski & Snowboard Festival

One of the biggest festivals in Whistler, this hugely popular nine-day celebration (www.wssf.com) includes daredevil demonstrations, outdoor concerts and a smile-triggering full-on party atmosphere.

May

Blossoms are opening across Vancouver and beyond, while the bears are stirring from their hibernation in more remote climes. Expect warmish bouts of sun in the south plus rain and late-season snow elsewhere.

BC farmers markets

Sprouting like post-thaw flowers, alfresco produce markets kick off this month, typically running to at least September. They're a great chance to sink your teeth into local apples, peaches and blueberries plus check out crafts and bakery treats. Listings at www.bcfarmers market.org.

Vancouver Craft Beer Week

Celebrating the region's surging microbrew scene, Vancouver's top booze event (www.vancouvercraftbeer week.com) showcases the thirsty work of BC's best beer makers with tastings, parties, dinners and an awards night. Arrive parched and drink deep.

June

Even in the colder parts of BC and Alberta, the sun will be out this month, making this the time to lace up your hiking boots and dive into the great outdoors without freezing your extremities.

Bard on the Beach

This joyously west coast approach to Shakespeare (www.bardonthebeach.org) features four plays staged in a lovely tented complex on Vancouver's mountain-framed waterfront. Runs to September but book ahead: it's a local favorite.

Vancouver International Jazz Festival

Mammoth music celebration (www.coastaljazz. com) staged in Gastown, Yaletown and around Vancouver over 10 days, with a generous helping of free outdoor shows complemented by superstar theater performances. Book in advance for top-drawer acts.

Penticton Elvis Festival

Dozens of hip-swinging impersonators of The King invade this small Okanagan town for a three-day celebration of all-things Elvis (www.penticton elvisfestival.com). It's a kitschtastic, eye-popping party whether or not you're a fan – although probably best not to tell anyone if you're not.

July

Summertime and the living is easy for visitors who enjoy warming their skin under sunny skies. It's also crowded, which means popular spots such as Banff and Jasper are at their busiest.

Canada Day Celebrations

The Canadian version of July 4 in the US, this is the country's flag-waving annual birthday party. Expect to see community celebrations across the region, with the biggest, including fireworks, in Vancouver at downtown's Canada Place.

Kokanee Crankworx

It's definitely summer in Whistler when the ski slopes become a bike park and this massive annual celebration of mountain-bike shenanigans (www.crank worx.com) kicks off. Expect displays of saddle-crunching prowess, live music and mud-splattered partying.

Calgary Stampede

North America's biggest rodeo event (www.calgary stampede.com) is a rocking cavalcade of cowboy culture where everyone finds their inner Stetson-wearer. Dive in for raging bulls, frenetic chuck-wagon races and barbecued steak.

August

The region's summer peak, the crowds (and hotel prices) are now at their height. Interior areas in BC can be hot and humid,

while the rest of the region is generally pleasantly warm and sunny.

Edmonton Fringe Theatre Festival

Canada's oldest and largest fringe fest (www.fringe theatreadventures.ca) lures thousands to the city's Old Strathcona neighborhood for a 10-day buffet of short but eclectic comic and dramatic performances. It's Edmonton's biggest annual party.

Discovery Days

The evocative pioneer-era streets of Dawson City are home to the Yukon's most popular annual event (p264), a colorful week-long party of parades, games, races and movie shows that recall the region's gold-rush heyday. Look out for the naughty can-can dancers.

Pacific National Exhibition

Vancouver's century-old PNE (www.pne.bc.ca) is one of Canada's best community festivals, a three-week-long showcase of farm animals, live music, horse and dog displays, naughty fast-food (go for the mini doughnuts) and a great fun-fair, complete with a kick-ass wooden roller coaster.

Pride Week

Canada's biggest and boldest pride event (www.vancouverpride.ca), this Vancouver party kicks off with a massive mardi gras–style parade that draws half-a-million oglers. Galas, live music, fashion shows and other saucy shenanigans keep things lively.

September

One of the best months to visit: the crowds have gone home, there are still long stretches of sunny weather, and the colors are starting to turn to fall's golden hues.

Vancouver International Film Festival

Starting at the end of September, this is the city's favorite movie-watching event (www.viff.org). Book ahead for two weeks of the world's best new indie, international and documentary flicks; consider a multiaccess pass for maximum screen-time.

October

Fall foliage is in full blaze across the region but temperatures are cooling off, while rain is returning to coastal communities that have forgotten where they put their umbrellas.

Fall Okanagan Wine Festival

The Oakanagan's biggest annual wine fest (www.thewinefestivals.com) encompasses 10 days of more than 150 events spread throughout the region's autumnal-hued rolling hills. Choose from vineyard tours, food-pairing seminars and gourmet dinners.

Banff Mountain Film and Book Festival

One of the Rockies' biggest festivals, this annual celebration (www.banffcentre.ca/mountainfestival) draws the culturally inclined as well as a clutch of world-renowned artists to readings, screenings and chin-stroking gatherings throughout the town.

November

The ski season starts to kick off for some resorts while the southern cities are unpacking their waterproof jackets. Temperatures are just a taste of what's to come for winter, though.

Cornucopia

Mid-November in Whistler means this indulgent multiday showcase (www.whistlercornucopia.com) of the region's great food and wine. It's also a chance to dress up and schmooze at decadent parties throughout the gabled resort village.

December

The region is in festive mood with a full advent calendar of Christmas events. Temperatures are dropping and the snow is back in many areas – strap on your skis in the Rockies, BC interior and beyond.

Santa Claus Parade

The best reason to stand outside in the cold in Vancouver, this huge two-hour parade (www.rogerssantaclausparade.com) includes marching bands, decorated floats, thousands of kids and an appearance by the jolly old elf himself.

itineraries

Whether you've got six days or 60, these itineraries can provide a starting point for the trip of a lifetime. Want more inspiration? Head online to lonelyplanet. com/thorntree to chat with other travelers.

10 Days
The Epic Rockies Roll

Kick off your Canadian Rockies road trip in the gateway city of **Edmonton**, spending a couple of days shopping, perusing museums and puttering around Old Strathcona. Then hit Hwy 16 westward for your first big drive: a half-day weave to **Jasper**. Check in for three nights, grab a beer at the Jasper Brewing Co and plan your wildlife watching around the region's lakes and mountains. Next up, it's time to move on southwards via the **Icefields Parkway,** Canada's most scenic drive. It's shadowed by looming crags and studded with inquisitive bighorn sheep peering at you from the clifftops. Stop off en route at the **Columbia Icefield** and take a hike or truck tour on the **Athabasca Glacier**. After lunch at the nearby **Icefield Centre**, continue southwards to **Lake Louise**: take photos and wander the shoreline, saving time for a visit to the equally dazzling **Moraine Lake** a short drive away. Back in the car, you'll soon be in **Banff**. Treat yourself to a few nights at a fancy hotel here and spend the rest of your visit hiking flower-covered alpine trails and marveling at the epic Unesco-listed landscapes.

Two Weeks
Circling BC – Vancouver to Vancouver

> Start your journey of discovery in **Vancouver**. Catch the BC Ferries vessel from Horseshoe Bay for the short ride to **Nanaimo**, where you can sink into 'island time' and start to enjoy Vancouver Island's laid-back culture – it's distinctly more independent and small-town than the Lower Mainland. After spending the night, head

north on Hwy 19, taking an eastward detour to waterfront **Telegraph Cove**. Take a whale-watching tour here – a taste of what's to come – and check in for a night in one of the restored telegraph station buildings.

Continue north on Hwy 16 the next morning and check in to **Port Hardy** for the night: if it's still daylight, consider an oceanfront hike. You'll have an early start to catch the **Discovery Coast Ferry** here the next morning (summer only) but it's well worth it: a languid 12 hours of coastline gazing with the ever-present promise of spotting whales, seals and more from your sun-dappled deck perch.

Arriving in tiny **Bella Coola**, which sits at the end of a long fjord, find rustic retreat for a few nights in the **Bella Coola Valley**. Spend your days exploring trails past huge old cedars and make the hike to pounding **Odegaard Falls**. Go for a river float and lose count of the grizzlies wandering the shores. When you leave, tackle The Hill, a thrill-ride for cars, and head east through the lonely **Chilcotin**. Stop at the alpine waters of **Nimpo Lake** or just take any little tributary road and lose civilization – what little there is – altogether. At **Williams Lake** say yee-ha to cowboy country.

Turn south on the **Cariboo Hwy** (Hwy 97), otherwise known as the Gold Rush Trail. The road follows the route of the first pioneers and gold-seekers who settled in the hardy conditions of BC's unforgiving interior. At **Lytton** go white-water rafting on the Fraser and Thompson Rivers. After these chilly waters, warm up with a soak in **Harrison Hot Springs**. From here it is an easy drive back to Vancouver on Hwy 1.

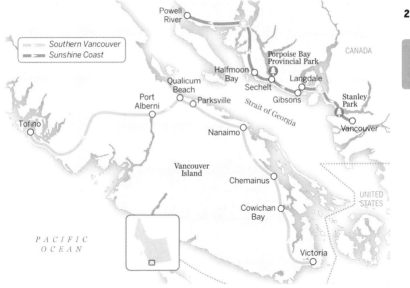

One Week
Southern Vancouver

> Start with two nights in **Victoria**, BC's provincial capital, giving yourself plenty of time to explore the museums, galleries and historic streets before departing northwards on day three via Hwy 1. Take your time weaving through the Malahat mountain region but save time for a long lunch in the idyllic waterfront community of **Cowichan Bay**. It'll be hard to tear yourself away (there are B&Bs in the area if you can't manage it) but worth it to continue north and reach **Chemainus**, a former logging town that's now adorned with dozens of murals. It's not far to your sleepover in **Nanaimo**, the island's second city, where there are some good restaurants and a popular museum. Next morning, you'll be off to check out the friendly oceanfront communities of **Parksville** and **Qualicum Beach** – ideal for beachcombing fans – before veering inland via Hwy 4 towards the dramatic west coast. **Port Alberni** is a handy en route lunch stop, but you'll likely be eager to thread through the winding mountain roads to **Tofino**. Spend at least three nights here soaking up BC's wild and wave-licked Pacific Ocean coastline.

Four Days
Sunshine Coast

> Head north from **Vancouver** on Hwy 99 through **Stanley Park** and make for West Van's Horseshoe Bay ferry terminal. Take the Sunshine Coast vessel to **Langdale** and roll off onto Hwy 101, the region's main artery. After a few minutes you'll be in artist-studded **Gibsons**, an ideal lunch stop – fish and chips at Molly's Reach is recommended. Check into your local B&B here, then take an early evening kayak tour on the glassy ocean. Rejoining Hwy 101 the next morning, continue on to **Sechelt**, where **Porpoise Bay Provincial Park** offers some lovely short hikes. If you're lucky, you'll also catch Saturday's Farmers & Artisans Market, a great way to hang with the locals and stuff your face. Drive past the town for tonight's accommodation: a luxury cliffside tent suite at Rockwater Secret Cove Resort in **Halfmoon Bay**. On the road again the next morning, you'll have a short ferry hop before arriving in the area's top town. **Powell River** combines old-school heritage, a funky young population and tons of outdoor activities. Stick around for a day or two of kayaking, hiking and mountain biking.

Top of the World Hwy
9 Dawson City
ALASKA
YUKON TERRITORY
NORTHWEST TERRITORIES
Kluane National Park
Whitehorse
GULF OF ALASKA
Haines Junction
Haines, AK
BRITISH COLUMBIA
ALBERTA
Smithers
Prince George
Prince Rupert
PACIFIC OCEAN
Barkerville
Williams Lake
Pemberton
Whistler
Vancouver
WASHINGTON
MONTANA

Due North
Yukon Bound

Six Days
Due North

From downtown **Vancouver**, drive through Stanley Park on Hwy 1 then join Hwy 99 northwards to **Whistler**. Spend the afternoon hiking or biking the summer trails and sleep over at one of the resort's grand hotels. Next morning, continue north via **Pemberton** – keep your eyes peeled for towering Mt Currie. You're now in the heart of Cariboo cowboy country but it's probably too late to swap your car for a horse. After a five-hour drive, stop for a night in a **Williams Lake** motel: time your visit for the June–July rodeo and you'll have a blast, or book a white-water rafting tour with a local operator. On Hwy 97 the next morning, you'll be en route to **Prince George**: the heart of northern BC's logging country is about three hours away but stop off – via Hwy 26 – at **Barkerville**, an evocative re-creation of an old pioneer town. After a Prince George layover, you'll need an early start for the four-hour Yellowhead Hwy drive to **Smithers**, an artsy little frontier town with plenty of good places to stay. Your final four-hour drive the next day delivers you eastward to lovely **Prince Rupert**, northern BC's best town.

Two Weeks
Yukon Bound

Spend a couple of days exploring **Prince Rupert** – the Museum of Northern BC and the North Pacific Historic Fishing Museum are must-sees – before rolling onto an Alaska Marine Highway ferry to **Haines, AK**. It's a two-day odyssey that the region's cruise ships will charge you a comparative arm and a leg for. Once you're back on dry land, spend a night in one of the many hotels in Haines. From here, you'll be (almost) on the doorstep of one of the world's largest protected wildernesses. Accessed 249km away via the BC town of **Haines Junction**, **Kluane National Park** is a vast Unesco-recognized realm of glaciers and mountains. Weave through the park and cross over again into Alaska briefly to access the **Top of the World Hwy**. Continue on your merry way and you'll reach **Dawson City**, the Yukon's coolest old-school town and center of gold-rush heritage. Stick around for a couple of nights to enjoy the heritage ambience, then continue southwards on the Klondike Hwy for 538km to **Whitehorse**, the territory's capital. There are enough museums and galleries here to keep you occupied for another Yukon night.

National & Regional Parks

Best for Hiking
Pacific Rim National Park Reserve; Banff, Jasper and Waterton Lakes National Parks.

Best for Skiing
Banff National Park; Strathcona, Seymour and Cypress Provincial Parks.

Best for Rock Climbing
Kootenay National Park; Horne Lake Caves Provincial Park.

Best for Wildlife Watching
Jasper, Banff, Wood Buffalo and Yoho National Parks.

Best for Kayaking
Gwaii Haanas and Gulf Islands National Park Reserves; Bowron Lake Provincial Park.

Best Unesco World Heritage Sites
Banff, Jasper and Yoho National Parks; Dinosaur Provincial Park.

Best National Historic Sites
Banff Park Museum; Head-Smashed-In Buffalo Jump; Gulf of Georgia Cannery Museum.

For some international visitors, towering sawtooth peaks, vast mirrored lakes and huge, wildlife-packed forests spring to mind when they try and imagine what Canada will be like. But here's a secret: what they're really imagining is British Columbia and the Rockies, the region where the country's most awe-inspiring, camera-luring landscapes come to life. Many of these natural treasures are protected in parks – from Unesco World Heritage sites like Banff and Jasper to breathtaking provincial gems such as Garibaldi and Strathcona – and for visitors the choice can be overwhelming. You'll find giant glaciers, expansive beaches, alpine meadows, remote islands, evocative historic sites and more, plus park-based activities ranging from hiking and kayaking to skiing and wildlife watching. But don't be discouraged by this brain-fuzzing excess of options; instead, peruse this chapter, underline a few personal recommendations and plan your visit accordingly. After your vacation, it's these breathtaking nature-based memories that will be imprinted on your mind like desktop wallpaper.

Where to Go
National Parks
These carefully protected parks of national importance – or international for those with Unesco World Heritage site designations – are the must-see attractions of this region. They typically have excellent visitor centers and do all they can to maintain a successful

balance between preserving the wilderness and enabling access for tourists.

Banff, designated Canada's first national park in 1885, offers something for everyone, which is just as well given the number of visitors it draws. But its grand size means you can still escape into the backcountry and be wowed by its sheer-faced glacier-cut peaks. It is often compared to its smaller sibling Jasper to the north, and while it's best to visit both, there is one main difference if you only have time for a single visit: Banff offers close proximity to dramatic mountains lapped by ethereally blue lakes, while Jasper is the region's center for watching incredible wildlife in its natural setting. And by wildlife, we mean the big kind: bears, wolves, moose et al. That's not to say there isn't great mountain scenery in Jasper or wildlife aplenty in Banff. But if you have to choose your visit, that's the way to do it.

High alpine adventure awaits around Rogers Pass in BC's Glacier National Park, while among the highlights of craggy and uncrowded Yoho National Park are spectacular glacier-fed lakes such as O'Hara and Emerald.

In BC's Kootenays region, a multitude of microclimates are crammed into the comparatively tiny Kootenay National Park, which straddles the border between the two provinces. It's the ideal spot for a soak at Radium Hot Springs. Alternatively, consider Mount Revelstoke National Park, where you can hike wildlife-studded trails to the summit for breathtaking views over the Selkirks.

While Banff and Jasper draw the most visitors, the province's other three national parks are also visually thrilling: sublimely tranquil Waterton Lakes, with its off-the-beaten-path location and network of alpine day hikes; giant Wood Buffalo, where the world's last free-roaming herd of wood bison

hang out; and Elk Island, a comparatively small park close to Edmonton and bristling with elk and plains bison.

The Yukon also has two remote national parks: Vuntut and Ivvavik.

For more information on the region's national park highlights, pick up a copy of Lonely Planet's *Banff, Jasper & Glacier National Parks*.

National Park Reserves

These are areas that have been earmarked as national parks, pending the settlement of aboriginal land claims. They are managed in much the same way as the national parks, with entry fees, visitor centers, and various environmental rules and regulations.

There are three national park reserves in BC. Protecting the fragile ecosystem of a small, representative portion of the Southern Gulf Islands, the Gulf Islands National Park Reserve includes delicate little islets, craggy reefs and stretches of coastline on 15 islands. It's the perfect spot for an idyllic island-hopping kayaking trip.

The northern BC islands of Haida Gwaii (Queen Charlotte Islands) are home to the Gwaii Haanas National Park Reserve and Haida Heritage Site. Remote and magical, they enable intrepid kayakers to explore the rich mysteries of the Haida culture. The area is at its most evocative when you suddenly come across rows of majestically rotting totem poles staring out across the ocean.

Located on the ragged Pacific Ocean coastline of western Vancouver Island, the Pacific Rim National Park Reserve combines wide sandy beaches with a continually frothy surf that dramatically whips the shoreline as if trying to snatch it. It's the heart of the region's stormwatching scene, and also a hotbed for surfing and wilderness hiking.

TOP PICKS FOR BEAUTY

It's like choosing the best muffin in the world's best bakery, but here's a very subjective list of five.

» Garibaldi Provincial Park (p76) Alpine beauty just 70km north of Vancouver.

» Gwaii Haanas National Park Reserve & Haida Heritage Site (p169) Almost like another world.

» Ruckle Provincial Park (p124) An island retreat.

» Tombstone Territorial Park (p267) The magnificent Arctic.

» Yoho National Park (p153) Puts the rocky in the Rockies.

PARK	TRAIL	LENGTH (KM)	LEVEL	PAGE
Banff	Lake Agnes	3.4	medium-hard	p223
Jasper	Discovery Trail	8	easy	p229
Pacific Rim	West Coast Trail	75	hard	p111
Waterton Lakes	Carthew-Alderson Trail	19	medium	p239
Yoho	Lake O'Hara Alpine Circuit	12	medium	p154

There are no park reserves in Alberta but the Yukon is the site of Kluane National Park and Reserve, a remote glacier-sliced region near the Alaska border that's home to Mount Logan, Canada's highest peak.

Provincial & Territorial Parks

Alberta has more than 500 provincial parks and protected areas (see www.albertaparks. ca for listings) while BC is home to almost double that number (visit www.bcparks. ca for information). Among the highlights are Alberta's fossil-rich Dinosaur Provincial Park and Writing-On-Stone Provincial Park, with its fascinating 3000-year-old aboriginal artworks.

Since the Yukon is not a province, its large parks (described in detail at www.yukon parks.ca) are called 'territorial parks.' These include the rugged, bird-studded Herschel Island Territorial Park – also known as Qikigtaruk to the native people who still hold it sacred – and Tombstone Territorial Park, a wild and windswept area of broad tundra-cloaked valleys and jaw-dropping hiking trails.

Alongside the region's provincial and territorial parks systems, there are hundreds of city parks and some of them are among western Canada's must-see highlights. These include Calgary's Prince Island Park and, in Vancouver, the spectacular waterfront Stanley Park, one of North America's finest urban greenspaces.

National Historic Sites

Buildings, forts and neighborhoods that recall or evoke important people, places and events of major heritage significance are designated by Parks Canada as national historic sites. These include Banff Springs Hotel – a handsome chateau-like property – and Banff Park Museum. See the Parks Canada website for comprehensive listings.

Among BC's 35 national historic highlights, Fort Langley provides a glimpse into the early days of the fur-trading pioneers. There are lots of interpretive programs here, especially in summer, and kids can enjoy panning for gold.

Head south of Vancouver to the Fraser River shoreline in Richmond. The area's Steveston fishing village is home to two sites: the excellent Gulf of Georgia Cannery Museum, where you can relive the sights and sounds of the region's once-mighty fish processing industry, and the nearby Britannia Heritage Shipyard, a gritty boatshed-lined reminder of the region's maritime heyday.

Among Alberta's 59 National Historic Sites, check out Fort Calgary for a taste of frontier life – complete with re-created buildings and costumed 'locals' – and the immersive Head-Smashed-In Buffalo Jump, a cultural interpretation center that evokes the heritage and traditions of the area's Blackfoot people. It's also a Unesco World Heritage site.

If you're Yukon-bound, hit the Chilkoot Trail and you'll be following the legendary route used by thousands during the Klondike Gold Rush. Also check out Dawson City. It's a funky and vibrant modern-day town colonizing mostly well-preserved streets of old-school stores, a dancehall and even a riverboat.

Plan Ahead

When to Go

Summer is the most popular time to visit western Canada's parks, but that can mean rubbing shoulders with waves of camera-wielding tour groups at hotspots like Banff, Japser and Lake Louise. There are three ways to deal with this and ensure the magic of your visit: when you arrive at the aforementioned must-see spots, head off the beaten path and onto a less-trafficked trail. Secondly, add some less-visited park gems to your visit – Yoho and Glacier, for example,

TOP 10 PROVINCIAL PARKS

Try to weave in a visit to some of these parks. You won't regret it...and you'll have major bragging rights when you get back home.

» **Bowron Lake Provincial Park** (p163) Home to one of the world's great paddling circuits: 116km through the Cariboo Mountains. Portages are easy but you have to re-serve your slot for the six- to 10-day adventure. Best feature: you look at the moose, the moose looks at you...

» **Dinosaur Provincial Park** (p235) A Unesco World Heritage site between Calgary and Medicine Hat, this is a pilgrimage spot for dinosaur fans. Hit the trails, enjoy the wildflowers and look out for fossil remains of T.rex and his associates. Best feature: it feels like a compact version of the Grand Canyon.

» **EC Manning Provincial Park** (p129) Right in the heart of the Cascade Mountain range east of Hope, this craggy wilderness comprises brooding forests and rolling rivers. Best feature: hiking and biking, skiing and boarding.

» **Garibaldi Provincial Park** (p76) A favorite spot for BC outdoor nuts, Garibaldi's alpine wilderness hikes showcase diverse lakeside flora and fauna amid the Coast Mountains. Best feature: winter cross-country ski routes.

» **Horne Lake Caves Provincial Park** (p108) A hotspot for regional spelunkers, experts come for the two caves that can be explored without a guide, while novices can take lessons. Best feature: families bonding underground.

» **Kokanee Glacier Provincial Park** (p159) A BC park with an actual visitor center. This is prime hiking country – one good four-hour trail through lush forest takes you to waterfalls fed by glaciers. Best feature: close to delightful Nelson.

» **Macmillan Provincial Park** (p109) The massively popular and easily accessible heart of the park is Cathedral Grove, a stirring pocket of massive old-growth trees that will turn you into an instant tree-hugger. Best feature: Douglas fir trees up to 3m in diameter.

» **Mt Seymour Provincial Park** (p71) A favorite Vancouver nature retreat in sum-mertime becomes one of the city's three ski resort options in winter. Best feature: escaping the big smoke in minutes.

» **Strathcona Provincial Park** (p118) Vancouver Island's largest provincial park and the region's oldest protected wilderness has got alpine meadows, glacial lakes and looming peaks. Best feature: large, woodsy lodge.

» **Writing-On-Stone Provincial Park** (p238) Not just a natural gem, this secluded park is home to ancient carvings and wall paintings produced by the region's long-ago Aboriginal residents. Best feature: trails to the amazing pictographs.

are great Rockies parks with a fraction of the visitor numbers of Banff and Jasper. Thirdly, consider visiting outside the summer peak. Locals will tell you they prefer late spring and early fall when there are no crowds, the colors are even more vibrant and the wild-life watching – from post-hibernation bears to rutting elk and bighorn sheep – is often spectacular.

Lowdown on Fees

National parks charge for entry, and you'll need to pay and display your pass in your car. Passes are purchased at toll-booth-style barriers in large parks like Banff and Jasper or at ticket machines or visitor cen-ters in parks like Vancouver Island's Pacific Rim National Park Reserve. Daily fees go up to adult/child/family $9.80/4.90/19.60. If you're planning on visiting several parks over a number of days or weeks, the Parks Canada Discovery Pass is recommended. It costs adult/child/family $67.70/33.30/136.40 and covers unlimited entry for 12 months to national parks and historic sites. A cheaper pass covers national historic sites only (adult/child/family $53/26.50/106.90). The family passes include entry for groups or families and generously applies to up to seven people (two adults only).

The BC Parks system does not charge admission. In addition, parking fees – which were first levied in 2002 – were scrapped across all BC parks in 2011.

The Yukon Parks system does not charge for entry to its parks.

To Stay or Not to Stay

If you just want to dip into western Canada's parks without leaving the conveniences of the region's biggest metropolis – and its swank hotels – there are several options within an hour's drive of Vancouver. Less than 30 minutes from downtown by car, the North Shore's provincial parks include Cypress and Seymour, both crisscrossed with summer hiking trails and both transformed into popular ski and snowboard areas in winter. You'll enjoy similar handy proximity on Vancouver Island, where hiking-friendly Goldstream Provincial Park and swimmer-luring Sooke Potholes Provincial Park are short drives from Victoria.

But if sleeping in the heart of the matter is your dream, there's a full range of options from luxe resorts to rolled-up foamies. The Fairmont chain offers some memorable top-end properties including Jasper Park Lodge, Chateau Lake Louise and Banff Springs. In the midrange, the eco-friendly Strathcona Park Lodge on Vancouver Island is a great way to encounter the wilderness.

But for many, camping under the stars is the way to go. This region is studded with park-based camping options, ranging from basic sites on beaches with little more than a shared fire ring and a pit toilet to large and highly popular sites in high-trafficked areas that are packed with facilities – shower blocks and guided interpretive tours, for example – and need to booked months in advance. Keep in mind that some services also charge reservation fees.

Camp it Up

» **Parks Canada** (www.pccamping.ca) campgrounds charge up to $30 per night and the busiest (mainly in the Rockies) take reservations, incurring an additional $10.80 fee.

» **BC Parks** (www.discovercamping.ca) manages hundreds of campgrounds with rates of up to $24 for the most highly developed.

PROTECTING NATURE: DOS & DON'TS

When you're out and about in BC, Alberta and the Yukon, there is a lot you can do to both respect and protect the precious environment around you. Although commonsense and awareness are your best guides, it's always useful to remember a few simple guidelines.

» Don't litter (this is a no-brainer, or so you would have thought...). Use the recycling bins that you'll find in hotels, parks and along the street. Carry out all of your trash from trails and parks, because most facilities are too underfunded and understaffed to make regular collections. And as a random act of goodness, if you see trash left by someone else, pick it up.

» Do stay on trails: they lessen the erosion caused by human transit. This especially goes for mountain-bikers. The best guides and tour companies are serious about preserving trails.

» Don't disturb animals or damage plants. Observe wildlife from a distance with binoculars.

» Don't feed the animals! Feeding the animals interferes with their natural diets. They can be susceptible to bacteria transferred by humans. Not only do they become more vulnerable to hunting and trapping, they may even stop seeking out their own natural food sources and become dependent on this human source. Every year bears have to be moved or even destroyed because they've become accustomed to a Cheetos handout and now see humans as a food source – or even as the food source.

» Do learn about wildlife and local conservation, environmental, and cultural issues before your trip and especially during your visit. Do ask questions and listen to what locals have to say. Lots of people are passionate about preserving this region – you'll find them and their organizations pretty much wherever you go.

About 70 popular parks offer reserved sites and reservations cost from $6 to $18 extra.

» **Alberta Parks** (www.reserve.albertaparks.ca) oversees dozens of campgrounds. Reservations can be made up to 90 days ahead (for a $12 fee) and nightly rates run from $5 to $23.

» **Yukon Parks** (www.yukonparks.ca) offers scores of government campgrounds in some breathtaking wilderness locations. Campsites are $12 per night but they are not bookable in advance.

On the Ground

Bears & Bugs

There are some precautions you should take to fully enjoy your western Canada park visits. Browse these possible hazards and take a few precautions before you stroll out into the wilderness.

Wildlife attacks on humans are rare but you need to be aware that you are going to be encroaching on areas that some scarily large critters call home. And while animals such as elk and deer may seem to be per-fectly used to all the cameras pointing their way in busy parks like Banff and Jasper, Parks Canada works very hard to keep animals and humans from becoming too used to each other. See (p308) for information on what to do if you encounter a bear in the wild – read this before you enter parks in this area.

During spring and summer, black flies and mosquitoes blight the interior and northern reaches of BC, Alberta and the Yukon. The cumulative effect of scores of irritated, swollen bites can wreck your trip. Building a fire will help keep them away, and camping in a tent with a zippered screen is a necessity. In clearings, along shorelines or anywhere there's a breeze you'll be safe, which is why Vancouver and the coast are relatively bug-free. Wherever you go, bring liquid repellents. DEET, a common ingredient, is both effective and essential. Get a product with at least 15% DEET and read the precautions carefully.

Wood ticks hop onto warm-blooded hosts from tall grasses and low shrubs throughout the region. They're most troublesome March through June. Protect your legs by

PARK TOUR OPERATORS

OPERATOR	ACTIVITIES	WHERE?	MORE INFORMATION...
Athabasca Glacier Icewalks	guided glacier hikes	Columbia Icefield	www.icewalks.com
Brewster	bus tours	Banff, Jasper and Columbia Icefield	www.brewster.ca
Discovery Banff Tours	guided tours of the region, including wildlife tours	Banff	www.banfftours.com
North Island Daytrippers	guided hikes to north Vancouver Island's remote parks	Northern Vancouver Island	www.islanddaytrippers.com
Queen Charlotte Adventures	single or multi-day guided boat and kayak tours	Queen Charlotte Islands	www.queencharlotteadventures.com
Tonquin Valley Adventures	multiday horse-back riding tours	Jasper	www.tonquinadventures.com
Up North Adventures	kayaking, guided bike trips and winter sports	Yukon	www.upnorthadventures.com
Yamnuska Mountain Adventures	guided rock climbing	Lake Louise	www.yamnuska.com

THREE HIDDEN BC GEMS

You won't encounter Banff-level crowds at these comparatively virginal BC parks, unless it's a group of marmots.

Never troubled by tour buses, remote Cape Scott Provincial Park (p122) is a ravishing natural beauty with fern-lined trails and the remains of an old Scandinavian village. Access is by logging roads and trails and it has some of BC's most awesome white-sand beaches.

A compact, rustic treat on Saltspring Island, Ruckle Provincial Park (p124) combines a fringe of copper-trunked arbutus trees with a grassy shoreline that's ideal for sunbathing and bird-watching.

Bounce along an access road for 136km and you reach the utterly isolated subalpine wonderland of Spatsizi Plateau Provincial Wilderness Park (p175), where you can enjoy backcountry hiking through some of BC's least-touched wilderness.

wearing gaiters or tucking your pants into socks. Give yourself, your children and pets a good going over after outdoor activities. If you find a tick burrowing into your skin it's most easily removed by grasping and pulling it, gently, straight up and out with a small pair of tweezers. Disinfect the bite site with rubbing alcohol. Save the tick in a small plastic or glass container if possible. That way, a doctor can inspect it if a fever develops or the area around the bite appears to be infected.

A tiny parasite found in some of BC's lakes can generate swimmer's itch, a pesky rash. However, warnings are usually posted at places where it's a problem. To help prevent itching, apply baby oil before you enter the water then dry yourself off completely with a towel after getting out.

Driving Tips

Weather and driving conditions can change rapidly in the parks and wilderness areas of western Canada. If you're driving in winter, expect snow. In addition, when you see an animal by the side of the road, the etiquette here is to slow down and alert other drivers by using your hazard lights.

regions at a glance

This book encompasses three diverse areas: the adjoining provinces of British Columbia and Alberta – which straddle the Rocky Mountains – plus the Yukon Territory, a remote northern wilderness next to Alaska. Each offers spectacular outdoor vistas and some once-in-a-lifetime experiences. But they also have distinctions that you'll want to know about before you plan your trip.

Southern coastal BC and the Rockies region attract the lion's share of visitors: the first for Vancouver – cosmopolitan metropolis and gateway to Whistler, Victoria and wider Vancouver Island; and the latter for the iconic national parks of Banff and Jasper, with their picture-postcard, wildlife-packed mountains. But if your idea of communing with nature means not seeing anyone else, the vast and unremitting Yukon may be your nirvana.

British Columbia

Coastline ✓✓✓
Food & Drink ✓✓
Activities ✓✓

Ocean Vistas

The vast, multifjorded BC coastline defines this region, whether you're strolling the Stanley Park seawall, hiking Vancouver Island's rugged West Coast Trail or reclining on a BC Ferries deck watching for passing orcas.

Locavores United

From Vancouver's top restaurant tables to produce-packed farmers markets throughout the province, BC's local bounty is a real draw. And seafood is the way to go, preferably coupled with a regional wine or beer.

Olympian Adrenalin

From ski resorts large and small to life-enhancing hiking, biking, kayaking and more, visitors will never run out of ways to challenge themselves in the great outdoors here. Start small with a forest stroll, and you'll be ziplining through the valleys in no time.

p36

Alberta

Wildlife Watching ✓✓✓
Cowboy Culture ✓✓
Scenic Drives ✓✓

Jasper Critters
There's wildlife throughout the Rockies but in Jasper you'll be closer than ever to a snuffling menagerie of elk, moose, bighorn sheep and, of course, bears (of the black as well as grizzly varieties). But it's a wolf sighting that will tingle your spine like nothing else.

Calgary Stampede
There's no better way to dive into cowboy culture than this giant summertime rodeo, a rip-roaring cavalcade of Stetson-donning western culture, man-versus-beast contests and steaks as big as cars. Saddle up.

Rocky Roads
A drive-through diorama of towering peaks, mammoth forests and glacier-fed lakes, the Rockies are idyllic car country. Among the wide, wildlife-lined highway highlights is the Icefields Parkway, a smooth, leisurely ribbon linking Banff and Jasper.

p178

Yukon Territory

History ✓✓
Raw Nature ✓✓✓
Activities ✓

Gold Rush
The imprint of the 1898 Klondike gold rush is indelible here, especially on the clapboard streets of old Dawson City. You wouldn't be surprised to see a wily-faced old geezer run the main drag proclaiming his discovery here – although if you do, it's probably time to stop drinking.

Spectacular Beauty
At remote Kluane National Park you won't have to jostle with the kind of crowds that flock to the Rockies. And you'll be rewarded for your persistence with a vast, Unesco-recognized wonderland of glacier-sliced mountains. Humbling is the word.

Frontier Kayaking
Re-create the early days of gritty pioneer exploration by traveling the way they used to: via canoe or kayak along the Yukon River. Gold panning along the way is optional.

p243

Look out for these icons:

 Our author's recommendation

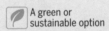 A green or sustainable option

 No payment required

See the Index for a full list of destinations covered in this book.

On the Road

British Columbia

Includes »

Best Places to Eat

» C Restaurant (p59)
» Araxi (p82)
» Bishop's (p62)
» Red Fish Blue Fish (p94)
» Tojo's (p62)

Best Places to Stay

» Wickaninnish Inn (p113)
» Lake O'Hara Lodge (p154)
» Free Spirit Spheres (p108)
» Nita Lake Lodge (p80)
» Loden Vancouver (p55)

Why Go?

Visitors to British Columbia are never short of superlatives when writing postcards home. It's hard not to be moved by towering mountain ranges, wildlife-packed forests and uncountable kilometers of coastline that slow your heart like a sigh-triggering spa treatment. But Canada's westernmost province is more than a nature-hugging diorama.

Cosmopolitan Vancouver is an animated fusion of cuisines and cultures from Asia and beyond, while vibrant smaller cities like Victoria and Kelowna are increasingly catching up with their own intriguing scenes. And for sheer character, it's hard to beat the province's kaleidoscope of quirky little communities, from rustic northern BC to the laid-back Southern Gulf Islands.

Wherever you head, the great outdoors will always be calling. Don't just point your camera at it. BC is unbeatable for the kind of life-enhancing skiing, kayaking, hiking and biking experiences you'll always remember fondly.

When to Go
Vancouver, BC

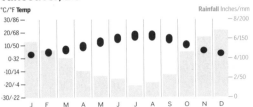

December– March Powder action on the slopes of Whistler and Blackcomb Mountains

July & August Beaches, BBQs and a plethora of outdoor festivals in Vancouver

September & October Great surfing and the start of storm-watching season in Tofino

Getting There & Around

BC's vastness is what strikes most visitors, the majority of whom fly into Vancouver or drive across the US border: it's a scary-sounding 1508km drive from Vancouver to Prince Rupert, for example. But while it's tempting to simply stick around in the big city and avoid the car, you won't really have been to the West Coast unless you head out of town.

Despite the distances, driving remains the most popular method of movement in BC. Plan your routes via the **Drive BC website** (www.drivebc.ca) and check out the 36 services covered by the **BC Ferries** (www.bcferries.com) system.

VIA Rail (www.viarail.com) operates three BC train services. One trundles across the north from the coastline to Jasper. Pick up the second in Jasper for a ride back to Vancouver. The third departs downtown Victoria, weaving up island to Courtenay.

PARKS & WILDLIFE

BC's eight national parks include snow-capped **Glacier** and the Unesco World Heritage sites of **Kootenay** and **Yoho**. The newer **Gulf Islands National Park Reserve** protects a fragile coastal region. See the National & Regional Parks chapter(p25) for further information.

The region's 850 provincial parks offer 3000km of hiking trails. Notables include **Strathcona** and remote **Cape Scott**, as well as the Cariboo's canoe-friendly **Bowron Lake** and the Kootenays' Matterhorn-like **Mt Assiniboine**. Check the website of **BC Parks** (www.bcparks.ca) for information.

Expect to spot some amazing wildlife. Ocean visitors should keep an eye out for Pacific gray whales, while land mammals – including elk, moose, wolves, grizzlies and black bear – will have most scrambling for their cameras. And there are around 500 bird varieties, including BC's provincial fowl the Steller's Jay.

Local Culture: Raise a Glass

BC has enjoyed a huge surge in local microbrewed beer, so don't miss out. Steel your taste buds for Surrey's **Central City Brewing** (www.centralcitybrewing.com) and their mildly malty Red Racer ESB. Alternatively, Kelowna's **Tree Brewing** (www.treebeer.com) produces a Hop Head Indian Pale Ale (IPA) that makes your eyes pop out. To prove that beer doesn't need to pack a punch, **Gulf Islands Brewing** (www.gulfislandsbrewery.com), based on Salt Spring Island, crafts Heatherdale Ale, an aromatic, heather-infused brew that's subtle, complex and seductive.

GUILT-FREE FISH & CHIPS

Seafood is BC's main dining choice. Support the sustainability of the region's aquatic larder by checking out restaurants operating under the Ocean Wise system – see www.oceanwise.ca.

Fast Facts

» Population: 4.5 million
» Area: 944,735 sq km
» Capital: Victoria
» Quirky fact: Home of the world's largest hockey stick (Duncan)

It's Official

BC's official flower is the Pacific dogwood. Also officially, its gemstone is jade and its mammal is the Kermode bear.

Resources

» Tourism BC (www.hellobc.com)
» Cycling BC (www.cyclingbc.net)
» British Columbia Beer Guide (www.bcbeer.ca)
» BC Government (www.gov.bc.ca)
» BC Wine Institute (www.winebc.com)
» WaveLength Magazine (www.wavelengthmagazine.com)
» Van Dop Arts & Cultural Guide (www.art-bc.com)
» Go BC (www.gobc.ca)
» Surfing Vancouver Island (www.surfingvancouverisland.com)

British Columbia Highlights

1 Stretch your legs on a seawall stroll around Vancouver's **Stanley Park** (p43) then enjoy a relaxing sunset at Third Beach

2 Surf up a storm (or just watch a storm) in **Tofino** (p112) on Vancouver Island's wild west coast

3 Slurp some celebrated tipples on an ever-winding **Okanagan Valley** (p132) winery tour

4 Ski the Olympian slopes at **Whistler** (p77) then enjoy a warming après beverage while you rub your aching muscles in the village

5 Explore the ancient and ethereal rainforest of the **Gwaii Haanas National Park Reserve** (p169) and kayak the coastline for a fish-eye view of the region

6 Putter around the lively Saturday Market on **Salt Spring Island** (p124) and scoff more than a few fruit and bakery treats

7 Indulge in some lip-smacking Asian hawker food at the **Summer Night Market** (p73) in Richmond and come away with some spicy takeout

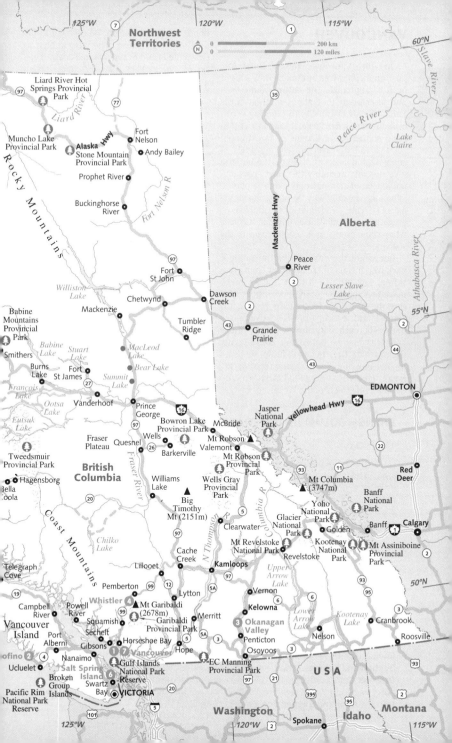

VANCOUVER

POP 578,000

Flying into Vancouver International Airport on a cloud-free summer's day, it's not hard to appreciate the nature-bound utopia description that sticks to this 'Lotus Land' like a wetsuit. Gently rippling ocean crisscrossed with ferry trails, the crenulated shorelines of dozens of forest-green islands and the ever-present sentinels of snow-dusted crags glinting on the horizon give this city arguably the most spectacular setting of any metropolis on the planet. Which is probably why there was no shortage of stirring TV visuals for the global coverage of the 2010 Winter Olympic Games, when some events took second place to the scenery.

But while the city's twinkling outdoor backdrop means you're never far from great skiing, kayaking or hiking, there's much more to Vancouver than appearances. Hitting the streets on foot means you'll come across a kaleidoscope of distinctive neighborhoods, each one almost like a village in itself. There's bohemian, coffee-loving Commercial Dr; the cool indie shops of hipster-hugging South Main (SoMa); the hearty character bars of old Gastown; and the colorful streets of the West End 'gayborhood.' And that's before you even get to the bustling artisan nest otherwise known as Granville Island or the forested seawall vistas of Stanley Park, Canada's finest urban green space. In fact, if this really is Lotus Land, you'll be far too busy checking it out to rest.

This diversity is Vancouver's main strength and a major reason why some visitors keep coming back for more. If you're a first timer, soak in the breathtaking vistas and hit the verdant forests whenever you can, but also save time to join the locals and do a little exploring off the beaten track; it's in these places that you'll discover what really makes this beautiful metropolis special.

History

The First Nations lived in this area for up to 16,000 years before Spanish explorers arrived in the late 1500s. When Captain George Vancouver of the British Royal Navy sailed up in 1792, he met a couple of Spanish captains who informed him of their country's land claim. The beach they met on is now called Spanish Banks. But by the early 1800s, as European settlers began arriving, the British crown had an increasing stranglehold.

BRITISH COLUMBIA ITINERARIES

Three Days

Once you've checked out the big-city sights and sounds of metropolis **Vancouver**, jump in the car and drive, via Hwys 99 and 17, to the Tsawwassen ferry terminal for a sigh-triggering boat trip to Swartz Bay on **Vancouver Island**. After docking (not before, please) continue your drive to **Victoria**, overnighting here and exploring the pretty capital and its historic buildings. Next day, drive north up the island on Hwy 1, stopping off at **Chemainus**, a former logging settlement that's reinvented itself as an 'art town.' Continue north for a late lunch and a night in **Nanaimo**, then, next morning, catch the ferry back to the Horseshoe Bay terminal in West Vancouver. It's a short drive from here back to your Vancouver starting point.

One Week

If you have the luxury of a whole week, follow the three-day itinerary to **Nanaimo** then continue north on Hwy 19 to the quaint seaside towns of **Qualicum Beach** and **Parksville**. Walk around, window-shop, absorb the atmosphere, before you continue on to **Comox** and take a ferry back to the mainland, arriving at **Powell River** on the Sunshine Coast. Wind southwards along the coast and forest road, taking a short-hop ferry at Earl's Cove to continue your drive, stopping off at quirky communities like **Sechelt** and **Roberts Creek**. Allow time to wander the charming waterfront village of **Gibsons**, before boarding the 45-minute ferry to Horseshoe Bay. If there's no need to hurry back downtown, divert to North Vancouver and the ever-popular **Grouse Mountain** and **Capilano Suspension Bridge** attractions.

Vancouver

BRITISH COLUMBIA

4 km
2 miles

To Horseshoe Bay (2km);
Bowen Island (7km);
Whistler (105km)

Bowen Island

Lighthouse Park

Burrard Inlet

Sandy West Cove Bay

Upper Levels Hwy

Marine Dr

Lions Gate Bridge

Stanley Park

First Narrows

Vancouver Harbour

Capilano Suspension Bridge

To Grouse Mountain (1km)

NORTH VANCOUVER

Mt Seymour Pkwy

Lynn Canyon Park

Mt Seymour Provincial Park

Indian Arm Provincial Park

Indian Arm

BELCARRA

ANMORE

Belcarra Regional Park

Coquitlam River

To Buntzen Lake (10km)

Noons Creek

Mary Hill By-Pass

PORT COQUITLAM

Barnston Island

Douglas Island

To Fort Langley (8km)

Tynehead Regional Park

Fraser Hwy

176th St

168th St

152nd St

88th Ave

SURREY

Green Timbers Urban Forest

King George Hwy

96th Ave

128th St

120th St

72nd Ave

Nordel Way

River Rd

DELTA

Delta Nature Reserve

Annacis Hwy

Annacis Island

NEW WESTMINSTER

Canada Way

Marine Way

Kingsway

Deer Lake

Burnaby Lake Regional Park

Burnaby Village Museum

BURNABY

Burnaby Mountain Conservation Area

Dollarton Hwy

Mt Seymour Hwy

Confederation Park

E Hastings St

Lougheed Hwy

Como Lake Ave

Mundy Park

Austin Ave

COQUITLAM

10th Ave

Central Park

Boundary Rd

Rupert St

Kerr St

Nanaimo St

Commercial Dr

Kingsway

Knight St

Main St

Cambie St

Queen Elizabeth Park

Oak St

SOUTH MAIN

Granville St

W Broadway

16th Ave

W 41st Ave

WEST SIDE

KITSILANO

Jericho Beach

Spanish Banks Beach Park

Point Grey

Museum of Anthropology

University Of British Columbia

Wreck Beach

UBC Botanical Garden

Marine Drive Foreshore Park

Pacific Spirit Regional Park

Musqueam Indian Reserve 2

Sea Island

Iona Island

Vancouver International Airport

RICHMOND

Richmond Nature Park

Bridgeport Rd

Mitchell Island

Richmond Fwy

Westminster Hwy

Blundell Rd

No 1 Rd

Steveston Hwy

STEVESTON

Gulf of Georgia Cannery

Kuan Yin Temple

Fraser River

Middle Arm Fraser River

North Arm Fraser River

South Arm Fraser River

Westminster Hwy

To Tsawwassen (15km);
Seattle (USA, 190km)

Strait of Georgia

English Bay

Burrard Inlet

Vancouver

See Downtown Vancouver Map (p46)

To Horseshoe Bay

Fur trading and a feverish gold rush soon redefined the region as a resource-filled Aladdin's cave. By the 1850s, thousands of fortune seekers had arrived, prompting the Brits to officially claim the area as a colony. Local entrepreneur 'Gassy' Jack Deighton seized the initiative in 1867 by opening a bar on the forested shoreline of Burrard Inlet. This triggered a rash of development – nicknamed Gastown – that became the forerunner of modern-day Vancouver.

But not everything went to plan. While Vancouver rapidly reached a population of 1000, its buildings were almost completely destroyed in an 1886 blaze – quickly dubbed the Great Fire, even though it only lasted 20 minutes. A prompt rebuild followed and the new downtown core soon took shape. Buildings from this era still survive, as does Stanley Park. Originally the town's military reserve, it was opened as a public recreation area in 1888.

Relying on its port, the growing city became a hub of industry, importing thousands of immigrant workers to fuel economic development. The Chinatown built at this time is still one of the largest in North America. But WWI and the 1929 Wall St crash brought deep depression and unemployment. The economy recovered during WWII, when shipbuilding and armaments manufacturing added to the traditional economic base of resource exploitation.

Growing steadily throughout the 1950s and 1960s, Vancouver added an NHL (National Hockey League) team and other accoutrements of a midsized North American city. Finally reflecting on its heritage, Gastown – by now a slum – was saved for gentrification in the 1970s, becoming a national historic site in 2010.

In 1986 the city hosted a highly successful Expo world's fair, sparking a wave of new development and adding the first of the mirrored skyscrapers that now define Vancouver's downtown core. A further economic lift was hoped for when the city staged the Olympic and Paralympic Winter Games in 2010. Even bigger than Expo, it was the city's chance to showcase itself to the world.

◉ Sights

Vancouver's most popular attractions are in several easily walkable neighborhoods, especially hot spots like Gastown, Chinatown, Stanley Park and Granville Island. Chichi Yaletown attracts fashionista window shoppers, while the real hipsters and bohemians are more likely to be found cruising SoMa and Commercial Dr. Laidback Kitsilano enjoys great beach access and leads out towards the tree-lined University of British Columbia (UBC) campus, a minitown of its own.

DOWNTOWN
Bordered by water on two sides and with Stanley Park on its tip, downtown Vancouver combines shimmering glass apartment and business towers with the shop-lined attractions of Robson St, the city's central promenade.

VANCOUVER IN...

One Day

Begin with a heaping breakfast at the **Templeton** before heading to the **Vancouver Art Gallery**. Next, take a window-shopping stroll along Robson St, then cut down to the waterfront for some panoramic sea and mountain vistas. Walk west along the **Coal Harbour** seawall and make for the dense trees of **Stanley Park**. Spend the afternoon exploring the beaches, totem poles and **Vancouver Aquarium** here before ambling over to the **West End** for dinner.

Two Days

Follow the one-day itinerary then, the next morning, head to clamorous **Chinatown**. Stop at the towering **Millennium Gate** and duck into the nearby **Dr Sun Yat-Sen Classical Chinese Garden** for a taste of tranquility. Check out the colorful stores (and tempting pork bun snacks) around the neighborhood before strolling south along Main St towards **Science World** for some hands-on fun, then hop on the SkyTrain at the nearby station. Trundle to Waterfront Station and take the scenic SeaBus over to North Vancouver's **Lonsdale Quay public market**. On your way back, drop in at Gastown's **Alibi Room** for a microbrew beer.

Vancouver Art Gallery ART GALLERY
(Map p46; www.vanartgallery.bc.ca; 750 Hornby St; adult/child $17.50/6.25, by donation 5-9pm Tue; ⊙10am-5pm Wed-Mon, to 9pm Tue) The VAG has dramatically transformed since 2000, becoming a vital part of the city's cultural scene. Contemporary exhibitions – often showcasing Vancouver's renowned photoconceptualists – are now combined with blockbuster international traveling shows. Check out **Fuse** (admission $19.50), a quarterly late-night party where you can hang out with the city's young arties over wine and live music.

Canada Place NOTABLE BUILDING
(Map p46; www.canadaplace.ca; 999 Canada Place Way) Shaped like a series of sails jutting into the sky over the harbor, this cruise-ship terminal and convention center is also a pier where you can stroll the waterfront for some camera-triggering North Shore mountain views. If you have kids in tow, duck inside for the **Port Authority Interpretation Centre** (www.portvancouver.com; admission free; ⊙8am-5pm Mon-Fri), a hands-on illumination of the city's maritime trade. Check out the grass-roofed expansion next door and the tripod-like **Olympic Cauldron**, a permanent reminder of the 2010 Games.

Bill Reid Gallery of Northwest Coast Art
ART GALLERY
(Map p46; www.billreidgallery.ca; 639 Hornby St; adult/child $10/5; ⊙11am-5pm Wed-Sun) Showcasing carvings, paintings and jewelry from Canada's most revered Haida artist, this is a comprehensive intro to Reid and his fellow First Nations creators. Hit the mezzanine floor and you'll be face-to-face with an 8.5m-long bronze of intertwined magical creatures, complete with impressively long tongues.

BC Place Stadium NOTABLE BUILDING
(Map p46; www.bcplacestadium.com; 777 Pacific Blvd) Site of 2010's Winter Olympic opening and closing ceremonies, the city's main arena was having a new retractable lid fitted during research for this book. On completion, it will host football's **BC Lions** and soccer's **Vancouver Whitecaps**. The **BC Sports Hall of Fame & Museum** (www.bcsportshalloffame.com) – a kid-friendly celebration of the province's sporting achievements – is also expected to reopen after the refurbishment.

GARDENS

» Dr Sun Yat-Sen Classical Chinese Garden (p45)
» VanDusen Botanical Garden (p51)
» Bloedel Floral Conservatory (p51)
» UBC Botanical Garden (p50)
» Nitobe Memorial Garden (p50)

Marine Building HISTORICAL BUILDING
(Map p46; 335 Burrard St) This elaborate, 22-story art deco gem is a tribute to the city's maritime past. Peruse the exterior of seahorses, lobsters and streamlined ships, then hit the lobby's stained-glass panels, zodiac-inlaid floor and brass-doored elevators. The British Empire's tallest building when completed in 1930, it now houses offices.

Vancouver Lookout NOTABLE BUILDING
(Map p46; www.vancouverlookout.com; 555 W Hastings St; adult/child $15/7; ⊙8:30am-10:30pm mid-May–Sep, 9am-9pm Oct–mid-May) Atop this 169m-high, needle-like viewing tower – accessed via twin glass elevators – you'll enjoy 360-degree vistas of city, sea and mountains unfurling around you. Tickets are pricey but are valid all day – return for a sunset view to get your money's worth.

STANLEY PARK
This magnificent 404-hectare park combines excellent attractions with a mystical natural aura. Don't miss a stroll or cycle (rentals near the W Georgia St entrance) around the 8.8km seawall: a kind of visual spa treatment fringed by a 150,000-tree temperate rainforest, it'll take you past the park's popular totem poles.

Vancouver Aquarium AQUARIUM
(www.vanaqua.org; adult/child $27/17, reduced in winter; ⊙9:30am-7pm Jul & Aug, 9:30am-5pm Sep-Jun) Home to 9000 water-loving critters – including wolf eels, beluga whales and mesmerizing jellyfish – there's also a walk-through rainforest of birds, turtles and a statue-still sloth. Check for feeding times and consider an **Animal Encounter trainer tour** (from $24). The newest draw here is the 4D Experience: a 3D movie theater with added wind, mist and aromas.

Miniature Railway RAILWAY
(☑604-257-8531; adult/child $6.19/3.10; ☺10am-6pm Jul-early Sep, reduced off-season) Families looking for a charming alternative to the city's bigger kid-friendly attractions should head to the heart of the park for a 15-minute railway trundle through the trees. This is also one of Vancouver's fave Christmas lures, when the grounds are decorated with Yuletide decorations and dioramas.

Second Beach & Third Beach BEACH
Second Beach is an ever-busy, family-friendly area on the park's western side, with a grassy playground, snack bar and a pitch-and-putt golf course. Its main attraction is the seasonal outdoor **swimming pool** on the waterfront. Third Beach is a more laid-back hangout, with plenty of large logs to sit against and catch possibly Vancouver's best sunset.

FREE **Lost Lagoon** NATURE RESERVE
Originally an extension of Coal Harbour, this tranquil, watery oasis is now colonized by indigenous plant and beady-eyed birdlife accessed via a shoreline trail. Drop into the **Nature House** (Map p46; www.stanleyparkecology.ca; admission free; ☺10am-7pm Tue-Sun May-Sep) for an introduction to the park's ecology and ask about the area **walks** (adult/child $10/5).

WEST END
A dense nest of low-rise older apartment buildings occupying a tangle of well-maintained residential streets, the West End is the city center's lively heart. Dripping with wooden heritage homes and lined on two sides by seawall promenades, it has plenty of dining and shopping options and is also the home of Vancouver's gay community.

Roedde House Museum MUSEUM
(Map p46; www.roeddehouse.org; 1415 Barclay St; admission $5; ☺1-4pm Tue-Sun mid-May-Aug, 1-4pm Mon, Wed, Thu & Sun, closed Tue & Fri Sep-Apr) For a glimpse of pioneer-town Vancouver, drop by this handsome 1893 timber-framed mansion. Packed with antiques, it's a superb re-creation of how well-heeled locals used to live. Sunday entry includes tea and cookies and costs $1 extra. Also check out the surrounding pre-served homes in **Barclay Heritage Sq.**

English Bay Beach BEACH
(Map p46; cnr Denman & Davie Sts) Whether it's a languid August evening with buskers, sunbathers and volleyballers, or a blustery November day with the dog walkers, this sandy curve is an unmissable highlight. Snap photos of the beach's towering **inukshuk sculpture** or continue along the bustling seawall into neighboring Stanley Park.

YALETOWN
An evocative, brick-lined former warehouse district transformed into swanky bars, restaurants and boutiques in the 1990s, pedestrian-friendly Yaletown is where the city's rich and beautiful come to see and be seen. Roughly bordered by Nelson, Homer, Drake and Pacific Sts, the past is recalled by the old rail tracks still embedded in many of the roads.

Roundhouse Community Arts & Recreation Centre NOTABLE BUILDING
(Map p46; www.roundhouse.ca; 181 Roundhouse Mews, cnr Davie St & Pacific Blvd) Yaletown's main cultural and performance space is housed in a refurbished Canadian Pacific Railway repair shed. This train-flavored heritage is recalled in a small on-site **museum** (www.wcra.org/engine374; admission free) housing one of the city's most important artifacts: engine No 374, the locomotive that pulled the first passenger train into Vancouver in 1887.

David Lam Park PARK
(Map p46; www.vancouverparks.ca; cnr Drake St & Pacific Blvd) A crooked elbow of landscaped waterfront at the neck of False Creek, this is a popular summertime hangout for Yale-townites. It's also a perfect launch point for a 2km stroll along the north bank of False Creek to Science World. You'll pass public artworks, slick glass towers and visiting birdlife, including blue herons.

FREE **Contemporary Art Gallery** ART GALLERY
(Map p46; www.contemporaryartgallery.ca; 555 Nelson St; ☺noon-6pm Wed-Sun) Focused on modern art – photography is particularly well represented – this small, purpose-built gallery showcases local and international works.

GASTOWN
Now a national historic site, the cobbled streets of Gastown are where the city began – look out for the jaunty bronze of early resident 'Gassy' Jack Deighton teetering on his whiskey barrel. Many heritage buildings remain, most now housing cool bars, restaurants or trendy shops. The landmark **steam clock** (Map p46) is halfway along Water St. A snapshot favorite, it's actually powered by electricity.

Vancouver Police Museum MUSEUM
(Map p46; www.vancouverpolicemuseum.ca; 240 E Cordova St; adult/student $7/5; ⊘9am-5pm) Charting the city's murky criminal past – complete with confiscated weapons, counterfeit currencies and a mortuary exhibit lined with wall-mounted tissue samples – this excellent little museum also runs recommended Sins of the City walking tours (adult/child $15/12) plus after-hours Forensics for Adults workshops ($12).

Science World at TELUS World of Science MUSEUM
(Map p46; www.scienceworld.ca; 1455 Quebec St; adult/child $21/14.25; ⊘10am-5pm Mon-Fri, 10am-6pm Sat & Sun) The two levels of hands-on science and natural-history exhibits here bring out the kid in everyone. An ideal place to entertain the family, there's also an **Omnimax Theatre** screening large-format documentaries. Explore without the kids at the regular adults-only After Dark ($19.75) events. During research, an outdoor science park was also being added to the site.

CHINATOWN

Adjoining Gastown, North America's third-largest Chinatown is a highly wanderable explosion of sight, sound and aromas. Check out the towering Chinatown Millennium Gate (cnr W Pender & Taylor Sts), the area's monumental entry point, and don't miss the bustling summer night market (Map p46). For more information on the area – including events like the summer festival and the annual New Year parade – visit www.vancouver-chinatown.com.

Dr Sun Yat-Sen Classical Chinese Garden GARDEN
(Map p46; www.vancouverchinesegarden.com; 578 Carrall St; adult/child $14/10; ⊘9:30am-7pm mid-Jun—Aug, 10am-6pm Sep & May—mid-Jun, 10am-4:30pm Oct-Apr) A tranquil break from clamorous Chinatown, this intimate 'garden of ease' reveals the Taoist symbolism behind the placing of gnarled pine trees and ancient limestone formations. Check out the less elaborate, but free, park next door.

SOUTH MAIN (SOMA) & COMMERCIAL DRIVE

Eschewing the fake tans of Robson St's mainstream shoppers, Vancouver's indie crowd has colonized an area of town that used to be a byword for down-at-heel. Radiating from the intersection of Main St and Broadway, South Main – also known as SoMa – is home to the city's carefully cultivated young alternative crowd: think skinny jeans and plaid shirts for guys and vintage chic and thick-framed spectacles for girls. Bohemian coffee shops, cool-ass bars, vegetarian eateries and one-of-a-kind boutiques – especially past the 20th Ave intersection – are blooming here.

Urban adventurers should also alight at the Broadway-Commercial SkyTrain station for a stroll north along funky Commercial Dr (www.thedrive.ca), where decades of European immigrants – especially Italians, Greeks and Portuguese – have created a United Nations of restaurants, coffee bars and exotic delis. The best spot in town to watch televised international soccer games among passionate fans, it's also a promenade of espresso-supping patio dwellers on languid afternoons when it's lined with young bohemians and student-types.

Punjabi Market SHOPPING AREA
Located on Main St, past 48th Ave, and also known as 'Little India,' this enclave of sari stores, bhangra music shops and some of the region's best-value curry buffet restaurants is a good spot for a spicy all-you-can-eat lunch followed by a restorative walkabout.

GRANVILLE ISLAND

Fanning out under the giant iron arches of Granville Bridge, this gentrified former industrial peninsula – it's not actually an island – is one of the best spots to spend a lazy afternoon. Studded with restaurants, bars, theaters and artisan businesses, it's usually crowded on summer weekends, as visitors chill out with the buskers and wrestle the seagulls for their fish and chips. For information and happenings, check www.granvilleisland.com.

Granville Island Public Market MARKET
(Map p46; Johnston St; ⊘9am-7pm) Granville Island's highlight is the covered Public Market, a multisensory smorgasbord of fish, cheese, fruit and bakery treats. Pick up some fixings for a picnic at nearby Vanier Park or hit the international food court (dine off-peak and you're more likely to snag a table). Edible BC (www.edible-britishcolumbia.com; tours $49) offers excellent market tours for the foodie-inclined.

Granville Island Brewing BREWERY
(Map p46; www.gib.ca; 1441 Cartwright St; tours $9.75; ⊘noon, 2pm & 4pm) A short tour of Canada's oldest microbrewery ends with four sample beers in the Taproom – often

BRITISH COLUMBIA VANCOUVER

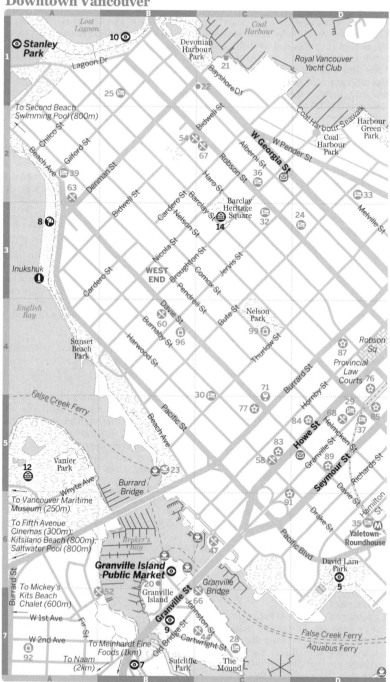

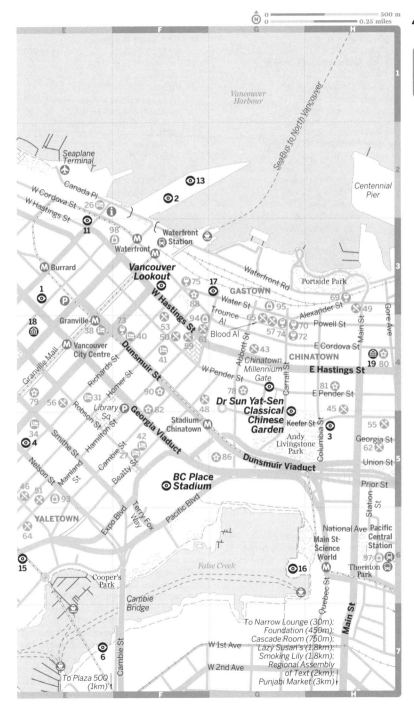

0 — 500 m
0 — 0.25 miles

Vancouver
Harbour

Seaplane
Terminal

Centennial
Pier

Canada Pl

W Cordova St
W Hastings St
26 ⊕ ❶

⊙13

⊙2

11

98

Waterfront
Station

Waterfront

Burrard

Vancouver
Lookout

⊕75

17 ⊙
GASTOWN
Water St

88

94

Trounce
Al
Blood Al

65
57 74
70
95
Powell St
72

Waterfront Rd

Portside Park

69
49

Main St

Gore Ave

1 ⊙
P

18

Granville

38

73

53
50

59

61

E Cordova St

43

19 80

CHINATOWN
E Hastings St

Vancouver
City Centre

41

Dunsmuir St

Richards St

Homer St

W Pender St

Chinatown
Millennium
Gate

Abbott St

Carrall St

78

79

56

31

Library
Sq
90

P
82

Georgia Viaduct

Robson St

Hamilton St

Stadium-
Chinatown

48

81
E Pender St

45

55

Dr Sun Yat-Sen
Classical
Chinese
Garden

Keefer St

3

Columbia St

Georgia St
62

34 ⊙

4 ⊙

Smithe St

Cambie St

42

27

Beatty St

Mainland
St

Nelson St

86

Andy
Livingstone
Park

Dunsmuir Viaduct

Union St

Prior St

46

51

93

BC Place
⊙ Stadium

National Ave

Pacific
Central
Station

YALETOWN

64

Pacific Blvd

Main St-
Science
World

97

Thornton
Park

15 ⊙

Expo Blvd

Terry Fox Way

False Creek

⊙16

Quebec St

Cooper's
Park

Cambie
Bridge

Main St

To Narrow Lounge (30m);
Foundation (450m);
Cascade Room (750m);
Lazy Susan's (1.8km);
Smoking Lily (1.8km);
Regional Assembly
of Text (2km);
Punjabi Market (3km)

To Plaza 500
(1km)

Cambie St

6 ⊙

W 1st Ave

W 2nd Ave

including summer-favorite Hefeweizen, mildly hopped Brockton IPA or the recommended Kitsilano Maple Cream Ale. You can buy takeout in the adjoining store – look for special-batch tipples like the popular Ginger Ale.

Downtown Historic Railway   RAILWAY
(Map p46; www.trams.bc.ca; adult/child $2/1; ⊙noon-6pm Sat, Sun & holidays Jun–mid-Oct) Once you've finished trawling the shops, hop aboard the Downtown Historic Railway, which runs clackety antique streetcars between the Granville Island entrance and the Canada Line Olympic Village SkyTrain station.

KITSILANO
A former hippy haven where the counterculture flower children grew up to reap professional jobs, 'Kits' is a pleasant neighborhood of wooden heritage homes, cozy coffee bars and highly browseable shops. Store-lined W 4th Ave is especially recommended for a lazy afternoon stroll. A short seawall amble from Granville Island, Vanier Park houses three museums and is a popular picnic haunt.

HR MacMillan Space Centre   MUSEUM
(www.hrmacmillanspacecentre.com; 1100 Chestnut St; adult/child $15/10.75; ⊙10am-5pm Jul & Aug, 10am-3pm Mon-Fri & 10am-5pm Sat & Sun Sep-Jun) Popular with kids, who hit the hands-on exhibits with maximum force, this high-tech space center offers the chance to battle aliens, design spacecraft and take a Mars-bound simulator ride. There's an additional **observatory** (admission free; ⊙weekends, weather permitting) and a **planetarium** running weekend laser shows ($10.75) with music by the likes of Pink Floyd.

Museum of Vancouver MUSEUM
(MOV; www.museumofvancouver.ca; 1100 Chestnut St; adult/child $12/8; ◷10am-5pm Tue-Sun, to 8pm Thu) The recently rebranded MOV has upped its game with cool temporary exhibitions and late-opening parties aimed at an adult crowd. There are still colorful displays on local 1950s pop culture and 1960s hippie counterculture, plus plenty of hands-on kids stuff, including weekend scavenger hunts.

Vancouver Maritime Museum MUSEUM
(www.vancouvermaritimemuseum.com; 1905 Ogden Ave; adult/child $11/8.50; ◷10am-5pm May-Aug, 10am-5pm Tue-Sat & noon-5pm Sun Sep-Apr) Combining dozens of intricate model ships with detailed re-created boat sections and a few historic vessels, the highlight here is the *St Roch*, an arctic patrol vessel that was the first to navigate the Northwest Passage in both directions.

Kitsilano Beach BEACH
(cnr Cornwall Ave & Arbutus St) Attracting a young crowd of buff Frisbee tossers and giggling volleyball players, the water here is fine for a dip but there's also a giant outdoor heated saltwater pool if you prefer.

UNIVERSITY OF BRITISH COLUMBIA
West from Kits on a 400-hectare forested peninsula, UBC (www.ubc.ca) is the province's largest university. Its concrete campus is surrounded by the University Endowment Lands, complete with accessible beach and forest areas and a smattering of visitor attractions.

TOP CHOICE **Museum of Anthropology** MUSEUM
(Map p41; www.moa.ubc.ca; 6393 NW Marine Dr; adult/child $14/12; ◷10am-5pm Wed-Mon & 10am-9pm Tue, closed Mon mid-Oct—mid-Jan) Recently renovated and expanded,

GREEN YOUR VANCOUVER VISIT

Apart from walking, using transit and picking up a **Green Zebra Guide** (www.green zebraguide.ca), a coupon book that gives you deals at local sustainable businesses, there are a couple of additional ways to add a shiny eco sheen to your Vancouver trip. Spearheaded by the Vancouver Aquarium and a growing menu of city restaurants, **Ocean Wise** (www.oceanwise.ca) encourages sustainable fish and shellfish supplies that minimize environmental impact. Visit its website for an ever-growing list of partic-ipating local restaurants and check menus for symbols indicating Ocean Wise dishes. A similar, smaller movement called the **Green Table Network** (www.greentable.net) can help you identify area restaurants that try to source all their supplies – not just seafood – from sustainable, mostly local sources.

Sustainability also has a chatty social side with **Green Drinks** (www.greendrinks. org), a monthly drop-in gathering for anyone interested in environmental issues. The meetings take place at Steamworks Brewing Company (p64) and usually attract more than 100 regulars for beer-fueled discussions on alternative energy, global warming and the sky-high price of tickets to Al Gore events.

For more tips on how to green your trip, check in with the online **Granville Maga-zine** (www.granvilleonline.ca), which is brimming with eco ideas. And if you need some extra inspiration, check out these cool, locally written books: *100-Mile Diet: A Year of Local Eating* by Alisa Smith and JB Mackinnon (2007), *Greater Vancouver Green Guide* by the UBC Design Centre for Sustainability (2009) and *The Greenpeace to Amchitka* by Robert Hunter (2004), which is a first-hand account of the inaugural protest voy-age from Vancouver that kick-started the world's biggest green movement.

Vancouver's best museum houses northwest coast aboriginal artifacts, including Haida houses and totem poles, plus non–First Na-tions exhibits like European ceramics and Cantonese opera costumes. The free guided tours are highly recommended, as is the ex-cellent artsy gift shop. Give yourself a couple of hours at this museum.

UBC Botanical Garden GARDEN
(Map p41; www.ubcbotanicalgarden.org; 6804 SW Marine Dr; adult/child $8/4; ☺9am-4:30pm Mon-Fri, 9:30am-4:30pm Sat & Sun, reduced off-season) A giant collection of rhododendrons, a fasci-nating apothecary plot and a winter green space of off-season bloomers are highlights of this 28-hectare complex of themed gar-dens. The additional **Greenheart Canopy Walkway** (www.greenheartcanopywalkway.com; adult/child $20/6; ☺9am-5pm) lifts visitors 17m above the forest floor on a 308m guided eco tour. Combined entry with Nitobe Me-morial Garden is adult/child $12/6.

Nitobe Memorial Garden GARDEN
(www.nitobe.org; 1895 Lower Mall; adult/child $8/4; ☺10am-4pm, reduced off-season) De-signed by a top Japanese landscape archi-tect, this lovely green space is a perfect example of the Asian nation's symbolic horticultural art form. Aside from some traffic noise and summer bus tours, it's a

tranquil retreat, ideal for quiet meditation. Combined entry with the botanical garden is adult/child $12/6.

Pacific Spirit Regional Park PARK
(Map p41; cnr Blanca & W 16th Aves) A stun-ning 763-hectare green space stretching from Burrard Inlet to the North Arm of the Fraser River, this is an idyllic spot to hug some trees and explore the 54km of walking, jogging and cycling trails. Visit the Park Centre on W 16th Ave for maps and further info.

WEST SIDE

A large, catch-all area covering City Hall and the heritage homes of Fairview, plus the strollable stores and restaurants of South Granville and beyond, there are sev-eral good reasons to visit this part of the city. And with the opening of the Canada Line SkyTrain link in 2009, it's much easier to reach and explore from downtown.

Queen Elizabeth Park PARK
(www.vancouverparks.ca) With sports fields, manicured lawns and formal gardens, this 52-hectare spot is a local favorite. Check out the synchronized fountains at the park's summit, where you'll also find a hulking Henry Moore bronze called *Knife Edge – Two Piece*. If you want to be taken out to the

ball game, the recently restored **Nat Bailey Stadium** is a popular summer-afternoon haven for baseball fans.

Bloedel Floral Conservatory GARDEN
(www.vancouverparks.ca; adult/child $4.76/ 2.43; ⏱9am-8pm Mon-Fri, 10am-9pm Sat & Sun May-Aug, 10am-5pm daily Sep-Apr) Cresting the hill in Queen Elizabeth Park, this domed conservatory has three climate-controlled zones housing 400 plant species, dozens of koi carp and many free-flying tropical birds, including parrots and macaws. At time of writing, the conservatory was under threat of closure so check before heading over.

VanDusen Botanical Garden GARDEN
(www.vandusengarden.org; 5251 Oak St; adult/ child $9.75/5.25; ⏱10am-4pm Nov-Feb, 10am-5pm Mar & Oct, 10am-6pm Apr, 10am-8pm May, 10am-9pm Jun-Aug, 10am-7pm Sep) Four blocks west of Queen Elizabeth Park, this garden offers a highly ornamental confection of sculptures, Canadian heritage flowers, rare plants from around the world and a popular hedge maze. The garden is one of Vancouver's top Christmas destinations, complete with thousands of twinkling fairy lights.

🏃 Activities

With a reputation for outdoorsy locals who like nothing better than an early morning 20km jog and a lip-smacking rice-cake breakfast, Vancouver is all about being active. Popular pastimes include running, biking and kayaking, while you're also just a short hop from some serious winter-sport action in North Vancouver and West Vancouver.

Hiking & Running

For arm-swinging strolls or heart-pounding runs, the 8.8km Stanley Park seawall is mostly flat – apart from a couple of up-hills where you could hang onto a pass-

ing bike. UBC's Pacific Spirit Regional Park (p50) is also a popular running spot, with tree-lined trails marked throughout the area. If you really want a workout, try North Vancouver's **Grouse Grind**, a steep, sweat-triggering slog up the side of Grouse Mountain that's been nicknamed 'Mother Nature's Stairmaster.' You can reward yourself at the top with free-access to the resort's facilities – although you'll have to pay $10 to get down on the Skyride gondola.

Cycling

Joggers share the busy Stanley Park seawall with cyclists (and in-line skaters), necessitating a one-way traffic system to prevent bloody pileups. The sea-to-sky vistas are breathtaking, but the exposed route can be hit with crashing waves and icy winds in winter. Since slow-moving, camera-wielding tourists crowd the route in summer, it's best to come early in the morning or late in the afternoon.

COAL HARBOUR SEAWALL STROLL

An idyllic waterfront weave starting at **Canada Place** and ending at **Stanley Park** (it's about 2km), this is a perfect, sigh-triggering amble for a sunny afternoon. You'll pass the new convention centre expansion, a gaggle of bobbling floatplanes and the grassy nook of **Harbour Green Park**, where you can catch a breathtaking mountain-framed vista that will have you pulling out your camera and setting it to 'panoramic' mode. Continue past the handsome *Light Shed* artwork – a replica of one of the many marine shacks that once lined this area – then look out for the cozy houseboats bobbling in the marina near the Westin Bayshore, the hotel where Howard Hughes holed up for three months in 1972. You'll soon be on the doorstep of Stanley Park, where you can extend your walk for 8.8km around the shoreline perimeter or retire for dinner to the restaurants crowding nearby Denman St.

Family-friendly Vancouver is stuffed with things to do with vacationing kids. Pick up a copy of the free *Kids' Guide Vancouver* flyer from racks around town and visit www. kidsvancouver.com for tips, resources and family-focused events. Car-hire companies rent car seats – legally required for young children here – for a few dollars per day, but you'll need to reserve in advance. If you're traveling around the city without a car, make sure you hop on the SkyTrain or SeaBus transit services or the miniferry to Granville Island: kids love 'em, especially the new SkyTrain cars, where they can sit up front and pretend they're driving. Children under five travel free on all transit. Child-care equipment – strollers, booster seats, cribs, baby monitors, toys etc – can be rented from the friendly folk at Wee Travel (604-222-4722; www.weetravel.ca). Your hotel can usually recommend a licensed and bonded babysitting service.

Stanley Park (p43) can keep most families occupied for a full day. If it's hot, make sure you hit the water park at Lumberman's Arch or try the swimming pool at Second Beach; also consider the **miniature railway** (p44). The park is a great place to bring a picnic, and its beaches – especially Third Beach – are highly kid-friendly. Save time for the **Vancouver Aquarium** (p43) and, if your kids have been good, consider a behind-the-scenes trainer tour.

The city's other educational family-friendly attractions include **Science World** (p45) and the **HR MacMillan Space Centre** (p48). If it's raining, you can also duck inside Canada Place for the hands-on **Port Authority Interpretation Centre** (p43).

If you time your visit right, the city has an array of family-friendly festivals, including the **Pacific National Exhibition**, the **Vancouver International Children's Festival** and the fireworks fiesta known as the **Celebration of Light**.

After circling the park to English Bay, energetic cyclists can continue along the north side of False Creek towards Science World, where the route heads up the south side of False Creek towards Granville Island, Vanier Park, Kitsilano Beach and, finally, UBC. This extended route, including Stanley Park, is around 25km. If you still have some energy, UBC's Pacific Spirit Regional Park (p50) has great forested bike trails, some of them with challenging uphills.

There's a plethora of bike and blade rental stores near Stanley Park's W Georgia St entrance, especially around the intersection with Denman St. One of these, Spokes Bicycle Rentals (Map p46; www.vancouverbik erental.com; 1798 W Georgia St), offers a handy free route map. Also pick up the *Greater Vancouver Cycling Map* ($3.95) from local convenience stores. It highlights designated routes around the region and includes resources for visiting bikers.

Kayaking & Windsurfing
It's hard to beat the joy of an early evening paddle around the coastline here, with the sun sliding languidly down the mirrored glass towers that forest the city like modern-day totem poles. With its calm waters,

Vancouver is a popular spot for both veteran and novice kayakers.

Headquartered on Granville Island, the friendly folk at Ecomarine Ocean Kayak Centre (Map p46; www.ecomarine.com; 1668 Duranleau St; rentals 2hr/day $36/69; 9am-6pm Sun-Thu & 9am-9pm Fri & Sat Jun-Aug, 10am-6pm daily Sep-May, closed Mon in Jan) offer equipment rentals and guided tours. Its Jericho Beach branch (Jericho Sailing Centre, 1300 Discovery St; 9am-dusk daily late Apr-Aug, 9am-dusk Sat & Sun Sep, closed Oct-mid-Apr) organizes events and seminars where you can rub shoulders with local paddle nuts.

For those who want to be at one with the sea breeze, Windsure Adventure Watersports (www.windsure.com; Jericho Sailing Centre, 1300 Discovery St; surfboard/skimboard rentals per hr $18.58/4.64; 9am-8pm Apr-Sep) specializes in kiteboarding, windsurfing and skimboarding and offers lessons and equipment rentals from its Jericho Beach base.

Swimming
Vancouver's best beaches – English Bay, Kitsilano Beach, Jericho Beach and Stanley Park's Second Beach and Third Beach – bristle with ocean swimmers in summer. For the nakedly inclined, UBC's Wreck Beach is the city's naturist haven.

Popular with families, there's an excellent – though often crowded – outdoor **swimming pool** near Second Beach in Stanley Park. Alternatively, Kitsilano Beach has a large heated outdoor **saltwater pool** (2305 Cornwall Ave; adult/child $5.10/2.52; ⏰7am-8:45pm mid-May–mid-Sep). If it's raining, you'll likely prefer the indoor **Vancouver Aquatic Centre** (Map p46; 1050 Beach Ave; adult/child $5.10/2.52; ⏰6:30am-9:30pm Mon-Fri, 8am-9pm Sat & Sun), which also has a sauna, whirlpool and diving tank.

☞ Tours

Architectural Institute of BC WALK
(☎604-683-8588 ext 333; www.aibc.ca; tours $5; ⏰1pm Tue-Sat Jul & Aug) Two-hour guided walks around the buildings of historic neighborhoods. Six tours available.

Vancouver Urban Adventures BIKE
(☎604-451-1600, 877-451-1777; www.vancouverurbanadventures.com; tours from $25) Alongside its extensive walking-tour program, it offers a five-hour guided bike ride ($75) around the city.

Accent Cruises BOAT
(Map p46; ☎604-688-6625; www.accentcruises.ca; 1698 Duranleau St; dinner cruise $60; ⏰May–mid-Oct) Popular sunset boat cruises with salmon buffet option. Departs from Granville Island.

Vancouver Trolley Company BUS
(☎604-801-5515, 888-451-5581; www.vancouvertrolley.com; adult/child $38/20) Red replica trolley buses offering hop-on-hop-off transportation around popular city stops.

Vancouver Tour Guys WALK
(☎604-690-5909; www.tourguys.ca) The scheduled walking tours of three area neighborhoods are free but gratuities (in the $5 to $10 range) are highly encouraged. Check the website for the ever-changing itinerary.

Harbour Cruises BOAT
(Map p46; ☎604-688-7246, 800-663-1500; www.boatcruises.com; north end of Denman St; adult/child $30/10; ⏰May-Oct) View the city, and some unexpected wildlife, from the water on a 75-minute harbor boat tour. Dinner cruises also available.

Big Bus BUS
(☎604-299-0700, 877-299-0701; www.bigbus.ca; adult/child $38/20) Hop-on-hop-off tourist bus covering 23 attractions. Two-day option also available.

★☆ Festivals & Events

Dine Out Vancouver FOOD
(www.tourismvancouver.com) Two weeks of three-course tasting menus ($18, $28 or $38) at area restaurants. Mid-January.

Chinese New Year COMMUNITY
(www.vancouver-chinatown.com) Festive kaleidoscope of dancing, parades and great food held in January or February.

Winterruption ARTS
(www.winterruption.com) Granville Island brushes off the winter blues with a music and performance festival around mid-February.

Vancouver Playhouse International Wine Festival WINE
(www.playhousewinefest.com) The city's oldest and best annual wine celebration takes place in late March.

Vancouver Craft Beer Week BEER
(www.vancouvercraftbeerweek.com) The first week of May sees a boozy roster of tastings, pairing dinners and tipple-fueled shenanigans.

Vancouver International Children's Festival CHILDREN'S
(www.childrensfestival.ca) Storytelling, performance and activities in the tents at Vanier Park in mid-May.

Bard on the Beach ARTS
(www.bardonthebeach.org) A season (June to September) of four Shakespeare-related plays in Vanier Park tents.

Vancouver International Jazz Festival MUSIC
(www.coastaljazz.ca) City-wide cornucopia of superstar shows and free outdoor events from mid-June.

Car Free Vancouver Day COMMUNITY
(www.carfreevancouver.org) Neighborhoods across the city turn over their main streets around mid-June for food, music and market stalls.

Dragon Boat Festival BOAT
(www.dragonboatbc.ca) In the third week of June, a two-day splashathon of boat-racing fun.

Vancouver Folk Music Festival MUSIC
(www.thefestival.bc.ca) Folk and world music shows at Jericho Beach in mid-July.

Celebration of Light FIREWORKS
(www.celebration-of-light.com) Free international fireworks extravaganza in English Bay from late July.

START COAL HARBOUR
FINISH ENGLISH BAY
DISTANCE 8.8KM
DURATION 3 HOURS

Walking Tour
Stanley Park

❯ Overlooking the glassy waters of ❶ **Coal Harbour**, follow the curving seawall path into the park, looking out for cyclists and in-line skaters who haven't yet grasped the route's dual-lane system. Keeping your gaze on the water, and looking for beady-eyed blue herons along the way, you'll soon reach the ❷ **Stanley Park Information Centre**, where you can pick up a map (and maybe an ice cream) for the rest of your trek. Pull out your camera for some photos of the nearby brightly painted ❸ **totem poles**, then turn around and shoot the downtown towers and maybe a floatplane or two skittering into the harbor. Continue on towards the ❹ **Nine O'clock Gun**, which still booms across the city every night, then wind northwards to ❺ **Brockton Point** with its little white-and-red lighthouse. This is where Arnold Schwarzenegger handed the torch to Sebastian Coe just before the Winter Olympics in 2010. The adjoining downhill stretch will bring you to the oft-photographed ❻ **Girl in a Wetsuit** sculpture and then the looming undercarriage of the towering ❼ **Lions Gate Bridge**. You'll get a blast of sea breeze as you round ❽ **Prospect Point** as well as some spectacular sea-to-sky vistas; pause here to reflect on the 2006 storm that uprooted many of the old trees in this area. Take out your camera again for some shots of ❾ **Siwash Rock**, a slender offshore outcrop that's part of First Nations legend. If your legs are feeling wobbly, it might be time for a break soon – a good opportunity to dig into that picnic you brought along (what do you mean you forgot?). Back on your feet, push on to ❿ **Third Beach**, where you can relax on a log and let the panoramic sea views roll over you. Pick up the pace after this break, strolling past the ⓫ **swimming pool at Second Beach** and hitting the home stretch to ⓬ **English Bay**, where ice-cream shops and restorative restaurants abound.

Pride Week COMMUNITY
(www.vancouverpride.ca) From late July, parties, concerts and fashion shows culminate in a giant pride parade.

MusicFest Vancouver MUSIC
(www.musicfestvancouver.com) Showcase of choral, opera, classical, jazz and world music performances in mid-August.

Pacific National Exhibition COMMUNITY
(www.pne.bc.ca) Family-friendly shows, music concerts and a fairground from mid-August.

Vancouver International Fringe Festival ARTS
(www.vancouverfringe.com) Wild and wacky theatricals at mainstream and unconventional Granville Island venues in mid-September.

Vancouver International Film Festival ARTS
(www.viff.org) Popular two-week showcase (from late September) of Canadian and international movies.

Vancouver International Writers & Readers Festival ARTS
(www.writersfest.bc.ca) Local and international scribblers populate literary seminars, galas and public forums from mid-October.

Eastside Culture Crawl ARTS
(www.eastsideculturecrawl.com) East Vancouver artists open their studios for three days of wandering visitors in late November.

Santa Claus Parade COMMUNITY
(www.rogerssantaclausparade.com) Christmas procession in mid-November, complete with the great man himself.

🛏 Sleeping

With around 25,000 metro Vancouver hotel, hostel and B&B rooms available, the region has plenty of options to suit all tastes and budgets. While rates peak in the summer months, there are some great deals available in fall and early spring, when the weather is often amenable and the tourist crowds reduced. The Tourism Vancouver (www.tourismvancouver.com) website lists options and packages while the province's Hello BC (www.hellobc.com) service provides further information and bookings. Be aware that hotels often charge $10 to $20 for overnight parking.

DOWNTOWN

Loden Vancouver BOUTIQUE HOTEL $$$
(Map p46; ☎604-669-5060, 877-225-6336; www.theloden.com; 1177 Melville St; r from $249; ❋⛆) The definition of class, the stylish Loden is the real designer deal. Its 70 rooms combine a knowing contemporary élan with luxe accoutrements like marble-lined bathrooms and those oh-so-civilized heated floors. The attentive service is top-notch, while the glam Voya is one of the city's best hotel bars. Hit the town in style in the hotel's complimentary London taxicab.

Fairmont Pacific Rim HOTEL $$$
(Map p46; ☎604-695-5300, 888-264-6877; www.fairmont.com/pacificrim; 1038 Canada Pl; r from $350; ❋⛆⛵) This chic 400-room property opened just in time for the Olympics. Check out the wraparound text-art installation on the exterior, then nip inside to the elegant white lobby. Many rooms have city views, while the ones with waterfront vistas will blow you away as you sit in your jetted tub. High-tech flourishes include iPod docks and Nespresso machines.

Victorian Hotel HOTEL $$
(Map p46; ☎604-681-6369, 877-681-6369; www.victorianhotel.ca; 514 Homer St; r with private bathroom from $149, with shared bathroom from $129) Housed in a pair of renovated older properties, the high-ceilinged rooms at this Euro-style pension combine glossy hardwood floors, a sprinkling of antiques, an occasional bay window and plenty of heritage charm. Most are en suite, with TVs and summer fans provided, but the best rooms are in the newer extension, complete with marble-floored bathrooms.

Urban Hideaway Guesthouse GUESTHOUSE $$
(Map p46; ☎604-694-0600; www.urban-hideaway.com; 581 Richards St; d/tw/loft $109/129/149; ⓔ) This supremely cozy home-away-from-home is a good-value, word-of-mouth favorite. Tuck yourself into one of the seven comfy rooms (the loft is our favorite) or spend your time in the lounge areas downstairs. Breakfast fixings (eggs, bacon et al) are provided: you cook it yourself in the well-equipped kitchen. Bathrooms are mostly shared, although the loft is en suite.

St Regis Hotel BOUTIQUE HOTEL $$$
(Map p46; ☎604-681-1135, 800-770-7929; www.stregishotel.com; 602 Dunsmuir St; r from $220; ❋ⓔ⛆) The rooms at this art-lined bou-

tique sleepover in the heart of downtown exhibit a loungey élan, with leather-look wallpaper, earth-tone bedspreads, flat-screen TVs and multimedia hubs. Check out the furniture, too: it's mostly reclaimed and refinished from the old Hotel Georgia. Rates include breakfast, a business center with free-use computers and access to the nearby gym.

Samesun Backpackers Lodge HOSTEL $
(Map p46; ☑604-682-8226, 877-972-6378; www.samesun.com; 1018 Granville St; dm/r $29.50/71; @✈) Expect a party atmosphere at this lively hostel in the heart of the Granville nightclub area – there's also a hopping on-site bar if you don't quite make it out the door. The dorms, complete with funky paint jobs, are comfortably small and there's a large kitchen plus a strong lineup of social events. Free continental breakfast.

Moda Hotel BOUTIQUE HOTEL $$
(Map p46; ☑604-683-4251, 877-683-5522; www.modahotel.ca; 900 Seymour St; d from $159; ✈) The old Dufferin Hotel has been reinvented as this white-fronted, designer-flecked boutique property one block from the Granville St party area. The new rooms have loungey flourishes like mod furnishings and bold paintwork, and the bathrooms have been given a swanky makeover.

HI Vancouver Central HOSTEL $
(Map p46; ☑604-685-5335, 888-203-8333; www.hihostels.ca/vancouver; 1025 Granville St; dm/r $33.50/83; ✸@✈) Opposite the Samesun, this labyrinthine former hotel has a calmer ambience, small dorms with sinks and many private rooms – some with en suites. Continental breakfast included.

L'Hermitage Hotel BOUTIQUE HOTEL $$$
(Map p46; ☑778-327-4100, 888-855-1050; www.lhermitagevancouver.com; 788 Richards St; r from $190; ✸) Another new boutique sleepover, the look is typically designer here but there are also some handy suites with full kitchens.

WEST END

TOP
CHOICE **Sylvia Hotel** HOTEL $$
(Map p46; ☑604-681-9321; www.sylviahotel.com; 1154 Gilford St; s/d/ste from $110/165/195) Generations of guests keep coming back to this ivy-covered gem for a dollop of old-world charm followed by a side order of first-name service. The lobby decor resembles a Bavarian pen-

sion – stained-glass windows and dark-wood paneling – and there's a wide array of comfortable room configurations to suit every need. The best are the 12 apartment suites, which include full kitchens and English Bay panoramas. If you don't have a room with a view, decamp to the main floor lounge to nurse a beer and watch the sunset.

Listel Vancouver BOUTIQUE HOTEL $$
(Map p46; ☑604-684-8461, 800-663-5491; www.thelistelhotel.com; 1300 Robson St; d from $169; ✸) Vancouver's self-described 'art hotel' is a graceful cut above the other properties at this end of Robson St. Attracting a grown-up gaggle of sophisticates with its gallery-style art installations (check the little hidden art space just off the lobby), the mood-lit rooms are suffused with a relaxing west-coast ambience. Adding to the artsy appeal, the on-site O'Doul's resto-bar hosts nightly live jazz.

Buchan Hotel HOTEL $$
(Map p46; ☑604-685-5354, 800-668-6654; www.buchanhotel.com; 1906 Haro St; r from $86) This cheery, tidy and good-value heritage sleepover near Stanley Park combines cheaper rooms – many with shared bathrooms, elderly furnishings and older blankets – with higher-quality and pricier en suites. The smiley front-desk staff is excellent and there are storage facilities for bikes and skis.

Riviera Hotel HOTEL $$
(Map p46; ☑604-685-1301, 888-699-5222; www.rivieraonrobson.com; 1431 Robson St; r from $119; ✈) Best of the slightly dinged but well-located apartment-style hotels crowding the Robson and Broughton intersection, the finest deals at this midsized concrete tower are the spacious one-bedroom suites. Complete with full kitchens and slightly scuffed furnishings, they easily fit small families. Free parking.

HI Vancouver Downtown HOSTEL $
(Map p46; ☑604-684-4565, 888-203-4302; www.hihostels.ca/vancouver; 1114 Burnaby St; dm $33.50/83.25) This quiet, purpose-built hostel has a more institutional feel than its Granville St brother. Dorms are all small and rates include continental breakfast.

Blue Horizon Hotel HOTEL $$
(Map p46; ☑604-688-1411, 800-663-1333; www.bluehorizonhotel.com; 1225 Robson St; d from $159; ✸@✉) Sleek and comfortable, this slender tower-block property has

Vancouver's gay and lesbian scene is part of the city's culture rather than a subsection of it. The legalization of same-sex marriages in BC has resulted in a huge number of couples using Vancouver as a kind of gay Vegas for their destination nuptials. For more information on tying the knot, visit www.vs.gov.bc.ca/marriage/howto.html.

Vancouver's West End district – complete with its pink-painted bus shelters, fluttering rainbow flags and hand-holding locals – houses western Canada's largest 'gayborhood,' while the city's lesbian contingent is centered more on Commercial Dr.

Pick up a free copy of *Xtra!* for a crash course on the local scene, and check www.gayvancouver.net, www.gayvan.com, and www.superdyke.com for pertinent listings and resources. In the evening, start your night off at the **Fountainhead Pub** (www.thefountainheadpub.com; 1025 Davie St), the West End's loudest and proudest gay bar, with its sometimes-raucous patio. Later, move on to the scene's biggest club: **Celebrities** (Map p46; www.celebritiesnightclub.com; 1022 Davie St). For an even bigger party, don't miss the giant annual **Pride Week** (p55) in late July, which includes Vancouver's biggest street parade.

Check the online directory of the **Gay & Lesbian Business Association of BC** (www.glba.org) or pick up its glossy free brochure for listings on all manner of local businesses, from dentists to spas and hotels. You can also drop in and tap the local community at the popular **Little Sister's Book & Art Emporium** (Map p46; www.littlesisters.ca; 1238 Davie St).

business hotel–like rooms. All are corner suites with balconies.

YALETOWN

Opus Hotel Vancouver BOUTIQUE HOTEL $$$
(Map p46; ☏604-642-6787, 866-642-6787; www.opushotel.com; 322 Davie St; d/ste from $210/400; ❄☎) Celebs looking for a place to be seen should look no further. The city's original designer boutique sleepover has been welcoming the likes of Justin Timberlake and that bald bloke from REM for years. The paparazzi magnets come for the chic suites, including feng-shui bed placements and luxe bathrooms with clear windows overlooking the streets (visiting exhibitionists take note). There's a stylish on-site resto-bar plus a small gym.

YWCA Hotel HOTEL $$
(Map p46; ☏604-895-5830, 800-663-1424; www.ywcahotel.com; 733 Beatty St; s/d/tr $69/86/111; ❄☎❖) One of Canada's best Ys, this popular tower near Yaletown is a useful option for those on a budget. Accommodating men, women, couples and families, it's a bustling place with a communal kitchen on every other floor and rooms ranging from compact singles to group-friendly larger quarters. All are a little institutionalized – think student study bedroom – but each has a sink and refrigerator.

Georgian Court Hotel HOTEL $$
(Map p46; ☏604-682-5555, 800-663-1155; www.georgiancourt.com; 773 Beatty St; r from $160; ❄☎) A recent makeover for this discreet, European-style property hasn't changed its classic approach to high service levels and solid, dependable amenities. The spruced-up standard rooms have new carpets and curtains but the apartment-style corner suites, with their quiet, recessed bedrooms, are recommended. There's a small on-site fitness room and the Swiss-flavored William Tell Restaurant draws plenty of outside diners.

GRANVILLE ISLAND & KITSILANO

Granville Island Hotel BOUTIQUE HOTEL $$
(Map p46; ☏604-683-7373, 800-663-1840; www.granvilleislandhotel.com; 1253 Johnston St; d from $159; ❄@☎) Hugging the quiet eastern tip of Granville Island, you'll be a five-minute walk from the public market here, with plenty of additional dining, shopping and theater options right on your doorstep. Characterized by contemporary west-coast decor, the rooms feature exposed wood and soothing earth tones. There's also a cool rooftop Jacuzzi, while the on-site brewpub makes its own distinctive beer (Jamaican Lager recommended).

Kitsilano Suites APARTMENT $$
(☏778-833-0334; www.kitsilanosuites.com; 2465 W 6th Ave; ste $149-229; ☎) Pretend you're a

Kits local at this shingle-sided arts-and-crafts house divided into three smashing self-catering suites. Although a century old, each is lined with modern appliances without spoiling their heritage feel: think hardwood floors, claw-foot bathtubs and stained-glass windows. Each has a full kitchen (a welcome pack is included so you can chef-up your first breakfast); there are shops and restaurants nearby on W 4th Ave.

HI Vancouver Jericho Beach HOSTEL $
(☑604-224-3208, 888-203-4303; www.hihostels. ca/vancouver; 1515 Discovery St; dm/r $20/76.25; ☺May-early Oct; @🛜) Resembling a Victorian hospital from the outside, this large hostel has a great outdoorsy location – especially if you're here for the sun-kissed Kitsilano vibe and the activities at nearby Jericho Beach (downtown is a 20-minute bus ride away). Rooms are basic, but extras include a large kitchen, licensed Jerry's Cove Café and bike rentals. Plan ahead and book one of the nine sought-after private rooms.

Mickey's Kits Beach Chalet B&B $$
(☑604-739-3342, 888-739-3342; www.mickeys bandb.com; 2142 W 1st Ave; d $135-175; 🛜🏠) Eschewing the heritage-home approach of most Kitsilano B&Bs, this modern, Whistler-style chalet has three rooms and a tranquil, hedged-in garden terrace. Rooms – including the gabled, top-floor York Room – are decorated in a comfortable contemporary style, but only the York has an en suite bathroom. It's a family-friendly place: the hosts can supply toys, cribs and help arrange babysitters. Includes continental breakfast.

UBC & WEST SIDE

Shaughnessy Village HOTEL $$
(☑604-736-5511; www.shaughnessyvillage.com; 1125 W 12th Ave; s/d $79/101; ⚓) This entertainingly kitsch sleepover – pink carpets, flowery sofas and nautical memorabilia – describes itself as a tower-block 'B&B resort.' Despite the old-school approach, it's perfectly shipshape, right down to its well-maintained rooms, which, like boat cabins, are lined with wooden cupboards and include microwaves, refrigerators and tiny en suites. Extras include cooked breakfasts, an outdoor pool and a large laundry room.

University of British Columbia Housing
HOSTEL, HOTEL $
(☑604-822-1000, 888-822-1030; www.ubccon ferences.com; hostel r from $35, apt from $49, ste

from $179; 🛜) You can pretend you're still a student by staying on campus at UBC. The wide variety of room types includes good-value one- or two-bed spots at the Pacific Spirit Hostel, private rooms in shared four-to six-bed apartments at Gage Towers (most with great views), and the impressive, hotel-style West Coast Suites with flat-screen TVs and slick wood-and-stone interiors. Most rooms available May to August only.

Plaza 500 HOTEL $$
(☑604-873-1811, 800-473-1811; www.plaza500. com; 500 W 12th Ave; r from $159; ✳🛜) With some great views overlooking the downtown towers and the looming North Shore mountains, rooms at the Plaza 500 have a contemporary business-hotel feel. It's a mod look that's taken to the max in Fig-Mint, the property's Euro-chic resto-bar. Rates include passes to a local gym, while the nearby Canada Line SkyTrain station can have you downtown in minutes.

🍴 Eating

Celebrated for an international diversity that even rival foodie cities like Toronto and Montréal can't match, Vancouver visitors can fill up on great ethnic dishes before they even start on the region's flourishing west-coast cuisine. To sample the best, just combine both approaches: try some of North America's finest sushi for lunch, then sample Fraser Valley duck or Vancouver Island lamb for a sophisticated dinner. Whatever you choose, don't miss the seafood – it's BC's greatest culinary asset.

With the city in the midst of a restaurant renaissance – barely a week goes by without a new eatery launching itself on the scene – you can tap into the latest vibe with the online reviews at www.urbandiner.ca or pick up a free copy of either *Eat Magazine* or *City Food*.

DOWNTOWN

Chambar EUROPEAN $$
(Map p46; ☑604-879-7119; www.chambar.com; 562 Beatty St; mains $14-29) This romantic, brick-lined cave – atmospherically lit by candles at night – is a great place for a lively chat among Vancouver's urban professionals. The sophisticated Euro menu includes perfectly prepared highlights like pan-seared scallops and velvet-soft lamb shank but delectable *moules et frites* are the way to go. An impressive wine and cocktail list (try a Blue Fig Martini) is coupled with a great Belgian beer menu. For more casual

fare, check out Medina Café, Chambar's daytime-only sister next door.

Templeton
BREAKFAST, BURGERS **$**

(Map p46; www.thetempleton.blogspot.com; 1087 Granville St; mains $8-12) A funky chrome-and-vinyl '50s diner with a twist, Templeton chefs up plus-sized organic burgers, addictive fries, vegetarian quesadillas and perhaps the best hangover cure in town – the 'Big Ass Breakfast.' Sadly, the mini jukeboxes on the tables don't work, but you can console yourself with a waistline-busting chocolate-ice-cream float. Beer here is of the local microbrew variety. Avoid busy weekend peak times or you'll be queuing for ages.

C Restaurant
SEAFOOD **$$$**

(Map p46; ☎604-681-1164; www.crestaurant.com; 1600 Howe St; mains $28-40) This pioneering west-coast seafood restaurant overlooking False Creek isn't cheap (lunch is cheaper, though) but its revelatory approach to fish and shellfish makes it possibly the city's best seafood dine-out. You'll be hard-pressed to find smoked salmon with cucumber jelly served anywhere else, but there's also a reverence for simple preparation that reveals the delicate flavors in dishes such as local side-stripe prawns and northern BC scallops.

Finch's
CAFE **$**

(Map p46; www.finchteahouse.com; 353 W Pender St; mains $3-8) Arrive off-peak and you might find a seat at one of the dinged old dining tables studding this buzzing corner cafe that has a 'granny-chic' look of creaky wooden floors and junk-shop bric-a-brac. You'll be joining in-the-know hipsters and creative types who've been calling this their local for years. They come for good-value breakfasts (egg and soldiers from $2.50) and a range of fresh-prepared baguette sandwiches and house-made soups.

La Bodega
MEDITERRANEAN **$$**

(Map p46; www.labodegavancouver.com; 1277 Howe St; small plates $8-12) It's all about the tasting plates at this country-style tapas bar, one of the most authentic Spanish restaurants in Vancouver. Pull up a chair, order a jug of sangria and decide on a few shareable treats from the extensive menu – if you're feeling spicy, the chorizo sausage hits the spot and the Spanish meatballs are justifiably popular. There's a great atmosphere, so don't be surprised if you find yourself staying for more than a few hours.

Japadog
ASIAN FUSION **$**

(Map p46; www.japadog.com; 520 Robson St; hotdogs $8-12) You'll have spotted the patient lineups at Vancouver's three Japadog fusion hotdog stands, but these celebrated, ever-*genki* Japanese expats have now opened a small storefront with a handful of tables. The short menu is almost the same – think turkey smokies with miso-mayo sauce and bratwursts with onion, daiko and soy – but there's also a naughty choc-banana dessert dog. Cash only.

Gallery Café
CAFE **$**

(Map p46; www.thegallerycafe.ca; 750 Hornby St; mains $5-10) The mezzanine level of the Vancouver Art Gallery is home to a chatty indoor dining area complemented by one of downtown's best and biggest outdoor patios. The food is generally of the salad and sandwiches variety, but it's well worth stopping in for a drink, especially if you take your coffee (or bottled beer) out to the parasol-forested outdoor area to top up your tan.

Gorilla Food
VEGETARIAN **$**

(Map p46; www.gorillafood.com; 436 Richards St; mains $4-7.50; ✐) This smashing little subterranean eatery is lined with woodsy flourishes and the kind of fresh-faced, healthy-living vegans who will make you want to adopt a new lifestyle. Organic raw food is the approach, which means treats such as seaweed wraps and pizza made from a dehydrated seed crust topped with tomato sauce, tenderized zucchini and mashed avocado.

WEST END

Raincity Grill
WEST COAST **$$$**

(Map p46; ☎604-685-7337; www.raincitygrill.com; 1193 Denman St; mains $17-30) This excellent English Bay restaurant was sourcing and serving unique BC ingredients long before the fashion for Fanny Bay oysters and Salt Spring Island lamb took hold. It's a great showcase for fine west-coast cuisine: the $30 three-course tasting menu (served between 5pm and 6pm) is a bargain and the weekend brunch is a local legend. If you're on the move, drop by the takeout window and pick up gourmet fish and chips for $10, then head to English Bay Beach for a picnic. Excellent wine list.

Guu With Garlic
JAPANESE **$$**

(Map p46; www.guu-izakaya.com; 1689 Robson St; mains $8-14) One of the many authentic Asian bistros, sushi spots and noodle joints at Robson St's West End tip, you'll be chilling with the ESL students at this cool-ass and ultra-welcoming *izakaya* (Japanese-style pub). Heaping hot pots and steaming noodle bowls are on offer but it's best to experiment with a few Japanese bar tapas plates like black cod with miso mayo, deep-fried egg pumpkin balls or a finger-lickin' basket of *tori-karaage* chicken that will make you turn your back on KFC forever.

Lolita's
MEXICAN $$
(Map p46; www.lolitasrestaurant.com; 1326 Davie St; mains $18-25) This lively cantina is ever-popular with in-the-know West Enders for good reason: a great place to find yourself late at night, its warm and mellow party vibe makes you feel like you're hanging out with friends in a bar at the beach. Turn your taste buds on with a few rounds of gold tequila or a fruity cocktail or three, but make sure you take a booze respite with some spicy, fusionesque fare, including the wonderful halibut tacos.

Sushi Mart
JAPANESE $
(Map p46; www.sushimart.com; 1686 Robson St; mains $6-10) You'll be rubbing shoulders with chatty young Asians at the large communal dining table here, one of the best spots in town for a sushi feast in a casual setting. Check the fresh-sheet blackboard showing what's available and then tuck into expertly prepared and well-priced shareable platters of all your fave *nigiri*, *maki* and sashimi treats.

YALETOWN

Blue Water Café
SEAFOOD $$$
(Map p46; ☑604-688-8078; www.bluewater cafe.net; 1095 Hamilton St; mains $22-44) Under chef Frank Pabst's expert eye, this high-concept seafood restaurant has become Vancouver's best posh oyster bar and the pinnacle of Yaletown fine dining. House music gently percolates through the brick-lined, cobalt-blue interior, while seafood towers, arctic char and BC sablefish grace the tables inside and on the patio outside. If you feel like an adventure, head for the semicircular raw bar and watch the whirling blades prepare delectable sushi and sashimi, served with the restaurant's signature soy-seaweed dipping sauce.

Glowbal Grill Steaks & Satay
FUSION $$
(Map p46; www.glowbalgrill.com; 1079 Mainland St; mains $17-40) Casting a wide net that catches the power-lunch, after-work and late-night fashionista crowds, this hip but unpretentious joint has a comfortable, lounge-like feel. Its menu of classy dishes fuses west-coast ingredients with Asian and Mediterranean flourishes – the prawn linguine is ace and the finger-licking satay sticks are a recommended starter. Check the glass-walled meat cellar on the counter and choose your desired steak cut.

Regional Tasting Lounge
FUSION $$
(Map p46; www.r.tl; 1130 Mainland St) An intimate, mood-lit dining room with an innovative menu approach: every three months it adds a new regional focus, which brings taste-bud-hugging treats from different parts of the world. Foodie focuses have included Italy, Spain, Greece and New Orleans, but there's always a selection of Pacific Northwest classics if you want to taste-trip BC, too. There's a three-course $29 tasting menu available daily.

GASTOWN

TOP CHOICE \ Judas Goat
FUSION $$
(Map p46; www.judasgoat.ca; 27 Blood Alley; small plates $6-10) This smashing 28-seat, mosaic-and-marble nook became a local foodie favorite soon after its 2010 opening. Named after the goats used to lead sheep off slaughterhouse trucks, it's nailed the art of small, simply prepared but invitingly gourmet tapas treats like beef brisket meatballs, lamb cheek wrapped in savoy cabbage and scallop tartare with pork rinds. Like its Salt Tasting Room brother next door, you'll find a good (although much shorter) wine and Spanish sherry drinks list. Arrive off-peak to avoid lineups: there's a 90-minute time limit for diners.

Acme Café
CAFE $
(Map p46; www.acmecafe.ca; 51 W Hastings St; mains $8-10) The black-and-white deco-style interior here is enough to warm up anyone on a rainy day – or maybe it's the retro-cool U-shaped counter. But it's not just about looks at this new neighborhood fixture. The hipsters flock here for good-value hearty breakfasts and heaping comfort-food lunches flavored with a gourmet flourish: meatloaf, chicken club and shrimp guacamole sandwiches are grand but why not drop by for an afternoon coffee and some house-baked fruit pie?

La Taqueria
MEXICAN $
(Map p46; www.lataqueria.ca; 322 W Hastings St; taco platters $7.50-9.50;☑) Arrive off-peak to

avoid the crush at this delightful hole-in-the-wall and you'll be able to grab a perch at the turquoise-colored counter. Listening to the grassroots Mexican soundtrack is the perfect accompaniment to a few superbly prepared soft tacos: go for the four-part combo (around $10) and choose from fillings like grilled fish, pork cheeks and house-marinated beef. Vegetarians have some tasty choices (the veggie combo is cheaper). Save room for a glass of cinnamony *horchata*.

Salt Tasting Room   CHEESE & CHARCUTERIE **$$**
(Map p46; www.salttastingroom.com; Blood Alley; small plates $8-15) Tucked along a cobbled back alley reputedly named after the area's former butcher trade, this atmospheric brick-lined wine bar offers around 100 interesting tipples, most of which are unusually offered by the glass. Beer fans will also find a small menu of treats, including the excellent Anchor Liberty Ale. From your communal table perch, peruse the giant blackboard of house-cured meats and regional cheeses, then go for a $15 tasting plate of three, served with piquant condiments – sharp, Brit-style piccalilli is best.

Nuba   MIDDLE EASTERN **$$**
(Map p46; www.nuba.ca; 207 W Hastings St; mains $8-19; 🖋) This hopping subterranean Lebanese restaurant attracts budget noshers and cool hipsters in equal measure. Try the good-value falafel plate ($9), heaped with hummus, tabbouleh, salad, pita and brown rice. It'll make you realize what wholesome, made-from-scratch food is supposed to taste like. More substantial fare – grilled lamb, Cornish hen etc – has also been added since the eatery moved from its hole-in-the-wall site across the street. Excellent service.

Deacon's Corner   CAFE **$**
(Map p46; www.deaconscorner.ca; 101 Main St; mains $6-13) The perfect Gastown combination of new gentrification and old-school good value, this lively neighborhood diner has been luring Vancouverites to a grubby part of town since opening day. They come for the large, hangover-busting breakfasts (biscuits with sausage, gravy and eggs is recommended if you want your weekly calorie intake in a single meal), while lunch options include good-value grilled sandwiches (go for the pulled pork) plus heaping fish and chips.

CHINATOWN

Bao Bei   ASIAN FUSION **$$**
(Map p46; www.bao-bei.ca; 163 Keefer St; mains $10-18) This chic-but-welcoming Chinese brasserie quickly hooked the hipsters when it opened in 2010. From its prawn and chive dumplings to its addictive short-rib-filled buns, it's brought a unique contemporary flair to eating out in the area, combined with an innovative approach to ingredients: top-of-the-range organic meat and sustainable seafood is used throughout. It's easy to find yourself seduced by the relaxed, candlelit ambience, especially if you hit the excellent cocktail menu.

Phnom Penh   VIETNAMESE **$$**
(Map p46; 244 E Georgia St; mains $8-18) Arrive early or late to avoid the queues at this locals' favorite eatery. The dishes here are split between Cambodian and Vietnamese soul-food classics, such as crispy frog legs, spicy garlic crab and prawn- and sprout-filled pancakes. Don't leave without sampling a steamed rice cake, stuffed with pork, shrimp, coconut and scallions, and washed down with an ice-cold bottle of Tsingtao.

Hon's Wun-Tun House   CHINESE **$$**
(Map p46; www.hons.ca; 268 E Keefer St; mains $6-18) Part of the city's favorite Chinese restaurant minichain, Hon's flagship Chinatown branch is suffused with inviting cooking smells and clamorously noisy diners. The giant, 300-plus items menu ranges from satisfying dim sum brunches to steaming wonton soups bobbing with juicy dumplings. For something different, try the congee rice porridge, a fancy-free, soul-food dish in seafood, chicken and beef varieties.

SOUTH MAIN (SOMA) & COMMERCIAL DRIVE

Chutney Villa   INDIAN **$$**
(www.chutneyvilla.com; 147 E Broadway; mains $8-18) Don't be surprised to get a hug from the owner when entering this warmly enveloping South Indian restaurant that lures savvy SoMa-ites with its lusciously spiced curries (lamb *poriyal* is a favorite), best served with fluffy dosas to mop them up. There's an outstanding Sunday-brunch combo of veggie curries and piping-hot Indian coffee, plus a drinks list of bottled Indian beers, on-tap BC brews and fresh lime cordial. Come hungry and expect to share and stay long.

Foundation
VEGETARIAN $$

(2301 Main St; mains $6-14; 🖋) This lively vegetarian (mostly vegan) noshery is where artsy students and chin-stroking young intellectuals like to hang. Despite the clientele, it's not at all pretentious (apart from the philosophical quotes on the walls) and its mismatched Formica tables are often topped with dishes like heaping Utopian Nachos, spicy black bean burgers or hearty house-made curries – called Revolutionary Rations on the menu. Vancouver's Storm Brewing beers are also served.

Havana
LATIN, FUSION $$

(www.havanarestaurant.ca; 1212 Commercial Dr; mains $10-20) The granddaddy of Drive dining has still got it, hence its buzzing patio on most summer nights. Combining a rustic Latin American ambience – peruse the graffiti signatures scratched into the walls – with a roster of satisfying Afro-Cuban-southern soul-food dishes, highlights range from yam fries to slow-roasted lamb curry and perfect platters of clams, mussels and oysters.

Reef
CARIBBEAN $$

(www.thereefrestaurant.com; 1018 Commercial Dr; mains $11-17) With its funkily bright interior, this is a perfect rainy-night haunt. The Caribbean soul-food menu includes heaping dishes like Bajan fried chicken and eye-poppingly spicy Jamaican curries, but don't ignore the cornmeal johnny cakes that usually arrive free at the table: you'll be planning your next visit as soon as you've finished them.

GRANVILLE ISLAND

Go Fish
SEAFOOD $$

(Map p46; 1505 W 1st Ave; mains $8-13) A two-minute walk west along the seawall from the Granville Island entrance, this wildly popular seafood shack is one of the city's best fish-and-chip joints, offering a choice of halibut, salmon or cod encased in crispy golden batter. The smashing (and lighter) fish tacos are highly recommended, while the ever-changing daily specials – brought in by the nearby fishing boats – often include praiseworthy scallop burgers or ahi tuna sandwiches. There's not much of a seating area, so pack your grub and continue along the seawall to Vanier Park for a picnic with the ever-watchful seagulls.

Agro Café
CAFE $

(Map p46; www.agrocafe.org; 1363 Railspur Alley; mains $6-10) Seemingly known only to locals and Emily Carr Uni students, this slightly hidden cafe is a smashing coffee stop with a Fair Trade commitment. But there's much more on offer here: tuck into a BC-brewed Back Hand of God Stout or a bulging ciabatta sandwich. And if you're hungry for a good start to the day, the heaping brekkies are a great fill-up (and a genuine good deal). In summer, sip your Americano outside and watch the Granville Island world go by.

Sandbar
SEAFOOD $$$

(Map p46; 🖋604-669-9030; www.vancouverdine.com; 1535 Johnston St; mains $18-35) West-coast seafood dominates at this adult-oriented, high-ceilinged restaurant under the Granville St Bridge. The oysters, best enjoyed on the rooftop deck, are recommended and the 1800-strong wine list is something to write home about. Live music is served up Thursday to Saturday when the urban professionals drop by to loosen their ties.

KITSILANO & WEST SIDE

Maenam
THAI $$

(www.maenam.ca; 1938 W 4th Ave; mains $15-18) A swish, contemporary reinvention of the Thai restaurant model, this is probably unlike any Thai eatery you've been to. Sophisticated, subtle and complex traditional and international influences flavor the menu in a room with a laid-back modern lounge feel. Inviting exploration, try the *geng panaeng neua* beef curry, a sweet, salty and nutty treat suffused with aromatic basil. The mains are great value, but why not share a few smaller plates (around the $8 to $10 range) instead?

Bishop's
WEST COAST $$$

(🖋604-738-2025; www.bishopsonline.com; 2183 W 4th Ave; mains $28-38) A pioneer of superb west-coast cuisine long before the 'locavore' fashion took hold, modest but legendary chef-owner John Bishop – he'll almost certainly drop by your table to say hi – is still at the top of his game in this charming, art-lined little restaurant. Served in an elegant, white-tablecloth room, the weekly changing menu can include stuffed rabbit loin, steamed smoked sablefish and the kind of crisp, seasonal veggies that taste like they've just been plucked from the ground.

Tojo's
JAPANESE $$$

(🖋604-872-8050; www.tojos.com; 1133 W Broadway; mains $19-26) Hidekazu Tojo's legendary skill with the sushi knife has created one of North America's most revered sushi restaurants. Among his exquisite dishes are favorites like lightly steamed monkfish, sautéed halibut cheeks and fried red tuna wrapped with seaweed and served with plum sauce. The maplewood sushi bar seats are more sought after than a couple of front-row Stanley Cup tickets, so reserve as early as possible and make sure you sample a selection or two from the sake menu.

Vij's　　　　　　　　　　　　　INDIAN **$$**
(www.vijs.ca; 1480 W 11th Ave; mains $18-26) Just off S Granville St, Vij's is the high-water mark of contemporary East Indian cuisine, fusing regional ingredients, subtle global flourishes and classic ethnic dishes to produce an array of innovative flavors. The unique results range from signature wine-marinated 'lamb popsicles' to savor-worthy dishes like halibut, mussels and crab in a tomato-ginger curry. Reservations not accepted.

Naam　　　　　　　　　　　VEGETARIAN **$$**
(www.thenaam.com; 2724 W 4th Ave; mains $8-14; 🖉) Luring city vegetarians for 30 years, this casual 24-hour eatery still has the ambience of a cozy hippy hangout. But the menu and weekend brunch queues show that these guys mean business, encouraging legions of repeat diners who keep coming back for stuffed quesadillas, hearty farmers breakfasts and sesame-fried potatoes with miso gravy. Live music is a nightly fixture and there's a convivial covered patio.

Bistrot Bistro　　　　　　　　FRENCH **$$**
(www.bistrotbistro.com; 1961 W 4th Ave; mains $14-19) A charming, snob-free neighborhood bistro with a casual contemporary feel, the menu here combines traditional French recipes with seasonal local ingredients and simple, flavor-revealing preparations. Expect hearty nosh like apple-sweetened pork tenderloin still simmering in its skillet and the kind of robust *boeuf bourguignon* that makes lesser chefs weep.

🍷 Drinking

Distinctive new lounges and pubs are springing up in Vancouver like persistent drunks at an open bar. Wherever you end up imbibing, check out some of the region's excellent craft brews, including tasty tipples from Driftwood Brewing, Howe Sound Brewing and Central City Brewing. Granville St, from Robson to Davie Sts, is a party district of mainstream haunts, but Gastown is your best bet for brick-lined character bars.

⌜TOP⌐
⌞CHOICE⌟ **Alibi Room**　　　　　　　　PUB
(Map p46; www.alibi.ca; 157 Alexander St) Vancouver's favorite craft-brew bar, this hopping brick-walled contemporary tavern

stocks a changing roster of about 25 mostly BC beers from celebrated breweries like Phillips, Driftwood, Old Yale, Crannog, Central City and beyond. Adventurous taste-trippers, Main St hipsters and old-lag Camra (Campaign for Real Ale) drinkers alike, enjoy the $9 'frat bat' of four sample tipples: choose your own or ask to be surprised. Food-wise, go for skinny fries with chili garlic vinegar or a bulging, Pemberton-sourced burger.

Six Acres　　　　　　　　　　　　BAR
(Map p46; www.sixacres.ca; 203 Carrall St) Perfect for a shared plate of finger food, it's just as easy to cover all the necessary food groups with the extensive beer selection here. There's a small, animated patio out front but inside is great for hiding in a candlelit corner and working your way through some exotic bottled brews, often including London Porter and the rather marvelous Draft Dodger from Phillips Brewing. Vancouver's coziest tavern, you can pull a board game from the shelf for an extended stay.

Railway Club　　　　　　　　　　PUB
(Map p46; www.therailwayclub.com; 579 Dunsmuir St) Accessed via an unobtrusive wooden door next to a 7-11, this is one of the city's friendliest drinkeries and you'll fit right in as soon as you roll up to the bar – unusually for Vancouver, you have to order at the counter. Expect regional microbrews from the likes of Tree Brewing and Central City (go for its ESB) and hit the hole-in-the-wall kitchen for late-night nosh, including burgers and quesadillas. There's an eclectic roster of live music every night.

Three Lions Café　　　　　　　　PUB
(www.threelionscafe.ca; 1 E Broadway) This small, Brit-owned gastropub has a dedicated local following. Pulling both Tetley and London Pride on tap, as well as a good array of bottled ciders, the service is excellent and the food (including great pies, Indian-style curries and a truly smashing lamb burger) is made to order from locally sourced ingredients. Drop by for its excellent weekend breakfast or try the ever-popular quiz night held every second Tuesday. Good spot to watch TV soccer games.

Cascade Room　　　　　　　　　BAR
(www.thecascade.ca; 2616 Main St) A warm and chat-noisy spot that's the perfect contemporary reinvention of a trad neighborhood bar. Choice bottled beers feature but the excellent 50-strong cocktail list is best: try a Cascade Room Cocktail of bourbon,

pressed apple, lime juice, vanilla bean, bitters and egg white. Food is of fine gastropub quality, with the wine-braised beef and bubble and squeak recommended. Drop by on Mondays for quiz night.

Irish Heather
PUB

(Map p46; www.irishheather.com; 210 Carrall St) One of Vancouver's best gastropubs, pull up a chair on the bar side – the floor is reclaimed Guinness barrels – and dip into a great list of Irish drafts and international bottled brews. Or head to the narrow room next door where the regular Long Table Series – beer and dinner for under $15 – has become a runaway success. A great spot for charcuterie plates or hearty, homemade fare like bangers and mash or steak and Guinness pie.

Narrow Lounge
BAR

(www.narrowlounge.com; 1893 Main St) Enter just around the corner on 3rd Ave – the red light above the door tells you if it's open – then descend into Vancouver's coolest small bar. Little bigger than a train carriage and lined with stuffed animal heads and junk-shop pictures, it's an atmospheric nook where the absence of windows means it always feels like midnight. Ask the friendly bar staff for recommendations – cocktails like the Bramble or beers such as Blue Buck Ale are popular.

UVA
BAR

(Map p46; www.uvawinebar.ca; 900 Seymour St) Possibly the city's best wine bar, this little nook combines a heritage mosaic floor and swanky white vinyl chairs that add a dash of mod class. Despite the cool look, there's a snob-free approach that will have you happily taste-tripping through a boutique drinks list carefully selected from old- and new-world delights. Combine with tasting plates from charcuterie to tangy cheese.

Steamworks Brewing Company
BREWERY

(Map p46; www.steamworks.com; 375 Water St) A giant Gastown microbrewery in a cavernous converted brick warehouse. The signature beer here is Lions Gate Lager, a good summer tipple. A favorite place for the city's after-work crowd, the pub downstairs can get noisy while the upstairs is all about serene views across to the North Shore. The menu is packed with pub classics, but the pizzas are a stand-out.

St. Augustine's
PUB

(www.staugustinesvancouver.com; 2630 Commercial Dr) Looking like a regular neighborhood sports bar from the outside, step inside for Vancouver's largest array of on-tap microbrews. Most are from BC but there's usually an intriguing selection or three from south of the border. Drop by for Monday evening's cask night and you'll find an extra special tipple on offer. Food is of the standard pub-grub variety.

Diamond
BAR

(Map p46; www.di6mond.com; 6 Powell St) Look for the unassuming entrance and head upstairs and you'll suddenly find yourself in one of Vancouver's best cocktail bars. This high-ceilinged heritage room is popular with local hipsters but it's never pretentious. Try the list of perfectly nailed cocktails plus some intriguing, Asian-focused tapas plates.

☆ Entertainment

Pick up the free *Georgia Straight* – or check www.straight.com – to tap local happenings. Event tickets are available from **Ticketmaster** (www.ticketmaster.ca) but **Tickets Tonight** (www.ticketstonight.ca) also sells half-price day-of-entry tickets. Clubbers should peruse the listings at www.clubvibes.com and www.clubzone.com. Live music shows are listed in the *Straight* and at www.livevan.com. For cinema listings, visit www.cinemaclock.com.

Nightclubs

Fortune Sound Club
NIGHTCLUB

(Map p46; www.fortunesoundclub.com; 147 E Pender St) The city's best club has transformed a grungy old Eastside location – formerly the legendary Ming's Chinese Restaurant – into a slick space with the kind of genuine staff and younger, hipster-cool crowd rarely seen in Vancouver nightspots. Slide inside and you'll find a giant dance floor bristling with party-loving locals out to have a great time. Expect a long wait to get in on weekends: it's worth it, though, for Happy Ending Fridays when you'll possibly dance your ass off.

Caprice
NIGHTCLUB

(Map p46; www.capricenightclub.com; 967 Granville St) Originally a movie theater – hence the giant screen evoking its Tinseltown past – upscale Caprice is one of the Granville strip's best mainstream haunts. The cavernous two-level venue is a thumping magnet for all the local preppies and their miniskirted girlfriends, while the adjoining resto-lounge is great if you need to rest your eardrums and grab a restorative cocktail and bite to eat. Expect to line up here on weekends

when the under-25s visiting from the suburbs dominate.

Republic
NIGHTCLUB

(Map p46; www.donnellynightclubs.ca; 958 Granville St) If you make it this far up Granville,
you're in for a loungey change of pace from
the noisy clubs at the Robson St end: Re-
public attracts those sophisticated over-25s
who have strayed all the way from Yaletown.
Start your visit with a cocktail on the 2nd-
floor patio while you look over the human
wreckage of staggering late-night drunks.
Then hit the dance floor, open nightly. Sunday is reggae and ska classics, while Saturday offers pulsing dance shenanigans.

Shine
NIGHTCLUB

(Map p46; www.shinenightclub.com; 364 Water
St) With music from electro to funky house
and hip-hop, Gastown's sexy subterranean
Shine attracts a younger crowd and is divided into a noisy main blue room and an
intimate cozy-cave red room with a 40ft
chill-out sofa. The club's Bonafide Saturday
indie disco and electro rave night is justifiably popular, while Wednesday's reggae,
glitch and dubstep is slightly more chill.

Live Music

Biltmore Cabaret
LIVE MUSIC

(www.biltmorecabaret.com; 395 Kingsway) One
of Vancouver's best alternative venues has
only been open in its present incarnation
for a few years but it's already a firm favorite. The SoMa crowd comes for the nightly
changing smorgasbord of Vancouver and
visiting indie bands that can range from
the Wintermitts to Tribal Soiree and Attack
in Black (what do you mean you've never
heard of them?). When there are no bands,
DJ, poetry and film nights keep things lively, as well as Sunday's highly popular Kitty
Nights burlesque show.

Commodore
LIVE MUSIC

(Map p46; www.livenation.com; 868 Granville St)
Up-and-coming local bands know they've
finally made it when they play the city's
best midsized music venue, a lovingly restored art deco ballroom that still has the
bounciest dance floor in town – courtesy of
stacks of tires placed under its floorboards.
If you need a break from your moshing shenanigans, collapse at one of the tables lining the perimeter, catch your breath with
a bottled Stella from the back bar then
plunge back in.

Media Club
LIVE MUSIC

(Map p46; www.themediaclub.ca; 695 Cambie St)
This intimate, low-ceilinged indie space
tucked underneath the back of the Queen
Elizabeth Theatre books inventive local
acts that mix and match the genres, so you
may have the chance to see electro-sym-
phonic or acoustic metal groups alongside
power pop, hip-hop and country bands –
although probably not on the same night.
A great place for a loud night out (earplugs
not supplied), this rivals the Railway Club
and the Rickshaw for catching up-and-coming Vancouver acts.

Yale
LIVE MUSIC

(Map p46; www.theyale.ca; 1300 Granville St)
Blues fans should head along Granville to
the Yale, a blowsy, unpretentious joint with
a large stage, devoted clientele and beer-
sticky dance floor. Many shows are free –
check the website for details.

Cellar Restaurant & Jazz Club
LIVE MUSIC

(www.cellarjazz.com; 3611 W Broadway) Chin-
stroking jazz nuts might find themselves
drawn to the subterranean Cellar Restaurant & Jazz Club, where serious tunes are
reverentially performed. Tuesday entry is
free and there are good beer specials.

Cinemas

Scotiabank Theatre
CINEMA

(Map p46; www.cineplex.com; 900 Burrard St)
Modern, nine-screen multiplex.

Cinemark Tinseltown
CINEMA

(Map p46; www.cinemark.com; 88 W Pender St)
Popular multiplex combining blockbusters
and art-house films.

Pacific Cinémathèque
CINEMA

(Map p46; www.cinematheque.bc.ca; 1131 Howe
St) Art-house cinema screening foreign
and underground movies.

Vancity Theatre
CINEMA

(Map p46; www.viff.org; 1181 Seymour St) State-
of-the-art facility screening festival and
art-house fare.

Fifth Avenue Cinemas
CINEMA

(www.festivalcinemas.ca; 2110 Burrard St)
Popular venue screening indie, foreign
flicks and blockbuster movies.

Theater & Classical Music

Vancouver Playhouse
THEATER

(Map p46; www.vancouverplayhouse.com; cnr
Hamilton & Dunsmuir Sts) Presenting a six-
play season at its large civic venue.

Arts Club Theatre Company THEATER
(www.artsclub.com) Popular classics and works by contemporary Canadian playwrights are at three venues around town.

Firehall Arts Centre THEATER
(Map p46; www.firehallartscentre.ca; 280 E Cordova St) An intimate studio venue presenting 'difficult' works to an artsy crowd.

Vancouver Symphony Orchestra LIVE MUSIC
(www.vancouversymphony.ca) Fusing complex and stirring recitals with crossover shows of movie music, opera and even Shakespearean sonnets. At venues around the city.

Sports

Vancouver Canucks SPORTS
(www.canucks.com) The city's NHL team is Vancouver's leading sports franchise. Book ahead for games at downtown's Rogers Arena, also known as GM Place (Map p46).

Vancouver Whitecaps SPORTS
(www.whitecapsfc.com) Playing at the temporary Empire Field stadium until BC Place is renovated, the city's professional soccer team hits the MLS big league in 2011.

BC Lions SPORTS
(www.bclions.com) Also playing at Empire Field until BC Place is ready, Vancouver's Canadian Football League (CFL) side is ever-hungry for Grey Cup triumph.

Vancouver Canadians SPORTS
(www.canadiansbaseball.com) Watching this fun baseball team play at Nat Bailey Stadium is all about hanging out in the sun with beer and a hotdog.

🔒 Shopping

Robson St is ideal for wanton chain-store browsing, but if you're aiming your credit cards at independent retailers in Vancouver, you'll have to dig a little deeper. If you prefer an edgier look, it's hard to beat the quirky SoMa boutiques between 19th and 23rd Aves. For window shopping, Granville Island, South Granville (especially from Broadway onwards) and Kitsilano's W 4th Ave usually hit the spot. But it's Gastown that's the up-and-comer: check out the streets radiating from Maple Tree Sq for some cool hipster shopping.

Regional Assembly of Text ACCESSORIES
(www.assemblyoftext.com; 3934 Main St) The epitome of South Main eccentricity, this ironic antidote to the digital age was founded by pen-and-paper-loving art-school grads. Ink-stained fans flock here to stock up on Little Otsu journals, handmade pencil boxes and American Apparel T-shirts printed with typewriter motifs. Check out the tiny under-the-stairs reading room showcasing cool underground art, and don't miss the monthly letter-writing club (7pm, first Thursday of every month), where you can sip tea, scoff cookies and hammer away on those vintage typewriters.

John Fluevog Shoes CLOTHING
(Map p46; www.fluevog.com; 65 Water St) The cavernous Gastown flagship of Vancouver's fave shoe designer (the smaller original store still operates on Granville), Fluevog's funky shoes, sandals and thigh-hugging boots have been a fashion since 1970. It's tempting to try something on – some of the footwear looks like Doc Martens on acid, while others could poke your eye out from 20 paces – but beware: falling in love can happen in an instant.

Mountain Equipment Co-op OUTDOOR GEAR
(www.mec.ca; 130 W Broadway) The cavernous granddaddy of Vancouver outdoor stores, with an amazing selection of mostly own-brand clothing, kayaks, sleeping bags and clever camping gadgets: MEC has been turning campers into fully fledged outdoor enthusiasts for years. You'll have to be a member to buy, but that's easy to arrange and only costs $5. Equipment – canoes, kayaks, camping gear etc – can also be rented here.

Smoking Lily CLOTHING
(www.smokinglily.com; 3634 Main St) Quirky art-school cool is the approach at this SoMa store, where skirts, belts and halter tops are whimsically accented with prints of ants, skulls or the periodic table. Men's clothing is slowly creeping into the mix, with some fish, skull and tractor T-shirts and ties. A fun spot to browse (the staff are friendly and chatty), it's hard to imagine a better souvenir than the silk tea cozy printed with a Pierre Trudeau likeness.

Deluxe Junk CLOTHING
(Map p46; www.deluxejunk.com; 310 Cordova St) A treasure trove of antique glories, from flapper dresses to sparkly evening shoes and even the occasional old-school wedding outfit, this is one of the city's best vintage-clothing stores. Mostly serving discerning females, there are also essential outfits for passing blokes, including cummerbunds and Hawaiian shirts (not usually worn to-

A tasty cornucopia of BC farm produce hits the stalls around Vancouver from June to October. Seasonal highlights include crunchy apples, lush peaches and juicy blueberries, while home-baked cakes and treats are frequent accompaniments. Don't be surprised to see zesty local cheese and a few arts and crafts added to the mix. To check out what's on offer, visit www.eatlocal.org.

» **East Vancouver Farmers Market** (Trout Lake Park north parking lot; ☺9am-2pm Sat mid-May–mid-Oct)

» **Kitsilano Farmers Market** (Kitsilano Community Centre, 2690 Larch St; ☺10am-2pm Sun mid-May–mid-Oct)

» **Main Street Station Farmers Market** (Map p46; Thornton Park, 1100 Station St; ☺3-7pm Wed early Jun-Sep)

» **UBC Farm Market** (UBC; ☺9am-1pm Sat mid-Jun–Sep)

» **West End Farmers Market** (Map p46; Nelson Park, btwn Bute & Thurlow Sts; ☺9am-1pm Sat mid-Jun–mid-Oct)

» **Winter Farmers Market** (Wise Hall, 1882 Adanac St; ☺10am-2pm 2nd & 4th Sat of month Nov-Apr)

gether). Check out the vintage cigarette holders – perfect for that 1940s dinner party you're time traveling back to.

Mink Chocolates   FOOD & DRINK
(Map p46; www.minkchocolates.com; 863 W Hastings St) Avoid the usual Canuck souvenirs of maple-syrup cookies and vacuum-packed salmon at this decadent designer chocolate shop in the downtown core. Trouble is, once you've selected a handful of choccy bonbons – little edible artworks embossed with prints of trees and coffee cups – you'll be lured to the drinks bar for a velvety hot chocolate. Next stop: years of addiction therapy.

Gravity Pope   CLOTHING
(www.gravitypope.com; 2205 W 4th Ave) One of a clutch of cool clothing stores strung along Kitsilano's highly browseable W 4th Ave, this unisex shop includes ultracool footwear on one side and and designer clothing for the pale and interesting set (think ironic tweed ties and printed halter tops) on the other. Don't spend all your dosh here, though: check out nearby **Vivid** and **Urban Rack**, too.

Rubber Rainbow Condom Company
                                        ACCESSORIES
(3851 Main St) Doing brisk business in its South Main location, this fun, funky condom and lube store serves all manner of experiment-inviting accessories, including studded, vibrating and 'full-fitting strawberry flavored' varieties. Ask for a selection pack if you're going to be in town for a while – you never know how lucky you might get.

Coastal Peoples Fine Arts Gallery
                                        SOUVENIRS
(Map p46; www.coastalpeoples.com; 1024 Mainland St) This sumptuous Yaletown gallery showcases a fine selection of Inuit and northwest coast aboriginal jewelry, carvings and prints. Focusing on the high-art side of aboriginal crafts, you'll find some exquisite items here that will likely have your credit card sweating within minutes.

Meinhardt Fine Foods   FOOD & DRINK
(www.meinhardt.com; 3002 Granville St) There's a great deli and a handy next-door takeout service at this South Granville cuisine-lover's paradise – the culinary equivalent of a sex shop for fine-food fans. Check out the narrow aisles of international condiments, then start building your ideal picnic from the impressive bread, cheese and cold-cuts selection.

Red Cat Records   MUSIC STORE
(www.redcat.ca; 4332 Main St) *High Fidelity*-style record store that's a 101 intro to Vancouver's underground music scene.

Wanderlust   BOOKSTORE
(www.wanderlustore.com; 1924 W 4th Ave) Extensive travel guides, maps and accessories.

Lazy Susan's   ACCESSORIES
(www.lazysusansonline.com; 3467 Main St) A fabulous display of must-have kitsch from 1950s greetings cards to sushi-shaped building blocks and Scrabble-tile rings and cufflinks.

Barbara-Jo's Books to Cooks BOOKSTORE
(Map p46; www.bookstocooks.com; 1740 W
2nd Ave) Foodie bookstore with a menu
of cooking classes.

Information

Internet Access

Internet Coffee (104 Davie St; per hr $3.25;
⊘9am-1:30am) Twenty terminals plus fax, CD-
burning and printing services.

Vancouver Public Library (www.vpl.vancouver.
bc.ca; 350 W Georgia St; free; ⊘10am-9pm
Mon-Thu, 10am-6pm Fri & Sat, noon-5pm Sun;
@🛜) Free internet access on library computers
plus free wi-fi access with a guest card from the
information desk.

Media & Internet Resources

CBC Radio One 88.1 FM (www.cbc.ca/bc)
Canadian Broadcasting Corporation's commer-
cial-free news, talk and music station.

City of Vancouver (www.vancouver.ca)
Resource-packed official city site with downloadable maps.

CKNW 980AM (www.cknw.com) News, traffic
and talk radio station.

Georgia Straight (www.straight.com) Free
listings newspaper.

Inside Vancouver (www.insidevancouver.ca)
Stories on what to do in and around the city.

Miss 604 (www.miss604.com) Vancouver's
favorite blogger.

Tyee (www.thetyee.ca) Local online news
source.

Vancouver is Awesome (www.vancouveri
sawesome.com) Vibrant, arts-focused online
magazine.

Vancouver Magazine (www.vanmag.com)
Glossy local trend mag.

Vancouver Sun (www.vancouversun.com)
City's main daily newspaper.

Medical Services

St Paul's Hospital (1081 Burrard St; ⊘24hr)
Downtown accident and emergency.

Shoppers Drug Mart (www.shoppersdrugmart.
ca; 1125 Davie St; ⊘24hr) Pharmacy chain.

Ultima Medicentre (www.ultimamedicentre.
ca; Bentall Centre, Plaza Level, 1055 Dunsmuir
St; ⊘8am-5pm Mon-Fri) Walk-in clinic, appoint-
ments unnecessary.

Money

RBC Royal Bank (www.rbc.com; 1025 W Georgia St; ⊘9am-5pm Mon-Fri) Main bank branch
with money-exchange services.

Vancouver Bullion & Currency Exchange
(www.vbce.ca; 800 W Pender St; ⊘9am-5pm
Mon-Fri) Often the best exchange rates in town.

Post

Canada Post main outlet (349 W Georgia St;
⊘8:30am-5:30pm Mon-Fri)

Georgia Post Plus (1358 W Georgia St;
⊘9:30am-6pm Mon-Fri, 10am-4pm Sat)

Howe Street postal outlet (732 Davie St;
⊘9am-7pm Mon-Fri, 10am-5pm Sat)

Tourist Information

Tourism Vancouver visitor centre (www.tour
ismvancouver.com; 200 Burrard St; ⊘8:30am-
6pm daily Jun-Aug, 8:30am-5pm Mon-Sat
Sep-May) Free maps, city and wider BC visitor
guides and a half-price theater ticket booth.

Getting There & Away

Air

Vancouver International Airport (www.yvr.ca) is
the main west-coast hub for airlines from Canada,
the US and international locales. It's in Richmond,
a 13km (30-minute) drive from downtown.

Domestic flights arriving here include regular
Westjet (www.westjet.com) and **Air Canada**
(www.aircanada.com) services. Linked to the
main airport by free shuttle bus, the South
Terminal receives BC-only flights from smaller
airlines and floatplane operators.

Several handy floatplane services can also
deliver you directly to the Vancouver waterfront's
Seaplane Terminal. These include frequent **Harbour Air Seaplanes** (www.harbour-air.com) and
West Coast Air (www.westcoastair.com) services
from Victoria's centrally located Inner Harbour.

Boat

BC Ferries (www.bcferries.com) services arrive at Tsawwassen – an hour's drive south of
downtown – from Vancouver Island's Swartz
Bay (passenger/vehicle $14/46.75, 1½ hours)
and Nanaimo's Duke Point (passenger/vehicle
$14/46.75, two hours). Services also arrive here
from the Southern Gulf Islands (p122).

Ferries also arrive at West Vancouver's Horseshoe Bay – 30 minutes from downtown – from
Nanaimo's Departure Bay (passenger/vehicle
$14/46.75, 1½ hours), Bowen Island (passenger/
vehicle $9.75/27.90, 20 minutes) and Langdale
(passenger/vehicle $12.85/43.20, 40 minutes)
on the Sunshine Coast.

Bus

Most out-of-town buses grind to a halt at Vancouver's **Pacific Central Station** (1150 Station
St). **Greyhound Canada** (www.greyhound.ca)
services arrive from Whistler (from $25, 2¾
hours), Kelowna (from $48, six hours) and Cal-
gary (from $79, 14 to 17 hours), among others.
Traveling via the BC Ferries Swartz Bay–Tsawwassen route, frequent **Pacific Coach Lines**
(www.pacificcoach.com) services trundle in
here from downtown Victoria (from $28.75, 3½

hours). PCL also operates services between Whistler, Vancouver and Vancouver International Airport (from $35, from 3½ hours). **Snowbus** (www.snowbus.com) also offers a winter-only ski bus service to and from Whistler ($30.95, three hours).

Quick Coach Lines (www.quickcoach.com) runs an express shuttle between Seattle and Vancouver, departing from downtown Seattle (US$40.85, four hours) and the city's Sea-Tac International Airport (US$54.15, 3½ hours).

Car & Motorcycle

If you're coming from Washington State in the US, you'll be on the I-5 until you hit the border town of Blaine, then on Hwy 99 in Canada. It's about an hour's drive from here to downtown Vancouver. Hwy 99 continues through downtown, across the Lions Gate Bridge to Horseshoe Bay, Squamish and Whistler.

If you're coming from the east, you'll probably be on the Trans-Canada Hwy (Hwy 1), which snakes through the city's eastern end, eventually meeting with Hastings St. If you want to go downtown, turn left onto Hastings and follow it into the city center, or continue on along the North Shore toward Whistler.

If you're coming from Horseshoe Bay, Hwy 1 heads through West Vancouver and North Vancouver before going over the Second Narrows Bridge into Burnaby. If you're heading downtown, leave the highway at the Taylor Way exit in West Vancouver and follow it over the Lions Gate Bridge toward the city center.

All the recognized car rental chains have Vancouver branches. Avis, Budget, Hertz and Thrifty also have airport branches.

Train

Trains trundle in from across Canada and the US at **Pacific Central Station** (1150 Station St). The Main Street-Science World SkyTrain station is just across the street for connections to downtown and the suburbs.

VIA Rail (www.viarail.com) services arrive from Kamloops North ($86, 10 hours), Jasper ($179, 20 hours) and Edmonton ($241, 27 hours), among others.

Amtrak (www.amtrak.com) US services arrive from Eugene (from US$67, 13½ hours), Portland (from US$50, eight hours) and Seattle (from US$35, 3½ hours).

Getting Around

To/From the Airport

SkyTrain's 16-station Canada Line (adult one-way fare to downtown $7.50 to $8.75) operates a rapid-transit train service from the airport to downtown. Trains run every eight to 20 minutes and take around 25 minutes to reach downtown's Waterfront Station.

If you prefer to cab it, budget $30 to $40 for the 30-minute taxi ride from the airport to your downtown hotel. For $10 to $20 more, consider arriving in style in a limo from **Aerocar Service** (www.aerocar.ca).

Bicycle

With routes running across town, Vancouver is a relatively good cycling city. Pick up a *Greater Vancouver Cycling Map* ($3.95) at convenience stores. Cyclists can take their bikes for free on SkyTrains, SeaBuses and rack-fitted transit buses. Additional maps and resources are available at the **City of Vancouver** (www.vancouver.ca/cycling) website.

Boat

Running mini vessels (some big enough to carry bikes) between the foot of Hornby St and Granville Island, **Aquabus Ferries** (www.theaquabus.com) services spots along False Creek as far as Science World. Its cutthroat rival is **False Creek Ferries** (www.granvilleislandferries.bc.ca), which operates a similar Granville Island service from the Aquatic Centre, plus additional ports of call around False Creek.

Car & Motorcycle

The rush-hour vehicle lineup to cross the Lions Gate Bridge to the North Shore frequently snakes far up W Georgia St. Try the alternative Second Narrows Bridge. Other peak-time hot spots to avoid are the George Massey Tunnel and Hwy 1 to Surrey.

Parking is at a premium downtown: there are few free spots available on residential side streets and traffic wardens are predictably predatory. Some streets have metered parking, but pay-parking lots (from $4 per hour) are a better proposition – arrive before 9am at some for early-bird discounts. Underground parking at either Pacific Centre shopping mall or the Central Library will have you in the heart of the city.

Public Transportation

The website for **TransLink** (www.translink.bc.ca) bus, SkyTrain and SeaBus services has a useful trip-planning tool, or you can buy the handy *Getting Around* route map ($1.95) from convenience stores.

A ticket bought on any of the three services is valid for 1½ hours of travel on the entire network, depending on the zone you intend to travel in. The three zones become progressively more expensive the further you journey. One-zone tickets are adult/child $2.50/1.75, two-zone tickets $3.75/2.50 and three-zone tickets $5/3.50. An all-day, all-zone pass costs $9/7. If you're traveling after 6:30pm or on weekends or holidays, all trips are classed as one-zone fares and cost $2.50/1.75. Children under five travel free on all transit services.

Bus

The bus network is extensive in central areas and many vehicles have bike racks. All are wheelchair accessible. Exact change is required since all buses use fare machines and change is not given.

99B-Line express buses operate between the Commercial-Broadway SkyTrain station and UBC. These buses have their own limited arrival and departure points and do not use the regular bus stops.

There is also a handy night-bus system that runs every 30 minutes between 1:30am and 4am across the Lower Mainland. The last bus leaves downtown Vancouver at 3:10am. Look for the night-bus signs at designated stops.

SeaBus

The aquatic shuttle SeaBus operates every 15 to 30 minutes throughout the day, taking 12 minutes to cross the Burrard Inlet between Waterfront Station and Lonsdale Quay. At Lonsdale there's a bus terminal servicing routes throughout North Vancouver and West Vancouver. Services depart from Waterfront Station between 6:16am and 1:22am Monday to Saturday (8:16am to 11:16pm Sunday). Vessels are wheelchair accessible and bike-friendly.

SkyTrain

The SkyTrain rapid-transit network consists of three routes and is a great way to move around the region: consider taking a spin on it, even if you don't have anywhere to go.

The original 35-minute Expo Line goes to and from downtown Vancouver and Surrey, via stops throughout Burnaby and New Westminster. The Millennium Line alights near shopping malls and suburban residential districts in Coquitlam and Burnaby. Opened in late 2009, the new Canada Line links the city to the airport and Richmond.

Expo Line trains run every two to eight minutes, with services departing Waterfront Station between 5:35am and 1:15am Monday to Friday (6:50am to 1:15am Saturday; 7:15am to 12:15am Sunday). Millennium Line trains run every five to eight minutes, with services departing Waterfront Station between 5:54am and 12:31am Monday to Friday (6:54am to 12:31am Saturday; 7:54am to 11:31pm Sunday). Canada Line trains run every eight to 20 minutes throughout the day. Services run from the airport to downtown between 5:10am and 12:57am and from Waterfront Station to the airport between 4:50am and 1:05am. If you're heading for the airport from the city, make sure you board a YVR-bound train – some are heading to Richmond, not the airport.

While SkyTrain ticket prices mirror the zones used across the TransLink network, there is one notable exception. Passengers departing on Canada Line trains from the airport are charged an extra $5 AddFare when purchasing their ticket from station vending machines. You do not have to pay this extra charge when traveling to the airport from downtown.

Taxi

Flagging a downtown cab shouldn't take long, but it's easier to get your hotel to call you one. Operators include **Vancouver Taxi** (☑604-871-1111), **Black Top & Checker Cabs** (☑604-731-1111) and **Yellow Cab** (☑604-681-1111). Taxi meters start at $3.05 and add $1.73 per kilometer.

LOWER MAINLAND

Metro Vancouver – often referred to as Greater Vancouver or the Lower Mainland – is chock-full of looming mountains, crenulated coastal parks, wildlife sanctuaries, historic attractions and characterful communities, mostly within a 45-minute drive of downtown Vancouver. North Vancouver and West Vancouver together make up the North Shore, located across Burrard Inlet from Vancouver proper. For more information on the North Shore, visit www.van couversnorthshore.com.

In contrast, Richmond (and its charming Steveston enclave) lies directly south of Vancouver via Hwy 99. It's now easily accessible from the city via the Canada Line SkyTrain route .

North Vancouver

POP 45,000

A commuter 'burb for downtown professionals, the city of 'North Van' rises from the waterfront from the SeaBus stop at Lonsdale Quay, where you'll find a popular public market. It also houses a couple of the region's top visitor attractions. For information on what to do here, visit the municipal website (www.cnv.org) or pick up the free *North Shore News* paper.

◉ Sights & Activities

Capilano Suspension Bridge PARK
(Map p41; www.capbridge.com; 3735 Capilano Rd; adult/child $29.95/10; ◐8:30am-8pm Jun-Aug, 9am-7pm May & Sep, reduced off-season) Walking gingerly across the world's longest (140m) and highest (70m) suspension bridge, swaying gently over the roiling waters of Capilano Canyon, remember that the steel cables you are gripping are embedded in huge concrete blocks on either side. That should steady your feet – unless the teenagers are stamp-

ing their way across. The region's most popular attraction – hence the summertime crowds – the grounds here include rainforest walks, totem poles and some smaller bridges strung between the trees.

Grouse Mountain PARK
(www.grousemountain.com; 6400 Nancy Greene Way; adult/child $39/13.95; ◷9am-10pm) This mountaintop perch is one of the region's most popular outdoor hangouts. In summer, Skyride gondola tickets to the top include access to lumberjack shows, alpine hiking trails and a grizzly-bear refuge. Pay extra for the zipline course ($105) or the new Eye of the Wind tour ($25), which takes you to the top of a 20-story wind turbine tower for spectacular views. In winter, Grouse is also a magnet for skiers and snowboarders.

FREE **Lynn Canyon Park** PARK
(Map p41; Park Rd; ◷7am-9pm May-Aug, 7am-7pm Sep-Apr) This free alternative to Capilano is a verdant North Van spot with its own slightly smaller suspension bridge. There are also plenty of excellent hiking trails and some great tree-hugging picnic spots. Check out the park's **Ecology Centre** (www.dnv.org/ecology; 3663 Park Rd; admission by donation; ◷10am-5pm Jun-Sep, 10am-5pm Mon-Fri, noon-4pm Sat & Sun Oct-May) for displays on the area's rich biodiversity.

Mt Seymour Provincial Park PARK
(Map p41; www.bcparks.ca; 1700 Mt Seymour Rd) A popular nature escape from the city, this ruggedly lovely, tree-lined park is suffused with summertime hiking trails that suit walkers of all abilities. Like Grouse, the area transforms in winter, when **Mt Seymour Resorts** (www.mountseymour. com) runs three lifts to take you skiing or snowboarding on its 21 runs. There's also a toboggan area and snow-tubing course.

Vancouver Eco Tours BUS TOUR
(◷604-290-0145; www.vancouverecotours.com; adult/child $65/55) Trundle around North Shore sights – Deep Cove, Grouse Mountain etc – in green biofuel vans. See the website for free tour options.

🛏 Sleeping & Eating

Pinnacle Hotel at the Pier HOTEL $$
(◷604-986-7437; www.pinnaclehotelatthepier. com; 138 Victory Ship Way; r from $169; ❄🛜🏊) North Van's swanky new Pinnacle is an excellent option if you want to stay on this side of the water and hop over to the city center on the SeaBus, just a few minutes' walk

away. Rooms are furnished with understated elegance – the hotel balances itself nicely between business and leisure travelers – with calming pastel hues favored over bold colors. Fitness buffs will enjoy the property's large gym and pool. Harbor-view rooms are recommended but they cost a little extra.

Grouse Inn MOTEL $$
(◷604-988-1701, 800-779-7888; www.grouse inn.com; 1633 Capilano Rd; s/d/ste from $79/99/129; ❄🐾) While it looks like a small shopping mall from the outside, this family-friendly motel is favored by winter skiers and summer wilderness explorers and is stuffed with amenities. It has a playground, outdoor pool and free continental breakfast. Rooms have bright and breezy interiors – especially if you like busy, 1980s-style bedspreads – and come in a wide array of configurations, including Jacuzzi suites and larger rooms for groups.

Burgoo Bistro FUSION $$
(www.burgoo.ca; 3 Lonsdale Ave; mains $8-16) With the feel of a cozy, rustic cabin, Burgoo's menu of comfort foods with a twist aims to warm up those North Van winter nights: the Guinness-infused Irish stew, spicy apricot lamb tagine or smile-triggering butter chicken with brown basmati rice would thaw a glacier from 50 paces. If all you fancy is a few beers, dip into the dark and hoppy Burgoo Brew or the blackcurranty Middle Mountain Black Mead. Live jazz on Sunday nights.

Observatory WEST COAST $$$
(◷604-998-4403; www.grousemountain.com; Grouse Mountain; mains $35-40) Clinging gamely to the top of Grouse Mountain, this fine dining spot serves up dishes of seared scallops and beef tenderloin along with the region's best views of nighttime Vancouver, twinkling in the valley far below.

Altitudes Bistro BURGERS, CANADIAN $$
(www.grousemountain.com; Grouse Mountain; mains $8-17) Adjoining the Observatory, the views here are almost as good and the atmosphere is decidedly more laid-back. Quality pub food in a ski-lodge setting.

❶ Getting There & Around

SeaBus vessels arrive at Lonsdale Quay from Vancouver's Waterfront Station ($3.50, 12 minutes) every 15 to 30 minutes throughout the day. From the bus terminal at the quay, bus 236 runs to Capilano Suspension Bridge then on to the base of Grouse Mountain.

Rocky Mountaineer Vacations runs its popular **Whistler Sea to Sky Climb** (www.rockymountaineer.com) train into North Vancouver from Whistler (from $129, three hours, once daily May to mid-October).

West Vancouver

POP 42,000

Adjoining North Vancouver, the considerably more wealthy 'West Van' is studded with multilevel mansions that cling to the cliff tops and look down – in more ways than one – across the region. It's a stop-off point on the drive from downtown to the Horseshoe Bay ferry terminal and points north to Whistler. You can check out all the parochial intrigue at the city council website (www.westvancouver.ca).

◉ Sights & Activities

Cypress Provincial Park   PARK
(www.bcparks.ca; Cypress Bowl Rd) Around 8km north of West Van along Hwy 99, Cypress Provincial Park offers great summertime hiking trails, including the fairly challenging Black Mountain Loop. In winter, the park's **Cypress Mountain** (www.cypressmountain.com) attracts well-insulated sporty types with its 38 ski runs and popular snowshoe trails. Site of the snowboard and freestyle skiing events at the 2010 Winter Olympic and Paralympic Games, it's one of the city's favorite snowbound playgrounds.

Lighthouse Park   PARK
(Map p41; cnr Beacon Lane & Marine Dr) Some of the region's oldest and most spectacular trees live within the 75-hectare Lighthouse Park, including a rare stand of original coastal forest and plenty of copper-trunked arbutus trees. About 13km of hiking trails crisscross the area, including a recommended trek that leads to Point Atkinson Lighthouse and some shimmering views across lovely Burrard Inlet. If you're driving from downtown, turn left on Marine Dr after crossing the Lions Gate Bridge.

Sewell's Sea Safari   TOUR
(☑604-921-3474; www.sewellsmarina.com; 6409 Bay St; adult/child $79/69; ⊗Apr-Oct) Head to the marina near Horseshoe Bay to get a seat on a rigid-hulled inflatable for a two-hour high-speed ride out to sea. With the spray in your face and the wind rattling your sunglasses, keep your eyes open for possible whale-pod sightings – barking seals and soaring eagles are almost guaranteed.

🛏 Sleeping & Eating

Lighthouse Park B&B   B&B $$
(☑604-926-5959,   800-926-0262;   www.lighthousepark.com; 4875 Water Lane; ste from $175) This elegant two-suite sleepover, complete with private entrances and a flower-decked courtyard, will have you feeling like a West Van aristo in no time. Each suite has a fridge and DVD player, as well as a decanter of sherry for that essential alfresco evening tipple. You can sober up with a stroll to nearby Point Atkinson Lighthouse.

Fraiche   WEST COAST $$$
(www.fraicherestaurant.ca;   2240   Chippendale Rd; mains $28-40) You'll fall in love with the panoramic shoreline views over the city even before you start eating at this swanky locals' favorite. Perfect Pacific Northwest is the approach here, with typical highlights on the seasonal menu including roasted Steelhead or Qualicum Bay scallops served with lobster ravioli. If you fancy a taste of the high life without the price, drop in for lunch when many dishes are under $20, or try the weekend brunch (Dungeness crab cakes recommended).

Salmon House on the Hill   SEAFOOD $$$
(www.salmonhouse.com; 2229 Folkestone Way; mains $22-30) The buttery-soft salmon dishes are always excellent, but there's also an ever-changing array of seasonal BC seafood, including delectable Fanny Bay oysters and Hecate Strait halibut.

DON'T MISS

WATERFRONT WALK FEST

Take bus 250 from downtown Vancouver and hop off along West Van's Marine Dr at the intersection with 24th St. Peruse the charming clutch of stores and coffee shops in Dundarave Village, then stroll downhill to the waterfront. Drink in the panoramic coastline views from Dundarave Pier, then weave eastwards along the shore-hugging Centennial Seawalk. On West Van's favorite promenade, you'll pass joggers, blue herons and public artworks before the 2km paved walkway comes to a stop. From here, head back up to the Marine Dr shops or weave over to Ambleside Park where you'll find a dramatic First Nations welcome figure facing the water.

Thai Pudpong THAI $
(www.thaipudpong.com; 1474 Marine Dr; mains $8-14) Locals' fave with sweet-and-sour classics like stir-fried squid and the excellent red curry beef.

Burnaby

POP 203,000

East of Vancouver, no-nonsense Burnaby is a residential suburb with a strip-mall feel. In addition, a handful of attractions aim to keep you away from the shops.

Offering a peaceful environment, minus the hectic energy of downtown, the pathways of Deer Lake Park (Map p41) crisscross the meadows and woodlands, circling the lake where fowl and other wildlife hang out. The adjoining Burnaby Village Museum (Map p41; www.burnaby villagemuseum.ca; 6501 Deer Lake Ave; adult/child/youth $10/5/7.50; ⊙11am-4:30pm May-Aug) colorfully recreates a BC pioneer town, complete with replica homes, businesses and a handsome 1912 carousel. To get directly there, take the Sperling Ave exit off Hwy 1 and follow the museum signs.

An ever-expanding homage to materialism, Metropolis at Metrotown (www.metropolisatmetrotown.com; ⊙10am-9pm Mon-Fri, 9:30am-9pm Sat, 11am-6pm Sun) is BC's biggest mall, with 470 wallet-luring stores. Savvy shoppers arrive early in the morning to beat the crowds then rest their weary credit cards at the sprawling food court – Indian, Japanese and Chinese cuisines are recommended. The mall is a 20-minute SkyTrain ride from downtown Vancouver; the mall is big enough to warrant its own eponymous station.

For information on the area, contact Tourism Burnaby (✆604-419-0377; www.tourismburnaby.com).

Richmond & Steveston

POP 174,000

The new Canada Line SkyTrain link has made the region's modern-day Chinatown much easier to reach from downtown Vancouver. Hop aboard and head down the line for a half-day of Asian shopping malls – centered on the Golden Village area – followed by a taste-trip through Chinese, Japanese and Vietnamese restaurants.

And don't miss the city's charming historic waterfront Steveston village, a popular destination for sunset-viewing locals with a penchant for great fish and chips. For information on both areas, log on to www.tourismrichond.com.

◉ Sights & Activities

TOP CHOICE Gulf of Georgia Cannery MUSEUM
(Map p41; www.gulfofgeorgiacannery.com; 12138 4th Ave; adult/child $7.80/3.90; ⊙10am-5pm daily) Illuminating the sights and sounds (and smells) of the region's bygone era of labor-intensive fish processing, this is an excellent museum in a former working cannery. Most of the machinery remains and there's an evocative focus on the people who used to work here. You'll hear recorded testimonies from old 'slimers' percolating through the air like ghosts and see large black-and-white blow-ups of the real staff who spent their days immersed in entrails. Take one of the free hourly tours, often run by former employees.

Summer Night Market MARKET
(www.summernightmarket.com; 12631 Vulcan Way; ⊙7pm-1am Fri & Sat, 7pm-midnight Sun mid-May–early Oct) Much larger than downtown's Chinatown version, thousands of hungry locals are lured here every weekend to check out the tacky vendor stands and – more importantly – the dozens of hawker food stalls. Don't eat before arriving and you can taste-trip through steaming Malaysian, Korean, Japanese and Chinese treats.

Britannia Shipyard MUSEUM
(www.britannia-hss.ca; 5180 Westwater Dr; ⊙10am-6pm Tue-Sun May-Sep, 10am-4pm Sat & noon-4pm Sun Oct-Apr) A fascinating museum site of creaky old sheds housing dusty tools, boats and reminders of the region's gritty maritime past.

Kuan Yin Temple NOTABLE BUILDING
(Map p41; www.buddhisttemple.ca; 9160 Steveston Hwy; admission free; ⊙9:30am-5:30pm) Modeled on Beijing's Forbidden City, this temple's highlight is its sumptuous Gracious Hall, complete with deep-red and gold exterior walls and a gently flaring orange porcelain roof.

🛏 Sleeping & Eating

Fairmont Vancouver Airport HOTEL $$
(✆604-207-5200, 866-540-1414; www.fairmont.com/vancouverairport; Vancouver International Airport; r from $169; ❋🔊🌊) You can't stay any closer to the airport than this luxury, amenity-laden hotel, reached by a walkway from the US departure hall. A great

IDYLLIC ISLAND JAUNT

Just because you've found yourself running out of road in shoreline West Vancouver, it doesn't mean you have to end your adventures. You can hit the Horseshoe Bay ferry terminal – with or without your car – for a quick hop over to **Bowen Island**. Once a favored summertime retreat for colonials looking for a seaside escape from the hard work of building the province, it's now populated by a friendly clutch of writers and artists.

Once you're there – the breathtaking crossing over the glassy, tree-lined water takes around 20 minutes – you'll find yourself in a rustically charming little community that suddenly feels a million miles from big city life. Drop into the **visitor centre** (www.bowenchamber.com; 432 Cardena Rd; ⊙10am-5pm Thu-Sun mid-May–early Sep, reduced off-season) for a crash course on what to do...then set about doing it.

Scenic kayaking tours are offered by **Bowen Island Sea Kayaking** (☑604-947-9266, 800-605-2925; www.bowenislandkayaking.com; rentals 3hr/day $45/70, tours from $65). But just strolling the many relatively easy forest trails – and stopping for a picnic overlooking the waterfront – is always a good idea.

You'll likely spend a lot of time clattering along the boardwalk area near the ferry dock. This is where you'll find **Doc Morgan's Restaurant & Pub** (mains $8-22), where the chatty patios overlook the park and the harbor. Pub grub is the main focus here and the fish and chips are recommended. If you enjoy yourself so much that you decide to stay, you're only a short stroll from the **Lodge at the Old Dorm** (☑604-947-0947; www.lodgeattheolddorm.com; 460 Melmore Rd; r $95-150), a character-filled B&B dripping with art deco and arts-and-crafts accents. The six rooms are bright and comfortable – the Lady Alexandra room with its own private garden is our favorite – and the continental buffet breakfast, served on a central counter in the kitchen, is full of yummy home-baked treats. In fact, you'll probably already be considering moving here permanently.

option for boarding your long-haul flight in a trance-like state of calm. The rooms are elegantly furnished with high-end flourishes, including remote-controlled drapes and marble-lined bathrooms.

Stone Hedge B&B　　　　B&B $$
(☑604-274-1070; www.thestonehedge.com; 5511 Cathay Rd; s/d from $125/140; ▓) This surprisingly peaceful B&B is named after the large stone wall and formidable cedar hedge surrounding the property. Rooms are tastefully lined with reproduction antiques and landscape paintings. The best feature is the chintzy guest lounge, which opens directly onto a large, secluded swimming pool.

Pajo's　　　　SEAFOOD $
(www.pajos.com; the Wharf, Steveston; mains $6-9) It's hard to think of a better spot to enjoy fish and chips than Steveston's boat-bobbling wharf. Luckily, this floating, family-run local legend fully delivers. Peruse the fresh catches on the backs of the nearby fishing boats, then follow your nose down the ramp to Pajo's little ordering hatch. You'll be greeted by a friendly face and a menu more extensive than your average chippy. Go the traditional fresh-fried cod,

salmon or halibut route (with secret-recipe tartar sauce) or mix things up with a yellowfin tuna burger and zucchini sticks.

Shanghai River Restaurant　　　CHINESE $$
(7381 Westminster Hwy; mains $6-18) Grab a seat overlooking the kitchen window at this cavernous contemporary northern Chinese eatery and you'll be mesmerized by the work that goes into folding what are among the best Vancouver-area dim-sum dumplings. Order shareable plates - one dish per person is best - and be careful not to squirt everyone with the delicate but ultrajuicy pork or shrimp dumplings. The braised duck and ham soup is a great winter warmer.

SEA TO SKY HIGHWAY

Otherwise known as Hwy 99, this picturesque cliffside roadway links the communities between West Vancouver and Lillooet and is the main route to Whistler from Vancouver and the Lower Mainland. Recently upgraded for the Olympics, the winding route has several worthwhile stops – especially if you're an outdoor-activity fan, history buff or lover of BC's variegated mountain landscape. 'The Mountain' radio station (107.1FM in Squamish, 102.1FM in Whistler) provides handy traffic and road-condition updates en route.

Squamish & Around

POP 15,000

Situated midway between Vancouver and Whistler, Squamish sits at the meeting point of ocean, river and alpine forest. Originally just a grungy logging town, it's now a popular base for outdoor activities, especially in summer. Head to the slick visitor center, named the Squamish Adventure Centre (☎604-815-4994, 866-333-2010; www.tourismsquamish.com; 38551 Loggers Lane; ⊙8am-8pm Jun-Sep, 9am-6pm Oct-May), to see what's on offer. It has lots of good info and maps on area hiking and biking trails.

⊙ Sights & Activities

Just before town, on Hwy 99, the Britannia Mine Museum (www.britanniaminemuseum. ca; adult/child $19.75/12.75; ⊙9am-4:30pm) is a popular stop. Once the British Empire's largest copper mine, it's been preserved with an impressive recent restoration. The underground train tour into the pitch-black mine tunnels is a highlight and there are plenty of additional kid-friendly exhibits – including gold panning – as well as a large artsy gift shop. Plans are afoot for enhanced attractions and facilities in the next few years, so check ahead to see what's new.

About 4km before you reach Squamish, you'll hear the rushing waters of Shannon Falls Provincial Park (www.bcparks.ca). Pull into the parking lot and stroll the short trail to BC's third-highest waterfall, where water cascades down a 335m drop. A few picnic tables make this a good stopping point for an alfresco lunch.

Continuing your drive, you'll soon see a sheer, 652m-high granite rock face looming ahead. Attracting hardy climbers, it's called 'The Chief' and it's the highlight of Stawamus Chief Provincial Park (www.bcparks. ca). You don't have to be geared up to experience the summit's breathtaking vistas: there are hiking routes up the back for anyone who wants to have a go. Consider Squamish Rock Guides (www.squamishrock guides.com; guided climbs half-/full day from $75/115) for climbing assistance or lessons.

The 100 or so trails around Squamish draw plenty of mountain-bike enthusiasts. The **Cheekeye Fan trail** near Brackendale has some easy forested rides, while downhill thrill seekers will prefer the **Diamond**

WORTH A TRIP

WHERE BC BEGAN

Little Fort Langley's tree-lined streets and 19th-century storefronts make it one of the Lower Mainland's most picturesque historic villages, ideal for an afternoon away from Vancouver. Its main historic highlight is the colorful Fort Langley National Historic Site (www.pc.gc.ca/fortlangley; 23433 Mavis Ave; adult/child $7.80/3.90; ⊙9am-8pm Jul & Aug, 10am-5pm Sep-Jun), perhaps the region's most important old-school landmark.

A fortified trading post since 1827, this is where James Douglas announced the creation of BC in 1858, giving the site a legitimate claim to being the province's birthplace. With costumed reenactors, re-created artisan workshops and a gold-panning area that's very popular with kids (they also enjoy charging around the wooden battlements) this is an ideal place for families who want to add a little education to their trips.

If you need an introduction before you start wading into the buildings, there's a surprisingly entertaining time-travel-themed movie presentation on offer. And make sure you check the website before you arrive: there's a wide array of events that bring the past evocatively back to life, including a summertime evening campfire program that will take you right back to the pioneer days of the 1800s.

If you're driving from Vancouver, take Hwy 1 east for 40km, then take the 232nd St exit north. Follow the signs along 232nd St until you reach the stop sign at Glover Rd. Turn right here, and continue into the village. Turn right again on Mavis Ave, just before the railway tracks. The fort's parking lot is at the end of the street.

If traveling by transit, take the SkyTrain from downtown to Surrey Central Station, then transfer to bus 501, 502 or 320 to Langley. Transfer in Langley to the C62 and alight at the intersection of 96 Ave and Glover Rd. The fort is a signposted 400m walk from here.

Head/Power Smart area, where the routes have inviting names like **Dope Slope** and **Icy Hole of Death**. Drop in on **Corsa Cycles** (www.corsacycles.com; 830-1200 Hunter Pl; bike rental per day $45; ◷9:30am-5:30pm) for rentals and trail advice. Also check the website of the **Squamish Off Road Cycling Association** (www.sorca.ca).

Historic-train nuts should continue just past town to the smashing **West Coast Railway Heritage Park** (www.wcra.org; 39645 Government Rd; adult/child $15/10; ◷10am-5pm). This large, mostly alfresco museum is the final resting place of BC's legendary *Royal Hudson* steam engine and has around 90 other historic railcars, including 10 working engines and the original prototype SkyTrain car. Check out the handsome new Roundhouse building, housing the park's most precious trains and artifacts.

If you prefer to travel under your own steam, **Squamish Spit** is a kiteboarding (and windsurfing) hot spot; the season runs from May to October. The website of the **Squamish Windsports Society** (www.squamishwindsports.com) is your first point of contact for weather and water conditions and information on access to the spit.

🛏 Sleeping & Eating

Howe Sound Inn & Brewing Company

INN $$

(☏604-892-2603; www.howesound.com; 37801 Cleveland Ave; r $119; 🕿) Quality rustic is the approach at this comfortable sleepover: rooms are warm and inviting with plenty of woodsy touches. There's an outdoor climbing wall where you can train for your attempt on the nearby Stawamus Chief and a sauna where you can recover afterwards. The downstairs brewpub is worth a visit even if you're not staying – yam fries and Oatmeal Stout are recommended.

Alice Lake Provincial Park   CAMPGROUND $

(☏800-689-9025; www.discovercamping.ca; campsites from $24) A large, family-friendly campground, 13km north of Squamish, with more than 100 sites. There are two shower buildings with flush toilets, and campers often indulge in activities like swimming, hiking and biking (rentals available). Consider an interpretive ranger tour through the woods (July and August only). Reserve ahead – this is one of BC's most popular campsites.

Squamish Inn on the Water   HOTEL $$

(☏604-892-9240, 800-449-8614; www.innonthewater.com; 38222 Hwy 99; d/r/ste from $28.50/79/139; 🕿) This attractive, lodge-style hotel, complete with hardwood floors and a sun-bathed riverfront patio, is just a short walk (via tunnel) to the downtown core. The lodge suites and rooms are contemporary and comfortable and there are also a few small, good-value dorm rooms with large bathrooms – you'll have to ask about these (and book ahead) since the hotel doesn't advertise them.

Grilled Fromage   SANDWICH SHOP $

(www.grilledfromage.com; 38134 Cleveland Ave; mains $4-9) If you thought a grilled cheese sandwich was just that, step inside this funkily painted spot and peruse the menu of more than 50 varieties. The Napoleon (Camembert and bacon on sourdough) is popular but go for the decadent High Roller (lobster and smoked Gruyère).

Sunflower Bakery Cafe   CAFE $

(www.sunflowerbakerycafe.com; 38086 Cleveland Ave; mains $4-9) This bright and breezy spot serves fresh wraps and bagel sandwiches plus an array of chunky cakes and bulging fruit pies that will have you committing to some heavy exercise. Good coffee pit stop.

❶ Getting There & Away

Greyhound Canada (www.greyhound.ca) buses arrive in Squamish from Vancouver ($17, 1½ hours, seven daily) and Whistler ($14, one hour, eight daily). Slightly more salubrious **Pacific Coach Lines** (www.pacificcoach.com) buses also arrive here from downtown Vancouver ($39.20, 1½ hours, up to eight daily).

Garibaldi Provincial Park

Visiting outdoor types often make a beeline for the 1950-sq-km **Garibaldi Provincial Park** (www.bcparks.ca), justly renowned for hiking trails colored by diverse flora, abundant wildlife and panoramic wilderness vistas. Summer hikers seem magnetically drawn here but the trails also double as cross-country ski routes in winter. There are five main trail areas – directions to each are marked by the blue-and-white signs you'll see off Hwy 99.

Among the park's most popular trails, the **Cheakamus Lake hike** (3km) is relatively easy with minimal elevation. Also in this area, and just outside the provincial park, the BC Forest Service's 30-sq-km **Whistler Interpretive Forest** offers a lot of summer activities, including kayaking, fishing and mountain biking. The trailhead is 8.5km from Hwy 99, opposite Function Junction at the south end of Whistler.

The **Elfin Lakes trail** (11km) is a lovely, relatively easy day hike. For overnighters, the trail continues on to the extinct volcano of Opal Cone. There's a first-come, first-served overnight shelter once you reach Elfin, and backcountry camping ($5) is available at Red Heather, 5km from the parking lot. The trailhead parking lot is 16km east of Hwy 99.

The **Garibaldi Lake hike** (9km) is an outstanding introduction to 'Beautiful BC' wilderness, fusing scenic alpine meadows and breathtaking mountain vistas. The bright aqua hue of the undisturbed lake contrasts with the dark, jagged peak of Black Tusk rising behind it. Backcountry campsites ($5) are further up the trail at Taylor Meadows, on the lake's western shoreline.

Brandywine Falls Provincial Park

A few kilometers north of Squamish and adjacent to Hwy 99, this tree-lined 143-hectare park (www.bcparks.ca) is centered on a spectacular 70m waterfall. A short stroll through the forest leads to a leg-jellying platform overlooking the top of the falls, where water drops suddenly out of the trees like a giant faucet. There are also great vistas over Daisy Lake and the mountains of Garibaldi Provincial Park. A 7km looped trail leads further through the dense forest and ancient lava beds to Cal-Cheak Suspension Bridge.

WHISTLER

POP 9200

Named for the furry marmots that populate the area and whistle like deflating balloons, this gabled alpine village is one of the world's most popular ski resorts. It was home to many of the outdoor events at the 2010 Winter Olympic and Paralympic Games, so feel free to slip on your skis and aim (if only in your imagination) for a gold medal of your own.

Nestled in the shade of the formidable Whistler and Blackcomb Mountains, the wintertime village has a frosted, Christmas card look. But summer is also a popular time, with Vancouverites and international travelers lured to the lakes and crags by a wide array of activities, from mountain biking to scream-triggering zipline runs.

Centered on four main neighborhoods – approaching via Hwy 99 from the south, you'll hit Creekside first – Whistler Village is the key hub for hotels, restaurants and shops. You'll find humbler B&B-type accommodations in the quieter Village North, while the Upper Village is home to some swanky hotels, clustered around the base of Blackcomb. Don't be surprised if you get lost when you're wandering around on foot, though there are plenty of street signs and lots of people around to help with directions.

◉ Sights

The dramatic wood-beamed Squamish Lil'wat Cultural Centre (www.slcc.ca; 4854 Blackcomb Way; adult/child/youth $18/8/11; ⊙9:30am-5pm) showcases two quite different First Nations groups – one coastal and one interior based – with museum exhibits and artisan presentations. Entry starts with a 15-minute movie and includes a self-guided tour illuminating the heritage and modern-day indigenous communities of the region. There's a wealth of art and crafts on display (check out the amazing two-headed sea serpent carving near the entrance) and the energetic young staff encourage plenty of questions about their twin cultures.

Perched just above the village on Blackcomb, Whistler Sliding Centre (www.whistler slidingcentre.com; 4910 Glacier Lane; adult/child $7/free; ⊙10am-5pm) hosted Olympic bobsled, luge and skeleton events and is now open to the public. You can wander exhibits and check out video footage from the track or take a general tour (adult/child $15/free) or behind-the-scenes tour (adult/child $69/59).

The recently revamped Whistler Museum (www.whistlermuseum.org; 4333 Main St; adult/child $7/4; ⊙11am-5pm) traces the area's dramatic development, with some colorful exhibits plus evocative photos of old skiing gear and the region's pre-resort days. There's also plenty of information on the 2010 Olympics if you missed it (as well as recollections of the previous Games bid).

If you're here in summer, head to the Upper Village and the plaza in front of the Fairmont Chateau Whistler for the lively Whistler Farmers Market (www.whistler farmersmarket.org; ⊙11am-4pm Sun, mid-Jun–mid-Oct), where you can peruse the arts and crafts and stuff your face with seasonal fruits and bakery treats.

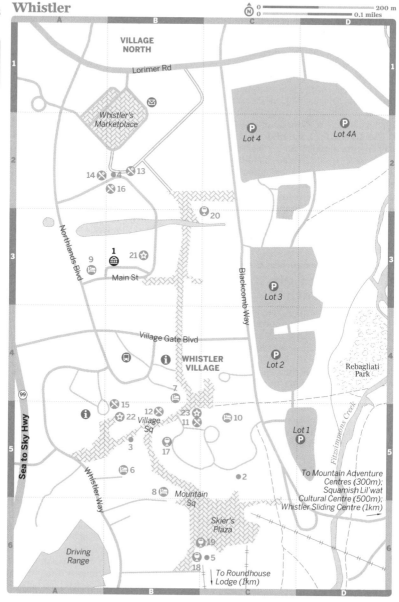

🏃 Activities

Skiing & Snowboarding

Comprising 38 lifts and almost 34 sq km of skiable terrain, criss-crossed with over 200 runs (more than half aimed at intermediate-level skiers), the **Whistler-Blackcomb** (www. whistlerblackcomb.com; 1-day lift ticket adult/child/youth $93/46/78) sister mountains were physically linked for the first time in 2009. The resort's mammoth 4.4km **Peak 2 Peak Gondola** includes the world's longest unsupported span and takes 11 minutes to

BRITISH COLUMBIA ACTIVITIES

shuttle wide-eyed powder hogs between the two high alpine areas, so you can hit the slopes on both mountains on the same day.

The winter season kicks off here in late November and runs to April on Whistler and June on Blackcomb – December to February is the peak. If you want to emulate your fave Olympic ski heroes, Whistler Creekside was the setting for all the 2010 downhill skiing events.

You can beat the crowds with an early-morning **Fresh Tracks ticket** (adult/child $17.25/12.60), which must be bought in advance at Whistler Village Gondola Guest Relations. The price includes a buffet breakfast at the Roundhouse Lodge up top. Night owls might prefer the evening **Night Moves** (adult/child $18/12) program operated via Blackcomb's Magic Chair lift after 5pm.

Snowboard fans should also check out the freestyle terrain parks, mostly located on Blackcomb, including the Snow Cross and the Big Easy Terrain Garden. There's also the popular Habitat Terrain Park on Whistler.

If you didn't bring you own gear, **Mountain Adventure Centres** (www.whistlerblackcomb.com/rentals; 1-day ski or snowboard rental adult/child from $46/32) has several equipment rental outlets around town. It offers online reservations – choose your favorite gear before you arrive – as well as lessons for ski and snowboard first timers.

Cross-country Skiing & Snowshoeing

A pleasant stroll or free shuttle bus away from the village, **Lost Lake** (www.crosscount ryconnection.bc.ca; day pass adult/child/youth $17/8.50/10; ⊙8am-9pm) is the hub for 22km of wooded cross-country ski trails, suitable for novices and experts alike. Around 4km of the trail is lit for nighttime skiing until 10pm and there's a handy 'warming hut' providing lessons and equipment rentals. Snowshoers are also well served in this area: you can stomp off on your own on 10km of trails or rent equipment and guides.

The **Whistler Olympic Park** (www.whistlerolympicpark.com; 5 Callaghan Valley Rd, Callaghan Valley) is 16km southwest of the village via Hwy 99. It hosted the 2010 Olympic biathlon, Nordic combined, cross-country skiing and ski jumping events. While the site was still being prepared on our visit after the Games, it's expected to become a prime area for public cross-country skiing and snowshoeing. Check the venue's website for the latest information.

For snowshoeing tours – including a three-hour fondue excursion – check in with **Outdoor Adventures Whistler** (www.adventureswhistler.com; 4205 Village Sq; adult/child from $69/39). Prices include equipment rentals and the company also offers a wide array of other tours and activities.

Mountain Biking

Taking over the melted ski slopes in summer and accessed via the lift at the village's south end, **Whistler Mountain Bike Park** (www.whistlerbike.com; 1-day pass adult/child/youth $53/29/47; ⊙10am-8pm mid-Jun–Aug, 10am-5pm May–mid-Jun & Sep–mid-Oct) offers barreling downhill runs and an orgy of jumps, beams and bridges twisting through 200km of well-maintained forested trails. You don't have to be a bike courier to stand the knee-buckling pace: easier routes are marked in green, while blue intermediate trails and black-diamond advanced paths are offered if you want to **Crank It Up** – the name of one of the park's most popular routes. The park stages well-attended **women's nights** on Mondays and Wednesdays.

Outside the park area, winding trails around the region include **Comfortably Numb** (a tough 26km with steep climbs and bridges), **A River Runs Through It** (suitable for all skill levels, it has teeter-totters and log obstacles), and the gentle **Valley Trail**, an easy 14km loop that encircles the village and its lake, meadow and mountain-chateau surroundings – this is recommended for first timers.

Hiking

With more than 40km of flower-and-forest alpine trails, most accessed via the Whistler Village Gondola, the region is ideal for those who like nature of the strollable variety. Favorite routes include the **High Note Trail** (8km), which traverses pristine meadows and has stunning views of the blue-green waters of Cheakamus Lake. Route maps are available at the visitor centre. Guided hikes are also offered by the friendly folk at Whistler Alpine Guides Bureau (www.whistler guides.com; 19-4314 Main St; guided hikes adult/child from $79/59), who can also help with rock-climbing and rap-jumping excursions.

Rafting

Tumbling waterfalls, dense forest and a menagerie of wildlife are some of what you might see as you lurch along the Elaho or Squamish Rivers on an adrenalin-charged half- or full-day rafting trip. Whistler River Adventures (www.whistlerriver.com; Whistler Village Gondola; adult/child/youth from $95/59/75) offers five paddle-like-crazy-or-you'll-never-make-it excursions, including the popular Green River trip, a white-water roller-coaster that'll have you whimpering and getting your pants wet just like a baby.

✪ Festivals & Events

WinterPRIDE   COMMUNITY
(www.gaywhistler.com) A week of gay-friendly snow action and late-night partying in early February.

TELUS World Ski & Snowboard Festival   SKIING
(www.wssf.com) In mid-April, a nine-day showcase of pro ski and snowboard competitions.

Kokanee Crankworx   BIKING
(www.crankworx.com) An adrenalin-filled celebration of bike stunts, speed and shenanigans in mid-July.

Cornucopia   FOOD, WINE
(www.whistlercornucopia.com) Bacchanalian mid-November food and wine fest.

Whistler Film Festival   ARTS
(www.whistlerfilmfestival.com) Four days of Canadian and independent movie screenings, plus industry schmoozing, in late November.

🛏 Sleeping

Winter is the peak for prices here, but last-minute deals can still be had if you're planning an impromptu overnight from Vancouver – check the website of Tourism Whistler (www.whistler.com) for room sales and packages. Most hotels extort parking fees (up to $20 daily) and some also slap on resort fees (up to $25 daily) – confirm these before you book.

TOP CHOICE **Nita Lake Lodge**   HOTEL **$$$**
(☎604-966-5700, 888-755-6482; www.nitalakelodge.com; 2135 Lake Placid Rd; r from $250; ☎) Adjoining Creekside train station – handy if you're coming up on the Rocky Mountaineer Sea to Sky Climb – this swanky timber-framed lodge is perfect for a pampering retreat. Hugging the lakeside, the chic but cozy rooms feature individual patios, rock fireplaces and bathrooms with heated floors and large tubs – they also have little kitchenettes with microwaves and fridges. There's a good on-site restaurant but a free shuttle can whisk you to the village if you want to dine further afield. Creekside lifts are a walkable few minutes away.

Adara Hotel   HOTEL **$$**
(☎604-905-4665, 866-502-3272; www.adara hotel.com; 4122 Village Green; r from $160; ❋☎) Unlike all those smaller lodges now claiming to be boutique hotels, the sophisticated and centrally located Adara was built from scratch as the real deal. Lined with sparse but knowing designer details – including fake antler horns in the lobby – the accommodations have spa-like bathrooms, flat-screen TVs and iPod docking stations (the

WIRED FOR FUN

Stepping out into thin air 70m above the forest floor might seem like a normal activity for a cartoon character but ziplining turns out to be one of the best ways to encounter the Whistler wilderness. Attached via a body harness to the cable you're about to slide down, you soon overcome your fear of flying solo. By the end of your time in the trees, you'll be turning midair summersaults and whooping like a banshee. The two cool courses operated by **Ziptrek Ecotours** (www.ziptrek.com; adult/child from $99/79) are strung between Whistler and Blackcomb mountains and operate in both winter and summer seasons. Its newer **TreeTrek guided canopy walk** (adult/child $39/29) is a gentle web of walkways and suspension bridges for those who prefer to keep their feet on something a little more solid than air. It's ideal for families.

front desk will loan you an iPod if you've left yours at home). Despite the ultracool aesthetics, service is warm and relaxed.

HI Whistler Hostel HOSTEL $
(☎604-962-0025; www.hihostels.ca; 1035 Legacy Way; dm/r $39/153; ☎◉) Replacing Whistler's former too-small HI, this smashing new hostel repurposes part of the 2010 Olympic athletes village near Function Junction – it's 7km south of town with transit bus access. The large, lodge-like building with its IKEA-esque furnishings includes 188 beds in four-bed dorms as well as 14 sought-after en suite private rooms. There's a well-equipped kitchen plus a BBQ deck and cafe.

Riverside RV Resort & Campground
CAMPGROUND $
(☎604-905-5533; www.whistlercamping.com; 8018 Mons Rd; tent sites/cabins/yurts $35/159/99; ◉) This warm and friendly RV property, a few minutes' drive past Whistler on Hwy 99, recently restored its tent camping spots and has also added some cool new yurts to its cozy cabins. The yurts have basic furnishings and electricity (bring your own sleeping bag) and they also have a dedicated service block with hot showers. The resort's on-site Junction Café serves great breakfasts (have the salmon eggs Benedict).

Crystal Lodge HOTEL $$
(☎604-932-2221, 800-667-3363; www.crystal-lodge.com; 4154 Village Stroll; d/ste from $130/175; ☀☀◉) Not all rooms are created equal at the Crystal, a central sleepover forged from the fusion of two quite different hotel towers. Cheaper rooms in the South Tower are standard motel-style – baths and fridges are the highlight – but those in the Lodge Wing match the splendid rock-and-beam lobby, complete with small balconies. Both share excellent proximity to village

restaurants and are less than 100m from the main ski lift.

Chalet Luise B&B $$
(☎604-932-4187, 800-665-1998; www.chaletluise.com; 7461 Ambassador Cres; r from $125; ☎) A five-minute trail walk from the village, this recently renovated, Bavarian-look pension has eight bright and sunny rooms – think pine furnishings and crisp white duvets – and a flower garden that's ideal for a spot of evening wine quaffing. Or you can just hop in the hot tub and dream about the large buffet breakfast coming your way in the morning. Free parking.

Edgewater Lodge HOTEL $$
(☎604-932-0688, 888-870-9065; www.edgewater-lodge.com; 8020 Alpine Way; r from $150; ☎) A few minutes' drive past Whistler on Hwy 99, this 12-room lakeside lodge is a nature lover's idyll and has a celebrated on-site restaurant. Each room overlooks the glassy water through a large picture window – sit in your padded window alcove and watch the ospreys or hit the surface with a kayak rental.

Blackcomb Lodge HOTEL $$
(☎604-935-1177, 888-621-1117; www.whistlerpremier.com; 4220 Gateway Dr; r/ste from $109/139; ☀◉☀) With an excellent Village Sq location, the top rooms here have deep leather sofas, dark-wood furnishings and full kitchens, while the standard rooms without kitchens are almost as comfortable. Very close to grocery and liquor stores.

UBC Whistler Lodge HOSTEL $
(☎604-822-5851; www.ubcwhistlerlodge.com; 2124 Nordic Dr; dm summer/winter $30/40) Up a steep hill in the Nordic residential neighborhood, facilities are basic and quirky (bunks are built into the walls; rooms are separated by curtains) but the rates are a bargain.

Fairmont Chateau Whistler HOTEL **$$$**
(☎604-938-8000, 800-606-8244; www.fairmont.
com/whistler; 4599 Chateau Blvd; r from $350)
Dramatic baronial lodge lobbies and com-
fortably palatial rooms, many with moun-
tain views. Close enough to enjoy ski-in,
ski-out privileges on Blackcomb.

Whistler Village Inn & Suites HOTEL **$$**
(☎604-932-4004, 800-663-6418; www.whistler
villageinnandsuites.com; 4429 Sundial Pl; d/ste
$119/139; ☒ ☷) Recently renovated twin-
lodge sleepover with rustic chic rooms
and a free breakfast buffet. Good central
location.

Pinnacle International Hotel HOTEL **$$**
(☎604-938-3218, 888-999-8986; www.whistler
pinnacle.com; 4319 Main St; d from $139; ☎☒☷)
Friendly, well-established, adult-oriented
lodge with Jacuzzi tubs in most rooms.

✘ Eating

RimRock Café WEST COAST **$$**
(☎604-932-5565; www.rimrockwhistler.com; 2117
Whistler Rd; mains $16-22) On the edge of
Creekside and accessible just off Hwy 99,
the menu at this locals' favorite includes
highlights like seared scallops, venison
tenderloin and a recommended Seafood
Trio of grilled prawns, ahi tuna and nut-
crusted sablefish. All are served in an intimate room with two fireplaces and a large,
flower-lined patio where you can laugh at
the harried highway drivers zipping past.

Araxi Restaurant & Lounge
WEST COAST **$$$**
(☎604-932-4540; www.toptable.ca; 4222 Village
Sq; mains $30-45) Whistler's best splurge
restaurant, Araxi chefs up an inventive
and exquisite Pacific Northwest menu plus
charming and courteous service. Try the
BC halibut and drain the 15,000-bottle
wine selection but save room for a dessert:
a regional cheese plate or the amazing
Okanagan apple cheesecake...or both.

Christine's Mountain Top Dining
CANADIAN **$$**
(☎604-938-7437; Rendezvous Lodge, Blackcomb
Mountain; mains $12-22) The best of the hand-
ful of places to eat while you're enjoying a
summertime summit stroll or winter ski
day on the slopes at Blackcomb Mountain.
Socked into the Rendezvous Lodge, try for
a view-tastic patio table and tuck into a seasonal seafood grill or a lovely applewood
smoked cheddar grilled cheese sandwich.
Reservations recommended.

Crepe Montagne FRENCH **$$**
(www.crepemontagne.com; 4368 Main St; mains
$8-14) This small, authentic creperie – hence
the French accents percolating among the
staff – offers a bewildering array of sweet
and savory buckwheat crepes with fillings
including ham, brie, asparagus, banana,
strawberries and more. Good breakfast
spot: go the waffle route and you'll be per-
fectly set up for a day on the slopes.

Beet Root Café CAFE **$**
(29-4340 Lorimer Rd; light mains $6-11) The
best home-style hangout in town, pull up
a cushion by the window, make yourself at
home and tuck into fresh-made soup, bulg-
ing sandwiches or the excellent breakfast
burritos. Stick around until you smell the
cookies emerging from the oven, then scoff
yourself into a happy stupor.

Gone Village Eatery CANADIAN **$**
(www.gonevillageeatery.com; 4205 Village Sq; mains
$6-12; ☎) Hidden behind Armchair Books,
this chatty, wood-floored haunt serves
hearty breakfast grub (have the omelet bur-
rito), lunch specials (sandwiches, falafel or
the $10 burger-and-beer deal do the trick)
and any-time-of-day baked treats (snag a
chewy toffee cookie). Also a good spot to fire
up your laptop and update your travel blog.

Roundhouse Lodge FAST FOOD **$**
(Whistler Mountain; mains from $6) Handily
located at the junction of several ski lifts,
most powder hogs hit the Roundhouse at
least once during their day atop Whistler
Mountain. The giant, food-court-style ap-
proach delivers plenty of choice, so you
shouldn't have any trouble stuffing your
face with burgers, pizza and fish and
chips. Alternatively, kick it up a notch with
Steeps Grill, a full-service Roundhouse
joint with great views and lip-smacking
seafood chowder.

Sachi Sushi JAPANESE **$$**
(106-4359 Main St; mains $8-22) Whistler's
best sushi spot doesn't stop at California
rolls. Serving everything from crispy pop-
corn shrimp to seafood salads and stom-
ach-warming udon noodles (the tempura
noodle bowl is best), this bright and breezy
eatery is a relaxing après hangout. Consider
a glass of hot sake on a cold winter day.

21 Steps Kitchen & Bar CANADIAN **$$**
(www.21steps.ca; St Andrews House; mains
$14-22) With small plates for nibblers, the
main dishes at this cozy upstairs spot have

a high-end comfort-food approach. Not a great place for vegetarians – unless you like stuffed Portobello mushroom – with steak, chops and seafood featuring heavily. Check out the great attic bar, a Whistlerite favorite.

Drinking & Entertainment

Garibaldi Lift Company PUB
(Whistler Village Gondola) The closest bar to the slopes – watch the powder geeks or bike nuts on Whistler Mountain skid to a halt from the patio – the GLC is a rock-lined cave of a place. It's the ideal spot to absorb a Kootenay Mountain Ale and a bulging GLC burger while you rub your muscles and exchange exaggerated stories about your epic battles with the mountain.

Whistler Brewhouse BREWERY
(www.markjamesgroup.com; 4355 Blackcomb Way) This lodge-like drinkery crafts its own beer on the premises and, like any artwork, the natural surroundings inspire the masterpieces, with names like Lifty Lager and Twin Peaks Pale Ale. It's an ideal pub if you want to hear yourself think, or if you just want to watch the game on one of the TVs. The food, including pasta, pizza and fish and chips, is superior to standard pub grub.

Amsterdam Café Pub PUB
(www.amsterdampub.com; Village Sq) A brick-lined party joint with a neighborhood-pub vibe, this bar is in the heart of the village action and offers lots of drinks specials – the Alexander Keith's Pale Ale is recommended. You can treat your hangover to a late breakfast the next day by coming in for a good-value fry-up.

Longhorn Saloon & Grill PUB
(www.longhornsaloon.ca; 4290 Mountain Sq) Fanning out near the base of Whistler Mountain with a patio that threatens to take over the town, this local legend feels like it's been here since the first skier turned up. The pub food is nothing special but it's hard to beat the atmosphere on a hopping winter evening.

Garfinkels NIGHTCLUB
(www.garfswhistler.com; 1-4308 Main St) Mixing mainstream dance grooves with a few live bands, Whistler's biggest club is ever-popular. Arrive early on weekends when it's especially packed.

Moe Joe's NIGHTCLUB
(www.moejoes.com; 4155 Golfer's Approach) More intimate than Garfinkels, this is the best place in town if you like dancing

yourself into a drooling heap. It's always crowded on Friday nights.

Village 8 Cinema CINEMA
(www.village8.ca; Village Stroll) Shows first-run flicks in the heart of the village.

Information

Pick up the *Pique* or *Whistler Question* newspapers for further local insights.

Armchair Books (www.whistlerbooks.com; 4205 Village Sq; ⊙9am-9pm) Central bookstore with strong travel section.

Custom House Currency Exchange (4227 Village Stroll; ⊙9am-5pm May-Sep, 9am-6pm Oct-Apr) Handy central exchange.

Northlands Medical Clinic (www.northlandsclinic.com; 4359 Main St; ⊙9am-5:30pm) Walk-in medical center.

Post office (106-4360 Lorimer Rd; ⊙8am-5pm Mon-Fri, 8am-noon Sat)

Public Library (www.whistlerlibrary.ca; 4329 Main St; ⊙11am-7pm Mon-Sat, 11am-4pm Sun; 🛜) Internet access per 10 minutes $2.50; register at front desk.

Whistler Activity Centre (4010 Whistler Way; ⊙10am-6pm) Recommendations and bookings for local activities.

Whistler visitor center (www.whistler.com; 4230 Gateway Dr; ⊙8am-8pm) Flyer-lined visitor center with friendly staff.

Getting There & Around

While most visitors arrive by road from Vancouver via Hwy 99, you can also fly in on a **Whistler Air** (www.whistlerair.ca) floatplane to Green Lake (from $149, 30 minutes, two daily May to September).

Greyhound Canada (www.greyhound.ca) buses arrive at Creekside and Whistler Village from Vancouver (from $25, 2¾ hours, seven daily) and Squamish ($14, one hour, eight daily).

SkyLynx motor coach services from **Pacific Coach Lines** (www.pacificcoach.com) also arrive from Vancouver (from $35, 3½ hours, six daily) and Vancouver International Airport and drop off at Whistler hotels. **Snowbus** (www.snowbus.com) operates a winter-only service from Vancouver ($21, three hours, two daily).

Train spotters can trundle into town on Rocky Mountaineer Vacations' **Whistler Sea to Sky Climb** (www.rockmountaineer.com), which winds along a picturesque coastal route from North Vancouver (from $129, three hours, one daily May to mid-October).

Whistler's **WAVE** (www.busonline.ca) public buses (adult/child/one-day pass $2/1.50/5) are equipped with ski and bike racks. In summer, there's a free service from the village to Lost Lake.

SUNSHINE COAST

Stretching 139km along the water from Langdale to Lund, the Sunshine Coast – separated from the Lower Mainland by the Coast Mountains and the Strait of Georgia – has an independent, island-like mentality that belies the fact that it's only a 40-minute ferry ride from Horseshoe Bay. With Hwy 101 linking key communities like Gibsons, Sechelt and Powell River, it's an easy and convivial region to explore and there are plenty of available activities to keep things lively: think kayaking and scuba diving with a side order of artists' studios for good measure. Check the website of Sunshine Coast Tourism (www.sunshinecoastcanada.com) for information and pick up a copy of the *Recreation Map & Attractions Guides* ($3) for activities around the region.

ℹ️ Getting There & Around

BC Ferries (www.bcferries.com) services arrive at Langdale, 6km northeast of Gibsons, from West Vancouver's Horseshoe Bay (passenger/vehicle $12.85/43.20, 40 minutes, eight daily). Reservations recommended in summer. **Sunshine Coast Transit System** (www.busonline.ca; adult/child $2.25/1.75) runs bus services from the terminal into Gibsons, Roberts Creek and Sechelt.

Malaspina Coach Lines (www.malaspinacoach.com) buses arrive twice daily (once a day offseason) from Vancouver, via the ferry, in Gibsons ($30, two hours), Roberts Creek ($32, 2½ hours), Sechelt ($40, three hours) and Powell River ($58, five to six hours). Rates include the ferry fare.

Gibsons

POP 4100

Your first port of call after docking in Langdale and driving on to town, Gibsons' pretty waterfront strip is named Gibsons Landing and it's a rainbow of painted wooden buildings perched over the marina. Famous across Canada as the setting for *The Beachcombers,* a TV show filmed here in the 1970s that fictionalized a town full of eccentrics, the place hasn't changed much since. Head up the incline from the water and you'll hit the shops on the main drag of Upper Gibsons and Hwy 101.

Once you've finished wandering the town, kayak rentals and tours are available from the friendly folk at Sunshine Kayaking (www.sunshinekayaking.com; Molly's Lane; rentals 4hr/24hr $40/75; ⊘9am-6pm Mon-Fri, 8am-6pm Sat & Sun). Its guided sunset ($65) and full-moon ($65) tours are especially recommended.

Your best bet for a bed in the area is Soames Point B&B (☑604-886-8599, 877-604-2672; www.soamespointbb.com; 1000B Marine Dr; d from $159), an immaculate and tranquil sleepover with breathtaking waterfront views. The large suite has a private entrance, vaulted ceilings and its own deck, a great spot for breakfast. At the end of the day, you can head down to the water where another deck, complete with seats and a BBQ, is ideal for a glass of wine.

While the best spot in town for a hearty breakfast and comfort food of the fish-

---

WORTH A TRIP

DETOUR TO COWBOY COUNTRY

The next town after Whistler on Hwy 99, friendly Pemberton (www.pemberton.ca) has a welcoming vibe and a distinctive provenance as a farming and cowboy region – which explains why the town's kitsch-cool mascot is a potato in a neckerchief called Potato Jack. Mosey on in and you'll find the area's valley location creates a milder climate than Whistler in winter – it's often much warmer in summer, too. Visitors, generally outdoorsy types, spend their time horse riding, with operators including Pemberton Stables (www.pembertonstables.ca; tours $45-120) and Adventures on Horseback (www.adventuresonhorseback.ca; 2hr tours from $75). But consider a little flying she-nanigans instead: Pemberton Soaring Centre (www.pembertonsoaring.com) offers 15-minute taster trips in two-person gliders (the pilot does all the work) for $94, while a spectacular 50-minute glide over the glaciers and snowcapped peaks costs $237. Sliding silently over the toy-town meadows and checking out the imposing mountains close up will likely be one of the highlights of your BC visit. Visit the town's website for a few more activity ideas. Better still, just drop into the ever-animated Pony Espresso (www.ponyespresso.ca; 1392 Portage Rd; mains $8-14), where the locals will be hanging out and chatting over fresh-made pasta and sandwich dishes. Time your visit for Thursday evening's beer and pizza night and you'll likely meet every Pembertonian in town.

and-chips variety is Molly's Reach (www.mollysreach.ca; 647 School Rd; mains $7-12), where you should certainly aim for a window seat, gourmet seafood fans shouldn't miss Smitty's Oyster House (www.smittysoysterhouse.com; 643 School Rd; mains $12-26), tucked just underneath. Regionally sourced and perfectly prepared treats here include Fanny Bay oysters and golden halibut fritters.

Drop by the visitor centre (604-886-2374, 866-222-3806; www.gibsonschamber.com; 417 Marine Dr; 9am-5pm Jul & Aug, reduced off-season) for information and resources.

Roberts Creek

POP 3100

Roberts Creek Rd, off Hwy 101, leads to the center of this former hippy enclave that retains a distinctly laid-back vibe. Follow the road through the village and amble out onto **Roberts Creek Pier**, overlooking the Strait of Georgia. Backed by a large waterfront park (there's a beach here at low tide), it's an idyllic spot to watch the natural world float by. West of town, Roberts Creek Provincial Park (www.bcparks.ca) is another beachfront picnic spot.

Exactly what a great hostel should be, the laid-back Up the Creek Backpackers (604-885-0384, 877-885-8100; www.upthecreek.ca; 1261 Roberts Creek Rd; dm/r $26/75; @) has small dorms, one private room and a predilection for recycling. The local bus stops just around the corner, so you're encouraged to arrive here by transit – loaner bikes are offered to get you around once you've unpacked.

For something a little more upmarket, the Artist & the Quiltmaker B&B (604-741-0702, 866-570-0702; www.theartistandthequiltmaker.com; 3173 Mossy Rock Rd; d from $125) is a three-room, Victorian-style property that's well worth a stop. Its large upstairs suite, complete with kitchenette, is popular with families but the lovely Renaissance Room is perfect for romantic canoodling.

For sustenance, the ever-popular Gumboot Restaurant (1041 Roberts Creek Rd; mains $7-14) is ideal for rubbing shoulders with the locals and scoffing a hearty dinner – check out those organic buffalo burgers and bulging, veggie-friendly Gumboot Garden sandwiches.

For more information on the area, visit www.robertscreek.com.

POP 8500

A useful base for active travelers, with plenty of hiking, biking, kayaking and diving opportunities, Sechelt is the second-largest town on the Sunshine Coast. It also has plenty of pit-stop amenities if you're just passing through.

With a good kayak launch site and a sandy, stroll-worthy beach, fir- and-cedar-forested Porpoise Bay Provincial Park (www.bcparks.ca) is 4km north of Sechelt along East Porpoise Bay Rd. There are trails throughout the park and an 84-site campground (www.discovercamping.ca; campsite $24) with handy hot showers.

For visiting paddlers (and pedalers), Pedals & Paddles (www.pedalspaddles.com; Tillicum Bay Marina; rentals 4hr/24hr $40/75) organizes kayak rentals or takes you on one of the tours of the inlet's wonderfully tranquil waters.

Alternatively, chat with local artists and growers at the summertime Sechelt Farmers & Artisans Market (www.secheltmarket.com; 8:30am-1:30pm Sat Apr-Sep), in the parking lot of the Raven's Cry Theatre, or stick around for the mid-August Sunshine Coast Festival of the Written Arts (www.writersfestival.ca).

If you feel like splurging on a sleepover, it's worth continuing your drive along Hwy 101 past Sechelt to Rockwater Secret Cove Resort (604-885-7038, 877-296-4593; www.rockwatersecretcoveresort.com; 5356 Ole's Cove Rd; r/cabin/ste/tent $209/209/249/419;), where the high-light accommodations are luxury tent suites perched like nests on a steep cliff. About as far from camping as you can get, each canvas-walled cabin has a heated rock floor, Jacuzzi tub and a private deck overlooking the bay. The resort has a good west-coast restaurant (mains $16 to $28), but if you want to hang out with the locals, head to the Lighthouse Pub (5764 Wharf Rd; mains $8-16), a lively neighborhood haunt where you can eavesdrop on debates about whether Gibsons is better than Powell River, while feasting on hearty pub grub and boat-bobbling waterfront vistas.

For information, drop by the visitor centre (604-885-1036, 877-885-1036; www.secheltvisitorcentre.com; 5790 Teredo St; 9am-5pm daily Jul & Aug, 9am-5pm Mon-Sat Jun & Sep, 10am-4pm Mon-Sat Oct-May).

SUNSHINE COAST GALLERY CRAWL

While you're pootling along Hwy 101, keep your eyes peeled for a jaunty purple flag or two fluttering in the breeze. The flags indicate that an artist is at work on the adjoining property. Pick up the *Sunshine Coast Purple Banner* flyer from area visitor centers and galleries and it will tell you where the artists are located – just in case you miss the flags – and if they're available for a drop-in visit – some prefer that you call ahead. The region is studded with art and crafts creators, working with wood, glass, clay, jewelry and just about everything else. For further information, check www.suncoastarts.com.

Powell River

POP 13,000

A short ferry hop along Hwy 101 brings you to this vibrant former resource town, which has a strong claim to being the heart and soul of the Sunshine Coast. Funkier than Sechelt and busier than Gibsons, Powell River is well worth a sleepover and is a hot spot for outdoor activities – drop by the **visitor centre** (☎604-485-4701, 877-817-8669; www.discoverpowellriver.com; 111-4871 Joyce Ave; ⊙9am-9pm Mon-Fri, 10am-6pm Sat & Sun May-Sep, 9am-5pm Mon-Fri Oct-Apr) for tips and information.

West of downtown, **Willingdon Beach City Park** is ideal for a waterfront picnic. The fascinating **Powell River Museum** (www.powellrivermuseum.ca; 4798 Marine Ave; adult/child $2/1; ⊙9am-4:30pm Jun-Aug, 9am-4:30pm Mon-Fri Sep-May) nearby houses a shack once occupied by Billy Goat Smith, a hermit who lived here (with his goats) in the early 1900s. Alternatively, hit the water with a kayak from **Powell River Sea Kayak** (www.bcseakayak.com; 3hr/12hr rental $35/44).

For a quirky, creaky-floored sleepover, the character-packed **Old Courthouse Inn** (☎604-483-4000, 877-483-4777; www.oldcourthouseinn.ca; 6243 Walnut St; s/d $94/109) occupies the town's former court chambers and police station. In keeping with the historic theme, its rooms are handsomely decorated with antique furnishings.

At the end of a long day of exploring, it's hard to beat a brew and a hearty meal at the **Shinglemill Pub & Bistro** (www.shinglemill.net; 6233 Powell Pl; mains $8-16). But if you're looking for something a little bit fancier, try the **Alchemist Restaurant** (www.alchemistrestaurant.com; 4680 Marine Ave; mains $19-33), where local seasonal ingredients are fused with French Mediterranean approaches to produce mouthwatering mains such as pan-seared scallops and rack of lamb served with goat-cheese ravioli. Save some room and time to sit back with the artisan cheese plate.

VANCOUVER ISLAND

The largest populated landmass off the North American coast – it's around 500km long and 100km wide – Vancouver Island is laced with colorful, often quirky communities, many founded on logging or fishing and featuring the word 'Port' in their name.

Despite the general distaste among residents for the 'too busy' mainland – a distaste that often comes from people who've never actually left the island – the locals are usually a friendly and welcoming bunch, proud of their region and its distinct differences. If you want to make a good impression, don't refer to the place as 'Victoria Island,' a frequent mistake that usually provokes involuntary eye rolls and an almost imperceptible downgrading of your welcome.

While Victoria itself – the history-wrapped BC capital that's stuffed with attractions – is the first port of call for many, it should not be the only place you visit here. Food and wine fans will enjoy weaving through the verdant Cowichan Valley farm region; those craving a laid-back, family-friendly enclave should hit the twin seaside towns of Parksville and Qualicum; outdoor-activity enthusiasts shouldn't miss the surf-loving west-coast area; and those who fancy remote backcountry far from the madding crowds should make for the north island region, an undiscovered gem that's among BC's most rewarding wilderness areas.

For an introduction to the island, contact **Tourism Vancouver Island** (☎250-754-3500; www.vancouverisland.travel) for listings and resources.

Victoria

POP 78,000

With a population approaching 350,000 when you add in the suburbs, this picture-postcard provincial capital was long touted as North America's most English city. This was a surprise to anyone who actually came from Britain, since Victoria promulgated a dreamy version of England that never really was: every garden (complete with the occasional palm tree) was immaculate; every flagpole was adorned with a Union Jack; and every afternoon was spent quaffing tea from bone-china cups.

Thankfully this tired theme-park version of Ye Olde England has gradually faded in recent years. Fuelled by an increasingly younger demographic, a quiet revolution has seen lame tourist pubs, eateries and stores transformed into the kind of bright-painted bohemian shops, wood-floored coffee bars and surprisingly innovative restaurants that would make any city proud. It's worth seeking out these enclaves on foot but activity fans should also hop on their bikes: Victoria has more cycle routes than any other Canadian city. Once you've finished exploring, there's also BC's best museum, a park that's licked with a windswept seafront and outdoor activities that include whale-watching and kayak adventures.

⊙ Sights

TOP\
CHOICE **Royal BC Museum** MUSEUM
(Map p92; www.royalbcmuseum.bc.ca; 675 Belleville St; adult/child $14.29/9.06; ⊘10am-5pm) At the province's best museum, start at the 2nd-floor natural-history showcase fronted by a beady-eyed woolly mammoth and lined with realistic dioramas – the forest of elk and grizzlies peeking from behind trees is highly evocative. Then peruse the First Peoples exhibit and its deep exploration of indigenous culture, including a fascinating mask gallery (look for the ferret-faced white man). The best area, though, is the walk-through recreated street that re-animates the early colonial city, complete with a chatty Chinatown, highly detailed stores and a little movie house showing Charlie Chaplin films. The museum also has an **IMAX theatre**.

FREE **Parliament Buildings** HISTORICAL BUILDING
(Map p92; www.leg.bc.ca; 501 Belleville St; ⊘8:30am-5pm daily May-Sep, 8:30am-5pm Mon-Fri Oct-Apr) Across from the museum, this surprisingly handsome (despite its glorious confection of turrets, domes and stained glass) building is the province's working legislature but it's also open to history-loving visitors. Peek behind the facade on a colorful 30-minute **tour** led by costumed Victorians, then stop for lunch at the 'secret' politicians' restaurant (see p95). Come back in the evening when the building's handsome exterior is lit up like a Christmas tree.

Art Gallery of Greater Victoria ART GALLERY
(Map p90; www.aggv.bc.ca; 1040 Moss St; adult/child $13/2.50; ⊘10am-5pm Mon-Wed, Fri & Sat, 10am-9pm Thu, noon-5pm Sun) Head east of downtown on Fort St and follow the gallery signs to find one of Canada's best Emily Carr collections. Aside from Carr's swirling nature canvases, you'll find an ever-changing array of temporary exhibitions. Check online for events, including lectures, presentations and even singles' nights for lonely arts fans.

Craigdarroch Castle MUSEUM
(Map p90; www.thecastle.ca; 1050 Joan Cres; adult/child $13.75/5; ⊘9am-7pm mid-Jun–Aug, 10am-4:30pm Sep–mid-Jun) If you're in this part of town checking out the gallery, don't miss this elegant turreted mansion a few minutes' walk away. A handsome, 39-room landmark built by a 19th-century coal baron with money to burn, it's dripping with period architecture and antique-packed rooms. Climb the tower's 87 steps (check out the stained-glass windows en route) for views of the snowcapped Olympic Mountains.

Victoria Bug Zoo ZOO
(Map p92; www.bugzoo.com; 631 Courtney St; adult/child/youth $9/6/8; ⊘10am-5pm Mon-Sat, 11am-5pm Sun, reduced off-season) The most fun your wide-eyed kids will have in Victoria without even realizing it's educational, step inside the bright-painted main room for a cornucopia of show-and-tell insect encounters. The excellent guides handle and talk about critters like frog beetles, dragon-headed crickets and the disturbingly large three-horned scarab beetles, before releasing their audience (not the insects) into the gift shop.

Beacon Hill Park PARK
(Map p92) Fringed by the crashing ocean, this dramatic green space is a great spot to weather a wild storm – check out the wind-swept trees along the cliff top. You'll also find one of the world's tallest totem poles, a Victorian cricket pitch and a marker for Mile 0 of Hwy 1, alongside a statue of Terry

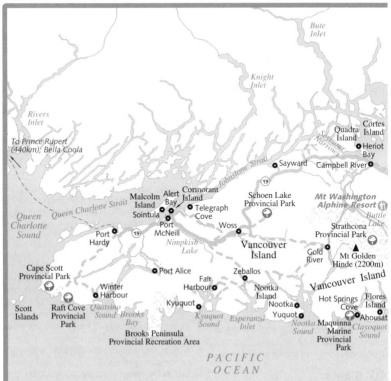

Fox, the one-legged runner whose attempted cross-Canada trek gripped the nation in 1981. If you're here with kids, check out the **children's farm** with its baby goats and wandering peacocks.

Emily Carr House   MUSEUM
(Map p90; www.emilycarr.com; 207 Government St; admission by donation; ⊙11am-4pm Tue-Sat May-Sep) The birthplace of BC's best-known painter, this bright-yellow, gingerbread-style house has plenty of period rooms and displays on the artist's life and work. There's an ever-changing array of local contemporary works on display but head to the **Art Gallery of Greater Victoria** (p87) if you want to see more of Carr's paintings.

🏃 Activities
Whale-watching
Raincoat-clad tourists head out by the boatload from Victoria throughout the May-to-October viewing season. The whales don't always show, so most excursions also visit the local haunts of elephant seal and sea lions.

Operators include the following:

Prince of Whales
(Map p92; ☎250-383-4884, 888-383-4884; www.princeofwhales.com; 812 Wharf St; adult/child $100/80) Long-established local operator.

Springtide Charters
(Map p92; ☎250-384-4444, 800-470-3474; www.springtidecharters.com; 1111 Wharf St; adult/child $99/69) Popular local operator.

Kayaking
Ambling around the coast of Vancouver Island by kayak is the perfect way to see the region, especially if you come across a few soaring eagles, lolling seals and an occasional starfish-studded beach. You can rent equipment for your own trek or join a tour of the area's watery highlights.

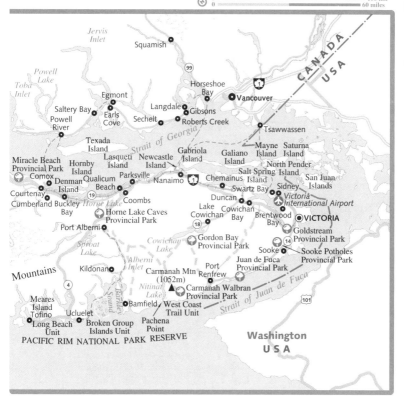

Some operators:

Ocean River Sports

(Map p92; ☎250-381-4233; www.oceanriver. com; 1824 Store St; rental 2 hr/24hr $30/48; ⏰9:30am-6pm Mon-Wed & Sat, 9:30am-8pm Thu & Fri, 10am-5pm Sun) Popular 2½-hour harbor tours ($65).

Sports Rent

(Map p92; ☎250-385-7368; www.portsrentbc. com; 1950 Government St; canoe rental 5hr/24hr $39/49; ⏰9am-5:30pm Mon-Thu, 9am-6pm Fri, 9am-5pm Sat, 10am-5pm Sun) Rents equipment like canoes as well as bikes, tents, wetsuits etc.

Scuba Diving

The region's dive-friendly underwater ecosystem includes many popular spots such as Ogden Point Breakwater and 10 Mile Point.

Some established equipment rental and guide operators:

Frank Whites Dive Store

(Map p92; ☎250-385-4713; 1620 Blanshard St; www.frankwhites.com; ⏰9am-5:30pm) Scuba equipment rentals and courses.

Ogden Point Dive Centre

(☎250-380-9119, 888-701-1177; www.divevictoria. com; 199 Dallas Rd; ⏰9am-6pm) Courses, rentals etc a few minutes from the Inner Harbour.

☞ Tours

Architectural Institute of BC WALK

(Map p92; ☎604-683-8588 ext 333, 800-667-0753; www.aibc.ca; 1001 Douglas St; tours $5; ⏰1pm Tue-Sat Jul & Aug) Five great-value, building-themed walking tours covering angles from art deco to ecclesiastical.

Harbour Air Seaplanes PLANE

(Map p92; ☎800-665-0212, 604-274-1277; www.harbour-air.com; tours from $99) For a bird's-eye Victoria view, the 30-minute floatplane tour from the Inner Harbour

BRITISH COLUMBIA VANCOUVER ISLAND

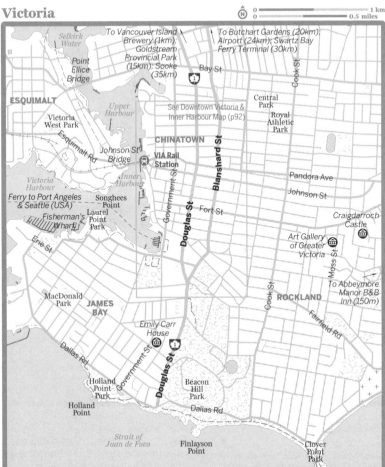

is fab – especially when it dive-bombs the water on landing.

Cycle Treks   BIKE
(Map p92; ☑250-386-2277, 877-733-6722; www.cycletreks.com; 1000 Wharf St; tours from $99; ⏰9:30am-6pm Mon-Sat) Leads six-hour seafront-themed cycling tours.

Vancouver Island Brewery   BREWERY
(Map p90; ☑250-361-0005; www.vanisland brewery.com; 2330 Government St; tour $6; ⏰3pm Fri & Sat) Offers 30-minute tours of the plant followed by four-sample tasting.

Big Bus Victoria   BUS
(Map p92; ☑250-389-2229, 888-434-2229; www.bigbusvictoria.ca; 811 Government St; adult/child $35/17) Offers 90-minute hop-on, hop-off tours around 22 local points of interest.

✹✸ Festivals & Events

Dine Around Stay in Town   FOOD
(www.tourismvictoria.com/dinearound) Three weeks of bargain *prix fixe* meals at many restaurants around the city; mid-February.

STROLLABLE 'HOODS

Sometimes you just need to abandon the guidebook and go for a wander. Luckily, compact and highly walkable downtown Victoria is ideal for that. Start your amble in **Chinatown**, at the handsome gate near the corner of Government and Fisgard Sts. One of Canada's oldest Asian neighborhoods, this tiny strip of businesses is studded with neon signs and traditional grocery stores, while **Fan Tan Alley** – a narrow passageway between Fisgard St and Pandora Ave – is a miniwarren of traditional and trendy stores hawking cheap and cheerful trinkets, cool used records and funky artworks. Consider a guided amble with **Hidden Dragon Tours** (www.oldchinatown. com; adult/child $29/14.50). Its three-hour evening lantern tour will tell you all about the area's historic opium dens and the hardships of 19th-century immigration.

Next up, head over to **Bastion Sq**, located between Government and Wharf Sts. Occupying the site of the old Fort Victoria, this pedestrianized plaza of scrubbed colonial strongholds is also home to the **Maritime Museum of British Columbia** (Map p92; www.mmbc.bc.ca; 28 Bastion Sq; adult/child/youth $12/6/7; ⊙9:30am-5pm mid-Jun–mid-Sep, 9:30am-4:30pm mid-Sep–mid-Jun), where 400 model ships illuminate the region's rich and salty nautical heritage.

Victoria Day Parade　　　　FIESTA
Mid-May street fiesta shenanigans with dancers and marching bands.

Victoria SkaFest　　　　MUSIC
(www.victoriaskafest.ca) Canada's largest ska music event, held in mid-July.

Victoria International Jazzfest　　JAZZ
(www.jazzvictoria.ca) Nine days of jazz performance in late June.

Moss Street Paint-In　　　　ART
(www.aggv.bc.ca) In mid-July 100 artists demonstrate their skills at this popular one-day community event.

Victoria Fringe Theater Festival　THEATER
(www.victoriafringe.com) Two weeks of quirky short plays staged throughout the city in late August.

🛏 Sleeping

From heritage B&Bs to midrange motels and swanky high-end sleepovers, Victoria is stuffed with accommodations options for all budgets. Off-season sees some great deals and Tourism Victoria's **room reservation service** (☑250-953-2033, 800-663-3883; www.tourismvictoria.com) can let you know what's available.

Swans Suite Hotel　　　HOTEL $$$
(Map p92; ☑250-361-3310, 800-668-7926; www.swanshotel.com; 506 Pandora Ave; d/ste $199/289; ☎) Across the street from the tiny railway station – you'll hear the train toot into town twice a day – this former old brick warehouse has been transformed into an art-lined boutique sleepover. Most rooms are spacious loft suites where you climb upstairs to bed in a gabled nook, and each is decorated with a comfy combination of wood beams, rustic chic furniture and deep leather sofas. The full kitchens are handy but continental breakfast is included.

Fairmont Empress Hotel　　HOTEL $$$
(Map p92; ☑250-384-8111, 866-540-4429; www.fairmont.com/empress; 721 Government St; r from $189; ❄@☂) Rooms at this ivy-covered, century-old Inner Harbour landmark are elegant but conservative and some are quite small, but the overall effect is grand and classy – from the Raj-style curry restaurant to the high tea sipped while overlooking the waterfront. Even if you don't stay, make sure you stroll through and soak up the ambience.

Parkside Victoria Resort & Spa HOTEL $$$
(Map p92; ☑250-716-2651, 866-941-4175; www.parksidevictoria.com; 810 Humboldt St; ste from $269; ☎☂) A slick new apartment-style hotel a couple of blocks from the Inner Harbour, with the comfortable, well-equipped rooms ideal if you want a home-style base steps from the city center. Full kitchens, balconies and a gym might make you want to move in permanently. There's also an on-site mini-cinema screening nightly free flicks.

Hotel Rialto　　　　　HOTEL $$
(Map p92; ☑250-382-4157, 800-332-9981; www.hotelrialto.ca; 653 Pandora Ave; r $139-249; ☎) Completely refurbished from the faded former budget hotel it used to be, the new Rialto is a well-located downtown option

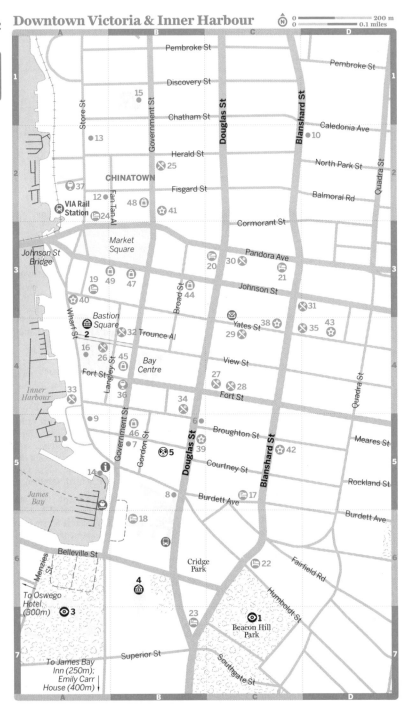

BRITISH COLUMBIA VANCOUVER ISLAND

BRITISH COLUMBIA VICTORIA

in an attractive century-old heritage building. Each of the 38 mod-decorated rooms has a fridge, microwave and flat-screen TV and some have tubs as well as showers. The lobby's tapas lounge is justifiably popular, whether or not you're staying here.

Oswego Hotel HOTEL **$$**
(☎250-294-7500, 877-767-9346; www.oswegovictoria.com; 500 Oswego St; d/ste from $159/229) Victoria's swankiest newer hotel is a designer lounge sleepover in a quiet residential location. Rooms come with granite floors, cedar beams and (in most units) small balconies. All have kitchens (think stainless steel) and deep baths, making them more like apartments than hotel suites. Cleverly, the smaller studio rooms have space-saving high-end Murphy beds.

Spinnakers Guesthouses B&B **$$**
(☎250-384-2739; www.spinnakers.com; 308 Catherine St; r/ste from $159/259; 🐾) A short stumble from its own celebrated brewpub (p96), this clutch of adult-oriented guesthouses combines luxury details with pampering home comforts. The Heritage House is a restored 1884 family home with antiques, fireplaces and private patios. The larger Garden Suites have a contemporary feel and a smattering of Asian design flourishes. Gourmet continental breakfast is included.

James Bay Inn INN **$$**
(☎250-384-7151, 800-836-2649; www.jamesbayinn.com; 270 Government St; r from $129) A few minutes' walk from the Emily Carr House, this quirky charmer has a well-maintained, retro feel. The charm might wear off when

you realize there's no elevator but once you lug your bags up the stairs, you'll find a vast array of room types: most have busy-patterned carpets and furniture that's old but not quite antique. There are some kitchenettes but the downstairs neighborhood bar also serves decent pub grub.

Ocean Island Inn
HOSTEL **$**

(Map p92; ☎250-385-1788, 888-888-4180; www. oceanisland.com; 791 Pandora Ave; dm/s/d from $27.50/30/55; @☎) This funky, multicolored sleepover is a labyrinth of dorms and private rooms – ask for one with a window. There's a large communal kitchen on the ground floor and a licensed lounge for quiz nights and open mikes. It also offers private, self-catering suites across town in a James Bay character house (from $128) – see www.oisuites.com for information.

HI Victoria Hostel
HOSTEL **$**

(Map p92; ☎250-385-4511, 888-883-0099; www. hihostels.ca; 516 Yates St; dm/d $31.50/78; @☎) A well-located, quiet hostel with two large single-sex dorms, three small co-eds and a couple of private rooms. While an extensive reno was being planned at the time of our visit, it's currently a little institutionalized with basic dorms, a large games room and a book-lined reading area. Free weekly city tours are offered.

Abbeymoore Manor
B&B **$$**

(☎250-370-1470, 888-801-1811; www.abbey moore.com; 1470 Rockland Ave; r from $165; ☎) A romantic 1912 arts-and-crafts mansion, Abbeymoore's handsome colonial exterior hides seven antique-lined rooms furnished with Victorian knickknacks. Some rooms have kitchens and jetted tubs.

Queen Victoria
HOTEL **$$**

(Map p92; ☎250-386-1312, 800-663-7007; www.qvhotel.com; 655 Douglas St; d/ste from $133/152; ✻☎) A well-maintained tower-block property near the Inner Harbour with rooms that have a business-hotel feel. All have balconies and handy fridges; some also have kitchenettes.

Chateau Victoria Hotel & Suites
HOTEL **$$**

(Map p92 ☎250-382-4221, 800-663-5891; www.chateauvictoria.com; 740 Burdett Ave; d/ ste/penthouse from $152/202/400; ✻@✻) There's a well-maintained '80s feel at this perfectly located tower-block hotel but the rooms are clean and many have handy kitchens. The hotel's top-floor restaurant has breathtaking views.

Eating

Formerly dominated by tourist traps serving nothing but poor-quality fish and chips, Victoria's dining scene has radically transformed in recent years. Pick up *Eat Magazine* (free) to see what's on the menu and keep in mind that hours are often extended ad hoc in summer.

⬆TOP⬆ CHOICE Fort Café
CANADIAN **$**

(Map p92; 742 Fort St; mains $6-10; ☎) This warm and inviting subterranean hipster haunt offers the perfect combination of great comfort food and cool digs. Among the heaping fresh-made nosh, the turkey avocado wraps and hot pepper beef sandwiches are stand-outs, while there's also a rare offering of all the Salt Spring Brewing beers on draft. Check out the Atari game system around the corner at the back, or drop in for Friday's massively popular quiz night (doors open 7:30pm). If you miss it, there's a shelf of board games to keep you busy. Also check out its cool-ass coffee-shop satellite called **Picnic** (506 Fort St).

Hernandéz
MEXICAN **$**

(Map p92; www.hernandezcocina.com; just off 750 Yates St; mains $5-8) Inauspiciously hidden in a covered passageway between Yates and View Sts, Victoria's best Mexican hole-in-the-wall has a queue of slavering locals as soon as it opens. Vegetarian options abound but the *huarache de pollo* – thick tortilla with chicken – is legendary and goes perfectly with a local Phillips Brewing beer. There are never enough available tables, so consider packing your butcher-paper parcel and heading to Beacon Hill Park for a picnic. Cash only.

Red Fish Blue Fish
SEAFOOD **$**

(Map p92; www.redfish-bluefish.com; 1006 Wharf St; mains $6-10) On the waterfront boardwalk at the foot of Broughton St, this freight-container takeout shack serves a loyal clientele who just can't get enough of its fresh-made sustainable seafood. Highlights like scallop tacones, wild salmon sandwiches, tempura battered fish and chips and the signature chunky Pacific Rim chowder all hit the spot: find a waterfront perch to enjoy your nosh but watch for hovering seagull mobsters.

Camille's
WEST COAST **$$**

(Map p92; ☎250-381-3433; www.camilles restaurant.com; 45 Bastion Sq; mains $18-26) A charming subterranean dining room with a lively, ever-changing menu reflecting whatever the chef can source locally and seasonally, perhaps ranging from pan-seared BC duck and sweet spot prawns to breathtaking desserts packed with local fruits and berries. With a great wine menu, this spot invites adventurous foodies to linger. Recommended for a romantic night out.

John's Place BREAKFAST, CANADIAN **$$**
(Map p92; www.johnsplace.ca; 723 Pandora Ave; mains $7-17) Victoria's best weekend brunch spot, this wood-floored, high-ceilinged heritage room is lined with funky memorabilia and the menu is a cut above standard diner fare. It'll start you off with a basket of addictive house-made bread, but save room for heaping pasta dishes or a Belgian waffle breakfast. And don't leave without trying a thick slab of pie from the case at the front.

Brasserie L'Ecole FRENCH **$$**
(Map p92; ✆250-475-6260; www.lecole.ca; 1715 Government St; mains $20-24) This country-style French bistro has a warm, casual atmosphere and a delectable menu. Locally sourced produce is de rigueur, so the dishes constantly change to reflect seasonal highlights like figs, salmonberries and heirloom tomatoes. We recommend the lamb shank, served with mustard-creamed root vegetables and braised chard. Beer fans will also love the bottled French, Belgian and Quebec brews.

Dutch Bakery BAKERY **$**
(Map p92; www.thedutchbakery.com; 718 Fort St; mains $4-7) A charming downtown institution that's been packing them in for decades with its Formica counter tops, old-lady ambience and simple light meals and cream-packed cakes. Chat up the regulars and they'll recommend a beef pie with potato salad followed by a fruit-pie chaser. Peruse the handmade candies near the entrance and pick up some marzipan teeth or sprinkle-topped chocolate coins for the road.

Pig BBQ Joint SANDWICH SHOP **$**
(Map p92; www.pigbbqjoint.com; 1325 Blanshard St; sandwiches $5-6) This vegetarian-free hole-in-the-wall is all about the meat, specifically bulging, Texas-style pulled-pork sandwiches (beef brisket and smoked-chicken variations are also offered). Expect lunchtime queues (better to arrive early or late) and consider perking up your order with a side of succulent cornbread or pail of house-made ice tea. Plans were afoot to open a second larger venue around the corner at the time of our visit – stay tuned.

Tibetan Kitchen ASIAN FUSION **$**
(Map p92; www.tibetankitchen.ca; 680 Broughton St; mains $7-15) Lunch specials are an excellent deal (check the board outside) at this cozy, wood-lined South Asian eatery. Start with some shareable openers like veggie pakoras and paneer poppers, then move on to fresh-made noodle and curry mains; there are plenty of vegetarian options but the slow-cooked, ginger-infused Shepta Beef is highly recommended. Whatever you end up trying, wash it down with a lip-smacking lychee lassi.

Legislative Dining Room CANADIAN **$$**
(Map p92; room 606 Parliament Buildings; mains $6-16) One of Victoria's best-kept dining secrets, the Parliament Buildings has its own subsidized restaurant where MLAs (and the public) can drop by for a silver-service menu of regional dishes, ranging from smoked tofu salads to velvety steaks and shrimp quesadillas. It's cash only and entry is via the security desk just inside the building's main entrance.

Zambri's ITALIAN **$$**
(Map p92; www.zambris.ca; 820 Yates St; mains $20-25) Run by a second-generation Italian chef, the menu here is far from traditional trattoria fare. Unassuming from the outside, the ever-changing dishes might range from a hearty squash soup with butter-fried sage to a mouth-melting sablefish, served with rapini and poached eggs. Consider the nightly three-course tasting menu or, for the budget minded, drop by for lunch instead.

ReBar VEGETARIAN, FUSION **$$**
(Map p92; www.rebarmodernfood.com; 50 Bastion Sq; mains $9-16; ✏) A laid-back local legend, ReBar mixes colorful interiors with a natty, mostly vegetarian menu. Carnivores will be just as happy to eat here, though, with hearty savory dishes such as shitake-tofu pot stickers, Thai green curry and heaping brunches – the salmon-topped bagel melt is great. There's also a wholesome specialty juice selection (try the orange, pear and cranberry).

 Drinking

One of BC's best beer towns, Victoria offers local craft brews and a frothy array of great watering holes. Look out for tipples by local lads Phillips Brewing and Driftwood Brewery. Repeated first-hand research was undertaken for these reviews.

Spinnakers Gastro Brewpub PUB
(www.spinnakers.com; 308 Catherine St) A pioneering craft brewer, this wood-floored smasher is a short hop from the Inner Harbour but it's worth it for tongue ticklers like copper-colored Nut Brown Ale and hoppy Blue Bridge Double IPA – named after the sky-blue span that delivers most quaffers to the door. Save room to eat: the seasonal dishes – many designed for beer pairing – often include sharable platters piled high with everything from wild salmon to Cortez Island clams.

Big Bad John's PUB
(Map p92; www.strathconahotel.com; 919 Douglas St) Easily missed from the outside because of the regulars piling into the much larger but fairly generic Sticky Wicket pub adjoining it, this evocative little hillbilly theme bar feels like you've stepped into the backwoods. But rather than some dodgy banjo players with mismatched ears, you'll find good-time locals enjoying the cave-like ambience of peanut-shell-covered floors and a ceiling dotted with grubby bras. Likely the most fun you'll have in any Victoria bar.

Canoe Brewpub PUB
(Map p92; www.canoebrewpub.com; 450 Swift St) The cavernous brick-lined interior here is popular on rainy days but the patio is the best in the city with its (usually) sunny views across to the Johnson St Bridge. Indulge in on-site-brewed treats like the hoppy Red Canoe Lager and the summer-friendly Siren's Song Pale Ale. Grub is also high on the menu here with stomach-stuffing lamb potpie and wild salmon tacos recommended.

Bard & Banker PUB
(Map p92; www.bardandbanker.com; 1022 Government St) This cavernous Victorian repro pub is handsomely lined with cut-glass lamps, open fireplaces and a long granite bar topped with 30 brass beer taps. Pull up a stool and taste-test Phillips Blue Buck, Nova Scotia's Alexander Keith's and the house-brand Robert Service Ale. There's nightly live music plus a nosh menu ranging from elevated pub standards to crisp-fried squid and an artisan cheese board.

Swans Brewpub PUB
(Map p92; www.swanshotel.com; 506 Pandora Ave) This chatty, wood-beamed brewpub was formerly a grain warehouse where freight trains rolled right into the building. Great tipples include the malty Apple-

ton Brown Ale, a distinctive brew that'll make you permanently turn your back on Budweiser. Make room for a naughty beer pairing of Riley Scotch Ale and dark chocolate truffles.

☆ Entertainment

Check the freebie *Monday Magazine* weekly for listings or head online to www.livevictoria.com.

Live Music & Nightclubs

Lucky Bar NIGHTCLUB
(Map p92; www.luckybar.ca; 517 Yates St) A Victoria institution, downtown's eclectic Lucky Bar offers live music from ska and indie to electroclash. There are bands here at least twice a week, while the remaining evenings are occupied by dance-floor club nights, including Wednesday's mod fest and Saturday's mix night.

Logan's Pub LIVE MUSIC
(www.loganspub.com; 1821 Cook St) A 10-minute walk from downtown, in Cook St Village, this sports pub looks like nothing special from the outside, but its roster of shows is a fixture of the local indie scene. Fridays and Saturdays are your best bet for performances but other nights are frequently also booked – check the online calendar to see what's coming up.

Sugar LIVE MUSIC
(Map p92; www.sugarnightclub.ca; 858 Yates St) A popular, long-standing club that's been hosting a wide array of local and visiting bands for years – expect everything from Bob Marley tribute acts to a thundering visit from the Dayglo Abortions. Usually only open Thursday to Saturday, the two-floored joint hosts DJ club nights when there's no live act on board.

Element NIGHTCLUB
(Map p92; www.elementnightclub.ca; 919 Douglas St) Conveniently located under the Sticky Wicket and Big Bad John's, Element is a mainstream club hangout known for its Saturday top 40, hip-hop and R&B night. Friday is also popular and there are additional fairly regular live acts.

Theater & Cinemas

Victoria's main stages, **McPherson Playhouse** (Map p92; www.rmts.bc.ca; 3 Centennial Sq) and the rococo-interiored **Royal Theatre** (Map p92; www.rmts.bc.ca; 805 Broughton St), each offer mainstream visiting shows and performances. The latter is also home of the **Victoria Symphony** (www.victoriasymphony.bc.ca) and **Pacific Opera Victoria** (www.pov.bc.ca). A 20-minute stroll from downtown, the celebrated **Belfry Theatre** (www.belfry.bc.ca; 1291 Gladstone Ave) showcases contemporary plays in its lovely former-church-building venue.

The city's main first-run cinema is **Cineplex Odeon** (Map p92; www.cineplex.com; 780 Yates St). Art-house flicks hit the screen at UVic's **Cinecenta** (www.cinecenta.com; University of Victoria), while the Royal BC Museum's **IMAX Theatre** (Map p92; www.imaxvictoria.com) shows larger-than-life documentaries and Hollywood blockbusters.

 ## Shopping

While Government St is a magnet for souvenir shoppers, those looking for more original purchases should head to the Johnson St stretch between Store and Government. Now designated as 'LoJo' (Lower Johnson), this old-town area is a hotbed of independent stores.

Smoking Lilly CLOTHING
(Map p92; www.smokinglily.com; 569 Johnson St) LoJo's signature shop is an almost-too-tiny boutique stuffed with eclectic garments and accessories that define art-school chic. Tops and skirts with insect prints are hot items, but there are also lots of cute handbags, socks and brooches to tempt your credit card.

Ditch Records MUSIC STORE
(Map p92; www.ditchrecords.com; 635 Johnson St) This narrow, *High Fidelity*–style shop is lined with tempting vinyl and furtive musos perusing the homemade racks of releases by bands like the Meatmen and Nightmares on Wax. With its threadbare carpet and cave-like feel, it's an ideal wet Monday afternoon hangout. And if it suddenly feels like time to socialize, you can book gig tickets here, too.

Munro's Books BOOKSTORE
(Map p92; www.munrobooks.com; 1108 Government St) Like a cathedral to reading, this high-ceilinged local legend lures browsers who just like to hang out among the shelves. There's a good array of local-interest tomes as well as a fairly extensive travel section at the back on the left. Check out the racks of bargain books, too – they're not all copies of *How to Eat String* from 1972.

Rogers' Chocolates FOOD & DRINK
(Map p92; www.rogerschocolates.com; 913 Government St) This charming, museum-like confectioner has the best ice-cream bars in town but repeat offenders usually spend their time hitting the menu of rich Victoria Creams, one of which is usually enough to substitute for lunch. Flavors range from peppermint to chocolate nut and they're good souvenirs, so long as you don't scoff them all before you get home.

Silk Road FOOD & DRINK
(Map p92; www.silkroadtea.com; 1624 Government St) A pilgrimage spot for regular and exotic tea fans, you can pick up all manner of leafy paraphernalia here. Alternatively, sidle up to the tasting bar to quaff some adventurous brews. There's also a small on-site spa where you can indulge in oil treatments and aromatherapy.

Salt Spring Soapworks ACCESSORIES
(Map p92; www.saltspringsoapworks.com; 575 Johnson St) Like a candy shop for soap fans, this kaleidoscopically colored nook is stuffed with pampering bath bombs, body butters and soaps, all made just across the water on Salt Spring. If you're looking for an unexpected souvenir for that bloke in your life, the tangy wild rhubarb soap is the top seller for men.

 ## Information

Downtown Medical Centre (622 Courtney St; ☉8:30am-5pm) Handy walk-in clinic.

Main post office (Map p92; 706 Yates St; ☉9am-5pm Mon-Fri) Near the corner of Yates and Douglas Sts.

Stain Internet Café (609 Yates St; per hr $3.50; ☉10am-2am) Central and late-opening internet spot.

Visitor centre (Map p92; www.tourismvictoria.com; 812 Wharf St; ☉8:30am-8:30pm Jun-Aug, 9am-5pm Sep-May) Busy, flyer-lined visitor center overlooking the Inner Harbour.

 ## Getting There & Away

Air

Victoria International Airport (www.victoriaairport.com) is 26km north of the city via Hwy 17. **Air Canada** (www.aircanada.com) services arrive here from Vancouver (from $73, 25 minutes, up to 21 daily) while **Westjet** (www.westjet.com) flights arrive from Calgary (from $129, 1½ hours, six daily). Both airlines offer competing connections across Canada.

Harbour Air Seaplanes (www.harbour-air.com) arrive in the Inner Harbour from downtown

Vancouver ($145, 35 minutes) throughout the day. Similar **Helijet** (www.helijet.com) helicopters arrive from Vancouver (from $149, 35 minutes).

Boat

BC Ferries (www.bcferries.com) arrive from mainland Tsawwassen (adult/child/vehicle $14/7/46.75, 1½ hours) at Swartz Bay, 27km north of Victoria via Hwy 17. Services arrive hourly throughout the day in summer but are reduced off-season.

Victoria Clipper (www.clippervacations.com) services arrive in the Inner Harbour from Seattle (adult/child US$93/46, three hours, up to three a day). **Black Ball Transport** (www.ferrytovictoria.com) boats also arrive from Port Angeles (adult/child/vehicle US$15.50/7.75/$55, 1½ hours, up to four daily) as do passenger-only **Victoria Express** (www.victoriaexpress.com) services (US$10, one hour, up to three daily).

Bus

Services terminating at the city's main **bus station** (Map p92; 700 Douglas St) include **Greyhound Canada** (www.greyhound.ca) routes from Nanaimo ($23.30, 2½ hours, four daily) and Port Alberni ($40.30, four to five hours, two daily), along with frequent **Pacific Coach Lines** (www.pacificcoach.com) services from Vancouver (from $28.75, 3½ hours) and Vancouver International Airport ($40.25, four hours).

Car & Motorcycle

Budget (www.budgetvictoria.com; 757 Douglas St)

Hertz (www.hertz.ca; 2253 Douglas St)

Train

The charming **VIA Rail** (www.viarail.com) *Malahat* train arrives in the city on the Johnson St Bridge from Courtenay ($53, five hours, once a day), with additional island stops in Nanaimo, Parksville and Chemainus, among others.

ⓘ Getting Around

To/From the Airport

AKAL Airporter (www.victoriaairporter.com) minibuses run between the airport and area hotels ($19, 30 minutes). The service meets all incoming and outgoing flights. In contrast, a taxi to downtown costs around $50, while transit bus 70 takes around 35 minutes, runs throughout the day and costs $2.50.

Bicycle

Victoria is a great cycling capital with plenty of routes criss-crossing the city and beyond. Check the website of the **Greater Victoria Cycling Coalition** (www.gvcc.bc.ca) for local resources. Bike rentals are offered by **Cycle BC Rentals** (Map p92; www.cyclebc.ca; 685 Humboldt St; per hr/day $7/24; ☺9am-6pm).

Boat

Victoria Harbour Ferry (Map p92; www.victoriaharbourferry.com; tickets from $5) covers the Inner Harbour, Songhees Park (for Spinnakers Brewpub), Reeson's Landing (for the LoJo shopping area) and other stops along the Gorge Waterway with its colorful armada of bath-sized little boats.

Public Transportation & Taxi

Victoria Regional Transit (www.busonline.ca) buses (tickets adult/child $2.50/1.65) cover a wide area from Sidney to Sooke, with some routes served by modern-day double deckers. Day passes (adult/child $7.75/5.50) are also available from convenience and grocery stores. Under-fives travel free.

Established taxi providers:

BlueBird Cabs (☑250-382-2222, 800-665-7055; www.taxicab.com)

Yellow Cab (☑250-381-2222, 800-808-6881; www.yellowcabofvictoria.ca)

Southern Vancouver Island

Not far from Victoria's madding crowds, southern Vancouver Island is a laid-back region of quirky little towns that are never far from tree-lined cycle routes, waterfront hiking trails and rocky outcrops bristling with gnarly Garry oaks. The wildlife here is abundant and impressive and you'll likely spot bald eagles swooping overhead, sea otters cavorting on the beaches and perhaps the occasional orca sliding silently by just off the coast.

SAANICH PENINSULA & AROUND

Home of Vancouver Island's main regional airport and its much busier ferry terminal, this peninsula north of Victoria has more to offer than just a way to get from here to there. A languid day trip from Victoria, waterfront Sidney offers bookstore browsing, while further afield you'll find BC's most popular garden attraction.

SIDNEY

At the northern end of Saanich Peninsula, seafront Sidney is studded with around a dozen used bookstores, enabling it to call itself the region's only 'Booktown.'

If the book angle floats your boat, you can spend a leisurely afternoon ducking into the likes of Tanner's (2436 Beacon Ave), with its massive magazine and large travel-book sections; and Beacon Books (2372 Beacon Ave), with its huge array of used tomes, all guarded by Rosabelle, the portly store cat.

ON YER BIKE

Bring your bike across on the ferry from the mainland and when you arrive in Swartz Bay you can hop on to the easily accessible and well-marked **Lochside Regional Trail** to downtown Victoria. The 29km mostly flat route is not at all challenging – there are only a couple of overpasses – and it's an idyllic, predominantly paved ride through small urban areas, waterfront stretches, rolling farmland and forested countryside. There are several spots to pick up lunch en route and, if you adopt a leisurely pace, you'll be in town within four hours or so. If you've been bitten by the biking bug, consider extending your trek past Victoria on the 55km **Galloping Goose Regional Trail**. Colonizing a former 1920s railway line, it's one of the island's most popular bike routes and it will take you all the way to rustic, waterfront Sooke. While longer than its sibling, it's similarly flat most of the way, which makes it popular with the not-quite-so-hardcore biking fraternity. You can access the trail by crossing over the Johnson St Bridge from downtown Victoria; the trailhead is on your right.

The cracking Shaw Ocean Discovery Centre (www.oceandiscovery.ca; 9811 Seaport Pl; adult/child $12/6; ⊙noon-5pm) is the town's kid-luring highlight. Enter through a dramatic Disney-style entrance – it makes you think you're descending below the waves – then step into a gallery of aquatic exhibits, including mesmerizing iridescent jellyfish, spiky sea cucumbers and a large touch tank brimming with purple starfish and gelatinous anemones. Continue your marine education aboard a whale-watching boat trek with Sidney's Sea Quest Adventures (www.seaquestadventures.com; 2537 Beacon Ave; adult/child $95/79), located a few steps away.

If the sight of fish just makes you hungry, head to the end of the town's short pier and tuck into some halibut and chips at Pier Bistro (2550 Beacon Ave; mains $10-16), which serves lovely waterfront views along with its nosh. Avoid deep-fried seafood altogether with an authentic Mexican alternative – the $9.95 three-part taco plate is best – at the cheery Carlos Express (2527 Beacon Ave; mains $8-10) nearby. It runs a larger sit-down eatery a couple of blocks away if you're ready for dinner. You can also join the gossiping locals at the art-lined Red Brick Café (2423 Beacon Ave; mains 4-8), where coffee and a large ginger snap makes for an ideal pit stop: the house-made soups, chili and pizzas are deservedly popular – check the specials board before you order.

If you decide to stick around, the new Sidney Pier Hotel and Spa (☑250-655-9445, 866-659-9445; www.sidneypier.com; 9805 Seaport Pl; d/ste $159/299; @) on the waterfront fuses west-coast lounge cool with beach pastel colors. Many rooms have shoreline views – some side-on – and each has local artworks lining the walls. Also check out the lobby's unmissable artifact: a large chunk of the *Sea Shepherd* Greenpeace vessel.

On your way into 'book town', drop by the visitor centre (☑250-656-7102; www.sidney.ca; 2295 Ocean Ave; ⊙10am-4pm) for tips on bookish and non-bookish pursuits.

Victoria Regional Transit (www.busonline.ca) bus 70 trundles into Sidney from Victoria ($2.50, one hour) throughout the day.

BRENTWOOD BAY

A 30-minute drive from Victoria via West Saanich Rd, the rolling farmlands of waterfront Brentwood Bay are chiefly known for Butchart Gardens (www.butchartgardens.com; 800 Benvenuto Ave; adult/child/youth $28.10/2.86/14.05; ⊙9am-10pm mid-Jun–Aug, reduced off-season), Vancouver Island's top visitor attraction. The immaculate grounds are divided into separate gardens where there's always something in bloom. Summer is crowded, with tour buses rolling in relentlessly, but evening music performances and Saturday night fireworks (July and August) make it all worthwhile. Tea fans take note: the **Dining Room Restaurant** serves a smashing afternoon tea, complete with roast-vegetable quiches and Grand Marnier truffles...leave your diet at the door.

If you have time, also consider nearby Victoria Butterfly Gardens (www.butterflygardens.com; 1461 Benvenuto Ave; adult/child/youth $12.50/6.50/11.50; ⊙9am-5:30pm May-Aug, reduced off-season), which offers a kaleidoscope of thousands of fluttering critters (from around 75 species) in a free-flying environment. As well as watching them flit about and land on your head, you can learn about ecosystem life cycles, as well as eye-balling exotic fish, plants and birds. Look out for Spike, the red-crowned puna ibis bird that likes strutting around the trails as if he owns the place.

SOOKE & AROUND

Rounding Vancouver Island's rustic southern tip towards Sooke (a 45-minute drive from Victoria), Hwy 14 is lined with twisted Garry oaks and unkempt hedgerows, while the houses – many of them artisan workshops or homely B&Bs – seem spookily hidden in the forest shadows.

Sharing the same building (and hours) as the visitor center, the fascinating Sooke Region Museum illuminates the area's rugged pioneer days. Check out Moss Cottage in the museum grounds: built in 1869, it's the oldest residence west of Victoria.

If you're also craving a few thrills, find your inner screamer on the eight-run forested zipline course (plus two suspension bridges) operated by Adrena LINE (www.adrenalinezip.com; 5128 Sooke Rd; adult/child $95/85). Its monthly full-moon zips are the most fun and if you don't have your own transport, it'll pick you up from Victoria.

A more relaxed way to encounter the natural world is the Sooke Potholes Provincial Park (www.bcparks.ca), a 5km drive from Hwy 14 (the turnoff is east of Sooke). With rock pools and potholes carved into the river base during the last ice age, it's a popular spot for swimming and tube floating and is ideal for a summer picnic. Camping is available through the website of the Land Conservancy (www.conservancy.bc.ca; tent site $21; May-Sep).

You'll find B&Bs dotted along the route here but, for one of the province's most delightful and splurge-worthy sleepovers, head to Whiffen Spit and Sooke Harbour House (250-642-3421, 800-889-9688; www.sookeharbourhouse.com; 1528 Whiffen Spit Rd; ste from $399). Paintings, sculptures and carved wood line its interiors. Some of the 28 rooms have fireplaces and steam showers and all have views across the wildlife-strewn waterfront – look for gamboling sea otters and swooping cranes.

You won't be disappointed with the hotel's celebrated restaurant but also consider checking the town's Edge Restaurant (6686 Sooke Rd; mains $9-19), an inauspicious-looking eatery that turns out to be a gourmet revelation. Seasonal regional ingredients are the approach and everything is made from scratch. The menu is ever-changing – spend some time perusing the chalkboard – but it often includes delectables like crispy tuna or braised beef short rib. The desserts (think apple spring rolls with whipped cream cheese) are dangerously good.

For local info, chat up the friendly folk at the Sooke visitor centre (250-642-6351, 866-888-4748; www.sooke-portrenfrew.com; 2070 Philips Rd; 9am-5pm, closed Mon in winter).

JUAN DE FUCA PROVINCIAL PARK

The 47km Juan de Fuca Marine Trail (www.juandefucamarinetrail.com) in Juan de Fuca Provincial Park (www.bcparks.ca) rivals the West Coast Trail (p111) as a must-do trek for outdoorsy island visitors. From east to west, its trailhead access points are China

TIME FOR A HIKE?

About 16km from Victoria, on the Island Hwy, abundantly scenic Goldstream Provincial Park (www.bcparks.ca), at the base of Malahat Mountain, makes for a restorative nature-themed day trip from the city. Dripping with ancient, moss-covered cedar trees and a moist carpet of plant life, it's known for its chum salmon spawning season (late October to December). Hungry bald eagles are attracted to the fish and bird-watchers come ready with their cameras. Head to the park's Freeman King visitor centre (250-478-9414; 9am-4:30pm) for area info and natural history exhibits.

Aside from nature watching, you'll also find great hiking here: marked trails range from tough to easy and some are wheelchair accessible. Recommended treks include the hike to 47.5m-high Niagara Falls (not that one) and the steep, strenuous route to the top of Mt Finlayson, one of the region's highest promontories. The visitor center can advise on trails and will also tell you how to find the park's forested campground (604-689-9025, 800-689-9025; www.discovercamping.ca; campsites $24) if you feel like staying over.

Beach, Sombrio Beach, Parkinson Creek and Botanical Beach.

It takes around four days to complete the route – the most difficult stretch is between Bear Beach and China Beach – but you don't have to go the whole hog if you want to take things easier. Be aware that some sections are often muddy and difficult to hike, while bear sightings and swift weather changes are not uncommon.

The route has several basic backcountry campsites and you can pay your camping fee ($5 per person) at any of the trailheads. The most popular spot to pitch your tent is the slightly more salubrious, family-friendly **China Beach Campground** (☎604-689-9025, 800-689-9025; www.discovercamping. ca; tent sites $24), which has pit toilets and cold-water taps but no showers. There's a waterfall at the western end of the beach and booking ahead in summer is essential.

Booking ahead is also required on the **West Coast Trail Express** (☎250-477-8700, 888-999-2288; www.trailbus.com) minibus that runs between Victoria, the trailheads and Port Renfrew (from $55, daily from May to September in each direction).

Conveniently nestled between the Juan de Fuca and West Coast Trails, Port Renfrew is a great access point for either route. Quiet and often stormy during the off-season, it's usually dripping with preparing or recuperating hikers in summer.

If you've had enough of your sleeping bag, try **Port Renfrew Resorts** (☎250-647-5541; www.portrenfrewresorts.com; 17310 Parkinson Rd; d from $159), a recently refurbished waterfront miniresort with motel-style rooms and some luxurious, wood-lined cabins. Wherever you lay your head, save time for dinner and a few brews on its pub-style restaurant patio.

For a respite from campground mystery-meat pasta, the nearby **Coastal Kitchen Café** (17245 Parkinson Rd; mains $8-14) serves fresh salads and sandwiches, plus burgers and pizzas. The seafood is the star attraction, especially the Dungencss crab and chips. Hikers are often found lolling around outside on the picnic tables here.

Port renfrew has several spots to stock up on supplies or just fraternize with other trekkers and it's worth dropping by the **visitor centre** (www.portrenfrew.com; ⊙10am-6pm May-Sep) on your left as you enter town.

Cowichan Valley

A swift Hwy 1 drive northwest of Victoria, the verdant Cowichan Valley region is ripe for discovery, especially if you're a traveling foodie or you're craving some outdoor activities. Contact **Tourism Cowichan** (☎250-746-1099, 888-303-3337; www.tourismcowichan. com) for maps and information.

DUCAN
POP 5000

Originally an isolated logging-industry railroad stop – the gabled station now houses a little museum – Duncan is the Cowichan Valley's main town (officially, it's a city). A useful base for exploring the region, it's known for its dozens of totem poles, which dot the downtown core like sentinels. Sports fans should also check out the community center, which is fronted by a latter-day totem: the recently refurbished World's Largest Hockey Stick (plus puck).

If your First Nations curiosity is piqued, head to the **Quw'utsun' Cultural & Conference Centre** (www.quwutsun.ca; 200 Cowichan Way; adult/child $13/6; ⊙10am-4pm Mon-Sat Jun-Sep) to learn about carving, beading and traditional salmon runs. Its **Riverwalk Café** serves authentic First Nations cuisine.

Alternatively, drive 3km north of town to the **BC Forest Discovery Centre** (www. discoveryforest.com; 2892 Drinkwater Rd; adult/child $15/10; ⊙10am-4:30pm Jun-early Sep, reduced off-season), complete with its pioneer-era buildings, logging machinery and a working steam train.

If you're hungry, time your visit well and sample some of the region's abundant produce (and baked treats) at downtown's giant **Duncan Farmers Market** (www. marketinthesquare.net; cnr Ingram St & Market Sq; ⊙9am-2pm Sat May-Nov).

The area's chatty hub, **Duncan Garage** (3330 Duncan St; mains $4-9) is a refurbished heritage building housing a bookshop, an organic grocery store and a lively cafe where brunches, baked treats and light lunches draw locals. For more substantial fare, **Craig Street Brew Pub** (www. craigstreet.ca; 25 Craig St; mains $11-15) is a wood-floored resto-bar serving quality comfort food like jambalaya pizza and excellent own-brewed beer – try the Shawnigan Irish Ale.

LAKE COWICHAN & AROUND

West of Duncan on Hwy 18, the waterfront town of Lake Cowichan is an ideal destination for outdoorsy types. Hugging the eastern end of the lake and the adjoining Cowichan River, the town marks the end of the Trans-Canada Trail, a mammoth hiking and biking route that runs across the country from Newfoundland. While you probably won't be taking on the whole thing, you can take a photo at the grand wooden marker and tell everyone back home that you did.

It's worth taking a few deep breaths at the ultraclear, tree-fringed lakefront – look out for elk and perhaps the occasional black bear – and you should also consider a swim or area hike here. Alternatively, check in for a kayak excursion with the friendly folks at Warm Rapids Inn & Kayak Centre (250-709-5543; www.warmrapidsinn.com). A great spot to learn kayaking, they'll take you out for a full-day, fully equipped course ($150) on the nearby river, tailored to your skill level. They also offer good-value home-style B&B accommodation (r $65-110), plus a cool self-contained yurt in the woods ($150).

COWICHAN BAY

'Cow Bay' to the locals, the region's most attractive pit stop is a colorful string of wooden buildings perched on stilts over a mountain-shadowed ocean inlet. It's well worth an afternoon of your time, although it might take that long to find parking on a busy summer day. Arrive hungry and drop into Hilary's Artisan Cheese (www.hilaryscheese.com; 1737 Cowichan Bay Rd) and True Grain Bread (www.truegrain.ca; 1725 Cowichan Bay Rd) for the makings of a great picnic.

Alternatively, let someone else do all the work with some hearty fish and chips from Rock Cod Café (www.rockcodcafe.com; 1759 Cowichan Bay Rd; mains $8-16), or push out the boat – not literally – with a multicourse regional tasting feast on the patio deck of the lovely Masthead Restaurant (www.themastheadrestaurant.com; 1705 Cowichan Bay Rd; mains $22-29), where seafood treats like prosciutto-wrapped snapper combine with sterling views and a great Cowichan Valley wine list.

After you're fully fueled, duck into the Maritime Centre (www.classicboats.org; 1761 Cowichan Bay Rd; admission by donation; 9am-dusk) to peruse some salty boat-building exhibits and intricate models. And if you really can't tear yourself away, stay for the night overlooking the water at the ever-friendly Cowichan Oceanview B&B (250-746-5669; www.cowichanoceanviewbb.com; 1778 Fenwick Rd; d $85-130;), where your smashing host Lorraine chefs up a great breakfast: if you're lucky it will include a blackberry smoothie of locally picked fruit. There are two rooms available, but the Lighthouse Room is recommended for its panorame bay vista and giant bathroom.

CARMANAH WALBRAN PROVINCIAL PARK

Home to some of BC's most elderly residents, the old-growth spruce and cedar trees in this magnificent but remote park (www.bcparks.ca) frequently exceed 1000 years. With an ancient and mythical ambience, it's a half-hour walk down the valley to commune with the tallest trees. However, the trails are primitive and are not intended for the unprepared.

COWICHAN WINE (& CIDER) COUNTRY

Eyebrows were raised when the Cowichan Valley region began proclaiming itself as Vancouver Island's version of Provence a few years back, but the wine snobs have been choking on their words ever since.

Favorite stops include Cherry Point Vineyards (www.cherrypointvineyards.com; 840 Cherry Point Rd, Cobble Hill; 10am-5pm), with its lip-smacking blackberry port; Averill Creek (www.averillcreek.ca; 6552 North Rd, Duncan; 11am-5pm May-Oct), with its view-tastic patio and lovely pinot noirs; and the ever-popular Merridale Estate Cidery (www.merridalecider.com; 1230 Merridale Rd, Cobble Hill; 10:30am-4:30pm), an inviting apple-cider producer offering six varieties as well as a new brandy-distilling operation.

If you can, time your visit for the three-day Cowichan Wine & Culinary Festival (www.wines.cowichan.net) in September, when regional producers showcase their wares in a series of tasty events.

For more information on the wineries of this area and throughout Vancouver Island, check www.wineislands.ca.

For those without a map looking for the main Carmanah Valley trailhead, follow South Shore Rd from Lake Cowichan to Nitinat Main Rd and bear left. Then follow Nitinat Main to Nitinat Junction and turn left onto South Main. Continue to the Caycus River Bridge and, just south of the bridge, turn right and follow Rosander Main (blue-and-white BC Parks signs reassuringly point the way) for 29km to the trailhead. Be aware that these are active logging roads, which means bumpy, often narrow tracks and the promise of a rumbling approach from a scary log truck – they have the right of way, so don't give them a hard time.

CHEMAINUS
POP 4500

After the last sawmill shut down in 1983, tiny Chemainus became the model for BC communities dealing with declining resource jobs. Instead of submitting to a slow death, town officials commissioned a giant wall mural depicting local history. More than three dozen additional artworks were later added and a new tourism industry was born. A popular day trip by train from Victoria, the town introduced its own currency in 2010 – pick up your Chemainus Dollars at local banks and you can use them around the area.

Stroll the Chemainus streets on a mural hunt and you'll pass artsy boutiques and tempting ice-cream shops. In the evening, the surprisingly large Chemainus Theatre (www.chemainustheatrefestival.ca; 9737 Chemainus Rd) stages professional productions – mostly popular plays and musicals to keep you occupied.

Developed in partnership with the theater – ask about show packages – the town's Chemainus Festival Inn (✐250-246-4181, 877-246-4181; www.festivalinn.ca; 9573 Chemainus Rd; r $139-249; ⊠) is like a midrange business hotel from a much larger town. Rooms are slick and comfortable and many include kitchens.

You can chat with the locals over coffee at the Dancing Bean Cafe (www.dancingbean.ca; 9885 Maple St; mains $6-9.50), an animated hangout with light meals (chicken sandwich recommended), live music most Saturdays and a good-value $2.22 breakfast special.

Check in at the visitor centre (✐250-246-3944; www.chemainus.bc.ca; 9796 Willow St; ⊙9am-5pm May-Oct, reduced off-season) for mural maps and further information.

Nanaimo
POP 79.000

Maligned for years as Vancouver Island's grubby second city, Nanaimo will never have the allure of tourist-magnet Victoria. But the 'Harbour City' has undergone its own quiet renaissance since the 1990s, with the downtown emergence of some good shops and eateries and a slick new museum. With its own ferry service from the mainland, the city is also a handy hub for exploring up-island.

◉ Sights & Activities

Nanaimo Museum   MUSEUM
(www.nanaimomuseum.ca; 100 Museum Way; adult/child/youth $2/0.75/1.75; ⊙10am-5pm mid-May–Aug, 10am-5pm Tue-Sat Sep–mid-May) Just off the Commercial St main drag, this shiny new museum showcases the region's heritage, from First Nations to colonial, maritime, sporting and beyond. Highlights include a strong Coast Salish focus and a walk-through evocation of a coal mine that's popular with kids. Ask at the front desk about summertime pub and cemetery tours.

Newcastle Island Marine Provincial Park   PARK
(www.newcastleisland.ca) Nanaimo's rustic outdoor gem offers tranquil hiking and cycling, as well as beaches and wildlife-spotting opportunities. Settled by the Coast Salish – and still part of their traditional territory - it was the site of shipyards and coal mines before becoming a popular short-hop summer excursion in the 1930s, when a teahouse was added. Accessed by a 10-minute ferry from the harbor (adult/child $4/3), there's a seasonal eatery and regular First Nations dancing displays.

Bastion   HISTORICAL BUILDING
(www.nanaimomuseum.ca; cnr Front & Bastion Sts; adult/child $1/free; ⊙10am-3pm Jun-Aug, reduced hrs May & Sep) Undergoing a renovation at the time of our visit, this waterfront wooden tower was built as a fortification by the Hudson's Bay Company in 1853 and moved to this spot in 1974. A brief but charming ceremony sees one of its cannons fired for tourists at noon – the polystyrene 'cannonball' can still shake a few ribs. Nearby is the site of the weekly Nanaimo Downtown Farmers Market (www.nanaimofarmersmarket.com; ⊙10am-2pm Fri May-Oct).

BRITISH COLUMBIA VANCOUVER ISLAND

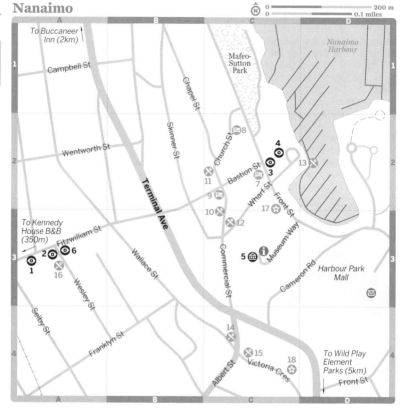

Old City Quarter NEIGHBORHOOD
(www.oldcityquarter.com; cnr Fitzwilliam & Wesley Sts) Amble uphill from the waterfront and within minutes you'll arrive at a few blocks of strollable heritage buildings colonized by independent stores, galleries and eateries. Highlights include **Artzi Stuff** (309B Wesley St), with its local jewelry and own-made silk scarves, and **A Wee Cupcakery** (www.aweecupcakery.com; 407 Fitzwilliam St), with its irresistible array of all-butter cakes, including a naughty Nanaimo Bar variety.

Just Dive In Adventures TOUR
(☑250-754-2241; www.justdiveinadventures.com; dive excursions/boat tours $95/79) Possibly the most fun you'll have in the water, snorkeling with seals is this operator's most popular excursion. You'll likely spot dozens of the playful critters and – possibly – a killer whale or two. Scuba diving is also offered: the regional waters are among the best in Canada for diving and wolf eels and Pacific

octopus sightings are common. If you prefer to watch without doing any work, try a marine safari boat tour instead.

Wild Play Element Parks AMUSEMENT PARK
(www.wildplay.com; 35 Nanaimo River Rd; adult/child from $40/20; ⊙10am-6pm mid-Jun–Aug, reduced off-season) This former bungee-jumping site has reinvented itself with five obstacle courses strung between the trees. Once you're harnessed, you can hit zip lines, rope bridges, tunnels and Tarzan swings, each aimed at different ability levels.

🛏 Sleeping

Painted Turtle Guesthouse HOSTEL $
(☑250-753-4432, 866-309-4432; www.paintedturtle.ca; 121 Bastion St; dm $26.12, r $45-98; @奈) This exemplary budget property in the heart of downtown combines four-bed dorms with family and private rooms. Hardwood floors and IKEA-esque furnishings abound, while facilities range from a

BRITISH COLUMBIA NANAIMO

large and welcoming kitchen to a laundry room and en suite showers. You can book local activities through the front desk but you might spend most of your time hanging around the fireplace in the lounge playing table football instead.

Kennedy House B&B B&B **$$**
(☎250-754-3389, 877-750-3389; www.kenne dyhouse.ca; 305 Kennedy St; r $85-125) Uphill from the waterfront, this is one of the few Nanaimo B&Bs nearish to the city center – in fact, it's close to the VIA Rail stop and the Old City Quarter. A restored and outwardly imposing 1913 heritage mansion, it has two lovely rooms, combining antique knickknacks and contemporary flourishes. Elegant, quiet and adult-oriented, there's a smashing cooked breakfast to rouse you from your morning slumber.

Buccaneer Inn MOTEL **$$**
(☎250-753-1246, 877-282-6337; www.buccaneer inn.com; 1577 Stewart Ave; s/ste from $79/149; 🖰) Handy for the Departure Bay ferry terminal, this family-run motel has an immaculate white paint job. The neat and tidy approach is carried over into the maritime-themed rooms, many of which have kitchenettes. Splurge on a spacious suite and you'll have a fireplace, full kitchen and flat-screen TV.

Coast Bastion Inn HOTEL **$$**
(☎250-753-6601, 800-663-1144; www.coastho tels.com; 11 Bastion St; r from $139; 🖰) Downtown's leading hotel has an unbeatable location overlooking the harbor, with most rooms having good views. Rooms have been refurbished with a lounge-modern élan in recent years, adding flat-screen

TVs and (in most rooms) small fridges. The lobby resto-bar is a popular hangout but there's also an on-site spa if you want to chillax.

Dorchester Hotel HOTEL **$$**
(☎250-754-6835, 800-661-2449; www.dorches ternanaimo.com; 70 Church St; r/ste from $119/129; 🖰) Waterfront tower hotel with business-hotel-style rooms and an exceedingly slow elevator.

Grand Hotel Nanaimo HOTEL **$$**
(☎250-758-3000, 877-414-7263; www.the grandhotelnanaimo.ca; 4898 Rutherford Rd; r from $149; @🐾) Edge-of-town business-style accommodation with some superior suites.

✗ Eating

TOP CHOICE **Gabriel's Café** FUSION **$**
(183 Commercial St; mains $4-8; 🖰) This well-located hole-in-the-wall is a revelation. Chat with the man himself behind the counter, then tuck into made-from-scratch treats like pulled-pork sandwiches with apple-cider BBQ sauce or the popular Thai green chili coconut curry, inspired by the owner's global travels. Vegetarians are well looked after – try the black-bean burger – while off-menu vegan dishes can be made on request. There's not much room to sit so consider a takeout: pick up a smoked salmon and cream-cheese breakfast bun and scoff it on the nearby waterfront. Don't miss the homemade green mint raspberry iced tea.

Penny's Palapa MEXICAN **$$**
(10 Wharf St H Dock; mains $8-12; ☉Apr-Oct) This tiny, flower-and-flag-decked floating hut and patio in the harbor is a lovely spot

First run in 1967 to mark the city's centennial, and now overseen by the Loyal Nanaimo Bathtub Society, the **World Championship Bathtub Race** (www.bathtubbing.com) is the region's biggest summer draw. In late July, the four days of marine-themed shenanigans include a street fair, a parade and a giant fireworks extravaganza, but the main event remains the big race where hundreds of salty sea dogs jump into customized bath-sized crafts – some adapted for upwards of $3000 – and embark on a grueling 58km course. Whizzing around Entrance and Winchelsea Islands, they finish – if they make it – at Departure Bay. Speedboat engines are standard for the 90-minute sprint, with thousands of spectators lining the bay for the spectacular finish. A dip in the tub will never seem the same again.

for an alfresco meal among the jostling boats. An inventive, well-priced menu of Mexican delights includes seasonal seafood specials – the signature halibut tacos are recommended – plus some good vegetarian options. Arrive early: the dining area fills rapidly on balmy summer evenings. Drinks- wise: it's all about the margaritas.

Wesley Street Restaurant WEST COAST **$$**
(www.wesleycafe.com; 321 Wesley St; mains $15-29; ☺lunch & dinner Tue-Sat) Like a transplant from Victoria, Nanaimo's best splurge-worthy dine-out showcases BC-sourced ingredients prepared with contemporary flair. The oft-changing menu is seasonal, but look out for Haida Gwaii salmon, Qualicum Bay scallops and Cowichan Valley duck. Take your time and savor. And if you're looking for a dinner deal, there's a three-course $30 special from Tuesday to Thursday.

Pirate Chips FAST FOOD **$**
(1 Commercial St; mains $4-10) Locals originally came here for the best fries in town – the curry topping is recommended – but they keep coming back for the funky ambience and quirky pirate-themed decor. It's an excellent late-night hangout: you can even indulge in poutine and deep-fried chocolate bars – although preferably not together: see p107 for the hospital location if you do.

Thirsty Camel Café MIDDLE EASTERN **$$**
(www.thirstycamelcafe.ca; 14 Victoria Cres; mains $8-14) Partake of a lip-smacking Middle Eastern feast at this sunny little family-owned joint, tucked into an elbow of Victoria Cres. Everything's house-prepared from scratch, which makes for hearty falafel pitas, addictive hummus and some spicy winter soups. The shareable platters (especially the spice-encrusted Persian chicken) are recommended and there are several excellent vegetarian options that even meat eaters will love.

Mon Petit Choux Café & Bakery BAKERY **$**
(120 Commercial St; mains $7-9) A chatty neighborhood hangout that has a surprisingly gourmet approach to its light meals. French-flecked favorites include roast chicken and cranberry compote sandwiches and an amazing Alsace pizza of smoked bacon and caramelized onions. Drop in for afternoon coffee and a dangerous roster of delectable bakery treats like cherry chocolate strudel and *pan au chocolat*.

Modern Café' CANADIAN **$$**
(221 Commercial St; mains $9-19; ☺9am-11pm) This reinvented old coffee shop has cool loungey interiors combining exposed brick and comfy booths or, if it's sunny, a sun-warmed outdoor patio. The menu has wraps, burgers and sandwiches that are a cut above standard diner fare and there are some small-plate options for those who just want to snack. It also recently opened a nightclub upstairs.

🍸 Drinking & Entertainment

Longwood Brewpub BREWERY
(www.longwoodbrewpub.com; 5775 Turner Rd) Incongruously located in a new strip mall development, this handsome stone and gabled resto-pub combines a surprisingly good food menu with some lip-smacking own-brewed beers. Try for a deck table and decide between recommended mains like Cajun chicken quesadilla or halibut and prawn wraps – vegetarians should hit the roasted vegetable lasagna. Beer-wise, you can't go wrong with the four 6oz taster glasses for $6.63 – make sure one of them is Russian Imperial Stout.

Dinghy Dock Pub PUB
(www.dinghydockpub.com; 8 Pirates Lane) Accessed via a mini-ferry hop, this lively pub and restaurant combo floating offshore

from Protection Island is an ideal place to rub shoulders with salty locals and knock back a few malty brews on the deck. The menu doesn't stretch far beyond classic pub fare but there's live music on weekends to keep your toes tapping. To get to the pub, take the 10-minute ferry (return $9) from the harbor.

Queen's Hotel   LIVE MUSIC
(www.thequeens.ca; 34 Victoria Cres) The city's best live music and dance spot, hosting an eclectic roster of performances and club nights, ranging from indie to jazz and country.

Port Theatre   THEATER
(www.porttheatre.com; 125 Front St) Presenting local and touring live-theater shows.

Avalon Cinema Centre   CINEMA
(Woodgrove Centre, 6631 N Island Hwy) Nanaimo's favorite blockbuster movie house is this 10-screen multiplex.

Information

Nanaimo Maps & Charts (250-754-2513; 8 Church St; 9am-5:30pm Mon-Sat, 10am-4pm Sat) Excellent bookstore with good array of maps and travel guides.

Nanaimo Regional General Hospital (250-754-2121; 1200 Dufferin Cres)

Post office (250-267-1177; Harbour Park Mall; 8:30am-5pm Mon-Fri)

Tourism Nanaimo (250-754-8141; www.tourismnanaimo.com; 2290 Bowen Rd; 9am-6pm May-Aug, reduced off-season) Edge-of-town site, with downtown satellite operation in the museum building.

Getting There & Away

Air
Nanaimo Airport (www.nanaimoairport.com) is 18km south of town via Hwy 1. **Air Canada** (www.aircanada.com) flights arrive here from Vancouver (from $98, 25 minutes) throughout the day.

Frequent **Harbour Air Seaplanes** (www.harbour-air.com) services arrive in the inner harbor from downtown Vancouver ($79, 25 minutes) and Vancouver International Airport ($67, 20 minutes).

Boat
BC Ferries (www.bcferries.com) from Tsawwassen (passenger/vehicle $14/46.75, two hours) arrive at Duke Point, 14km south of Nanaimo. Services from West Vancouver's Horseshoe Bay (passenger/vehicle $14/46.75, one hour 35 minutes) arrive at Departure Bay, 3km north of the city center via Hwy 1.

Bus
Greyhound Canada (www.greyhound.ca) buses arrive from Victoria ($23.30, 2½ hours, four daily), Campbell River ($30.80, three hours, two daily), Port Alberni ($25.80, 1½ hours, two daily) and Tofino ($46.30, four hours, two daily).

Train
The daily **VIA Rail** (www.viarail.com) *Malahat* train trundles in from Victoria ($27, 2½ hours), Parksville ($20, 35 minutes) and Courtenay ($27, two hours), among other places.

Getting Around

Downtown Nanaimo, around the harbor, is highly walkable, but after that the city spreads out and a car or strong bike legs are required. Be aware that taxis are expensive here.

Nanaimo Regional Transit (www.busonline.ca) buses (single trip/day pass $2.25/5.75) stop along Gordon St, west of Harbour Park Mall. Bus 2 goes to the Departure Bay ferry terminal. No city buses run to Duke Point.

Nanaimo Airporter (www.nanaimoairporter.com) provides door-to-door service ($26) to downtown from both ferry terminals.

Parksville & Qualicum

Previously called Oceanside, this mid-island region has reverted to using its twin main towns as its moniker, mainly because no one could tell where Oceanside was just by hearing its name.

 Sights & Activities

Coombs Old Country Market   MARKET
(www.oldcountrymarket.com; 2326 Alberni Hwy, Coombs; 9am-7pm Jul & Aug, reduced off-season) The mother of all pit stops, this ever-expanding menagerie of food and crafts is centered on a large store stuffed with bakery and produce delectables. It attracts huge numbers of visitors on balmy summer days, when cameras are pointed at the grassy roof where a herd of goats spends the season. Nip inside for giant ice-cream cones, heaping pizzas and the deli makings of a great picnic, then spend an hour wandering the attendant stores clustered around the site.

Milner Gardens & Woodland   GARDEN
(www.milnergardens.org; adult/child/youth $10/free/6; 2179 W Island Hwy, Qualicum Beach; 10am-5pm daily May-Aug, 10am-5pm Thu-Sun Apr & Sep) An idyllic summertime attraction combining rambling forest trails shaded by centuries-old trees and flower-packed gardens planted with magnificent

rhododendrons. Meander down to the 1930s **tearoom** on a stunning bluff overlooking the water. Tuck into afternoon tea ($8.75, 1pm to 4pm) on the porch and drink in views of the bird-lined shore and snow-capped peaks shimmering on the horizon.

World Parrot Refuge NATURE RESERVE
(www.worldparrotrefuge.org; 2116 Alberni Hwy, Coombs; adult/child $12/8; ☺10am-4pm) Rescuing exotic birds from captivity and nursing them back to health, this excellent educational facility preaches the mantra that parrots are not pets. Pick up your earplugs at reception and stroll among the enclosures, each alive with recovering (and very noisy) birds. Don't be surprised when some screech a chirpy 'hello' as you stroll by.

Horne Lake Caves Provincial Park PARK
(www.hornelake.com; tours adult/child from $20/17; ☺10am-5pm Jul & Aug, reduced off-season) Horne Lake Caves Provincial Park is a 45-minute drive from Parksville (take Hwy 19 towards Courtenay, then exit 75 and proceed for 12km on the gravel road) but it's worth it for BC's best spelunking. Two caves are open to the public for self-exploring, or you can take a guided tour of the spectacular Riverbend Cave – look out for the 'howling wolf' and 'smiling Buddha' formations.

🛏️ Sleeping & Eating

TOP
CHOICE **Free Spirit Spheres** CABINS $$
(☎250-757-9445; www.freespiritspheres. com; 420 Horne Lake Rd, Qualicum Bay; cabins from $125) Suspended by cables in the trees, this clutch of three spherical treehouses enables guests to cocoon themselves in the forest canopy. Compact inside, Eve is smaller and basic, while Eryn and Melody are lined like little boats with built-in cabins, nooks and mp3 speakers. Sleeping here is all about communing with nature (TVs are replaced with books), but that doesn't mean you have to give up creature comforts: guests receive a basket of baked goodies on arrival and there's a ground-level facilities block with sauna, BBQ and hotel-like showers. Book early for summer.

Inn the Estuary B&B $$
(☎250-468-9983; www.inntheestuary.com; 2991 Northwest Bay Rd, Nanoose Bay; ste $175; ☜) Hidden off the road, this lovely, retreat-style B&B is as close to waterfront nature as you can get: its two self-contained suites have huge picture windows overlooking the bay's wildlife sanctuary wetlands and all you'll be able to hear are chirping birds and the rustle of occasional deer in the woods. The contemporary chic rooms have fireplaces, kitchens and jetted outdoor tubs, while free loaner bikes and kayaks are also available.

Crown Mansion BOUTIQUE HOTEL $$
(☎250-752-5776; www.crownmansion.com; 292 E Crescent Rd, Qualicum Beach; r from $145; ☜) A sumptuous family home built in 1912, this handsome white-painted mansion was restored to its former glory and opened as a unique hotel in 2009. Recall past guests Bing Crosby and John Wayne as you check out the family crest in the library fireplace, then retire to your elegant room with its heated bathroom floor and giant bed. Rates include continental breakfast – arrive early and snag the window table.

Blue Willow Guest House B&B $$
(☎250-752-9052; www.bluewillowguesthouse. com; 524 Quatna Rd, Qualicum Beach; s/d/ste

WORTH A TRIP

SAY CHEESE...AND THEN MOO

Nibble on the region's 'locavore' credentials at **Morningstar Farm** (www.morningstar farm.ca; 403 Lowry's Rd, Parksville; admission free; ☺9am-5pm Mon-Sat), a small working farmstead that's also a family-friendly visitor attraction. Let your kids run wild checking out the cowsheds and cheese makers – most will quickly fall in love with the roaming pigs, goats and chickens so you can expect some unusual Christmas pressie requests when you get back home. But it's not just for youngsters here: head to the **Little Qualicum Cheeseworks** shop, where samples of the farm's curdy treats (as well as its own-cured bacon) are provided – this is a great place to pick up picnic supplies. The creamy, slightly mushroomy brie is a bestseller but the Qualicum Spice is recommended: it's flavored with onion, garlic and sweet red pepper. Better still, the farm recently opened **Mooberry Winery**, where you can pair your cheese with blueberry, cranberry or gooseberry fruit wines.

$120/130/140) A surprisingly spacious Victorian-style cottage, this lovely B&B has a book-lined lounge, exposed beams and a fragrant country garden. The two rooms and one self-contained suite are lined with antiques and each is extremely homely. The attention to detail carries over to the gourmet breakfast: served in the conservatory, it's accompanied by finger-licking home-baked treats.

Fish Tales Café   SEAFOOD **$$**
(www.fishtalescafe.com; 336 W Island Hwy, Qualicum Beach; mains $8-21) This Qualicum fixture has the look of an old-school English teashop but it's been reeling in visitors with its perfect fish and chips for years. It's worth exploring the non-deep-fried dishes – the two-person platter of scallops, shrimp, smoked salmon and mussels is recommended – and, if you arrive early enough, you can grab a table in the garden.

Shady Rest   CANADIAN **$$**
(3109 W Island Hwy, Qualicum Beach; mains $10-19) A laid-back neighborhood bar perched over the shell-strewn beach on Qualicum's main drag, this casual hangout is popular with locals and visitors. Drop by for some perfectly prepared pub grub – try the excellent halibut burger – and a couple of restorative beers (Sea Dog Amber Ale is recommended). Hearty weekend brunches are also available.

❶ Information

Find out more about the region – which also includes rustic Coombs – by checking with the local **tourism board** (☑250-248-6300, 888-799-3222; www.visitparksvillequalicumbeach.com) or visiting the friendly folks at **Qualicum Beach visitor centre** (☑250-752-95326; www.qualicum.bc.ca; 2711 W Island Hwy; ⊕8:30am-6:30pm mid-May–mid-Sep, 9am-4pm Mon-Sat mid-Sep–mid-May).

❶ Getting There & Away

Greyhound Canada (www.greyhound.ca) services arrive in Parksville from Victoria ($35.80, three to four hours, five daily), Nanaimo ($14.90, 40 minutes, four daily) and Campbell River ($27.30, two hours, two daily), among other towns. The same buses, with similar times and rates, serve Qualicum Beach.

The daily **VIA Rail** (www.viarail.com) *Malahat* train arrives in Parksville from Victoria ($34, 3½ hours), Nanaimo ($20, 40 minutes) and Courtenay ($20, one hour 20 minutes), among others. The same train, with similar times and rates, serves Qualicum Beach.

Port Alberni
POP 17,500
Although its key fishing and forestry sectors have been declining for decades, Alberni – handily located on Hwy 4 between the island's east and west coasts – is a good location for outdoor exploration. Additionally, there are some intriguing historic attractions and an unexpected winery.

◉ Sights & Activities

Cathedral Grove   PARK
(www.bcparks.ca) Between Parksville and Port Alberni, the spiritual home of tree huggers is a mystical highlight of MacMillan Provincial Park. Often overrun with summer visitors – try not to knock them down as they scamper across the highway in front of you – its accessible forest trails wind through a dense canopy of vegetation, offering glimpses of some of BC's oldest trees, including centuries-old Douglas firs more than 3m in diameter. Try hugging that.

Alberni Valley Museum   MUSEUM
(www.alberniheritage.com; 4255 Wallace St; admission by donation; ⊕10am-5pm Tue-Sat, to 8pm Thu) Lined with eclectic aboriginal and pioneer-era exhibits, this is a fascinating local attraction. The section on the West Coast Trail shows how the route was once a life-saving trail for shipwreck victims. History fans should also hop aboard the town's **Alberni Pacific Railway** (adult/child/youth $30/15/22.50) to **McLean Mill**. A national historic site, it's Canada's only working steam-powered sawmill.

Emerald Coast Vineyards Wine Shop   WINERY
(www.emeraldcoastvineyards.ca; 2787 Alberni Hwy; ⊕noon-5pm Tue-Sun May-Sep, noon-4pm Thu-Sat Oct-Apr) This handsome wood-gabled, family-run winery building looks like it should be somewhere else but it's an indication that Alberni is moving on from its gritty past. Step inside for free tastings made from locally grown grapes: the dessert-like blueberry port is well worth a sip or three.

Wild West Watersports   WATERSPORTS
(www.wildwestwatersports.com; 4255 Wallace St) Colonizing a grubby former corner of the old waterfront mill site, this local operator is taking full advantage of the area's predilection for exposed wind currents with kiteboarding and windsurfing rentals and lessons. Kayak rentals are also available.

MV Francis Barkley TOUR
(www.ladyrosemarine.com; 5425 Argyle St; return trip $50-74) With the sale of the venerable *Lady Rose*, it's left to the *MV Francis Barkley* to take passengers on idyllic day cruises up Barkley Sound.

Batstar Adventure Tours TOUR
(www.batstar.com; 4785 Beaver Creek Rd) From guided bike trips into the wilderness to multiday kayak odysseys around the Broken Group Islands, these guys can get you outdoors…and then some.

Sleeping & Eating

Hummingbird Guesthouse B&B $$
(250-720-2111, 888-720-2114; www.hummingbirdguesthouse.com; 5769 River Rd; ste $125-160;) With four large suites and a giant deck (complete with hot tub), this modern B&B has a home-away-from-home feel – just ask Jasper the languid house cat. There's a shared kitchen on each of the two floors but the substantial cooked breakfast should keep you full for hours. Each suite has satellite TV, one has its own sauna and there's a teen-friendly games room out back.

Fat Salmon Backpackers HOSTEL $
(250-723-6924; www.fatsalmonbackpackers.com; 3250 Third Ave; dm $21-25; @) Driven by energetic, highly welcoming owners, this funky, eclectic backpacker joint offers four-to eight-bed dorms with names like 'Knickerbocker' and 'Mullet Room.' There are lots of books, free tea and coffee and a kitchen bristling with utensils. Make sure you say hi to Lily, the world-famous house dog.

Arrowvale Riverside Campground & Cottages CAMPGROUND $
(250-723-7948; www.arrowvale.ca; 5955 Hector Rd; campsite/cottage $25/149) About 6km west of Alberni, along the Somass River, the Arrowvale offers showers, a playground and heaping fruit pies in its on-site cafe. For those who've had enough of camping, there are two comparatively luxe river-view cottages with fireplaces and Jacuzzi tubs. Kids will enjoy the farm animals (check their bags for smuggled baby goats when you leave).

All Mex'd Up MEXICAN $
(5440 Argyle St; mains $3-9; May-Sep) A funky and highly colorful little Mexican shack near the waterfront – it's decorated with chili-shaped fairy lights – with everything made from scratch. Pull up a stool and tuck into a classic array of made-with-love tacos, quesadillas and big-ass burritos.

Information

For tips, visit the **Alberni Valley visitor centre** (250-724-6535; www.albernivalleytourism.com; 2533 Port Alberni Hwy; 8am-6pm mid-May–Aug, reduced off-season) on your way into town.

Getting There & Away

Greyhound Canada (www.greyhound.ca) buses arrive here from Victoria ($46.30, four to five hours, three daily), Nanaimo ($25.80, 1½ hours, two daily) and Tofino ($29.40, two hours, two daily), among others.

Pacific Rim National Park Reserve

A wave-crashing waterfront and brooding, mist-covered trees ensure that the **Pacific Rim National Park Reserve** (www.pc.gc.ca/pacificrim; park pass adult/child $7.80/3.90) is among BC's most popular outdoor attractions. The 500-sq-km park comprises the northern Long Beach Unit, between Tofino and Ucluelet; the Broken Group Islands in Barkley Sound; and, to the south, the ever-popular West Coast Trail.

LONG BEACH UNIT

Attracting the lion's share of visitors, Long Beach Unit is easily accessible by car along the Pacific Rim Hwy. Wide sandy beaches, untamed surf, lots of beachcombing nooks and a living museum of old-growth rainforest are the main reasons for the summer tourist clamor.

The **Wickaninnish Interpretive Centre** (Wick Rd; admission included with park pass fee) was being redesigned during your visit to the region: check ahead and consider a visit if it's open, since it's a great introduction to the park.

If you're inspired to take a stroll, try one of the following trails, keeping your eyes peeled for swooping bald eagles and shockingly large banana slugs. Safety precautions apply on all trails in the region: tread carefully over slippery surfaces and never turn your back on the mischievous surf.

Long Beach Great scenery along the sandy shore (1.2km; easy).

Rainforest Trail Two interpretive loops through old-growth forest (1km; moderate).

Schooner Trail Through old- and second-growth forests with beach access (1km; moderate).

Shorepine Bog Loops around a moss-layered bog (800m; easy and wheelchair-accessible).

South Beach Through forest to a pebble beach (800m; easy to moderate).

Spruce Fringe Trail Loop trail featuring hardy Sitka spruce (1.5km; moderate).

Wickaninnish Trail Shoreline and forest trail (2.5km; easy to moderate).

🛏 Sleeping & Eating

Green Point Campground   CAMPGROUND **$**
(📞250-689-9025, 877-737-3783; www.pccamping.ca; campsites $34.40; ⊗mid-Mar–mid-Oct) Between Ucluelet and Tofino, on the Pacific Rim Hwy, Green Point Campground encourages lots of novice campers to try their first night under the stars. Extremely popular in the summer peak (book ahead), its 105 tent sites are located on a forested terrace, with trail access to the beach. Expect fairly basic facilities: the faucets are cold but the toilets are flush.

Wickaninnish Restaurant   WEST COAST **$$**
(www.wickaninnish.ca; mains $16-28) You can make up for roughing it with a rewarding meal in the interpretive centre at the Wickaninnish Restaurant, where the crashing surf views are served with fresh-catch local seafood. If you're just passing through, drop by the complex's **Beachfront Café** (snacks $3-5; ⊗9am-6pm Mar-Sep) for a snack or an ice-cold Wickaccino.

ℹ Information

First-timers should drop by the **Pacific Rim visitor centre** (📞250-726-4600; www.pacificrimvisitor.ca; 2791 Pacific Rim Hwy; ⊗10am-4pm, reduced off-season) for maps and advice on exploring this spectacular region. If you're stopping in the park, you'll need to pay and display a pass, available here or from the yellow dispensers dotted along the highway.

ℹ Getting There & Around

Tofino Bus (www.tofinobus.com; one way/return/day pass $10/15/21) runs a 'Beach Bus' service linking points throughout the area.

BROKEN GROUP ISLANDS UNIT

Comprising some 300 islands and rocks scattered across 80 sq km around the entrance to Barkley Sound, the Broken Group is a serene natural wilderness beloved of visiting kayakers – especially those who enjoy close-up views of gray whales, harbor porpoises and multitudinous birdlife. Com-

passes are required for navigating here, unless you fancy paddling to Hawaii.

If you're up for a trek, **Lady Rose Marine Services** (www.ladyrosemarine.com) will ship you and your kayak from Port Alberni to its Sechart Whaling Station Lodge (three hours away) in Barkley Sound on the *MV Francis Barkley*. The lodge rents kayaks (per day $40 to $60) if you'd rather travel light and it offers accommodation (single/double $150/235, including all meals).

From there, popular paddle destinations include Gibraltar Island, one hour away, with its sheltered campground and explorable beaches and tidal pools. Willis Island (1½ hours from Sechart) is also popular. It has a campground and, at low tide, you can walk to the surrounding islands. Remote Benson Island (four hours from Sechart) has a campground, grazing deer and a blowhole.

Camping fees are $9.80 per night, payable at Sechart or to the boat-based staff who patrol the region – they can collect additional fees from you if you decide to stay longer. The campgrounds are predictably basic and have solar composting toilets, but you must carry out all your garbage. Bring your own drinking water since island creeks are often dry in summer.

WEST COAST TRAIL UNIT

Restored after a major 2006 storm, the 75km West Coast Trail is BC's best-known hiking route. It's also one of the toughest. Not for the uninitiated, there are two things you'll need to know before tackling it: it will hurt and you'll want to do it again next year.

Winding along the wave-licked rainforest shoreline between trailhead information centers at Pachena Bay, 5km south of Bamfield on the north end, and Gordon River, 5km north of Port Renfrew on the southern tip, the entire stretch takes between six and seven days to complete. Open May to September, access to the route is limited to up to 60 overnight backpackers each day. All overnighters must pay a trail-user fee ($127.50) plus $30 to cover the two short ferry crossings on the route. **Reservations** (📞250-387-1642, 800-435-5466; www.parks canada.gc.ca/pacificrim; nonrefundable reservation fee $24.50) are required for the mid-June to mid-September peak season but not for the off-peak periods. All overnighters must attend a 1½-hour orientation session before departing.

If you don't have a reservation, some permits are kept back for a daily wait-list system: six of each day's 26 available spaces are set aside at 1pm to be used on a first-come, first-served basis at each trailhead. If you win this lottery you can begin hiking that day, but keep in mind that you might wait a day or two to get a permit this way in the peak season.

If you don't want to go the whole hog (you wimp), you can do a day hike or even hike half the trail from Pachena Bay, considered the easier end of the route. Overnight hikers who only hike this end of the trail can leave from Nitinat Lake. Day hikers are exempt from the large trail-user fee but they need to get a free day-use permit at one of the trailheads.

West Coast Trailers are a hardy bunch and must be able to manage rough, slippery terrain, stream crossings and adverse, suddenly changing weather. There are also more than 100 little (and some not-so-little) bridges and 70 ladders. Be prepared to treat or boil all water and cook on a lightweight camping stove (you'll be bringing in all your own food). Hikers can rest their weary muscles at any of the basic campsites along the route, most of which have solar-composting outhouses. It's recommended that you set out from a trailhead at least five hours before sundown to ensure you reach a campsite before nightfall – stumbling around in the dark is the prime cause of accidents on this route.

West Coast Trail Express (www.trailbus. com) runs a daily shuttle (May to September) to Panchena Bay from Victoria ($85, six hours) and Nanaimo ($95, four hours). It also runs a service to Gordon River from Victoria ($60, 2½ hours) and Bamfield ($75, 3½ hours). Check the website for additional stops and reserve ahead in summer.

Tofino

POP 1650

Transforming rapidly in recent years from a sleepy hippy hangout into a soft-eco resort town (it's like the Whistler of Vancouver Island), Tofino is the region's most popular outdoor hangout. It's not surprising that surf fans and other visitors keep coming: packed with activities and blessed with stunning beaches, Tofino sits on Clayoquot (clay-kwot) Sound, where forested mounds rise from roiling waves

that batter the coastline in a dramatic, ongoing spectacle. A short drive south of town, the **visitor centre** (☑250-725-3414; www.tourismtofino.com; 1426 Pacific Rim Hwy; ☺10am-6pm May-Sep, reduced off-season) has detailed information on area accommodations, hiking trails and hot surf spots. There's also a satellite branch in town at 455 Campbell St.

◉ Sights

Tofino Botanical Gardens　　　　GARDEN
(www.tbgf.org; 1084 Pacific Rim Hwy; 3-day admission adult/child/youth $10/free/6; ☺9am-dusk) Check out what coastal temperate rainforests are all about by exploring the flora and fauna at the Tofino Botanical Gardens, complete with a frog pond, forest boardwalk, native plants and an ongoing program of workshops and field trips. There's a $1 discount for car-free arrivals. This is also the new home of the **Raincoast Interpretive Centre** (www.raincoast education.org).

Maquinna Marine Provincial Park　　PARK
(www.bcparks.ca) One of the most popular day trips from Tofino, the highlight here is **Hot Spring Cove**. Tranquility-minded trekkers travel to the park by Zodiac boat or seaplane, watching for whales and other sea critters en route. From the boat landing, 2km of boardwalks lead to the natural hot pools.

Meares Island　　　　　　　　　PARK
Visible through the mist and accessible via kayak or tour boat from the Tofino waterfront, Meares Island is home to the Big Tree Trail, a 400m boardwalk through old-growth forest that includes a stunning 1500-year-old red cedar. The island was the site of the key 1984 Clayoquot Sound antilogging protest that kicked off the region's latter-day environmental movement.

Ahousat　　　　　　　　　　　　PARK
Situated on remote Flores Island and accessed by tour boat or kayak, Ahousat is the mystical location of the spectacular Wild Side Heritage Trail, a moderately difficult path that traverses 10km of forests, beaches and headlands between Ahousat and Cow Bay. There's a natural warm spring on the island and it's also home to a First Nations band. A popular destination for kayakers, camping of the no-facilities variety is allowed here.

🏃 Activities

Surfing

Live to Surf
(www.livetosurf.com; 1180 Pacific Rim Hwy; board rental 6hr $25) Tofino's original surf shop also supplies skates and skimboards.

Pacific Surf School
(www.pacificsurfschool.com; 430 Campbell St; board rental 6hr/24hr $15/20) Offering rentals, camps and lessons for beginners.

Surf Sister
(www.surfsister.com; 625 Campbell St) Introductory lessons for boys and girls plus women-only multiday courses.

Kayaking

Rainforest Kayak Adventures
(www.rainforestkayak.com; 316 Main St; multiday courses & tours from $685) Specializes in four-to-six-day guided tours and courses.

Remote Passages
(www.remotepassages.com; Wharf St; tours from $64) Gives short guided kayaking tours around Clayoquot Sound and the islands.

Tofino Sea Kayaking Co
(www.tofino-kayaking.com; 320 Main St; tours from $60) Offers short guided paddles, including a popular four-hour Meares Island trip, plus rentals (from $40).

Boat tours

Jamie's Whaling Station
(www.jamies.com; 606 Campbell St; adult/child $99/65) Whale, bear and sea-lion spotting tours.

Ocean Outfitters
(www.oceanoutfitters.bc.ca; 421 Main St; adult/child $79/59) Popular whale-watching tours, with bear and hot-springs treks also offered.

Tla-ook Cultural Adventures
(www.tlaook.com; tours from $44) Learn about aboriginal culture by paddling an authentic dugout canoe.

🛏 Sleeping

Wickaninnish Inn   HOTEL $$$
(☎250-725-3100, 800-333-4604; www.wickinn. com; Chesterman Beach; r from $399) Cornering the market in luxury winter storm-watching packages, 'the Wick' is worth a stay any time of year. Embodying nature with its recycled wood furnishings, natural stone tiles and the ambience of a place grown rather than constructed, the sumptuous guest rooms have push-button gas fireplaces, two-person hot tubs and floor-to-ceiling windows. The region's most romantic sleepover, it's high-end but never pretentious and has a truly awesome waterfront restaurant.

Pacific Sands Beach Resort   HOTEL $$$
(☎250-725-3322, 800-565-23224; www.pacif icsands.com; 1421 Pacific Rim Hwy; r/villa from $220/450) The chic but nevertheless laid-back Pacific Sands has great lodge rooms but its stunning waterfront villas are even better. Great for groups, these huge timber-framed houses open directly onto the beach and include kitchens, stone fireplaces, slate and wood floors and ocean-view bedrooms with private decks. Built on pillars to preserve rainforest root systems, it also has energy-efficient heating systems. It'll drop you off and pick you up in town with its courtesy cars.

Chesterman Beach B&B   B&B $$$
(☎250-725-3726; www.chestermanbeach.net; 1345 Chesterman Beach Rd; ste from $185; ☎) Located among a string of B&Bs, this classy, adult-oriented spot leads the way. The two main rooms have their own private entrances and amazing access to the beach just a few steps away (you'll be lulled to sleep by the waves at night). The smaller Lookout suite is our favorite, with its cozy, wood-lined ambience and mesmerizing beach vistas. There's also a separate cottage at the back of the property that's good for small groups.

Inn at Tough City   HOTEL $$
(☎250-725-2021; www.toughcity.com; 350 Main St; d $169-229; ☎) Near the heart of the action and monikered after the town's old nickname, this quirky brick-built waterfront inn offers eight wood-floored en suite rooms, most with balconies and some with those all-important Jacuzzi tubs. Room five has the best views – look out for the bright-red First Nations longhouse across the water. Built from recycled wood, bricks and stained-glass windows from as far away as Scotland (ask co-owner Crazy Ron about the project), there's also an excellent on-site sushi bar.

Sauna House B&B   B&B $$
(☎250-725-2113; www.saunahouse.net; 1286 Lynn Rd; r/cabin $115/135) On a tree-lined street of secluded B&Bs just across from Chesterman Beach, this rustic nook includes a gabled loft above the main property and a small,

self-contained cabin out back. The tranquil, wood-lined cabin is recommended: it has a small kitchenette, a sunny deck that's great for breakfast (included in rates and usually featuring home-baked muffins) and its own compact sauna – the perfect place to end a strenuous day of hiking.

Whalers on the Point
Guesthouse HOSTEL **$**
(250-725-3443; www.tofinohostel.com; 81 West St; dm $32, r $85-135; @) This excellent HI hostel is the Cadillac of backpacker joints. Close to the center of town, but with a secluded waterfront location, it's a comfy wood-lined place with a lounge overlooking the shoreline that is an idyllic spot to watch the natural world drift by. The dorms are mercifully small and some double-bed private rooms are also available. Facilities include a granite-countered kitchen, BBQ patio, games room and a wet sauna. Reservations essential in summer.

Clayoquot Field Station HOSTEL **$$**
(250-725-1220; www.tbgf.org; 1084 Pacific Rim Hwy; dm/r $32/85; @) In the grounds of the botanical gardens, this immaculate and quiet wood-built education center has a selection of four-bed dorm rooms, a large kitchen and an on-site laundry. There are also two private suites (the larger one has a kitchen and is ideal for families). A great sleepover for nature lovers, with rates including entry to the gardens.

Eating

TOP CHOICE TacoFino MEXICAN **$**
(www.tacofino.com; 1180 Pacific Rim Hwy; mains $4-10) Arrive off-peak at this massively popular, orange-painted taco truck or you'll be waiting a while for your made-from-scratch nosh. It's worth it, though: these guys have nailed the art of great Mexican comfort food. Pull up an overturned yellow bucket – that's the seating – and tuck into sustainable fish tacos or bulging burritos stuffed with chicken. Even better are the tasty pulled-pork *gringas* and the ever-popular taco soup. Whatever you have, wash it down with a zinging lime-mint freshie: it's so sharply minty, your eyes will pop out.

Sobo SEAFOOD **$$**
(www.sobo.ca; 311 Neill St; mains $6-14) Before TacoFino ruled the vending-cart world, Sobo – it means 'sophisticated bohemian' – was the king with its legendary purple truck. It was so successful it's now upgrad-

ed to its own wildly popular bistro-style restaurant. Fish tacos and crispy shrimp cakes remain, but new treats at the table include Vancouver Island seafood stew and roasted duck confit pizza.

Shelter WEST COAST **$$$**
(www.shelterrestaurant.com; 601 Campbell St; mains $25-39) An exquisite west-coast eatery with international accents. Our menu favorite here is the shrimp and crab dumplings. There's a strong commitment to local, sustainable ingredients – the salmon is wild and the sablefish is trap-caught – and there are plenty of nonfishy options for traveling carnivores, including a delectable char-grilled pork chop dish.

Schooner on Second SEAFOOD **$$**
(www.schoonerrestaurant.ca; 331 Campbell St; mains $12-28) Family-owned for 50 years, this local legend has uncovered many new ways to prepare the region's seafood: halibut stuffed with shrimp, brie and pine nuts is recommended (as are the giant breakfasts). Or try the giant Captain's Plate blowout of salmon, scallops et al.

Getting There & Around

Orca Airways (www.flyorcaair.com) flights arrive at Tofino Airport from Vancouver International Airport's South Terminal ($206, 55 minutes, one to four daily).

Greyhound Canada (www.greyhound.ca) buses arrive from Port Alberni ($29.40, two hours, two daily), Nanaimo ($46.30, four hours, two daily) and Victoria ($70.70, six to seven hours, three daily), among other towns.

Tofino Bus (www.tofinobus.com) 'Beach Bus' services roll in along Hwy 4 from Ucluelet ($15, 40 minutes, up to three daily).

Ucluelet

POP 1500

Driving on Hwy 4's winding mountain stretch to the west coast, you'll suddenly arrive at a junction sign proclaiming that Tofino is 33km to your right, while just 8km to your left is Ucluelet (yew-klew-let). Sadly, most still take the right-hand turn. Which is a shame, since sleepier 'Ukee' – often regarded as the ugly sister of the two – has more than a few charms of its own and is a good reminder of what Tofino used to be like before tourism took over. For information, head to the **visitor centre** (250-726-2485; www.ucluelet.travel; 200 Main St; 9:30am-4:30pm), hidden up the ramp at the back of the building.

⊙ Sights & Activities

Tucked in a little waterfront cabin, **Ucluelet Aquarium** (www.ucluletaquarium.org; Main St Waterfront Promenade; adult/child $5/2; ⏱10am-6pm Mar-Oct) is an excellent small attraction, often crammed with wide-eyed kids. The emphasis is on biodiversity education, using pinkie-finger touch tanks teeming with colorful local marine life, including purple starfish and alien-like anemones – the octopus is the star attraction, though. All the critters are here temporarily on a catch-and-release program. Bold plans are afoot for a much bigger facility – watch this space.

Starting at the intersection of Peninsula and Coast Guard Rds, then winding around the wave-slapped cliffs past the lighthouse (get your camera out here) and along the craggy shoreline fringing the town, the 8.5km **Wild Pacific Trail** (www.wildpacific trail.com) offers smashing views for hikers of Barkley Sound and the Broken Group Islands. Seabirds are abundant and it's a good storm-watching spot – stick to the trail or the crashing waves might pluck you from the cliffs.

If you're not too tired, **Majestic Ocean Kayaking** (www.oceankayaking.com; 1167 Helen Rd; tours from $67) can lead you around the harbor or Barkley Sound on a bobbling kayak trek. And if you want to practice the ways of surfing, check in with **Relic Surf Shop** (www.relicsurfshop.com; 1998 Peninsula Rd; 3hr lesson/rentals per day from $74/40); it offers lessons and rentals. Alternatively, rent some wheels from the friendly team at **Ukee Bikes** (www.ukeebikes.com; 1559 Imperial Lane; per hr/24hr $5/25) and cycle over to Tofino to see what all the fuss is about.

🛏 Sleeping & Eating

Surfs Inn Guesthouse   HOSTEL $
(☑250-726-4426; www.surfsinn.ca; 1874 Peninsula Rd; dm/ste/cottage $28/159/259; ☎) While this blue-painted clapboard house on a small hill contains three homey little dorm rooms, a well-equipped kitchen and is high on friendliness, it's the two refurbished cabins out the back that attract many: one is larger, self-contained and great for groups of up to six; while the other is divided into two suites with kitchenettes. Each cottage has a BBQ and surf packages are available if you want to hit the waves.

Black Rock Oceanfront Resort   HOTEL $$$
(☑250-726-4800, 877-762-5011; www.blackrock resort.com; 596 Marine Dr; r from $179) Just to prove that Tofino doesn't have all the swanky resorts, this slick new sleepover combines lodge, cottage and beach-house accommodation, all wrapped in a contemporary wood and stone west-coast look. Many rooms have great views of the often dramatically stormy surf and there's also a vista-hugging restaurant specializing in regional nosh.

C&N Backpackers   HOSTEL $
(☑250-726-7416, 888-434-6060; www.cnnback packers.com; 2081 Peninsula Rd; dm/r $25/65; ☎) They're very protective of their hardwood floors here, so take off your shoes at the door of this calm and well-maintained hostel. The dorms are mostly small and predictably basic, but private rooms are also available and there's a spacious downstairs kitchen. The highlight is the landscaped, lounge-worthy garden overlooking the inlet, complete with hammocks and a rope swing.

Ukee Dogs   CANADIAN $
(1576 Imperial Lane; mains $4-7) Focused on home-baked treats and comfort foods, this bright and breezy, good-value eatery offers hotdogs of the gourmet variety (go for the Canuck dog) and great pies from steak and curry to salmon wellington. Drop by in the afternoon for coffee and sprinkle-topped cakes and come back in the morning for the best breakfast in town: the sausage scrambler. Cash only.

ℹ Getting There & Around

Greyhound Canada (www.greyhound.ca) buses arrive from Port Alberni ($27.30, 1½ hours, two daily), Nanaimo ($46.30, three to four hours, two daily) and Victoria ($64.70, five to seven hours, three daily), among others.

Tofino Bus (www.tofinobus.com) 'Beach Bus' services roll in along Hwy 4 from Tofino ($15, 40 minutes, up to three daily).

Denman & Hornby Islands

Regarded as the main Northern Gulf Islands, **Denman** (www.denmanisland.com) and **Hornby** (www.hornbyisland.net) share laidback attitudes, artistic flair and some tranquil outdoor activities. You'll arrive by ferry at Denman first from Buckley Bay on Vancouver Island, then you hop from Denman across to Hornby. Stop at **Denman Village**, near the first ferry dock, and pick up a free map for both islands

Denman has three provincial parks: **Fillongley**, with easy hiking and beachcombing; **Boyle Point**, with a beautiful walk to the lighthouse; and **Sandy Island**, only accessible by water from north Denman. Consider timing your visit for a free Saturday tour of **Denman Island Chocolate Factory** (www.denmanislandchocolate.com), which must be reserved in advance. Note, though: there are no samples on offer.

Among Hornby's provincial parks, **Tribune Bay** features a long sandy beach with safe swimming, while **Helliwell** offers notable hiking. **Ford's Cove**, on Hornby's south coast, offers the chance for divers to swim with six-gill sharks. The island's large **Mt Geoffrey Regional Park** is criss-crossed with hiking and mountain-biking trails.

For kayaking rentals contact **Denman Hornby Canoes & Kayaks** (www.denmanpaddling.ca; 4005 East Rd, Denman Island; 3/6hr $35/50), or **Hornby Island Outdoor Sports** (www.hornbyoutdoors.com; 5875 Central Rd, Hornby Island) for kayak (per three hours $42) and bike rentals (per hour/day $15/45).

🛏 Sleeping & Eating

Sea Breeze Lodge　　　　　　　HOTEL **$$**
(☑250-335-2321, 888-516-2321; www.seabreezelodge.com; 5205 Fowler Rd, Hornby Island; adult/child/youth $165/75/115; 🖶) This 12-acre retreat, with 16 cottages overlooking the ocean, has the feel of a Spanish villa with a Pacific Rim twist. Rooms are comfortable rather than palatial and some have fireplaces and full kitchens. You can swim, kayak and fish or just flop lazily around in the cliff-side hot tub. Rates – reduced for those under 17 – are per person and include three daily meals.

Hawthorn House B&B　　　　　　B&B **$$**
(☑250-335-0905; 3375 Kirk Rd, Denman Island; r $95-110) Handily located near the ferry dock and a short walk from the main Denman Village shops and services, this rustic garden property has three cozy rooms that can each be adapted for small groups. The best is the cottage room, located in a separate cabin and with a little kitchenette and an ocean-view porch. Cooked breakfast included.

Cardboard House　　　　　　　　BAKERY **$**
(2205 Central Rd, Hornby Island; mains $4-8) It's easy to lose track of time at this old shingle-sided farmhouse that combines a hearty bakery, pizza shop and cozy cafe. It's impossible not to stock up on a bag full of oven-fresh muffins, cookies and croissants for the road, but stick around for an alfresco lunch in the adjoining orchard, which also stages live music Wednesday and Sunday evenings in summer.

Island Time Café　　　　　　　CAFE **$**
(3464 Denman Rd, Denman Island; mains $7-9) This village hangout specializes in fresh-from-the-oven bakery treats like muffins and scones (plus organic coffee), as well as bulging breakfast wraps and hearty house-made soups. The pizza is particularly recommended, and all is served with a side order of gossip from the chatty locals. If the sun is cooperating, sit outside and catch some rays.

ℹ Getting There & Away

BC Ferries (www.bcferries.com) services arrive throughout the day at Denman from Buckley Bay (passenger/vehicle $8.35/19.55, 10 minutes). Hornby Island is accessed by ferry from Denman (passenger/vehicle $8.35/19.55, 10 minutes).

Comox Valley

Comprising the towns of Comox, Courtenay and Cumberland, this is a temperate region of rolling mountains, alpine meadows and colorful communities. A good base for outdoor adventures, its activity-triggering highlight is Mt Washington. Drop by the area **visitor centre** (☑250-334-3234, 888-357-4471; www.discovercomoxvalley.com; 2040 Cliffe Ave, Comox; ⊙9am-5pm mid-May–Aug, 9am-5pm Mon-Sat Sep–mid-May) for tips.

◉ Sights & Activities

The main reason for winter visits, **Mt Washington Alpine Resort** (www.mountwashington.ca; lift ticket adult/child winter $59/31, summer $37.50/25) is the island's skiing mecca, with its 60 runs, snowshoeing park and 55km of cross-country ski trails. But there are also some great summer activities here, including horseback riding, fly-fishing and some of the region's best biking and alpine hiking trails. Visit www.discovermountwashington.com for more activity suggestions.

Known for its life-sized replica of an elasmosaur – a prehistoric marine reptile first discovered in the area – the excellent **Courtenay & District Museum & Palaeontology Centre** (www.courtenaymuseum.ca; 207 Fourth St; admission by donation; ⊙10am-

5pm Mon-Sat, noon-4pm Sun mid-May–mid-Sep, 10am-5pm Tue-Sat mid-Sep–mid May) also houses First Nations exhibits and provides a colorful introduction to the region's pioneering past. You can hunt for your own fossils along the banks of the Puntledge River on a guided summertime fossil tour (adult/child $25/15).

Outdoor types should also make for Miracle Beach Provincial Park (www.bcparks.ca), home to some excellent hiking trails and tranquil beaches. Alternatively, Courtenay's Pacific Pro Dive & Surf (www.scubashark.com; 2270 Cliffe Ave; scuba package rental per day $75) can help with scuba lessons and equipment rentals, while Comox's Simon's Cycles (www.simoncycle.com; 1841 Comox Ave; rental $30) offers bike rentals.

🛏 Sleeping & Eating

Riding Fool Hostel   HOSTEL $
(☑250-336-8250, 888-313-3665; www.ridingfool.com; 2705 Dunsmuir Ave, Cumberland; dm/r $23/55; @🛜) One of Vancouver Island's best backpacker joints, Riding Fool is a restored heritage building with immaculate wooden interiors, a large kitchen and lounge area and the kind of neat and tidy private rooms often found in hotels. Bicycle rentals are available at the downstairs shop: this is a great hostel in which to hang out with the mountain-bike crowd.

Shantz Haus Hostel   HOSTEL $
(☑250-703-2060, 866-603-2060; www.shantzhostel.com; 520 Fifth St, Courtenay; dm/r $25/58; @🛜🐾) This peaceful little hostel feels like staying in a favorite aunt's house. Luckily, she's quite a cool aunt: her two dorms are small and cozy, while her two private rooms are ideal for families. The bathrooms are the antithesis of institutionalized hostels and there's a full kitchen, fireplace common room and sunny deck with BBQ. Give Jake the house cat a little attention.

Mad Chef Café   CANADIAN, FUSION $$
(www.madchefcafe.net; 492 Fitzgerald Ave, Courtenay; mains $8-20) Bright and colorful neighborhood eatery serving a great selection of made-from-scratch meals: this is a good place for a salad, since they're heaping and crispy-fresh. Sharers should go for the Mediterranean plate, piled high with olives, hummus, pitta and lovely own-made bruschetta. Gourmet duck or salmon burgers are also popular.

Atlas Café   FUSION $$
(www.atlascafe.ca; 250 Sixth St, Courtenay; mains $12-18) Courtenay's favorite dine-out has a pleasing modern bistro feel with a taste-tripping global menu fusing Asian, Mexican and Mediterranean flourishes. Check out the gourmet fish tacos plus ever-changing seasonal treats. Good vegetarian options, too.

Kingfisher Oceanside Resort   HOTEL $$
(☑250-338-1323, 800-663-7929; www.kingfisherspa.com; 4330 Island Hwy, Courtenay; r/ste $145/220; @🛜) Comfortable waterfront lodge with spa. Many rooms have full kitchens and shoreline balconies.

Cona Hostel   HOSTEL $
(☑250-331-0991, 877-490-2662; www.theconahostel.com; 440 Anderton Ave, Courtenay; d/r $25/58; @🛜) Cozy, orange-painted riverfront hostel with large kitchen and BBQ patio. Runs a Mt Washington shuttle in winter.

Waverley Hotel Pub   BURGERS $$
(www.waverleyhotel.ca; 2692 Dunsmuir Ave, Cumberland; mains $8-14) Come for hearty pub grub and stick around for live bands on the kick-ass little stage.

Campbell River

POP 29,500

Southerners will tell you this marks the end of civilization on Vancouver Island, but Campbell River is a handy drop-off point for wilderness tourism in Strathcona Provincial Park and is large enough to have plenty of attractions and services of its own. The visitor centre (☑250-830-1115, 877-286-5705; www.campbellriver.travel; 1235 Shoppers Row; ☺9am-6pm Mon-Sat, 10am-4pm Sun) can fill you in.

◉ Sights & Activities

The recommended Museum at Campbell River (www.crmuseum.ca; 470 Island Hwy; adult/child $6/4; ☺10am-5pm daily May-Sep, noon-5pm Tue-Sun Oct-Apr) showcases aboriginal masks, an 1890s pioneer cabin and video footage of the world's largest artificial, non-nuclear blast: an underwater mountain in Seymour Narrows that caused dozens of shipwrecks before it was blown apart in a controlled explosion 1958.

Since locals claim the town as the 'Salmon Capital of the World' you should wet your line off the downtown Discovery Pier (rod rentals $6 per day) or just stroll along with the crowds and see what everyone else has caught. Much easier than catching your own lunch, you can also buy fish and chips here.

🛏 Sleeping & Eating

Heron's Landing HOTEL **$$**

(☑250-923-2848, 888-923-2849; www.herons landinghotel.com; 492 S Island Hwy; r from $145; @🛜) Superior motel-style accommodation with renovated rooms, including large loft suites ideal for families.

Heritage River Inn MOTEL **$$**

(☑250-286-6295, 800-567-2007; www.heritage riverinn.com; 2140 N Island Hwy; r from $80; 🌢) Quiet motel north of downtown with sauna, Jacuzzi and gazebo-covered BBQs. Rates include continental breakfast.

Royal Coachman Inn BURGERS **$$**

(84 Dogwood St; mains $8-18) Brit-style pub serving BC and cross-Canada brews and a large array of grub from burgers to Thai ginger salad.

ℹ Getting There & Around

Campbell River Airport (www.crairport.ca) gets **Pacific Coastal Airlines** (www.pacific-coastal. com) flights from Vancouver International Airport ($208, 45 minutes, up to seven daily).

Greyhound Canada (www.greyhound.ca) services arrive from Port Hardy, ($48.30, 3½ hours, daily), Nanaimo ($35.80, three hours, two daily), Victoria ($57.60, six to 10 hours, three daily) and beyond.

Campbell River Transit (www.buslonline.ca; adult/child $1.75/1.50) operates local buses throughout the area.

Strathcona Provincial Park

Driving inland from Campbell River on Hwy 28, you'll soon come to BC's oldest protected area and also Vancouver Island's largest **park** (www.bcparks.ca). Centered on Mt Golden Hinde, the island's highest point (2200m), Strathcona is a magnificent pristine wilderness criss-crossed with trail systems that deliver you to waterfalls, alpine meadows, glacial lakes and looming mountain crags.

On arrival at the main entrance, get your bearings at **Strathcona Park Lodge & Outdoor Education Centre** (www.strath cona.bc.ca). A one-stop shop for park activities, including kayaking, guided treks, yoga camps, ziplining and rock climbing (all-in adventure packages are available, some aimed specifically at families), this is a great place to rub shoulders with other outdoorsy types – head to the **Whale Dining Room** or **Canoe Club Café** eateries for a fuel up.

The lodge also offers good **accommodation** (r/cabin from $136/175), which, in keeping with its low-impact approach to nature and commitment to eco-education, is sans telephones and TVs. Rooms range from basic college-style bedrooms to secluded timber-framed cottages. If you are a true back-to-nature fan, there are also several campsites available in the park. Alternatively, consider pitching your tent at **Buttle Lake Campground** (☑604-689-9025, 800-689-9025; www.

WORTH A TRIP

QUADRA ISLAND HOP

A short skip across the water with **BC Ferries** (www.bcferries.com; passenger/vehicle $8.35/19.55), rustic Quadra is a popular jaunt from Campbell River. Drop into the **visitor information booth** (www.quadraisland.ca; ⊙9am-4pm Jun-Sep) in the parking lot of the Quadra Credit Union near the ferry dock for some tips on your visit.

The island's fascinating **Nuyumbalees Cultural Centre** (www.nuyumbalees.com; 34 Weway Rd; adult/child $10/5; ⊙10am-5pm May-Sep) illuminates the heritage and traditions of the local Kwakwaka'wakw First Nations people, showcasing carvings and artifacts and staging traditional dance performances. Alternatively, the sandy beaches and clear waters of **Rebecca Spit Provincial Park** (www.bcparks.ca) offer idyllic swimming. For paddle nuts, **Quadra Island Kayaks** (www.quadraislandkayaks. com; tours from $59, rentals per day $40) can get you out on the glassy waters around the coastline; it provides rentals as well as lessons and guided tours (sunset paddle recommended). If you just want to hang out with the locals, head to **Spirit Sqare** where, in summer, performers entertain alfresco.

If you've fallen in love and want to stay, the handsome **Heriot Bay Inn & Marina** (☑250-285-3322, 888-605-4545; www.heriotbayinn.com; Heriot Bay; r/tent site from $99/24) has motel-style rooms, rustic cabins and tent spots, while the lovely, wood-lined **Quadra Island Boutique Hostel** (☑250-285-3198; www.quadraislandhostel. com; 653 Green Rd; dm/r $28/60) has small rooms, friendly hosts, a hot tub and a tree-fringed BBQ deck. What are you waiting for?

discovercamping.ca; tent site $24). The swimming area and playground here make this a good choice for families.

Notable park hiking trails include **Paradise Meadows Loop** (2.2km), an easy amble in a delicate wildflower and evergreen ecosystem; and **Mt Becher** (5km), with its great views over the Comox Valley and mountain-lined Strait of Georgia. The 9km **Comox Glacier Trail** is quite an adventure but is only recommended for advanced hikers. Around Buttle Lake, easier walks include **Lady Falls** (900m) and the trail along **Karst Creek** (2km), which winds past sinkholes, percolating streams and tumbling waterfalls.

North Vancouver Island

Down-islanders (which means anyone below Campbell River) will tell you, 'There's nothing up there worth seeing,' while locals here will respond, 'They would say that, wouldn't they?' Parochial rivalries aside, what this giant region, covering nearly half the island, lacks in towns, infrastructure and population, it more than makes up for in rugged natural beauty. Despite the remoteness, some areas are remarkably accessible to hardy hikers, especially along the North Coast Trail.

Spotting black bears feasting on roadside berries soon becomes commonplace up here, but you'll also appreciate many of the quirky locals who color the region: northerners have a hardy, independent streak that marks them out from the south-island softies. For further information on the region, check in with Vancouver Island North (www.vancouverislandnorth.ca).

TELEGRAPH COVE

Originally just a one-shack telegraph station, charming Telegraph Cove has successfully reinvented itself in recent decades as a visitor magnet. Its pioneer-outpost feel is enhanced by the dozens of wooden buildings standing around the marina on stilts, but the place can get ultracrowded in summer. The road into the area was paved a few years back, encouraging a new hotel and housing development.

Head first along the boardwalk to the smashing Whale Interpretive Centre (www.killerwhalecentre.org; suggested donation $2; ⊙May-Sep), bristling with hands-on artifacts and artfully displayed skeletons of cougars, sea otters and a giant fin whale.

You can also see whales of the live variety just offshore: this is one of the island's top marine-life viewing regions and Stubbs Island Whale Watching (www.stubbs-island.com; adult/child $94/84; ⊙May-Sep) will get you up close with the orcas on a boat trek – you might also see humpbacks, dolphins and sea lions. Its sunset cruise is a highlight. For a bear alternative, Tide Rip Grizzly Tours (www.tiderip.com; $288; ⊙mid-May–Sep)

AND FINALLY...THE NORTH COAST TRAIL

If your response to the famed West Coast Trail (p111) is 'been there, done that,' it's time to strap on your hiking boots for the north-island equivalent, a 43km route that opened to itchy hikers in 2008. You can start on the western end at Nissen Bight, but you'll have to hike in 15km on the established (and relatively easy) Cape Scott Trail to get there. From Nissen Bight, the trail winds eastwards to Shushartie Bay. You'll be passing sandy coves, deserted beaches and dense, wind-whipped rainforest woodland, as well as a couple of river crossings on little cable cars. The trail is muddy and swampy in places so there are boardwalks to make things easier. The area is home to elk, deer, cougars, wolves and black bears (make sure you know how to handle an encounter before you set off), while offshore you're likely to spot seals, sea lions, sea otters and grey whales. Like its west-coast sibling, the North Coast Trail is for experienced and well-equipped hikers only. There are backcountry campsites at Nissen Bight, Laura Creek and Shuttleworth Bight and the route should take five to eight days.

The Holberg Cape Scott trailhead is 63km from Port Hardy and is accessible on well-used logging roads. You can drive there yourself or take the dedicated North Coast Trail Shuttle (www.northcoasttrailshuttle.com; $70). Once you're done at the Shushartie Bay end, you can pick up a Cape Scott Water Taxi (www.capescottwater taxi.ca; $80) back to Port Hardy. You must book both the shuttle and the boat ahead of time – the shuttle company can also help you book the water taxi.

Reservations are not required for the North Coast Trail.

DON'T MISS

BEST LITTLE COOKHOUSE IN THE NORTH

The winding, tree-lined Hwy 19 stretch between mid-island Campbell River and north-island Port Hardy is studded with little communities (as well as a few black bears feasting on roadside berries). If it's mealtime when you arrive around tiny Sayward, drop into the legendary **Cable Cookhouse** (1741 Sayward Rd; mains $8-20). This seemingly age-old cafe is uniquely cocooned in 2.7km of steel logging cables, a reminder of the area's hardy resource-industry past. Inside, cool 1950s frescoes of logging-camp scenes adorn the back walls. But you haven't just come here to look, so make sure you unnotch your belt and hit the menu. An ideal spot to kick-start your day, tuck into the heaping Loggers Breakfast of eggs, bacon et al. Better still, drop by for lunch: the salmon melt sandwich and oyster burger are excellent. And if you can resist the thick slabs of own-made fruit pie on the counter, you're doing better than most. In fact, the Cable Cookhouse is where many diets come to die.

leads full-day trips to local beaches and inlets in search of the area's furry residents.

The established **Telegraph Cove Resorts** (250-928-3131, 800-200-4665; www.telegraphcoveresort.com; campsite/cabin from $27/115) provides accommodations in forested tent spaces and a string of rustic cabins on stilts overlooking the marina. The nearby and much newer **Dockside 29** (250-928-3163, 877-835-2683; www.telegraphcove.ca; r $140-175) is a good, motel-style alternative. Its rooms have kitchenettes with hardwood floors and waterfront views.

The **Killer Whale Café** (mains $14-18; May-Sep) is the cove's best eatery – the salmon, mussel and prawn linguini is recommended. The adjoining **Old Saltery Pub** is an atmospheric, wood-lined nook with a cozy central fireplace and tasty Killer Whale Pale Ale. It's a good spot to sit in a corner and pretend you're an old sea salt – eye patch and wooden leg optional.

PORT MCNEILL
POP 2600

Barreling down the hill almost into Broughton Straight, Port McNeill is the north island's second-largest community, making it a useful supply stop for travelers.

More a superior motel than a resort, the hilltop **Black Bear Resort** (250-956-4900, 866-956-4900; www.port-mcneill-accommodation.com; 1812 Campbell Way; d/tw/ste $135/155/235; @🖥️🐾) overlooks the town and is conveniently located across from shops and restaurants. The standard rooms are small but clean and include microwaves and fridges; full-kitchen units are also available and there's a new on-site spa. Rates include a large continental-breakfast buffet.

If you're still hungry, the nearby **Bo-Banees** (1705 Campbell Way; mains $7-15) restaurant serves burritos, burgers and Lucky Lager – the logger's favorite beer. The chicken quesadilla is a winner here.

Drop by the gabled **visitor center** (250-956-3131; www.portmcneill.net; 1594 Beach Dr; 9am-5pm Mon-Fri, 10am-3pm Sat, reduced off-season) for regional info, then stop in at the **museum** (351 Shelley Cres; 10am-5pm Jul-Sep, 1-3pm Sat & Sun Oct-Jun) to learn about the area's logging-industry heritage.

Greyhound Canada (www.greyhound.ca) buses arrive in Port McNeill from Port Hardy ($14.90, 30 minutes, daily), Campbell River ($42, 2½ hours, daily) and Nanaimo ($70.70, six hours, daily).

Regular **BC Ferries** (www.bcferries.com) services also arrive from Alert Bay and Sointula (passenger/vehicle $9.75/22.75) but times and schedules vary – see the website for details.

ALERT BAY
POP 550

Located on Cormorant Island, this visitor-friendly village has an ancient and mythical appeal. Its First Nations community and traditions are still prevalent, but its blend with an old pioneer fishing settlement makes it an even more fascinating day trip from Port McNeill. Drop by the **visitor center** (250-974-5024; www.alertbay.ca; 116 Fir St; 9am-4:30pm Mon-Fri, reduced off-season) for an introduction.

The highly recommended **U'mista Cultural Centre** (250-974-5403; www.umista.ca; 1 Front St; adult/child $8/1; 9am-5pm daily May-Aug, 9am-5pm Tue-Sat Sep-Apr) showcases an impressive collection of Kwakwaka'wakw masks and other potlatch items originally confiscated by Canada's federal government. Singing, dancing and BBQs are often held here, while modern-day totem-pole carvers usually work their magic out front. One of the world's tallest totem poles was carved on site in the 1960s and is appropriately placed on the front lawn of the **Big House**, which hosts traditional dances in July and August. Also drop into Culture Shock Interactive Gallery (www.cultureshockgallery.ca; 10A Front St) for some exquisite artwork souvenirs.

If the ocean is calling you, Seasmoke Whale Watching (www.seaorca.com; adult/child $95/85) offers a five-hour whale-watching trek on its yacht, including afternoon tea.

PORT HARDY
POP 3800

Settled by Europeans in the early 1800s, this small north-island settlement is best known as the arrival/departure point for BC Ferries Inside Passage trips. It's also a handy gear-up spot for the North Coast Trail.

◉ Sights & Activities

Before you leave town on a long hike, check into the new Quatse Salmon Stewardship Centre (www.thesalmoncentre.org; 8400 Byng Rd; adult/child $5/2; ⊙10am-5pm Wed-Sun mid-May–Sep) to learn all about the life cycle of local salmon. The kid-friendly facility has lots of critters in tanks and was also working on a new theater room at the time of our visit. The friendly staff will answer all your salmon-related questions.

Port Hardy is a great access point for exploring the north-island wilderness and hikers can book a customized guided tour with the friendly folk at North Island Daytrippers (www.islanddaytrippers.com). For those who prefer to paddle, Odyssey Kayaking (www.odysseykayaking.com; rentals/tours from $40/99) can take you on guided tours around Malei Island, Bear Cove and Alder Bay or leave you to your own devices with a full-day rental. For dive fans, Catala Charters (www.catalacharters.net; dive trips from $150) options include trips to Browning Passage. Dripping with octopus, wolf eels and corals, it's one of BC's top cold-water dive sites.

🛏 Sleeping & Eating

Ecoscape Cabins   CABIN **$$**
(☏250-949-8524; www.ecoscapecabins.com; 6305 Jensen Cove Rd; cabins $125-175; 🛜) A clutch of immaculate cedar-wood cabins, divided between three compact units –

with flat-screens, microwaves and sunny porches (ideal for couples) – and three roomier hilltop units with swankier furnishings, BBQs and expansive views. There's a tranquil retreat feel to staying here and you should expect to see eagles swooping around the nearby trees. Deer are not uncommon, too.

North Coast Trail Backpackers Hostel   HOSTEL **$**
(☏250-949-9441, 866-448-6303; www.porthardyhostel.webs.com; 8635 Granville St; dm/r from $24/58) Colonizing a former downtown storefront, this labyrinthine hostel is a warren of small and larger dorms, overseen by a friendly couple with plenty of tips about how to encounter the region – they'll even pick you up from the ferry if you call ahead. The hostel's hub (a hangout for house dog Luke) is a large rec room and, while the kitchen is small, a coffee shop was being added at the time of our visit.

Bear Cove Cottages   CABIN **$$**
(☏250-949-7939, 877-949-7339; www.bearcovecottages.ca; 6715 Bear Cove Hwy; d $149; 🛜) A string of eight comfy cabins, all with kitchenettes and views across the water (and the road) from your deck . There's a well-maintained motel feel but the rooms have handy extras like small Jacuzzi tubs and corner fireplaces – you can also borrow a BBQ to make full use of your patio.

Escape Bistro & Gallery   CANADIAN **$$**
(8405 Byng Rd; mains $16-22) Just across from the Salmon Stewardship Centre, this excellent reinvention of a once-tired resto-bar is a revelation. The old-school dining room (try for a booth) has been enlivened with local artworks and there's live Friday and Saturday guitar music to keep things animated. The menu combines simple home-cooked dishes with lip-smacking European fare like Hungarian goulash and Vienna schnitzel – go for Friday's pork-roast special. Excellent service.

Café Guido   CAFE **$**
(7135 Market St; mains $5-7; 🛜) A friendly locals' hangout where you'll easily end up sticking around for an hour or two, especially if you hit the loungey sofas with a tome purchased from the bookstore downstairs. Grilled paninis are the way to go for lunch (try the Nero) but there's always a good soup special. Then nip upstairs to the surprisingly large and diverse craft shop.

ℹ Information

Head to the **visitor center** (☎250-949-7622; www.porthardy.travel; 7250 Market St; h9am-5pm Jun-Aug, 9am-5pm Mon-Fri Sep-May) for local info, including comprehensive North Coast Trail maps ($9.95). Say hi to the stuffed otter while you're checking your email at the terminal (per half-hour $2.50).

ℹ Getting There & Around

Pacific Coastal Airlines (www.pacific-coastal. com) services arrive from Vancouver ($235, 1¼ hours, up to three daily).

Greyhound Canada (www.greyhound.ca) buses roll in from Port McNeill ($14.90, 45 minutes, daily), Campbell River ($48.30, 3½ hours, daily) and Nanaimo ($73, seven hours, daily).

BC Ferries (www.bcferries.com) arrive from Prince Rupert (passenger/vehicle $170/390, 15 hours, schedules vary) through the spectacular Inside Passage.

North Island Transportation (nit@island.net) operates a handy shuttle ($8) to/from the ferry terminal via area hotels.

CAPE SCOTT PROVINCIAL PARK

It's more than 550km from the comparatively metropolis-like streets of down-island Victoria to the nature-hugging trailhead of this remote park (www.bcparks.ca) on Vancouver Island's crenulated northern tip. But if you really want to experience the raw, ravishing beauty of BC – especially its unkempt shorelines, breeze-licked rainforests and stunning sandy bays animated with tumbling waves and beady-eyed seabirds – this should be your number-one destination.

Hike the well-maintained, relatively easy 2.5km San Josef Bay Trail and you'll stroll from the shady confines of the trees right onto one of the best beaches in BC; a breathtaking, windswept expanse of roiling water, forested crags and the kind of age-old caves that could easily harbor lost smugglers. You can camp right here on the beach or just admire the passing ospreys before plunging back into the trees.

With several wooded trails to tempt you – most are aimed at well-prepared hikers with plenty of gumption – the forest offers moss-covered yew trees, centuries-old cedars and a soft carpet of sun-dappled ferns covering every square centimeter.

Between the giant slugs that seem to own the place, you'll also spot historic plaques showing that this unlikely area was once settled by Scandinavian pioneers who arrived here from Europe on a promise from the government of a main road link from down-island. Now mostly reclaimed by the forest, the evocative, crumbling shacks of these settlers, most of whom eventually left when the promised road failed to materialize, can still be seen almost hidden in the dense undergrowth.

One of the area's shortest trails (2km), in adjoining **Raft Cove Provincial Park** (www. bcparks.ca), brings you to the wide, crescent beach and beautiful lagoons of Raft Cove. You're likely to have the entire 1.3km expanse to yourself, although the locals also like to surf here (it's their secret, so don't tell anyone).

Hiking much further in the region is not for the uninitiated or unprepared. But if you really want to go for it, consider hitting the relatively new **North Coast Trail** (p119).

SOUTHERN GULF ISLANDS

Stressed-out Vancouverites tired of languishing on their favorite Stanley Park beach or trying to find the city's best sushi restaurants often seek solace in the restorative arms of the rustic Southern Gulf Islands, conveniently strung like a necklace of enticing pearls between the mainland and Vancouver Island. Once colonized by hippy-dippy Canadian dropouts and fugitive US draft dodgers, Salt Spring, Galiano, Mayne, Saturna and North and South Pender Islands are the natural retreat of choice for many in the region.

Not all the islands are created equal, of course. Salt Spring is recommended if you want a sojourn where you don't have to sacrifice on great restaurants; Galiano is popular if you fancy a wood cabin, scenic nooks and outdoor activities; and remote Saturna is ideal if you really need to escape from the tourist hordes dogging your every step. Wherever you decide to head, the soothing relaxation begins once you step on the ferry to get here: time suddenly slows, your heart rate drops to hibernation level and the scenery of forested isles and glassy water slides by like a slow-motion nature documentary.

During your ferry trip, pick up a free copy of the *Gulf Islands Driftwood* (www. gulfislandsdriftwood.com) newspaper for local info, listings and happenings.

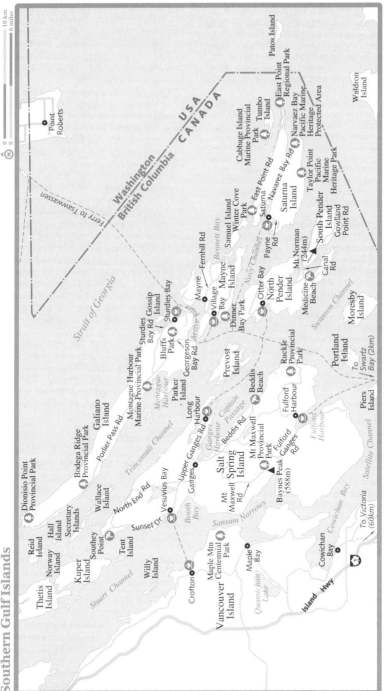

Southern Gulf Islands

ℹ️ Getting There & Around

Serving the main Southern Gulf Islands, **BC Ferries** (www.bcferries.com) operates direct routes from Vancouver Island's Swartz Bay terminal to Salt Spring and North Pender. From North Pender, you can connect to Mayne, Galiano or Salt Spring. From Mayne, you can connect to Saturna.

From the mainland, there is a direct service from Tsawwassen to Galiano, which then connects to North Pender. There are also direct weekend services from Tsawwassen to both Mayne (Sunday only) and Salt Spring (Friday to Sunday). For more frequent services to these and the other islands, you will need to travel from Tsawwassen to Swartz Bay, then board a connecting ferry. For island hopping, consider a handy SailPass (four-/seven-day pass $199/239). It covers ferry travel around the region on 20 different routes.

Gulf Islands Water Taxi (www.saltspring. com/watertaxi) runs walk-on ferries between Salt Spring, North Pender and Saturna (one way/return $15/25) and between Salt Spring, Galiano and Mayne (one way/return $15/25), twice daily from September to June and once a day in July and August.

Salt Spring Air (www.saltspringair.com) floatplane services arrive throughout the Southern Gulf Islands from downtown Vancouver and Vancouver International Airport. Check the website for its many schedules and fares. Similar services are offered by **Seair Seaplanes** (www.seairseaplanes.com).

Salt Spring Island

POP 10,500

A former hippie enclave that's now the site of many rich vacation homes, pretty Salt Spring justifiably receives the majority of Gulf Island visitors. The heart of the community is Ganges, also the location of the **visitor center** (☎250-537-5252; www. saltspringtourism.com; 121 Lower Ganges Rd; ⊙9am-5pm Jul & Aug, reduced off-season).

◉ Sights & Activities

If you arrive on a summer weekend, the best way to dive into the community is at the thriving **Saturday Market** (www. saltspringmarket.com; Centennial Park, Ganges; ⊙8am-4pm Sat Apr-Oct), where you can tuck into luscious island-grown fruit and piquant cheeses while perusing locally produced arts and crafts. Visit some of these artisans via a free downloadable **Studio Tour Map** (www.saltspringstudiotour. com). One of the best is the rustic **Blue Horse Folk Art Gallery** (www.bluehorse. ca; 175 North View Dr; ⊙10am-5pm Sun-Fri Mar-Dec), with, among other cool creations, its funky carvings of horses. The friendly owners recently opened an on-site **B&B** (www.bloomorganicbandb.com; d $150) if you feel like sticking around.

If you haven't eaten your fill at the market, drop into **Salt Spring Island Cheese** (www.saltspringcheese.com; 285 Reynolds Rd) for a self-guided tour of the facilities. Be sure to check out the miniature ponies before sampling up to 10 curdy treats in the winery-style tasting room.

Pick a favorite cheese then add to your picnic-in-the-making with a bottle from **Salt Spring Vineyards** (www.saltspringvine yards.com; 151 Lee Rd; ⊙11am-5pm mid-Jun–Aug, reduced off-season), where you can sample a few tipples until you find the one you like best – it could be the rich blackberry port.

Pack up your picnic and head over to **Ruckle Provincial Park** (www.bcparks.ca), a southeast gem with ragged shorelines, gnarly arbutus forests and sun-kissed farmlands. There are trails here for all skill levels, with Yeo Point making an ideal pit stop.

It's not all about hedonism on Salt Spring, of course. If you crave some activity, touch base with **Salt Spring Adventure Co** (www.saltspringadventures.com; 124 Upper Ganges Rd; tours from $50). It can kit you out for a bobbling kayak tour around Ganges Harbour.

🛏️ Sleeping

Love Shack CABIN $$
(☎250-653-0007, 866-341-0007; www.oceanside cottages.com; 521 Isabella Rd; cabins $135) If Austin Powers ever comes to Salt Spring, this is where he'll stay. A groovy waterfront nook, where the hardest part is leaving, this cozy cottage has a lava lamp, a collection of vintage cameras and a record player plus albums (Abba to Stan Getz). With plenty of artsy flourishes, the kitchen is stocked with organic coffee and the private deck is ideal for watching the sunset in your velour jumpsuit.

Lakeside Gardens CABIN $$
(☎250-537-5773; www.lakesidegardens resort .com; 1450 North End Rd; cabana/cottage $75/135; ⊙Apr-Oct) A rustic wooded retreat where nature is the main attraction, this tranquil, family-friendly clutch of cottages and cabanas is ideal for low-key fishing,

swimming and boating. The cabanas are basic – think camping in a cabin – with fridges, outdoor BBQs and solar-heated outdoor showers, while the larger cottages have TVs, en suites and full kitchens.

Wisteria Guest House B&B **$$**
(☑250-537-5899, 888-537-5899; www.wisteria guesthouse.com; 268 Park Dr; r/cottage $129/159) A home-style B&B with welcoming cats and dogs, there are six guest rooms here (some with shared bathrooms) and a pair of private-entrance studios, plus a small cottage space that has its own compact kitchen facilities. The property is surrounded by a rambling, flower-strewn garden that lends an air of tranquility. An excellent cooked breakfast is served in the large communal lounge.

Harbour House Hotel HOTEL **$$**
(☑250-537-5571, 888-799-5571; www.salt springharbourhouse.com; 121 Upper Ganges Rd; s & d from $129; 🛜) Great Ganges location and a combination of motel-style and superior rooms with Jacuzzis.

Seabreeze Inne MOTEL **$$**
(☑250-537-4145, 800-434-4112; www.sea breezeinne.com; 101 Bittancourt Rd; s & d from $119; 🛜) Immaculate motel up the hill from Ganges; rates include continental breakfast and outdoor hot tub.

✕ Eating & Drinking

Tree House Café CAFE **$$**
(www.treehousecafe.ca; 106 Purvis Lane; mains $11-18) A magical outdoor cafe in the heart of Ganges, you'll be sitting in the shade of a large plum tree as you choose from a menu of comfort pastas, Mexican specialties and gourmet burgers – the Teriyaki salmon burger is recommended, washed down with a hoppy bottle of Salt Spring Pale Ale. Live music every night in summer.

Barb's Buns CAFE **$**
(121 McPhillips Ave; mains $6-9) Good wholesome treats are the menu mainstays here, with heaping pizza slices, hearty soups and bulging sandwiches drawing the lunch crowd, many of them grateful vegetarians. Others repeatedly fail to resist the mid-afternoon lure of organic coffee, cookies, cakes and, of course, Barb's lovely buns.

Raven Street Market Café CANADIAN **$$**
(www.ravenstreet.ca; 321 Fernwood Rd; mains $8.50-18) A favorite haunt of north-island locals, this neighborhood eatery has a comfort-food

menu with a gourmet twist. Adventurous pizzas include herbed lamb and artichoke, while the awesome seafood-and-sausage gumbo combines mussels, tiger prawns and chorizo sausage with a secret Creole recipe. There's a little shop here, too, so you can pick up some local wine for breakfast.

Restaurant House Piccolo WEST COAST **$$$**
(www.housepiccolo.com; 108 Hereford Ave; mains $20-28) White tablecloth dining – duck is recommended – along with Salt Spring's best wine list.

Oystercatcher Seafood Bar & Grill
SEAFOOD **$$**
(100 Manson Rd; mains $8-16) Delectable local seafood, especially the oysters and salmon.

ℹ Getting There & Around

BC Ferries, Gulf Island Water Taxis and Salt Spring Air operate services to Salt Spring (see p124). The island's three ferry docks are at Long Harbour, Fulford Harbour and Vesuvius Bay. Water taxis and floatplanes arrive in Ganges Harbour.

If you don't have your own car, **Salt Spring Island Transit** (www.busonline.ca; adult/under-5 $2/free) runs a five-route mini-shuttle service around the island, connecting to all three ferry docks. Bus 4 runs from Long Harbour to Ganges. Alternatively, **Amber Taxi Co** (☑250-537-3277) provides a local cab service.

North & South Pender Islands

POP 2200

Once joined by a sandy isthmus, the North and South Penders are far quieter than Salt Spring and attract those looking for a quiet, retreat approach to their vacation. With pioneer farms, old-time orchards and almost 40 coves and beaches, the Penders – now linked by a single-lane bridge – are a good spot for bikers and hikers. For visitor information check www.penderislandchamber.com.

⊙ Sights & Activities

Enjoy the sand at **Medicine Beach** and **Clam Bay** on North Pender as well as **Gowlland Point** on the east coast of South Pender. Just over the bridge to South Pender is **Mt Norman Regional Park**, complete with a couple of hikes that promise grand views of the surrounding islands. There's a regular Saturday farmers market (☺Apr-Nov) in the community hall and a smaller one at the Driftwood Centre, the region's not-very-big commercial hub.

Dozens of artists call Pender home and you can chat with them in their galleries and studios by downloading a pair of free maps from **Pender Creatives** (www.pender creatives.com) that reveal exactly where they're all at. Not surprisingly, most are on North Pender.

You can hit the water with a paddle (and hopefully a boat) with the friendly team at **Pender Island Kayak Adventures** (www. kayakpenderisland.com; Otter Bay Marina; tours adult/child from $45/30). If you prefer recreation of the bottled variety, consider a tasting at **Morning Bay Vineyard** (www. morningbay.ca; 6621 Harbour Hill; ⊙10am-5pm Wed-Sun, reduced off-season), a handsome post-and-beam-built winery where the grapes are grown on a steep 20-step terrace. Its recommended Gewurztraminer-Riesling blend is light and crisp.

🛏 Sleeping

Poet's Cove Resort & Spa   HOTEL $$$
(☑250-629-2100, 888-512-7638; www.poetscove. com; 9801 Spalding Rd, Bedwell Harbour, South Pender; r from $250; ☒) A luxurious harbor-front lodge with arts-and-crafts-accented rooms, most with great views across the glassy water. Some of Chichi extras include a full-service spa and an activity center that books ecotours and fishing excursions around the area. There's also an elegant west coast restaurant (Aurora), where you can dine in style. As well as this, the resort offers kayak treks plus a full-treatment spa, complete with that all-important steam cave.

Inn on Pender Island   HOTEL $$
(☑250-629-3353; 800-550-0172; www.innon pender.com; 4709 Canal Rd; r/cabins $99/149) A rustic lodge with motel-style rooms and a couple of cozy, wood-lined cabins, you're surrounded here by verdant woodland, which explains the frequent appearance of wandering deer. The lodge rooms are neat and clean and share an outdoor hot tub, but the waterfront cabins have barrel-vaulted ceilings, full kitchens and little porches out front. There's also an on-site restaurant.

Shangri-La Oceanfront B&B   B&B $$$
(☑250-629-3808, 877-629-2800; www.pend erislandshangrila.com; 5909 Pirate's Rd; d from $185) It's all about escaping and relaxing at this three-unit waterfront property where each room has its own outdoor hot tub for drinking in the sunset through the trees. You'll have your own private entrance plus pampering extras like thick robes, large individual decks and a sumptuous breakfast. Our fave room is the Lost in Space suite, where the walls are painted with a glowing galaxy theme.

Arcadia by the Sea   CABIN $$
(☑250-629-3221, 877-470-8439; www.arca diabythesea.com; 1329 MacKinnon Rd; d $125-225; ⊙May-Sep; ☒) Tranquil, adults-only sleepover with three homely cottages (each with kitchen and deck). Free ferry pickup.

Pior Centennial Park   CAMPGROUND $
(☑604-689-9025, 800-689-9025; www.discov ercamping.ca; campsite from $15; ⊙mid-May–mid-Oct) Nestled among trees, this fairly basic campground has a cold-water pump, pit toilets and picnic tables.

🍴 Eating

Pender Island Bakery Café   BAKERY $
(Driftwood Centre, 1105 Stanley Point Dr; mains $6-16) The locals' fave coffeehouse, there's much more to this chatty nook than regular joe. For a start, the java is organic, as are many of the bakery treats, including some giant cinnamon buns that will have you wrestling an islander for the last one. Gourmet pizzas are a highlight – the Gulf Islander (smoked oysters, anchovies, spinach and three cheeses) is best – while heartier fare includes spinach and pine nut pie and a bulging seafood lasagna.

Hope Bay Café   SEAFOOD $$
(4301 Bedwell Harbour Rd; mains $16-24) Seafood rules (closely followed by the sterling views across Plumper Sound) at this laidback, bistro-like spot a few minutes from the Otter Bay ferry dock. The fish and chips are predictably good but dig deeper into the menu for less-expected treats like stuffed pork shoulder, herb-crusted wild BC salmon and the excellent bouillabaisse that's brimming with mussels, scallops, salmon and cod.

Aurora   WEST COAST $$$
(☑250-629-2115; www.poetscove.com; Poet's Cove Resort & Spa; mains $18-34) Seasonal and regional are the operative words at this fine-dining eatery. Allow yourself to be tempted by a Salt Spring goat-cheese tart starter but save room for main dishes like the local seafood medley of crab, scallops and mussels. Dinner reservations are recommended, but if you can't get in here, head to the resort's Syrens lounge bar.

❶ Getting There & Around

BC Ferries, Gulf Island Water Taxis and Salt Spring Air operate services to Pender (see p124). Ferries stop at North Pender's Otter Bay, where most of the islands' population resides. If you don't have a car, and your accommodations can't pick you up, catch a **Pender Island Taxi** (✆250-629-3555).

Saturna Island

POP 325

Small and suffused with tranquility, Saturna is a lovely nature retreat that's remote enough to deter casual visitors. Almost half the island, laced with curving bays, stunning rock bluffs and towering arbutus trees, is part of the Gulf Islands National Park Reserve and the only crowds you're likely to come across are the feral goats that have called this their munchable home for decades. If you've had enough of civilization, this is the place to lose it. The Saturna Island Tourism Association (www.saturna tourism.com) website has a downloadable map. Bring cash with you – there are no ATMs (and only two shops) here.

On the north side of the island, Winter Cove Park has a white-sand beach that's popular for swimming, boating and fishing. If you're here for Canada Day (July 1), you should also partake of the island's main annual event in the adjoining Hunter Field. This communal Lamb Barbecue (www.saturnalambbarbeque.com; adult/child $20/10), complete with live music, sack races, beer garden and a smashing meatlovers feast, is centered on a pagan fire pit surrounded by dozens of staked-out, slow-roasting sheep.

Walk off your meat belly the next day with a hike up Mt Warburton Pike (497m), where you'll spot wild goats, soaring eagles and restorative panoramic views of the surrounding islands: focus your binoculars and you might spy a whale or two sailing quietly along the coast.

Wine fans can also partake of tastings and tours at Saturna Island Winery (www. saturnavineyards.com; 8 Quarry Rd; ◷11:30am-4:30pm), which also has an on-site **bistro** that's only open for lunch.

If you're been inspired by the gentler pace of life to stick around, Breezy Bay B&B (✆250-539-5957; www.saturnacan.net/breezy; 131 Payne Rd; d $95) is a century-old still-working farmhouse property with its own private beach. The main house has wooden floors, stone fireplaces and even an old library, while your room – with shared bathroom – will be fairly basic but clean and comfortable. Breakfast is in a window-lined room overlooking a garden. Alternatively, Saturna Lodge (◷250-539-2254, 866-539-2254; www.saturna.ca; 130 Payne Rd; d $119-149; ☍) is an elegant, six-room country inn, combining landscaped gardens with close proximity to the waterfront. Rates include breakfast.

❶ Getting There & Around

BC Ferries, Gulf Island Water Taxis and Salt Spring Air operate services to Saturna (see p124). The ferry docks at Lyall Harbour on the west of the island. A car is not essential here since some lodgings are near the ferry terminal, but there are no taxis or shuttle services to get you around. Only bring your bike if you like a challenge: Saturna is a little too hilly for casual pedalers.

Mayne Island

POP 900

Once a stopover for gold rush miners (who nicknamed it 'Little Hell') on their way to the mainland, Mayne is the region's most historic island. Long past its importance as a commercial hub, it now houses a colorful clutch of resident artists. For further information, visit www.mayneislandchamber.ca.

The heritage Agricultural Hall in Miners Bay hosts the lively farmers market (◷10am-1pm Sat Jul-Sep) of local crafts and produce, while the nearby Plumper Pass Lock-up (◷11am-3pm Fri-Mon late Jun-early Sep) is a tiny museum that originally served as a jailhouse.

Among the most visit-worthy galleries and artisan studios on the island is Mayne Island Glass Foundry (www.mayne islandglass.com; ◷10am-5pm Jun-Sep, reduced off-season), where recycled glass is used to fashion new jewelry and ornaments – pick up a cool green-glass slug for the road.

The south shore's Dinner Bay Park has a lovely sandy beach, as well as a Japanese Garden. Built by locals to commemorate early-20th-century Japanese residents, it's immaculately landscaped and is lit up with fairy lights at Christmas.

For paddlers and pedalers, Mayne Island Kayaking (www.kayakmayneisland.com; 563

Arbutus Dr; rentals 2hr/8hr from $40/60, tours from $50) offers rentals and tours.

If it's time to eat, head to **Wild Fennel Restaurant** (574 Fernhill Rd; mains $16-20), which specializes in seasonal fresh ingredients. The menu changes constantly, but hope for the Crab Three Ways – crab served in salad, bisque and lollipop form.

If you're just too lazy to head back to the mainland, **Mayne Island Resort** (866-539-5399; www.mayneislandresort.com; 494 Arbutus Dr; r/cottage from $99/225; 🔊🏊) combines ocean-view rooms in a century-old inn with swanky new luxe beach cottages. There's also a large resto-bar and a new spa.

❶ Getting There & Around

BC Ferries, Gulf Island Water Taxis and Salt Spring Air operate services to Mayne (see p124). For transportation around the island, call **MIDAS Taxi** (☑250-539-3132).

Galiano Island

POP 1100

Named after a Spanish explorer who visited in the 1790s, the bustling ferry end of Galiano is markedly different to the rest of the island, which becomes ever more forested and tranquil as you continue your drive from the dock. Supporting the widest ecological diversity of the Southern Gulf Islands – and regarded by some as the most beautiful – this skinny landmass offers a bounty of activities for visiting marine enthusiasts and landlubbers alike.

Once you've got your bearings – ie driven off the ferry – head for **Montague Harbour Marine Provincial Park** for trails to beaches, meadows and a cliff carved by glaciers. In contrast, **Bodega Ridge Provincial Park** is renowned for its eagle, loon and cormorant bird life and has some spectacular drop-off viewpoints.

The protected waters of **Trincomali Channel** and the more chaotic waters of **Active Pass** satisfy paddlers of all skill levels. **Gulf Island Kayaking** (www.seakayak.ca; 3hr/day rental from $38/75, tours from $55) can help with rentals and guided tours.

If you're without a car, or you just want to stretch your legs, you can explore the island with a bike from **Galiano Bicycle** (www.galianoisland.com/galianobicycle; 4hr/day $25/30).

Fuel up on food and local gossip at **Daystar Market Café** (96 Georgeson Bay Rd; mains $4-10), a funky hangout that serves hearty salads, thick sandwiches and fruit smoothies. Alternatively, down a pint or three at the venerable **Hummingbird Pub** (www.hummingbirdpub.com; 47 Sturdies Bay Rd; mains $8-12), where pub grub on the patio is always a good idea.

Among the places to sleep on the island, sophisticates will enjoy **Galiano Inn** (☑250-539-3388, 877-530-3939; www.galianoinn.com; 134 Madrona Dr; r $249-299; 🔊), a Tuscan-style villa with 10 elegant rooms, each with a fireplace and romantic oceanfront terrace. Adult, sophisticated and soothing, it's close to the Sturdies Bay ferry dock. Those craving a nature-hugging retreat will likely enjoy **Bodega Ridge** (250-539-2677, 877-604-2677; www.bodegaridge.com; 120 Manastee Rd; d $200; 🔊), a tranquil woodland clutch of seven cabins at the other end of the island. Each has three bedrooms and is furnished in rustic country fashion.

The main clutch of businesses and services is around the ferry dock at Sturdies Bay and includes a garage, post office, bookstore and **visitor info booth** (www.galianoisland.com; 2590 Sturdies Bay Rd; �
Jul & Aug).

❶ Getting There & Around

BC Ferries, Gulf Island Water Taxis and Salt Spring Air operate services to Galiano (see p124). Ferries arrives at the Sturdies Bay dock.

FRASER & THOMPSON VALLEYS

Vancouverites looking for an inland escape shoot east on Hwy 1 through the fertile plains of places like Abbotsford. Most just whiz past this farmland and you should too – unless you have a hankering to see a turnip in the rough.

About 150km east of Vancouver, Hope has a good **visitor center** (☑604-869-2021; www.hope.ca; 919 Water Ave; �
9am-5pm) with plenty of information about the local provincial parks and the region. This is also where the road does a three-way split. Hwy 1 continues spectacularly north, literally through the vertical walls of the beautiful Fraser Canyon. From Lytton, it follows the Thompson River and the terrain slowly smoothes out and becomes drier, foreshadowing the ranchlands of the Cariboo region to the north beyond Cache Creek. Hwy 5 shoots its multilane expanse 200km north-

east to the commercial center of Kamloops. The Crowsnest Hwy (Hwy 3) takes a circuitous and pretty course east through rugged EC Manning Provincial Park and on to Osoyoos and the southern Okanagan Valley.

Note that on weekends and other busy times, Hwy 1 west of Hope can get traffic-clogged.

EC Manning Provincial Park

After the farmlands of the Lower Mainland, this 708-sq-km provincial park (☎604-795-6169; www.bcparks.ca), 30km southeast of Hope, is a hint of bigger – much bigger – things to come in the east (think Rocky Mountains). It packs in a lot: dry valleys; dark, mountainous forests; roiling rivers; and alpine meadows. It makes a good pause along Hwy 3 but don't expect solitude as there are scores of folk from the burgs west seeking the same.

The following hiking choices are easily reached from Hwy 3:

Dry Ridge Trail Crosses from dry interior to alpine climate; excellent views and wildflowers (3km round trip, one hour).

Canyon Nature Trail Nice loop trail with a river crossing on a bridge (2km, 45 minutes).

Lightning Lake Loop The perfect intro: a level loop around this central lake. Look for critters in the evening (9km, two hours).

Manning is a four-seasons playground. Manning Park Resort (☎250-840-8822, 800-330-3321; www.manningpark.com) offers downhill skiing and snowboarding (adult/child day pass $45/30) and 100km of groomed trails for cross-country skiing and snowshoeing. It also has the only indoor accommodations throughout the park. The 73 somewhat-pricey units (from $150) are a mix of rooms in the lodge and cabins. All provide the use of the requisite hot tub.

You can pitch your tent at Coldspring, Hampton or Mule campgrounds (campsites $21) or the more popular Lightning Lake campground (☎reservations 800-689-9025; www.discovercamping.ca; campsites $28), which takes reservations. There are 10 backcountry campgrounds (campsites per person $5) for overnight hikers that are normally not accessible before late June.

The park's **visitor center** (☉8:30am-4:30pm Jun-Sep, 8:30am-4pm Mon-Fri Oct-May) is 30km inside the western boundary and has detailed hiking descriptions and a relief model of the park and nearby beaver ponds.

Greyhound Canada (☎800-661-8747; www.greyhound.ca) has buses from Vancouver ($46, three to four hours, two daily).

Fraser River Canyon

The name alone makes Spuzzum a fun stop along Hwy 1 on its way to Cache Creek, 85km west of Kamloops. The road shadows the swiftly flowing Fraser River and, as you'd expect, white-water rafting is huge here. The grand scenery and several good provincial parks make this a winning trip.

Just north of Spuzzum, **Alexandra Bridge Provincial Park** (☎604-795-6169; www.bcparks.ca) makes a scenic stop; you can picnic while gazing at the historic 1926 span. Further north, the ecologically diverse **Stein Valley Nlaka'pamux Heritage Park** (www.bcparks.ca) is managed with the Lytton First Nation. It offers some excellent long-distance hiking through dry valleys and snow-clad peaks amid one of the best-preserved watersheds in lower BC.

Fraser & Thompson Valleys

White-water rafting down the Fraser and its tributaries' fast-flowing rapids is popular and a number of companies near Lytton lead trips. One-day trips cost from $120 per adult.

Kumsheen Rafting Resort (☑800-663-6667; www.kumsheen.com) offers a variety of trips and funky accommodations in tent-cabins ($100). **Hyak River Rafting** (☑800-663-7238; www.hyak.com) covers all the main waterways.

Kamloops

POP 83,200

If you've opted to follow Hwy 1 to the east to the Rockies and Banff, Kamloops makes a useful break in the journey. Motels abound and there's a walkable historic center. Historically, the Shuswap First Nation found the many rivers and lakes useful for transportation and salmon fishing. Traders set up camp for fur hunting in 1811.

Hwy 1 cuts eastwest through town, linking Vancouver with the Rockies, while Yellowhead Hwy (Hwy 5) heads northeast to Jasper and southwest to Vancouver via Merritt (this stretch is called the Coquihalla Hwy). The focus of the downtown area is tree-lined Victoria St, which is a lively place on sunny days; very busy train tracks separate the wide Thompson River from the downtown area. Franchises and malls line the highlands along Hwy 1.

◉ Sights & Activities

Using Victoria St as your anchor, stroll downtown, stopping at the art gallery and museum.

Kamloops Museum   MUSEUM
(☑250-828-3576; www.kamloops.ca/museum; cnr Seymour St & 2nd Ave; adult/child $3/1; ⊙9:30am-4:30pm Tue-Sat, until 7:30pm Thu) Kamloops Museum is in a vintage building and has a suitably vintage collection of historic photographs. Come here for the scoop on river-namesake David Thompson and a new floor dedicated to kids.

Kamloops Heritage Railway HISTORIC TRAIN
(☑250-374-2141; www.kamrail.com; 510 Lorne St; adult/child from $17/10) Across the train tracks from downtown, the Kamloops Heritage Railway runs 70-minute train rides powered by steam engine.

Kamloops Art Gallery   ART GALLERY
(☑250-377-2400; www.kag.bc.ca; 465 Victoria St; adult/child $5/3; ⊙10am-5pm Mon-Wed, Fri & Sat, 10am-9pm Thu) Suitably loft-like in feel, the Kamloops Art Gallery has an emphasis on contemporary Western and aboriginal works by regional artists.

British Columbia Wildlife Park   ZOO
(☑250-573-3242; www.bczoo.org; adult/child $13/10; ⊙9:30am-4:30pm) Parents may look longingly at the cages used to corral unruly critters at the British Columbia Wildlife Park, 17km east of Kamloops on Hwy 1. Captives include bears and cougars.

Paul Lake Provincial Park   PARK
(☑250-819-7376; www.bcparks.ca) On the often-hot summer days, the beach at Paul Lake Provincial Park beckons and you may spot falcons and coyotes. There is a 20km mountain-biking loop. It's 24km north of Kamloops via Hwy 5.

🛏 Sleeping

Older and cheaper motels can be found along a stretch of Hwy 1 east of downtown. Columbia St, from the center up to Hwy 1 above town, has another gaggle of chain and indie motels. The nearby parks have good camping.

Plaza Heritage Hotel   HOTEL $$
TOP CHOICE (☑250-377-8075, 877-977-5292; www.plazaheritagehotel.com; 405 Victoria St; r $110-250; ❁❋❂) You'll think you've fallen into a Laura Ashley seconds bin at this 66-room six-story classic that's little changed since its opening in 1928. In a town of bland modernity in the lodging department, the Plaza reeks character. Excellent free breakfasts.

South Thompson Inn   INN $$
(☑250-573-3777, 800-797-7713; www.stigr.com; 3438 Shuswap Rd; r $140-300; ❋❂❁) Some 20km west of town (via Hwy 1), this ranch-like waterfront sleepover is perched on the banks of the South Thompson and set amid rolling grasslands. Its 57 rooms are spread between the wood-framed main building, a small manor house and some converted stables.

Scott's Inn   MOTEL $$
(☑250-372-8221; www.scottsinn.kamloops.com; cnr 11th Ave & Columbia St; r from $90; ❋◉❂❁) Unlike many budget competitors, Scott's is close to the center. The 51 rooms are motel-standard but extras include an indoor pool, hot tub, cafe and rooftop sun deck.

DESTINATION	FARE	DURATION	FREQUENCY (PER DAY)
Vancouver	$64	5hr	7
Calgary	$90	10hr	4
Jasper	$61	6hr	2
Prince George	$77	7hr	4
Kelowna	$34	2½-4hr	3

✖ Eating & Drinking

Look for the free booklet *Farm Fresh*, which details the many local producers you can visit. Local farmers markets are held in the morning on Wednesday (corner of 5th Ave and Victoria St) and Saturday (corner of 2nd Ave and St Paul St). Victoria St is the place for nightlife.

Hello Toast　　　　　　　　　　CAFE $
(☑250-372-9322; 428 Victoria St; mains $5-9; ☺8am-5pm Mon-Sat; ☑) As opposed to Good Morning Croissant, this veggie-friendly, organic cafe offers whole grains for some, and fried combos of bacon and eggs or burgers for others. Nice open front and sidewalk tables.

Chapter's Viewpoint Restaurant　FUSION $$
(☑250-374-3224; 610 Columbia St; mains $14-24; ☺11:30am-10pm Mon-Fri, 5-10pm Sat & Sun) The patio overlooking Kamloops is the best place to be on a balmy summer evening. The menu features sirloin steak and poached salmon but the New Mexican route is recommended.

Commodore　　　　　　　　　　PUB $$
(☑250-851-3100; 369 Victoria St; ☺5pm-late Mon-Wed & Sat, from 11am Thu-Fri) Old-feeling pub with a long menu that highlights fondue, the Com is the place on Friday nights for live jazz and funk. Other nights, DJs spin pretty much anything.

Kelly O'Bryan's　　　　　　　　PUB $
(☑250-828-1559; 244 Victoria St; meals $8-10; ☺noon-late) A classic fake-Irish bar (yes, that's a real category these days), this one has solid bar chow, good pints and a laughable number of employees wearing kilts (Scottish? Irish? Whatever!).

❶ Information

The **visitor center** (☑250-374-3377, 800-662-1994; www.tourismkamloops.com; 1290 W Hwy 1, exit 368; ☺8am-6pm daily summer, 9am-6pm Mon-Fri rest of year; ☜) is just off Hwy 1, overlooking town. There's internet access here ($1 per 10 minutes, free wi-fi).

❶ Getting There & Around

Seven kilometers northwest of town, **Kamloops Airport** (YKA; ☑250-376-3613; www.kamloopsairport.com) has daily service to/from Vancouver and Calgary.

Greyhound Canada (☑800-661-8747; www.greyhound.ca) is about 1km southwest of the center off Columbia St W.

VIA Rail (☑888-842-7245; www.viarail.ca) serves Kamloops North Station – 11km from town – with the tri-weekly *Canadian* on its run from Vancouver (9½ hours) to Jasper (9½ hours) and beyond. Fares vary greatly by season and class of service.

Kamloops Transit System (☑250-376-1216; www.transitbc.com/regions/kam; adult/child $2/1.50) runs local buses.

For a taxi, call **Yellow Cabs** (☑250-374-3333).

Around Kamloops

The hills looming northeast of Kamloops are home to **Sun Peaks Resort** (☑800-807-3257; www.sunpeaksresort.com; lift tickets adult/child $73/36). This ever-growing resort boasts 122 ski runs (including some 8km-long powder trails), 11 lifts and a pleasant base-area village. In summer, lifts (adult/child $39/23) provide access to more than two dozen mountain-bike trails.

Those saving their cash for the slopes and/or trails choose the **Sun Peaks Hostel** (☑250-578-0057; www.sunpeakshostel.com; 1140 Sun Peaks Rd; dm/d from $30/70; ☜) over the various lodges, B&Bs and luxury condos.

Past the resort road, Hwy 5 continues north toward the Alberta border and Jasper National Park (440km from Kamloops). Along the way (125km from Kamloops) it passes near Wells Gray Provincial Park (p164), one of BC's finest and a haven for those who really want to get away from civilization.

OKANAGAN VALLEY

It is hard to know which harvest is growing faster in this fertile and beautiful valley: tourists or fruit. Certainly, bounty abounds in this ever-more-popular lovely swath midway between Vancouver and Alberta. The moniker 'Canada's Napa Valley' is oft repeated and somewhat apt. The 180km-long Okanagan Valley is home to dozens of excellent wineries, whose vines spread across the terraced hills, soaking up some of Canada's sunniest weather.

This recent emphasis on highbrow refreshments contrasts with the valley's traditional role as a summertime escape for generations of Canadians, who frolic in the string of lakes linking the Okanagan's towns. And while retirees mature slowly in the sun, so do orchards of peaches, apricots and other fruits that may not have the cachet of grapes but which give the air a perfumery redolence at the peak of summer.

Near the US border, Osoyoos is almost arid but things soon become greener heading north. Near the center, Kelowna is one of the fastest growing cities in Canada. It's a heady mix of culture, lakeside beauty and fun. In July and August, however, the entire valley can seem as overburdened as a grapevine right before the harvest. For many, the best time to visit is late spring and early fall, when the crowds are manageable.

Summer days are usually dry and hot, with the nights pleasantly cool. Winters are snowy but dry, making nearby Big White an attraction for skiers and snowboarders.

Osoyoos

POP 5100

Once-modest Osoyoos is on the brink of change, as it embraces an upscale and developed future as part of the new Okanagan Valley. The town takes its name from the First Nation word 'soyoos,' which means 'sand bar across,' and if the translation is a bit rough, the definition is not: much of the town is indeed on a narrow spit of land that divides Osoyoos Lake. It is ringed with beaches and the waters irrigate the lush farms, orchards and vineyards that line Hwy 97 going north out of town.

Nature's bounty aside, this is the arid end of the valley and locals like to say that the town marks the northern end of Mexico's Sonoran Desert; much of the town is done up in a manner that loses something across two borders. From the cactus-speckled sands to the town's cheesy faux tile-and-stucco architecture, it's a big change from the BC image of pine trees and mountains found in both directions on Hwy 3.

◎ Sights & Activities

Osoyoos Lake is one of the warmest in the country. That, together with the sandy beaches, means great swimming. Many lakeside motels and campgrounds hire out kayaks, canoes and small boats. For sweeping valley views go just 3km east of town up Hwy 3. About 8km west of town on Hwy 3, look for **Spotted Lake**, a weird natural phenomenon that once would have made a kitschy roadside attraction. In the hot summer sun, the lake's water begins to evaporate, causing its high mineral content to crystallize and leave white-rimmed circles of green on the water.

TOP CHOICE **Osoyoos Desert Centre** NATURE PARK (☎250-495-2470; www.desert.org; off Hwy 97; adult/child $7/5; ◎9:30am-4:30pm mid-May–mid-Sep, call other times) Hear the rattle of a snake and the songs of birds at the Osoyoos Desert Centre, 3km north of town, which has interpretive kiosks along raised boardwalks that meander through the dry land. The nonprofit center offers 90-minute guided tours throughout the day. Special gardens focus on delights like delicate wildflowers. Note that, even here, condo development encroaches like sand dunes.

Nk'Mip Desert & Heritage Centre MUSEUM (☎250-495-7901; www.nkmipdesert.com; 1000 Rancher Creek Rd; adult/child $12/8; ◎9:30am-8pm Jul & Aug, to 4pm Jun & Sep, call other times) Part of a First Nations empire, the Nk'Mip Desert & Heritage Centre, off 45th St north of Hwy 3, features cultural demonstrations and guided tours of the sandy highlights. It also has a desert golf course, a noted winery, a resort and more.

🛌 Sleeping

The eastern edge of the lake is lined with campgrounds. More than a dozen modest motels line the narrow strip of land that splits Osoyoos Lake (beware of shabby older properties). Many cluster around Hwy 3 and there's another clump on the southwest shore near the border. Chains can be found at the junction. Rates plummet in winter.

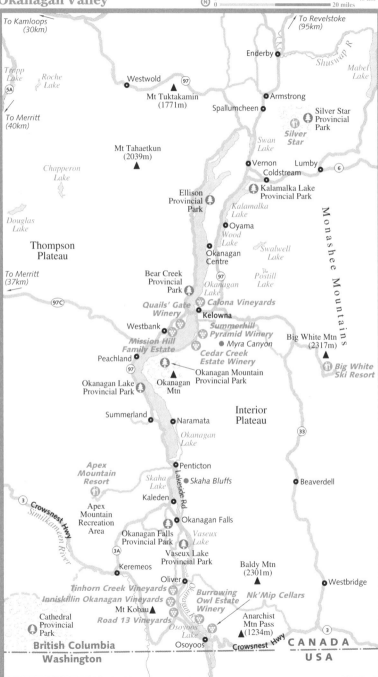

0 / 40 km
0 / 20 miles

To Kamloops (30km)

To Revelstoke (95km)

Enderby

Shuswap R

Tripp Lake

Roche Lake

Westwold

97

Mt Tuktakamin (1771m)

Armstrong

Spallumcheen

Silver Star Provincial Park

Silver Star

Mabel Lake

To Merritt (40km)

5A

Mt Tahaetkun (2039m)

Swan Lake

Vernon

Coldstream

Lumby

6

Chapperon Lake

Kalamalka Lake Provincial Park

Ellison Provincial Park

Kalamalka Lake

Douglas Lake

Oyama

Wood Lake

Swalwell Lake

Thompson Plateau

Okanagan Centre

Monashee Mountains

To Merritt (37km)

Bear Creek Provincial Park

Okanagan Lake

Postill Lake

97C

Quails' Gate Winery

Calona Vineyards

Kelowna

Summerhill Pyramid Winery

Big White Mtn (2317m)

Westbank

Mission Hill Family Estate

Myra Canyon

Cedar Creek Estate Winery

Big White Ski Resort

Peachland

97

Okanagan Mountain Provincial Park

Okanagan Lake Provincial Park

Okanagan Mtn

Interior Plateau

Summerland

Naramata

Okanagan Lake

33

Apex Mountain Resort

Penticton

Skaha Lake

Skaha Bluffs

Lakeside Rd

Beaverdell

Kaleden

3

Crowsnest Hwy

Similkameen River

Apex Mountain Recreation Area

Okanagan Falls

Okanagan Falls Provincial Park

Vaseux Lake

Vaseux Lake Provincial Park

Baldy Mtn (2301m)

Keremeos

Oliver

Westbridge

Tinhorn Creek Vineyards

Inniskillin Okanagan Vineyards

Burrowing Owl Estate Winery

Nk'Mip Cellars

Cathedral Provincial Park

3A

Mt Kobau

Road 13 Vineyards

Anarchist Mtn Pass (1234m)

3

British Columbia

Keremeos

Osoyoos Lake

Osoyoos

Crowsnest Hwy

CANADA

Washington

USA

Avalon Inn MOTEL $$
(☑250-495-6334, 800-264-5999; www.avalon inn.ca; 9106 Main St; r $100-180; ✳@🛜) Away from the lake but close to the best restaurants, this 20-unit motel has large rooms and gardens that get more ornate by the year. Some rooms have kitchens.

Sandy Beach Motel MOTEL $$
(☑250-495-6931, 866-495-6931; www.sandy beachmotel.com; 6706 Ponderosa Dr; r $140-280; ✳@) Free rowboats and a volleyball court set the cheery tone at this 25-unit beachside place just north of Hwy 3. Bungalows and a two-story block surround a shady lawn with BBQs.

White Horse B&B B&B $$
(☑250-495-2887; www.thewhitehorsebb.com; 8000 Hwy 3 East; r $90-130; ✳) The gourmet breakfasts here taste even better when enjoyed on the patio with its views of the valley. The three rooms have a separate entrance and are plush. It's about 2km east of town, up the hill.

Nk'Mip Campground & RV Resort
CAMPGROUND $
(☑250-495-7279; www.campingosoyoos.com; tent/RV sites from $29/38) Over 300 sites at this year-round resort off 45th St north of Hwy 3.

✖ Eating

Wildfire Grill FUSION $$
(☑250-495-2215; 8526 Main St; mains $15-25; ⊙11am-10pm Mon-Fri, 9am-11pm Sat & Sun) Wildfire serves up a range of global cuisines from its open kitchen. Tables in the courtyard are always in demand, especially on long summer nights. There's a stylish lounge area for enjoying the local wine bounty by the glass.

Bibo MEDITERRANEAN $$
(☑250-495-6686; 8316 Main St; mains $10-25; ⊙11am-10pm) Rich-feeling and oh-so-dark, Bibo feels like a smooth cabernet. Tapas and wines by the glass are the stars; opt for the locally sourced charcuterie plate. DJs spin till midnight on weekends.

Diamond Steakhouse STEAKHOUSE $$
(☑250-495-6223; 8903 Main St; mains $15-25; ⊙dinner) This timeless '60s supper club serves Greek-accented steak and seafood to diners humming Dean Martin while lounging in commodious booths. The steaks draw diners from afar, as does the seafood and the endless wine list.

Osoyoos Gelato GELATO $
(☑250-495-5425; Watermark Beach Resort, cnr Main St & Park Place; treats from $2; ⊙10am-10pm summer) Downtown near the lake, there are always at least 24 splendid housemade flavors.

ℹ Information

Visitor center (☑250-495-5070, 888-676-9667; www.destinationosoyoos.com; cnr Hwys 3 & 97; ⊙9am-5pm) This large center has internet access, maps and books, and it can book regional tours and accommodation.

ℹ Getting There & Away

Greyhound Canada (☑800-661-8747; www. greyhound.ca; visitor center, cnr Hwys 3 & 97) runs to Vancouver ($70, eight hours, twice daily) and through the valley to Kelowna ($25, 2½ hours, once daily).

Around Osoyoos

West of Osoyoos, Hwy 3 follows the rugged Similkameen Valley for 47km to **Keremeos**, a cute town surrounded by orchards.

About 30km west of Keremeos is **Cathedral Provincial Park** (☑604-795-6169; www. bcparks.ca), a 330-sq-km mountain wilderness that's a playground for the truly adventurous. The park offers excellent backcountry camping ($5) and hiking around wildflower-dappled alpine expanses and turquoise waters.

Oliver

POP 4500
Once a humdrum fruit-picking center, Oliver is now a center for organic produce and wine. Shortly after leaving Osoyoos for the 20km drive north, Hwy 97 plunges through orchard after orchard laden with lush fruits. Roadside stands display the ripe bounty and many places will let you pick your own. The route earns its moniker 'The Golden Mile' for both produce and wine. See the boxed text, p140, for details on the latter.

The **visitor center** (☑250-498-6321; www. sochamber.ca; 36250 93rd St; ⊙9am-5pm daily May-Sep, 9am-5pm Mon-Fri Oct-Apr) is in the old train station near the center of town. It has excellent regional info and walking/biking maps, including of the 10km **Golden Mile Walking Trail**.

The small roads through the vineyards around Oliver are made for exploring on a bike. Double O Bikes (②250-498-8348; www.doubleobikes.com; 35653 Main St; per day from $15; ⊙9:30am-5pm Tue-Sat) has tons of advice.

🛏 Sleeping & Eating

Oliver's vibrant farmers market (Lion's Park; ⊙8:30am-12:30pm Sat Jul-Sep) showcases local foodstuffs and is just off Hwy 97.

Burrowing Owl Guest House
BOUTIQUE HOTEL $$$
(②250-498-0620, 877-498-0620; www.bovwine.ca; Road 22; r $180-350; ❄@🗟⊠) One of the Okanagan's best wineries has 10 rooms with patios facing southwest over the vineyards. There's a big pool, hot tub, king-size beds and corporate mission-style decor. The Sonora Room (mains $12-25) is noted for its fusion cuisine. It's 13km south of Oliver, off Hwy 97.

Mount View Motel
MOTEL $
(②250-498-3446; www.mountviewmotel.net; 34426 97th St; r $70-120; ❄🗟) Close to the center of town, seven units sunbathe around a flower-bedecked motor court. All have kitchens – and corkscrews.

Cantaloupe Annie's
CAFE $
(②250-498-2955; 34845 97th St; meals from $6; ⊙9:30am-5:30pm Mon-Sat, 11am-3pm Sun summer; 🗟) For a splendid picnic, peruse the deli cases at this cafe famous for its local specials, smoked meats and fruit-based desserts.

Medici's Gelateria
GELATO $
(②250-498-2228; 9932 350th Ave; treats from $2; ⊙8am-6pm) Frozen delights so good, you'll want to worship – and you can easily, given this is an old church. Good coffee plus soups, paninis and more made with local produce.

Oliver to Penticton

About 10km north of Oliver on Hwy 97, nature reasserts itself. Vaseux Wildlife Centre (②250-494-6500; ⊙dawn-dusk) has a 300m boardwalk for viewing oodles of birds (it's not just humans migrating here), bighorn sheep, mountain goats or some of the 14 species of bat. You can also hike to the **Bighorn National Wildlife Area** and the **Vaseux Lake National Migratory Bird Sanctuary**, with more than 160 bird species. The lake itself is an azure gem, well framed by sheer granite cliffs.

If you're not in a hurry, small roads on the east side of Skaha Lake between Okanagan Falls and Penticton are much more interesting (wineries and views) than Hwy 97.

Penticton
POP 32,900

Not as frenetic as Kelowna, Penticton combines the idle pleasures of a beach resort with its own edgy vibe. Long a final stop in life for Canadian retirees (which added a certain spin to its Salish-derived name Pen-Tak-Tin, meaning 'place to stay forever'), the town today is growing fast, along with the rest of the valley.

Penticton makes a good base for your valley pleasures. There are plenty of activities and diversions to fill your days even when you don't travel further afield. Ditch Hwy 97, which runs west of the center, for Main St and the attractively walkable downtown area, which extends about 10 blocks southward from the picture-perfect lakefront; avert your eyes from the long stretch of strip malls and high-rise condos further south.

◉ Sights

Okanagan Beach boasts about 1300m of sand, with average summer water temperatures of about 22°C. If things are jammed, there's often quieter shores at 1.5km-long Skaha Beach, south of the center.

IT'S TIME FOR FRUIT

Roadside stands and farms where you can pick your own fruit line Hwy 97 between Osoyoos and Penticton. Major Okanagan Valley crops and their harvest times:

Strawberries Mid-June to early July

Raspberries Early to mid-July

Cherries Mid-June to mid-August

Apricots Mid-July to mid-August

Peaches Mid-July to mid-September

Pears Mid-August to late September

Apples Early September to late October

Table Grapes Early September to late October

SS Sicamous   HISTORICAL SITE
(☑250-492-0405; 1099 Lakeshore Dr W; adult/child $5/1; ☺9am-9pm May-Oct, 10am-4pm Mon-Fri Nov-Apr) Right on the sand, the SS *Sicamous* hauled passengers and freight on Okanagan Lake from 1914 to 1936. Now restored and beached, it has been joined by the equally old tugboat, *SS Naramata.*

Casabella Princess   BOAT TOUR
(☑250-492-4090; www.casabellaprincess.com; adult/child $20/10; ☺varies, May-Sep) If the *Sicamous* stimulates your inner seaman, enjoy a one-hour, open-air lake tour on a faux stern-wheeler. There are multiple daily sailings at summer's peak.

Penticton Museum   MUSEUM
(☑250-490-2451; 785 Main St; admission by donation; ☺10am-5pm Tue-Sat) Inside the library, the Penticton Museum has delightfully eclectic displays, including the de rigueur natural-history exhibit with stuffed animals and birds plus everything you'd want to know about the Peach Festival.

Art Gallery of Southern Okanagan
                               ART GALLERY
(☑250-493-2928; 199 Marina Way; admission $2; ☺10am-5pm Tue-Sat) The beachfront Art Gallery of Southern Okanagan displays a diverse collection of regional, provincial and national artists.

🏃 Activities

The paved **Okanagan River Channel Biking & Jogging Path** follows the rather arid channel that links Okanagan Lake to Skaha Lake. But why pound the pavement when you can float? Classic cheesy resort diversions like minigolf await at the west end of Okanagan Beach.

Watersports

Coyote Cruises (☑250-492-2115; 215 Riverside Dr; rental & shuttle $11; ☺10am-4:30pm Jun-Aug) rents out inner tubes that you can float to a midway point on the channel. Coyote Cruises buses you back to the start near Okanagan Lake (if you have your own floatable, it's $5 for the bus ride).

There are several watersports rental places on Okanagan Lake. If it floats you can rent it, including kayaks for $20 an hour and ski boats for $280 for four hours.

Castaways (☑250-490-2033; Penticton Lakeside Resort, 21 Lakeshore Dr)

Pier Water Sports (☑250-493-8864; Rotary Park, Lakeshore Dr W)

Mountain Biking & Cycling

Long dry days and rolling hills add up to perfect conditions for mountain biking. Get to popular rides by heading east out of town, toward Naramata (p138). Follow signs to the city dump and Campbell's Mountain, where you'll find a single-track and dual-slalom course, both of which aren't too technical. Once you get there, the riding is mostly on the right-hand side, but once you pass the cattle guard, it opens up and you can ride anywhere.

For cycling, try the route through Naramata and onto the Kettle Valley Rail Trail (p144); other good options are the small, winery-lined roads south of town and east of Skaha Lake.

Rent bikes and pick up a wealth of information at **Freedom – The Bike Shop** (☑250-493-0686; www.freedombikeshop.com; 533 Main St; bikes per day $40). **Fun City** (☑250-462-1151; 1070 Lakeshore Dr; bikes per day $40) lives up the promise of its name with maps of self-guiding tours.

Rock Climbing

Propelled by the dry weather and compact gneiss rock, climbers from all over the world come to the **Skaha Bluffs** to enjoy a seven-month climbing season to more than 400 bolted routes. The local climbing group, **Skaha.org** (www.skaha. org), has comprehensive info on the bluffs, which are on Smythe Dr off Lakeside Rd on the east side of Skaha Lake. In 2010, **BC Parks** (www.bcparks.ca) assumed control of the site; learn more of future plans online.

Skaha Rock Adventures (☑250-493-1765; www.skaharockclimbing.com; 1-day intros from $120) offers advanced, technical instruction and introductory courses for anyone venturing into a harness for the first time.

Skiing & Snowboarding

Apex Mountain Resort (☑877-777-2739, conditions 250-487-4848; www.apexresort.com; lift tickets adult/child $60/37), 37km west of Penticton off Green Mountain Rd, is one of Canada's best small ski resorts. It has more than 68 downhill runs for all ability levels, but the mountain is known for its plethora of double-black-diamond and technical runs (the drop is over 600m). It is usually quieter than nearby Big White Mountain.

✿ Festivals & Events

It seems like Penticton has nothing but crowd-drawing festivals all summer long.

Elvis Festival   CULTURAL

(www.pentictonelvisfestival.com) Dozens of Elvis impersonators could be your idea of heaven or hound-dog hell, especially the afternoon of open-mike sing-alongs. Held in late June.

Peach Festival   FRUIT

(✆800-663-5052; www.peachfest.com) The city's premier event is basically a week-long party in early August that has taken place since 1948, loosely centered on crowning a Peach Queen.

Pentastic Jazz Festival   MUSIC

(✆250-770-3494; www.pentasticjazz.com) More than a dozen bands perform at five venues over three days in early September.

🛏 Sleeping

Lakeshore Dr West and South Main St/Skaha Lake Rd are home to most of the local motels. The Okanagan Beach strip is the most popular area. The visitor center has a long list of B&Bs. Expect off-season discounts.

Spiller Estate B&B   B&B $$

(✆250-490-4162, 800-610-3794; www.holman langwineries.com; 475 Upper Bench Rd; r $140; ☉May-Oct; ❀) Just 2km east of the centre, on the road to Naramata, this four-room half-timbered 1930s lodge is on the grounds of its namesake winery. You can smell the peaches ripening from the shady grounds, which are a short jaunt from Munson Mountain.

Rochester Resort   MOTEL $$

(✆250-493-1128, 800-567-4904; www.pentic ton.com/rochester-resort; 970 Lakeshore Dr W; r $140-300; ❀☎🛜) The unassuming 1970s design extends to the modest beige and avocado decor. But you'll have little time to linger indoors, what with all the fun nearby. All 36 units have kitchens. Some have two bedrooms, others have lake views from their balconies.

Tiki Shores Beach Resort   MOTEL $$

(✆250-492-8769, 866-492-8769; www.tikishores .com; 914 Lakeshore Dr W; condos $140-300; ❀🛜) This lively resort has 40 condo-style units with separate bedrooms and kitchens. Throw your own toga party in one of the 'Roman theme units,' and throw your soiled post-bacchanalia ware into the handy guest laundry.

Park Royal RV Resort   CAMPGROUND $

(✆250-492-7051; www.parkroyal.ipenticton.com; 240 Riverside Dr; RV sites from $45) Right near the busy end of Okanagan Beach, the 40 sites here are set among shady lawns.

HI Penticton Hostel   HOSTEL $

(✆250-492-3992; www.hihostels.ca; 464 Ellis St; dm/r from $24/60; ❀@🛜) This 47-bed hostel is near the center in a heavily used old house; it arranges all sorts of activities, including wine tours.

🍴 Eating

Penticton definitely has its share of good eats. Stroll around Main and Front Sts in the center and you will find numerous choices. The **farmers market** (✆250-583-9933; Main St; ☉8am-noon Sat May-Oct) hosts large numbers of local organic producers and runs a few blocks south of the lake.

TOP CHOICE **Amante Bistro**   FUSION $$

(✆250-493-1961; www.amantebistro.com; 483 Main St; mains $10-30; ☉11am-2pm & 5-10pm Mon-Sat) There's intimate dining for those who want to enjoy a changing seasonal menu of carefully prepared dishes like small pizzas with Poplar Grove blue cheese or a slow-roasted pork belly with scallops; local produce stars. Excellent Okanagan wine list.

Salty's Beachouse   SEAFOOD $$

(✆250-493-5001; 1000 Lakeshore Dr W; mains $12-25; ☉5-10pm Apr-Oct) You expect deep-fried but what you get is a nuanced menu of seafood with global accents. Typical is Cayman Island chowder, which is rich and multifaceted. Dine under the stars on the patio or enjoy the lake views from the upper level.

Il Vecchio Deli   DELI $

(✆250-492-7610; 317 Robinson St; sandwiches $5; ☉10am-4pm Mon-Sat) The smell that greets you as you enter confirms your choice. The best lunch sandwiches in town can be consumed at a couple of tables in this atmospheric deli but will taste better on a picnic. Choices are amazing; we like the garlic salami with marinated eggplant sandwich.

Fibonacci   CAFE $

(✆250-770-1913; 219 Main St; meals from $7; ☉8am-10pm Mon-Sat; 🛜) You see the large brass coffee roaster right when you enter this downtown cafe that serves up lots of healthy Mediterranean fare. Thin-crust pizzas are made with local produce. At night there's a rotating line-up of art-house films, comedy acoustic and open mike.

Dream Cafe
FUSION $$

(☑250-490-9012; 67 Front St; mains $8-26; ☺8am-late Tue-Sun) The heady aroma of spices envelopes your, well, head as you enter this pillow-bedecked, upscale-yet-funky bistro. Asian and Indian flavors mix on the menu, which has many veggie options. On many nights there's live acoustic guitar by touring pros; tables outside hum all summer long.

Theo's
GREEK $$

(☑250-492-4019; www.eatsquid.com; 687 Main St; mains $10-25; ☺11am-10pm) The place for locals on match.com second dates, serving up authentic Greek island cuisine in the atmospheric dark and fire-lit interior or out on the patio. The Garithes Uvetsi is a symphony of starters that will please two.

Drinking & Entertainment

Look for local Cannery Brewing beers around town; the seasonal Blackberry Porter is fresh and smooth. Many dinner places also feature live entertainment some nights and most have good lounges.

The Hooded Merganser (☑250-493-8221; Penticton Lakeside Resort, 21 Lakeshore Dr) is a stylish over-the-water pub with walls of glass overlooking docks and the lake. It's popular through the year. Just ashore, the Barking Parrot (☑250-493-8221; Penticton Lakeside Resort, 21 Lakeshore Dr) has a vast patio with heaters that extend the season almost to winter. Cover bands rock the weekends.

Shopping

Purchase the best local artistic efforts at the Lloyd Gallery (☑250-492-4484; 18 Front St; ☺9:30am-5:30pm Mon-Sat), which bursts with the colors of the valley and is one of several on the block. Stock up on reading material amid the stacks of used titles at the appropriately named Book Shop (☑250-492-6661; 242 Main St).

ℹ Information

The visitor center (☑250-493-4055, 800-663-5052; www.tourismpenticton.com; 553 Railway St, cnr Hwy 97 & Eckhardt Ave W;☺8am-8pm May-Sep, 10am-6pm Oct-Apr) is one of BC's best. There's free internet and a whole room devoted to the BC Wine Information Centre with regional wine information, tasting and sales.

ℹ Getting There & Around

Penticton Regional Airport (YYF; ☑250-492-6042; www.cyyf.org) Daily flights by Air Canada Jazz to Vancouver (one hour).

Greyhound Canada (☑800-661-8747; www.greyhound.ca; 307 Ellis St) Services within the Okanagan Valley as well as routes to Vancouver ($76, seven hours, two daily) and Kamloops ($50, four hours, one daily).

Penticton Transit (☑250-492-5602; www.bctransit.com; single trip/day pass $2/4) Runs between both waterfronts.

Penticton to Kelowna

A lakeside resort town 18km north of Penticton on Hwy 97, Summerland features some fine 19th-century heritage buildings on the hillside above the ever-widening and busy highway. The Kettle Valley Steam Railway (☑877-494-8424; www.kettlevalleyrail.org; 18404 Bathville Rd; adult/child $21/13; ☺mid-May–mid-Oct) is an operating 16km remnant of the famous railway (p144). Ride behind old steam locomotives in open-air cars and enjoy orchard views.

Hugging the lake below Hwy 97, some 25km south of Kelowna, the little town of Peachland is good for a quick, breezy stroll. Smart stoppers will pause longer at the Blind Angler Grill (☑250-767-9264; 5899A Beach Ave; mains $8-25; ☺9am-9pm), a shack-like place overlooking a small marina. What's lost in structural integrity is more than made up for in food quality: breakfasts shine, burgers are superb and night-time ribs and halibut are sublime.

Between Peachland and Kelowna, urban sprawl becomes unavoidable, especially through the billboard-lined nightmare of Westbank.

WORTH A TRIP

SCENIC DRIVE TO NARAMATA

On all but the busiest summer weekends, you can escape many of Penticton's mobs by taking the road less traveled, 18km north from town along the east shore of Okanagan Lake. The route is lined with more than 20 wineries as well as farms producing organic lavender and the like. There are lots of places to hike, picnic, bird-watch or do whatever else occurs to you in beautiful and often secluded surroundings. Naramata is a cute little village. This is a good route for cycling and at several points you can access the Kettle Valley Rail Trail (p144).

Kelowna

POP 120,300

A kayaker paddles past scores of new tract houses on a hillside: it's an iconic image for fast-growing Kelowna, the unofficial 'capital' of the Okanagan and the sprawling centre of all that's good and not-so-good with the region.

Entering from the north, the ever-lengthening urban sprawl of tree-lined Hwy 97/ Harvey Ave seems to go on forever. Once past the ceaseless waves of chains and strip malls, the downtown is a welcome reward. Museums, culture, nightlife and the park-lined lakefront feature. About 2km south of the center, along Pandosy Ave, is Pandosy Village, a charming and upscale lakeside enclave.

Kelowna, an Interior Salish word meaning 'grizzly bear,' owes its settlement to a number of missionaries who arrived in 1858, hoping to 'convert the Natives.' Settlers followed and in 1892 the town was established. Industrial fruit production was the norm until the wine industry took off 20 years ago.

⊙ Sights

CITY PARK & PROMENADE

The focal point of the city's shoreline, this immaculate downtown park is home to manicured gardens, water features and **Hot Sands Beach**, where the water is a respite from the summer air. Among the many statues (the visitor center has a good guide) look for the one of the **Ogopogo**, the lake's mythical – and hokey – monster. Restaurants and pubs take advantage of the uninterrupted views of the lake and forested shore opposite. North of the marina, **Waterfront Park** has a variegated shoreline and a popular open-air stage.

CULTURAL DISTRICT

Be sure to pick up the Cultural District walking-tour and public-art brochures at the visitor center and visit www.kelownamuseums.ca.

Located in the old Laurel Packing House, the **BC Orchard Industry Museum** (☑250-763-0433; 1304 Ellis St; admission by donation; ☉10am-5pm Mon-Sat) recounts the Okanagan Valley from its ranchland past, grazed by cows, to its present, grazed by tourists. The old fruit packing-crate labels are works of art. It reopened in 2011 after a major restoration.

In the same building, the knowledgeable staff at the **Wine Museum** (☑250-868-0441; admission free; ☉10am-6pm Mon-Sat, 11am-5pm Sun) can recommend tours, steer you to the best wineries for tastings and help you fill your trunk with the many local wines on sale.

The airy **Kelowna Art Gallery** (☑250-979-0888; www.kelownaartgallery.com; 1315 Water St; admission $3; ☉10am-5pm Tue, Wed, Fri & Sat, 10am-9pm Thu, 1-4pm Sun) features local works. Nearby, **Turtle Island Gallery** (☑250-717-8235; 115-1295 Cannery Lane) sells and displays works by Aboriginal artists.

The **Okanagan Heritage Museum** (☑250-763-2417; 470 Queensway Ave; admission by donation; ☉10am-5pm Mon-Sat) looks at centuries of local culture in an engaging manner that includes a First Nations pit house, a Chinese grocery and a Pandosy-era trading post.

Behind the museum, the exquisite grounds of **Kasugai Gardens** (admission free; ☉9am-6pm) are good for a peaceful stroll.

🏃 Activities

The balmy weather makes Kelowna ideal for fresh-air fun, whether on the lake or in the surrounding hills.

You can rent speedboats (starting at $60 per hour), arrange fishing trips and cruises or rent windsurfing gear at **Kelowna Marina** (☑250-861-8001; www.kelownamarina.ca), at the lake end of Queensway Ave. Windsurfers take to the water from the old seaplane terminal, near the corner of Water St and Cawston Ave.

You'll find great hiking and mountain-bike riding all around town. The 17km **Mission Creek Greenway** is a meandering, wooded path following the creek along the south edge of town. The western half is a wide and easy expanse, but to the east the route becomes sinuous as it climbs into the hills.

Knox Mountain, which sits at the northern end of the city, is another good place to hike or ride. Along with bobcats and snakes, the 235-hectare park has well-maintained trails and rewards visitors with excellent views from the top.

👉 Tours

TOP CHOICE **Monashee Adventure Tours** (☑250-762-9253; www.monasheeadventuretours.com) Offers scores of biking and hiking tours of the valley, parks, Kettle Valley Rail Trail (from $80) and wineries. Many tours are accompanied by entertaining

OKANAGAN VALLEY WINERIES

The abundance of sunshine, fertile soil and cool winters have allowed the local wine industry to thrive. Kelowna and the region north are known for whites like pinot grigio. South, near Penticton and Oliver, reds are the stars, especially the ever-popular merlots.

A majority of the over 100 wineries are close to Hwy 97, which makes tasting a breeze. Most offer tours and all will gladly sell you a bottle or 20 (in fact many of the best wines are only sold at the wineries). A growing number feature excellent cafes and bistros that offer fine views and complex regional fare to complement what's in the glass.

Festivals

Okanagan seasonal **wine festivals** (www.thewinefestivals.com) are major events, especially the one in fall. For more on the winter festival and ice wine, see p303. The usual dates are fall (early October), winter (mid-January), spring (early May) and summer (early August).

Information

Two good sources of information on Okanagan Valley wines are the **BC Wine Information Centre** (p138) in Penticton's visitor center and the **Wine Museum** (p139) in Kelowna. *John Schreiner's Okanagan Wine Tour Guide* is an authoritative guidebook.

Tours

There are numerous companies that let you do the sipping while they do the driving.

Club Wine Tours (☑250-762-9951, 866-386-9463; www.clubwinetours.com; 3-7hr tours $65-125) The signature tour includes four wineries and lunch in a vineyard.

Distinctly Kelowna Tours (☑250-979-1211, 866-979-1211; www.wildflowersandwine.com; 3-7hr tours $80-140) Offers winery tours by valley region, plus hikes through the scenic hills followed by a winery lunch and agricultural tours.

Visiting the Wineries

At wineries open for visitors, you can expect to taste wine, but the experience varies greatly. Some places have just a couple of wines on offer, others offer dozens of vintages. Some tasting rooms are just glorified sales areas, others have magnificent views of the vineyards, valley and lakes. Some charge, others are free.

Among the dozens of options, the following (listed north to south) are recommended. Summerhill Pyramid and Cedar Creek Estate are south of Kelowna along the lake's east shore. The rest of the wineries can be reached via Hwy 97.

local guides. Prices include a bike, lunch and shuttle to the route. The same shuttle can also be used by independent riders looking for one-way transport. In winter, snowshoe tours are offered.

🛏 Sleeping

As in the rest of the Okanagan Valley, accommodations here can be difficult to find in summer if you haven't booked. At other times, look for bargains. The visitor center lists dozens of area B&Bs. Chain motels dominate Harvey Ave/Hwy 97 going east. Rates fall as you head along the strip but you pay the price by being in less-than-salubrious surroundings.

Hotel Eldorado   HOTEL **$$$**
(☑250-763-7500, 866-608-7500; www.hotelel doradokelowna.com; 500 Cook Rd; r $180-400; ✲@🛜🏊) This historic lakeshore retreat, south of Pandosy Village, has 19 heritage rooms where you can bask in antique-filled luxury. A modern low-key wing has 30 more rooms and six opulent waterfront suites. It's classy, artful and funky all at once. Definitely the choice spot for a luxurious getaway.

Royal Anne Hotel   HOTEL **$$**
(☑250-763-2277, 888-811-3400; www.royalan nehotel.com; 348 Bernard Ave; r $100-200; ✲@🛜) Location, location, location are the three amenities that count at this otherwise unexciting, older five-story motel in the heart of

Calona Vineyards (☎250-762-3332; www.calonavineyards.ca; 1125 Richter St, Kelowna; ⊗9am-6pm summer, 10am-5pm winter) Near Kelowna's Cultural District, and one of BC's largest producers, Calona was the first in the Okanagan Valley (it started in 1932).

Summerhill Pyramid Winery (☎250-764-8000; www.summerhill.bc.ca; 4870 Chute Lake Rd, Kelowna) On Kelowna's eastern shore, wines are aged in a huge pyramid.

Cedar Creek Estate Winery (☎250-764-8866; www.cedarcreek.bc.ca; 5445 Lakeshore Rd, Kelowna; ⊗10am-6pm Apr-Oct, 11am-5pm Nov-Mar) Known for excellent tours as well as Ehrenfelser, a refreshing fruity white wine. The **Vineyard Terrace** (mains $10-15; ⊗11:30am-3pm Jun–mid-Sep) is good for lunch.

Quails' Gate Winery (☎250-769-4451; www.quailsgate.com; 3303 Boucherie Rd, Kelowna; ⊗10am-5pm) A small winery with a huge reputation; known for its pinot noir and sauvignon blanc. The **Old Vines Restaurant** (mains $10-20; ⊗11am-9pm) is among the best.

Mission Hill Family Estate (☎250-768-7611; www.missionhillwinery.com; 1730 Mission Hill Rd, Westbank; ⊗10am-5pm) Go for a taste of one of the blended reds (try the Bordeaux) or the thirst-quenching pinot gris. Luncheons at the **Terrace** (mains $24-27; ⊗11am-3pm mid-May–mid-Sep) are a seasonal treat.

Tinhorn Creek Vineyards (☎250-498-3743; www.tinhorn.com; 32830 Tinhorn Creek Rd, Oliver; ⊗9am-5pm) Near the junction of Hwy 97 and Road 7 on the Golden Mile. Notable reds and whites include the top-tier Oldfield series, namesake of owner Sandra Oldfield.

Inniskillin Okanagan Vineyards (☎250-498-6663; www.inniskillin.com; Road 11 W, Oliver; ⊗10am-6pm May-Oct, 10am-5pm Mon-Fri Nov-Apr) BC's first producer of Zinfandel is also home to the elixirs known as ice wines.

Road 13 Vineyards (☎250-498-8330; www.road13vineyards.com; 13140 316A Ave, Road 13, Oliver; ⊗10am-5:30pm Apr-Oct) Its very drinkable reds and whites win plaudits. The no-frills vibe extends to the picnic tables with gorgeous views and the motto: 'It's all about dirt.'

Burrowing Owl Estate Winery (☎250-498-0620; www.bovwine.ca; 100 Burrowing Owl Pl, Oliver; ⊗10am-5pm Apr-Oct) Wine with an eco-accent that includes organic grapes. This Golden Mile landmark includes a hotel and the Sonora Room restaurant (p135).

Nk'Mip Cellars (☎250-495-2985; www.nkmipcellars.com; 1400 Rancher Creek Rd, Osoyoos; ⊗) Excellent winery owned by an entrepreneurial First Nations band. Simple meals with aboriginal touches like corn bread are served at the **Patio** (mains $16-18; ⊗11:30am-8pm May-Sep).

town. Rooms have standard modern decor, fridges and huge, openable windows.

Travelodge Kelowna MOTEL **$$**
(☎250-763-7771, 800-578-7878; www.travelodge.com; 1627 Abbott St; r $90-180; ❉@🅿) Perfectly located downtown and across from City Park, this 52-room motel is as unadorned as a grapevine in winter. There is a decent outdoor pool and a hot tub.

Prestige Hotel MOTEL **$$**
(☎250-860-7900, 877-737-8443; www.prestigeinn.com; 1675 Abbott St; r $120-250; ❉@🅿) This 66-room place has a great location across from City Park and once you're inside, you can't see the rather hideous exterior. The rooms are just fine, in an upscale-motel sort

of way (nice soap, LCD TVs, piles of decorative pillows etc).

Willow Creek Family Campground
  CAMPGROUND **$**
(☎250-762-6302; www.willowcreekcampground.ca; 3316 Lakeshore Rd; tent/RV site $30/45; 🅿) Close to Pandosy Village and a beach, this 87-site facility has a laundry; tent sites are on a grassy verge.

Kelowna SameSun International Hostel HOSTEL **$**
(☎250-763-9814, 877-562-2783; www.samesun.com; 245 Harvey Ave; dm/r from $28/80; ❉@🅿) Near the center and the lake, this purpose-built hostel has 88 dorm beds plus private rooms. Activities include BBQs year-round.

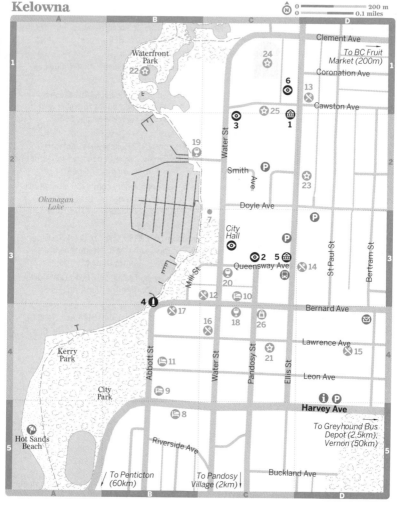

✕ Eating

Many of Kelowna's restaurants take full advantage of the local bounty of foodstuffs. But don't let the feel of Vancouver East cause you to go all continental in your dining time: 8pm is late. The local microbrewer, **Tree Brewing**, has an excellent range of beers that are widely sold around

Food Purveyors

The **farmers market** (☏250-878-5029; cnr Springfield Rd & Dilworth Dr; ◷8am-1pm Wed & Sat Apr-Oct) has over 150 vendors, including many with prepared foods. Local artisans also display their wares. It's off Hwy 97. Another **market** (◷4-8pm Thu) is held at the Dolphins statue parking lot.

TOP CHOICE **BC Fruit Market** (☏250-763-8872; 816 Clement Ave; ◷9am-5pm Mon-Sat) is like a county fair. Right inside the local fruit-packing cooperative, with dozens upon dozens of the Okanagan's best fruits on display and available for tasting; prices are half that in supermarkets.

At first glance, **Guisachan Village** (2355 Gordon Dr) may look like a humdrum strip mall but closer inspection reveals that it is a culinary mecca of fine-food purveyors, including the following:

Codfathers Seafood Market　SEAFOOD **$**
(250-763-3474; 9am-7pm) There's fresh fish of course but picnickers love the array of smoked salmon and other smoked goods. A small cafe serves chowders, fish and chips etc.

L&D Meats & Deli　DELI **$**
(250-717-1997; 9:30am-6pm Mon-Sat) Arrays of smoked meats and other deli items; good choice of deliciously good sandwiches.

Okanagan Grocery　BAKERY **$**
(250-862-2811; 9:30am-5:30pm Tue-Sat) Artisan and organic bakery with breads from baguettes to croissants.

Restaurants & Cafes

TOP CHOICE **RauDZ**　FUSION **$$**
(250-868-8805; www.raudz.com; 1560 Water St; mains $12-25; 5-10pm) Noted chef Rod Butters returns with this casual bistro that is a temple to Okanagan produce and wine. The dining room is as airy and open as the kitchen and the seasonal menu takes global inspiration for Med-infused dishes good for sharing, as well as steaks and seafood. Suppliers include locally renowned Carmelis goat cheese.

Rotten Grape　TAPAS **$$**
(250-717-8466; 231 Bernard Ave; mains $8-15; 5pm-midnight Wed-Sun) Enjoy flights of local wines without the fru-fru in the heart of town. If you utter 'tannin, the hobgoblin of pinot' at any point, be quiet and eat some of the tasty tapas (from $10).

Mamma Rosa　ITALIAN **$$**
(250-763-4114; 561 Lawrence Ave; mains $12-25; 5-10pm Tue-Sun) Okay, the red-and-white checked tablecloths are plastic, but that just makes wiping up your slobber that much easier. And slobber you will over big bowls of excellent homemade pasta (about 100 varieties it seems) and more. Customize by adding meatballs, broccoli, anchovies etc.

Bean Scene　CAFE **$**
(250-763-1814; 274 Bernard Ave; coffee $2; 6:30am-10pm;) Has a great bulletin board to check up on local happenings while you munch on a muffin. A quieter location, **Bean Scene North** (250-763-4022; 1289 Ellis St; 6am-6pm;), offers caffeinated respite in the Cultural District.

La Bussola　ITALIAN **$$**
(250-763-3110; 1451 Ellis St; mains $15-30; 5-10pm Mon-Sat) The Cultural District location is fitting. Since 1974 Franco and Lauretta Coccaro have worked to perfect their Italian supper house. The menu

DON'T MISS

KETTLE VALLEY RAIL TRAIL

The famous **Kettle Valley Rail Trail** vies with wine drinking and peach picking as the attraction of choice for visitors (smart ones do all three).

Once stretching 525km in curving, meandering length, the railway was built so that silver ore could be transported from the southern Kootenays to Vancouver. Finished in 1916, it remains one of the most expensive railways ever built on a per-kilometer basis. It was entirely shut by 1989 but it wasn't long before its easy grades (never over 2.2%) and dozens of bridges were incorporated into the Trans Canada Trail.

Of the entire KVR Trail, the most spectacular stretch is close to Kelowna. The 24km section through the **Myra Canyon** has fantastic views of the sinuous canyon from **18 trestles** that span the gorge for the cliff-hugging path. That you can enjoy the route at all is something of a miracle as 12 of the wooden trestles were destroyed by fire in 2003. But all are rebuilt; much credit goes to the Myra Canyon Trestle Restoration Society (www.myratrestles.com). The broad views take in Kelowna and the lake. Although much fire damage remains, you can see alpine meadows reclaiming the landscape.

To reach the area closest to the most spectacular trestles, follow Harvey Ave (Hwy 97) east to Gordon Dr. Turn south and then go east 2.6km on KLO Rd and then join McCulloch Rd for 7.4km after the junction. Look for the Myra Forest Service Rd, turn south and make a winding 8.7km climb on a car-friendly gravel road to the parking lot.

Myra Canyon is just part of an overall 174km network of trails in the Okanagan that follow the old railway through tunnels, past Naramata and as far south as Penticton and beyond. You can easily access the trail at many points or book hiking and cycling tours (p139). Myra Canyon Bike Rentals (☎250-878-8763; www.myracanyonrental. com; half-day from $40; ☺May–mid-Sep) has bike rentals; confirm by calling in advance.

---

spans the boot, from pesto to red sauce, veal to seafood. Dine on the flower-bedecked sidewalk tables or in the stylish dining room.

🍷 Drinking

Sturgeon Hall   PUB
(☎250-860-3055; 1481 Water St; ☺11am-midnight Mon-Sat) Fanatical fans of hockey's Kelowna Rockets feast on excellent burgers and thin-crust pizza while quaffing brews at the bar or outside at sidewalk tables. In season, every TV shows hockey.

Doc Willoughby's   PUB
(☎250-868-8288; 353 Bernard Ave; ☺11:30am-2am) Right downtown, this pub boasts a vaulted interior lined with wood and tables on the street; perfect for a drink or a meal. The beer selection is excellent, including brews from Tree Brewing and Penticton's Cannery Brewing.

Rose's Waterfront Pub   PUB
(☎250-860-1141; Delta Grand Okanagan Hotel, 1352 Water St) Part of the upscale end of the waterfront, the vast lakeside terrace is the place for sunset drinks and snacks – from several hours before to several hours after.

☆ Entertainment

Downtown Kelowna boasts several ever-changing clubs, mostly at the west end of Leon and Lawrence Aves. Free summer nighttime concerts take place in **Kerry Park** on Friday and Saturday and on Waterfront Park's **Island Stage** on Wednesday.

Blue Gator   LIVE MUSIC
(☎250-860-1529; www.bluegator.net; 441 Lawrence Ave; ☺Tue-Sun) Blues, rock, acoustic jam and more at the valley's sweaty temple of live music and cold beer.

Kelowna Rockets   SPORTS
(☎250-860-7825; www.kelownarockets.com; tickets from $20) Kelowna Rockets is the much-beloved local WHL hockey team, playing in the flashy 6000-seat **Prospera Place Arena** (☎250-979-0888; cnr Water St & Cawston Ave).

Kelowna Actors Studio   THEATER
(☎250-862-2867; www.kelownaactorsstudio. com; 1379 Ellis St; tickets from $45) Enjoy works as diverse as *The Producers* and *Same Time Next Year* at this dinner theater with serious ambitions.

Rotary Centre for the Performing Arts VENUE
(250-717-5304, tickets 250-763-1849; 421 Cawston Ave) There's galleries, a theatre, cafe, craft workshops and live classical music.

Shopping

The many food purveyors offer locally produced items that make excellent gifts. Mosaic Books (250-763-4418; 411 Bernard Ave) is an excellent independent bookstore, selling maps (including topographic ones) and travel guides, plus books on aboriginal history and culture.

❶ Information

Many downtown cafes have wi-fi access.

Kelowna General Hospital (250-862-4000; 2268 Pandosy St, cnr Royal Ave; 24hr)

Kelowna Library (250-762-2800; 1380 Ellis St; 10am-5:30pm Mon, Fri & Sat, 10am-9pm Tue-Thu, noon-4pm Sun Oct-Mar) Visitors enjoy one hour of free online access.

Postal outlet (250-868-8480; 571 Bernard Ave; 9am-5pm Mon-Sat)

Visitor center (250-861-1515, 800-663-4345; www.tourismkelowna.com; 544 Harvey Ave; 8am-7pm daily summer, 8am-5pm Mon-Fri & 10am-3pm Sat & Sun winter) Near the corner of Ellis St; excellent touring maps.

❶ Getting There & Away

From **Kelowna airport** (YLW; 250-765-5125; www.kelownaairport.com), **Westjet** (www.westjet.com) serves Vancouver, Victoria, Edmonton, Calgary and Toronto. **Air Canada Jazz** (www.aircanada.com) serves Vancouver and Calgary. **Horizon Air** (www.alaskaair.com) serves Seattle. The airport is a long 20km north of the center on Hwy 97.

Greyhound Canada (800-661-8747; www.greyhound.ca; 2366 Leckie Rd) is inconveniently east of the downtown area, off Hwy 97. City buses 9 and 10 make the run from Queensway station in the downtown (every 30 minutes between 6:30am and 9:45pm).

❶ Getting Around
To/From the Airport

Kelowna Airport Shuttle (250-888-434-8687; www.kelownashuttle.com) costs $12 to $15 per person. Cabs cost about $30.

Bus

Kelowna Regional Transit System (250-860-8121; www.busonline.ca) runs local bus services. The one-way fare in the central zone is $2. A day pass for all three zones costs $5.50. All the downtown buses pass through **Queensway station** (Queensway Ave, btwn Pandosy & Ellis Sts). Service is not especially convenient.

Car & Taxi

All major car-rental companies are at Kelowna airport. Taxi companies include **Kelowna Cabs** (250-762-4444/2222).

Big White Ski Resort

Perfect powder is the big deal at Big White Ski Resort (250-765-8888, 800-663-2772, snow report 250-765-7669; www.bigwhite.com; 1-day lift pass adult/child $71/35), located 55km east of Kelowna off Hwy 33. With a vertical drop of 777m, it features 16 lifts and 118 runs that offer excellent downhill and backcountry skiing, while deep gullies make for killer snowboarding. Because of Big White's isolation, most people stay up here. The resort includes numerous restaurants, bars, hotels, condos, rental homes and a hostel. The resort has lodging info and details of the ski-season Kelowna shuttle.

Vernon

POP 59,200

The Okanagan glitz starts to fade before you reach Vernon. Maybe it's the weather. Winters have more of the traditional inland BC bite and wineries are few. But that doesn't mean the area is without its charms. The orchard-scented valley is surrounded by three lakes – Kalamalka,

REGIONAL BUS DISTANCES FROM KELOWNA

DESTINATION	FARE	DURATION	FREQUENCY (PER DAY)
Penticton	$22	1¼hr	4
Kamloops	$39	3hr	3
Vancouver	$78	6hr	6
Calgary	$110	10hr	1

Okanagan and Swan – that attract fun seekers all summer long. Downtown Vernon has some good eateries and is enlivened by over 30 wall murals ranging from schmaltzy to artistic. Most of the shops are found along 30th Ave (known as Main St). Confusingly, 30th Ave is intersected by 30th St in the middle of downtown, so mind your streets and avenues.

◉ Sights & Activities

The beautiful 9-sq-km **Kalamalka Lake Provincial Park** (☑250-545-1560; www.bcparks.ca) south of town lies on the eastern side of this warm, shallow lake. The park offers great swimming at Jade and Kalamalka Beaches, good fishing and a network of mountain-biking and hiking trails. There's also excellent rock climbing at cougar-free Cougar Canyon.

Ellison Provincial Park, 16km southwest of Vernon on Okanagan Lake, is western Canada's only freshwater marine park; scuba diving is popular here and gear (scuba, snorkeling and kayaks) can be rented from **Innerspace Watersports** (☑250-549-2040; www.innerspacewatersports.com; 3103 32nd St). Ellison is also known for its world-class rock climbing. To get to Ellison from downtown, go west on 25th Ave, which soon becomes Okanagan Landing Rd. Follow that and look for signs to the park.

Two fun attractions make hay from local agriculture. **Davison Orchards** (☑250-549-3266; www.davisonorchards.ca; 3111 Davison Rd; ◷daylight hrs May-Oct) has tractor rides, homemade ice cream, fresh apple juice, winsome barnyard animals and more.

Next door, **Planet Bee** (☑250-542-8088; www.planetbee.com; 5011 Bella Vista Rd; admission free; ◷daylight hrs May-Oct) is a working honey farm where you can learn all the sweet secrets of the nectar and see a working hive up close. Follow 25th Ave west, turn north briefly on 41st St, then go west on Bella Vista Rd and watch for signs.

⌂ Sleeping

Accommodations are available in all price ranges. The visitor center has information on local B&Bs.

Beaver Lake Mountain Resort
CAMPGROUND, INN **$**
(☑250-762-2225; www.beaverlakeresort.com; 6350 Beaver Lake Rd; campsites from $27, cabins $55-170; ⊚) Set high in the hills east of

Hwy 97, about midway between Vernon and Kelowna, this postcard-perfect lakeside resort has a range of rustic log and more luxurious cabins that sleep up to six people.

Tiki Village Motel
MOTEL **$$**
(☑250-503-5566, 800-661-8454; www.tikivillagevernon.com; 2408 34th St; r $80-150; ✳☎☀) Hide your brother's Game Boy in the pool wall and he'll never find it again. Another ode to the glory days of concrete blocks, the Tiki has suitably expansive plantings and 30 rooms with an unintended *Mad Men* vibe.

Schell Motel
MOTEL **$**
(☑250-545-1351, 888-772-4355; www.schellmotel.ca; 2810 35th St; r $70-140; ✳☎☀) Another vision in artful concrete blocks, this immaculate indie motel has a welcoming pool, BBQ, a sauna, fridges and some kitchens. The 32 rooms are ideally central but out of range of the 32nd St roar.

Ellison Provincial Park
CAMPGROUND **$**
(☑800-689-9025, information only 250-494-6500; www.discovercamping.ca; campsites $30; ◷Apr-Oct) Some 16km southwest of Vernon on Okanagan Landing Rd, this is a great place. The 71 campsites fill up early, so reserve.

✗ Eating

The evening **farmers market** (☑250-546-6267; cnr 48th Ave & 27th St; ◷4-8pm Fri) adds class to the Village Green Mall parking lot at the north end of town. There are also morning **markets** (3445 43rd Ave; ◷8am-noon Mon & Thu), just west of Hwy 97.

Talkin Donkey
CAFE **$**
(☑250-545-2286; 3923 32nd St; meals $7; ◷7am-9pm, until 11pm Fri; ☎) When they talk about 'drinking responsibly' at this local institution, they mean ensuring that your coffee is fair trade. A good chunk of the proceeds at this funky coffeehouse with a spiritual edge goes to charity. Tap your Birkenstock-clad toes to Friday-night folk music.

Blue Heron Waterfront Pub
CAFE **$$**
(☑250-542-5550; 7673 Okanagan Landing Rd; mains $8-25; ◷11am-late Apr-Oct) Southwest of town, sweeping views of Okanagan Lake from the big patio keep things hopping all summer long. The meaty fare of excellent steaks and burgers is leavened by cheesy fare such as nachos.

DESTINATION	FARE	DURATION	FREQUENCY (PER DAY)
Kelowna	$19	1hr	6
Kamloops	$30	2hr	3
Vancouver	$75	7½hr	3
Calgary	$85	9hr	1

Eclectic Med   MEDITERRANEAN **$$**
(☑250-558-4646; 2915 30th Ave; mains $12-25; ☺noon-9pm) The name sums up the menu, which brings a Mediterranean accent to local standards like Alberta steaks, lake fish and lots of valley veggies. Plates are artfully presented.

🔒 Shopping

Bookland   BOOKSTORE
(☑250-545-1885; 3400 30th Ave) Topo maps, travel guides and books on activities in the Okanagan Valley and BC. Excellent selection of local works, magazines and newspapers.

ℹ Information

Visitor center (☑250-545-3016, 800-665-0795; www.tourismvernon.com; 701 Hwy 97 S; ☺8:30am-6pm May-Oct, 10am-4pm Nov-Apr) The office is 2km south of the town centre.

ℹ Getting There & Around

Greyhound Canada (☑800-661-8747; www.greyhound.ca; 3102 30th St, cnr 31st Ave) runs services listed in box.

Vernon Regional Transit System (☑250-545-7221; fares $2) buses leave downtown from the bus stop at the corner of 31st St and 30th Ave. For Kalamalka Lake, catch bus 1 or 6; for Okanagan Lake, bus 7.

North of Vernon

Attractions are few in this area, which is more notable for its major highway connections. Just north of Vernon, beautiful Hwy 97 heads northwest to Kamloops via tree-clad valleys punctuated by lakes, while equally lovely Hwy 97A continues northeast to Sicamous and Hwy 1. Armstrong, 23km north of Vernon, is a cute little village.

SILVER STAR

Classic inland BC dry powder makes Silver Star (☑250-542-0224, 800-663-4431, snow report 250-542-1745; www.skisilverstar.com; 1-day lift ticket adult/child $71/35) a very popular ski resort. The 115 runs have a vertical drop of 760m; snowboarders enjoy a half-pipe and a terrain park. In June the lifts haul mountain bikers and hikers up to the lofty green vistas.

All manner of accommodations can be reserved through the resort. Samesun Lodge (☑250-545-8933, 877-562-2783; www.samesun.com; 9898 Pinnacles Rd; dm/r from $30/80; @☎) runs a very popular and almost posh backpacker hotel.

To reach Silver Star, take 48th Ave off Hwy 97. The resort is 20km northeast of Vernon.

SHUSWAP REGION

Rorschach-test-like Shuswap Lake anchors a somewhat bland but pleasing region of green, wooded hills, farms and two small towns, Sicamous and Salmon Arm. The latter has the area's main visitor center (☑250-832-2230, 877-725-6667; www.shuswap.bc.ca; 200 Hwy 1; ☺8am-8pm daily May-Aug, 10am-5pm Mon-Fri Sep-Apr).

The area is home to several lake-based provincial parks and is a popular destination for families looking for outdoor fun. The main attraction, though, is the annual spawning of sockeye salmon at Roderick Haig-Brown Provincial Park (☑250-851-3000; www.bcparks.ca), just off the highway via Squilax. This 10.59-sq-km park protects both sides of the Adams River between Shuswap Lake and Adams Lake, a natural bottleneck for the bright-red sockeye when they run upriver every October. The fish population peaks every four years, when as many as four million salmon crowd the Adams' shallow riverbed – the next big spawn is due in 2014.

Puttering about the lake on a **houseboat** is a convivial way to explore the Shuswap, especially during the height of summer, when the lake fills with people hoping to wash away their urban cares. Most rent by the week (from $2000) and can sleep upward of 10 people. Contact the visitor center for listings of houseboat operators.

THE KOOTENAYS & THE ROCKIES

Ahhhh. You just can't help saying it as you ponder the plethora of snow-covered peaks in the Kootenay Region of BC. Deep river valleys cleaved by white-water rivers, impossibly sheer rock faces, alpine meadows and a sawtooth of white-dappled mountains stretching across the horizon inspire awe, action or mere contemplation.

Coming from the west, the mountain majesty builds as if choreographed from above. The roughly parallel ranges of the Monashees and the Selkirks striate the West Kootenays with the Arrow Lakes adding texture. Appealing towns like Revelstoke and Nelson nestle against the mountains and are centers of year-round outdoor fun. The East Kootenays cover the Purcell Mountains region below Golden, taking in Radium Hot Springs and delightful Fernie. The Rockies climb high in the sky to the border with Alberta.

BC's Rocky Mountains parks (Mt Revelstoke, Glacier, Yoho and Kootenay) don't have the – no pun intended – high profile of Banff and Jasper National Parks over the border, but for many that's an advantage. Each has its own spectacular qualities, often relatively unexploited by the Banff-bound hordes.

Across this richly textured region, look for grizzly and black bear, elk, moose, deer, beaver, mountain goats and much more. Pause to make your own discoveries.

Revelstoke

POP 8000

Gateway to serious mountains, Revelstoke doesn't need to toot its own horn – the ceaseless procession of trains through the center does all the tooting anyone needs. Built as an important point on the Canadian Pacific transcontinental railroad that first linked eastern and western Canada, Revelstoke echoes not just with whistles but with history. The compact center is lined with heritage buildings yet it's not a museum piece; there's a vibrant local arts community and most locals take full advantage of the boundless opportunities for hiking, kayaking and, most of all, skiing. It's more than worth a long pause as you pass on Hwy 1, which bypasses the town centre to the northeast. The main streets include 1st St and Mackenzie Ave.

◎ Sights

Grizzly Plaza, between Mackenzie and Orton Aves, is a pedestrian precinct and the heart of downtown, where free live-music performances take place in the evenings throughout July and August. While outdoor activities are Revelstoke's real draw card, a stroll of the center and a pause at the museums is a must.

TOP CHOICE Revelstoke Railway Museum
MUSEUM

(☎250-837-6060; www.railwaymuseum.com; adult/child $10/2; ⊙9am-8pm summer, 11am-4pm Fri-Tue winter) Revelstoke Railway Museum, in an attractive building across the tracks from the town center, contains restored steam locomotives, including one of the largest steam engines ever used on Canadian Pacific Railway (CPR) lines. Photographs and artifacts document the construction of the CPR, which was instrumental – actually essential – in linking eastern and western Canada.

Revelstoke Museum
MUSEUM

(☎250-837-3067; 315 1st St W; adult/child $4/2; ⊙9am-5pm Mon-Sat, 1-4pm Sun May-Sep, 1-4pm Mon-Fri Oct-Apr) Revelstoke Museum holds a permanent collection of furniture and historical odds and ends, including mining, logging and railway artifacts that date back to the town's establishment in the 1880s. Also keep a look out for the many historical plaques mounted on buildings around town.

🏃 Activities

Winter

Sandwiched between the vast but relatively unknown Selkirk and Monashee mountain ranges, Revelstoke draws serious snow buffs looking for vast landscapes of crowd-free powder. It's where North America's first ski jump was built (1915).

Just 6km southeast of town, the **Revelstoke Mountain Resort** (☎888-837-2188; www.revelstokemountainresort.com; 1-day lift ticket adult/child $75/26) has ambitions to become the biggest ski resort this side of the Alps. But given its seemingly endless virgin slopes only opened in 2008, it has a ways to go. In the meantime you can, in one run (out of 52), ski both 700m of bowl and 700m of trees. The vertical drop is 1713m, greater than Whistler's.

Although the resort is making bowls accessible that were once helicopter or cat only, there are myriad more that are still remote. **Mica Heliskiing** (☑877-837-6191; www.micaheli.com; 207 Mackenzie Ave) is one of several companies offering trips; costs begin at $1200 per day.

For **cross-country skiing** (www.revelstokenordic.org), head to the Mt MacPherson Ski Area, 7km south of town on Hwy 23. You'll pay a mere $6 to use the 22km of groomed trails.

Free Spirit Sports (☑250-837-9453; 203 1st St W) rents a wide variety of winter gear, including essential avalanche equipment.

Summer

All that white snow turns into white water come spring and rafting is big. **Apex Rafting Co** (☑250-837-6376, 888-232-6666; www.apexrafting.com; 112 1st St E; adult/child $85/69) runs kid-friendly two-hour guided trips on the Illecillewaet River in spring and summer. **Natural Escapes Kayaking** (☑250-837-7883; www.naturalescapes.ca) leads tours, offers lessons and rent kayaks ($35 for two hours).

Mountain biking is huge here, as it is across the region. Pick up a copy of the *Biking Trail Map* from the visitor center or **Skookum Cycle & Ski** (☑250-814-0090; www.skookumcycle.com; 118 Mackenzie Ave), where you can rent bikes.

🛏 Sleeping

Revelstoke has a good selection of places to stay. Only truck spotters will gravitate to those out on Hwy 1. Several motels and cute B&Bs (the visitor center has lists) are right in the center.

Swiss Chalet Motel MOTEL **$$**
(☑250-837-4650, 888-272-4538; www.swisschaletmotel.com; 1101 Victoria Rd; r $80-160; ✴@🛜) It's a short walk to the center from this cheery family-run motel, which includes an especially generous continental breakfast (one of the muffins here would make a dozen at many chains). The 22 rooms have fridges.

Regent Inn HOTEL **$$**
(☑250-837-2107, 888-245-5523; www.regentinn.com; 112 1st St E; r $120-200; ✴🛜🏊) The poshest place in town is not lavish but is comfy. The 50 modern rooms bear no traces of the hotel's 1914 roots (and exterior). The restaurant and lounge are both good and popular. Many bob the night away in the outdoor hot tub.

Revelstoke Lodge MOTEL **$$**
(☑250-837-2181; 888-559-1979; www.revelstokelodge.com; 601 1st St W; r $70-150; ✴@🛜🏊) This 42-room, pink-hued motel overcomes its inherent flaws, such as an all-encompassing parking area and stark cinder-block construction, thanks to its location. Check out a room or two to find one with recent paint and watch out for dark ones.

Blanket Creek Provincial Park CAMPGROUND **$**
(☑800-689-9025; www.discovercamping.ca; campsites $21) This park, 25km south of Revelstoke along Hwy 23, includes over 60 campsites with flush toilets and running water. There's a playground and a waterfall is nearby.

SameSun Budget Lodge HOSTEL **$**
(☑250-837-4050, 877-562-2783; www.samesun.ca; 400 2nd St W; dm/r from $25/60; @🛜) Ramble though the numerous rooms in this perennial backpacker favorite. The 80 beds are often full, so book ahead. Expanded patios fill with a jovial international crowd.

🍴 Eating & Drinking

The **farmers market** (☉8am-1pm Sat) sprawls across Grizzly Plaza. Mt Begbie Brewing makes good local microbrews that are available around town.

TOP CHOICE **Woolsey Creek** FUSION **$$**
(☑250-837-5500; 604 2nd St W; mains $10-20; ☉5-10pm) The food at this lively and fun place is the artistic result of two women, Sylvie and Sophie, and their passion for inventive fare. There are global influences across the menu (you won't go wrong with the prosciutto-stuffed chicken) and a fine wine list. Excellent starters encourage sharing and lingering on the large patio.

La Baguette BAKERY **$**
(☑250-814-7088; Garden St; snacks from $3; ☉7am-7pm Thu-Tue) Delicious new bakery near Victoria Rd has luscious, French-style goods plus paninis and coffees.

Modern Bakeshop & Café CAFE **$**
(☑250-837-6886; 212 Mackenzie Ave; mains from $5; ☉7am-5pm Mon-Sat; 🛜) Try a *croque-monsieur* (grilled ham-and-cheese sandwich) or an elaborate pastry for a taste of Europe at this cute art moderne cafe. Many items are made with organic ingredients.

The Cabin BAR **$**
(☑250-837-2144; 200 E 1st St; ☉5pm-midnight) Bowling alley, bar, outdoor gear store and

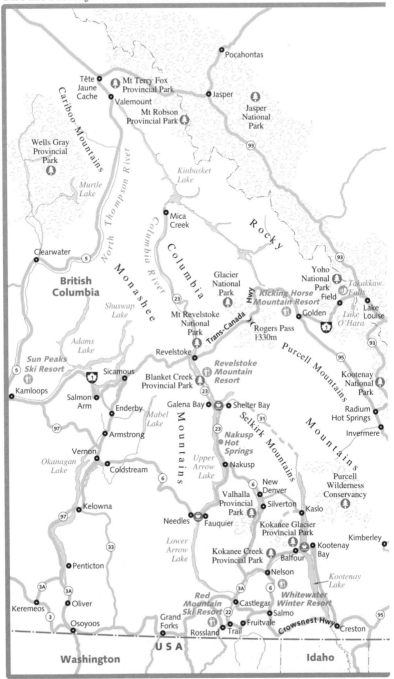

art gallery. A groovy chill spot with a few
snacks to go with the beers.

ℹ Information

The main **visitor center** (☎250-837-5345, 800-
487-1493; www.seerevelstoke.com; 206 Campbell Ave; ⊙9am-4pm Mon-Fri) is open year-round.
But during summer, go to the larger seasonal
visitor center (110 Mackenzie Ave; ⊙9am-9pm
Jun-Aug, 10am-6pm May & Sep). It has parking
and internet access ($1 per 10 minutes).

A **Parks Canada regional office** (☎250-837-
7500; revglacier.reception@pc.gc.ca; 301 3rd St;
⊙8am-4:30pm Mon-Fri) has in-depth info about
nearby Mt Revelstoke and Glacier National Parks.

ℹ Getting There & Away

Greyhound Canada (☎800-661-8747; www.
greyhound.ca; 1899 Fraser Dr) is west of town,
just off Hwy 1. It has storage lockers. Buses go
east to Calgary ($62, six hours, three daily) via
Banff, and west to Vancouver ($95, 10 hours,
three daily) via Kamloops or Kelowna.

Revelstoke Shuttle (☎888-569-1969; www.
revelstokeconnection.com) has daily shuttles
to/from Kelowna ($84, 2½ hours).

Mt Revelstoke National Park

Grand in beauty if not in size (only 260
sq km), this national park (www.pc.gc.ca/
revelstoke), just northeast of its namesake
town, is a vision of peaks and valleys – many
all but untrod.

From the 2223m summit of Mt Revelstoke, the views of the mountains and the
Columbia River valley are excellent. To as-
cend here, take the 26km Meadows in the
Sky Parkway, 1.5km east of Revelstoke off
the Trans-Canada Hwy (Hwy 1). Open after the thaw (usually June to September),
this paved road winds through lush cedar
forests and alpine meadows and ends at

DON'T MISS

TWO PERFECT WALKS

Easily accessible, **Skunk Cabbage
Trail**, 28km east of Revelstoke on Hwy
1, is a 1.2km boardwalk along the Illecillewaet River. It is lined with its huge
namesakes. Another 4km east, the **Giant Cedars Boardwalk** winds a 500m
course up and down and all around a
grove of huge old-growth cedars.

ⓘ AVALANCHE WARNING

The Kootenays are the heart of avalanche country, which kill more people in BC each year than any other natural phenomenon. The toll is high every year; a 2010 disaster at an extreme snowmobiling meet near Revelstoke claimed three lives and injured at least 30.

Avalanches can occur at any time and even on terrain that seems relatively flat. Roughly half the people caught in them don't survive. It's vital that people venturing out onto the snow make inquiries about conditions first; if an area is closed don't go there. Whether you're backcountry ski touring or simply hiking in the alpine region, you'll want to rent a homing beacon; most outdoor shops can supply one.

In Revelstoke, the Canadian Avalanche Centre is operated by the Canadian Avalanche Association (CAA; ☑250-837-2435, 24hr info 800-667-1105; www.avalanche.ca). It analyzes avalanche trends, weather patterns and issues forecasts for the Kootenays and beyond.

Balsam Lake, within 2km of the peak. From here, walk to the top or take the free shuttle, which runs from 10am to 4pm daily.

There are several good hiking trails from the summit. You can camp only in designated backcountry campsites, and you must have a $10 Wilderness Pass camping permit (in addition to your park pass), which, along with lots of useful information, is available from **Parks Canada in Revelstoke** (p151) or from the **Rogers Pass Centre** (p152) inside Glacier National Park. Admission to both Mt Revelstoke and Glacier National Parks (the two are administered jointly) is adult/child $8/4 per day.

Glacier National Park

To be really accurate, this 1350-sq-km park (www.pc.gc.ca/glacier) should be called 430 Glaciers National Park; the annual snowfall here can be as much as 23m. Because of the sheer mountain slopes, this is one of the world's most active avalanche areas. For this reason, skiing, caving and mountaineering are regulated; you must register

with park wardens before venturing into the backcountry. Call for a daily avalanche report (☑250-837-6867) in season. Admission to this and Mt Revelstoke National Park (the two are administered jointly) is adult/child $8/4 per day.

Whether you travel by car, bus, trail or bicycle (more power to you), Rogers Pass will likely rank as one of the most beautiful mountain passes you'll ever traverse. Be sure to pause at the Hemlock Grove Trail, 54km west of Revelstoke, where a 400m boardwalk winds through an ancient hemlock rainforest.

Spend some time with the CPR dioramas at the informative Rogers Pass Centre (☑250-814-5233; ◑8am-8pm mid-June–Aug, 7am-5pm other times), 72km east of Revelstoke. The center shows films about the park and organizes guided walks in summer. As a bonus, there's an excellent bookstore run by the Friends of Mt Revelstoke & Glacier National Parks (www.friendsrevglacier.com).

Across from the center, the 50-room Glacier Park Lodge (☑250-837-2126, 888-567-4477; www.glacierparklodge.ca; r $100-140; ❄☎☂) has a cafe, gas station and coin laundry.

Not far from here are the park's two campgrounds: Illecillewaet and Loop Brook (per campsite $22; ◑Jul-Sep). Both have running water and flush toilets.

Golden

POP 3900

Golden is well situated for the national parks – there are six nearby – and for more immediate pleasures, like white-water rafting – the Kicking Horse River converges with the Columbia here. Don't just breeze past the strip of franchised yuck on Hwy 1 or you'll miss the tidy little town center down by the tumbling river.

Expect delays for years to come on Hwy 1 east of Golden as the road is reconstructed from scratch (see www.kickinghorsecanyon.ca).

🏃 Activities

Golden is the center for **white-water rafting** trips on the turbulent and chilly Kicking Horse River. Powerful grade III and IV rapids, and breathtaking scenery along the sheer walls of the Kicking Horse Valley, make this rafting experience one of

North America's best. Full-day trips on the river average about $105; half-day trips are about $65. Local operators include Alpine Rafting (☑250-344-6778, 888-599-5299; www.alpinerafting.com).

Over 60% of the 106 ski runs at Kicking Horse Mountain Resort (☑250-439-5400, 866-754-5425; www.kickinghorseresort.com; 1-day lift pass adult/child from $74/35) are rated advanced or expert. With 1260 vertical meters and a snowy position between the Rockies and the Purcells, the resort's popularity grows each year. It's 14km from Golden on Kicking Horse Trail.

🛌 Sleeping & Eating

There are scores of chain motels along Hwy 1; check with the chamber of commerce for B&Bs. In the walkable center, 9th Ave N is good for cafes, bakeries and shops. The farmers market (⊗2-7pm Wed Jul & Aug) is next to the chamber of commerce.

Chancellor Peak Chalets   INN $$$
(☑800-644-8888, 250-344-7038; www.chancellorpeakchalets.com; 2924 Kicking Horse Rd; cabins $195-265) 'What a find!' is a common response among guests to this riverside retreat. The 18 log chalets have two levels and sleep up to six. There are soaker tubs, full kitchens and all the nature you can breathe in. The chalets are 25km east of Golden, off Hwy 1.

Mary's Motel   MOTEL $$
(☑250-344-7111, 866-234-6279; www.marysmotel.com; 603 8th Ave N; r $80-140; ✳🏠🏊) In town, right on the roaring river, Mary's has 81 rooms spread across several buildings; get one with a patio. There are more choices nearby.

Sander Lake Campground   CAMPGROUND $
(☑250-344-6517; www.rockies.net/~bsander; campsites $15-18) This campground, located 12km southwest of Golden off Hwy 95, has a bucolic location amid trees and hills. There are 27 sites and three log cabins ($80).

Kicking Horse Grill   CANADIAN $$
(☑250-344-2330; www.thekickinghorsegrill.ca; 1105 9th St S; mains $20-30; ⊗5-9pm) Dishes at this creative log cabin change depending on the season, although excellent steaks and trout are always on the menu. See if you can try for a table outside under the huge tree.

> ### ℹ WINTER ROAD CONDITIONS
> For up-to-date road conditions on the Trans-Canada Hwy (Hwy 1) and across the province, consult DriveBC (☑800-550-4997; www.drivebc.ca). This is essential in winter when storms can close roads for extended periods.

ℹ Information

Unfortunately, the shiny **visitor center** (☑250-344-7711; ⊗9am-6pm), 1km east on Hwy 1 from the Hwy 95 turnoff into Golden, mostly ignores the immediate region. For local info, visit the **Golden Chamber of Commerce** (☑250-344-7125, 800-622-4653; www.goldenchamber.bc.ca; 500 10th Ave N; ⊗10am-6pm Mon-Sat Jun-Aug, 10am-4pm Mon-Fri Sep-May).

ℹ Getting There & Away

Greyhound Canada (☑800-661-8747; www.greyhound.ca; Husky Travel Centre, 1050 Trans-Canada Hwy) serves Vancouver ($124, 11 to 13 hours, three daily) and Calgary ($48, four hours, three daily) via Banff.

Yoho National Park

Fed by glaciers, the ice-blue Kicking Horse River plows through the valley of the same name. The surging waters are an apt image for this dramatic national park (☑250-343-6783; www.pc.gc.ca/yoho; adult/child $10/5), home to looming peaks, pounding waterfalls, glacial lakes and patches of pretty meadows.

Although the smallest (1310 sq km) of the four national parks in the Rockies, Yoho is a diamond in the (very) rough. This wilderness is the real deal; it's some of the continent's least tarnished.

East of Field on Hwy 1 is the Takakkaw Falls road (⊗late Jun-early Oct). At 254m, Takakkaw is one of the highest waterfalls in Canada. From here Iceline, a 20km hiking loop, passes many glaciers and spectacular scenery.

This World Heritage site protects the amazing Cambrian-age fossil beds on Mt Stephen and Mt Field. These 515-million-year-old fossils preserve the remains of marine creatures that were some of the earliest forms of life on earth. You can only get to the fossil beds by guided hikes, which

WORTH A TRIP

NORTHERN LIGHTS WOLF CENTRE

The **Northern Lights Wolf Centre** (☎250-344-6798; www.northernlight-swildlife.com; adult/child $10/6; ⏰10am-6pm) is a refuge in the wild for wolves born into captivity. Visitors can expect to meet a resident wolf or two and learn about their complex and human-like family structure. The goal of the centre is to educate people about wolves, which are still being hunted to extinction to protect both cattle and even other endangered species. The centre is just west of Golden, 5km off the Trans-Canada. Look for signs or call.

are led by naturalists from the **Yoho Shale Geoscience Foundation** (☎800-343-3006; www.burgess-shale.bc.ca; tours from $75). Reservations are essential.

Near the south gate of the park, you can reach pretty **Wapta Falls** along a 2.4km trail. The easy walk takes about 45 minutes each way.

The three campgrounds within Yoho all close from October to April. Only the **Kicking Horse Campground** (campsites $28) has showers, making its 88 sites the most popular. Nearby, right at the turnoff to Yoho Valley Rd, the quieter **Monarch Campground** (campsites $18) offers 44 basic sites. Appealing **Takakkaw Falls Campground** (campsites $18), 13km along the gravel Yoho Valley Rd, has 35 walk-in (200m) campsites for tents only.

The isolated **HI-Yoho National Park** (Whiskey Jack Hostel; ☎403-670-7580, 866-762-4122; www.hihostels.ca; dm $26-28; ⏰Jul-Sep) offers 27 dorm-style beds. It's 13km off Hwy 1 on Yoho Valley Rd, just before the Takakkaw Falls Campground and close to the falls itself.

LAKE O'HARA

Perched high in the mountains east of Field, **Lake O'Hara** is worth the significant hassle involved in reaching the place, which is an encapsulation of the whole Rockies. Compact wooded hillsides, alpine meadows, snow-covered passes, mountain vistas and glaciers are all wrapped around the stunning lake. A basic day trip is

worthwhile, but stay overnight in the backcountry and you'll be able to access many more trails, some quite difficult, all quite spectacular. The **Alpine Circuit** (12km) has a bit of everything.

To reach the lake, you can take the **shuttle bus** (adult/child $15/7.50; ⏰mid-Jun–early Oct) from the Lake O'Hara parking lot, 15km east of Field on Hwy 1. A quota system governs bus access to the lake and limits permits for the 30 backcountry campsites. You can freely walk the 11km from the parking area, but no bikes are allowed. The area around Lake O'Hara usually remains snow-covered or very muddy until mid-July.

Make reservations for the **bus trip** (☎250-343-6433) or for **camping** (backcountry permit adult $10) up to three months in advance. Given the popularity of Lake O'Hara, reservations are basically mandatory (unless you want to walk). However, if you don't have advance reservations, six day-use seats on the bus and three to five campsites are set aside for 'standby' users. To try to snare these, call ☎250-343-6433 at 8am the day before.

Lake O'Hara Lodge (☎250-343-6418; www.lakeohara.com; r per person per night from $280, 2-night minimum) has been leaving guests slack jawed for over 80 years. The only place to stay at the lake tent-free, the lodge is luxurious in a rustic way. Its environmental practices are lauded.

FIELD

Don't go past Field without stopping. Right off Hwy 1, this historic railroad town has a dramatic overlook of the river and is a quaint yet unfussy place. Many of its buildings date from the early days of the railways, when it was the Canadian Pacific Railway's headquarters for exploration and, later, for strategic planning when engineers were trying to solve the problem of moving trains over Kicking Horse Pass (see the results from a Hwy 1 lookout 8km east of Field).

Field has more than 20 B&Bs. **Fireweed Hostel** (☎250-343-6999, 877-343-6999; www.fireweedhostel.com; 313 Stephen Ave; dm $30-40, r $80-160; @☎) has four spotless rooms.

TOP CHOICE **Truffle Pigs Bistro and Kicking Horse Lodge** (☎250-343-6303; www.trufflepigs.com; 100 Centre St; r $100-200, mains $8-25; ☎) is a legendary cafe serving inventive, high-concept bistro fare that's locally sourced and usually organic. The inn across the street has 14 rooms with the same cheeky style as the bistro.

Greyhound Canada buses stop at the park info center on Hwy 1 on their trips west to Golden ($20, 1½ hours, three daily) and beyond and east to Banff ($25, 1½ hours, three daily).

Information

At Yoho National Park Information Centre (☏250-343-6783; off Hwy 1, Field; ◷9am-4pm Sep-Apr, 9am-5pm May & Jun, 9am-7pm Jul & Aug), pick up the free *Backcountry Guide*; its map and trail descriptions give an excellent overview. Rangers can advise on itineraries and conditions. Alberta Tourism staffs a desk here in summer.

Mt Assiniboine Provincial Park

Between Kootenay and Banff National Parks lies this lesser-known and smaller (39-sq-km) provincial park (www.bcparks.ca), part of the Rockies' Unesco World Heritage site. The pointed peak of Mt Assiniboine (3618m) – often referred to as Canada's Matterhorn – and its near neighbors have become a magnet for experienced rock climbers and mountaineers. Backcountry hikers revel in its meadows and glaciers.

The park's main focus is crystal-clear Lake Magog, which is reachable on a 27km trek from Banff National Park. At the lake there's the commercially operated Mt Assiniboine Lodge (☏403-678-2883; www.canadianrockies.net/assiniboine; r per person from $260), a campground (campsites $10) and some huts (per person $20), which may be reserved through the lodge. Helicopter transport is $130 to $160 each way.

Kootenay National Park

Shaped like a lightning bolt, Kootenay National Park (☏250-347-9505; www.pc.gc.ca/kootenay; adult/child $10/5) is centered on a long, wide, tree-covered valley shadowed by cold, gray peaks. Encompassing 1406 sq km, Kootenay has a more moderate climate than the other Rocky Mountains parks and, in the southern regions especially, summers can be hot and dry (which is a factor in the frequent fires). It's the only national park in Canada to contain both

glaciers and cacti. From BC you can create a fine driving loop via Kootenay and Yoho National Parks. See p155 for details on the main park visitor center.

The short interpretive Fireweed Trail loops through the surrounding forest at the north end of Hwy 93. Panels explain how nature here is recovering from a 1968 fire. Some 7km further on, Marble Canyon has a pounding creek flowing through a nascent forest. Another 3km south on the main road is the short, easy trail through forest to ochre pools known as the Paint Pots. Panels describe both the mining history of this rusty earth and its past importance to Aboriginal people.

Learn how the park's appearance has changed over time at the Kootenay Valley Viewpoint, where informative panels vie with the view. Just 3km south, Olive Lake makes a perfect picnic or rest stop. A lakeside interpretive trail describes some of the visitors who've come before you.

Radium Hot Springs

Lying just outside the southwest corner of Kootenay National Park, Radium Hot Springs is a major gateway to the whole Rocky Mountains national park area. The Kootenay National Park & Radium Hot Springs Visitor Center (☏250-347-9331, 800-347-9704; www.radiumhotsprings.com; 7556 Main St E/Hwy 93/95; ◷9am-7pm May-Sep, 9am-5pm Oct-Apr) has internet access, an excellent display on the park and is staffed with Parks Canada rangers.

Radium boasts a large resident population of **bighorn sheep**, which often wander through town, but the big attraction is the hot springs (☏250-347-9485; adult/child $7/6; ◷9am-11pm mid-May–early Oct, noon-9pm rest of yr), 3km north of town. The hot springs' pools are quite modern and can get very busy in summer. The water comes from the ground at 44°C, enters the first pool at 39°C and hits the final one at 29°C.

Radium glows with lodging – some 30 motels at last count. Highly recommended is Misty River Lodge B&B (☏250-347-9912; www.mistyriverlodge.bc.ca; 5036 Hwy 93; r $60-100). Directly outside the park gate, this five-room B&B has owners who are enthusiastic about the parks and ready to share their knowledge with guests; bicyclists are welcomed.

Radium Hot Springs to Fernie

South from Radium Hot Springs, Hwy 93/95 follows the wide Columbia River valley between the Purcell and Rocky Mountains. It's not especially interesting, unless you're into the area's industry (building ski resorts), agriculture (golf courses) or wild game (condo buyers).

At Skookumchuk, 90km south of Radium Hot Springs, a gravel road heads eastwards to **Top of the World Provincial Park** (☑250-422-4200; www.bcparks.ca), which has hiking trails and backcountry camping ($5) and cabins ($15 to $30). The highlight is a 6km hike or bike ride from the end of the road to the simply named **Fish Lake**, which is filled with just that.

South of Skookumchuk, the road forks. Go left and after 31km you'll reach Hwy 3 for Fernie. Go left on Hwy 95A and you'll come to **Fort Steele Heritage Town** (☑250-426-7342; www.fortsteele.ca; adult/child summer $15/5, less other times; ☺9:30am-6:30pm Jul & Aug, 9:30am-5pm Apr-Jun, Sep & Oct, 10am-4pm Nov-Mar), a re-created 1880s town that's an order of magnitude less irritating than many of similar ilk.

From here it's 95km to Fernie along Hwys 93 and 3.

Fernie

POP 4700

Surrounded by mountains on four sides – that's the sheer Lizard Range you see looking west – Fernie defines cool. Once devoted solely to lumber and coal, the town has used its sensational setting to branch out. Skiers love the more-than-8m of dry powder that annually hits the runs easily seen from town. In summer this same dramatic setting lures scores of hikers and mountain bikers.

Despite the town's discovery by pleasure seekers, it still retains a down-to-earth vibe, best felt in the cafes, bars, shops and galleries along Victoria/2nd Ave in the historic center, three blocks south of Hwy 3/7th Ave. Fernie was the location of *Hot Tub Time Machine*, a farcical 2010 film that starred John Cusack and Chevy Chase.

◉ Sights

Fernie experienced a devastating fire in 1908 (one of many disasters), which resulted in a brick-and-stone building code.

Thus today you'll see numerous fine **early-20th-century buildings**, many of which were built out of local yellow brick, giving the town an appearance unique in the East Kootenays. Get a copy of *Heritage Walking Tour* ($5), a superb booklet produced by the **Fernie Museum** (☑250-423-7016; 491 2nd Ave; admission by donation; ☺10am-5:30pm).

Located in the old CPR train station, the **Arts Station** (☑250-423-4842; 601 1st Ave; ☺vary) has a small stage, galleries and studios for some of the many local artists.

🏃 Activities

In fall, eyes turn to the mountains for more than their beauty: they're looking for snow. A five-minute drive from downtown Fernie, fast-growing **Fernie Alpine Resort** (☑250-423-4655, 877-333-2339, snow conditions 250-423-3555; www.skifernie.com; 1-day pass adult/child $75/25) boasts 114 runs, five bowls and almost endless dumps of powder. Most hotels run shuttles here daily.

Mountain biking is almost as big as skiing. From easy jaunts in **Mt Fernie Provincial Park** (www.bcparks.ca), which is a mere 3km from town, to legendary rides up and down the hills in and around the ski resort (which runs lifts in summer), Fernie has lots for riders. Many come just to tackle the legendary **Al Matador**, which drops over 900m before finishing in the terrific Three Kings trail. Get a copy of the widely available *Fernie Mountain Bike Map* and check out the **Crank Fernie** (www.crankfernie.com) website. **Ski & Bike Base** (☑250-423-6464; www.skibase.com; 432 2nd Ave) is but one of many excellent gear-rental and supply places along 2nd Ave. Mountain bikes start at $30 per day.

The Elk River is a classic white-water river, with three grade IV rapids and 11 more grade IIIs. It passes through beautiful country and you can often see large wildlife. Several outfits, such as **Mountain High River Adventures** (☑250-423-5008, 877-423-4555; www.raftfernie.com), offer day trips for about $120 or half-day floats for $60.

Great hiking trails radiate in all directions from Fernie. The excellent and challenging **Three Sisters hike** (20km) winds through forests and wildflower-covered meadows, along limestone cliffs and scree slopes. Get directions at the visitor center.

🛏 Sleeping

Being a big ski town, Fernie's high season is winter. You'll have most fun staying in the center, otherwise **Fernie Central Reservations** (☏800-622-5007; www.ferniecentralreservations.com) can book you a room at the ski resort.

HI Raging Elk Hostel   HOSTEL $
(☏250-423-6811; www.ragingelk.com; 892 6th Ave; dm/r from $26/60; @) Wide decks allow plenty of inspirational mountain gazing at this well-run central hostel that has good advice for those hoping to mix time on the slopes and/or trails with seasonal work. The pub is a hoot.

Mt Fernie Provincial Park   CAMPGROUND $
(☏800-689-9025; www.discovercamping.ca; campsites $21) Only 3km from town, it has 40 sites, flush toilets, waterfalls and access to mountain-bike trails.

Park Place Lodge   HOTEL $$
(☏250-423-6871, 888-381-7275; www.parkplacelodge.com; 742 Hwy 3; r $90-200; ✳@☲) The nicest lodging close to the center, its 64 comfortable rooms have high-speed internet, fridges, microwaves and access to an indoor pool. Some have balconies and views.

Red Tree Lodge   MOTEL $$
(☏250-423-4622, 800-977-2977; www.redtreelodge.com; 1101 7th Ave; r $80-150; ✳☎☲) Unprepossessing but ideally located, this two-story motel has refurbished rooms, with a touch of style. There's a hot tub, a full shared kitchen, some balconies and lots of mountain views.

✖ Eating & Drinking

Cincott Farms Organic Market
(☏250-423-5564; 851 7th Ave; ◷8am-8pm) is like a daily farmers market. Look for the good ales of Fernie Brewing Co at most local pubs. The Arts Station sometimes has live music by local bands.

Blue Toque Diner   CAFE $
(☏250-423-4637; 500 Hwy 3; mains $8; ◷8:30am-3:30pm) Part of the Arts Station, the menu features lots of seasonal and organic vegetarian specials. This is the place for breakfast.

Rip 'n' Richards Eatery   PIZZA $$
(☏250-423-3002; 301 Hwy 3; mains $10-15; ◷11am-11pm) Enjoy the views of the Elk River and surrounding peaks from the deck. But save some attention for the long menu of good burgers, salads and pizza.

Mug Shots Bistro   BAKERY $
(☏250-423-8018; 591 3rd Ave; mains $5; ◷8am-5pm; @☎) Always buzzing, it offers coffee, baked goods, sandwiches and internet access.

🛍 Shopping

Polar Peek Books   BOOKSTORE
(☏250-423-3736; 592 2nd Ave) An eclectic mix of books, with a good section of local interest. Great recommendations.

ℹ Information

The **visitor center** (☏250-423-6868; www.ferniechamber.com; 102 Commerce Rd; ◷9am-6pm summer, 9am-5pm Mon-Fri winter) is east of town off Hwy 3, just past the Elk River crossing. Good displays about the area; the Fernie Museum is also a good info source.

ℹ Getting There & Around

Shuttles operate between town and the ski resort.

Airport Shuttle Express (www.airportshuttleexpress.com) To/from Calgary airport (adult/child $114/94, four hours) in ski season.

Greyhound Canada (☏250-423-6811; HI Raging Elk Hostel, 892 6th Ave) Buses west to Kelowna ($115, 11½ hours, two daily) via Cranbrook and Nelson ($68, six hours, two daily) and east to Calgary ($70, 5½ to seven hours, two daily).

The Shuttle (☏250-423-4023; theshuttle-fernie@hotmail.com) To/from Calgary airport (adult/child $120/90, 4½ hours) in winter.

Kimberley

POP 5900

When big-time mining left Kimberley in 1973, a plan was hatched to turn the little mountain village (altitude 1113m) into a tourist destination with a Bavarian theme. The center was turned into a pedestrian zone named the **Platzl**, locals were encouraged to prance about in lederhosen and dirndls and sausage was added to many a menu. Now, over three decades later, the shtick is fading like memories of the war. There's still a bit of fake half-timbering about, you can get a schnitzel and there is summertime dancing aimed at the tour-bus crowds, but mostly it's a diverse place that makes a worthwhile detour off Hwy 95 between Cranbrook and Radium Hot Springs.

The **visitor center** (☑250-427-3666; www.kimberleychamber.com; 270 Kimberley Ave; ☺10am-6pm daily Jun-Aug, 10am-6pm Mon-Sat Sep-May) sits in the large parking area behind the Platzl.

Take a 15km ride on **Kimberley's Underground Mining Railway** (☑250-427-7365; www.kimberleysundergroundmining railway.ca; Gerry Sorensen Way; adult/child $18/7; ☺11am-3:30pm mid-May–mid-Sep) as the tiny train putters through the steep-walled Mark Creek Valley toward some sweeping mountain vistas. At the end of the line, you can take a chairlift up to the **Kimberley Alpine Resort** (☑250-427-4881, 877-754-5462; www.skikimberley.com; 1-day lift pass adult/child $65/18). In winter, the resort has over 700 hectares of skiable terrain, mild weather and 80 runs.

Cranbrook

POP 19,800

The area's main center, 31km southeast of Kimberley, **Cranbrook** is a dusty crossroads. However, it has one great reason for stopping: the **Canadian Museum of Rail Travel** (☑250-489-3918; www.trains deluxe.com; adult/child $16/8; ☺10am-6pm summer, 10am-5pm Tue-Sat winter), which has some fine examples of classic Canadian trains, including the luxurious 1929 edition of the *Trans-Canada Limited,* a legendary train that ran from Montréal to Vancouver.

Hwy 3/95 bisects the town and is a grim, treeless strip of motels. But just south, **Elizabeth Lake Lodge** (☑250-426-6114; www.elizabethlakelodge.com; 590 Van Horn St S/Hwy3/95; campsites/r from $24/90; ❈@☎) stars with its lakeside location, stylish

CHECK YOUR WATCH

It is a constant source of confusion that the East Kootenays lie in the Mountain Time Zone along with Alberta – unlike the rest of BC, which falls within the Pacific Time Zone. West on Hwy 1 from Golden, the time changes at the east gate of Glacier National Park. Going west on Hwy 3, the time changes between Cranbrook and Creston. Mountain Time is one hour ahead of Pacific Time.

rooms and fun-filled mini-golf course based on BC history.

Cranbrook to Rossland

Hwy 3 twists and turns its way 300km from Cranbrook to Osoyoos at the south end of the Okanagan Valley. Along the way it hugs the hills close to the US border and passes eight border crossings. As such, it's a road of great usefulness, even if the sights never quite live up to the promise.

Creston, 123km west of Cranbrook, is known for its many orchards and as the home of Columbia Brewing Co's Kokanee True Ale. But both of these products are mostly shipped out, so you should do the same. Hwy 3A heads north from here for a scenic 80km to the Kootenay Lake Ferry (see the boxed text, p161), which connects to Nelson. This is a fun journey.

The **Creston Valley Wildlife Management Area** (☑250-402-6900; www.creston wildlife.ca; admission free; ☺dawn-dusk), 11km west of Creston, is a good place to spot oodles of birds, including blue herons, from the 1km boardwalk.

Some 85km west of Creston, **Salmo** is notable mostly as the junction with Hwy 6, which runs north for a bland 40km to Nelson. The Crowsnest Hwy splits 10km west. Hwy 3 bumps north through **Castlegar**, which is notable for having the closest large airport to Nelson and a very large pulp mill. Hwy 3B dips down through the cute little cafe-filled town of **Fruitvale** and industrial **Trail**.

Rossland

POP 3500

About 10km west of Trail, Rossland is a world apart. High in the Southern Monashee Mountains (1023m), this old mining village is one of Canada's best places for mountain biking. A long history of mining has left the hills crisscrossed with old trails and abandoned rail lines – all of which are prefect for riding.

The **visitor center** (☑250-362-7722, 888-448-7444; www.rossland.com; ☺9am-5pm mid-May–mid-Sep) is located in the **Rossland Museum** building, at the junction of Hwy 22 (from the US border) and Hwy 3B.

Mountain biking is the reason many come to Rossland. Free-riding is all the rage as the ridgelines are easily accessed and there are lots of rocky paths for plunging downhill. The **Seven Summits Trail** is a 30.4km single track along the crest of the Rossland Range. The Kootenay Columbia Trails Society (www.kcts.ca) has tons of info, including downloadable maps.

Good in summer for riding, Red Mountain Ski Resort (☑250-362-7384, 800-663-0105, snow report 250-362-5500; www.redresort.com; 1-day lift pass adult/child $64/32) draws plenty of ski bums in winter. Red, as it's called, includes the 1590m-high Red Mountain and 2040m-high Granite Mountain, for a total of 485 hectares of challenging, powdery terrain.

Hwy 3B curves through awesome alpine scenery before rejoining Hwy 3 28km northwest of Rossland. The road then wends its way 170km west to Osoyoos through increasingly arid terrain.

Nelson

POP 9300

Nelson is reason enough to visit the Kootenays and should be on any itinerary in the region. Tidy brick buildings climb the side of a hill overlooking the west arm of deep-blue Kootenay Lake, and the waterfront is lined with parks and beaches. The thriving cafe, art and nightlife culture is simply a bonus. However, what really propels Nelson over the top is its personality: a funky mix of hippies, characters, creative types and rugged individualists. You can find all these along Baker St, the pedestrian-friendly main drag where wafts of patchouli mingle with hints of fresh-roasted coffee.

Born as a mining town in the late 1800s, in 1977 a decades-long heritage-preservation project began. Today there are more than 350 carefully preserved and restored period buildings. Nelson is an excellent base for hiking, skiing and kayaking the nearby lakes and hills.

◉ Sights

Almost a third of Nelson's historic buildings have been restored to their high- and late-Victorian architectural splendor. Pick up the superb *Heritage Walking Tour* booklet from the visitor center. It gives details of over two dozen buildings in the center and offers a good lesson in Victorian architecture. The *Artwalk* brochure lists the many public-art displays.

Touchstones Nelson (☑250-352-9813; 502 Vernon St; adult/child $10/4; ⊙10am-5pm Mon-Wed, Fri & Sat, to 8pm Thu, noon-4pm Sun Jun-Aug, closed Mon Sep-May) combines engaging historical displays with art in Nelson's grand old city hall (1902).

By the iconic Nelson Bridge, Lakeside Park is both a flower-filled, shady park and a beach. From the center, follow the Waterfront Pathway, which runs all along the shore (its western extremity past the airport has a remote river vantage). You can walk one way to the park and ride Streetcar 23 (adult/child $3/2; ⊙11am-5pm daily Jun–mid-Sep, Sat & Sun May & mid-Sep–mid-Oct) the other way. It follows a 2km track from Lakeside Park to the wharf at Hall St.

🏃 Activities

Kayaking

The natural (meaning undammed) waters of Kootenay Lake are a major habitat for kayaks. ROAM (☑250-354-2056; www.roamshop.com; 639 Baker St) sells gear, offers advice and works with the noted Kootenay Kayak Company (☑250-505-4549; www.kootenaykayak.com; rentals per day from $40, tours from $80). Kayaks can be picked up at ROAM or Lakeside Park.

Hiking

The two-hour climb to Pulpit Rock, practically in town, affords fine views of Nelson and Kootenay Lake, and excellent hikes abound in two parks in the Selkirk Mountains north across the lake. Kokanee Creek Provincial Park (☑250-825-4212; www.bcparks.ca), 20km northeast off Hwy 3A, has several trails heading away from the visitor center. Kokanee Glacier Provincial Park (☑trail conditions 250-825-3500; www.bcparks.ca) boasts 85km of some of the area's most superb hiking trails. The fantastic 4km (two-hour) hike to Kokanee Lake on a well-marked trail can be continued to the treeless, boulder-strewn expanse around the glacier.

Mountain Biking

Mountain-bike trails wind up from Kootenay Lake along steep and challenging hills, followed by vertigo-inducing downhills. Pick up *Roots Rocks Rhythm* ($15), which details 70 trails, from Sacred Ride (☑250-362-5688; www.sacredride.ca; 213B Baker St; rentals per day $45-55).

Skiing & Snowboarding

Known for its heavy powdery snowfall, **Whitewater Winter Resort** (☎250-354-4944, 800-666-9420, snow report 250-352-7669; www.skiwhitewater.com; 1-day lift ticket adult/child $57/35), 12km south of Nelson off Hwy 6, has the same small-town charm as Nelson. Lifts are few but so are the crowds, who enjoy a drop of 396m on 46 runs.

🛏 Sleeping

By all means stay in the heart of Nelson so you can fully enjoy the city's beat. The visitor center has lists of B&Bs in heritage homes near the center.

TOP CHOICE **Hume Hotel** HOTEL $$
(☎250-352-5331, 877-568-0888; www.humehotel.com; 422 Vernon St; r $80-150; @🖅) This 1898 classic hotel is reclaiming its former grandeur. The 43 rooms (beware of airless ones overlooking the kitchen on sultry nights) vary in quality; ask for the huge corner rooms with views of the hills and lake. Rates include a delicious breakfast, and it has several appealing nightlife venues.

HI Dancing Bear Inn HOSTEL $
(☎250-352-7573, 877-352-7573; www.dancingbearinn.com; 171 Baker St; dm $22-26, r $50-60; ☺@🖅) The brilliant management here offers advice and smoothes the stay of guests in the 14 shared and private rooms (all share bathrooms). Gourmet kitchen and a library.

Cloudside Inn INN $$
(☎250-352-3226, 800-596-2337; www.cloudside.ca; 408 Victoria St; r $100-160; ❄@🖅) Live like a silver baron at this vintage mansion where the six rooms are named after trees. Luxuries abound, and a fine patio looks over the terraced gardens.

Victoria Falls Guest House INN $$
(☎250-352-2297; www.victoriafallsguesthouse.com; cnr Victoria & Falls Sts; r $110-130; 🖅) The wide porch wraps right around this festive yellow renovated Victorian. The four rooms have sitting areas and cooking facilities. Decor ranges from cozy antique to family-friendly bunk beds.

Mountain Hound Inn GUESTHOUSE $$
(☎250-352-6490, 866-452-6490; www.mountainhound.com; 621 Baker St; r $80-110; ❄@) The 19 rooms are small but have an industrial edge – to go with the cement-block walls. It also offers in-room high-speed internet.

WhiteHouse Backpacker Lodge HOSTEL $
(☎250-352-0505; www.white-house.ca; 816 Vernon St; dm $25, r from $50-60; @🖅) Relax on the broad porch overlooking the lake at this comfy heritage house. You'll get all the pancakes you can cook yourself for breakfast.

City Tourist Park CAMPGROUND $
(☎250-352-7618; campnels@telus.net; 90 High St; campsites from $20; ☺May-Oct) Just a five-minute walk from Baker St, this small campground has 40 shady sites.

🍴 Eating

Stroll the Baker St environs and you'll find a vibrant mix of eateries.

Nelson has two **farmers markets**: one is in the **centre** (cnr Josephine & Baker Sts; ☺9:30am-3pm Wed Jul-Sep); the other in **Cottonwood Falls Park** (☺8am-2pm Sat May-Oct) is both the largest in the region and next to a waterfall.

TOP CHOICE **All Seasons Cafe** FUSION $$
(☎250-352-0101; www.allseasonscafe.com; 620 Herridge Lane; mains $15-30; ☺5-10pm Mon-Sat) Sitting on the patio under the little lights twinkling in the huge maple above is a Nelson highlight (in winter, candles provide the same romantic flair). The eclectic menu changes with the seasons. The wine list is iconic.

Bibo FUSION $$
(☎250-352-2744; 518 Hall St; mains $10-25; ☺noon-11pm) Bibo is all exposed brick inside, while outside, a hillside terrace looks down to the lake. Small plates celebrate local produce: go nuts and design your own cheese and charcuterie plate. The short list of mains includes steaks and seafood.

Dominion Cafe BAKERY $
(☎250-352-1904; 334 Baker St; mains $5) A little gem of a bakery-cafe, the chairs are as rickety as the ancient decor; the metaphors continue as the dining area is as small as the menu. But items like the organic, vegan bumbleberry square are sublime.

Oso Negro CAFE $
(☎250-532-7761; 604 Ward St; coffee from $2; ☺7am-5pm; @) This local favorite corner cafe roasts its own coffee. Outside there are tables in a garden that burbles with water features amid statues.

Busaba Thai Cafe THAI $$
(☎250-352-2185; 524 Victoria St; mains $10-20; ☺11am-10pm) The iced Thai coffee here can turn around a hot day. The rich details of the interior have the lush elegance of a

Bangkok gift shop where you'd actually buy something. The food is authentic and best enjoyed on the patio under the stars.

 Drinking

Look for the organic ales of the Nelson Brewing Co.

Library Lounge BAR
(250-352-5331; Hume Hotel, 422 Vernon St; 11am-late) This refined space in the classic hotel (p160) has some good sidewalk tables where you can ponder the passing parade. There's live jazz most nights. Downstairs, the Spiritbar nightclub aspires to something more metropolitan.

The Royal PUB
(250-352-1269; 330 Baker St; 11am-2am) A popular bar right on Baker St. Listen to bands under the high ceilings inside or kick back on the deck.

 Shopping

Otter Books BOOKSTORE
(250-352-7525; 398 Baker St) New books and maps.

Isis Exotica ACCESSORIES
(250-352-0666; 582 Ward St) The place to feel the local vibe: sex toys and oils in a feminist setting.

 Information

The **visitor center** (250-352-3433, 877-663-5706; www.discovernelson.com; 225 Hall St; 8:30am-6pm daily May-Oct, 8:30am-5pm Mon-Fri Nov-Apr) contains good information about the region.

Many cafes have internet access. **Nelson Library** (250-352-6333; 602 Stanley St; 11am-8pm Mon & Wed, 11am-6pm Tue & Thu-Sat) has free access.

Listen to the Nelson beat on **Kootenay Co-op Radio** (FM93.5).

 Getting There & Around

Castlegar Airport (YCG; www.castlegar.ca/airport.php) Closest airport to Nelson.

Greyhound Canada (250-352-3939; Chahko-Mika Mall, 1128 Lakeside Dr) Buses to Calgary ($120, 11 to 13 hours, two daily) via various south Kootenays cities, and Vancouver ($130, 12 to 13 hours, two daily) via Kelowna ($65, 5½ hours).

Nelson Transit System Buses (250-352-8201; www.bctransit.ca; fare $1.75) Main stop: the corner of Ward and Baker Sts. Buses 2 and 10 serve Chahko-Mika Mall and Lakeside Park.

Queen City Shuttle (250-352-9829; www.kootenayshuttle.com; one way adult/child $24/12) Links with Castlegar Airport (one hour).

Nelson to Revelstoke

Heading north from Nelson, there are two options – both scenic – for reaching Revelstoke. Hwy 6 heads west for 16km before turning north at South Slocan. The road eventually runs alongside pretty Slocan Lake for about 30km before reaching New Denver. You'll see some dramatic rock faces,

KOOTENAY FERRIES

The long Kootenay and Upper and Lower Arrow Lakes necessitate some scenic ferry travel. All **ferries** (www.th.gov.bc.ca/marine/ferry_schedules.htm) are free. On busy summer weekends you may have to wait in a long line for a sailing or two before you get passage.

Kootenay Lake Ferry (250-229-4215) sails between Balfour on the west arm of Kootenay Lake (34km northeast of Nelson) and Kootenay Bay, where you can follow Hwy 3A for the pretty 80km ride south to Creston. It is a 35-minute crossing. In summer the ferry leaves Balfour every 50 minutes between 6:30am and 9:40pm, and Kootenay Lake from 7:10am to 10:20pm.

Needles Ferry (250-837-8418) crosses Lower Arrow Lake between Fauquier (57km south of Nakusp) and Needles (135km east of Vernon) on Hwy 6; the trip takes five minutes and runs every 30 minutes in each direction. This is a good link between the Okanagan Valley and the Kootenays.

Upper Arrow Lake Ferry (250-837-8418) runs year-round between Galena Bay (49km south of Revelstoke) and Shelter Bay (49km north of Nakusp) on Hwy 23. The trip takes 20 minutes and runs from 6am to 11pm every hour on the hour from Shelter Bay and every hour on the half-hour between 6:30am and 11:30pm from Galena Bay.

cool vistas of snow-clad peaks rising from the lake and little else with this option, which is 97km in total between Nelson and New Denver.

Heading north and east from Nelson on Hwy 3A is probably the most interesting route. After 34km there is the dock for the **Kootenay Lake Ferry** (p161) at Balfour. This ride is worth it even if you're not going anywhere, because of the long lake vistas of blue mountains rising sharply from the water.

At Balfour the road becomes Hwy 31 and follows the lake 34km north to Kaslo, passing cute little towns along the way.

KASLO

A cute little lake town that's a good stop, Kaslo is a low-key gem. The visitor center (☎250-353-2525; www.klhs.bc.ca; 324 Front St; ◷9am-5pm mid-May–mid-Oct) can help with info on the myriad ways to kayak and canoe the sparkling blue waters right outside. Next door, the 1898 SS Moyie (adult/child $8/4; ◷9am-5pm mid-May–mid-Oct) has been restored. There's a range of accommodations in and around town, plus some good ice-cream stands.

NEW DENVER

Wild mountain streams are just some of the natural highlights on Hwy 31A, which goes up and over some rugged hills. At the end of this twisting 47km road, you reach New Denver, which seems about five years away from ghost-town status. But that's not bad as this historic little gem slumbers away peacefully right on the clear waters of Slocan Lake. The Silvery Slocan Museum (☎250-358-2201; www.newdenver.ca; 202 6th Ave; ◷9am-5pm mid-Jun–Sep) is also home to the very helpful visitor center. Housed in the 1897 Bank of Montreal building, it features well-done displays from the booming mining days, a tiny vault and an untouched tin ceiling.

Both New Denver and the equally sleepy old mining town of Silverton, just south, have excellent cafes. They are also good for arranging access to Valhalla Provincial Park (www.bcparks.ca), a 496-sq-km area that's one of BC's most attractive and underappreciated parks. Like the famous photo of Diana sitting alone in front of the Taj Mahal, the park sits in grand isolation on the west side of Slocan Lake: you'll need a boat to access the many trails and remote campsites.

Making the loop from Nelson via Hwys 6 and 31 through New Denver is an excel-

lent day trip. Otherwise, if you're headed to Revelstoke, continue north 47km on Hwy 6 from New Denver to Nakusp through somewhat bland rolling countryside.

NAKUSP

Right on Upper Arrow Lake, both Nakusp and the chain of lakes were forever changed by BC's orgy of dam building in the 1950s and 1960s. The water level here was raised and the town had to be moved, which is why it now has a sort of 1960s-era look. It does have some attractive cafes and a tiny museum.

Nakusp Hot Springs (☎250-265-4528; www.nakusphotsprings.com; adult/child $9/free; ◷9:30am-9:30pm), 12km northeast of Nakusp off Hwy 23, feel a bit artificial after a revamp. However, you'll forget this as you soak away your cares amid an amphitheater of trees. Ditch the car and walk here on the beautiful 8km **Kuskanax Interpretive Trail** from Nakusp.

From Nakusp you could head west on Hwy 6 to Vernon (p145) in the Okanagan Valley – a 245km drive that includes the Needles Ferry. Or head north 55km on Hwy 23 to the Upper Arrow Lake Ferry (p161) and the final 48km to Revelstoke.

CARIBOO, CHILCOTIN & COAST

This vast and beautiful region covers a huge swath of BC north of the Whistler tourist hordes. It comprises three very distinct areas. The **Cariboo** region includes numerous ranches and terrain that's little changed from the 1850s when the 'Gold Rush Trail' passed through from Lillooet to Barkerville. There are two noteworthy provincial parks here: untamed Wells Gray and canoe-happy Bowron Lake.

Populated with more moose than people, the **Chilcotin** lies to the west of Hwy 97, the region's north–south spine. Its mostly wild, rolling landscape has a few ranches and some aboriginal villages. Hwy 20 travels west from Williams Lake to the spectacular Bella Coola Valley – a bear-and-wildlife-filled inlet along the coast.

Much of the region can be reached via Hwy 97 and you can build a circle itinerary to other parts of BC via Prince George in the north. The Bella Coola Valley is served by ferry from Port Hardy on Vancouver Island (p121), which makes for cool circle-route itineraries.

There is a daily Greyhound Canada (☎800-661-8747; www.greyhound.ca) service along Hwy 97 to/from Prince George.

Williams Lake to Prince George

Cattle and lumber have shaped **Williams Lake**, the hub for the region. Some 206km north of the junction of Hwys 1 and 97, this small town has a pair of small museums and numerous motels. The best reason to stop is the superb Discovery Centre (☎250-392-5025; www.williamslakechamber. com; 1660 Broadway S, off Hwy 97; ☺9am-5pm summer, 9am-4pm rest of year), a visitor center in a huge log building. It has full regional info and the lowdown for trips west to the coast on Hwy 20.

Quesnel, 124km north of Williams Lake on Hwy 97, is all about logging. There are some good motels and cafes in the tidy, flower-lined center. From Quesnel, Hwy 26 leads east to the area's main attractions, Barkerville Historic Town and Bowron Lake Provincial Park.

North of Quesnel it's 116km on Hwy 97 to Prince George (p173).

Barkerville & Around

In 1862 Billy Barker, previously of Cornwall, struck gold deep in the Cariboo. Soon Barkerville sprung up, populated by the usual fly-by-night crowds of whores, dupes, tricksters and just plain prospectors. Today you can visit more than 125 restored heritage buildings in Barkerville Historic Town (☎888-994-3332; www. barkerville.ca; adult/child $14/4.25; ☺8am-8pm mid-May–Sep). In summer, people dressed in period garb roam through town, and if you can tune out the crowds it feels more authentic than forced. It has cafes and a couple of B&Bs. At other times of year you can visit the town for free but don't expect to find much open – possibly a plus.

BOWRON LAKE PROVINCIAL PARK

The place heaven-bound canoeists go when they die, Bowron Lake Provincial Park (www.bcparks.ca) is a fantasyland of 10 lakes surrounded by snowcapped peaks. Forming a natural circle with sections of the Isaac, Cariboo and Bowron Rivers, its 116km canoe circuit is one of the world's finest. There are eight portages, with the longest (2km) over well-defined trails.

The whole circuit takes between six and 10 days, and you'll need to be completely self-sufficient. It's generally open mid-May to October. September is an excellent choice, both for the bold colors of changing leaves and lack of summertime crowds.

The BC Parks website has a downloadable document with everything you'll need to know for planning your trip, including mandatory reservations (which book up months in advance).

If you'd rather leave the details to others, Whitegold Adventures (☎250-994-2345, 866-994-2345; www.whitegold.ca; Hwy 26, Wells) offers four- to eight-day guided paddles of Bowron Lake. A full circuit costs $1800 per person.

To get to the park by car, turn off Hwy 26 just before Barkerville and follow the 28km gravel Bowron Lake Rd.

Sleeping

All the following are near the start of the circuit. The lodges rent gear, kayaks and canoes.

» Bowron Lake Provincial Park Campground (campsites $16) Has 25 simple sites.

» Bowron Lake Lodge (☎250-992-2733, 800-519-3399; www.bowronlakelodge.com; campsites $28, r $40-80; ☺May-Sep) Picture-perfect and right on the lake, there are cabins and motel rooms.

» Becker's Lodge (☎250-992-8864, 800-808-4761; www.beckerslodge.ca; r 2 nights $80-220) Log chalets are inviting inside and out.

Near Barkerville, quirky Wells has accommodations, restaurants and a general store. The visitor center (250-994-2323, 877-451-9355; www.wellsbc.com; 4120 Pooley St; 9am-6pm May-Sep), in an old storefront, has details.

Barkerville is 82km east of Quesnel, at the end of Hwy 26.

Wells Gray Provincial Park

Plunging 141m onto rocks below, Helmcken Falls – Canada's fourth-highest – is but one of the undiscovered facets of Wells Gray Provincial Park (www.bcparks.ca), itself an undiscovered gem.

BC's fourth-largest park is bounded by the Clearwater River and its tributaries, which define the park's boundaries. Highlights for visitors include five major lakes, two large river systems, scores of waterfalls and most every kind of BC land-based wildlife.

Most people enter the park via the town of Clearwater on Hwy 5, 123km north of Kamloops. From here a 36km paved road runs to the park's south entrance. Part-gravel, Wells Gray Rd then runs 29km into the heart of the park. Many hiking trails and sights such as Helmcken Falls are accessible off this road, which ends at Clearwater Lake.

You'll find opportunities for **hiking**, **cross-country skiing** or **horseback riding** along more than 20 trails of varying lengths. Rustic backcountry campgrounds dot the area around four of the lakes. To rent canoes, contact Clearwater Lake Tours (250-674-2121; www.clearwaterlaketours.com; canoes per day from $50), which also leads treks.

There are three vehicle-accessible campgrounds (250-674-2194; campsites $14) in the park, all with pit toilets but no showers. One of the woodsiest, the 50-site Pyramid Campground (May-Oct) is just 5km north of the park's south entrance and close to Helmcken Falls. There's plenty of backcountry camping (per person $5).

Clearwater has stores, restaurants and a slew of motels, including Dutch Lake Resort (250-674-3351, 888-884-4424; www.dutchlake.com; 361 Ridge Dr, Clearwater; campsites from $25, r $100-220), which has cabins, motel units and 65 campsites. Rent a canoe and practice for greater fun in the park.

Wells Gray Guest Ranch (250-674-2792, 866-467-4346; www.wellsgrayranch.com; campsites $15, r $75-130) has 12 cozy rooms in cabins and the main lodge building. It's 27km north of Clearwater.

The Clearwater visitor center (250-674-2646; www.wellsgray.ca; 425 E Yellowhead Hwy, cnr Clearwater Valley Rd; 9am-7pm daily Jul & Aug, 9am-7pm Mon-Fri Apr-Jun & Sep-Dec;) is a vital info stop for the park; it books rooms.

Chilcotin: Highway 20

Meandering over the lonely hills west of the Chilcotin, Hwy 20 runs 450km from Williams Lake to the Bella Coola Valley. Long spoken about by drivers in the sort of hushed tones doctors use when describing a worrisome stool specimen, the road has been steadily improved and today is more than 90% paved. However, the section that's not is a doozy. Known as the Hill, this perilous 30km stretch of gravel is 386km west of Williams Lake. It descends 1524m from Heckman's Pass to the valley (nearly sea level) through a series of tortuous switchbacks and 10% to 18% grades. However, by taking your time and using low gear you'll actually enjoy the stunning views (just make certain that's not as you plunge over the side). And it's safe for all vehicles – tourists engorged with testosterone from their SUVs (sport-utility vehicles) are humbled when a local in a Chevy beater zips past.

Driving the road in one go will take about six hours. You'll come across a few aboriginal villages as well as gravel roads that lead off to the odd provincial park and deserted lake. Check with the visitor center at Williams Lake (p163) for details of these and available services.

Bella Coola Valley

Leaving the dry expanses of the Chilcotin, you're in for a surprise when you reach the bottom of the hill. The Bella Coola Valley is at the heart of Great Bear Rainforest (p165), a lush land of huge stands of trees, surging white water and lots of bears. It almost feels like Shangri-La – without the monks. But it is a spiritual place: Nuxalk First Nations artists are active here, and for many creative types from elsewhere this is literally the end of the road.

The valley stretches 53km to the shores of the North Bentinck Arm, a deep, glacier-fed fjord that runs 40km inland from the Pacific Ocean. The two main towns, Bella Coola on the water and Hagensborg 15km

It's the last major tract of coastal temperate rainforest left on the planet. The Great Bear Rainforest is a wild region of islands, fjords and towering peaks. Covering 64,000 sq km (or 7% of BC), it stretches south from Alaska along the BC coast and Haida Gwaii to roughly Campbell River on Vancouver Island (which isn't part of the forest). The forests and waters are remarkably rich in life: whales, salmon, eagles, elk, otter and more thrive here. Remote river valleys are lined with forests of old Sitka spruce, Pacific silver fir and various cedars that are often 100m tall and 1500 years old.

As vast as it is, however, the Great Bear is under great threat. Less than 40% is protected and the BC government keeps missing deadlines for protection plans. Meanwhile mineral and logging companies are eyeing the forest, while others want to build a huge pipeline. Among the many groups fighting to save this irreplaceable habitat is the **Raincoast Conservation Foundation** (www.raincoast.org). The website www.savethegreatbear.org is a good source of info.

From Bella Coola, you can arrange boat trips and treks to magical places in the Great Bear, including hidden rivers where you might see a rare Kermode bear, a white-furred offshoot of the black bear known in tribal legend as the 'spirit bear' and the namesake of the rainforest.

east, almost seem as one, with most places of interest in or between the two. Most places aimed at visitors are open May to September; check for dates beyond that. Both the visitor center and your accommodations can point you to guides and gear for skiing, mountain biking, fishing, rafting and much more. Services like car repair, ATMs, laundry and groceries are available.

◉ Sights & Activities

Spanning the Chilcotin and the east end of the valley, the southern portion of **Tweedsmuir Provincial Park** (☎250-398-4414; www.bcparks.ca) is the second-largest provincial park in BC. It's a seemingly barely charted place perfect for challenging backcountry adventures. Many hikes and canoe circuits can only be reached by floatplane. Get details at the Williams Lake (p163) or Bella Coola Valley (p166) visitor centers. **Day hikes** off Hwy 20 in the valley follow trails into lush and untouched coastal rainforest.

A good, short hike just west of Hagensborg can be found at **Walker Island Park** on the edge of the wide and rocky Bella Coola River floodplain. Leaving the parking area you are immediately in the middle of a grove of cedars that are 500 years old. But there's really no limit to your activities here. You can hike into the hills and valleys starting from roads or at points only reachable by boat along the craggy coast.

The valley is renowned for bears. **Kynoch West Coast Adventures** (☎250-982-2298;

www.coastmountainlodge.com) specializes in critter-spotting float trips down local rivers (from $80) and wilderness hikes.

🛌 Sleeping & Eating

There are dozens of B&Bs and small lodges along Hwy 20. Many offer evening meals; otherwise there are a couple of cafes and motels in Bella Coola.

Coast Mountain Lodge   INN **$$**
(☎250-982-2298; www.coastmountainlodge.com; 1900 Hwy 20, Hagensborg; r $95-150; @⟩) The 14 rooms are huge, and many have kitchen facilities. There's also a cute coffee bar with an internet terminal. The owners also run Kynoch West Coast Adventures, and guests can rent minivans (per day $55).

Bella Coola's Eagle Lodge   GUESTHOUSE **$$**
(☎250-799-5587, 866-799-5587; www.eaglelodgebc.com; 1103 Hwy 20, Bella Coola; campsites $10-18, r $80-190; @⟩) Experts in the local area own this three-room lodge. It overlooks a verdant expanse; there are 10 campsites.

Bailey Bridge Campsite & Cabins   CAMPGROUND **$**
(☎250-982-2342; www.baileybridge.ca; Salloompt River Rd; campsites $18-25, cabins from $70) Near the namesake bridge, 27 nicely shaded campsites and six cabins dot the riverbank. A small store will sell gear and supplies.

ℹ Information

Bella Coola Valley Visitor Information (☏250-799-5202, 866-799-5202; www.bellacoola.ca; 628 Cliff St, Bella Coola; ☺8am-4:30pm mid-Jun–mid-Sep Sun-Fri) can help you sort out the many joys of the valley.

ℹ Getting There & Away

BC Ferries (☏888-223-3779; www.bcferries. com; adult/child $170/8, car from $340) runs the Discovery Coast route, which links Bella Coola and Port Hardy on Vancouver Island several times a week in summer. The journey takes from 13 to 34 hours, depending on stops. Best are the direct 13-hour trips as the usual boat, the aging *Queen of Chilliwack*, does not have cabins. Unfortunately, BC Ferries seems to be doing its best to ignore this route (except for raising fares substantially).

There are no buses along Hwy 20 to Williams Lake, although you can go by charter plane. **Pacific Coastal Airlines** (☏800-663-2872; www.pacificcoastal.com) has daily flights to/from Vancouver (one way from $234, one hour).

NORTHERN BC

Northern BC is where you will truly feel that you've crossed that ethereal border to some place different. Nowhere else are the rich cultures of Canada's Aboriginal people so keenly felt, from the Haida on Haida Gwaii to the Tsimshians on the mainland. Nowhere else does land so exude mystery, whether it's the storm-shrouded coast and islands or the silent majesty of glaciers carving passages through entire mountain ranges.

And nowhere else has this kind of promise. Highways like the fabled Alaska or the awe-inspiring Stewart-Cassiar inspire adventure, discovery or even a new life. Here, your place next to nature will never be in doubt; you'll revel in your own insignificance.

Prince Rupert

POP 14,700

People are always 'discovering Prince Rupert.' And what a find it is. This fascinating city with a gorgeous harbor is not just a transportation hub (ferries go south to Vancouver Island, west to Haida Gwaii and north to Alaska) but a destination in its own right. It has two excellent museums, fine restaurants and a culture that draws much from its aboriginal heritage.

It may rain 220 days a year but that doesn't stop the drip-dry locals enjoying activities in the misty mountains and waterways. Originally the dream of Charles Hays (who built the railroad here before going to a watery grave on the *Titanic*), Rupert (as it's called) always seems one step behind a bright future. But finally its ship may have come in – literally. A new container port speeds cheap tat from China to bargain-desperate Americans and each year huge cruise ships on the Inside Passage circuit drop off their hordes to 'discover' Rupert's authentic appeal.

⊙ Sights

A short walk from the center, **Cow Bay** is a delightful place for a stroll. The eponymous spotted decor is everywhere but somehow avoids seeming clichéd. There are shops, cafes and a good view of the waterfront, especially from the cruise ship docks at the Atlin Terminal.

TOP CHOICE **Museum of Northern BC** MUSEUM (☏250-624-3207; www.museumof northernbc.com; 100 1st Ave W; adult/child $6/2; ☺9am-5pm mid-May–Aug, 9am-5pm Tue-Sat Sep–mid-May) Don't miss the Museum of Northern BC, which resides in a building styled after an aboriginal longhouse. The museum shows how local civilizations enjoyed sustainable cultures that lasted for thousands of years – you might say they were ahead of their time. The displays include a wealth of excellent Haida, Gitksan and Tsimshian art and plenty of info on totem poles. Special tours of the museum and the bookshop are excellent.

Totem Poles MONUMENT
You'll see totems all around town: two flank the statue of Charlie Hays beside City Hall on 3rd Ave. To witness totem-building in action, stop by the **Carving Shed**, next door to the courthouse. For more, see p170.

🏃 Activities

Skeena Kayaking (☏250-624-5246; www. skeenakayaking.ca; rentals per 24hr $90) offers both rentals and custom tours of the area, which has a seemingly infinite variety of places to put in the water.

Beginning at a parking lot on the Yellowhead Hwy, 3km south of town, a flat

4km loop trail to Butze Rapids has interpretive signs. Other walks here are more demanding.

Pike Island (Laxspa'aws) is a small island past Digby Island, outside of the harbor. Thriving villages were based there as long as 2000 years ago, and remnants and evidence can be seen today. Further afield, Khutzeymateen Grizzly Bear Sanctuary is home to more than 50 of the giants. Both can only be reached with tours.

Tours

Prince Rupert Adventure Tours
BOAT, WILDLIFE

(☑250-627-9166; www.adventuretours.net; Atlin Terminal; adult/child from $55/50) Offers boat tours that circle Kaien Island (May to October) plus whale tours. Its Khutzeymateen trips are amazing.

Seashore Charters
BOAT, WILDLIFE

(☑250-624-5645, 800-667-4393; www.seashorecharters.com; Atlin Terminal; adult/child from $60/44) Half-day trips to Laxspa'aws that include a 40-minute boat ride each way; also offers Khutzeymateen, harbor, whale and wildlife tours.

🛏 Sleeping

Rupert has a range of accommodations, including more than a dozen B&Bs, but when all three ferries have pulled in, competition gets fierce: book ahead.

Crest Hotel
HOTEL **$$**

(☑250-624-6771, 800-663-8150; www.cresthotel.bc.ca; 222 1st Ave W; r $100-300; ✳@🛜) Prince Rupert's premier hotel has harbor-view rooms that are worth every penny, right down to the built-in bay-window seats. Avoid the smallish rooms overlooking the parking lot. Suites are downright opulent.

Eagle Bluff B&B
B&B **$$**

(☑250-627-4955; www.eaglebluff.ca; 201 Cow Bay Rd; r $50-120; @) Ideally located on Cow Bay, this B&B on a pier is in a heritage building that has a striking red and white paint job. Inside, however, the seven rooms have decor best described as home-style; some share bathrooms.

Inn on the Harbour
MOTEL **$$**

(☑250-624-9107, 800-663-8155; www.innontheharbour.com; 720 1st Ave W; r $85-160; 🛜) Sunsets may dazzle you to the point that you

NORTH PACIFIC HISTORIC FISHING MUSEUM

About 20km south of Prince Rupert, the North Pacific Historic Fishing Museum (☑250-628-3538; www.cannery.ca; 1889 Skeena Dr; adult/child $12/6; ⏱noon-4:30pm Tue-Sun May, Jun & Sep, 11am-5pm Jul & Aug), near the town of Port Edward, explores the history of fishing and canning along the Skeena River. The fascinating all-wood complex was used from 1889 to 1968; exhibits document the miserable conditions of the workers. Hours are not always reliable so confirm before your visit. Prince Rupert Transit has bus service to the site.

don't notice the humdrum exterior at this modern, harbor-view motel. The 49 rooms have been revamped.

Pioneer Hostel
HOSTEL **$**

(☑250-624-2334, 888-794-9998; www.pioneerhostel.com; 167 3rd Ave E; dm $25-30; r $50-60; 🖨🛜) Spotless compact rooms, accented with vibrant colors. Small kitchen and BBQ facilities out back; provides free bikes and ferry/train pickups.

Black Rooster Roadhouse
HOSTEL **$**

(☑250-627-5337; www.blackrooster.ca; 501 6th Ave W; dm $25, r $25-85; @🛜) Renovated house just up the hill from the center, with a patio and a bright common room. Call for shuttle pickup.

Prince Rupert RV Campground
CAMPGROUND **$**

(☑250-624-5861; www.princerupertrv.com; 1750 Park Ave; tent/RV sites from $27/35; @) Located near the ferry terminal, it has 88 sites, hot showers, laundry and flush toilets.

🍴 Eating & Drinking

Halibut and salmon fresh from the fishing fleet appear on menus all over town.

Charley's Lounge
PUB **$$**

(☑250-624-6771; Crest Hotel, 222 1st Ave W; mains $8-20; ⏱noon-late) Locals flock to trade gossip while gazing out over the harbor from the heated patio. The pub menu features some of Rupert's best seafood.

Cow Bay Café   FUSION $$
(☎250-627-1212; 205 Cow Bay Rd; mains $10-20; ☺11:30am-9pm) The inventive menu at this well-known bistro changes twice daily; there are always a half-dozen mains and desserts to tempt. Dine outside on the harbor.

Smiles Seafood   SEAFOOD $
(☎250-624-3072; 113 Cow Bay Rd; mains $6-20; ☺11am-9pm) Since 1934 Smiles has served classic, casual seafood meals. Slide into a vinyl booth or sit out on the deck.

Cowpuccino's   CAFE $
(☎250-627-1395; 25 Cow Bay Rd; coffee $2; ☺7am-8pm) A funky local cafe where the coffee will make you forget the rain.

Breakers Pub   PUB $
(☎250-624-5990; 117 George Hills Way; meals $8; ☺11am-late; 🛜) Right on the water at Cow Bay, take in the big views of the fishing boats while the skippers grouse at the bar. The food is fine (good fish sandwiches) and you can play darts or shoot pool.

🛍 Shopping

See the bounty of Rupert's vibrant creative community at the artist-run Ice House Gallery (☎250-624-4546; Atlin Terminal; ☺noon-5pm Tue-Sun). Rainforest Books (☎250-624-4195; 251 3rd Ave W) has a good selection of new and used.

ℹ Information

Java Dot Cup (☎250-622-2822; 516 3rd Ave W; per hr $3; ☺7:30am-9pm; 🛜) Internet access plus a decent cafe.

Visitor center (☎250-624-5637, 800-667-1994; www.tourismprincerupert.com; Museum of Northern BC, 100 1st Ave W; ☺9am-5pm daily mid-May–Aug, 9am-5pm Tue-Sat Sep–mid-May) Visitor services are limited to a rack of brochures and the front desk at the museum.

ℹ Getting There & Away

The ferry and train terminals are 3km southwest of the center.

Air

Prince Rupert Airport (YPR; ☎250-622-2222; www.ypr.ca) is on Digby Island, across the harbor from town. The trip involves a bus and ferry; pickup is at the Highliner Hotel (815 1st Ave) two hours before flight time. Confirm all the details with your airline or the airport.

Air Canada Jazz (☎888-247-2262; www.aircanada.com) and **Hawkair** (☎800-487-1216;

www.hawkair.ca). Check-in for the former is at the airport; for the latter, at Highliner Hotel.

Bus

Greyhound Canada (☎800-661-8747; www.greyhound.ca; 112 6th St) buses depart for Prince George ($120, 10 hours) once a day.

Ferry

Alaska Marine Highway System (☎250-627-1744, 800-642-0066; www.ferryalaska.com) has one or two ferries each week to the Yukon gateways of Haines (passenger/car $160/374, cabins from $120) and Skagway, Alaska: a spectacular albeit infrequent service (see the boxed text, p175).

BC Ferries (☎250-386-3431; www.bcferries.com) Inside Passage run to Port Hardy (adult $100-170, child fare 50%, car $220-390, cabin from $85, 15 to 25 hours) is hailed for its amazing scenery. There are three services per week in summer, one per week in winter on the new *Northern Expedition*. The Haida Gwaii service goes to Skidegate Landing (adult $33-39, child fare 50%, car $115-140, seven hours) six times per week in summer and three times a week in winter on the *Northern Adventure*.

Train

VIA Rail (www.viarail.ca; BC Ferries Terminal) operates tri-weekly to/from Prince George (12½ hours) and, after an overnight stop, Jasper in the Rockies.

ℹ Getting Around

Prince Rupert Transit (☎250-624-3343; www.bctransit.com; adult/child $1.25/1) Infrequent service to the ferry port and North Pacific Historic Fishing Village ($2.50). The main bus stop is at the ratty Rupert Square Mall on 2nd Ave.

Skeena Taxi (☎250-624-5318) To/from the ferries is about $12.

Haida Gwaii

Haida Gwaii, which means 'Islands of the People,' offers a magical trip for those who make the effort. Attention has long focused on their many unique species of flora and fauna to the extent that 'Canada's Galapagos' is a popular moniker. But each year it becomes more apparent that the real soul of the islands is the Haida culture itself. Long one of the most advanced and powerful First Nations, the Haida suffered terribly after Westerners arrived.

Now, however, their culture is resurgent and can be found across the islands in myriad ways beyond their iconic totem poles. Haida reverence for the environment is protecting the last stands of superb old-growth rainforests, where the spruce and cedars are some of the world's largest. Amidst this sparsely populated, wild and rainy place are bald eagles, bears and much more wildlife. Offshore, sea lions, whales and orcas abound.

In 2010 two events further confirmed the islands' resurgence. The name used by Europeans since their arrival in the 18th century, Queen Charlotte Islands, was officially ditched; and the federal government moved forward with its plans to make the waters off Haida Gwaii a marine preserve.

A visit to the islands rewards those who invest time to get caught up in their allure, their culture and their people – plan on a long stay. The number-one attraction here is remote **Gwaii Haanas National Park Reserve**, which makes up the bottom third of the archipelago. Named the top park in North America by *National Geographic Traveler* for being 'beautiful and intact,' it is a lost world of Haida culture and superb natural beauty.

Haida Gwaii forms a dagger-shaped archipelago of some 450 islands lying 80km west of the BC coast, and about 50km from the southern tip of Alaska. Mainland ferries dock at Skidegate Landing on Graham Island, the main island for 80% of the 5000 residents and commerce. The principal town is Queen Charlotte City (QCC), 7km west of Skidegate. The main road on Graham Island is Hwy 16, which is fully paved. It links Skidegate with Masset, 101km north, passing the small towns of Tlell and Port Clements.

Graham Island is linked to Moresby Island to the south by a ferry from Skidegate Landing. The airport is in Sandspit on Moresby Island, 12km east of the ferry landing at Aliford Bay. The only way to get to Gwaii Haanas National Park Reserve, which covers the south part of Moresby Island, is by boat or floatplane.

⊙ Sights & Activities

The Haida Gwaii portion of the **Yellowhead Hwy** (Hwy 16) heads 110km north from QCC past Skidegate, Tlell and Port Clements. The latter was where the famous golden spruce tree on the banks of the Yakoun River was cut down by a de-

mented forester in 1997. The incident is detailed in the best-selling *The Golden Spruce* by John Vaillant, one of the best books on the islands and the Haida culture in print.

All along the road to Masset, look for little seaside pullouts, oddball boutiques and funky cafes that are typical of the islands' character.

TOP CHOICE **Gwaii Haanas National Park Reserve & Haida Heritage Site**

PARK

This huge Unesco World Heritage site encompasses Moresby and 137 smaller islands at the southern end of the islands. It combines a time-capsule look at abandoned Haida villages, hot springs, amazing natural beauty and some of the continent's best kayaking.

Archaeological finds have documented more than 500 ancient Haida sites, including villages and burial caves throughout the islands. The most famous village is SGaang Gwaii (Ninstints) on Anthony Island, where rows of weathered **totem poles** stare eerily out to sea. Other major sights include the ancient village of Skedans, on Louise Island, and Hotspring Island, where you can soak away the bone-chilling cold in natural springs. The sites are protected by Haida Gwaii watchmen, who live on the islands in summer.

Access to the park is by boat or plane only. A visit demands a decent amount of

DON'T MISS

HAIDA HERITAGE CENTRE AT QAY'LLNAGAAY

One of the top attractions in the north is this marvelous cultural centre (☑250-559-7885; www.haidaheritage centre.com; Skidegate; adult/child $15/5; ⊙9am-6pm Jun-Aug, 11am-5pm Tue-Sat Sep-May). With exhibits on history, wildlife and culture, just by itself it would be enough reason to visit the islands. The rich traditions of the Haida are fully explored in galleries, programs and work areas where contemporary artists create new works such as the totem poles lining the shore.

advance planning and usually requires several days. From May to September, you must obtain a reservation, unless you're with a tour operator.

Contact **Parks Canada** (☑250-559-8818; www.pc.gc.ca/gwaiihaanas; Haida Heritage Centre at Qay'llnagaay, Skidegate; ☉8:30am-noon & 1-4:30pm Mon-Fri) with questions. The website has links to the **essential annual trip planner**. Anyone who has not visited the park during the previous three years must attend a free orientation at the park office (all visitors also must register).

The number of daily reservations (☑877-559-8818) is limited: plan well in advance. There are user fees (adult/child $20/10 per night). Nightly fees are waived if you have a Parks Canada Season Excursion Pass. A few much-coveted standby spaces are made available daily: call Parks Canada.

The easiest way to get into the park is with a tour company. Parks Canada can provide you with lists of operators; tours last from one day to two weeks. Many can also set you up with **rental kayaks** (average per day/week $60/300) and gear for independent travel.

Moresby Explorers (☑250-637-2215, 800-806-7633; www.moresbyexplorers.com; Sandspit) has one-day tours from $205 as well as much longer ones. It rents kayaks and gear.

Queen Charlotte Adventures (☑250-559-8990, 800-668-4288; www.queencharlotte adventures.com) offers lots of one- to 10-day trips using boats and kayaks. It has a six-day kayak trip to the remote south for $1620. It rents kayaks and gear.

Yakoun Lake   NATURAL ATTRACTION

Hike about 20 minutes through ancient stands of spruce and cedar to pristine Yakoun Lake, a large wilderness lake towards the west side of Graham Island. A small beach near the trail is shaded by gnarly Sitka alders. Dare to take a dip in the bracing waters or just enjoy the sweeping views.

The trailhead to the lake is at the end of a rough track that is off a branch from the main dirt and gravel logging road between

---

ONE TALL TALE

Though most Aboriginal groups on the northwest coast lack formal written history as we know it, centuries of traditions manage to live on through artistic creations such as totem poles.

Carved from a single cedar trunk, totems identify a household's lineage in the same way a family crest might identify a group or clan in Britain, although the totem pole is more of a historical pictograph depicting the entire ancestry.

Unless you're an expert, it's not easy to decipher a totem. But you can start by looking for the creatures that are key to the narrative. Try to pick out the following.

Beaver Symbolizes industriousness, wisdom and determined independence.

Black bear Serves as a protector, guardian and spiritual link between humans and animals.

Eagle Signifies intelligence and power.

Frog Represents adaptability, the ability to live in both natural and supernatural worlds.

Hummingbird Embodies love, beauty and unity with nature.

Killer whale Symbolizes dignity and strength (often depicted as a reincarnated spirit of a great chief).

Raven Signifies mischievousness and cunning.

Salmon Typifies dependable sustenance, longevity and perseverance.

Shark Exemplifies an ominous and fierce solitude.

Thunderbird Represents the wisdom of proud ancestors.

Two excellent places both to see totem poles and learn more are the Haida Heritage Centre at Qay'llnagaay (p169) at Skidegate and the Museum of Northern BC (see p166) in Prince Rupert.

QCC and Port Clements. It runs for 70km, watch for signs for the lake; on weekdays check in by phone (☑250-557-6810) for logging trucks.

Naikoon Provincial Park PARK
(☑250-626-5115; www.bcparks.ca) A substantial proportion of the island's northeastern side is devoted to the magnificent 726-sq-km Naikoon Provincial Park. This beautiful park combines sand dunes and low sphagnum bogs, surrounded by stunted and gnarled lodgepole pine, and red and yellow cedar. The **beaches** on the north coast feature strong winds, pounding surf and flotsam from across the Pacific. If you're keen on a hike, the beaches can be reached via the stunning 26km-long Tow Hill Rd, east of Masset. A 21km loop **trail** traverses a good bit of the park to/from Fife Beach at the end of the road.

🛏 Sleeping

Small inns and B&Bs are mostly found on Graham Island. There are numerous choices in QCC and Masset, with many in between and along the spectacular north coast. Naikoon Provincial Park has two campgrounds (campsites $16), including a dramatic windswept one on deserted Agate Beach, 23km east of Masset.

Premier Creek Lodging INN $
(☑250-559-8415, 888-322-3388; www.qcislands.net/premier; 3101 3rd Ave, QCC; dm $25, r $35-100; @) Dating from 1910, this friendly lodge has eight beds in a hostel building out back and 12 rooms in the main building, ranging from tiny but great-value singles to spacious rooms with views and porches. There's high-speed internet.

All The Beach You Can Eat CABINS $$
(☑604-313-6192; www.allthebeachyoucaneat.com; 15km marker Tow Hill Rd; cabins $85-120) On beautiful North Beach, two cabins are perched in the dunes, back from the wide swath of sand that runs for miles east and west. One, the sweet little Sweety Pie, has views that seem to reach to Japan. Like two other properties with rental cabins out here, there is no electricity; you cook and see with propane. It's off the grid and out of this world.

Copper Beech House B&B $$
(☑250-626-5441; www.copperbeechhouse.com; 1590 Delkatla Rd, Masset; r from $100) David Phillips has created a legendary B&B in

a rambling old house on Masset Harbor. It has three unique rooms and there's always something amazing cooking in the kitchen.

🍴 Eating & Drinking

The best selection of restaurants is in QCC, although there are also a few places in Skidegate, Tlell and Masset. Ask at the visitor centers about local Haida feasts, where you'll enjoy the most amazing salmon, blueberries and more you've ever had. You may need to adjust your belt buckles afterwards! Good supermarkets are found in Skidegate and Masset.

Queen B's CAFE $
(☑250-559-4463; 3201 Wharf St, QCC; mains $3-10; ⏰9am-5pm) This funky place excels at baked goods, which emerge from the oven all day long. There are tables with water views outside and lots of local art inside.

Ocean View Restaurant SEAFOOD $$
(☑250-559-8503; Sea Raven Motel, 3301 3rd Ave, QCC; mains $10-25; ⏰11am-9pm) Good fresh seafood (try the halibut) is the specialty at this casual dining room, where some tables look out to the harbor.

Rising Tide Bakery BAKERY, CAFE $
(☑250-557-4677; ⏰8am-5pm Wed-Sun Jun-Aug; 🔊) Loved by locals and visitors alike for its cliché-defying cinnamon rolls made with flour ground on site. Also delicious soups and sandwiches.

Moon Over Naikoon BAKERY $
(☑250-626-5064; 17km marker Tow Hill Rd; ⏰8am-5pm Jun-Aug) Embodying the spirit of this road to the end of everything, this tiny community center–cum–bakery has a kaleidoscopic collection of artworks and stuff found on the beach.

ℹ Information

Either download or pick up a free copy of the encyclopedic annual *Guide to the Haida Gwaii* (www.queencharlotteislandsguide.com). A good website for information is www.haidagwaiitourism.ca. **Parks Canada** (www.pc.gc.ca/gwaiihaanas) also has much information online.

QCC visitor center (☑250-559-8316; www.qcinfo.ca; 3220 Wharf St, QCC; ⏰8:30am-9pm daily Jul & Aug, 9am-5pm Tue-Sat Oct-Apr, 9am-5pm May, Jun & Sep) is handy, although there's been a recent encroachment of gift items. Get a free copy of *Art Route*, a guide to more than 40 studios and galleries. A desk at Sandspit Airport opens for incoming flights.

Getting There & Away

The BC Ferries service from Prince Rupert is the most popular way to reach the islands.

Air

The main airport for Haida Gwaii is at **Sandspit** (YZP; ☑250-559-0052) on Moresby Island. Please note that reaching the airport from Graham Island is extremely time-consuming: if your flight is at 3:30pm, you need to line up at the car ferry at Skidegate Landing at 12:30pm (earlier in summer). It's wise to plan ahead. There's also a small airport at **Masset** (YMT; ☑250-626-3995).

Air Canada Jazz (☑888-247-2262; www.aircanada.com) Daily between Sandspit and Vancouver.

Hawkair (☑800-487-1216; www.hawkair.ca) Daily service from Sandspit to Vancouver.

North Pacific Seaplanes (☑800-689-4234; www.northpacificseaplanes.com) Links Prince Rupert with Masset (from $260) and anyplace else a floatplane can land.

Pacific Coastal Airlines (☑800-663-2872; www.pacific-coastal.com) Masset to Vancouver several times per week.

Ferry

BC Ferries (☑250-386-3431; www.bcferries.com) Prince Rupert to/from Skidegate Landing (adult $33-39, child fare 50%, car $115-140, seven hours) runs six times a week in summer, three per week in winter on the *Northern Adventure*. You may find that cabins are useful for overnight schedules (from $85), particularly if want to stretch out in comfort.

Getting Around

Off Hwy 16, most roads are gravel or worse.

BC Ferries (adult/child $9/4.50, cars from $20, 20 minutes, almost hourly 7am to 10pm) operates a small car ferry linking the two main islands at Skidegate Landing and Alliford Bay. Schedules seem designed to inconvenience air passengers.

Eagle Transit (☑877-747-4461; www.haidagwaii.net/eagle) meets flights and ferries. The fare from the airport to QCC is $27.

Renting a car can be as expensive ($60 to $100 per day) as bringing one over on the ferry. **Budget** (☑250-637-5688; www.budget.com) has locations at the airport and QCC. **Rustic Car Rentals** (☑250-559-4641, 877-559-4641; citires@qcislands.net; 605 Hwy 33, QCC) is also in Masset.

Prince Rupert to Prince George

You can cover the 725km on Hwy 16 between BC's Princes in a day or a week. There's nothing that's an absolute must-see, but there's much to divert and cause you to pause if so inclined. Scenery along much of the road (with a notable exception) won't fill your memory card but it is a pleasing mix of mountains and rivers.

PRINCE RUPERT TO SMITHERS

For the first 150km, Hwy 16 hugs the wide and wild Skeena River. This is four-star scenic driving and you'll see glaciers and jagged peaks across the waters. However, tatty Terrace is nobody's idea of a reward at the end of the stretch.

From Terrace, Hwy 16 continues 93km east to Kitwanga, where the **Stewart-Cassiar Hwy** (Hwy 37) strikes north towards the Yukon and Alaska.

Just east of Kitwanga you reach the **Hazelton** area (comprising New Hazelton, Hazelton and South Hazelton), the center of some interesting aboriginal sites, including 'Ksan Historical Village & Museum (☑250-842-5544; www.ksan.org; admission $2; ◐9:30am-4:30pm Mon-Fri Oct-May, 9am-5pm Apr-Sep). This re-created village of the Gitksan people features longhouses, a museum, various outbuildings and totem poles.

SMITHERS

Smithers, a largish town with a cute old downtown, is roughly halfway between the Princes. The visitor center (☑250-847-5072, 800-542-6673; www.tourismsmithers.com; 1411 Court St; ◐9am-6pm May-Sep, 9am-5pm Mon-Fri Oct-Apr) can steer you to excellent mountain biking, white-water rafting and climbing. Great hiking is found at nearby Babine Mountains Provincial Park (☑250-847-7329; www.bcparks.ca; backcountry campsites per person $5), a 324-sq-km park with trails to glacier-fed lakes and subalpine meadows.

The Smithers Guesthouse (☑250-847-4862; www.smithersguesthouse.com; 1766 Main St; dm from $24, r $60-82; @◐) is close to the center. Rooms are basic, but the welcome is warm. Main St has several good cafes. Mountain Eagle Books & Bistro (☑250-847-5245; 3775 3rd St; ◐9am-6pm Mon-Sat; ◐) has books and info on the area's thriving folk-music scene. The tiny cafe has veggie soup and lunches.

SMITHERS TO PRINCE GEORGE

South and west of Smithers, after 146km you pass through Burns Lake, the center of a popular fishing district. After another 128km, at Vanderhoof, Hwy 27 heads 66km north to Fort St James National Historic Site (☑250-996-7191; www.pc.gc.ca; adult/child $8/4; ⊙9am-5pm May-Sep), a former Hudson's Bay Company trading post that's on the tranquil southeastern shore of Stuart Lake and has been restored to its 1896 glory. From Vanderhoof, the 100km to Prince George passes through a region filled with the dead trees seen across the north. These bright-red specimens are victims of mountain pine beetles, whose explosive population growth is linked to comparatively milder winters due to climate change.

Prince George

POP 84,300

In First Nations times, before outsiders arrived, Prince George was called Lheidli T'Enneh, which means 'people of the confluence,' an appropriate name given that the Nechako and Fraser Rivers converged here. Today the name would be just as fitting, although it's the confluence of highways that matters most. A lumber town since 1807, it is a vital BC crossroads and you're unlikely to visit the north without passing through at least once.

Hwy 97 from the south cuts through the center of town on its way north to Dawson Creek (360km) and the Alaska Hwy. Hwy 16 becomes Victoria St as it runs through town westward to Prince Rupert (724km), and east to Jasper (380km) and Edmonton. The downtown, no beauty-contest winner, is compact and has some good restaurants. Still, you'll do well to nab your 40 winks, enjoy some chow and hit the road.

◉ Sights

Exploration Place (☑250-562-1612; www.theexplorationplace.com; Fort George Park; adult/child $9/6; ⊙9am-6pm), southeast of downtown (follow 20th Ave east of Gorse St), has various kid-friendly galleries devoted to science plus natural and cultural history.

Cottonwood Island Nature Park has walks alongside the river and is home to the small Prince George Railway & Forestry Museum (☑250-563-7351; www.pgrfm.bc.ca; 850 River Rd; adult/child $6/3; ⊙10am-5pm mid-May–mid-Oct), which honors choo-choos, the beaver and local lore.

🛏 Sleeping

Hwy 97/Central St makes an arc around the center, where you'll find legions of motels and big-box stores. The Bed & Breakfast Hotline (☑250-562-2222, 877-562-2626; www.princegeorgebnb.com) arranges bookings in your price range (from $50 to $100). Most provide transportation from the train or bus station.

Economy Inn   MOTEL $
(☑250-563-7106, 888-566-6333; www.economyinn.ca; 1915 3rd Ave; r $60-95; ✳ 🐾) Close to the center, this simple blue-and-white motel has 30 clean rooms and a whirlpool. Celebrate your savings with a scrumptious Dairy Queen Peanut Buster Parfait across the street.

Esther's Inn   MOTEL $$
(☑250-562-4131, 800-663-6844; www.esthersinn.com; 1151 Commercial Cres; r $80-120; ✳ @ ⚓) Do you seek a tiki? The faux Polynesian theme extends through the 118 rooms. Have hot times in the three Jacuzzis. It's out on the Hwy 97 bypass.

Travelodge Goldcap   MOTEL $$
(☑250-563-0666, 800-663-8239; www.travelodgeprincegeorge.com; 1458 7th Ave; r $75-130; ✳ @ 🐾) A real barker in the beauty department, the Travelodge is nicer on the inside (isn't everything?). The 77 rooms are motel-standard but huge. Better yet, it's steps from good restaurants and bars.

Bee Lazee Campground   CAMPGROUND $
(☑250-963-7263, 866-679-6699; www.beelazee.ca; 15910 Hwy 97S; campsites $20-27; ⊙May-Sep; 🐾 ⚓) About 10km south of town, this RV-centric place features full facilities, including free hot showers, a pool and laundry.

🍴 Eating & Drinking

The farmers market (cnr George St & 3rd Ave; ⊙8:30am-2pm Sat May-Sep) is a good place to sample some of the array of local foods and produce.

REGIONAL BUS DISTANCES FROM PRINCE GEORGE

DESTINATION	FARE	DURATION	FREQUENCY (PER DAY)
Dawson Creek	$72	5-6½hr	2
Jasper	$65	5hr	1
Prince Rupert	$120	10hr	1
Vancouver	$96	12hr	2

Cimo   MEDITERRANEAN **$$**
(☑250-564-7975; 601 Victoria St; mains $10-25; ☺noon-2pm Mon-Fri, 5-10pm Mon-Thu, until 11pm Fri & Sat) The pesto and other excellent Mediterranean dishes here never disappoint. Dine (or enjoy just a glass of BC wine) in the stylish interior or out on the patio. There's live jazz heard here many nights.

Thanh Vu   ASIAN **$**
(☑250-564-2255; 1778 Hwy 97 S; mains $8-15; ☺11am-9pm) This local favorite is situated out on the Hwy 97 strip. The Vietnamese food is tasty and fresh – it's better than most Asian food you'll find north of greater Vancouver.

White Goose Bistro   FUSION **$$**
(☑250-561-1002; 1205 3rd Ave; mains $8-25; ☺11:30am-10pm) A touch of class downtown, chef Ryan Cyre cooks up surprising treats like lobster nachos in addition to more classic bistro fare at this white-tablecloth restaurant. Lunch sees salads, sandwiches and pastas.

🛍 Shopping

Books & Company   BOOKSTORE
(☑250-563-6637; 1685 3rd Ave; ☺8am-6pm Mon, Wed & Sat, 8am-9pm Thu, 8am-10pm Fri, 10am-5pm Sun; 🖥) The best bookstore in northern BC; it has a convivial cafe.

ℹ Information

Visitor center (www.tourismpg.com) Station (☑250-562-3700, 800-668-7646; VIA Rail Station, 1300 1st Ave; ☺8am-8pm May-Sep, 8:30am-5pm Oct-Apr); branch (☑250-563-5493; cnr Hwy 97 & Hwy 16; ☺8am-8pm May-Aug) The excellent train station visitor center can make bookings like ferry tickets. Internet access per 30 minutes is $3.50.

ℹ Getting There & Away

Prince George Airport (YXS; ☑250-963-2400; www.pgairport.ca) is on Airport Rd, off Hwy 97. **Air Canada Jazz** (www.aircanada.com) and **Westjet** (www.westjet.com) serve Vancouver.

Greyhound Canada (☑800-661-8747; www.greyhound.ca; 1566 12th Ave)

VIA Rail (www.viarail.ca; 1300 1st Ave) heads west three times a week to Prince Rupert (12½ hours) and east three times a week to Jasper (7½ hours) and further east; through passengers must overnight in Prince George.

ℹ Getting Around

Major car rental agencies have offices at the airport.

Prince George Transit (☑250-563-0011; www.busonline.ca; fare $2) Operates local buses.

Prince George Taxi (☑250-564-4444)

Prince George to Alberta

Look for lots of wildlife along the 380km stretch of Hwy 16 that links Prince George with Jasper, just over the Alberta border. The major attraction along the route actually abuts Jasper National Park, but on the BC side of the border. **Mt Robson Provincial Park** (☑250-964-2243; www.bcparks.ca) has steep glaciers, prolific wildlife and backcountry hiking that is unfortunately overshadowed by its famous neighbor. **McBride** is good for a pause.

Stewart-Cassiar Highway

Like the promises of a politician, the Stewart-Cassiar Hwy (Hwy 37) just gets better each year. But unlike those promises, it's not full of holes. Much improved, this 700km road is a viable and ever-more-popular route between BC and the Yukon and Alaska (see the boxed text, p175). But it's more than just a means to get from Hwy 16 (Meziadin Junction) in BC to the Alaska Hwy in the Yukon (7km west of Watson Lake), it's a window onto one of the largest remaining wild and wooly parts of the province. And it's the road to Stewart, the very worthwhile detour to glaciers, and more (see boxed text, p176).

Less than 2% of the road is unsealed gravel and it's suitable for all vehicles. At any point you should not be surprised to see bears, moose and other large mammals.

There's never a distance greater than 150km between gas stations and you'll find the occasional lodge and campground. But note that many places keep erratic hours and are only open in summer. The Stewart-Cassiar Tourism Council (www.stewart cassiar.com) is a good source of info. BC provides road condition reports (☑800-550-4997; www.drivebc.ca). When it's dry in summer, people drive from Stewart or even Smithers to Watson Lake in a single day, taking advantage of the long hours of daylight. But this a real haul, so prepare.

Dease Lake, 488km north of Meziadin Junction, is the largest town and has year-round motels, stores and services.

Among the many natural wonders, Spatsizi Plateau Provincial Wilderness Park (☑250-771-4591; www.bcparks.ca) is accessed by a rough, 28km gravel road from Tatogga, about 150km north of Meziadin Junction. The park is undeveloped and isolated. The trails are often little more than vague notions across the untouched landscape. You'll need to be both highly experienced and self-sufficient to tackle this one.

Boya Lake Provincial Park (☑250-771-4591; www.bcparks.ca; campsites $16) is less than 90km from the provincial border. This serene little park surrounds Boya Lake, which seems to glow turquoise. You can camp on the shore.

Alaska Highway

As you travel north from Prince George along Hwy 97, the mountains and forests give way to gentle rolling hills and farmland. Nearing Dawson Creek (360km) the

NORTH TO THE YUKON

From BC there are three main ways to go north (or south!) by vehicle. All are potentially good choices, so you have several ways of creating a circle itinerary to the Yukon and possibly Alaska.

Alaska Highway

Fabled and historic, the Alaska Hwy, from its start point in Dawson City (364km northeast of Prince George) through northeast BC to Watson Lake (944km), is being somewhat eclipsed by the Stewart-Cassiar Hwy. Still, it's an epic drive, even if the sections to Fort Nelson are bland. It's most convenient for those coming from Edmonton and the east.

Stewart-Cassiar Highway

The Stewart-Cassiar (Hwy 37; see p174) runs 700km through wild scenery from the junction with Hwy 16, 240km east of Prince Rupert and 468km west of Prince George. A side trip to the incomparable glaciers around Stewart is easy. This route is convenient for people from most of BC, Alberta and the western US. It ends at the Alaska Hwy, near Watson Lake in the Yukon.

Alaska Marine Highway System

We love the car ferries run by the state of Alaska along the Inside Passage (www.ferryalaska.com). Free of frills, they let you simply relax and view one of the world's great shows of marine life while enjoying the same scenery cruise-ship passengers spend thousands more to see. You can take a three-day ride on boats from Bellingham, Washington (north of Seattle) to Haines and Skagway in southeast Alaska, on the Yukon border. Or catch the ferries in Prince Rupert (see p168) for service to the same two towns (you could link this to the BC Ferries route from Port Hardy). The ferries – especially cabins – fill up fast in summer, so reserve.

WORTH THE TRIP: STEWART & HYDER

Awesome. Yes it's almost an automatic cliché, but when you gaze upon the **Salmon Glacier**, you'll understand why it was coined in the first place. This horizon-spanning expanse of ice is more than enough reason to make the 67km detour off Hwy 37 (the turnoff is 158km north of Meziadin Junction). In fact, your first confirmation comes when you encounter the iridescent blue expanse of the **Bear Glacier** looming over Hwy 37A.

The sibling border towns of **Stewart, BC** and **Hyder, Alaska** sit on the coast at the head of the Portland Canal. Stewart, the more business-like of the pair, has the visitor center (☎250-636-9224, 888-366-5999; www.stewart-hyder.com; 222 5th Ave; ☺9am-6pm Jun-Sep, limited hr winter) and excellent places to stay and eat.

Among several campgrounds and motels, the real star is Ripley Creek Inn (☎250-636-2344; www.ripleycreekinn.com; 306 5th Ave; r $55-125; @☎). The 39 rooms are stylishly decorated with new and old items and there's a huge collection of vintage toasters (!) and the excellent **Bitter Creek Cafe**.

Hyder ekes out an existence as a 'ghost town.' Some 40,000 tourists come through every summer, avoiding any border hassle from US customs officers because there aren't any (although going back to Stewart you'll pass through beady-eyed Canadian customs). It has muddy streets and two businesses of note: the **Glacier Inn**, a bar you'll enjoy if you ignore the touristy 'get Hyderized' shot-swilling shtick and Seafood Express (☎250-636-9011), which has the tastiest seafood ever cooked in a school bus (this is Hyder).

The Salmon Glacier is 33km beyond Hyder, up a winding dirt road that's okay for cars when it's dry. Some 3km into the drive, you'll pass the **Fish Creek viewpoint**, an area alive with bear and doomed salmon in late summer.

---

landscape resembles the prairies of Alberta. There's no need to dawdle.

From **Chetwynd** you can take Hwy 29 along the wide vistas of the Peace River valley north via Hudson's Hope to join the Alaska Hwy north of Fort St John.

Dawson Creek is notable as the starting point (Mile 0) for the Alaska Hwy and it capitalizes on this at the Alaska Highway House (☎250-782-4714; 10201 10th St; admission by donation; ☺9am-5pm daily May-Sep, 9am-5pm Mon-Fri Oct-Apr), an engaging little museum in a vintage building overlooking the milepost. The nearby downtown blocks make a good stroll and there is a walking tour of the old buildings. The visitor center (☎250-782-9595, 866-645-3022; www.tourismdawsoncreek.com; 900 Alaska Ave; ☺8am-5:30pm May-Aug, 10am-5pm Tue-Sat Sep-Apr; ☎) has the usual listings of accommodations. Note that this corner of BC stays on Mountain Standard Time year-round, so in winter the time is the same as Alberta, one hour later than BC. In summer the time is the same as Vancouver.

Now begins the big drive. Heading northwest from Dawson Creek, Fort St John is a stop best not started; in fact the entire 430km to **Fort Nelson** gives little hint of the wonders to come.

Fort Nelson's visitor center (☎250-774-2541; www.northernrockies.ca; 5500 50th Ave N; ☺8am-8pm daily May-Sep, 8:30am-4:30pm Mon-Fri Oct-Apr) has good regional information for the drive ahead. The town itself is in the midst of a boom brought on by the exploitation of the region's vast oil-filled lands. This is the last place of any size on the Alaska Hwy until Whitehorse – most 'towns' along the route are little more than a gas station and motel or two.

Around 140km west of Fort Nelson, Stone Mountain Provincial Park (☎250-427-5452; www.bcparks.ca; campsites $14) has hiking trails with backcountry camping and a campground. The stretches of road here often have dense concentrations of wildlife: moose, bears, bison, wolves, elk and much more. The Alaska Hwy now rewards whatever effort it took getting this far.

A further 75km brings you to Muncho Lake Provincial Park (www.bcparks.ca; campsites $16), centered on the emerald-green lake of the same name and boasting spruce forests, vast rolling mountains and some truly breathtaking scenery. There are two campgrounds by the lake, plus a few lodges scattered along the highway through the park, including **Northern Rockies Lodge** (☎250-776-3481, 800-663-5269; www.northern-rockies-lodge.com; campsites from $35, r $80-200).

Finally, **Liard River Hot Springs Provincial Park** (☎250-427-5452; www.bcparks.ca) has a steamy ecosystem that allows a whopping 250 species of plants to thrive (and, after a long day in the car, you will too, in the soothing waters). The park's **campground** (☎800-689-9025; www.discovercamping.ca; campsites $17) has 52 campsites. From here it's 220km to Watson Lake and the Yukon.

Alberta

Best Places to Eat

» Da-De-O (p189)

» Catch (p201)

» Coyote's Deli & Grill
(p219)

» Last Chance Saloon
(p235)

Best Places to Stay

» Prince of Wales Hotel
(p239)

» Moraine Lake Lodge
(p225)

» Fairmont Banff Springs
(p218)

» Centro Motel (p199)

Why Go?

In Alberta first impressions often lie. Here, landlocked in central Canada's spectacular hinterland, the Wild West sidles up to the Middle East and blue-eyed sheiks in Stetsons break bread with eco-conscious snowboarders in second-hand Gortex. But, to get a true feel for Canada's most caustic and contradictory province you need to avert your gaze momentarily from its Saudi Arabian–sized oil deposits and take a look through a wider lens. Sitting awkwardly alongside Fort McMurray's tar sands lies the world's third-oldest national park (Banff), its second-largest protected area (Wood Buffalo), numerous Unesco World Heritage sites and enough dinosaur remains to warrant a *Jurassic Park* sequel.

Alberta's urban areas are of patchier interest. Get-rich-quick Calgary is a young, audacious and constantly evolving metropolis that still feels strangely soulless to some, while archrival Edmonton is a cultural dark horse with more annual festivals than any other Canadian city.

When to Go
Edmonton

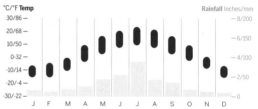

July Prime time for festivals with Edmonton Street Performers and the Calgary Stampede

July-September Banff and Jasper trails are snow-free, making a full range of hikes available

December-February Winter sports season in the Rocky Mountains

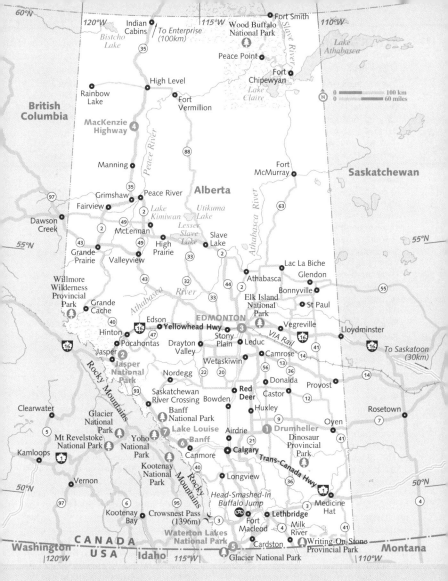

Map labels (north to south, west to east):

60°N · 120°W · 115°W · 110°W

Indian Cabins · To Enterprise (100km) · Fort Smith · Wood Buffalo National Park · Lake Athabasca

Bistcho Lake · 35 · Peace Point · Fort Chipewyan · Lake Claire

High Level · Fort Vermillion · Slave River

Rainbow Lake · MacKenzie Highway · 4 · 88 · Peace River

British Columbia · Manning · Fort McMurray · Saskatchewan

35 · Grimshaw · Peace River · Alberta · 63

97 · Fairview · Lake Kimiwan · Utikuma Lake · 55°N

Dawson Creek · 49 · McLennan · Lesser Slave Lake · Slave Lake · 55

43 · 49 · High Prairie · 33 · 2

Grande Prairie · Valleyview · 2 · Lac La Biche · Glendon

Willmore Wilderness Provincial Park · 43 · 32 · Athabasca River · Athabasca · 44 · 2 · Bonnyville

Grande Cache · 40 · Edson · Yellowhead Hwy · 33 · Elk Island National Park · St Paul

16 · Hinton · 16 · EDMONTON · 3 · Vegreville · 16 · Lloydminster

Jasper · 47 · Pocahontas · Drayton Valley · Stony Plain · Leduc · VIA Rail · To Saskatoon (30km)

2 · Jasper National Park · Wetaskiwin · 41 · 14

Rocky Mountains · Nordegg · 22 · 20 · Camrose · 13 · 36 · 14

93 · Saskatchewan River Crossing · Bowden · 56 · Donalda · Provost

Clearwater · Banff National Park · Red Deer · Castor · 12

Glacier National Park · Lake Louise · 7 · Huxley · 9 · Oyen · Rosetown

5 · Mt Revelstoke National Park · Banff · 6 · Airdrie · 1 · Drumheller · 41 · 7

Kamloops · 1 · Yoho National Park · Canmore · 21 · Calgary · Dinosaur Provincial Park

Vernon · Kootenay National Park · 40 · Longview · Trans-Canada Hwy · 36 · 1

97 · 6 · 95 · Crowsnest Pass (1396m) · Head-Smashed-In Buffalo Jump · 3 · Medicine Hat · 4

Kootenay Bay · Waterton Lakes National Park · 5 · 3 · Fort Macleod · Lethbridge

Washington · CANADA · USA · Idaho · Cardston · Writing-On-Stone Provincial Park · Montana

Milk River · 4 · 41 · 50°N

Glacier National Park · 5

100 km / 60 miles

Alberta Highlights

1 Explore the Jurassic remnants of **Drumheller** (p233) and call into the **Royal Tyrrell Museum of Palaeontology** (p234)

2 Get up early and make fresh tracks on a rugged cross-country skiing trail in chilly, wintery **Jasper National Park** (boxed text, p230)

3 Take in a festival and unlock the bohemian bonhomie of historic **Old Strathcona** (boxed text, p187) in Edmonton

4 Head north on the **MacKenzie Highway** (p241) into a pure, untamed, boreal wilderness

5 Get above the tree line on the **Carthew-Alderson Trail** (p239) in Waterton Lakes National Park,

6 Relax in **Banff Upper Hot Springs** (p215) after a hike

7 Enjoy a brew in the **Lake Agnes Teahouse** (p226) high above bluer than blue Lake Louise

One Week

Spend the day in **Calgary** exploring the sites from the 1988 Winter Olympics and grab a meal on trendy 17th Ave. The next day, get into dino mode by taking a day trip to Drumheller and visiting the **Royal Tyrrell Museum of Palaeontology**. Back in Calgary, go for a wander through the neighborhoods of Kensington and Inglewood and fight for a table at world-class **Rouge**.

Wake early and head west. Stop first in **Canmore** before continuing into Banff National Park and arriving in **Banff Town**. Hike up Sulphur Mountain, ride back down on the **Banff Gondola** and finish off at the bottom with a soak in **Banff Upper Hot Springs**.

After a stay in Banff, continue north to **Lake Louise**, stopping for the view outside the Chateau. Find time for the short, steep hike to the **Lake Agnes Teahouse**, then continue the drive to the **Columbia Icefield**. Get ready to stop every five minutes to take yet another amazing photograph.

Roll into **Jasper** and splash out on the **Park Place Inn**. After some much-needed sleep, stop off at **Maligne Canyon** on the way to **Maligne Lake**, where a short hike might bag you a bear or a moose. Escape the mountains and head to **Edmonton**. Once there dive into the **Old Strathcona** neighborhood, finishing your Alberta adventure with a plate of smoking hot jambalaya at **Da-De-O**.

The Complete Rockies

Follow the One Week itinerary, but include side trips into **Kananaskis Country**, the **Icefields Parkway** and north to **Grande Cache** to see the start of the mountains. Also tack on some time down south heading to **Waterton Lakes National Park**, experiencing this less-visited mountain paradise.

History

Things may have started off slowly in Alberta, but it's making up for lost time. Human habitation in the province dates back 7500 years – the aboriginal peoples of the Blackfoot, Kainaiwa (Blood), Siksika, Peigan, Atsina (also called Gros Ventre), Cree, Tsuu T'ina (Sarcee) and Assiniboine tribes all settled here in prehistoric times, and their descendants still do. These nomadic peoples roamed the southern plains of the province in relative peace and harmony until the middle of the 17th century, when the first Europeans began to arrive.

With the arrival of the Europeans, Alberta began to change and evolve – the impact of these new arrivals was felt immediately. Trading cheap whiskey for buffalo skins saw the start of the decline of both the buffalo and the traditional ways of the indigenous people. Within a generation, the aboriginal peoples were restricted to reserves and the buffalo all but extinct.

In the 1820s, the Hudson's Bay Company set up shop in the area and European settlers continued to trickle in. By 1870 the North West Mounted Police (NWMP) – the predecessor of the Royal Canadian Mounted Police (RCMP) – had built forts within the province to control the whiskey trade and maintain order. And it was a good thing they did, because 10 years later the railway reached Alberta and the trickle of settlers turned into a gush.

These new residents were mostly farmers, and farming became the basis of the economy for the next century. Vast riches of oil and gas were discovered in the early 20th century, but it took time to develop them. At the conclusion of WWII there were 500 oil wells; by 1960, there were 10,000, by which time the petroleum business was the biggest in town.

From humble pastoral beginnings to one of the strongest economies in the world, Alberta has done alright for itself.

Land & Climate

The prairies to the east give way to the towering Rocky Mountains that form the western edge of Alberta. That mountainous spine forms the iconic scenery for which the province is known. The eastern foothills eventually peter out, melding into the flatland.

Alberta is a sunny sort of place; any time of year you can expect the sun to be out. Winters can be cold, when the temperature can plummet to a bone-chilling -20°C. Climate change has started to influence snowfall, with the cities receiving less and less every year.

Summers tend to be hot and dry, with the warmest months being July and August, where the temperature sits at a comfortable 25°C. The 'June Monsoon' is, as you'd expect from the nickname, often rain-filled, while the cooler temperatures and fall colors of September are spectacular.

Chinook winds often kick up in the winter months. These warm westerly winds blow in from the coast, deposit their moisture on the mountains and give Albertans a reprieve from the winter chill, sometimes increasing temperatures by as much as 20°C in one day!

 Getting There & Around

Alberta is easily accessible by bus, car, train and air. The province shares an international border with Montana, USA and provincial borders with the Northwest Territories (NWT), British Columbia (BC) and Saskatchewan.

Air

The two major airports are in Edmonton and Calgary, and there are daily flights to both from major hubs across the world. Carriers serving the province include Air Canada, American Airlines, British Airways, Delta, Horizon Air, KLM, United Airlines and WestJet.

Bus

Greyhound Canada has bus services to Alberta from neighboring provinces and Greyhound has services from the USA. Destinations from Edmonton include Winnipeg ($148, 18 hours, three daily), Vancouver ($133, 17 hours, five daily), Prince George ($84, 10 hours, daily), Hay River ($173, 16 hours, six times weekly) and Whitehorse ($191, 29 hours, one daily). From Calgary, destinations include Kamloops ($82, 10 hours, four daily), Regina ($71, 10 hours, two daily), Saskatoon ($87, nine hours, four daily), Vancouver ($90, 15 hours, five daily) and Winnipeg ($152, 20 hours, two daily). Times can vary greatly, based upon connections, and fares can be reduced by booking in advance.

Moose Travel Network (p326) runs a variety of trips in western Canada. Most start and finish in Vancouver, but along the way hit the highlights of the mountain parks and other Alberta must-sees. In winter it operates ski-focused tours that are a great option for carless ski bums. During the summer months trips depart daily and for the winter season a few times per week.

Car

Alberta was designed with the automobile and an unlimited supply of oil in mind. There are high-quality, well-maintained highways and a network of back roads to explore. Towns for the most part will have services, regardless of the population. Be aware that in more remote areas, especially in the north, those services could be a large distance apart. Fill up the gas tank where possible and be prepared.

In winter, driving can be a real challenge; roadways are maintained, but expect them to be snow-covered after a snowfall. Drivers here are hardy, so roads rarely close. Use common sense, slow down and check the forecast and road conditions before venturing out.

Train

Despite years of hard labor, countless work-related deaths and its aura as one of the great feats of 19th-century engineering, Alberta's contemporary rail network has been whittled down to just two regular passenger train services. **VIA Rail** (www.via.ca) runs the thrice-weekly *Canadian* from Vancouver to Toronto which passes through Jasper and Edmonton in both directions. Edmonton to Vancouver costs $225 and takes 27 hours; Edmonton to Toronto costs $405 and takes 55 hours. The Toronto-bound train stops in Saskatoon, Winnipeg and Sudbury Junction.

The thrice-weekly *Skeena* travels from Jasper to Prince Rupert, BC ($117, 32 hours).

The legendary Canadian Pacific Railway, the western section of which operates from Calgary to Vancouver via Banff, is primarily a freight line these days. Its only 'passenger service' is on luxury train journeys run by **Royal Canadian Pacific** (www.royalcanadianpacific.com) and **Rocky Mountaineer** (www.rockymountaineer.com) costing from $2000 for six-day excursions.

ALBERTA FAST FACTS

» Population: 3,724,832

» Area: 642,317 sq km

» Capital: Edmonton

» Quirky fact: The Albertosaurus was a relative of the T.rex that was first discovered in the Horseshoe Canyon in 1884

EDMONTON

POP 730,000

First-time visitors to Alberta bracing themselves for another underwhelming central Canadian city are often flummoxed by Edmonton. Despite advance publicity regaling everything from dirty oil sands to North America's largest mall, Alberta's often ignored capital is more refined than many outsiders imagine. Sure, there are the glitzy petroleum-funded towers of downtown, predictable urban sprawl and plenty of SUV-clogged highways to negotiate, but in contrast to its longtime archrival to the south (Calgary), Edmonton has carved a distinctive cultural niche. Count on a large annual calendar of festivals, the redbrick and vaguely bohemian neighborhood of Old Strathcona, some little-heralded Ukrainian heritage, and a huge swath of riverside parkland that cuts through the downtown district like a pair of green lungs.

The North Saskatchewan River divides Edmonton in half. To the north is the downtown area, which is centered on 101st Ave, or Jasper Ave as it is called. To the south is Old Strathcona, once a separate city but now an independently minded neighborhood devoid of high-rises and overflowing with art, culture and style.

Giant-sized West Edmonton Mall is to the west, hidden in suburbia and best experienced in small doses.

History

The Cree and Blackfoot tribes can trace their ancestry to the Edmonton area for 5000 years. It wasn't until the late 18th century that Europeans first arrived in the area. A trade outpost was built by the Hudson's Bay Company in 1795, which was dubbed Fort Edmonton.

Trappers, traders and adventurers frequented the fort, but it wasn't until 1870, when the government purchased Fort Ed and opened up the area for pioneers, that Edmonton saw its first real growth in population. When the railway arrived in Calgary in 1891, growth really started to speed up.

REGIONAL DRIVING DISTANCES

Calgary to Banff: 130km
Banff to Jasper: 290km
Edmonton to Calgary: 300km

Gold was the first big boom for the area – not gold found in Alberta, but gold in the Yukon. Edmonton was the last stop in civilization before dreamers headed north to the Klondike. Some made their fortunes, most did not; some settled in Edmonton and the town began to grow.

In the 1940s, WWII precipitated the construction of the Alaska Hwy and the influx of workers further increased the population. Ukrainians and other Eastern European immigrants came to Edmonton in search of work and enriched the city.

Edmonton is again the hub for those looking to earn their fortune in the north. But it isn't gold or roads this time – it's oil.

◎ Sights & Activities

Royal Alberta Museum MUSEUM
(Map p183; www.royalalbertamuseum.ca; 12845 102nd Ave; adult/child $10/5; ◎9am-5pm) Exhibits in Edmonton's leading museum include sections on insects and diamonds, and a lauded display of Alberta's First Nations' culture. The highlight, however, is the 'Wild Alberta' gallery which splits the province into different geographical zones and displays plants and animals from each. The museum – in operation since 1967 – is situated high on a bluff to the west of downtown in a modern granite building that was visited and renamed by Queen Elizabeth II during Alberta's centenary in 2005.

TOP CHOICE Art Gallery of Alberta ART GALLERY
(Map p184; www.youraga.ca; 2 Sir Winston Churchill Sq; adult/child $12/8; ◎11am-7pm Tue-Fri, 10am-5pm Sat & Sun, closed Mon) With the opening of this fantastic new art gallery in January 2010, Edmonton at last gained a modern signature building to emulate any great city and doubled the display space of its less-exalted predecessor, the Edmonton Art Gallery. Looking like a giant glass and metal space helmet, the new futuristic structure in Churchill Sq is an exhibit in its own right that houses over 6000 historical and contemporary works of art, many of which have a strong Canadian bias. Additional plush facilities include a 150-seat theater, shop and restaurant.

FREE Alberta Government House
HISTORIC BUILDING
(Map p183; 12845 102nd Ave; tours free; ◎11am-4:30pm Sun & holidays) When you finish exploring the Royal Alberta Museum head next door (Sundays and holidays only) to Govern-

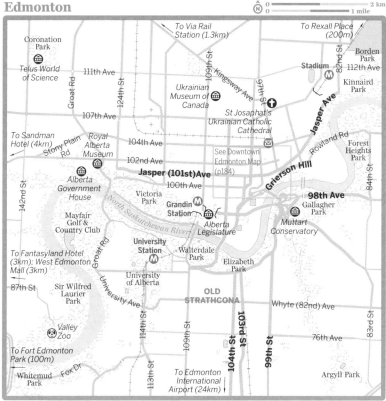

N 0 ——— 2 km
   0 ——— 1 mile

To Via Rail Station (1.3km)
To Rexall Place (200m)
Coronation Park
Telus World of Science
111th Ave
Borden Park
Stadium
82nd St
112th Ave
Kinnaird Park
124th St
109th St
Kingsway Ave
97th St
Groat Rd
107th Ave
Ukrainian Museum of Canada
St Josaphat's Ukrainian Catholic Cathedral
Jasper Ave
To Sandman Hotel (4km)
Stony Plain Rd
Royal Alberta Museum
104th Ave
See Downtown Edmonton Map (p184)
Rowland Rd
Forest Heights Park
84th St
102nd Ave
Grierson Hill
Jasper (101st)Ave
100th Ave
142nd St
Alberta Government House
Victoria Park
98th Ave
Gallagher Park
North Saskatchewan River
Grandin Station
Alberta Legislature
Muttart Conservatory
Mayfair Golf & Country Club
Groat Rd
University Station
Walterdale Park
Elizabeth Park
To Fantasyland Hotel (3km); West Edmonton Mall (3km)
University of Alberta
OLD STRATHCONA
87th St
Sir Wilfred Laurier Park
University Ave
114th St
109th St
103rd St
104th St
99th St
Whyte (82nd) Ave
83rd St
Valley Zoo
76th Ave
To Fort Edmonton Park (100m)
Whitemud Park
Fox Dr
113th St
To Edmonton International Airport (24km)
Argyll Park

ment House, an opulent mansion and the former residence of the lieutenant governor. Steeped in history and tirelessly preserved, you'd never guess that it's nearing its centennial birthday (in 2013). The artwork alone is worth visiting – the walls are lined with stunning works by Alberta artists.

FREE Alberta Legislature   NOTABLE BUILDING
(Map p183; www.assembly.ab.ca; cnr 97th Ave & 107th St; admission free; ⊙8:30am-5pm) Home to politicians, debate and some surprisingly good art is the Alberta Legislature. Where Fort Edmonton once stood, the Leg is a grand old building. With its iconic dome and marble interiors, it has grown to become a local landmark. There are free 45-minute tours (every hour) to take you behind the scenes and the grounds themselves are a splendid place to spend a warm day. To hook up with a tour, head to the interpretive center/gift shop in the pedway at 10820 98th Ave.

Fort Edmonton Park   HISTORIC SITE
(off Map p183; www.fortedmontonpark.ca; cnr Fox & Whitemud Drs; adult/child $13.75/7; ⊙10am-6pm May-Sep; ⏹) Originally built by the Hudson Bay Company in 1795, Fort Edmonton was moved several times before being finally dismantled in 1915. This newer riverside reconstruction began life in the 1960s and captures the fort at its 1846 apex. Onsite are mock-ups of Edmonton's city streets at three points of their historical trajectory: 1885, 1905 and 1920. A vintage steam train and streetcar link all the exhibits, and costumed guides are there to answer questions and add some flavor.

Muttart Conservatory   GARDEN
(Map p183; www.muttartconservatory.ca; 9626 96A St; adult/child $10.50/5.25; ⊙10am-5pm Mon-Fri, 11am-5pm Sat, Sun & holidays) Looking like some sort of pyramid-shaped, glass bomb shelter, the Muttart Conservatory is actually a botanical garden that sits south

ALBERTA EDMONTON

of the river off James MacDonald Bridge. Each of the four pyramids holds a different climate region and corresponding foliage. It's an interesting place to wander about, especially for gardeners, plant fans and those in the mood for something low-key.

Sir Winston Churchill Square LANDMARK (Map p184) The subject of a controversial facelift designed to tie in with the city's 2005 centennial, this public space is a Europeanlike plaza where people can meet, hang out and relax (outside temperature permitting). The square's former green areas have been replaced with a small amphitheater, a fountain and a cafe. Around the perimeter is a quadrangle of important buildings, including the City Hall, the Provincial Court and the impressive new Art Gallery of Alberta (p182).

Ukrainian Heritage Sites HISTORICAL SITE With a huge Ukrainian population and a long history of immigration, there are a few places around town to learn about the culture of the old country and its transplantation in Canada. These sites are found north of downtown and can be combined into a single outing:

St Josaphat's Ukrainian Catholic Cathedral (Map p183; www.stjosaphat.ab.ca; 10825 97th St at 108th Ave; admission free; ☉by appointment)

Ukrainian Canadian Archives & Museum of Alberta (9543 110th Ave; admission by donation; ☉10am-5pm Tue-Fri, noon-5pm Sat)

Ukrainian Museum of Canada (Map p183; 10611 110th Ave; admission free; ☉9:30am-4pm Mon-Fri May-Aug)

Alberta Railway Museum MUSEUM (www.railwaymuseum.ab.ca; 24215 34th St; adult/child $5/2; ☉10am-5pm mid-May–early Sep) This museum, on the northeast edge of the city, has a collection of more than 50 railcars, including steam and diesel locomotives and rolling stock, built and used between 1877 and 1950. It also has a col-

Art Gallery
of Alberta

M Churchill
Station

97th St

99th St

☆15 11

Grierson Hill

North Saskatchewan River

●1

Low Level
Bridge

◎ **Top Sights**
Art Gallery of Alberta E1

◎ **Sights**
1 Edmonton Queen F4

🛏 **Sleeping**
2 Alberta Place Suite Hotel...................C3
3 Crowne Plaza......................................C4
4 Fairmont Hotel Macdonald................D3
5 Go Backpackers..................................C4
6 Matrix A4
7 Sutton Place Hotel.............................D1
8 Union Bank Inn....................................D3

✖ **Eating**
9 Blue Plate Diner B2
10 Characters...B2
11 Hardware Grill E2
Madison's Grill ....(see 8)
12 Russian Tea Room...............................B3

◯◯ **Drinking**
13 Pub 1905 ....A3
14 Three Bananas....................................D2

✦ **Entertainment**
15 Citadel Theatre E2
16 Halo Lounge..A3
17 New City Suburbs...............................D3

lection of railway equipment, old train stations and related buildings. On weekends, volunteers fire up some of the old engines and you can ride along for $4 (the diesel locomotives run every Sunday in season; the 1913 steam locomotive gets going only on holiday weekends). To get there, drive north on 97th St (Hwy 28) to Hwy 37, turn right and go east for 7km to 34th St, then turn right and go south about 2km.

North Saskatchewan River Valley   PARK
Edmonton has more designated urban parkland than any other city in North America, most of it contained within an interconnected riverside green belt that effectively cuts the metropolis in half. The green zone is flecked with lakes, bridges, wild areas, golf courses, ravines and approximately 160km worth of cycling and walking trails. It is easily accessed from downtown.

A fine way to get a glimpse of the downtown core from the river is to take a ride

on the **Edmonton Queen** (Map p184; www.edmontonqueen.com; 9734 98th Ave; 1hr cruise from $17.95, dinner cruise $49.95; ⊙May-Sep). This modern stern-wheeler will take you for an hour-long cruise up- or downriver, depending on the mood of the captain. There is often onboard live entertainment to keep the mood festive.

West Edmonton Mall   SHOPPING MALL
(off Map p183; www.westedmontonmall.com; 170th St; ⊙10am-9pm Mon-Fri, to 6pm Sat, noon-6pm Sun; 👪) A kitsch lover who is tired of Vegas could still have a field day in West Edmonton Mall. Not content to simply be a shopping mall, this urban behemoth has the world's largest waterslides, an equipped indoor wave pool, a full-sized amusement park, a skating rink, two, yes, two minigolf courses, a fake reef with real seals swimming around, a petting zoo, a hotel and 800 stores thrown in as a bonus. Stroll through Chinatown, grab a meal on the delightfully unauthentic Bourbon St, or go for a skate or bungee jump. Then dive into the sea of chain retail shops.

EDMONTON SIGHTS & ACTIVITIES

☞ Tours

Several companies offer half-day tours of Edmonton ($40 to $65) or longer tours that explore outlying areas. **Magic Times Tours** (Map p183; ☎780-940-7479; www.magictimes.ca; Suite 309B, 9815 96A St) Does three-hour tours of all the main sights, including the river valley, Alberta Legislature and Old Strathcona.

Edmonton Ghost Tours (www.edmontonghosttours.com; per person $10; ☺9.30pm Mon-Thu Jul & Aug) Offers spooky walking tours starting from 10322 83rd Ave in Old Strathcona. No booking is required – just turn up 15 minutes early.

✯✯ Festivals & Events

Edmonton has many festivals throughout the year. Following are some highlights.

International Street Performers Festival   THEATER
(www.edmontonstreetfest.com; ☺2nd week Jul) Sometimes the best theater is outside – international performers all alfresco.

Edmonton's Capital Ex   FAIR
(www.capitalex.ca; ☺late Jul) For years, Klondike Days was the big summer festival in Edmonton. It has now morphed into the Capital Ex, with less of a focus on gold rush history and a move to contemporary fun. Live music, rides and a nugget's worth of olden days fun are the highlights of this evolving event.

Edmonton Fringe Theatre Festival
            THEATER
(www.fringetheatreadventures.ca; ☺mid-Aug) An 11-day program of live alternative theater on three outdoor stages in the parks and on the streets. Many shows are free and no ticket costs more than $10. There's no booking – you choose a theater and stand in line. The festival draws half a million people each year to Old Strathcona.

Canadian Finals Rodeo   RODEO
(www.canadianfinalsrodeo.ca; tickets $16-46; ☺early Nov) The Canadian Finals Rodeo is the biggest indoor pro rodeo in Canada. With good bucking stock and the top cowboys there to test their skills, this is a great event to check out, especially if you missed the Calgary Stampede.

🛌 Sleeping

Edmonton has a better range of independent accommodations than some Canadian cities. Options include a trio of boutique hotels, a couple of cheap hostels and a centrally located B&B. Downtown is business oriented with more generic accommodations. If you are in town mainly to visit the West Edmonton Mall, then staying in or near it is feasible, but the digs there are definitely leaning toward the touristy side of the spectrum. Expect to pay between $90 and $125 for a comfortable room at a midrange place.

TOP CHOICE Matrix   BOUTIQUE HOTEL $$
(Map p184; ☎780-429-2861; www.matrixedmonton.com; 10001 107th St; r Mon-Fri $135, Sat & Sun $170; ℗@🐾) One of a triumvirate of Edmonton boutique hotels (along with the Varscona and the Metterra), the Matrix is the new kid on the block (opened in 2007) that claims to serve the 'sophisticated traveler,' with cool minimalist architecture punctuated with woody color accents and plenty of handy modern gadgets. In keeping with its boutique image, there's free wine and cheese every evening at 5:30pm.

Fairmont Hotel Macdonald   HOTEL $$$
(Map p184; ☎780-424-5181; www.fairmont.com; 10065 100th St; r from $300; ℗@🏊) Stealing the best nook in town (as it always does) Edmonton's historic Fairmont Hotel exhibits the usual array of intricate stucco, Italian marble, ornate chandeliers and lush carpets. In the early 20th century it was one in a luxurious chain of railway hotels that dotted the cross-continental line from east to west. Preserved in all its regal glory, it's still fit for monarchs and for *you* if you can stretch to the $300-plus asking price. The regularly renovated rooms with all the expected amenities are almost worth the premium price.

Varscona   BOUTIQUE HOTEL $$
(☎780-434-6111; www.varscona.com; 8208 106th St, cnr Whyte Ave; r from $145; ℗@🐾) Right in the heart of Old Strathcona (Map p184), this charming hotel styles itself as 'casually elegant,' suggesting you can roll up either in a tracksuit or a business suit – or some kind of combination of the two. With the coolest neighborhood in town right on the doorstep, your ability to stick your finger on the collective pulse of Edmonton is made all the easier. Breakfast, parking and evening wine and cheese are thrown in to sweeten the deal.

Metterra   BOUTIQUE HOTEL $$
(☎780-465-8150; www.metterra.com; 10454 Whyte Ave; r Mon-Fri $149, Sat & Sun $179; ℗@🐾) If you can wade through the un-

OLD STRATHCONA

A roguish alternative to gigantic West Edmonton Mall and its wannabe satellites, Old Strathcona (Map p183) is what keeps the city interesting, a constantly evolving strip of redbrick 'Victorian' buildings that was saved from the developer's bulldozer in the 1970s and successfully reinvented as an antidote to the big box blandness ubiquitous elsewhere. Centered on 82nd Ave (colloquially known as Whyte Ave), Edmonton's collective pulse palpitates here in bohemian dive bars, cocktail lounges, vegetarian-biased eating joints, fringe theaters, vintage magazine shops and all kinds of other countercultural trends, ideas and fashion statements.

Situated 800m south of the North Saskatchewan River, Old Strathcona began life as a separate settlement in the 1880s with the coming of the Canadian Pacific Railway. Following a series of catastrophic fires in other prairie cities, Strathcona's lawmakers passed a decree in 1902 requiring all future buildings to be made of brick, which means much of the original building stock has survived to the present day intact.

When the Canadian Northern railway reached Edmonton in 1905 much of the town's business moved north and, in 1912, Strathcona residents voted to reluctantly amalgamate with their cocky new sibling. But Strathcona's dwindling importance turned out to be a blessing in disguise. In the 1970s, when Edmonton's downtown was being rebuilt with oil money, Strathcona was mysteriously overlooked. It was an oversight that ultimately saved it. The area enjoyed a cultural renaissance in the late 1980s, and in 2007 its historical value was recognized when it was granted provincial heritage status.

creative hotel brochure blurb ('urban oasis,' 'contemporary decor,' 'traditional hospitality'), you'll find that the Met is actually a decent place to stay and a fitting reflection of the happening entertainment district (Old Strathcona) in which it sits. The modern, luxurious interior is accented with Indonesian artifacts hinting at the owner's secret penchant for all things Eastern.

Union Bank Inn   BOUTIQUE HOTEL **$$$**
(Map p184; ☑780-423-3600; www.unionbankinn.com; 10053 Jasper Ave; r from $199; P✳@🛜) This posh boutique hotel on Jasper Ave, in a former bank building dating from 1910, is an upmarket masterpiece. With just 34 rooms, the staff will be at your beck and call, and the in-room fireplaces make even Edmonton's frigid winters almost bearable. There's an equally fancy restaurant – Madison's Grill (p189) – on the ground floor.

HI-Edmonton Hostel   HOSTEL **$**
(☑780-988-6836, 877-467-8336; www.hihostels.ca; 10647 81st Ave; dm/d $29/65; P@🛜) Right in the heart of Old Strathcona, this busy hostel is a safe bet. The rooms are a bit jam-packed with bunks and it feels somewhat like a converted old people's home (which is fitting seeing as it used to be a convent), but the location and price are hard to beat.

Hotel Selkirk   HOTEL **$$**
(☑780-496-7227; www.hotelselkirk.com; 1920 St, Fort Edmonton Park; r from $124; P✳🛜) If you're into the idea of visiting the past at Fort Edmonton, why not take it to the next level and spend the night? This historic hotel has period decorated rooms from the roaring 20s and staying here gives you free entry into the fort and its surrounds. There's an on-site restaurant and English high tea on offer during the summer.

Alberta Place Suite Hotel   HOTEL **$$**
(Map p184; ☑780-423-1565; www.albertaplace.com; 10049 103rd St; studio/ste $112/137; P@🛜☸) What was once an apartment building is now a suite hotel with a range of hotel room–style apartments spanning from studios to family suites. Well located and refreshingly mid-price, all rooms have private kitchen facilities, work desks and well-designed if austere furnishings. On the communal level, there's a pool and fitness center.

Glenora Inn B&B   B&B **$$**
(☑780-488-6766; www.glenorabnb.com; 12327 102nd Ave; r without/with bathroom $70/100; P@🛜) A B&B of the frilly Victorian variety, Glenora inhabits the burgeoning West End strip of 124th St. The building (of

EDMONTON FOR CHILDREN

Edmonton is nothing if not kid friendly and there are plenty of family-oriented things to do. **Telus World of Science** (Map p183; www.edmontonscience.com; 11211 142nd St; adult/child $13.95/11.95; ☉10am-7pm; ▣) is a great place to start. With an emphasis on interactive displays, there are a million things to discover, all under one roof. Fight crime with the latest technology, see what living on a spacecraft is all about, go on a dinosaur dig and explore what makes the human body tick. Young and old will have a blast and maybe even learn something at the same time. The center also includes an IMAX theater (extra cost) and an observatory with telescopes (no extra cost).

The **Valley Zoo** (Map p183; www.valleyzoo.ca; 13315 Buena Vista Rd; adult/child $10.50/5.25; ☉9:30am-4pm, to 6pm May-Sep; ▣), with more than 100 exotic, endangered and native animals, is another option. Kids will enjoy the petting zoo, camel and pony rides, miniature train, carousel and paddleboats. If you want to brave the zoo in the frigid winter, admission costs are reduced.

Fort Edmonton Park (p183) has a small amusement park for kids, while West Edmonton Mall (p185) could keep even the most hyperactive seven-year-old distracted for weeks.

1912 vintage, meaning it's 'historic' by Edmonton standards, though not technically 'Victorian') also houses a shop and a downstairs bistro where inn dwellers can procure a complimentary breakfast. There's a communal parlor and an outdoor patio for when the weather's less arctic.

Sutton Place Hotel HOTEL $$
(Map p184; ☎780-428-7111; www.suttonplace.com; 10235 101st St; s & d from $159; ▣@≋) Part of a chain – albeit a small one – the upmarket Sutton Place lacks the intimacy of smaller hotels. Aside from classy rooms replete with glitz and glamour there are numerous additional facilities here. The indoor water park is fantastic, and there are restaurants, cocktail lounges and a casino on the grounds. Look out for cheap specials.

Crowne Plaza HOTEL $$
(Map p184; ☎780-428-6611; www.chateaulacombe.com; 10111 Bellamy Hill; r from $120; ▣✳@☎) While aimed at the business crowd, this tidy hotel is a good place to check for some good deals. Make sure you request a room up high with a river view. The rooms are nice with balconies on some, which is great in the summer though pointless come winter.

Fantasyland Hotel HOTEL $$$
(off Map p183; ☎780-444-3000, 800-737-3783; www.fantasylandhotel.com; 17700 87th Ave; r $188-288; ▣✳@≋▣) As if West Ed wasn't surreal enough, this adjoining hotel is

something to behold. There are standard rooms, but the real draw is the themed rooms. With 13 themes to choose from – Africa to igloo, Roman to Polynesian – it's hard to pick just one. Barely staying on the cool side of kitsch, it's a big hit with families. It also has a wide variety of bedding options to suit any imaginable situation. There are bunk beds for kids, sitting beside the Jacuzzi, a round king-sized for mum and dad, and a mirror on the ceiling so everyone can keep an eye on each other – nice.

Go Backpackers HOSTEL $
(Map p184; ☎780-423-4146; www.gohostels.ca; 10209 100th Av NW; dm/d $30/88; ▣@☎) In a new location just south of Jasper Ave, Go has more breathing space than the HI with four- to six-bed dorms, private rooms, a TV room, kitchen and on-site pub.

Sandman Hotel HOTEL $$
(off Map p183; ☎780-483-1385; www.sandmanhotels.com; 17635 Stony Plain Rd; r from $119; ▣@≋) OK, it's a chain, but at least it's a Canadian one. This branch is close to the West Ed Mall and has a swimming pool, restaurant and decent rooms at a good price.

Rainbow Valley Campground & RV Park CAMPGROUND $
(☎780-434-5531, 888-434-3991; www.rainbow-valley.com; 13204 45th Ave; tent/RV sites $28/32; ☉mid-Apr–mid-Oct; ▣) For an inner-city camping spot this one is pretty

good. It's in a good location to get to 'The Mall' and keep some distance from it at the same time.

✖ Eating

Edmonton's food scene reflects its multiculturalism though you're never far from the default dinner, Alberta beef. If you're willing to hunt around, you can get a quality meal at any price, without ever having to succumb to a franchised restaurant. The most varied and economical place to eat is in Old Strathcona on or around its arterial road, Whyte Ave (Map p183). Here, you can traverse the globe gastronomically from Iran to India as well as choose from plenty of good vegetarian options. The best downtown nexus is Jasper Ave, the main road that slices through downtown. The up-and-coming option is the rejuvenated warehouse district centered north of Jasper Ave on 104th St.

Downtown

Taste of Ukraine
UKRAINIAN **$$**

(off Map p184; www.tasteofukraine.com; 12210 Jasper Ave) There's mum in the kitchen, the eldest son behind the bar, the chatty daughter waiting tables, and dad out back updating the books. Taste of Ukraine is a true family affair and a friendly one at that. The real test, of course, is the food but you don't need to be a Tolstoy-reading Cossack to realize that the cabbage rolls, sauerkraut, buckwheat, fresh bread and vodka shots are spot on.

🥄 Blue Plate Diner
FUSION, VEGETARIAN **$$**

(Map p184; www.blueplatediner.ca; 10145 104th St; mains $12-18; ✐) In the revitalized 104th St warehouse district, this vegetarian-biased diner serves healthy food in hearty portions. And there's style too. Cool colored lighting and exposed brickwork embellish the atmospheric interior, meaning you can eat your tofu and lentils without feeling as if you've joined a hippy commune. Try the tofu stir-fry or steak sandwich and enjoy larger-than-average plates of crisp, locally grown vegetables.

Madison's Grill
FUSION **$$$**

(Map p184; ☎780-401-2222; www.unionbankinn. com; 10053 Jasper Ave; mains from $26; ⊙8am-10pm Mon-Thu, to 11pm Fri & Sat, to 8pm Sun) Located in the Union Bank Inn and continuing the same high standards of service and quality, delicate meats and seafood are prepared here with flair. The dining room is elegant, the service is top-notch and the wine pairing menu goes for a wallet-stretching $50.

Characters
FUSION **$$$**

(Map p184; ☎780-421-4100; www.characters.ca; 10257 105th St; mains from $27; ⊙11:30am-2pm & 5:30-10:30pm Mon-Sat) What you expect is a loud, clamorous family-run restaurant full of old mafiosi hitmen. What you get is an upmarket bistro with a 20-page menu, professional service and dishes such as Chilean sea bass and ahi tuna. Not many characters, but plenty of fancy food.

Hardware Grill
STEAKHOUSE **$$$**

(Map p184; ☎780-423-0969; www.hardwaregrill. com; 9698 Jasper Ave; mains $36-48; ⊙5pm-late Mon-Sat) When you really want to impress even yourself, head to this plush oasis high on a bluff above the river in what is traditionally the seedier part of town. The Hardware occupies an old (for Edmonton) redbrick building that has retained its more elegant features and spruced up the rest. Signposts promise an ambitious triumvirate of 'comfort, flavor and panache,' a boast at least partly fulfilled in expertly prepared duck breast, lamb rack and Alberta beef.

Russian Tea Room
RUSSIAN **$$**

(Map p184; www.therussiantearoom.ca; 10312 Jasper Ave; mains $11-18) Bowls of borscht, a vast array of teas and some decent snacks are only half the story here. Darkly lit with an eerie bordello feel, the Russian Tea Room is also the haunt of various psychics who sit at dimly lit tables and tell the fortunes (tarot cards, tea leaves and palm-reading) of superstitious passing punters. It's surprisingly popular.

High Level Diner
CANADIAN **$**

(www.highleveldiner.com; 10912 88th Ave; mains $6-15; ⊙8am-10pm Mon-Thu, to 11pm Fri & Sat, 9am-9pm Sun) Want to catch up with some locals over eggs? This friendly, popular eatery right beside the river is a great way to start the day.

Old Strathcona & Around

📍 Da-De-O
CAJUN **$$**
TOP CHOICE

(www.dadeo.ca; 10548A Whyte Ave; mains $10-16; ⊙11:30am-11pm Mon, Tue & Thu-Sat, noon-10pm Sun, closed Wed) A classic diner restaurant serving Cajun food, Da-De-O competes for the prize of Edmonton's most memorable eating joint. With retro jukeboxes, art-deco lighting and some jazz etchings on the wall, the decor is eye-catching and interesting, while the food – oysters, jambalaya and filling po'boys – is the stuff of Louisiana legend. The perennial highlight is the spice-dusted sweet potato fries. Forget the Big Easy. Save the airfare and eat here.

Café Mosaics VEGETARIAN **$**
(10844 Whyte Ave; mains $6-12; ⊙9am-9pm Mon-Sat, 11am-2:30pm Sun;) A Strathcona institution, this arty, activist-frequented vegetarian-vegan haunt is a meat-free zone that has taken a page out of San Francisco's book: how to make vegetable dishes both interesting and tasty. The results are invariably good. As a litmus test, check the number of carnivores who take a day off meat to come here. Try the tofu curry, cowgirls' breakfast or Moroccan chickpea soup. There's even a special meat-free kids' menu.

Upper Crust Café CANADIAN **$**
(www.cafeuppercrust.ca; 10909 86th Ave; mains $8-16; ⊙11am-9pm Mon-Fri, 9am-9pm Sat) What was once just plain old home cooking has now been rebranded as 'comfort food,' ie basic, untechnical flavors and an eating experience that reminds you of your mum, gran – or both. Cottoning on to this nostalgic need, Upper Crust, tucked into the front of a nondescript, shabby-looking apartment building, effortlessly serves up such simple concoctions as chili con carne, pan-fried chicken in mushroom sauce (remember that?) and rainbow trout.

Origin India INDIAN **$$**
(www.theoriginindia.com; 10511 Whyte Ave; mains $13-16) Jumping on the burgeoning Indian fusion bandwagon, Origin India embraces a chic modern look while staying true to its origins – *dal makhani,* butter chicken and spicy paneer.

Tokyo Noodle Shop & Sushi Bar JAPANESE **$**
(10736 Whyte Ave; mains from $7.25; ⊙11:30am-9:30pm Mon-Thu, to 10:30pm Fri & Sat, noon-9pm Sun) Good sushi and noodles by the gallon. Nothing fancy, but that's the point.

🍸 Drinking

Nightlife is best found either on Whyte Ave (Map p183), with its bohemian feel, or downtown on Jasper Ave, with more inner-city flavored watering holes. The scene is fun and energetic and the locals are keen to integrate.

Three Bananas CAFE
(Map p184; www.threebananas.ca; Sir Winston Churchill Sq, 9918 102nd Ave) This bookish coffee bar in Churchill Sq with its mosaic walls and Warhol-esque banana prints is a good place to grab a caffeine hit on the way to the new art museum.

Black Dog Freehouse PUB
(www.blackdog.ca; 10425 Whyte Ave) Insanely popular with all types, the Black Dog is essentially a pub with a couple of hidden extras: a rooftop patio, known as the 'wooftop patio,' with heaters (naturally, this is Alberta), a traditional ground-floor bar (normally packed cheek to jowl on weekday nights), and a basement that features live music and occasional parties. The sum of the three parts has become a rollicking Edmonton institution.

Elephant & Castle PUB
(www.elephantcastle.com; 10314 Whyte Ave) What passes for damn ordinary in London (where the Elephant & Castle is a rather grotesque shopping center) is strangely exotic in Edmonton. A red phone box, velvety bar stools and the smell of beer emanating from the thick, carpeted floor add British authenticity to this sporty drinking nook where you can watch Man United do battle with Chelsea et al.

Block 1912 CAFE
(10361 Whyte Ave) A regal attempt at a genuine Torinese coffee bar on Whyte Ave, this inviting place allows you to recline on European-style sofas and armchairs and enjoy your coffee with a range of snacks – or even a gelato. There's a small bar open evenings.

Two Rooms Cafe CAFE
(10324 Whyte Ave) Another laid-back Strathcona joint that could have been transplanted from some libertine European city, Two Rooms has a tiny wood-furnished interior, street-side patio and – most importantly – good coffee.

Devlin's Martini Lounge BAR
(10507 Whyte Ave) Trendy but with a mixed-age demographic, Delvin's is all black leather couches, fruity cocktails and office escapees on a girls' night out. There's a limited tapas menu and big windows where you can sit and watch the insomniac action on Whyte Ave.

O'Byrne's PUB

(10616 Whyte Ave) Get lost in the labyrinth of rooms in this popular Irish pub. Lots of varieties on tap and live music keep the place interesting.

Pub 1905 PUB

(Map p184; 10525 Jasper Ave) A popular local watering hole with a happening happy hour and plethora of TVs makes this a choice spot to catch an Oilers game.

☆ Entertainment

See and *Vue* are free local alternative weekly papers with extensive arts and entertainment listings. For daily listings, see the entertainment section of the *Edmonton Journal* newspaper.

For concentrated club-hopping, Whyte Ave and Old Strathcona (Map p183) are the places to head.

Princess Theatre CINEMA

(10337 Whyte Ave; tickets Mon & weekend matinees $5, other times adult/student & child $8/6) The Princess is a grand old theater that defiantly sticks her finger up at the mall-housed multiplexes that are dominant elsewhere. Dating from the pre-talkie days (1915) it screens first-run, art-house and cult classics.

Blues on Whyte LIVE MUSIC

(www.bluesonwhyte.ca; 10329 Whyte Ave) This is the sort of establishment your mother warned you about: dirty, rough, but still somehow cool. It's a great place to check out some live music; blues and rock are the standards here. The small dance floor is a good place to shake a leg and let your hair down. What more do you need? Just don't bring your mother.

Halo Lounge NIGHTCLUB

(Map p184; 10538 Jasper Ave) A small, clamorous basement nightclub with Brit-biased music ranging from mod to alt rock, Halo has a kind of '70s lava lamp feel. The dance floor is compact and rarely empty.

New City Suburbs NIGHTCLUB

(Map p184; www.newcitycompound.com; 10081 Jasper Ave) Taking up residence in an old theater, this nightclub is a great venue for live punk rock, mod sounds, Buzzcocks reunions and straight rock and roll. It has frequent live bands, comedy nights and theme nights that are popular with the college crowd.

Citadel Theatre THEATER

(Map p184; www.citadeltheatre.com; 9828 101A Ave; tickets from $45; ⊙Sep-May) Presents contemporary and classic live theater by Edmonton's foremost company.

New Varscona Theatre THEATER

(www.varsconatheatre.com; 10329 83rd Ave; tickets from $14) Hiding in the fringes, the Varscona puts on edgy productions from its Strathcona home base.

Jubilee Auditorium THEATER

(1455 87th Ave) The place to check out the **Edmonton Opera** (☑780-424-4040; www.edmontonopera.com; tickets from $24; ⊙Oct-Apr). Otherwise, this is a great venue for live performances of every kind.

Gay & Lesbian Venues

Buddy's Nite Club NIGHTCLUB

(off Map p184; www.buddysedmonton.com; 11725B Jasper Ave) The font of wet T-shirt comps, drag shows and ominous-sounding 'dance your pants off' nights, Buddy's is ever popular with gay men.

Sports

Edmonton Oilers SPORTS

(www.edmontonoilers.com; tickets from $38.50) The Oilers are the local National Hockey League (NHL) team – the season runs from October to April. Games are played at oft-renamed **Rexall Place** (off Map p183; 7424 118th Ave NW), once the stomping ground of 'The Great One,' former ice-hockey pro Wayne Gretzky.

Edmonton Eskimos SPORTS

(www.esks.com; adult/child from $43/21.50) The Eskimos take part in the Canadian Football League (CFL) from July to October at **Commonwealth Stadium** (11000 Stadium Rd).

🏠 Shopping

Old Strathcona (Map p183) is the best area for unique independent stores – vintage magazines, old vinyl, retro furnishings and the like. If you're in search of the opposite – ie big chains selling familiar brands – sift through the 800-plus stores in West Edmonton Mall (p185).

Avenue Guitars MUSIC STORE

(10550 Whyte Ave) You can warm your fingers plucking opening stanzas to 'Stairway to Heaven' in Old Strathcona's premier music store. It sells custom-made and collector's guitars and all the usual suspects.

Old Strathcona Farmers' Market
FOOD & DRINK

(10310 83rd Ave at 103rd St; ◷8am-3pm Sat, noon-5pm Tue Jul & Aug) This not-to-be-missed indoor market offers everything from organic food to arts and crafts, and hosts some 130 vendors. Everyone comes here on Saturday morning – it's quite the scene.

Movie Poster Shop
SOUVENIRS

(8126 Gateway Blvd NW) Essential browsing for anyone who ever fantasized about having a rare black-and-white print of Steve McQueen/Natalie Wood/Mick Jagger on their wall.

Junque Cellar
ACCESSORIES

(10442 Whyte Ave) What is plain old junk to some is retro-cool to others. Sift through the typewriters, lava lamps, old phones, comics, clothes and other flashbacks of erstwhile pop culture.

ⓘ Information

Café Dabar (10816 Whyte Ave; internet per hr $5; ◷9am-10pm Mon-Sat, 11am-7pm Sun) Free wi-fi if you buy something.

Custom House Global Foreign Exchange (10104 103rd Ave) Foreign currency exchange.

Edmonton Tourism (9990 Jasper Ave; ◷8am-5pm) Friendly place with tonnes of flyers and brochures.

Main post office (9808 103A Ave)

Police, Ambulance & Fire (☎911)

Police Dispatch Line (☎780-423-4567) For nonemergencies.

Royal Alexandra Hospital (☎780-477-4111; 10240 Kingsway Ave) Has a 24-hour trauma center.

Stanley A Milner Public Library (7 Sir Winston Churchill Sq; ◷9am-9pm Mon-Fri, to 6pm Sat, 1-5pm Sun) Lots of free internet terminals.

ⓘ Getting There & Away
Air

Edmonton International Airport (YEG; www.edmontonairports.com) is about 30km south of the city along the Calgary Trail, about a 45-minute drive from downtown.

Bus

The large **bus station** (Map p184; 10324 103rd St) has Greyhound Canada services to numerous destinations, including Jasper ($67, 4½ hours, four daily), Calgary ($51, from 3½ hours, from 10 daily) and Yellowknife (22 hours, one daily). For more information on buses to other provinces in Canada, see p181.

Red Arrow (www.redarrow.ca) buses stop at the Holiday Inn Express hotel (10010 104th St) and serve Calgary ($67, three to 3½ hours, at least four daily), Fort McMurray ($81, five hours, one daily) and Banff ($127, seven hours, two daily). The buses are a step up, with plugs for your laptop, leather seats and more legroom for taller people.

Car

All the major car-rental firms have offices at the airport and around town. **Driving Force** (www.thedrivingforce.com; 11025 184 St) will rent, lease or sell you a car. Check the website; it often has some good deals.

Train

The small **VIA Rail station** (www.viarail.ca; 12360 121st St) is rather inconveniently situated 5km northwest of the city center near Edmonton City Centre Airport. The *Canadian* travels three times a week east to Saskatoon, Winnipeg and Toronto and west to Jasper, Kamloops and Vancouver. At Jasper, you can connect to Prince George and Prince Rupert. For fares see p181.

ⓘ Getting Around
To/From the Airport

City buses unfortunately don't make it all the way to the airport, so your best option is to jump on a **Sky Shuttle Airport Service** (www.edmontonskyshuttle.com; adult/child $18/10). It runs three different routes that service hotels in most areas of town, including downtown and the Strathcona area.

A cab fare from the airport to downtown will cost about $50.

Car & Motorcycle

There is metered parking throughout the city. If you're staying in Old Strathcona, most hotels offer complimentary parking to guests. Visitors can park their car for the day and explore the neighborhood easily on foot. Edmonton also has public parking lots, which cost about $12 per day or $1.50 per half hour; after 6pm you can park for a flat fee of about $2.

Public Transportation

City buses and a 10-stop tram system – the Light Rail Transit (LRT) – cover most of the city. The fare is $2.75 (day passes $8.25). Buses operate at 30-minute intervals between 5:30am and 1:30am. Check out the excellent transit planning resources at www.edmonton.ca. Daytime travel between Churchill and Grandin stations on the LRT is free.

Between mid-May and early October you can cross the High Level Bridge on a streetcar ($4 round-trip, every 30 minutes between 11am and 10pm). The vintage streetcars are a great way to travel to the Old Strathcona Market (103rd St at 94th Ave), where the line stops. Or go from Old Strathcona to the downtown stop, next to the Grandin LRT Station (109th St between 98th and 99th Aves).

Taxi

Two of the many taxi companies are **Yellow Cab** (☎780-462-3456) and **Alberta Co-Op Taxi** (☎780-425-2525). The fare from downtown to the West Edmonton Mall is about $25. Flagfall is $3.60, then it's $0.20 for every 150m.

AROUND EDMONTON

East of Edmonton

When Edmontonians want to get away from it all and retreat back to nature, **Elk Island National Park** (www.pc.gc.ca/eng/pn-np/ab/elkisland/index.aspx; adult/6-16yr/senior $7.80/3.90/6.80; ☺dawn-dusk) is often their first port of call. This 194-sq-km park is home to much native wildlife, such as elk, plains bison and a small herd of the threatened wood bison. At just 45km east of Edmonton on the Yellowhead Hwy (Hwy 16), it's convenient for weekend getaways, meaning the **campgrounds** (tent & RV sites $25.50, campfire permits $8.80) are quite popular. Some of the park's campgrounds close from early October to May.

There is ample opportunity to get some exercise here, too: hiking, canoeing and cycling are popular in the summer, while snowshoeing and cross-country skiing are the things to do after the snow flies. When you arrive, stop in at the visitors center at the entrance to get all the information you might need for enjoying the park.

The **Ukrainian Cultural Heritage Village** (8820 112th St; adult/7-17yr/senior $8/4/7; ☺10am-6pm mid-May–early Sep, 10am-6pm Sat & Sun early Sep–mid-Oct), 50km east of Edmonton on Hwy 16 (3km east of Elk Island National Park), is an exact replica of a turn-of-the-century Ukrainian town, paying homage to the 250,000 Ukrainian immigrants who came to Canada in the late 19th and early 20th centuries. Many settled in central Alberta, where the landscape reminded them of the snowy steppes of home. Among the exhibits are a dozen or so structures, including a restored pioneer home and an impressive Ukrainian Greek Orthodox church. The staff are dressed in period garb and are in character, too, adding a slice of realism and fun to the day.

South of Edmonton

Located halfway between Edmonton and Calgary on Hwy 2 is **Red Deer**. This growing community boasts an agricultural heritage and benefits from its proximity to the two major centers. Beyond being a rest stop and an all-else-fails place to stay during the tourist season, there is very little for the traveler here. Red Deer is about 1½ hours away from either city, and accommodations will not be as tight nor as expensive. For more information, contact the **Red Deer Visitor & Convention Bureau** (www.tourismreddeer.net; 30 Riverview Park), or just drive through the city where you'll have your pick of chain establishments.

West of Edmonton

Heading west from Edmonton toward Jasper, Hwy 16 is a gorgeous drive through rolling wooded hills that are especially beautiful in fall. Accommodations are available along the way. Greyhound buses ply the route.

Hinton is a small, rough-around-the-edges town carved from the bush. The pervasive logging industry keeps the majority of the town's population gainfully employed. There is some good mountain biking to be found here; cruise into the info center for more information on trails. If there is snow on the ground, the **Athabasca Lookout Nordic Centre** offers winter visitors beautiful groomed ski trails up to 25km long. It also has illuminated night skiing on a 1.5km trail, plus a 1km luge run. There's a user fee of $5. For more information, contact the **Hinton Tourist Information Centre** (☎780-865-2777), off Hwy 16.

Just north of Hinton lies the tiny settlement of **Grande Cache**. There is little of interest in this small industry town, only a few overpriced hotels aimed at expense account–wielding natural resources workers. However, the drive along Hwy 40 between Hinton and Grande Cache is spectacular, with rolling forested foothills, lakes and abundant wildlife.

CALGARY

POP 1,065,000

Brash, bold and dripping in oil money, it's easy to pour scorn on flashy Calgary, as some do. A slightly-less-frenetic but colder version of desert Dubai, this nebulous, hard-to-grasp prairie city has grown up so fast that last week (let alone last month) can seem like ancient history.

Livable but sometimes characterless, prosperous but economically precarious, super-modern but not always pretty, 21st-century Calgary isn't a place that any unbiased out-of-towner is likely to fall in love with (although the locals can be fanatically loyal). Most visitors either come here on business and deposit their briefcases in one of a plethora of generic business hotels, or arrive in outdoor garb and use it as a springboard for the more alluring attractions of K-Country and Banff. But itinerants holed up on longer stopovers (unexpected or otherwise) needn't break into a cold sweat. Shoehorned among the Stetsons and SUVs of downtown, there's a decent dining scene, an excellent museum, remnants of the 1988 Winter Olympics and – contrary to popular belief – a good (and expanding) public transportation system.

Cowboys led Calgary's first incarnation in the early 1900s, paving the way for what has become one of the world's biggest rodeos – the Calgary Stampede. The oil barons piled in next, after the first big Alberta oil strike in 1947, and brought with them a boom-bust economic cycle that has been both the city's blessing and curse. These days, the bulk of new arrivals are here to make fast money rather than immerse themselves in Calgary's cultural splendor. If you've arrived looking for the soul of the city it could be a long and fruitless search. If it's youthful nightlife, chic restaurants, clean streets and a well-paid job you're after, you might just get lucky.

History

From humble and relatively recent beginnings, Calgary has been transformed into a cosmopolitan modern city that has hosted an Olympics and continues to wield huge economic clout. Before the growth explosion, the Blackfoot people called the area home for centuries. Eventually they were joined by the Sarcee and Stoney tribes on the banks of the Bow and Elbow Rivers.

By the time the 1870s rolled around, the NWMP built a fort and called it Fort Calgary after Calgary Bay on Scotland's Isle of Mull. The railroad followed a few years later and, buoyed by the promise of free land, settlers started the trek west to make Calgary their home.

Long a center for ranching, the cowboy culture was set to become forever intertwined with the city. For the initial stages of the 20th century, Calgary simmered along, growing slowly. Then in the 1960s everything changed. Overnight, ranching was seen as a thing of the past and oil was the new favorite child. With the 'black gold' seeming to bubble up from the ground nearly everywhere in Alberta, Calgary became the natural choice of place to set up headquarters.

The population exploded and the city began to grow at an alarming rate. As the price of oil continued to skyrocket, it was good times for the people of Cowtown. The '70s boom stopped dead at the '80s bust. Things slowed and the city diversified.

The 21st century began with an even bigger boom. House prices have gone through the roof, there is almost zero unemployment and the economy is growing 40% faster than the rest of Canada. Not bad for a bunch of cowboys.

◎ Sights

TOP CHOICE Glenbow Museum   MUSEUM
(www.glenbow.org; 130 9th Ave SE; adult/student & youth/senior $14/9/10; ◎9am-5pm Fri-Wed, to 9pm Thu) For a town with such a short history, Calgary does a fine job in telling it at the commendable Glenbow Museum that traces the legacy of Calgary and Alberta both pre- and post-oil. Contemporary art exhibitions and stunning artifacts dating back centuries fill its halls and galleries. With an extensive permanent collection and an ever-changing array of traveling exhibitions, there is always something for the history buff, art lover and pop culture fanatic to ponder. The best museum in the province – hands down.

Fort Calgary Historic Park   HISTORIC PARK
(www.fortcalgary.com; 750 9th Ave SE; adult/child/senior $10.50/6.50/9.50; ◎9am-5pm) In 1875 Calgary was born at Fort Calgary. If only the NWMP who first called Fort Calgary home could see it now. Luckily their efforts have been restored for posterity. There are preserved buildings to walk through,

the chance to dress up like a Mountie and even a jail to get locked up in.

Calgary Zoo
ZOO

(www.calgaryzoo.ab.ca; 1300 Zoo Rd NE; adult/child/senior $18/10/16; ☺9am-6pm) More than 900 animals from around the world, many in enclosures simulating their natural habitats, make this Calgary's most popular attraction. Besides the animals, the zoo has a **Botanical Garden** with changing garden displays, a **tropical rainforest**, a good **butterfly enclosure** and the 6½-hectare **Prehistoric Park**, featuring fossil displays and life-sized dinosaur replicas in natural settings. Picnic areas dot the zoo and a cafe is on-site. During winter, when neither you nor the animals will care to linger outdoors, the admission price is reduced. To get here, take the C-Train east to the Zoo stop.

Heritage Park Historical Village
HISTORIC PARK

(www.heritagepark.ab.ca; 1900 Heritage Dr SW at 14th St SW; adult/child $19/14; ☺9.30am-5pm mid-May–early Sep, 9.30am-5pm Sat & Sun early Sep–mid-Oct) Want to see what Calgary used to look like? Head down to this historical park and step right into the past. With a policy that all buildings within the village are from 1915 or earlier, it really is the opposite of modern Calgary. There are 10 hectares of recreated town to explore, with a fort, grain mill, church, school and lots more. You can ride on the steam train, catch a trolley and even go for a spin on the SS *Moyie*, the resident stern-wheeler, as it churns around the Glenmore Reservoir. Heritage Park has always been a big hit with the kiddies and is a great place to soak up Western culture. To get there, take the C-Train to Heritage station, then bus 20.

FREE Inglewood Bird Sanctuary
NATURE RESERVE

(2425 9th Ave SE; admission free; ☺dawn-dusk) Get the flock over here and look out for some foul play at this nature reserve. With more than 260 bird species calling the sanctuary home, you are assured of meeting some feathered friends. It's a peaceful place with walking paths and benches to observe the residents. There is a small **interpretive center** (admission free, donations appreciated; ☺10am-4pm) to give you some more information about the birds, complete with displays that are popular with the young ones.

FREE Calgary Chinese Cultural Centre
MUSEUM

(197 1st St SW; admission free; ☺9am-9pm) Inside this impressive landmark building, built by skilled Chinese artisans in 1993, you'll find a magnificent 21m-high dome ornately painted with 561 dragons and other imagery. Its design was inspired by Beijing's Temple of Heaven. The 2nd and 3rd floors frequently house changing art and cultural exhibitions. Downstairs, the **museum** (adult/senior & child $2/1; ☺11am-5pm) holds Chinese art and artifacts, including a collection of replica terracotta soldiers.

Prince's Island Park
PARK

For a little slice of Central Park in the heart of Cowtown, take the bridge over to this island, with grassy fields just made for tossing the Frisbee, bike paths and ample space to stretch out. During the summer months, you can catch a Shakespeare production in the park's natural grass amphitheater. Watch yourself around the river: the water is cold and the current is strong and not suitable for swimming. The bridge to the island from downtown is at the north end of 3rd St SW, near the Eau Claire Market shopping area.

Fish Creek Provincial Park
PARK

(admission free; ☺8am-dark) Cradling the southwest edge of Calgary, this huge park is a sanctuary of wilderness hidden within the city limits. Countless trails intertwine to form a labyrinth to the delight of walkers, mountain bikers and the many animals who call the park home. Severe flooding in the park in the mid-2000s washed away many bridges and, in many cases, severely impacted on the landscape. The park is slowly returning to normal with the assistance of the city and Mother Nature. There are numerous access points to the park, which stretches 20km between 37th St in the west and Bow River in the east. From downtown, take bus 3 via Elbow Dr.

Calgary Tower
NOTABLE BUILDING

(101 9th Ave SW; adult/youth $14/10; ☺observation gallery 9am-9pm) This 1968 landmark tower is an iconic feature of the Calgary skyline, though it has now been usurped by six taller buildings. There is little doubt that the aesthetics of this once-proud concrete structure have passed into the realm of kitsch, but, love it or hate it, the slightly

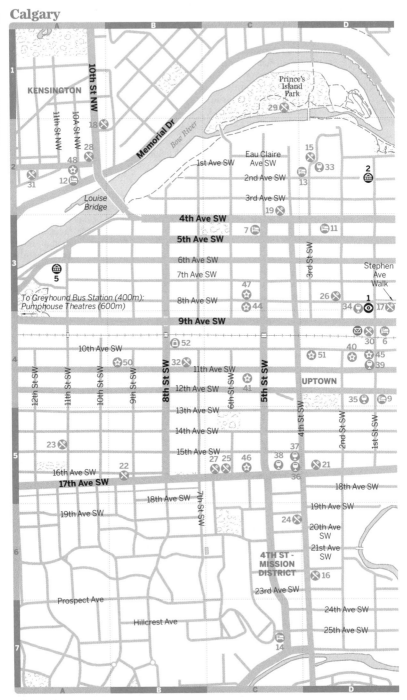

ALBERTA CALGARY

KENSINGTON

10th St NW

11th St NW

10A St NW

18

28

48

31

12

Louise Bridge

Memorial Dr

Bow River

Prince's Island Park

29

1st Ave SW

Eau Claire Ave SW

2nd Ave SW

3rd Ave SW

15

13

33

2

19

4th Ave SW

5th Ave SW

7

11

6th Ave SW

7th Ave SW

3rd St SW

Stephen Ave Walk

5

To Greyhound Bus Station (400m);
Pumphouse Theatres (600m)

8th Ave SW

47

44

26

34

17

1

9th Ave SW

10th Ave SW

52

30

6

12th St SW

11th St SW

10th St SW

9th St SW

8th St SW

50

32

11th Ave SW

6th St SW

5th St SW

40

51

45

39

UPTOWN

12th Ave SW

41

4th St SW

2nd St SW

1st St SW

35

9

13th Ave SW

14th Ave SW

23

22

15th Ave SW

27 25

46

37

38

21

36

16th Ave SW

17th Ave SW

18th Ave SW

7th St SW

18th Ave SW

19th Ave SW

19th Ave SW

24

20th Ave SW

21st Ave SW

4TH ST - MISSION DISTRICT

16

Prospect Ave

Hillcrest Ave

23rd Ave SW

24th Ave SW

25th Ave SW

14

phallic 191m structure is a fixture of the downtown area. The views from the top are fantastic and there is even a revolving restaurant so you won't miss a thing. Back in '88, the Olympic flame burned brightly on top of the tower.

Other Museums MUSEUMS

For stunning contemporary artwork, stop in at the **Art Gallery of Calgary** (www.artgallerycalgary.org; 117 8th Ave SW; adult/child $5/2.50; ⊙10am-5pm Tue-Sat). What it lacks in floor space, it more than makes up for with the standard of work on display.

To learn the history of Calgary's first inhabitants, the Tsuu T'ina (Sarcee) people, check out the **Tsuu T'ina Culture Museum** (3700 Anderson Rd SW; admission $3; ⊙9am-4pm Mon-Fri). Take MacLeod Trail South to Anderson Rd, turn west and follow for 5km to the museum.

Those with an interest in the military will enjoy the **Museum of the Regiments** (4520 Crowchild Trail SW; adult/student $6/3; ⊙9:30am-4pm), a very thorough overview of Calgary's military background and its role in Canadian conflicts over the years. Follow Crowchild Trail to Flanders Ave, about 3km south of downtown.

🏃 Activities

Though, ostensibly, it appears to be designed purely for the automobile, Calgary actually has over 400km of trails within its city limits. The best of them parallel the Bow River, meaning you can bisect the city free of road interference. To plan your route, check out the *Calgary Pathway & Bicycle Route Map,* available from the **Calgary Parks & Recreation Department office** (3rd fl, 205 8th Ave SE) and from most bike shops.

For rentals, the **Outdoor Programs Centre** (www.calgaryoutdoorcentre.ca; 2500 University Dr NW) at the University of Calgary, 7km from downtown, has top-quality bikes and just about anything else you might need.

Canada Olympic Park SPORTS

(www.canadaolympicpark.ca; 88 Canada Olympic Rd SW) In 1988 the Winter Olympics came to Canada for the first time. Calgary played host and many of the events were contested at Canada Olympic Park. Located near the western edge of town along Hwy 1, you won't be able to miss the distinctive 70m and 90m ski jumps crowning the skyline. Check out the **Olympic Hall of Fame** (admission $6; ⊙9am-5pm May-Sep, 10am-4pm

Oct-Apr) and learn about some great Canadian athletes and the story of the Calgary games. If you are feeling more daring, you can go for a 60-second **bobsleigh ride** (per ride $135) with a professional driver on a 120kmh Olympic course. It could be the most exhilarating and expensive minute of your life. Alternatively, you can take a trip along a **zip-line** (tickets $55) from the top of the ski jump. In winter you can go for a **ski**, or strap on a **snowboard** and hit the sphincter-tightening super-pipe. Summer is for **mountain biking** (hill ticket/lesson $22), when you can ride the lift-serviced trails till your brakes wear out.

Olympic Oval   ICE SKATING
(www.ucalgary.ca/oval; skating adult/child $6/4) Keeping with the Olympic spirit, head to the University of Calgary and go for a skate on Olympic Oval. Used for the speed skating events at the Olympics, it offers public skating on the long track and has skates available to rent.

👉 **Tours**
The cheapest way to tour town is to take bus 10 ($2.75) from along 6th Ave. This bus goes on a 2½-hour circular route past old and new areas and the city's highest point, with views to the foothills, the university and some wealthy districts in the northwest.

Hammerhead Tours   CULTURE
(☑403-590-6930; www.hammerheadtours.com; tours $45-135) Has a variety of tour options to choose from, including city tours and trips to the Columbia Icefield, Drumheller, Banff and more.

✷✷ Festivals & Events

For a year-round list of the city's events, go to www.tourismcalgary.com/e-cvb/coe/main.cfm. The big festival in Calgary is the annual Calgary Stampede, held every July.

Calgary International Children's Festival   CHILDREN
(www.calgarychildfest.org; Epcor Centre for the Performing Arts, 205 8th Ave SE; admission $9; ⊘late May) Kids have all the fun at this annual event, with music, performers and all sorts of kidding around.

Carifest   CARIBBEAN
(www.carifestcalgary.com; Stephen Ave & Prince's Island Park; ⊘early Jun) The Caribbean comes alive right here in Calgary. Concerts, food stalls, street parties and stuff for the kids.

Calgary Stampede   RODEO
(www.calgarystampede.com; tickets from $24; ⊘2nd week Jul) Billed as the greatest outdoor show on earth and fast approaching its 100th anniversary, Calgary's Stampede is world famous. Events include a daily rodeo with bucking broncos, steer wrestling, barrel racing and, of course, bull riding. At night there's a grandstand show and the ever-popular chuckwagon races. It's a great time to visit Calgary, when civic spirits are on a yearly high with live music, stampede breakfasts and a rowdy party atmosphere permeating the city. Book ahead for accommodations during this event.

Calgary Folk Music Festival   MUSIC
(www.calgaryfolkfest.com; ⊘late Jul) Ray Charles once said that all music is folk music; that statement is celebrated at this annual four-day event featuring great live music every summer on Prince's Island. Top-quality acts from around the globe make the trek to Cowtown for this groovy event. There's heaps of fun to be had hanging out on the grass listening to the sounds of summer with 12,000 close friends.

🛏 Sleeping

Finding a family-run nonchain hotel in Calgary used to be like finding a water hole in Death Valley, but the opening of a trio of boutique hotels during 2009 and '10 has provided some welcome relief.

Downtown hotels are notoriously expensive, although many run frequent specials. Business-orientated hotels are often cheaper over weekends. Hotels near the western edge of town are concentrated into an area called, appropriately, Motel Village (corner of Crowchild Trail NW and Banff Trail NW). Every chain hotel you can think of has a property here, so if you are looking for a deal, investigate this area.

The prices quoted in this section are normal for summer; during the Stampede, demand causes rates to rise and availability to plummet. If you are heading here during that time be sure to book ahead.

TOP CHOICE Centro Motel   MOTEL $$
(☎403-288-6658; www.centromotel.com; 4540 16th Ave NW; r from $99; P❈@🗢) A 'boutique motel' sounds like an oxymoron until you descend on the brand-new Centro 7km northwest of Calgary's real 'centro' on the Trans-Canada Hwy (Hwy 1). Taking an old motel building in March 2010 and making it over with modern boutique features, the indie owners have left no detail missing, from light fittings to bathrobes to the

---

CALGARY FOR CHILDREN

Calgary is a very kid-friendly destination, with most attractions having a portion aimed at the younger set. These are some highlights with kids in mind.

You'll wish science class was as fun as the **Telus World of Science** (www.calgary science.ca; 701 11th St SW; adult/child/family $15/12/49; ⊘9:30am-5:30pm). Kids get a big bang out of this user-friendly and very interactive science center. There is a giant dome, where light shows depicting the cosmos are projected, and a whole raft of other things to discover. Plans are in the works to move on from the current Bow River location, so it's best to phone ahead.

Children of all ages will enjoy **Calaway Park** (www.calawaypark.com; adult/child/family $27/21/70; ⊘10am-7pm Jul-early Sep, 5-9pm Fri, 10am-7pm Sat & Sun late May-Jul, 11am-6pm Sat & Sun early Sep-early Oct), western Canada's largest outdoor family amusement park. It features 30 rides from wild to mild, live stage entertainment, 22 food vendors, 28 different carnival games, a trout-fishing pond and an interactive maze. To get there, head 10km west of the city on Hwy 1.

flower baskets hanging from the walkways. Additional bonuses include a complimentary breakfast and free phone calls to anywhere in Canada and the US.

Hotel Alma
BOUTIQUE HOTEL **$$**

(☑403-220-3203; www.hotelalma.ca; 169 University Gate NW; r from $129; 🛜) Get ready for something different. Operated and run by the University of Calgary and situated on the campus (7km from downtown), the Alma opened in October 2009 with small Euro-style rooms decked out boutique fashion and located in an old student residence. Guests get access to all on-campus facilities that include everything from a gym to a florist, plus there's free long-distance phone calls (within North America).

Hotel Le Germain
BOUTIQUE HOTEL **$$$**

(☑403-264-8990; www.germaincalgary.com; 899 Centre St SW; d from $279; P @🛜) At last, a posh boutique hotel to counteract the bland assortment of franchise inns that service downtown Calgary. Germain is actually a member of a franchise, albeit a small French-Canadian one, but the style (check out the huge glass wall in reception) is verging on opulent, while the 24-hour gym, in-room massage, complimentary newspapers and funky lounge add luxury touches. Even better, the hotel is efficiently built and has a long list of conservation policies.

Hotel Arts
BOUTIQUE HOTEL **$$$**

(☑403-266-4611, 800-661-9378; www.hotelarts.ca; 119 12th Ave SW; ste from $250; P ✳@🛜🏊) Setting a new standard in Calgary, this boutique hotel plays hard on the fact that it's not part of an international chain. Aimed at the modern discerning traveler with an aesthetic eye, there are hardwood floors, thread counts Egyptians would be envious of and art on the walls that should be in a gallery.

Fairmont Palliser
HOTEL **$$$**

(☑403-262-1234, 800-441-1414; www.fairmont.com/palliser; 133 9th Ave SW; r from $200; P @🏊) Cut from the same elegant cloth as other Fairmont hotels, the Palliser is easily the most stunning place to bed down in Calgary. With crystal chandeliers, marble columns, wood-inlaid arched ceiling domes and antique furniture, the interior has a deep regal feel to it, unlike anything else within the city limits. Classic, beautiful and worth every penny.

Twin Gables B&B
B&B **$$$**

(☑403-271-7754; www.twingables.ca; 611 25th Ave SW; s/d $185/225; P @) In a lovely old home, this B&B features hardwood floors, stained-glass windows, Tiffany lamps and antique furnishings. The three rooms are tastefully decorated, and the location across from the Elbow River provides opportunities for serene walks.

International Hotel
HOTEL **$$$**

(☑403-265-9600; www.internationalhotel.ca; 220 4th Ave SW; ste from $250; P @🛜🏊) All 35 floors of this property were recently renovated and the results are uplifting. Large living spaces with great city views are standard, while the sweet suites may have the comfiest beds you'll ever pay to sleep on.

Sheraton Suites Calgary Eau Claire
HOTEL **$$$**

(☑403-266-7200, 800-325-3535; www.sheraton.com; 255 Barclay Pde SW; ste from $299; P ✳@🛜🏊) With a great location and overflowing with amenities, this business-oriented hotel should satisfy even the fussiest of travelers. The staff love to go the extra mile in this all-suite hotel. Valet parking, a pool and a beautiful interior top it all off.

HI-Calgary
HOSTEL **$**

(☑403-269-8239; www.hostellingintl.ca/Alberta; 520 7th Ave SE; dm from $30, r from $75; @🛜) For the budget-minded, this pleasant hostel is one of your only options for the price in Calgary. Fairly standard bunk rooms and a few doubles are available. It has a kitchen, laundry, games room and internet facilities; it's a popular crossroads for travelers and a good place to make friends, organize rides and share recommendations. Be careful at night in this area – you are only a couple of blocks from both a homeless shelter and the roughest bar in town.

Carriage House Inn
INN **$$**

(☑403-253-1101; www.carriagehouse.net; 9030 Macleod Trail S; r from $135; P ✳@🏊) When you first arrive here, the tired exterior is less than inspiring, but inside things perk up. Recent renovations have done wonders in bringing the Carriage House back up to speed. The rooms are tidy and it's close to lots of eating and shopping options.

Kensington Riverside Inn
BOUTIQUE HOTEL **$$$**

(☑403-228-4442; www.kensingtonriversideinn.com; 1126 Memorial Dr NW; r from $260; P🛜) This impressive boutique-style hotel in

Kensington is a delight; a refined attitude permeates the smart-looking, beautifully finished property. The rooms are elegant and sport river views. Highly recommended.

Five
HOTEL $$

(☑403-451-5551; www.5calgary.com; 618 5th Ave SW; r from $89; P@�sⓢ) Five is a middle-of-the-road downtown option with various pros (friendly staff, gym, kitchenettes in rooms) and cons (slightly worn rooms, dodgy 1970s architecture). Weigh them up and make your choice.

Calaway RV Park
CAMPGROUND $

(☑403-240-3822; www.calawaypark.com; Hwy 1; tent & RV sites from $24; Pⓢ) The youngsters will love camping at the amusement park, not too far from town to drive. During the Stampede it runs a shuttle into town.

Calgary West Campground
CAMPGROUND $

(☑403-288-0411; www.calgarycampground. com; Hwy 1; tent/RV sites $29/42; P@ⓢⓢⓢ) Just west of Calgary, near Canada Olympic Park, this campground is close to the city and has good facilities.

✖ Eating

If Calgary is a 'fast-moving city' then its burgeoning restaurant scene is supersonic. Eating establishments come and go here like thieves in the night making gastronomic Top 10s out-of-date before critics can even tweet them. The overall culinary trend is one of constant improvement in terms of both quality and eclecticism. Where solitary cows once roamed, vegetables and herbs now prosper, meaning that trusty old stalwart, Alberta beef, is no longer the only thing propping up the menu.

You will find good eat streets in the neighborhoods of Kensington, Inglewood, Mission and 17th Ave, and downtown on Stephen St.

Downtown

TOP CHOICE \ **Catch**
SEAFOOD $$

(☑403-206-0000;www.catchrestaurant. ca; 100 8th Ave SW; mains $17-27) The problem for any saltwater fish restaurant in landlocked Calgary is that, if you're calling it fresh, it can't be local. Overcoming the conundrum, Catch, situated in an old bank building in Stephen St, flies its 'fresh catch' in daily from both coasts (BC and the Maritimes). You can work out the carbon-offsets for your lobster, crab and oysters on one of three different floors: an oyster bar, a dining room or an upstairs atrium.

(☑403-271-7874; www.rushrestaurant.com; 207 9th Av SW; mains from $25) Not to be confused with the so-bad-they're-almost-good Canadian rock band of the same name, Rush the restaurant is a decidedly cooler affair with glass walls, gold millwork and not a long-haired head-banger in sight. Food-wise, this is gastronomy from the top drawer with intelligent wine pairings, and a chef's tasting menu winning almost universal plaudits. Opt for the foie gras or the halibut and enjoy the complimentary canapés and petit fours.

✐ Blink
FUSION $$

(☑403-263-5330; www.blinkcalgary.com; 111 8th Ave SW; mains from $20) Blink multiple times but you still won't miss this trendy city center gastro haven where an acclaimed British chef oversees an ever-evolving menu of fine dishes that yell out that well-practised modern restaurant mantra of 'fresh, seasonal and local.' The decor is all open-plan kitchens and exposed brick, and you can delve even deeper into the culinary process through regular cooking classes (last Sunday of the month; $125).

Peter's Drive-In
BURGERS $

(www.petersdrivein.com; 219 16th Ave NE; mains $2.50-5; ◷9am-midnight) In 1962 Peter's opened its doors and locals have been flocking there ever since to a largely unchanged menu of super-thick shakes, burgers off the grill and fries that make no pretence of being healthy. It's a true drive-in, so either bring the car along or be happy to eat on the lawn out front.

1886 Buffalo Cafe
BREAKFAST $

(187 Barclay Pde SW; ◷6am-3pm Mon-Fri, 7am-3pm Sat & Sun) Calgary needs more places like Buffalo Cafe, a salt-of-the-earth diner in the high-rise dominated city center that the realty lords forgot to knock down. The wooden shack construction dates from the late 19th century and once belonged to the Bow River Lumber Company. These days it's more famous for its huevos rancheros.

Metropolitan Grill
MEDITERRANEAN $$

(☑403-263-5432; www.themetropolitangrill.ca; 317 8th Ave SW; mains from $15; ◷11am-1am) With a prime location on Stephen Ave Walk, the Met Grill is a trendy and tasty place to savor dinner. Specializing in North American dishes with a fancy twist, the patio out front is a perfect location to have some lunch and take in the views of all the beautiful people.

River Café   FUSION $$$

(☎403-261-7670; www.river-cafe.com; Prince's Island Park; mains $24-50; ☺11am-11pm Mon-Fri, 10am-11pm Sat & Sun) This organic, free-range and undeniably upscale restaurant that has won a litany of culinary awards is situated on the surprisingly leafy confines of Prince's Island in the middle of the Bow River. The menu is eclectic and determined by season and availability of ingredients with everything originating from either Alberta or BC. With 24 hours notice they can prepare you a picnic hamper in the summer months to enjoy in the nearby park.

Caesar's Steak House   STEAKHOUSE $$$

(512 4th Ave SW; steaks from $35; ☺11am-midnight) Well, why wouldn't you? You're in the heart of beef country, so it's only polite to sink your teeth into some prime Alberta AAA steak.

The King and I   THAI $$

(www.kingandi.ca; 822 11th Ave SW; mains from $12; ☺11:30am-10:30pm Mon-Thu, to 11:30pm Fri, 4:30-11:30pm Sat, 4:30-9:30pm Sun) Not just a movie with Yul Brynner, but Bangkok-good Thai food, too. This downtown classic with an exotic atmosphere is popular with groups. Try the curries or the pad thai – both are fantastic.

17th Avenue & Mission

Le Chien Chaud   FAST FOOD $

(www.lechienchaud.com; 3-2015 4th St SW; hot dogs $5; ☺11am-8pm Mon-Sat, noon-6pm Sun) 'Gourmet hot dogs' sounds like a greasy joke, but these ones are rather delicious. With more varieties of tube-steak than anyone previously thought possible, Le Chien Chaud can even cater to vegetarians.

Nellie's Kitchen   BREAKFAST $

(738B 17th Ave SW; mains $6.50-9; ☺7:30am-3:30pm Mon-Fri, 8am-3:30pm Sat & Sun) Nellie's has long been a favorite place to start the day, catch up with friends and attempt to quell a hangover. Humungous breakfasts, bottomless coffee and funky style are the hallmarks of this 17th Ave stalwart. Nellie's is a growing empire these days, but the original is still the best.

Melrose Café & Bar   CANADIAN $$

(www.melrosecalgary.com; 730 17th Ave SW; mains $9-15; ☺11am-midnight Mon-Fri, 10am-1am Sat & Sun) Right in the epicenter of Calgary cool on 17th Ave, Melrose has been starting and finishing nights out since it was the in thing to go there and watch *Melrose Place* (how times have changed). The gourmet pizzas are good to split over one of the many beers available on tap. The patio is legendary, full of lounging, posing locals.

🖋 Farm   FUSION $$

(www.farm-restaurant.com; 1006 17th Ave SW; shared dish $12-19; ☺11.30am-10pm Mon-Fri, 10.30am-11pm Sat, 10.30am-10pm Sun) Raising the excitement bar on 17th Ave, Farm is a new 'tasting kitchen' for fine meats, beer, wine and particularly cheese. The menu is about attention to detail, back-to-the-land purity and a genuine love of good food.

Antonio's Garlic Clove   ITALIAN $$

(www.garlicclove.net; 2206 4th St SW; mains from $20; ☺5pm-late) They take their garlic seriously here – it's in *everything* from the appetizers right through to dessert. Flavorful and obviously aromatic dishes are the hallmark of this authentic Italian eatery. Make sure you try the garlic beer.

Galaxie Diner   BREAKFAST $

(www.galaxiediner.com; 1413 11th St SW; mains $5-9; ☺7am-3pm Mon-Fri, to 4pm Sat & Sun) Classic no-nonsense '50s-style diner that serves all-day breakfasts. Squeeze into one of the half-dozen tables or grab a pew at the bar.

Cilantro   ITALIAN $$

(www.crmr.com; 17th Ave SW; mains from $16; ☺11am-10pm Mon-Thu & Sun, to 11pm Fri, 5-11pm Sat) Great Italian food, big wine glasses and nice decor put the finishing touches on a good meal at small and intimate Cilantro.

Kensington

Osteria de Medici   ITALIAN $$$

(☎403-283-5553; www.osteria.ca; 201 10th St NW; mains from $21) Italian restaurants are ubiquitous in North America, but few are as good as their home-country counterparts. Fortunately, the grandiose Medici is one of an authentic minority with uncomplicated renditions of classic Italian dishes such as veal marsala and *linguine alla vongole* (mussels). The secret? The proprietor is from Molise (east of Rome) and half of the clientele are from Hollywood (if you believe the blurb).

Sushi Club   JAPANESE $$

(1240 Kensington Rd NW; mains from $10; ☺11:30am-2pm & 5-9pm Mon, Wed, Thu & Fri) This could well be the best sushi in town; at the very least it's right up there. It's perhaps a bit on the pricey side, but you get what you pay for. It has a great lunch special, where a massive spread costs under $10.

Broken Plate   MEDITERRANEAN $$
(www.brokenplate.ca; 302 10th St NW; mains from $15) One of three Greek-themed restaurants in the city (all under the same name), this one, in the independently minded neighborhood of Kensington, is the original and best. Excellent pastas, pizzas and traditional Greek fare are enthusiastically consumed in the open, light-filled dining area. And yes, they break plates to dancing waiters Friday and Saturday nights.

Inglewood
Rouge   FUSION $$$
(☑403-531-2767; www.rougecalgary.com; 1240 8th Ave SE; mains $36-80) Calgary cuisine has recently been a tale of two 'R's – Rush (p201) and Rouge, with the latter becoming the city's most celebrated restaurant with its inclusion in the prestigious 2010 S Pellegrino World's Top 100 Restaurants list (rated at No 60 – the highest in Canada). Located in a historic 1891 mansion in Inglewood, it's expensive and hard to get into, but once inside you're on hallowed ground. Enjoy the inspired, creative and sustainable food choices and exceptional fit-for-a-king service.

 ## Drinking

For bars hit 17th Ave NW, with a slew of martini lounges and crowded pubs, and 4th St SW, with a lively after-work scene. Other notable areas include Kensington Rd NW and Stephen Ave (a six-block downtown stretch of 8th Ave).

Hop In Brew   PUB
(www.hopinbrew.com; 213 12th Ave SW) Imagine if you took an old house, turned it into a dive bar, and then threw a great party every weekend. Tucked down a quiet street just off the main drag, the Hop In Brew has got some style. The converted house has a bar upstairs and down, a pool table up top and winding steps right through the middle. There are good tunes, grungy atmosphere and plenty on tap.

Ming   BAR
(520 17th Ave SW) 'Serving all comrades until 2am' says the sign, hinting that Ming might not be conservative Calgary's most traditional bar. Contrarians, lefties and people with their tongues stuck firmly in

their cheeks sit down inside beneath the pop-art image of Chairman Mao and sip on Che Guevara cocktails in what is one of 17th Ave's trendiest watering holes.

Barley Mill   PUB
(www.barleymill.net; 201 Barclay Pde SW) This freestanding structure adjacent to Eau Claire Market is a favorite after-work stop for the downtown working stiffs. There's a big summer patio and the festive atmosphere keeps it popular year-round.

Ship & Anchor   PUB
(534 17th Ave SW) The Ship is an uberclassic Calgary institution, an all-time favorite of uni students, people who think they're hip and indie music fans. With plentiful beers on tap, the shadowy interior is a cozy winter hideaway, while the picnic table-filled patio is Posing Central come summertime.

Flames Central   BAR
(www.flamescentral.com; 219 8th Ave SW) The place to be to catch a hockey game on the big screen. The huge interior of what used to be a cinema has been transformed into the sports bar to end all sports bars. With more TVs than an electronics shop, you'll definitely get a good view of the game, even when they're playing the Oilers. There is an on-site restaurant and it has concerts from time to time.

Rose & Crown   PUB
(www.roseandcrowncalgary.ca; 1503 4th St SW) This British-style pub feels like it could hold most of Britain. Multileveled and popular, it's a good place to meet and greet some new-found friends.

Vicious Circle   BAR
(www.viciouscircle.ca; 1011 1st St SW) Dark and moody, cocktails and martinis, comfy couches and a stylish atmosphere – check it out.

★ Entertainment

You can see the money walking Calgary's streets after dark: beautiful, well-dressed 20-somethings in stretch limos, noisy stag nights in corporate bars, high-heeled girls in skimpy party dresses defying minus 20°C temperatures. People like to go out here; and they like to dress up, too. Leave your fleece in Vancouver and borrow someone's ironing board.

For complete entertainment guides, pick up a copy of *ffwd*, the city's largest entertainment weekly.

Whiskey NIGHTCLUB

(www.thewhiskeynightclub.com; 341 10th Ave SW) Here lie all the unbeatable facets of an ubertrendy nightclub: surly bouncers, a big list of entry rules, long freezing cold lines, a chill-out bar, music from the '80s onwards, and plenty of beautiful people showing off on the dance floor.

Broken City MUSIC VENUE

(www.brokencity.ca; 613 11th Ave SW) If you fancy a bit of rock and roll and are looking for a club with a 4/4 heartbeat, then Broken City is your scene. Indie rock, alt country and punk all do the rounds and get the crowds going. Gigs are usually on Thursday and Friday nights.

HiFi Club NIGHTCLUB

(www.hificlub.ca; 219 10th Ave SW) The HiFi is a hybrid. Rap, soul, house; electro, funk; the dance floor swells nightly to the sounds of live DJs who specialize in making you sweat. Check out Sunday Skool, the weekly soul and jazz session or Saturday night's showcase for touring bands and DJs.

Kaos MUSIC VENUE

(718 17th Ave SW) Jazz lovers unite at Kaos for nightly live music. The hip older crowd is a nice relief from the pubescent atmosphere found at some nightspots around town.

Marquee Room MUSIC VENUE

(www.theuptown.com; 612 8th Ave SW) Upstairs from the Uptown Cinema, this stylish joint is quickly becoming one of Calgary's hot spots. Great for live bands and DJs.

Epcor Centre for the Performing Arts

THEATER

(www.epcorcentre.org; 205 8th Ave SE) This is the hub for live theater in Calgary with four theaters and one of the best concert halls in North America.

Loose Moose Theatre Company THEATER

(1229 9th Ave SE) Guaranteed to be a fun night out, Loose Moose specializes in improv comedy and audience participation.

Plaza Theatre CINEMA

(1113 Kensington Rd NW) Right in the heart of Kensington, the Plaza shows art-house flicks and cult classics – it's where you'll end up doing the 'Time Warp' (again!).

Globe Cinema CINEMA

(617 8th Ave SW) Specializing in foreign films and Canadian cinema, both often hard to find in mainstream movie houses.

Paramount Chinook CINEMA

(6455 MacLeod Trail SW) Located in Chinook Centre shopping mall, the Paramount has 17 screens, so there must be something on worth seeing. There is an IMAX theater on-site, too.

Pumphouse Theatres THEATER

(www.pumphousetheatres.ca; 2140 Pumphouse Ave SW) Set in what used to be, you guessed it, the pumphouse, this theater company puts on avant-garde, edgy and entertaining productions.

Jubilee Auditorium THEATER

(www.jubileeauditorium.com/southern; 1415 14th Ave NW) You can hang with the upper crust at the ballet or rock out to a good concert, all under the one roof.

Gay & Lesbian Venues

Pick up a copy of *Outlooks* (www.outlooks. ca), a gay-oriented monthly newspaper distributed throughout the province. The website offers an extensive gay resource guide to Calgary and beyond.

Twisted Element NIGHTCLUB

(www.twistedelement.ca; 1006 11th Ave SW) Consistently voted the best gay dance venue by the local community, this club has weekly drag shows, karaoke nights and DJs spinning nightly.

Calgary Eagle BAR

(www.calgaryeagle.com; 424A 8th Ave SE) Billed as Calgary's leather bar, this place is popular with the fetish-inclined.

Back Lot BAR

(209 10th Ave SW) This one's for boys mainly. There's a patio and drink specials while you take in the view.

Sports

Calgary Flames SPORTS

(☑403-777-0000; tickets from $15) Archrival of the Edmonton Oilers, the Calgary Flames play ice hockey from October to April at the **Saddledome** (Stampede Park). Make sure you wear red to the game and head down to 17th Ave afterwards, or the 'Red Mile' as they call it during playoff time.

Calgary Stampeders SPORTS

(☑403-289-0258; tickets from $27; ☺Jul-Sep) The Calgary Stampeders, part of the CFL, play at **McMahon Stadium** (1817 Crowchild Trail NW) in northwest Calgary.

Shopping

Shopping in Calgary can be a disjointed affair. There are several hot spots, but these districts are reasonably far apart. The Kensington area and 17th Ave SW have a good selection of interesting, fashionable clothing shops and funky trinket outlets. Stephen Ave Walk is another highlight; the pedestrian mall has a good selection of shops, bookstores and atmosphere.

Alberta Boot Co CLOTHING
(www.albertaboot.com; 50 50th Ave S; boots $235-1700) Visit the factory and store run by the province's only Western boot manufacturer and pick up a pair of your choice made from kangaroo, ostrich, python, rattlesnake, lizard, alligator or boring old cowhide.

Chinook Centre MALL
(www.chinookcentre.com; 6455 Macleod Trail SW) If you're in need of some retail therapy, Chinook, just south of downtown, is a good place to get your treatment. Chain retail shops, department stores, a movie theater and lots of greasy food are all present and accounted for.

Mountain Equipment Co-Op OUTDOOR GEAR
(MEC; 830 10th Ave SW) MEC is the place to get your outdoor kit sorted before heading into the hills. It has a huge selection of outdoor equipment, travel gear, active clothing and books.

Smithbilt Hats CLOTHING
(www.smithbilthats.com; 1103 12th St SE) Ever wondered how a cowboy hat is made? Well, here is your chance to find out. Smithbilt has been shaping hats in the traditional way since you parked your horse out front.

 # Information

Alberta Children's Hospital (☑403-955-7211; 2888 Shaganappi Trail NW) Emergency room open 24 hours.

Calforex (304 8th Ave SW) Currency exchange facilities. Banks seem to live at every corner downtown; look to 17th Ave or Stephen Ave Walk if one isn't within sight. Many branches are open on Saturday and bank machines are open 24/7.

Hard Disk Café (638 11th Ave SW; internet per hr $5; ☺7am-7pm Mon-Thu, to 9pm Fri)

Main post office (207 9th Ave SW)

Police, Ambulance & Fire (☑911)

Police Dispatch Line (☑403-266-1234) For nonemergencies.

Rockyview General Hospital (☑403-943-3000; 7007 14th St SW) Emergency room open 24 hours.

Tourism Calgary (www.tourismcalgary.com; 101 9th Ave SW; ☺8am-5pm) Operates a visitors center in the base of the Calgary Tower. The staff will help you find accommodations. Information booths are also available at both the arrivals and departures levels of the airport.

Getting There & Away

Air

Calgary International Airport (YYC; www.calgaryairport.com) is about 15km northeast of the center off Barlow Trail, a 25-minute drive away. For more information on flights into Calgary, see p181.

Bus

The Greyhound Canada **bus station** (877 Greyhound Way SW) has services to Banff ($29, two hours, six daily) and Edmonton ($51, from 3½ hours, 10 or more daily). It also serves Drumheller and Lethbridge. For information on fares to other parts of Canada, see p192. **Red Arrow** (www.redarrow.pwt.ca; 205 9th Ave SE) runs luxury buses to Edmonton ($60, 3½ hours, seven daily).

Car

All the major car-rental firms are represented at the airport and downtown. For more information on car hire, see p324.

Train

Inexplicably, Calgary welcomes no passenger trains (which bypass the city in favor of Edmonton and Jasper). Instead, you get **Rocky Mountaineer Railtours** (www.rockymountaineer.com), which runs expensive cruise-shiplike rail excursions (two-day tours per person from $1400).

Getting Around

To/From the Airport

Sundog Tours (☑403-291-9617; tickets adult/child $15/8) runs every half-hour from around 8:30am to 9:45pm between all the major downtown hotels and the airport.

You can also go between the airport and downtown on public transportation. From the airport, take bus 57 to the Whitehorn stop (northeast of the city center) and transfer to the C-Train; reverse that process coming from downtown. This costs only $2.75, and takes between 45 minutes and an hour.

A taxi to the airport costs about $35 from downtown.

Car & Motorcycle

Parking in downtown Calgary is an absolute nightmare. Luckily, downtown hotels generally have garages, and extortionately high-priced private lots are available for about $20 per day. There is also metered parking at about $1 per 45 minutes (free after 6pm and on Sunday). Thankfully, outside the downtown core, parking is free and easy to find.

Public Transportation

Calgary Transit (www.calgarytransit.com) is efficient and clean. You can choose from the Light Rapid Transit (LRT) rail system, also known as the C-Train, and ordinary buses. One fare entitles you to transfer to other buses or C-Trains. The C-Train is free in the downtown area along 7th Ave, between 10th St SW and 3rd St SE. If you're going further or need a transfer, buy your ticket from a machine on the C-Train platform. Most of the buses run at 15- to 30-minute intervals daily. There is no late-night service. The C-Train and bus fare per single/day is $2.75/8.25. The C-Train is currently adding a new line to access the west of the city, which is due to open in 2012.

Taxi

For a cab, call **Checker Cabs** (☑403-299-9999) or **Yellow Cab** (☑403-974-1111). Fares are $3 for the first 150m, then $0.20 for each additional 150m.

BANFF & JASPER NATIONAL PARKS

While Italy has Venice and Florence, Canada has Banff and Jasper, legendary natural marvels that are as spectacular and vital as anything the ancient Romans ever built. But, don't think these protected areas have no history. Of the thousands of national parks scattered around the world today, Banff, created in 1885, is the third oldest while adjacent Jasper was only 22 years behind. Situated on the eastern side of the Canadian Rockies, the two bordering parks were designated Unesco World Heritage sites in 1984, along with BC's Yoho and Kootenay, for their exceptional natural beauty coupled with their manifestation of important glacial and alluvial geological processes. In contrast to some of North America's wilder parks, they both support small towns that lure between 2 to 5 million visitors each year. Despite all this, the precious balance between humans and nature continues to be delicately maintained – just.

Visiting the Park

Visitors come here for all sorts of reasons: to ski, climb and hike on the mountains, to raft and kayak the rivers, to camp among the trees, or explore on their mountain bikes. But most come simply to look, and to stand in awe of the sheer beauty of this amazing place.

As you pass through this special area, you are under the ever-watchful eye of the animals that call it home. This is the place to see the Canadian Rockies' Big Five: deer, elk, moose, wolf and bear. (But only if you're lucky: they don't pose for everyone's photos.)

The one-day park entry fee (for entry to both parks) is $9.80/4.90 per adult/child; the passes are good until 4pm the following day.

History

Banff National Park, Canada's first park, became the template for conservation. When Jasper joined the park system just over a century ago, this corridor of conservation was complete. Within that protected zone, the small towns of Banff and Jasper have emerged. These two towns, where development is frozen and the idea of ecotourism has been around since the 1880s, have lived in harmony with the surrounding wilderness for decades.

Banff is far from a secret these days – crowds are inevitable and you will have to share those scenic lookouts. But most will agree that's a small price to pay for a part of this country that will remain in your thoughts long after you bid the mountains *au revoir*.

Kananaskis Country

Kananaskis, or K-Country as the locals call it, is a mountainous Shangri-la with all the natural highlights of Banff National Park, but with almost no clamor. Driving the scenic and sparsely trafficked Hwy 40, you are treated to blankets of pine forest interspersed with craggy peaks and the odd moose in the verge. At an impressive 4000 sq km, it's a hefty tract of landscape to try and take in. Luckily, there is a network of hiking trails to get you into the backcountry and away from the roads. Hikers, cross-country skiers, bikers and climbers – mainly in-the-know Albertans – all lust over these hills which are the perfect combination of wild, accessible, unspoiled and inviting.

From the eastern edge of the mountains you can drive the paved Hwy 40 to the Kananaskis lakes, before turning down onto the unsealed Smith-Dorian Rd to complete the drive to Canmore. Or if you can, continue along Hwy 40 all the way to Highwood House – this scenic drive is definitely the road less traveled and well worth exploring; be aware this portion of the road is closed over winter.

🏃 Activities

K-Country is also C-Country. Cowboy-up and go for a ride with **Boundary Ranch** (🖉403-591-7171; www.boundaryranch.com; Hwy 40; rides from $40; ⊙mid-May–mid-Oct), which will take you for a trail ride that could last anywhere from an hour to days.

Purpose-built to host the alpine skiing events in the '88 Olympics, **Nakiska** (www.skinakiska.com; Hwy 40), five minutes' drive south of Kananaskis Village, is a racer's

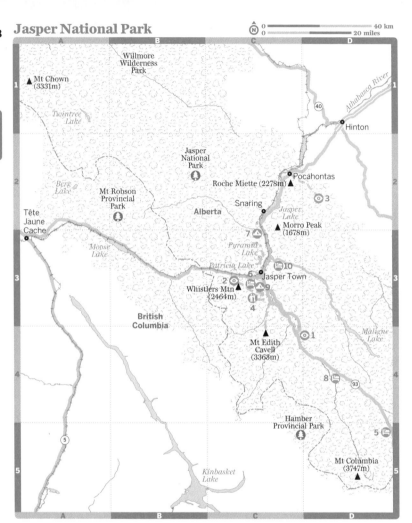

dream and top Canadian skiers still train here. K-Country's other ski resort, Fortress Mountain, has been closed on and off (mainly off) since 2004.

The Kananaskis River has class II and III rapids and is popular with white-water rafting companies operating out of Banff (see p217).

🛏 Sleeping & Eating

Proof of Kananaskis' get-away-from-it-all ethos came when it was selected to host the first post-9/11 G8 summit when security was particularly high. The likes of Tony Blair, Jacques Chirac and Vladimir Putin were bivouacked at the **Delta Lodge at Kananaskis** (☎403-591-7711; www.delta hotels.com; r from $219). The amazing scenery, tip-top facilities and isolation were a big hit with the world leaders, except Texan George W Bush who, oddly, opted to fly out of cowboy country and return to American soil – every night. Delta's pricey **Fireweed Grill** (Delta Lodge; mains $20-30) does baked river fish and AAA Alberta steak.

If you can't afford G8 prices, get the full Kananaskis experience by sleeping under

Jasper National Park

the stars at the **Boulton Creek Campground** (☑403-591-7226; Kananaskis Lakes Rd; powered/nonpowered sites $20/30; ⊙mid-May–Oct).

ⓘ Information

About 8km from Hwy 1 along Hwy 40 is the **Barrier Lake Information Centre** (☑403-673-3985; www.tpr.alberta.ca/parks; ⊙9am-4pm, to 5pm May-Sep), which has loads of info and sells backcountry camping permits.

Canmore

A former mining town, Canmore was once the quiet alternative to the mass tourism of Banff. Then, after one too many 'best kept secret' travel articles, everybody started coming here for a little peace and quiet. Despite the commotion, the soul of the town has remained intact and Canmore, although not national park protected, has been developed sensibly and sustainably – so far. At just 26km from Banff and on the cusp of Kananaskis Country, it's at the crossroads of some of the most magnificent scenery you will ever see. For those seeking a mountain holiday with slightly less glitz, more of a rugged feel and less pretension, Canmore can still cut it.

◉ Sights & Activities

Canmore excels in two particular mountain activities: cross-country skiing and mountaineering.

Cross-country Skiing
Both winter and summer are prime times at the **Canmore Nordic Centre** (www.canmore

nordic.com; 1988 Olympic Way). Used for the cross-country skiing events at the 1988 Olympics, the Nordic Centre is arguably the best facility of its kind in Canada and the training ground for many national champions. It offers ski rentals and lessons for the uninitiated and a network of trails that would keep an Olympian busy for days.

Mountain Biking
Once the snow melts, the Nordic Centre's trails transform into some of the best mountain biking around, with over 80km of off-road to test your skills. Close to here, the Rundle Riverside and Spray River/Goat Creek trails both head north to Banff Town (see p216).

Rock Climbing
Canmore is one of the premier rock-climbing destinations in the Rockies. In the summer, there are numerous climbing crags such as Cougar Creek, Grassi Lakes and Grotto Canyon all within a relatively short distance of each other. For those looking for multipitch rock, the limestone walls of Mt Rundle and Mt Yamnuska are local classics with routes of all grades. In the colder months, Canmore is the place to be for frozen waterfall climbing – learn at the Junkyards, practise on Grotto Falls or take the final exam on The Terminator.

If you are keen to give climbing in any of its forms a try, talk to **Yamnuska Mountain Adventures** (www.yamnuska.com; Suite 200, Summit Centre, 50 Lincoln Park), which will provide expert instruction, qualified guides and all the gear you might need. Yamnuska also offers longer courses for those wanting to gain the skills necessary to spend some serious time in the hills.

🛏 Sleeping

Canmore Clubhouse   HOSTEL $
(☑403-678-3200;   www.alpineclubofcanada.ca; Indian Flats Rd; dm from $36; ℗) Steeped in climbing history and mountain mystique, the Alpine Club of Canada's beautiful hostel sits on a rise overlooking the valley. You'll find all of the usual hostel amenities here, along with a sauna. The Alpine Club offers classes in mountaineering and maintains several backcountry huts. The Clubhouse is a great place to find climbing partners or just soak up the spirit of adventure. Located 5km south of town, it's an inconvenient 45-minute walk or pleasant five-minute drive away.

ALBERTA'S NATIONAL PARKS – A GROUNDBREAKING QUINTET

Alberta's five national parks are remarkable not just for their environmental steward-ship, but for the pioneering role they have played in the development of Canada's (and the planet's) bid to protect pristine land for future generations. Banff, formed in 1885, was Canada's first and the world's third national park and acted as a meta-phoric litmus test for subsequent ecological management, while Waterton (1895), Jasper (1907), Elk Island (1913) and Wood Buffalo (1922) provided four more testing grounds for Canada's still nascent National Parks Service in the first quarter of the 20th century.

All of Alberta's parks bar Elk Island double up as Unesco World Heritage sites. Yet, despite such impressive billing, Banff, Jasper and Waterton support infrastructures unheard of in many other North American parks, particularly in the US. Common to each are sizeable resort towns, commercial ski areas, thirsty golf courses, popular franchise restaurants and long-running and often feisty debates about how to man-age ecological integrity alongside the right of recreation for all. With the arguments still raging, the fate of Alberta's parks could well be a harbinger for the long-term fu-ture of protected areas worldwide.

Windtower Lodge & Suites HOTEL **$$**
(☑403-609-6600; www.windtower.ca; 160 Kananaskis Way; d/ste $169/239; P@🛜) Named for the stunning rock feature only a few kilometers to the east, this modern and well-appointed hotel is a good option. The rooms are a bit small, so spending a bit more on a suite is a good idea. Some rooms have fine views of the Three Sisters and all have access to the hot tub and fit-ness center.

✖ Eating

The Wood STEAKHOUSE **$$**
(www.thewood.ca; 838 8th St; mains $12-29) Plenty of wood and a big fireplace create a relaxed, sophisticated vibe in this log build-ing in Canmore's town center. If you're hav-ing a day off from AAA Alberta steak (not easy here), plump for the excellent salmon burger with a Dijon tartar relish.

Grizzly Paw PUB **$$**
(www.thegrizzlypaw.com; 622 Main St; mains $13-20) Yes, it's a microbrewery (offering six year-round beers) and yes, it serves food (including wings, burgers and shep-herd's pie), meaning this funky gastro-pub is a Rocky Mountain rarity.

Quarry PUB **$$$**
(www.quarrydininglounge.com; 718 Main St; mains $17-32) This posh brasserie with an open kitchen viewable from a wrap-around bar creates European-influenced food with some subtle surprises, includ-ing Moroccan tagine, homemade terrine and spaghetti carbonara.

ℹ Information

Canmore Library (950 8th Ave) For free internet and wi-fi; best to book ahead to get a computer.

Canmore Visitor Information Centre (www.discoveralberta.com; 2801 Bow Valley Trail; ⊙8am-8pm) Just off Hwy 1.

ℹ Getting There & Away

Canmore is easily accessible from Banff Town and Calgary from Hwy 1. The **Banff Airporter** (www.banffairporter.com) runs up to 10 buses a day to/from Calgary Airport ($52) and Banff ($15). Slightly cheaper is **Greyhound Canada** (www.greyhound.ca) with connections to Down-town Calgary ($25), Banff Town ($12.50) and all stops west as far as Vancouver ($138). The bus stops in 8th St and had no official depot at time of writing. You must buy your tickets online.

Icefields Parkway

Paralleling the Continental Divide for 230km between Lake Louise and Jasper Town, plain old Hwy 93 has been wisely rebranded as the Icefields Parkway (or the slightly more romantic 'Promenade des Glaciers' in French) as a means of somehow preparing people for the majesty of its sur-roundings. And what majesty! The high-light is undoubtedly the humungous Co-lumbia Icefield and its numerous fanning glaciers, and this dynamic lesson in erosive geography is complemented by weeping waterfalls, aquamarine lakes, dramatic mountains and the sudden dart of a bear, an elk, or was it a moose?

Completed in 1940, most people ply the Parkway's asphalt by car, meaning it can get busy in July and August. For a clearer vision consider taking a bus or, even better, tackling it on a bike – the road is wide, never prohibitively steep, and sprinkled with plenty of strategically spaced campgrounds, hostels and hotels.

◉ Sights

Every bend in the road reveals a view seemingly more stunning than the last. There are lakes and glaciers galore – too many to mention. Here are some favorites.

Peyto Lake ✕ NATURAL SITE

This is the sort of scenery you come to the Canadian Rockies to find. This bluer than blue glacier-fed lake has been photographed more than Brangelina. Don't let the inevitable zoo of people deter you – the view is one of the best anywhere. The lake is best visited in early morning, between the time the sun first illuminates the water and the first tour bus arrives. From the bottom of the lake parking lot, follow a paved trail for 15 minutes up a steady gradual incline to the wooden platform overlooking the lake. From here you can continue up the paved trail, keeping right along the edge of the ridge. At the junction of three trails, follow the middle trail until you reach an unmarked dirt road; if you continue down it for about 2.5km you'll find yourself in a serene rocky bowl with a stream running through the center.

The Weeping Wall ✕ NATURAL SITE

Just before you get to the Big Bend – you'll know it when you get there – you'll come across The Weeping Wall. The towering rock wall sits just above the east side of the highway. In the summer months it is a sea of waterfalls, with tears of liquid pouring from the top creating a veil of moisture. Come winter, it's a whole different story. The water freezes up solid to form an enormous sheet of ice. The vertical football field is a popular playground for ice climbers who travel from around the globe to test their mettle here. Scaling the wall is a feather in the cap for the alpinists lucky enough to clamber to the top. Be sure to observe the ice from the safety of the roadside lookout; falling chunks of ice the size of refrigerators are not uncommon.

Columbia Icefield ✕ MUSEUM

About halfway between Lake Louise Village and Jasper Town you'll encounter the only accessible section of the vast Columbia Icefield, which contains about 30 glaciers and is up to 350m thick. This remnant of the last ice age covers 325 sq km on the plateau between Mt Columbia (3747m) and Mt Athabasca (3491m). It's the largest icefield in the Rockies and feeds the North Saskatchewan, Columbia, Athabasca, Mackenzie and Fraser River systems with its meltwaters.

The mountainous sides of this vast bowl of ice are some of the highest in the Rockies, with nine peaks higher than 3000m.

Be sure to stop here at the **Icefield Centre** (☏780-852-6288; admission free; ⏰9am-6pm May–mid-Oct). The downstairs **Glacial Gallery** explains the amazing science of glaciers and provides a comprehensive snapshot of the area's history. On the main level you can have a friendly chat with the rangers from **Parks Canada** (☏780-852-6288), who can advise you on the various camping options and climbing conditions and answer any of the questions you might have regarding the park.

Athabasca Glacier ✕ NATURAL SITE

The tongue of the Athabasca glacier runs from the Columbia Icefield almost down to the road opposite the Icefield Centre and can be visited on foot or in specially designed buses. The glacier has retreated about 1.6km in the last 150 years. To reach its toe walk or drive 1km to a small parking lot and the start of the 0.6km **Forefield Trail**. While it is permitted to stand on a small roped section of the ice, do not attempt to cross the warning tape. Many do, but the glacier is riddled with crevasses and there are fatalities nearly every year.

The best way to experience the Columbia Icefield is to walk on it. For that you will need the help of **Athabasca Glacier Icewalks** (☏780-852-5595, 800-565-7547; www.icewalks.com; Icefield Centre), which supplies all the gear you'll need and a guide to show you the ropes. It offers a three-hour tour (adult/child $60/30; departing 10:40am daily June to September), and a six-hour option ($70/35) on Sunday and Thursday for those wanting to venture further onto the glacier.

The other far easier (and more popular) way to get on the glacier is via a 'Snocoach' ice tour offered by **Brewster** (☑877-423-7433; www.brewster.ca; adult/child $49/24; ⊗tours every 15-30min 9am-5pm May-Oct). For many people this is the defining experience of their Columbia Icefield visit. The large hybrid bus-truck grinds a track onto the ice where it stops to allow you to go for a short walk in a controlled area on the glacier. Dress warmly and wear good shoes. Tickets can be bought at the Icefield Centre or online.

Athabasca Glacier to Jasper Town

SCENIC HIGHWAY

As you snake your way through the mountains on your way to Jasper, there are a few places worth stopping at. **Sunwapta Falls** and **Athabasca Falls**, closer to Jasper, are both worth a stop. The latter is the more voluminous and is at its most ferocious in the summer when it's stoked with glacial meltwater. A less-visited spot is idyllic blue-green **Horseshoe Lake**, revered by ill-advised cliff-divers. Don't be tempted to join them.

At Athabasca Falls, Hwy 93A quietly sneaks off to the left. Take it. Literally the road less traveled, this old route into Jasper offers a blissfully traffic-free experience as it slips serenely through deep, dark woods and past small placid lakes and meadows.

🛏 Sleeping & Eating

The Icefields Parkway is punctuated with a good batch of well-camouflaged hostels and lodges. Most are close to the highway in scenic locations. There are also numerous primitive **campgrounds** (per night $15.70) in the area. Good options are Honeymoon Lake, Joans Creek, Mt Kerkeslin, Waterfowl Lakes and Wilcox Creek Campgrounds.

Mosquito Creek International Hostel

HOSTEL $

(☑403-670-7589; www.hihostels.ca; dm member/nonmember $23/27; P) Don't let the name put you off – Mosquito Creek, 26km north of Lake Louise, is a perfect launching pad for backcountry adventures, the sauna is an ideal flop-down-and-do-nothing end to the day and the adjacent river just adds to the atmosphere. The hostel sometimes closes in winter, so call ahead.

Rampart Creek International Hostel

HOSTEL $

(☑403-670-7589; www.hihostels.ca; dm member/nonmember $23/27; P) Rampart, 11km north of the Saskatchewan River Crossing, has long been a popular place with climbers, cyclists and other troublemakers. The tiny crag at the back is good fun for a bouldering session, and the 12 bunks and facilities are clean and cozy. Then there's the sauna – more lethargy. Call first in winter in case it's closed.

🏄 Beauty Creek International Hostel

HOSTEL $

(Map p208; ☑780-852-3215; www.hihostels.ca; Icefields Parkway; dm member/nonmember $23/27; ⊗check-in 5-10pm) Forget the lack of electricity, propane-powered lights, outside loos and well-drawn water, and home in on the all-you-can-eat pancake breakfast and poetry-inspiring scenery.

Sunwapta Falls Resort

HOTEL $$$

(Map p208; ☑888-828-5777; www.sunwapta.com; r from $209; P @) A handy Icefields pit stop 53km south of Jasper townsite, Sunwapta offers a comfortable mix of suites and lodge rooms cocooned in pleasant natural surroundings. There's a home-style restaurant and gift shop on-site that are popular with the tour-bus crowd.

Columbia Icefield Chalet

HOTEL $$$

(☑877-423-7433; Icefield Centre, Icefields Parkway; r from $260; ⊗May-Oct; P) Panoramic views of the glacier are unbelievable at this chalet – if only the windows were a bit bigger. You are in the same complex as the madness of the Icefield Centre, so it can feel like you are staying in a shopping mall at times. But after all the buses go away for the night, you are left in one of the most spectacular places around. A nothing-to-write-home-about cafeteria shares the complex.

Num-Ti-Jah Lodge

INN $$$

(☑403-522-2167; www.num-ti-jah.com; d $275; P) Standing like a guardian of Bow Lake, the historic Num-Ti-Jah Lodge is full to the brim with character and backcountry nostalgia. Carved wood interior decor, animal heads and photos from the golden age adorn the walls. The rooms are tidy, if a little small. The lodge restaurant (mains from $14, three-course dinner $45) has an extensive wine list.

Banff Town

Like the province in which it resides, Banff is something of an enigma. A resort town with souvenir shops, nightclubs and fancy restaurants is not something any national park purist would want to claim credit for. But, looks can be misleading. First, Banff is no ordinary town. It developed historically, not as a residential district, but as a service center for the park that surrounds it. Second, the commercialism of Banff Ave is delusory. Wander five minutes in either direction and (though you may not initially realize it) you're in wild country, a primeval food chain of bears, elk, wolves and bighorn sheep. Banff civilized? It's just a rumor.

History

While most mountain towns have their roots in the natural resource industry, Banff was created in the late 1800s with tourism in mind. The railway arrived first, then the Cave and Basin hot springs were discovered and the potential to make some money became evident. First came the hordes of wealthy Victorians, staying at the Banff Springs Hotel and soaking in the soothing waters. Everything changed in 1911 when the road finally reached the town and the doors were flung open to the masses.

Banff continued to grow as more tourists arrived and services aimed at not just the upper class began to take root. Town developers have long been frustrated by the inclusion of the townsite within the national park. This has meant that building restrictions are tight, new development has ceased and the future of building in Banff is both a political and ecological hot potato. Actually living in Banff is a challenge: the federal government owns all the land, only those employed can take up residence and businesses are obligated to provide accommodations for their employees.

Though the infrastructure and size of the town remains fixed, the number of tourists has continued to spiral skywards. For as long as the town has been incorporated, locals have bickered about tourism. While they may pay everyone's wages, the visitors overrun the town and move it away from the quiet mountain town it once was.

◉ Sights

TOP CHOICE **Whyte Museum of the Canadian Rockies**
MUSEUM
(www.whyte.org; 111 Bear St; adult/child $8/5; ☺10am-5pm) The century-old Whyte Museum is more than just a rainy-day option. There is a beautiful gallery displaying some great pieces on an ever-changing basis. The permanent collection tells the story of Banff and the hearty men and women who forged a home among the mountains. Attached to the museum is an archive with thousands of photographs spanning the history of the town and park; these are available for reprint. The museum also gives out leaflets for a self-guided **Banff Culture Walk**.

Banff Gondola
LANDMARK
(Mountain Ave; adult/6-15yr $29/14; ☺8:30am-9pm summer, reduced hours rest of year) In summer or winter you can summit a peak near Banff thanks to the Banff Gondola, whose four-person enclosed cars glide you up to the top of Sulphur Mountain in less than 10 minutes. Named for the thermal springs that emanate from its base, this peak is a perfect viewing point and a tick-box Banff attraction. There are a couple of restaurants on top plus an extended hike on boardwalks to Sanson Peak, an old weather station. Some people hike all the way up on a zigzagging 5.6km trail. You can travel back down on the gondola for half price and recover in the hot springs.

Cave & Basin National Historic Site
HISTORIC SITE
(Cave Ave; adult/child $4/3; ☺9am-6pm May-Oct, 11am-4pm Mon-Fri, 9:30am-5pm Sat & Sun Nov-Apr) Aboriginals have known about this hot spot for 10,000 years. The Cave & Basin is a great place to sniff around and discover how Banff National Park came into being. In 1883, three railway workers found the hot springs and discovered a thermal gold mine. Quickly throwing up a shack to charge bathers for their thermal treatments, the government soon stepped in and decided to declare Banff Canada's first national park in order to preserve the springs. You can't swim here any more, but there's an indoor museum (temporarily closed at the time of research) and an interpretive walk along boardwalks to the springs and cave vent. The 2.5km **Marsh Loop Trail** across the park's only natural river marsh also starts here.

Banff Town

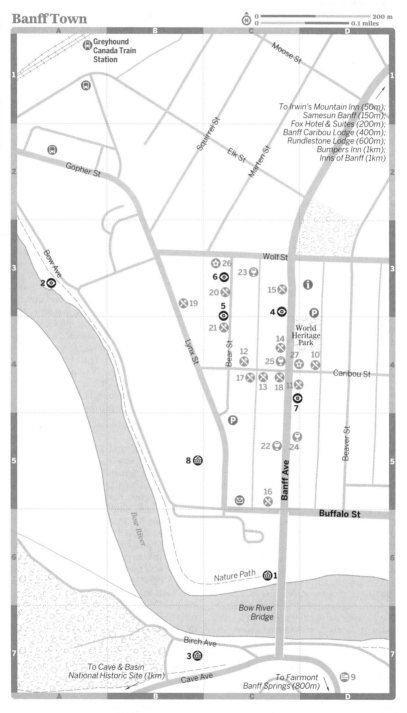

Greyhound Canada Train Station

Moose St

To Irwin's Mountain Inn (50m);
Samesun Banff (150m);
Fox Hotel & Suites (200m);
Banff Caribou Lodge (400m);
Rundlestone Lodge (600m);
Bumpers Inn (1km);
Inns of Banff (1km)

Gopher St

Squirrel St

Elk St

Marten St

Wolf St

Bow Ave

Lynx St

Bear St

Banff Ave

Beaver St

Caribou St

World Heritage Park

Buffalo St

Bow River

Nature Path

Bow River Bridge

Birch Ave

To Cave & Basin
National Historic Site (1km)

Cave Ave

To Fairmont
Banff Springs (800m)

Sights

1. Banff Park Museum C6
2. Blue Canoe A3
3. Buffalo Nations Luxton Museum B7
   Canadian Rockies Rafting
      Company .... (see 4)
   Discover Banff Tours .... (see 4)
4. GyPSy Guide C3
5. Hydra River Guides C3
6. Snowtips/Bactrax C3
7. Warner Guiding & Outfitting C4
8. Whyte Museum of the Canadian
      Rockies B5

Sleeping

9. Banff Y Mountain Lodge D7

Eating

Bison Mountain Bistro .... (see 21)
10. Bruno's Cafe & Grill D4
11. Cows C4

12. Coyote's Deli & Grill C4
13. Eddie Burger & Bar C4
14. Evelyn's Coffee Bar C4
15. Giorgio's Trattoria C3
16. Le Beaujolais C5
17. Magpie & Stump C4
18. Maple Leaf Grille C4
19. Melissa's Restaurant B3
20. Saltlik C3
21. Wild Flour C4

Drinking

22. Elk & Oarsman C5
23. St James's Gate Old Irish Pub C3
24. Tommy's Neighbourhood Pub C5
25. Wild Bill's Legendary Saloon C4

Entertainment

Hoodoo Club .... (see 18)
26. Lux Cinema Centre C3
27. Rose & Crown C4

Banff Upper Hot Springs SPA
(Mountain Ave; adult/student $7.30/6.30; ☺9am-11pm May-Sep, 10am-10pm Sun-Thu, 10am-11pm Fri & Sat Oct-Apr) You'll find a soothing (if often crowded) hot pool, steam room, spa and excellent mountain views at these hot springs, near the Banff Gondola, 4km south of town. The water emerges from the spring at 47°C; in winter it has to be cooled to 39°C before entering the pool, but in spring the snowmelt does that job. In addition to the pool, you can indulge in a massage or an aromatherapy wrap. Bathing suits, towels and lockers can be rented.

Lake Minnewanka NATURAL SITE
Lake Minnewanka, pronounced mini-won-ka, as in Willy Wonka, not mini-wanker, as Australian visitors enjoy saying, sits 13km east of Banff Town, making it a popular escape from downtown. The scenic recreational area features plenty of hiking, swimming, sailing, boating and fishing opportunities. The nonchallenging trail around the lake is a good option for a walk; the path is easy to follow and popular. **Minnewanka Lake Cruises** (www.explorerockies.com/minnewanka; adult/child $44/19; ☺5-9 departures 10am-6pm mid-May–early Oct) offers a 60-minute interpretive cruise on the lake giving plenty of insight into the region's history and geology. You can also fish here or hike to the Alymer Lookout trail

for spectacular lake and mountain views. A Brewster bus can transport you to the lake for an extra fee. See the Minnewanka Lake Cruises website for details.

Banff Park Museum MUSEUM
(93 Banff Ave; adult/child $3.95/1.95; ☺10am-6pm May-Sep, 1-5pm Oct-Apr) Occupying an old wooden Canadian Pacific Railway building dating from 1903, this museum is a national historic site. Its exhibits – a taxidermic collection of animals found in the park, including grizzly and black bear, plus a tree carved with graffiti dating from 1841 – have changed little since the museum opened a century ago.

Buffalo Nations Luxton Museum MUSEUM
(www.buffalonationsmuseum.ca; 1 Birch Ave; adult/6-12yr/senior & student $8/2.50/6; ☺11am-6pm) The Luxton Museum tells the story of the first inhabitants of the Banff area with some interesting displays and artifacts. Traditional clothing and historic photographs populate the display cabinets, and there's a life-sized replica of a sun dance ceremony and a few other well-put-together displays.

🏃 Activities

Canoeing & Kayaking

Despite a modern penchant for big cars, canoe travel is still very much a quintessential Canadian method of transportation. The best options near Banff Town are **Lake Minnewanka** and nearby **Two Jack Lake**, both to the northeast, or – closer to the town itself – the **Vermilion Lakes**. Unless you have your own canoe, you'll need to rent one; try **Blue Canoe** (☑403-760-5007; cnr Wolf St & Bow Ave; rental 1st hr/additional hours $34/20).

Cycling

There are lots of riding options around Banff, both on road and on selected trails. Popular routes around Banff Town include **Sundance** (7.4km round-trip) and **Spray River Loop** (12.5km); either is good for families. **Spray River & Goat Creek** (19km one way) and **Rundle Riverside** (14km one way) are both A to Bs with start/finish points near Canmore. The former is pretty straightforward; the latter is more challenging with ups and downs, and potential for thrills and spills. **Bactrax** (www.snowtips-bactrax.com) can organize a shuttle to the trailheads.

Serious road cyclists should check out Hwy 1A between Banff and Lake Louise; the rolling hills and quiet road here are a roadie's dream. Parks Canada publishes the brochure *Mountain Biking & Cycling Guide – Banff National Park,* which describes trails and regulations.

Snowtips/Bactrax (www.snowtips-bactrax .com; 225 Bear St; rentals per hr/day from $10/35) has a barn full of bikes to rent and will also take you on a tour to one of the plethora of bike trails in the Banff area ($20 per hour).

Hiking

Hiking is Banff's tour de force and the main focus of many travelers' visit to the area. The trails are easy to find, well signposted and maintained enough to be comfortable to walk on, yet rugged enough to still get a wilderness experience.

In general, the closer to Banff Town you are, the more people you can expect to see and the more developed the trail will be. But regardless of where in the park you decide to go walking, you are assured to be rewarded for your efforts.

Before you head out, check at the Banff Information Centre (p221) for trail conditions and possible closures. Keep in mind that trails are often snow-covered much later into the summer season than you might realize, and bear trail closures are a possibility, especially in berry season (June to September).

One of the best hikes from the town center is the **Bow River Falls and the Hoodoos Trail** which starts by the Bow River Bridge and tracks past the falls to the Hoodoos, weird rock spires caused by wind and water erosion. The trail plies its way around the back of Tunnel Mountain through forest and some river meadows and is 10.2km return.

You can track the north shore of Lake Minnewanka for kilometers on a multi-use trail that is sometimes closed due to bear activity. The classic hike is to walk as far as the **Alymer Lookout** just shy of 10km one way. Less taxing is the 5.6km return hike to **Stewart Canyon**, where you can clamber down rocks and boulders to the Cascade River.

Some of the best multiday hikes start at the Sunshine parking lot where skiers grab the gondola in winter. From here you can plan two- to four-day sorties up over Healy Pass and down to **Egypt Lake**, or get a bus up to Sunshine Village where you can cross the border into BC and head out across Sunshine Meadows and **Mount Assiniboine Provincial Park**.

The best backcountry experience is arguably the **Sawback Trail** that travels from Banff up to Lake Louise the back way over 74km, six primitive campsites and three spectacular mountain passes.

Check out Lonely Planet's *Banff, Jasper & Glacier National Parks* guide for more details about more single-day and multiday hikes.

Horseback Riding

Banff's first western explorers – fur traders and railway engineers – penetrated the region primarily on horseback and you can recreate this pioneering spirit on guided rides with **Warner Guiding & Outfitting** (☑403-762-4551; www.horseback.com; 132 Banff Ave; 1hr rides from $40) which will fit you out with a trusty steed and lead you along narrow trails for part of the day. Instruction and guiding are included; a sore backside is more or less mandatory for beginners. Grin and bear it. If you're really into it, opt for the six-day Wildlife Monitoring Adventure Expeditions out to limited-access areas accompanied by a Parks Canada researcher.

Skiing & Snowboarding

Strange though it may seem, there are three ski areas in the national park, two of them in the vicinity of Banff Town. Large, snowy

Sunshine Village is considered world-class. Tiny Norquay, a mere 5km from the center, is your half-day, family-friendly option.

Sunshine Village (www.skibanff.com; day ski passes $75) straddles the Alberta-BC border. Though slightly smaller than Lake Louise in terms of skiable terrain it gets much bigger dumpings of snow, or 'Champagne powder' as Albertans like to call it (up to 9m annually). Aficionados laud Sunshine's advanced runs and lengthy ski season, which lingers until Victoria Day weekend in late May. A high-speed gondola whisks skiers up in 17 minutes to the village which sports Banff's only ski-in hotel, the Sunshine Mountain Lodge.

Ski Banff@Norquay (www.banffnorquay. com; Mt Norquay Rd; lift tickets $46), just 6km north of downtown Banff, has a long history of entertaining Banff visitors. The smallest and least visited of the three local hills, this is a good place to body-swerve the major show-offs and hit the slopes for a succinct half day.

Local buses shuttle riders from Banff hotels to both resorts (and Lake Louise) every half hour during the season.

White-Water Rafting

The best rafting is outside the park (and province) on the Kicking Horse River in Yoho National Park, BC. There are class IV rapids here, meaning big waves, swirling holes and a guaranteed soaking. Lesser rapids are found on the Kananaskis River and the Horseshoe Canyon section of the Bow River. The Bow River around Banff is better suited to mellower float trips.

The following companies all have representation in the park. They offer tours starting at around $79. Factor in $15 more for a Banff pickup.

Canadian Rockies Rafting Company (☑403-763-2007; www.chinookraft.com; 215 Banff Ave)

Hydra River Guides (☑403-762-4554; www. raftbanff.com; 211 Bear St)

Wild Water Adventures (☑403-522-2211; www.wildwater.com) Has a desk at the Chateau Lake Louise, but will pick up from Banff for a fee.

👉 Tours

GyPSy Guide   SELF-DRIVE
(☑403-760-8200; www.gpstourscanada.com; Sundance Mall, 215 Banff Ave; per day $40) The future of guided travel is right here in Banff

with GyPSy Guide. The GyPSy is a handheld GPS device that you take in your car and guides you around the area. There is a lively running commentary that broadcasts through your stereo, pointing out highlights as you travel. All you have to do is follow the directions and you get a great self-guided tour of the area – Banff, Lake Louise, Columbia Icefield, Jasper and Calgary are all included on the tour. Best of all, if you get tired of the tour guide you can always turn it off.

Discover Banff Tours   WILDLIFE, SIGHTSEEING
(☑403-760-5007; www.banfftours.com; Sundance Mall, 215 Banff Ave; tours $39-145) Discover Banff has a great selection of tours to choose from: three-hour Banff Town tours, sunrise and evening wildlife tours, Columbia Icefield day trips and even a 10-hour grizzly bear tour, where if you don't see a bear you get your money back.

🎊 Festivals & Events
The town's biggest annual event is the dual **Banff Mountain Book Festival** and **Banff Mountain Film Festival** (www.banffcentre. ca/mountainfestival), held consecutively in late October and early November. Attracting the cream of the mountain culture aficionados, this event is a must-do for the armchair adventurer and mountain guru alike.

🛏 Sleeping
Compared with elsewhere in the province, accommodations in Banff Town are fairly costly and, in summer, often hard to find. The old adage of the early bird catching the worm really holds true here, and booking ahead is strongly recommended.

The Banff/Lake Louise Tourism Bureau tracks vacancies on a daily basis; check the listings at the Banff Information Center. You might also try **Enjoy Banff** (☑1-888-313-6161; www.enjoybanff.com), which books rooms for more than 75 different lodgings.

Camping in Banff National Park is popular and easily accessible. There are 13 campgrounds to choose from, most along the Bow Valley Parkway or near Banff Town.

TOP CHOICE **Fairmont Banff Springs**   HOTEL $$$
(☑403-762-2211; www.fairmont.com/ banffsprings; 405 Spray Ave; r from $337; P@🛜🏊) Imagine crossing a Scottish castle with a French chateau and then plonking it in the middle of one of the world's most spectacular (and accessible) wilderness

areas. Rising like a Gaelic Balmoral above the trees at the base of Sulphur Mountain and visible from miles away, the Banff Springs is a wonder of early 1920s revivalist architecture and one of Canada's most iconic buildings. Wandering around its museumlike interior, it's easy to forget that it's also a hotel. On a par with its opulent common areas, rooms here are suitably exquisite even if the prices fall into the once-in-a-lifetime 'second-honeymoon' bracket.

Banff Rocky Mountain Resort HOTEL **$$**
(☑403-762-5531; www.bestofbanff.com; 1029 Banff Ave; r from $119; P☎🌐⛱) Being 4km out of town at the far, far end of Banff Ave is a small price to pay for the preferential prices and excellent all-round facilities here (including a hot tub, pool, tennis courts and cafe-restaurant). Added to this is the greater sense of detachment, quiet tree-filled grounds (it never feels like a 'resort') and generously sized bedrooms with sofas, desks and extra beds. There's a free shuttle into town (hourly) or you can walk or cycle 4km along the Legacy Trail.

Rimrock Resort Hotel HOTEL **$$$**
(☑403-762-3356; www.rimrockresort.com; 300 Mountain Ave; r queen/king $275/365; P@☎⛱) Further up the hill but slightly further down the price bracket than the Fairmont is the Rimrock, another plush spectacularly located hotel next door to the hot springs which gets understandably overshadowed by its famous neighbor. Controversially located in a wildlife corridor on the slopes of Sulphur Mountain, the views here are nonetheless inspiring. Mountain decadence coats the chalet-like interior, the restaurant (Eden) is considered fine dining, and the rooms almost match the stunning outdoor vistas. Worth every penny.

Tunnel Mountain Village CAMPGROUND **$**
(☑877-737-3783; www.pccamping.ca; Tunnel Mountain Rd; tent/RV sites $27.40/38.20; P) It's hard to imagine this campground filling its nearly 1000 sites, but come summer it's bursting at the seams with holidaymakers from around the globe. Located at the top of Tunnel Mountain with sites among the trees, it's not nearly as grim as it sounds. Part of it is open during winter, too, so if you want to sleep under canvas at -20°C, they'll let you do it here.

HI-Banff Alpine Centre HOSTEL **$**
(☑403-762-4122; www.hihostels.ca; 801 Hidden Ridge Way; dm/d from $40/135; P@☎) Banff's best hostel is near the top of Tunnel Mountain and well away from the madness of Banff Ave. Walkers will find the commute a good workout, and their efforts will not go unrewarded. The buildings are finished in classic mountain lodge style but without classic mountain lodge prices. There are clean, comfortable accommodations in bunk rooms and a few doubles; fireplaces in the common areas and good views top it all off. The public bus runs right by the front door, so don't let the location deter you.

Fox Hotel & Suites HOTEL **$$$**
(☑800-760-8500; www.bestofbanff.com; 461 Banff Ave; d from $220; P@☎⛱) Banff's newest hotel opened in 2007 and justifies its four-star billing with an eye for the aesthetic and great attention to detail. Bright, modern rooms have retro-patterned wallpaper and unique interesting wall-prints, while the reception has enough trickling water to invoke flashbacks of Rome. The crème de la crème is the inspired recreation of the Cave & Basin springs in the hot tub area with an open hole in the roof that gives out to the sky. The bar-restaurant is called Chilis and serves, among other things, excellent margaritas. The town is a 10-minute walk away.

Banff Caribou Lodge HOTEL **$$**
(☑403-762-5887; www.bestofbanff.com; 521 Banff Ave; d/ste $149/229; P@☎⛱) One of the posher places in the locally run Banff Lodging Co empire (who don it three-and-a-half stars), the Caribou fits the classic stereotype of a mountain lodge with its log and stone exterior, giant lobby fireplace and general alpine coziness. Aside from 189 comfy rooms, you get free local bus passes here, a heated underground car park, an on-site Keg Steakhouse, and a hard-to-avoid spa with various pools and treatment rooms.

Inns of Banff HOTEL **$$**
(☑403-762-4581; www.bestofbanff.com; 600 Banff Ave; r from $129; P@☎⛱) The last hotel on Banff Ave and slightly out of the hustle and bustle, there are some good deals to be found here. Though the architecture is a little passé, there are loads of facilities including both indoor and outdoor pools, ski and bike rentals, and a Japanese restaurant.

Rundlestone Lodge HOTEL **$$$**
(☑403-762-2201; www.rundlestone.com; 537 Banff Ave; d/ste from $179/339; P☎⛱) This place is filled with pseudo old-English

charm, complete with Masterpiece Theater chairs in the lobby. The standard rooms are fairly, well... standard; but splash out for a family or Honeymoon suite that comes with a kitchen, fireplace and loft. The centrally located indoor pool is a nice feature and the obligatory Banff hotel restaurant – this one's called Toloulous – makes a game attempt at food with a Creole twist.

Samesun Banff HOSTEL **$**
(☎403-762-5521; www.banffhostel.com; 449 Banff Ave; dm/d $32/129; P@☎) One of a quintet of western Canada hostels (the other four are in BC), the Samesun is zanier, edgier and a little cheaper than the other local budget digs. Features include a large central courtyard with barbecue, compact four- or eight-person dorms, an on-site bar, complimentary breakfast plus a selection of hotel-style rooms in an adjacent 'chalet' (they're billed as four-star standard though they're not quite the Fox). The clientele is international, backpacker and young (or young at heart).

Irwin's Mountain Inn HOTEL **$$**
(☎403-762-4566; www.irwinsmountaininn.com; 429 Banff Ave; d from $149; P@☎☎) A marginal drop in price and quality on the upper echelons of Banff Ave lands you in Irwin's where the rooms are verging on motel-like and the decor is more 'plastic' than granite. Not surprisingly, the place is popular with families who take advantage of the hot tub, steam room, fitness center and complimentary continental breakfast.

Banff Y Mountain Lodge HOSTEL **$**
(☎403-762-3560; www.ymountainlodge.com; 102 Spray Ave; dm $33, d with shared/private bathroom $88/99; P@☎) The YWCA is Banff's swankiest hostel option offering dorm rooms along with private family-orientated accommodations down by the river.

Bumpers Inn MOTEL **$$**
(☎403-762-3386; www.bumpersinn.com; 603 Banff Ave; r from $125; P☎) Banff provides a rare no-frills motel in bog standard Bumpers, which offers zero pretension, but plenty of financial savings. The town is a 15-minute walk away.

Two Jack Lakeside CAMPGROUND **$**
(Minnewanka Loop Dr; tent sites from $27.40; ☺mid-May–mid-Sep; P) Right on Two Jack Lake and the most scenic of the Banff area campgrounds, Lakeside fills its 74 nonreservable sites quickly.

✖ Eating

Banff dining is more than just hiker food. Sushi and foie gras have long embellished the restaurants of Banff Ave and some of the more elegant places will inspire dirty hikers to return to their hotel rooms and take a shower before pulling up a pew. Aside from the establishments below, many of Banff's hotels have their own excellent on-site restaurants that welcome nonguests. AAA Alberta beef makes an appearance on even the most exotic à la carte.

TOP CHOICE **Coyote's Deli & Grill** FUSION **$$**
(www.coyotesbanff.com; 206 Caribou St; lunch mains $8-14, dinner mains $20; ☺7:30am-10:30pm) Coyote's is best at lunchtime when you can bunk off hiking and choose a treat from the deli and grill menu inflected with a strong southwestern slant. Perch on a stool and listen to the behind-the-bar banter as you order up flatbreads, seafood cakes, quesadillas or some interesting soups (try the sweet potato and corn chowder).

Eddie Burger & Bar BURGERS **$$**
(www.theeddieburgerbar.ca; Caribou St; burgers $13) Avoid the stereotypes. The Eddie might appear pretentious (black leather seats and mood lighting), and its name may contain the word 'burger,' but it welcomes all types (including exhausted hikers and kids) and its gourmet meals-in-a-bun are subtler and far less greasy than your standard Albertan patty. Try the Spicy Italian or the Mexican and water it down with a Kokanee beer.

Melissa's Restaurant STEAKHOUSE **$$**
(www.melissasrestaurant.com; 218 Lynx St; pizzas/steaks from $18/21; ☺7am-10pm) Melissa's is a casual ketchup-on-the-table type of place in an old heritage building dating from 1928. It's huge in the local community and has an equally huge selection of food and price ranges. Nonetheless, its brunch, dinnertime steaks and deep-dish pizzas are probably its most defining dishes.

Maple Leaf Grille CANADIAN **$$$**
(www.banffmapleleaf.com; 137 Banff Ave; mains $20-40) With plenty of local and foreign plaudits, the Maple Leaf eschews all other pretensions in favor of one defining word: 'Canadian.' Hence, the menu is anchored by BC salmon, East Coast cod, Albertan beef and Okanagan Wine Country salad... you get the drift. All very patriotic – and tasty.

Giorgio's Trattoria   ITALIAN $$

(www.giorgiosbanff.com; 219 Banff Ave; mains from $16; ☉5-10pm) Slightly fancier than your average salt-of-the-earth trattoria, Giorgio's, nonetheless, serves up authentic Italian classics like osso bucco risotto and a fine pear and gorgonzola pizza mixed with the odd Alberta inflection (Buffalo papardelle!). The interior is elegant and there are prices to go with it (especially the wines).

Bison Mountain Bistro   FUSION $$

(www.thebison.ca; 211 Bear St; lunch mains from $11, dinner mains from $18; ☉11am-late Mon-Fri, 10am-late Sat & Sun) The Bison might look like it's full of trendy, well-off Calgarians dressed in expensive hiking gear, but its prices are actually very reasonable (nothing over $20). And rather than saturating the menu in AAA Alberta beef, there are big salads here and weird starch-heavy pizzas with butternut squash and rosemary potato toppings. The modern decor is set off by an outdoor patio and ground-floor boutique deli that serves up gourmet cheese and other such delights.

Le Beaujolais   FRENCH $$$

(☎403-762-2712; www.lebeaujolaisbanff.com; Banff Ave at Buffalo St; 3-/6-course meals $68/95; ☉6-10pm) Stick the word 'French' in the marketing lingo and out come the ironed napkins, waiters in ties, snails (billed as 'escargot' because it makes them sound so much more palatable) and elevated prices. Beaujolais might not be everybody's post-hiking cup of tea, but if you just came here to gaze romantically at the mountains, why not do it over wild boar, bison and foie gras.

Evelyn's Coffee Bar   CAFE $

(201 Banff Ave; mains $6; ☉6.30am-11pm) Pushing Starbucks onto the periphery, Evelyn's parades four downtown locations all on or within spitting distance of Banff Ave. Dive in to any one of them for wraps, pies and – best of all – its own selection of giant homemade cookies.

Bruno's Cafe & Grill   BREAKFAST, BURGERS $

(304 Caribou St; mains from $10; ☉8am-10pm) While other joints stop serving breakfasts at 11am, Bruno's keeps going all day replenishing the appetites of mountain men (and women) as it once replenished its one-time Swiss guide owner, Bruno Engler. A kind of greasy spoon meets pub, the walls are decorated with antique ski gear and the crowd at the next table could well be last night's live band refueling for tonight's gig.

The formidable Mountain Breakfast ($17) is served in a basket and requires a Mt Rundle-sized appetite.

Saltlik   STEAKHOUSE $$

(www.saltliksteakhouse.com; 221 Bear St; mains from $18; ☉11am-2am) With rib-eye in citrus rosemary butter and peppercorn NY striploin on the menu, Saltlik is clearly no 'Plain Jane' steakhouse knocking out flavorless T-bones. No, this polished dining room abounds with rustic elegance and a list of steaks the length of many establishments' entire menu. In a town not short on steak-providers, this could be No 1.

Magpie & Stump   MEXICAN $$

(203 Caribou St; mains $9-14; ☉noon-2am) Classic musty cantina full of dreadlocked Sol-swigging snowboarders where you feel it's almost your dinnertime duty to demolish an overloaded plate of oven-finished chicken enchiladas with a tangy side relish.

⬚ Wild Flour   CAFE $

(www.wildflourbakery.ca; 211 Bear St; mains from $5; ☉7am-7pm; ⬚) Banff's antidote to Tim Hortons is heavy on organic, vegan and frankly strange-looking cakes, pastries and cinnamon buns backed up with free-trade, organic coffee. They also bake their own bread.

Cows   ICE CREAM $

(www.cows.ca; 134 Banff Ave; ice cream from $3.50; ☉11am-9pm) A Prince Edward Island import, Cow's ice cream is legendary out east but this is one of only two branches in western Canada. Bypass the tacky T-shirts and choose from 32 extra-creamy flavors.

⬚ Drinking & Entertainment

Throw a stone in Banff Ave and you're more likely to hit a gap-year Australian than a local. For drinking and entertainment, follow the Sydney accents to local watering holes or look through the listings in the 'Summit Up' section of the weekly *Banff Crag & Canyon* newspaper.

TOP CHOICE St James's Gate Olde Irish Pub   PUB

(www.stjamesgatebanff.com; 205 Wolf St; mains from $10; ☉11am-1am Sun-Thu, to 2am Fri & Sat) As Celts pretty much opened up western Canada and gave their name to the town of Banff, it's hardly surprising to find an Irish pub in the park and rather a good one at that. Aside from stout on tap and a healthy selection of malts, St James's offers classic pub grub such as burgers and stew.

Tommy's Neighbourhood Pub PUB
(www.tommysneighbourhoodpub.com; 120 Banff Ave) Tommy's pub grub menu stretches to crab cakes and spinach artichoke dip. More importantly for traditionalists there's good draft beer, a darts board, and plenty of opportunity to meet the kind of globe-trotting mavericks who have made Banff their temporary home.

Wild Bill's Legendary Saloon BAR
(www.wbsaloon.com; 201 Banff Ave) Cowboys – where would Alberta be without them? Check this bar out if you're not into line-dancing, calf-roping, karaoke and live music of the twangy Willy Nelson variety. The saloon is named after Wild Bill Peyto, a colorful 'local' character who was actually born and raised in that not-so-famous cowboy county of Kent in England.

Elk & Oarsman PUB
(www.elkandoarsman.com; 119 Banff Ave) Up-stairs with a crow's-nest view of Banff Ave, this is the town's most refined pub. The rooftop patio is prime real estate in the summer and the kitchen will fix you up with some good food if you so desire.

Rose & Crown PUB
(www.roseandcrown.ca; 202 Banff Ave) Banff's oldest pub (since 1985!) is a fairly standard British-style boozer with pool tables and a rooftop patio. Out of all the town's drinking houses, it is best known for its live music, which raises the rafters seven nights a week – everything from communal singalongs to Seattle grunge.

Hoodoo Club NIGHTCLUB
(137 Banff Ave) If you came to Banff to go nightclubbing look no further than this chic joint where you can drink, dance and pose not a mile from where wild animals roam.

Banff Centre THEATER
(www.banffcentre.ca; 107 Tunnel Mountain Dr) A cultural center in a national park? Banff never ceases to surprise. This is the cultural hub of the Bow Valley – con-certs, art exhibitions and the popular Banff Mountain Film Festival are all held here.

Lux Cinema Centre CINEMA
(229 Bear St) The local movie house screens first-run films.

Information

There are coin-fed internet terminals (per hour $6) in malls and hotels throughout town.

Banff Information Centre (www.parkscanada. gc.ca/banff; 224 Banff Ave; ◷8am-8pm Jun-Sep, 9am-5pm Oct-May) Offices for Parks Canada.

Banff/Lake Louise Tourism Bureau (www. banfflakelouise.com; ◷8am-8pm May-Sep, 9am-noon & 1-5pm Oct-Apr) In the same build-ing as the Banff Information Centre; advice on services and activities in and around Banff.

Banff Warden Office Dispatch Line (✆403-762-1470) Open 24 hours for nonemergency backcountry problems.

Custom House Currency Exchange (211 Banff Ave; ◷9am-10pm) In the Park Ave Mall.

Main Post Office (204 Buffalo St; ◷8:30am-5:30pm Mon-Fri, 9am-5pm Sat)

Mineral Springs Hospital (✆403-762-2222; 301 Lynx St; ◷24hr) Emergency medical treatment.

Underground (211 Banff Ave; internet per hr $6) Numerous terminals.

Getting There & Away
The nearest airport is in Calgary.

Greyhound Canada (327 Railway Ave) oper-ates buses to Calgary ($29, two hours, six daily), Vancouver ($130, 14 hours, five daily) and points in between.

Brewster Transportation (www.brewster. ca) will pick you up from your hotel and services Jasper ($66, 4¾ hours, daily) and Lake Louise ($15, one hour, multiple buses daily).

SunDog Tour Co (www.sundogtours.com) also runs transport between Banff and Jasper (adult/child $59/35, four hours, daily).

All of the major car-rental companies (see p324) have branches in Banff Town. During sum-mer all the cars might be reserved in advance, so call ahead. If you're flying into Calgary, reserving a car at the airport (where the fleets are huge) may yield a better deal than waiting to pick up a car when you reach Banff Town.

Getting Around
Shuttle buses operate daily year-round be-tween Calgary International Airport and Banff. Buses are less frequent in the spring and fall. Companies include **Brewster Transportation** (www.brewster.ca) and **Banff Airporter** (www. banffairporter.com). The adult fare for both is around $50 one way and $98 round-trip.

Banff Transit (✆403-762-1215) runs four hybrid 'Roam' buses on two main routes. Stops include Tunnel Mountain, the Rimrock Resort Hotel, Banff Upper Hot Springs, Fairmont Banff

ANN MORROW: EXTERNAL RELATIONS OFFICER – BANFF NATIONAL PARK

What challenges does Banff National Park face?

Like every national park, Banff exists to protect the health and sustainability of its natural heritage, while providing opportunities to enjoy the activities and discoveries that are possible in this wild and wonderful place. We have grizzly bears, cougars and wolves in the park, and more than 3 million visitors a year, so one challenge is teaching people how to be 'nature-smart' here in the Rocky Mountains: how to give wild animals the space that they need to survive. To allow wildlife to wander freely through their natural ranges, Parks Canada has also built wildlife overpasses and underpasses all along the Trans-Canada Hwy, which traverses the park.

Does the park actively market for new visitors?

Banff gets a lot of promotion, from national, regional and local tourism organizations to Parks Canada to travel guidebooks. We have something very special here – it's our job to share this treasure with all Canadians, and the world (we're also a Unesco World Heritage site). At the same time we have a legal mandate to protect the ecological health of the park for the future generations. Our park management plan, created in consultation with tourism, environmental, community and aboriginal groups, directs us to meet high standards of resource protection, visitor experience and education in the park.

Is Banff too commercialized?

Some people think so. For others it's the easy accessibility of Banff, and the services the town offers, that make this Canada's favorite (as well as first and most famous) national park. What locals love about Banff is that you can head out and enjoy an awe-inspiring, wilderness experience on any of our 1500km of trails in the park, then return to town for sushi and maybe a ballet.

How do you enjoy Banff?

For me it's about being open to the gifts that nature chooses to give, the magical moments that can happen at any time of year, in any weather or any part of the park. Rocky Mountain nature has its own rules and rhythms that you can only get to know by really paying attention over time, and that's part of the appeal. Even though I've lived here most of my life, every time I get outside I'm inspired in some way.

Springs and all the hotels along Banff Ave. Route maps are printed on all bus stops. Buses start running at 6:30am and finish at 11pm; the fare is $2/1 per adult/child.

Taxis can easily be hailed on the street, especially on Banff Ave. Otherwise call **Banff Taxi** (☑ 403-762-4444). Taxis are metered.

Lake Louise

Famous for its teahouses, grizzly bears, grand hotel, skiing, Victoria Glacier, hiking and lakes (yes, plural), Lake Louise is what makes Banff National Park the phenomenon it is, an awe-inspiring natural feature that is impossible to describe without resorting to shameless clichés. Yes, there is a placid turquoise-tinted lake

here; yes, the natural world feels (and is) tantalizingly close; and yes, the water is surrounded by an amphitheater of finely chiseled mountains that Michelangelo couldn't have made more aesthetically pleasing. Then there are the much commented-on 'crowds,' plus a strangely congruous (or incongruous – depending on your viewpoint) lump of towering concrete known as Chateau Lake Louise. But, frankly, who cares about the waterside claustrophobia? Lake Louise isn't about dodging other tourists. It's about viewing what should be everyone's god-given right to see.

When you're done with gawping, romancing or pledging undying love to your partner on the shimmering lakeshore, try hiking up into the mountainous amphitheater behind. Lake Louise also has a widely lauded ski resort and some equally enticing cross-country options. Thirteen kilometers to the southeast along a winding seasonal road is another spectacularly located body of water, Moraine Lake that some heretics claim is even more beguiling than its famous sibling.

The village of Lake Louise, just off Hwy 1, is little more than an outdoor shopping mall, a gas station and a handful of hotels. The object of all your yearnings is 5km away by car or an equitable distance on foot along the pleasantly wooded Louise Creek trail, if the bears aren't out on patrol (check at the visitors center).

The **Lake Louise Visitor Centre** (Samson Mall, Lake Louise village; ⊘9am-8pm May-Sep, to 5pm Oct & Apr, to 4pm Nov-Mar) has some good geological displays, a Parks Canada desk and a small film theater.

The Bow Valley Parkway between Banff Town and Lake Louise is a slightly slower but much more scenic drive than Hwy 1.

◉ Sights

Lake Louise   NATURAL SITE
Named for Queen Victoria's otherwise anonymous fourth daughter (who also lent her name to the province), Lake Louise is a place that requires multiple viewings. Aside from the standard picture-postcard shot (blue sky, even bluer lake), try visiting at six in the morning, at dusk in August, in the October rain or after a heavy winter storm.

You can rent an unethically priced canoe from the **Lake Louise Boathouse** (per hr $45; ⊘9am-4pm Jun-Oct) and go for a paddle around the lake. Don't fall overboard – the water is freezing.

Moraine Lake   NATURAL SITE
The scenery will dazzle you long before you reach the spectacular deep-teal colored waters of Moraine Lake. The lake is set in the Valley of the Ten Peaks, and the narrow winding road leading to it offers views of these distant imposing summits. With little hustle or bustle and lots of beauty, many people prefer the more rugged and remote setting of Moraine Lake to Lake Louise. There are some excellent day hikes from the lake, or rent a boat at the **Moraine Lake Boathouse** (per hr $40; ⊘9am-4pm Jun-Oct) and paddle through the glacier-fed waters.

Moraine Lake Rd and its facilities are open from June to early October.

Lake Louise Sightseeing Gondola
(www.lakelouisegondola.com; 1 Whitehorn Rd; round-trip adult/child $25.95/12.95; ⊘9am-5pm) To the east of Hwy 1, this sightseeing gondola will lever you to the top of Mt Whitehorn, where the views of the lake and Victoria Glacier are phenomenal. At the top, there's a restaurant and a Wildlife Interpretive Centre where you can partake in 45-minute **guided hikes** (per person $5; ⊘11am, 1pm & 3pm).

🏃 Activities

Hiking
In Lake Louise beauty isn't skin-deep. The hikes behind the stunning views are just as impressive. Most of the classic walks start from Lake Louise and Moraine Lake. Some are straightforward, while others will give even the most seasoned alpinist reason to huff and puff.

From Chateau Lake Louise, two popular day walks head out to alpine-style teahouses perched above the lake. The shorter but slightly harder hike is the 3.4km grunt past **Mirror Lake** up to the Lake Agnes Teahouse (see p226) on its eponymous body of water. After tea and scones you can trek 1.6km further and higher to the view-embellished **Big Beehive** lookout and Canada's most unexpectedly sited gazebo. Continue on this path down to the Highline Trail to link up with the **Plain of Six Glaciers**, or approach it independently from Chateau Lake Louise along the lakeshore (5.6km one way). Either way, be sure to get close enough for ice-crunching views of the Victoria Glacier. There's another teahouse on this route that supplements its brews with thick-cut sandwiches and spirit-lifting mugs of hot chocolate with marshmallows.

From Moraine Lake, the walk to **Sentinel Pass**, via the stunning **Larch Valley**, is best in the fall when the leaves are beginning to turn. A strenuous day walk with outstanding views of Mt Temple and the surrounding peaks, the hike involves a steep scree-covered last push to the pass If you're lucky you might spy some rock climbers scaling The Grand Sentinel – a 200m-tall rock spire nearby.

Shorter and easier, the 6km out-and-back **Consolation Lakes Trail** offers that typical Banff juxtaposition of crowded parking lot disappearing almost instantly into raw, untamed wilderness.

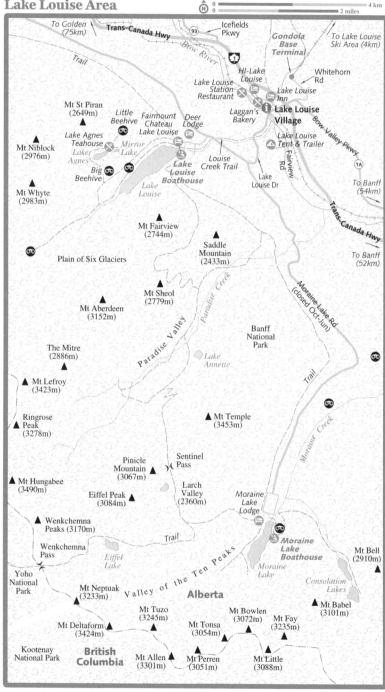

In recent years there has been a lot of bear activity in the Moraine Lake area. Because of this, a minimum group size of four has been imposed by the park on some hikes during berry-gathering season (June to September). If you're arriving solo, check on the noticeboard in the information center in Lake Louise for other hikers looking to make up groups.

Rock Climbing

The Back of the Lake is one of the classic crags in the Canadian Rockies. Steep, edgy limestone is the hallmark of this stellar rock-climbing area. The access is a dream: just stroll along the lakeside path until you see a route that tickles your fancy and away you go. There are both traditional climbs and sport routes. For nonclimbers, this is a great area to observe some rock stars at close range and even ask them a few questions. From a climber's perspective, the only downside to this awesome cragging spot are the tourists who insist on watching like you're a zoo animal and the inane questions they ask.

There is a multitude of alpine climbing adventures to be had in the Lake Louise area. Classic snow and ice routes such as Mt Temple and Fairview draw climbers from around the world. Check with Parks Canada for details on conditions and access. For a guided experience, talk to Canmore-based Yamnuska Mountain Adventures (☎866-678-4164; www.yamnuska.com). Its staff can meet you in Lake Louise and show you the ropes.

Skiing & Snowboarding

Lake Louise Ski Area (www.skilouise.com; lift tickets from $75), 60km west of Banff Town, is marginally larger than Sunshine Village but gets less natural snow. The ample runs containing plenty of beginner and intermediate terrain are on four separate mountains, so it's closer to a European ski experience than anything else on offer in Canada. The front side is a good place to get your ski legs back with a good selection of simpler stuff and fantastic views. On the backside there are some great challenges to find, from the knee-pulverizing moguls of Paradise Bowl to the high-speed cruising of the Larch area. Make sure you grab a deck burger at the Temple Lodge – it's all part of the whole experience.

🛏 Sleeping

Lake Louise has a campground, a hostel, a couple of mid-priced inns, and a handful of places that fall into the 'special night' category for many travelers.

TOP CHOICE Moraine Lake Lodge   HOTEL $$$

(☎800-522-2777; www.morainelakelodge.com; d $345-599; ☺Jun-Sep; P) Few people would shirk at an opportunity to hang around Moraine Lake for a day or three – and here's your chance. Though nearly as pricey as the Chateau, you'll get a totally different experience here: think small, intimate, personal, private and with famously good service. While billed as rustic (ie no TVs), the rooms and cabins offer mountain-inspired luxury with real fireplaces and balconies overlooking *that* view. There's a fine-dining restaurant on-site which wins equal plaudits.

Fairmont Chateau Lake Louise   HOTEL $$$

(☎403-522-3511; www.fairmont.com; Lake Louise Dr; d from $450; P@🛜🐾) The opulent twin of Banff Springs enjoys one of the world's most enviable locations on the shores of Lake Louise. Originally built by the Canadian Pacific Railway in the 1890s, the hotel was added to in 1925 and 2004. While opinions differ on its architectural merits, few deny the luxury and romance of its facilities that include a spa, fine dining, a mini-museum, fine views and an unforgettably grandiose decor. Rooms are comfortable, if a little generic.

HI-Lake Louise   HOSTEL $

(☎403-522-2200; www.hihostels.ca; Village Rd; dm/d from $34/99; P) This is what a hostel should be – clean, friendly, affordable and full of interesting travelers. The building itself is a stunning example of Rockies architecture, with raw timber and stone melding to a rustic aesthetic masterpiece. The dorm rooms are fairly standard, but beware of the private rooms: they are on the small side and a bit overpriced.

Deer Lodge   HOTEL $$

(☎403-410-7417; www.crmr.com; 109 Lake Louise Dr; r from $119; P) Tucked demurely behind the Chateau Lake Louise, the Deer Lodge is another historic throwback dating from the 1920s. But, although the rustic exterior and creaky corridors can't have changed much since the days of bobbed hair and F Scott Fitzgerald, the refurbished rooms are another matter, replete with new comfy beds and smart boutique-like furnishings. TV addicts, beware – there aren't any.

Lake Louise Inn HOTEL **$$**
(403-522-3791; www.lakelouiseinn.com; 210 Village Rd; d from $119; P @ ✈) A large, sprawling resort situated close to the village which has its merits, including a pool, restaurant and a tiny historic tearoom. The posher, less motel-like rooms in block five have the best views.

Lake Louise Tent & Trailer CAMPGROUND **$**
(403-522-3833; off Lake Louise Dr; tent/RV sites $27.40/32.30; mid-May–Oct; P) This is the closest campground to the village and your best option if you plan to sleep in a million-star hotel. It's a vast place that has great views of Mt Temple. Steer clear of the sites near the railroad tracks as the thundering trains do wonders for keeping you up all night.

✗ Eating

If you can't scrape together the $39 necessary for afternoon tea in the Lakeview Lounge at the Chateau Lake Louise, reconvene to one of the following.

TOP CHOICE **Lake Agnes Teahouse** CAFE **$**
(Lake Agnes Trail; snacks from $3; Jun-Oct) You thought the view from Lake Louise was good? Wait till you get up to this precariously perched alpine-style teahouse that seems to hang in the clouds beside ethereal Lake Agnes and its adjacent waterfall. The small log cabin runs on gas power and is hike-in only (3.4km uphill from the Chateau). Perhaps it's the thinner air or the seductiveness of the surrounding scenery but the rustic $6 tea and scones here taste just as good as the $39 spread at the Chateau Lake Louise.

Lake Louise Station Restaurant
CANADIAN **$$**
(mains from $14; 11:30am-9:30pm) Restaurants with a theme have to be handled so carefully – thankfully this railway-inspired eatery, at the end of Sentinel Rd, does it just right. You can either dine in the station among the discarded luggage or in one of the dining cars, which are nothing short of elegant. The food is simple yet effective. A must-stop for trainspotters.

Laggan's Bakery BAKERY **$**
(403-522-2017; Samson Mall; mains from $5; 6am-8pm) Laggan's (named after Lake Louise's original settlement) is a cafeteria/bakery with limited seating that's famously busy in the summer. The pastries and savories aren't legendary, but they're handy hiking snacks and tend to taste better the hungrier you get. The pizza bagels are worth a special mention.

ℹ Getting There & Around

The bus terminal is basically a marked stop at Samson Mall. The easiest way to get here from Banff is by car or Greyhound bus. See p221 for bus service details.

Jasper Town & Around

Take Banff, half the annual visitor count, increase the total land area by 40%, and multiply the number of bears, elk, moose and caribou by the power of three. The result: Jasper, a larger, less-trammeled more wildlife-rich version of the other Rocky Mountains parks whose rugged backcountry wins admiring plaudits for its vertiginous river canyons, adrenalin-charged mountain-bike trails, rampartlike mountain ranges and delicate ecosystems.

Most people enter Jasper Town from the south via the magnificently Gothic Icefields Parkway that meanders up from Lake Louise amid foaming waterfalls and glacier-sculpted mountains, including iconic Mt Edith Cavell, easily visible from the townsite. Another option is to take a legendary VIA train from either Edmonton or BC through foothills imbued with fur-trading and aboriginal history.

Stacked up against Canada's other national parks, Jasper scores highly for its hiking, pioneering history (it's the country's eighth-oldest park), easy-to-view wildlife and hut-to-hut backcountry skiing possibilities. Similarly, bike enthusiasts consistently laud it as having one of the best single-track cycling networks in North America.

◉ Sights

Jasper Tramway   LANDMARK
(Map p208; www.jaspertramway.com; Whistlers Mountain Rd; adult/child $29/15; Apr-Oct) If the average, boring views from Jasper just aren't blowing your hair back, go for a ride up this sightseeing tramway which is open 9am to 8pm from June to August and closes earlier in the shoulder seasons. The vista is sure to take your breath away, with views, on a clear day, of the Columbia Icefield 75km to the south. From the top of the tram you can take the steep 1.5km hike to the summit of Whistlers Mountain where

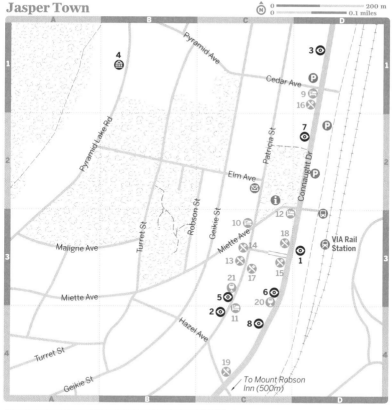

Jasper Town

the outlook is even better. The tramway is about 7km south of Jasper Town along Whistlers Mountain Rd, off the Icefields Parkway.

Miette Hot Springs SPA
(Map p208; www.parkscanada.gc.ca/hotsprings; Miette Rd; adult/child/family $6.05/5.15/18.45; ⊙10:30am-9pm late May-Jun) A good spot for a

soak is the remote Miette Hot Springs, 61km northeast of Jasper off Hwy 16, near the park boundary. The soothing waters are kept at a pleasant 39°C and are especially enjoyable when the fall snow is falling on your head and steam envelops the crowd. There are a couple of hot pools and a cold one, too – just to get the heart going – so it's best to stick a toe in before doing your cannonball. Opening hours are slightly longer in high summer.

You can hike 1km from the parking lot to the **source** of the springs which is overlooked by the original aquacenter built in the 1930s.

Patricia & Pyramid Lakes NATURAL SITE
There's nothing like seeing the mountains reflected in a small deserted alpine lake. These two lakes, a convenient 7km from town, fit that order nicely. Abundant activities are available on the water, with canoes, kayaks and windsurfers available for rent. For those wanting to stay dry, there are hiking and horseback riding trails, too. Keep your eyes peeled for animals – these are prime spotting locations.

Lakes Annette & Edith NATURAL SITE
On the opposite side of the highway to the town, Lakes Annette and Edith are popular for water activities in the summer and skating in the winter. If you're brave and it's very hot, Annette is good for a quick summer dip – just remember the water was in a glacier not too long ago! Edith is more frequented by kayakers and boaters. Both are ringed by cycling/hiking trails and picnic areas. The trail that circumnavigates Lake Annette is wheelchair accessible.

Jasper Town to Maligne Lake SCENIC DRIVE
The inspiring 46km drive between Jasper and Maligne Lake is well worth doing. The road twists and turns and it would seem that at every corner there is an opportunity to see some wildlife. This is one of the best places in Jasper to look for deer, elk, moose and, if you're lucky, bear. The best time to see wildlife is early in the morning.

Maligne Canyon NATURAL SITE
A steep, narrow gorge shaped by a river flowing at its base, this canyon at its narrowest is only a few meters wide and drops a stomach-turning 50m beneath your feet. Crossed by six bridges, various trails lead out from the parking area on Maligne Lake Rd. In the winter, waterfalls freeze solid into sheets of white ice and are popular with ice climbers.

Maligne Lake NATURAL SITE
Almost 50km from Jasper at the end of the road that bears its name, 22km-long Maligne Lake is the recipient of a lot of hype. It is billed as one of the most beautiful lakes within the park and there's no denying its aesthetics: the baby-blue water and a craning circle of rocky, photogenic peaks are feasts for the eyes. Although the north end of the lake is heavy with the summer tour bus brigade, most of the rest of the shoreline is accessible only by foot or boat – hence it's quieter. Numerous campgrounds are available lakeside and are ideal for adventurous kayakers and backcountry hikers. Moose and grizzly bears are also sometimes seen here.

The **Maligne Lake Boathouse** (boat rentals per hr/day $30/90) rents canoes for a paddle around the lake. Not many people paddle all the way to Spirit Island – the lake's most classic view – it would take you all day. If you are really keen to see it, **Maligne Tours** (Map p227; ☎780-852-3370; www.malignelake.com; 627 Patricia St; adult/child $55/27.50; ☉10am-5pm May-Oct) will zip you out there. The company runs a 1½-hour boat tour to the island.

Jasper-Yellowhead Museum & Archives MUSEUM
(Map p227; www.jaspermuseum.org; 400 Pyramid Lake Rd; admission $5; ☉10am-5pm summer, 10am-5pm Thu-Sun rest of year) Poke your head into this museum if it's raining, snowing or too hot. Even if the weather is nice, it does an ample job of telling the Jasper story and the stories of those who arrived here to make it into the town it is today.

🏃 Activities

Cycling
Single-track mountain biking is Jasper's forte and most routes are within striking distance of the townsite. Flatter, on-road options include the long-distance grunt along the Icefields Parkway. The holy grail for experienced off-road bikers is the **Valley of the Five Lakes**, varied and scenic with plenty of places where you can let rip. For more information, get a copy of *Mountain Biking Guide, Jasper National Park* from the Jasper Information Centre.

Vicious Cycle (Map p227; www.viciouscycle canada.com; 630 Connaught Dr; per day from $24;

9am-6pm) can sort out bike rentals and offer additional trail tips.

Hiking

Even when judged against other Canadian national parks, Jasper's trail network is mighty, and with comparatively fewer people than its sister park to the south, you've a better chance of seeing more wildlife and less humans.

Initiate yourself on the interpretative Discovery Trail, an 8km easy hike that encircles the townsite highlighting its natural, historical and railway heritage.

Other short, less radical trails include the 3.2km Mary Schäffer Loop by Maligne Lake named for one of the earliest European visitors to the area; the Old Fort Loop (3.5km) to the site of an old fur-trading post; and the 9km Mina and Riley Lakes Loop that leads out directly from the townsite.

Further away and slightly harder is the famous 9.1km Path of the Glacier Trail below the impressive face of Mt Edith Cavell that takes you to the foot of the Angel Glacier through the flower-scattered Cavell meadows.

The blue riband multiday hike is the Skyline Trail, unusual in that almost all of its 46km are on or above the tree line, affording amazing cross-park views. The hike is usually split over two days, starting at Maligne Lake and emerging near Maligne Canyon on Maligne Lake Rd. You can pitch your tent in a campground or stay in the historic Shovel Pass Lodge.

The leaflet *Day-Hikers' Guide to Jasper National Park* has descriptions of most of the park's easy walks, while the backcountry visitors' guide *Jasper National Park* details longer trails and backcountry campsites and suggests itineraries for hikes of two to 10 days. If you're hiking overnight, you must obtain a backcountry permit (per person per night $10, or buy a season pass for $69) from Parks Canada in the Jasper Information Centre.

Horseback Riding

Incredible fully guided summer pack trips head into the roadless Tonquin Valley where you are bivouacked in the backcountry (but comfortable) Tonquin Amethyst Lake Lodge. The trips are run by Tonquin Valley Adventures (www.tonquinadventures.com; 3-/4-/5-day trips $795/1050/1295) and include accommodations, meals and complimentary fishing trips on Amethyst Lake.

Rock Climbing

Despite a preponderance of sedimentary rock, Jasper lures a large number of aspiring rock climbers. If you want a popular crag with an easy approach head out to the Rock Gardens located up the trail from 5th Bridge off Maligne Lake Rd. For traditional options, look to Roche Miette and Morro Peak. The more ambitious opt to summit Mt Edith Cavell. As with most Rockies climbing, a helmet and good route-finding skills are essential.

Those looking to learn the ropes can try Peter Amann (☑780-852-3237; www.incentre.net/pamann; 2-day courses $160), something of a Jasper legend who will introduce you to the sport with a two-day beginner course. If you just need equipment, visit Gravity Gear (Map p227; www.gravitygearjasper.com; 618 Patricia St).

Skiing & Snowboarding

Jasper National Park's only downhill ski area is Marmot Basin (Map p208; www.skimarmot.com; Marmot Basin Rd; full-day pass adult/child $72/58), which lies 19km southwest of town off Hwy 93A. Though not legendary, the presence of 86 runs and the longest high-speed quad chair-lift in the Rockies, mean Marmot is no pushover and its relative isolation compared to the trio of ski areas in Banff means shorter lift lines.

On-site are some cross-country trails and a predictably expensive day lodge, but no overnight accommodations. Seriously cold weather can drift in suddenly off the mountains, so dress with this in mind.

White-water Rafting

There's nothing like a glacial splashdown to fight the summer heat. The Jasper area has lots of good rafting opportunities, from raging to relaxed on the Maligne, Sunwapta and Athabasca Rivers. The season runs from May to September.

Maligne Rafting Adventures (Map p227; www.raftjasper.com; 616 Patricia St; trips from $59) Everything from float trips to class II and III adventures, plus the option of overnight trips.

Rocky Mountain River Guides (Map p227; www.rmriverguides.com; 626 Connaught Dr; trips from $59) Fun for beginners or experienced river-runners.

JASPER IN WINTER

Half of Jasper shuts down in the winter; the other half just adapts and metamorphoses into something just as good (if not better) than its summertime equivalent. Lakes become skating rinks, hiking and biking routes (and some roads) become cross-country skiing trails, waterfalls become ice climbs, and – last but by no means least – prices become far more reasonable.

The best natural outdoor skating rink is on Lac Beauvert in front of the Fairmont Jasper Park Lodge, an area that is floodlit after dark. More skating can be found 6km northeast of the townsite on Pyramid Lake.

The park has an incredible 200km of cross-country skiing trails. Routes less prone to an early snow melt are the **Pyramid Lake Fire Road**, the **Meeting of the Waters** (along a closed section of Hwy 93A), the **Moab Lake Trail** and the **Mt Edith Cavell Road**. Relatively safe, but dramatic backcountry skiing can be found in the Tonquin Valley where you can overnight in a couple of lodges. See www.tonquinvalley.com for more details.

Slightly less athletic is the iconic three-hour **Maligne Canyon Ice-walk** offered by **Jasper Adventure Centre** (Map p227; www.jasperadventurecentre.com; 618 Connaught Dr; adult/child $55/25), a walk through a series of frozen waterfalls viewable from December to April. Extremists tackle these slippery behemoths with rappels and ice axes.

🕏 Tours

There is a variety of tour companies and booking centers in Jasper. They run a whole host of tours, including trips to the icefields, train rides, boat rides, wildlife viewing, rafting, horseback riding and more.

Brewster Gray Line SIGHTSEEING
(Map p227; www.brewster.ca; 607 Connaught Dr)

Jasper Walks & Talks HIKES
(Map p227; www.walksntalks.com; 626 Connaught Dr)

SunDog Tour Company SIGHTSEEING
(Map p227; www.sundogtours.com; Connaught Dr)

🛏 Sleeping

Despite its reputation as a quiet antidote to Banff, Jasper's townsite still gets busy in the summer. Book ahead or consider visiting in the less crowded late winter/early spring shoulder season when the deserted mountainscapes (best accessed on cross-country skis) take on a whole new dimension.

Accommodations in Jasper are generally cheaper than Banff, but that's not really saying much. Jasper's 10 park campgrounds are open from mid-May to September/October. One (Wapiti) is partly open year-round. Four of them take reservations. For information, contact **Parks Canada** (☑780-852-6176; 500 Connaught Dr) at the Jasper Information Centre.

Several places outside the town proper offer bungalows (usually wooden cabins) that are only open in summer. There are considerable winter discounts.

TOP CHOICE **Park Place Inn** BOUTIQUE HOTEL $$$
(Map p227; ☑780-852-9970; www.parkplaceinn.com; 623 Patricia St; r from $229; @) Giving nothing away behind its rather drab exterior among a parade of downtown shops, the Park Place is a head-turner as soon as you ascend the stairs to its plush open lobby. The 14 self-proclaimed heritage rooms are well deserving of their superior status with marble surfaces, fine local art, claw-foot baths and a general air of refinement and luxury. The service is equally professional.

Fairmont Jasper Park Lodge HOTEL $$$
(☑780-852-3301, 800-441-1414; www.fairmont.com/jasper; 1 Old Lodge Rd; r from $500; ℗@☎) Sitting on the shore of Lake Beauvert and surrounded by manicured grounds and mountain peaks, this classic old lodge is deservedly popular. With a country-club-meets-1950s-holiday-camp air, the amenity-filled cabins and chalets are a throwback to a more opulent era. The lodge's gem is its main lounge, open to the public, with stupendous lake views. It's filled with log furniture, chandeliers and fireplaces and is the best place in town to write a postcard over

a quiet cocktail. There are often off-season discounts.

Tekarra Lodge
HOTEL $$

(☎780-852-3058; www.tekarralodge.com; Hwy 93A; d from $169; ☺May-Oct; Ⓟ) The most atmospheric cabins in the park are set next to the Athabasca River amid tall trees and splendid tranquility. Hardwood floors, wood-paneled walls plus fireplaces and kitchenettes inspire coziness. It's only 1km from the townsite, but has a distinct backcountry feel.

Whistlers Inn
HOTEL $$$

(Map p227; ☎780-852-9919; www.whistlersinn. com; cnr Connaught Dr & Miette Ave; r $195; @☎☎) A central location and above standard rooms give Whistlers an edge over many of its rivals. The rooftop hot tub alone is worth spending the night for – watch the sun dip behind the hills as the recuperative waters soak away the stress of the day. What more could you ask for?

Astoria Hotel
HOTEL $$$

(Map p227; ☎780-852-3351; www.astoriahotel. com; 404 Connaught Dr; d from $207; ☎) With its gabled Bavarian roof the Astoria is one of the town's most distinctive pieces of architecture and one of an original trio of Jasper hotels that has been owned by the same family since the 1920s. Journeyman rooms are functional and comfortable, and are bolstered by the presence of a downstairs bar (De'd Dog) and restaurant (Papa George's).

Athabasca Hotel
HOTEL $$

(Map p227; ☎780-852-3386; www.athabascaho tel.com; 510 Patricia St; r without/with bathroom $99/175; Ⓟ@☎) If you can take the stuffed moose heads, noisy downstairs bar-nightclub and service that is sometimes as fickle as the mountain weather, you'll have no problems at the Athabasca (or Atha-B, as it's known). Centrally located with an attached restaurant and small, but comfortable, rooms (many with shared bathroom) it's been around since 1929 and is probably the best bargain in town.

Coast Pyramid Lake Resort
HOTEL $$$

(☎780-852-4900; www.coasthotels.com; Pyramid Lake Rd; d from $249; Ⓟ) This large property has fantastic views of the lake and great access to it. The design is a bit strange, with a huge swath of concrete driveway bisecting the hotel. The chalet-style buildings fan up the hill, giving most rooms an unencumbered view of the lake. Ample opportunities for lake fun abound, with canoes for rent and a small beach to hang out on. The prices are a bit on the high side and it would do well to improve some of the finishing touches. The resort is closed October to April.

YHA Maligne Canyon
HOSTEL $

(Map p208; ☎1-877-852-0781; www.hihostels. ca; Maligne Lake Rd; dm $23; Ⓟ) Well positioned for winter cross-country skiing and summer sorties along the Skyline Trail, this very basic hostel is poised a little too close to the road to merit a proper 'rustic' tag. Die-hards can get back to nature with six-bed dorms, outhouse toilets and regular visits to the water pump.

Whistlers Campground
CAMPGROUND $

(Map p208; Whistlers Rd; tent/RV sites $22/36; ☺early May–mid-Oct; Ⓟ) Ever spent the night with 780 other campers? Well, here is your chance. This mini camping city isn't particularly private, but it is the closest option to Jasper Town. Unbelievably, it regularly fills up in the high season. There are interpretive programs, flush toilets and fire pits.

HI-Jasper
HOSTEL $

(Map p208; ☎780-852-3215; www.hihostels.ca; Whistlers Mountain Rd; dm/d $26/65; Ⓟ@☎) It would be easy to take a disliking to this hostel. With dorm rooms that sleep upward of 40 people, giving it that distinctive refugee camp feel, and a location just far enough from town that the walk is a killer, it's already two strikes down. Despite all of this though, it's a great place to stay. The proximity of roommates and relative isolation foster a real community feel, and the nice interior, friendly staff and pristine surroundings make it that much better.

Mount Robson Inn
MOTEL $$$

(off Map p227; ☎780-852-3327; www.mount robsoninn.com; 902 Connaught Dr; r from $255; Ⓟ✳@☎) A clean, plush place laid out motel-style on the edge of Jasper Town which offers hot tubs, on-site restaurant and a substantial complimentary breakfast.

Snaring River Campground
CAMPGROUND $

(Map p208; Hwy 16; tent sites $15; ☺mid-May–mid-Sep; Ⓟ) Situated 17km north of Jasper Town, this basic campground – the park's most primitive and isolated – is the perfect antidote to the busy campgrounds found elsewhere in the park.

Eating

Jasper's cuisine is mainly hearty post-hiking fare supplemented with a couple of fine-dining spots. Most of the restaurants are located in the town around Connaught Dr and Patricia St. Outlying nexuses such as Maligne Lake and The Whistlers have cafeteria-style restaurants that close in the winter.

TOP CHOICE The Other Paw
CAFE, BAKERY $

(Map p227; 610 Connaught Dr; mains $2; ⊙7am-10pm) An offshoot of The Bear's Paw, a larger cafe around the corner, The Other Paw offers the same insanely addictive mix of breads, pastries, muffins and coffee, but it stays open longer, plus it's right opposite the train station. The aromatic memory of its white chocolate and raspberry scones is enough to jerk your senses into action during the last few kilometers of a lengthy hike/bike/ski.

Fiddle River Seafood Co
SEAFOOD $$

(Map p227; 620 Connaught Dr; mains from $18; ⊙5-10pm) Being almost 1600km from the sea makes some customers understandably leery, but Jasper's premier seafood joint is no slouch. Pull up a seat near the window and tuck into one of the innovative creations, such as pumpkin seed-crusted trout.

Coco's Café
CAFE $

(Map p227; 608 Patricia St; mains from $5; ⊙8am-4pm) Coco's versus The Other Paw is a toss-up, though the former might just pip it on the breakfast front. There's not much room inside, but plenty of bodies are content to cram in to plan hikes, trade bear sightings or compare rucksack burns. Ethical eaters are well catered for with tofu scrambles and fair-trade coffee.

Andy's Bistro
FUSION $$$

(Map p227; ☑780-852-3323; 622 Patricia St; mains from $22; ⊙5-11pm) Following a new trend for fine-dining in outdoor adventure areas (led by Whistler), Andy's is one of two posh Jasper options where you can take off your filthy hiking boots and quaff one of 70 wines. The European-inspired menu (escargot, vol-au-vents, pan-fired veal) has various Indian and Asian inflections.

Something Else
MEDITERRANEAN, STEAKHOUSE $$

(Map p227; 621 Patricia St; mains $13-24) Essentially a Greek restaurant, Something Else wears many hats (American, Italian, Cajun) and doesn't always succeed. What it *is* good for is space (even on a Saturday night), decent beer, menu variety, copious kids' options and the good old homemade Greek stuff. Try the lamb or chicken souvlaki.

Jasper Pizza Place
PIZZA $

(Map p227; 402 Connaught Dr; mains from $8; ⊙11am-11pm) Ask a local (if you can find one) where to grab a cheap meal and, even money, they'll mention this place. There's a method to the queuing madness, if you're prepared to stick around long enough to fight for a table. Not surprisingly, the much-sought-after pizzas are rather good.

View Restaurant
FAST FOOD $

(Maligne Lake Lodge; snacks from $4; ⊙9am-7pm) On first impressions this aptly named restaurant (behold the view!) at the head of Maligne Lake is just another overpriced cafeteria for tourists. But, beyond the sandwiches, soups and summer jobbers, this place serves up some of the best pastries, muffins and cinnamon buns in the park.

Villa Caruso
STEAKHOUSE $$

(Map p227; 640 Connaught Dr; mains from $21; ⊙11am-11:30pm) Carnivore, piscatorian and vegetarian needs are all catered for here. Plush wood trimmings and great views are the perfect appetizer for a fine meal out.

Edith Cavell
FUSION $$$

(☑780-852-6052; Jasper Park Lodge, 1 Old Lodge Rd; 2-/3-/4-course meals $90/110/130; ⊙6-9pm) Fine dining set among the beautiful surroundings of the Jasper Park Lodge with breathtaking views and a menu that is equally awe-inspiring.

🍷 Drinking

Pete's on Patricia
NIGHTCLUB

(Map p227; 614 Patricia St) Jasper's most authentic nightclub has some scarily concocted theme nights with a heavy metal vent. DJs spin anything from hip-hop to top 40 – head upstairs after 10pm once it gets going.

Jasper Brewing Co
BREWERY, PUB

(Map p227; www.jasperbrewingco.ca; 624 Connaught Dr) Open since 2005, this brew-pub uses glacial water to make its fine ales including the signature Rockhopper IPA or – slightly more adventurous – the Rocket Ridge Raspberry Ale. It's a sit-down affair with TVs and a good food menu.

Atha-B Pub   BAR, NIGHTCLUB
(Map p227; Athabasca Hotel, 510 Patricia St) Nightclubbing in a national park is about as congruous as wildlife-viewing in downtown Toronto. Bear this in mind before you hit the Atha-B, a pub-slash-nightclub off the lobby of the Athabasca Hotel where mullets are still high fashion and the carpet's probably radioactive.

ⓘ Information

Jasper Information Centre (www.parkscan ada.gc.ca/jasper; 500 Connaught Dr; ⊘8am-7pm Jun-Sep, 9am-4pm Oct-May) Informative office in historic 'parkitecture' building.

Jasper Municipal Library (500 Robson St; internet per hr $5)

Post office (Map p227; 502 Patricia St, cnr Elm Ave; ⊘9am-5pm Mon-Fri)

Seton General Hospital (Map p227; ☑780-852-3344; 518 Robson St)

ⓘ Getting There & Around

Bus

The **bus station** (www.greyhound.ca; 607 Connaught Dr) is at the train station. Greyhound buses serve Edmonton ($59, from 4½ hours, four daily), Prince George ($64, five hours, one daily), Kamloops ($70, six hours, two daily) and Vancouver ($115, from 11½ hours, two daily).

Brewster Transportation (www.brewster. ca), departing from the same station, operates express buses to Lake Louise village ($60, 4½ hours, at least one daily) and Banff Town ($70, 5½ hours, at least one daily).

The **Maligne Valley Shuttle** (www.ma lignelake.com) runs a May to October bus from Jasper Town to Maligne Lake via Maligne Canyon. Fares are one-way/return $20/40.

Car

International car-rental agencies (p324) have offices in Jasper Town.

If you're in need of a taxi, call **Jasper Taxi** (☑780-852-3600), which has metered cabs.

Train

VIA Rail (www.viarail.ca) offers tri-weekly train services west to Vancouver ($168, 20 hours) and east to Toronto ($456, 62 hours). In addition, there is a tri-weekly service to Prince Rupert, BC ($117, 32 hours). Call or check at the **train station** (607 Connaught Dr) for exact schedule and fare details.

SOUTHERN ALBERTA

The national parks of Banff and Jasper and the cities of Calgary and Edmonton grab most of the headlines in Alberta, leaving the expansive south largely forgotten. Here flat farmland is interrupted by deep coulees or canyons that were caused by flooding at the end of the last ice age. Another symbolic feature of the landscape is the towering hoodoos, funky arid sculptures that look like sand-colored Seussian realizations dominating the horizon. History abounds in both the recent Head-Smashed-In Buffalo Jump and the not-so-recent Dinosaur Provincial Park, two areas preserving the past that have attained Unesco World Heritage status.

Natural wonders are plentiful in this sleepy corner of the province. The dusty dry badlands around Drumheller open up into wide open prairies to the east that stretch all the way to the Cyprus Hills of western Saskatchewan. To the west there is Waterton Lakes National Park with some of the most spectacular scenery in the Rockies – yet still under the radar of most visitors.

Drumheller

Founded on coal but now committed to another subterranean resource – dinosaur bones – Drumheller is a small (some would say 'waning') town set amid Alberta's enigmatic badlands that is central axis on the so-called Dinosaur Trail. While paleontology is a serious business here (the nearby Royal Tyrrell Museum is as much research center as tourist site), Drumheller has cashed in on its Jurassic heritage – sometimes shamelessly. Aside from mocked-up stegosauruses on almost every street corner and dino-related prefixes to more than a few business names, there's the large matter of a 26m high fiberglass T.rex that haunts a large tract of downtown (see p234).

But don't let the paleontological civic pride deter you – once you get beyond the kitsch, the town itself is has a certain je ne sais quoi. The summers are hot and the deep-cut river valley in which Drumheller sits provides a much-needed break to the monotony of the prairies. Hoodoos dominate this badland landscape which has featured in many a movie, Westerns mainly.

The **tourist information center** (60 1st Ave W; ☉10am-6pm) is close to the aforementioned T-Rex.

◉ Sights & Activities

Dinosaur Trail, Horseshoe Canyon & Hoodoo Drive
SCENIC DRIVE

Drumheller is on the Dinosaur Trail, a 48km loop that runs northwest from town and includes Hwys 837 and 838; the scenery is quite worth the drive. Badlands and river views await you at every turn. The loop takes you past **Midland Provincial Park** (no camping), where you can take a self-guided hike; across the Red Deer River on the free, cable-operated **Bleriot Ferry**, which has been running since 1913; and to vista points – including the eagle's-eye **Orkney Viewpoint** – overlooking the area's impressive canyons.

Horseshoe Canyon, the most spectacular chasm in the area, is best seen on a short drive west of Drumheller on Hwy 9. A large sign in the parking lot explains the geology of the area, while trails lead down into the canyon for further exploration. There are helicopter rides if you're flush.

The 25km Hoodoo Drive starts about 18km southeast of Drumheller on Hwy 10; the road only goes one way so you must return by the same route. Along this drive you'll find the best examples of **hoodoos**: weird, eroded, mushroomlike columns of sandstone rock. This area was the site of a once-prosperous coal-mining community, and the **Atlas Mine** is now preserved as a provincial historic site. Take the side trip on Hwy 10X (which includes 11 bridges in 6km) from Rosedale to the small community of **Wayne**, population 27 and fast approaching ghost town status.

TOP CHOICE Royal Tyrrell Museum of Palaeontology
MUSEUM

(www.tyrrellmuseum.com; adult/youth $10/6, ☉9am-9pm mid-May–Sep, 10am-5pm Oct–mid-May) This fantastic museum is one of the preeminent dinosaur museums on the planet. It's not an overstatement to say that no trip to Alberta is complete without a visit to this amazing facility. Children will love the interactive displays and everyone will be in awe of the numerous complete dino-skeletons. There are opportunities to get among the badlands on a guided tour and to discover your own dino treasures either on a guided hike or a dinosaur dig. You'll feel like you've stepped behind the scenes of *Jurassic Park* – and in many ways this is the *real* Jurassic Park.

World's Largest Dinosaur
LANDMARK

(60 1st Ave W; admission $3; ☉10am-6pm) Warning – cheesy tourist attraction ahead! In a town filled to the brim with dinosaurs, this T.rex is the king of them all and features in the *Guinness Book of Records*. Standing 26m above a parking lot, it dominates the Drumheller skyline. It's big, not-at-all scary and cost over a million bucks to build, which explains the admission price to go up the 106 steps for the view from its mouth. Kids love it and, truth be told, the view is pretty good. Ironically, the dinosaur isn't even Jurassically accurate; at 46m long, it's about 4.5 times bigger than its extinct counterpart.

🛏 Sleeping

The quality of accommodations is limited in Drumheller, so it's best to book ahead to ensure you're not stuck with something you don't like, or worse, nothing at all.

Heartwood Inn & Spa
INN $$

(☑403-823-6495; www.innsattheartwood.com; 320 N Railway Ave E; d $119-279; @) Standing head and shoulders above most of the accommodations in town, this lovely country inn is awesome. The small rooms are luxurious, comfortable and tastefully done. It has an on-site spa facility that will welcome you like a queen or king. All the rooms have Jacuzzis, and there are romance packages available where the staff decorate your room with candles and rose petals, draw you a bath made for two and let you handle the rest.

River Grove Campground & Cabins
CAMPGROUND $

(☑403-823-6655; www.camprivergrove.com; 25 Poplar St; campsites from $26, cabins from $80, tepees $60; ☉May-Sep; P☀) Right in town and close to the big dinosaur, this is a pleasant campground with lots of amenities. The tent facilities are alright, with a few shady trees to try and keep you cool in the hot summer sun. You can even rent a tepee for the night, although the Stoney people likely didn't have concrete floors in theirs.

Taste the Past B&B
B&B $$

(☑403-823-5889; 281 2nd St W; s/d $95/115; ℗)
This converted turn-of-the-century house
has evolved into a cozy downtown B&B. All
rooms have a private bathroom and there
is a shared facility downstairs. With only
three rooms, this feels more like staying
with friends – and by the end of your stay,
that's often what it is.

✗ Eating

TOP CHOICE Last Chance Saloon
BAR $

(Hwy 10X, Wayne; mains from $4.50;
⊙11:30am-midnight) In a land partial to
fast-food franchises the words 'there's no-
where else remotely like it' are an under-
hand compliment. For a taste of something
completely different, take the 15-minute
drive from Drumheller to the tiny town of
Wayne to find this former hell-raising bar-
hotel turned Harley Davidson hangout.
Last Chance is a classic Western saloon,
but without a hint of tourist kitsch. Check
out the mining relics, Brownie cameras,
old cigarette tins, fully functioning band-
box, and the brick that somebody probably
tossed through the window circa 1913.
The food is almost an afterthought – bog
standard burgers with optional beans or
fries – but it'll fill you up and give you a
little longer to ponder the unique off-beat
atmosphere.

Whif's Flapjack House
CANADIAN $

(801 N Dinosaur Trail; mains $6-10; ⊙6am-2pm)
The name is the menu: waffles, hamburg-
ers, ice cream, flapjacks and salad. Big por-
tions, a miniature train track suspended
from the ceiling, and good value are all
found at this local greasy spoon.

Sizzling House
CHINESE, THAI $

(www.sizzlinghouse.com; 160 Centre St; mains
from $9; ⊙11am-9pm) The exterior of this
unusual Thai and Chinese combo restau-
rant screams 'run away!' but the redone
interior is nice enough and the food sur-
prisingly good. With an exotic mélange of
wonton soups, tom yum goong, Manchu
beef and Chang Mai vegetables you'll be
laughing all the way back to Bangkok – or
Beijing.

O'Shea's Eatery & Ale House
PUB $

(www.osheasalehouse.com; 600B, 680 2nd St;
mains from $10; ⊙11am-11pm) With everything
from Irish-style pub fare to steaks and
pasta dishes, everyone will find something
to chew on here. Hardwood floors, stained-
glass windows and high ceilings give the
meal a somewhat unneeded Gothic feel.
There is a pub here, too, if you are looking
for something more relaxed.

ℹ Getting There & Away

Greyhound Canada runs buses from the **bus
station** (308 Centre St) to Calgary ($38, 1¾
hours, two daily) and Edmonton ($68, seven
hours, two daily).

Hammerhead Tours (p198) runs a full-day tour
($90) from Calgary to the Drumheller badlands
and Royal Tyrrell Museum.

Dinosaur Provincial Park

Where *The Lost World* meets *Little House
on the Prairie,* Dinosaur Provincial Park
(www.dinosaurpark.ca; off Hwy 544; admission
free; ⊙9am-6pm mid-May–mid-Sep, 10am-5pm
mid-Sep–mid-May) isn't just the Grand Can-
yon in miniature, it's also a Unesco World
Heritage site. The final resting place of
thousands of dinosaurs, it's a stellar spot to
check out some fossils. It's halfway between
Calgary and Medicine Hat, and some 48km
northeast of Brooks. From Hwy 1, take Sec-
ondary Hwy 873 to Hwy 544.

The park comes at you by surprise as the
chasm in which it lives opens before your
feet from the grassy plain. A dehydrated
fantasy landscape, there are hoodoos and
colorful rock formations aplenty. Where 75
million years ago dinosaurs cruised around
a tropical landscape, it's now a hot and bar-
ren place to be. Make sure you dress for the
weather with sunscreen and water at the
ready.

The 81-sq-km park begs to be explored,
with wildflowers, the odd rattler in the
rocks and, if you're lucky, maybe even a
T.rex. This isn't just a tourist attraction,
but a hotbed for science; paleontologists
have uncovered countless skeletons, which
now reside in many of the finest museums
around the globe.

There are five short interpretive hiking
trails to choose from and a driving loop
runs through part of the park, but to pre-
serve the fossils, access to 70% of the park is
restricted. The off-limits areas may be seen
only on guided hikes (adult/child $14/8) or
bus tours (adult/child $12/8), which operate
from late May to October. The hikes and
tours are popular, and you should reserve a
place by calling ☑403-378-4344.

The park's **visitors center** (☎403-378-4342; adult/child $3/2; ◷8:30am-5pm mid-May–Sep, 9am-4pm Oct-Apr) has a small yet effective series of dino displays. Some complete skeletons and exhibits on the practicalities of paleontology are worthy of a look.

The park's **campground** (☎403-378-3700; tent/RV sites $23/29, reservations $10; ⓅP) sits in a hollow by a small creek. The ample tree cover is a welcome reprieve from the volcanic sun. Laundry facilities and hot showers are available, as well as a small shop for last-minute supplies. This is a popular place, especially with the RV set, so best to phone ahead.

Head-Smashed-In Buffalo Jump

The story behind the place with the strangest name of any attraction in Alberta is one of ingenuity and resourcefulness and is key to the First Nations' (and Canada's) cultural heritage. For thousands of years, the Blackfoot people used the cliffs near the town of Fort Macleod to hunt buffalo. **Head-Smashed-In Buffalo Jump** (www.head-smashed-in.com; Spring Point Rd/Secondary Hwy 785; adult/child $9/5; ◷10am-5pm) was a marvel of simple ingenuity. When the buffalo massed in the open prairie, braves from the tribe would gather and herd them toward the towering cliffs. As the animals got closer, they would be funneled to the edge and made to stampede over it to their doom, thus ensuring the survival of the tribe. For the Blackfoot, the buffalo was sacred; to honor the fallen prey, every part of the animal was used.

The displays at the interpretive centre are fascinating and well presented at this World Heritage Listed site. Despite being slightly out of the way, it's most definitely worth the excursion. The site, about 18km northwest of Fort Macleod and 16km west of Hwy 2, also has a snack bar and a network of walking trails.

Lethbridge

Right in the heart of southern Alberta farming country sits the former coal-mining city of Lethbridge, divided by the distinctive coulees of the Oldman River. Though there isn't a lot to bring you to the city, copious parkland, a couple of good historic sites and an admirable level of civic pride might keep you longer than you first intended. There are ample hiking opportunities in the Oldman River Valley, a 100m-deep coulee bisected by the proverbial Eiffel Tower of steel railway bridges, and the largest of its kind in the world. The downtown area, like many North American downtowns, has made a good stab at preserving its not-so-ancient history. To the east, less-inspiring Mayor McGrath Dr (Hwy 5) is a chain-store-infested drag that could be Anywhere, North America.

◉ Sights & Activities

Nikka Yuko Japanese Garden   GARDEN
(www.nikkayuko.com; cnr Mayor Mcgrath Dr & 9th Ave S; adult/youth $7/4; ◷9am-5pm, to 8pm Jul & Aug) The Nikka Yuko Japanese Garden is the perfect antidote if the stresses of the road are starting to show. The immaculate grounds interspersed with ponds, flowing water, bridges, bonsai trees and rock gardens form an oasis of calm amid the bustle of everyday life, and authentic Japanese structures sit among the grassy mounds. Take your time, sit a while and let the Zenlike atmosphere take you on a journey.

Indian Battle Park   PARK
(3rd Ave S) In the coulee between the east and west sides of the city, Indian Battle Park, west of Scenic Dr and named after a famous 1870 battle between the Blackfoot and the Cree, is no ordinary manicured green space. Instead, this is an expansive, surprisingly wild place astride the Oldman River that is strafed with trails, wildlife and some unsung mining history. Impossible to miss in the middle of it all is 96m-high, 1623m-long **High Level Bridge**, the largest trestle bridge in the world, built in 1909 to carry the railway across the deep coulee to the prairies on the other side.

Almost directly under the bridge, the **Helen Schuler Coulee Centre & Lethbridge Nature Reserve** (admission free; ◷10am-6pm Jun-Aug, 1-4pm Sep-May) contains a small interpretive center and is the starting point for various nature trails on the reserve's 80 wooded hectares along the river. It runs special nature programs in the summer. At the other end of the car park is the **Coalbanks Interpre-**

tive kiosk, an open-air shelter containing an impressive stash of information on Lethbridge's early mining history. Trails nearby lead to gazebos, picnic areas and viewpoints.

Also within the park is **Fort Whoop-Up** (www.fortwhoopup.com; adult/child $7/3; ☺10am-5pm Tue-Sat), a replica of Alberta's first and most notorious illegal whiskey trading post. Around 25 of these outposts were set up in the province between 1869 and 1874 to trade whiskey, guns, ammunition and blankets for buffalo hides and furs from the Blackfoot tribes. Their existence led directly to the formation of the NWMP, who arrived in 1874 at Fort Macleod to bring law and order to the Canadian west.

Sir Alexander Galt Museum   MUSEUM
(www.galtmuseum.com; 320 Galt St; adult/child $5/3; ☺10am-6pm) The story of Lethbridge is continued at the Sir Alexander Galt Museum, encased in an old hospital building (1910) on the bluff high above the river. Interactive kid-oriented displays sit beside a small gallery with contemporary and historical art that will interest the bigger kids. The view from the lobby out onto the coulee is great and free.

🛏 Sleeping

A huge selection of chain hotels from fancy to thrifty can be found on Hwy 5. Take your pick.

Lethbridge Lodge   HOTEL $$
(☎403-328-1123; www.lethbridgelodge.com; 320 Scenic Dr S; r from $109; 🅿@🛜) Like most Canadian hotels, the rooms here are clean if a little unmemorable, but the atrium, on the other hand, is something else. All the rooms look down into the fake-foliage-filled interior, complete with winding brick pathways, a kidney-shaped pool and water features. The Cotton Blossom Lounge sits among the jungle and is good fun – the piano player is stranded on a small island – and the pseudo Italian facade of the rooms completes the bizarre picture.

Ramada Hotel & Suites   HOTEL $$
(☎403-380-5050;   www.ramadalethbridge. ca; 2375 Hwy 5 S; r from $110; @🛜🏊) From a jungle (Lethbridge Hotel) to a 400,000-liter water feature! This slightly out-of-the-box Ramada has an indoor water park complete with dueling waterslides, wave pool and special kids area. All the standard stuff is here, too, and despite the wacky selling features, the Ramada retains a sense of class. Nonguests can pay to use the water park (adult/child $10/6).

Henderson Lake Campground
                              CAMPGROUND $
(☎403-328-5452; www.hendersoncampground. com; 3419 Parkside Dr; tent & RV sites from $25; 🅿) It may be in need of a bit of a clean up, but the central location of this campground is hard to beat. Right beside the lake it shares its name with and near to town, you are right among the action. There are tent sites, a shop and a laundry.

Eating

Ric's Grill   STEAKHOUSE $$$
(☎403-317-7427; www.ricsgrill.com; 103 Mayor Mcgrath Dr; mains $19-40) Ever eaten in a water tower – or an ex-water tower to be more precise? Well, here is your chance. Ric's sits 40m high above the prairie in the old Lethbridge water tower (decommissioned in 1999). Turned into a restaurant in 2004, the curved interior affords great views of the city. There is a lounge on one level and a classy dining room upstairs. The steaks are thick and the wine list long; best to reserve a good spot as it's deservedly popular.

Mocha Cabana Café   CAFE $$
(www.mochacabana.ca; 317 4th St; lunch from $12; ☺7am-9pm, to 11pm Fri & Sat; 🛜) Austere from the outside, the multifunctional Mocha is anything but within. Billing itself as a coffee lounge, wine bar, patio and music venue, it grabs 'best in Lethbridge' prize in each genre. The bright interior has an appealing European ambience and the substantial lunchtime salads are fantastic.

Round Street Café   CAFE $
(427 5th St S; sandwiches $7; ☺7am-6pm Mon-Sat) A simple but effective indie coffee bar near the Greyhound depot with a fine line in cinnamon buns and thick-cut sandwiches, plus free internet browsing rights.

ℹ Information

Main Post Office (☎403-382-4604; 704 4th Ave S)

Main Tourist Office (www.chinookcountry. com; 2805 Scenic Dr S, at Mayor Mcgrath Dr S; ☺9am-5pm)

ℹ Getting There & Around

Air

The **Lethbridge airport** (✆403-329-4474; 417 Stubb Ross Rd), a short drive south on Hwy 5, is served by commuter affiliates of Air Canada. Six or seven flights per day go to Calgary.

Bus

Greyhound Canada (✆403-327-1551; 411 5th St S) goes to Calgary ($48, three hours, five daily) and Regina ($103, from 14½ hours, two daily).

For detailed information about local bus services, call the **Lethbridge Transit Infoline** (✆403-320-4978/3885). The downtown bus terminal is on 4th Ave at 6th St. Local bus fares are $2.

Writing-On-Stone Provincial Park

Perhaps the best thing about this **park** (admission free; ⊙tours 9am-6pm mid-May–mid-Sep, 10am-5pm mid-Sep–mid-May) is that it really isn't on the way to *anywhere*. For those willing to get off the main thoroughfare and discover this hidden gem, all efforts will be rewarded. It's named for the extensive carvings and paintings made by the Plains Indians more than 3000 years ago on the sandstone cliffs along the banks of Milk River. There is an excellent self-guided interpretive trail that takes you to some of the more spectacular viewpoints and accessible pictographs.

The best art is found in a restricted area (to protect it from vandalism), which you can only visit on a guided tour with the park ranger. Other activities possible here include canoeing and swimming in the river in summer and cross-country skiing in winter. Park wildlife amounts to more than 160 bird species, 30 kinds of mammals, four kinds of amphibians and three kinds of reptiles, not to mention the fish in the river. Pick up tickets for tours at the park entrance, from the naturalist's office. Tours generally run Saturday and Sunday at 2pm from May to October (adult/child $12/8).

The park's riverside **campground** (✆403-647-2877; tent/RV sites from $21/27) has 64 sites, running water, showers and flush toilets and is popular on weekends.

The park is southeast of Lethbridge and close to the US border; the Sweetgrass Hills of northern Montana are visible to the south. To get to the park, take Hwy 501 42km east of Hwy 4 from the town of Milk River.

Waterton Lakes National Park

Who? What? Where? The name **Waterton Lakes National Park** (adult/child & senior per day $7.80/3.90) is usually prefixed with a vexed question rather than a contented sigh of recognition. While its siblings to the north – Canmore, Banff and Jasper – hemorrhage with tourists and weekend warriors, Waterton is a pocket of tranquility. Sublime. Established in 1895 and now part of a Unesco World Heritage site, Unesco Biosphere Reserve and International Peace Park (with Glacier National Park in the US), 525-sq-km Waterton Lakes lies in Alberta's southwestern corner. Here the prairies meet the mountains and the relief from the flat land is nothing short of uplifting. The park is a sanctuary for numerous iconic animals – grizzlies, elk, deer and cougar – along with 800-odd wildflower species.

The town of **Waterton**, a charming alpine village with a winter population of about 40, provides a marked contrast to larger, tackier Banff and, to a lesser extent, Jasper. There is a lifetime's worth of outdoor adventure to discover here. Highlights include serene Waterton Lake, the regal 1920s-era Prince of Wales Hotel, and the immediacy of the high-alpine hiking terrain; you can be up above the tree line less than one hour from the townsite.

Sitting right on the US border and next to the immense **Glacier National Park**, this is a good spot to forge neighborly relations with the people to the south. You can even flash your passport and do a polycountry backcountry adventure. Together the two parks comprise Waterton-Glacier International Peace Park. Although the name evokes images of binational harmony, in reality each park is operated separately, and entry to one does not entitle you to entry to the other.

For more information on Glacier National Park, see the excellent US National Park Service website at www.nps.gov/glac.

◉ Sights & Activities

A highlight for many visitors is a boat ride with **Waterton Shoreline Cruises** (www.watertoncruise.com; one way adult/child $23/12; ⊙May-Oct) across the lake's shimmering waters to the far shore of Goat Haunt, Montana, USA. The 45-minute trip is scenic and there is a lively commentary as you go. Grab your passport before you jump on the often rather full boats, as they dock in the USA for about half an hour.

Those looking to stretch their legs are in luck – Waterton is a hiker's haven. With over 225km of walking tracks, you'll run out of time before you run out of trails. The trails are shared with bikes and horses (where permitted), and once the snow flies, cross-country skis will get you to the same places. The 17km walk to Crypt Lake is a standout – there's a 20m tunnel, a stream that materializes out of the ground and a ladder to negotiate. The only way to get to the trailhead is by boat. Waterton Shoreline Cruises leave the town's marina in the morning and pick up the weary at the Crypt Lake trailhead in the afternoon (adult/child $18/9).

Another example of Waterton's 'small is beautiful' persona is the 19km Carthew-Alderson Trail, often listed as one of the best high alpine day hikes in North America. The Tamarack Shuttle runs every morning in the summer to the trailhead by Cameron Lake (reservations recommended). From here you hike back over the mountains to the townsite.

🛌 Sleeping

The park has three Parks Canada vehicle-accessible campgrounds, none of which takes reservations. Backcountry campsites are limited and should be reserved through the visitors center.

TOP CHOICE **Prince of Wales Hotel** HOTEL $$$
(☑403-859-2231; www.princeofwaleswaterton.com; Prince of Wales Rd; r from $234; ☉mid-May–Sep; P🐾) You can't come to Waterton and not check out this iconic alpine landmark. Situated to take full advantage of the best view in town, this hotel is nothing short of spectacular. When seen from a distance, the serene scene is perhaps the most photogenic in all the Canadian Rockies. Up close, the old girl is starting to show her age but she's aging like a fine wine. The grand lobby is illuminated with a chandelier worthy of a Scottish castle and the elevator is the oldest working example in North America. The rooms are small but retain the classic feel of this historic hotel. There's antique porcelain in the bathrooms and views that justify the $200-plus asking price.

Bayshore Inn HOTEL $$$
(☑403-859-2211; www.bayshoreinn.com; 111 Waterton Ave; r $199; ☉Apr–mid-Oct; P@🐾) Taking the prize as the biggest hotel in the downtown area, the Bayshore is nothing if not centrally located. With rooms that back right onto the lake and only a couple of steps away from the shops, this is a popular option. The lake views are great, but be sure to book early if you want to see them.

Aspen Village Inn HOTEL $$
(☑403-859-2255; www.aspenvillageinn.com; 111 Windflower Ave; r from $135; P🐾🚶) Aspen is a more economical, family-friendly version of the Bayshore. Rooms are in two main buildings and several cottage units. Bonuses include a kids' play area, a barbecue and picnic area, and the sight of wild deer grazing the grass outside your room.

Waterton Glacier Suites HOTEL $$$
(☑403-859-2004; www.watertonsuites.com; 107 Windflower Ave; ste from $225; P@🐾🏊) With amenities aplenty, these suites have two fireplaces, whirlpool tubs, microwaves and fridges. The rooms are spotless and the rock-and-log exterior looks the part, too. It's open all year round – come winter you'll appreciate those dual fireplaces.

Waterton Townsite Campground CAMPGROUND $
(☑877-737-3783; Hwy 5; unserviced/full-service $22.50/38.20; ☉mid-May–mid-Oct; P) Dominating the southern end of Waterton village, the town campground isn't ideal, but it's a means to an end. Consisting mainly of an enormous gopher hole-infested field aimed at RV campers, it has all the charm of a camping area at a music festival. There are some treed sites near the edges, but by midsummer you'll be lucky to get anything. Book ahead for this one.

HI-Waterton HOSTEL $
(☑403-859-2151; Cameron Falls Dr at Windflower Ave; dm from $31; r from $93, ☉mid-May–Nov; P@🏊) If you want a cheap place to stay in the park that isn't under canvas, the hostel is your sole option. Small dorms that sleep four weary travelers are clean and come with adjoining bathrooms, and there is a small communal kitchen. Check ahead as it's sometimes block-booked.

Bear Mountain Motel MOTEL $$
(☑403-859-2366; www.bearmountainmotel.com; 208 Mount View Rd; r from $95; P) Small,

bog-standard motel rooms in a central location. Throw in friendly, knowledgeable owners and you're laughing all the way to the ATM.

Crandell Mountain Campground

CAMPGROUND **$**

(403-859-5133; Red Rock Pkwy; tent & RV sites $22; ⊙mid-May–Sep; **P**) For a more rustic alternative to the townsite, head out to this secluded camping spot a few minutes' drive from the park gates.

✗ Eating

Waterton specializes in unsophisticated but filling cuisine, ideal for topping up your energy both pre- and post-hike. Everything is contained within the townsite.

Zum's Eatery   CANADIAN **$$**

(116B Waterton Ave; mains from $13) Good home-style cooking of the burger, pizza, and fish and chips variety is brought to you by hard-up students working their summer breaks. The lack of sophisticated flavors is made up for by the character of the decor; several hundred North American license plates embellish almost every centimeter of wall.

Waterton Bagel & Coffee Co   CAFE **$**

(309 Windflower Ave; bagels from $5; ⊙10am–10pm) A godsend if you've just staggered out of the wilderness, this tiny caffeine stop has a handful of window stools, life-saving peanut butter and jam bagels, and refreshing frappuccinos.

Pizza of Waterton   PIZZA **$**

(103 Fountain Ave; pizzas from $10) Fine pizza 'to go' (the lakeside calls on warm summer evenings), or in the informal interior where you can wash it down with a cold Canadian beer.

🍷 Drinking & Entertainment

Thirsty Bear Saloon   PUB

(www.thirstybearsaloon.com; Main St) Wild nights in the wilderness happen in this large pub/performance space aided by live music, karaoke, good beer and mildly inebriated young ladies in cowboy hats.

ℹ Information

Waterton Visitor Centre (⏹403-859-5133; www.parkscanada.gc.ca/waterton; ⊙8am–7pm early May–early Oct) is across the road from the Prince of Wales Hotel. It's the central stop for information.

ℹ Getting There & Around

Waterton lies in Alberta's southwestern corner, 130km from Lethbridge and 156km from Calgary. The one road entrance into the park is in its northeastern corner along Hwy 5. Most visitors coming from Glacier and the USA reach the junction with Hwy 5 via Hwy 6 (Chief Mountain International Hwy) from the southeast. From Calgary, to the north, Hwy 2 shoots south toward Hwy 5 into the park. From the east, Hwy 5, through Cardston, heads west and then south into the park.

There is no public transportation from Canadian cities outside the park. However, a shuttle service operated by **Glacier Park Inc** (www.glacierparkinc.com) offers daily transport from Prince of Wales Hotel to Glacier Park Lodge in Montana, USA from May to September. Here you can link up with the Amtrak train network.

A hiker's shuttle operates around the park in the summer, linking Cameron Lake with the townsite and the US border at Chief Mountain. It leaves from **Tamarack Outdoor Outfitters** (214 Mount View Rd) in the townsite.

Crowsnest Pass

West of Fort Macleod the Crowsnest Hwy (Hwy 3) heads through the prairies and into the Rocky Mountains to Crowsnest Pass (1396m) and the British Columbian border. The Pass, as it is commonly known, is a string of small communities just to the east of the BC border. What you'll find most remarkable is the story of the town of **Frank**. In 1903, Frank was almost completely buried when 30 million cubic meters (some 82 million tonnes worth) of nearby Turtle Mountain collapsed and killed around 70 people. There was much local speculation over the incident. The coal mine dug into the base of the mountain was to blame, some say. But the mining didn't stop; this black gold was the ticket to fortune for the entire region some hundred years ago. Eventually the demand for coal decreased, and after yet more tragedy below the earth, the mines shut down for good.

Frank Slide Interpretive Centre (www.frankslide.com; adult/child $9/5; ⊙10am–5pm), 1.5km off Hwy 3 and 27km east of the BC border, overlooks the Crowsnest Valley. It's an excellent interpretive center that helps put a human face on the tragedy of the Frank landslide, with many interesting displays about mining, the railroad and the early days of this area. There's also a fantastic film dramatizing the tragic events of

1903. Most of the staff can trace their roots to the area and thus the slide.

NORTHERN ALBERTA

Despite the presence of the increasingly infamous oil sands, the top half of Alberta is little visited and even less known. Once you travel north of Edmonton, the population drops off to Siberian levels and the sense of remoteness is almost eerie.

If it's solitude you seek, then this is paradise found. Endless stretches of pine forests seem to go on forever, nighttime brings aurora borealis displays that are better than any chemical hallucinogens, and it is here you can still see herds of buffalo.

This is also where the engine room of the Alberta economy lives. The oil sands near Fort McMurray are one of the largest oil reserves in the world. This helps to import workers from every corner of Canada and export oil earning the province millions of dollars – per hour.

The Cree, Slavey and Dene were the first peoples to inhabit the region, and many of them still depend on fishing, hunting and trapping for survival. The northeast has virtually no roads and is dominated by Wood Buffalo National Park, the Athabasca River and Lake Athabasca. The northwest is more accessible, with a network of highways connecting Alberta with northern BC and the NWT.

Peace River & Around

Alaska here we come! Heading northwest along Hwy 43 leads to the town of Dawson Creek, BC, and mile zero of the Alaska Hwy. Dawson is a whopping 590km from Edmonton, so it's a long way to go to check out this isolated section of northern Alberta. Along the way you'll pass through Grande Prairie, the base of operations for the local agricultural industry and home to chuckwagon legend Kelly Sutherland. If you decide to spend the night, most of the accommodations are centered on 100th St and 100th Ave.

Peace River is so named because the warring Cree and Beaver Indians made peace along its banks. The town of Peace River sits at the confluence of the Heart, Peace and Smoky Rivers. It has several motels

and two campgrounds. Greyhound Canada buses leave daily for the Yukon and NWT. West out of town, Hwy 2 leads to the Mackenzie Hwy.

Mackenzie Highway

The small town of Grimshaw is the official starting point of the Mackenzie Hwy (Hwy 35) north to the NWT. There's not much here except for the mile-zero sign and a few shops. The relatively flat and straight road is paved for the most part, though there are stretches of loose gravel or earth where the road is being reconstructed.

The mainly agricultural landscape between Grimshaw and Manning gives way to endless stretches of spruce and pine forest. Come prepared as this is frontier territory and services become fewer (and more expensive) as the road cuts northward through the wilderness. A good basic rule is to fill your tank any time you see a gas station from here north.

High Level, the last settlement of any size before the NWT border, is a center for the timber industry. Workers often stay in the motels in town during the week. The only service station between High Level and Enterprise (in the NWT) is at Indian Cabins.

Lake District

From St Paul, more than 200km northeast of Edmonton, to the NWT border lies Alberta's immense lake district. Fishing is popular (even in winter, when there is ice-fishing) but many of the lakes, especially further north, have no road access and you have to fly in.

St Paul is the place to go if you are looking for little green people. The flying-saucer landing pad, which is still awaiting its first customer, is open for business. Residents built the 12m-high circular landing pad in 1967 as part of a centennial project and as a stunt to try to generate tourism (it's billed as the world's largest, and only, UFO landing pad) to the remote region. It worked: UFO enthusiasts have been visiting ever since.

Hwy 63 is the main route into the province's northeastern wilderness interior. The highway, with a few small settlements and campgrounds on the way, leads to Fort

McMurray, which is 439km northeast of Edmonton. Originally a fur-trading outpost, it is now home to one of the world's largest oilfields. The town is pretty rough and the accommodations are aimed at unhoused oilfield workers, so it's not really a prime holiday spot. The story of how crude oil is extracted from the vast tracts of sand is told at the **Oil Sands Discovery Centre** (515 MacKenzie Blvd; adult/child $6/4; ☺9am-5pm Tue-Sat).

Wood Buffalo National Park

This huge park is best accessed from Fort Smith in the NWT.

In Alberta, the only access is via air to Fort Chipewyan. In winter, an ice road leads north to Peace Point (which connects to Fort Smith), and another road links the park to Fort McMurray.

Yukon Territory

Best Places to Eat

» Drunken Goat Taverna (p264)

» Klondike Kate's (p265)

» Klondike Rib & Salmon Bake (p250)

» Giorgio's Cucina (p250)

Best Places to Stay

» High Country Inn (p250)

» Edgewater Hotel (p250)

» Bombay Peggy's (p264)

» Klondike Kate's (p264)

Why Go?

The name Yukon is evocative as well as descriptive: adventure, the far north, wilderness, moose. How can you even hear 'Yukon' and not feel a stirring within? This vast and thinly populated wilderness – most four-legged species far outnumber humans – has a grandeur and beauty only appreciated by experience.

Few places in the world today have been so unchanged over the course of time. Aboriginal people, having eked out survival for thousands of years, hunt and trap as they always have. The Klondike Gold Rush of 1898 was the Yukon's high point of population, yet even its heritage is ephemeral, easily erased by time.

Any visit will mean much time outdoors. Canada's five tallest mountains and the world's largest ice fields below the Arctic are all within Kluane National Park. Canoe expeditions down the Yukon River are epic. You'll appreciate the people; join the offbeat vibe of Dawson City and the bustle of Whitehorse.

When to Go
Dawson City

Winter Days of snowy solitude from November to April end when the river ice breaks up.

Summer Summers, spanning June to August, are short but warm, even hot.

September You can feel the north winds coming. Trees erupt in color, crowds thin, things close.

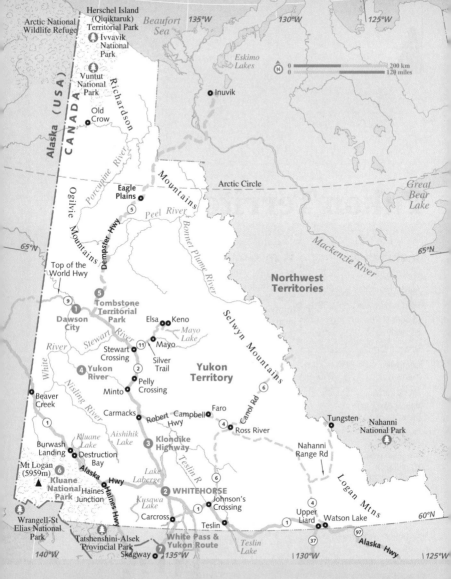

Yukon Territory Highlights

1. Get caught up in the modern vibe of **Dawson City** (p260), Canada's funkiest historic town

2. Spend an extra day in surprising **Whitehorse** (p246), where culture abounds

3. Count moose on the **Klondike Highway** (p257) – they may outnumber cars

4. Live the dream of kayakers and canoeists by paddling the legendary **Yukon River** (p248)

5. Lose yourself – not literally! – in **Tombstone Territorial Park** (p267), where the grandeur of the north envelops you

6. Find one of the 100 unnamed glaciers in **Kluane National Park** (p254) and give it a name

7. Sit back and enjoy the ride on the fabled **White Pass & Yukon Route** (p258)

YUKON TERRITORY FAST FACTS

» Population: 32,000

» Area: 483,450 sq km

» Capital: Whitehorse

» Quirky fact: Home to Robert Service, the poet who immortalized the Yukon through works like *The Shooting of Dan McGrew* and *The Cremation of Sam McGee*

History

There's evidence that humans were eating animals in the Yukon some 15,000 to 30,000 years ago, depending on your carbon-dating method of choice. However, it's widely agreed that these people were descended from those who crossed over today's Siberia while the land bridge was in place. There's little recorded history otherwise, although it's known that a volcanic eruption in AD 800 covered much of the southern Yukon in ash. Similarities to the Athapaskan people of the southwest US have suggested that these groups may have left the Yukon after the volcano ruined hunting and fishing.

In the 1840s Robert Campbell, a Hudson's Bay Company explorer, was the first European to travel the district. Fur traders, prospectors, whalers and missionaries all followed. In 1870 the region became part of the Northwest Territories (NWT). But it was in 1896 when the Yukon literally hit the map, after gold was found in a tributary of the Klondike River, near what was to become Dawson City. The ensuing gold rush attracted upwards of 40,000 hopefuls from around the world. Towns sprouted overnight to support the numerous wealth-seekers, who were quite unprepared for the ensuing depravities (see the boxed text, p259).

In 1898 the Yukon became a separate territory, with Dawson City as its capital. Building the Alaska Hwy (Hwy 1) in 1942 opened up the territory to development. In 1953 Whitehorse became the capital, because it had the railway and the highway. Mining continues to be the main industry, followed by tourism.

Local Culture

The 30,000-plus hardy souls who live in the Yukon Territory take the phrase 'rugged individualist' to heart. It's hard to stereotype but safe to say that the average Yukoner enjoys the outdoors (in all weather conditions!), relishes eating meats seldom found on menus to the south and has a crack in their truck's windshield (caused by one of the many dodgy roads).

Of course the independence of Yukoners comes at a price to the rest of Canada. More than 70% of the territory's annual revenue each year comes from the federal government and it has been used to fund all manner of services at relatively comfortable levels. Whitehorse, for instance, has a range of cultural and recreational facilities that are the envy of southern Canadian communities many times its size. More than 5000 people have government jobs.

Thanks to the Yukon's long isolation before WWII, the 14 First Nations groups have maintained their relationship to the land and their traditional culture, compared to groups forced to assimilate in other parts of Canada. They can be found across the territory and in isolated places like Old Crow, living lives not fundamentally changed in centuries. It's not uncommon to hear various aboriginal dialects spoken by elders.

Light – or the lack thereof – does play an important role in local life. Many people

EXTREME YUKON

Tough conditions spawn tough contests.

» **Yukon Quest** (www.yukonquest.com) This legendary 1600km dog-sled race goes from Whitehorse to Fairbanks, Alaska, through February darkness and -50°C temperatures. Record time: 10 days, two hours, 37 minutes.

» **Yukon River Quest** (www.yukonriverquest.com) The world's premier canoe and kayak race, which covers the classic 742km run of the Yukon River from Whitehorse to Dawson City in June. Record times include team canoe (39 hours, 32 minutes) and solo kayak (44 hours, 14 minutes).

» **Klondike Trail of '98 Road Relay** (www.klondikeroadrelay.com) Some 100 running teams of 10 each complete the overnight course from Skagway to Whitehorse in September.

KILL YOUR DINNER...

Worried that the increasing sophistication of Whitehorse was causing Yukoners to become too citified (read: Southern or south of the Yukon border), *Up Here*, the award-winning magazine of Canada's North, offered the following suggestions to avoid going soft.

Be Northern. Build a house out of town. Wear moosehide and sealskin. Park your car in your yard. Pee by the highway. Take your dog to work. Smoke 'em if you've got 'em. Say 'the Yukon' (What gutless bureaucrat dropped the 'the'?). Jaywalk. Commute on your quad. Look people in the eye. Don't shave – and ladies, that goes for you. Curse. Spit. Enter without knocking. Eat bannock, dry-meat and tea. Build campfires in your yard. Shop at the dump. Call the rest of the world 'Outside.' Kill your cellphone. Kill your dinner. And stop acting like a goddamn Southerner.

Up Here (www.uphere.ca)

adjust to the radical variations in daylight through the year just fine but others do not. Every year you hear of long-time residents and newcomers alike who one day (often in February) announced enough was enough and moved south for good.

Parks

The Yukon has a major Unesco World Heritage site. Raw and forbidding, Kluane National Park sits solidly within the Yukon abutting Tatshenshini-Alsek Provincial Park in British Columbia (BC), while Glacier Bay and Wrangell-St Elias National Parks are found in adjoining Alaska.

The Yukon has four territorial parks (www.yukonparks.ca), but much of the territory itself is park-like and government campgrounds can be found throughout. Tombstone Territorial Park is both remote yet accessible via the Dempster Hwy, so that you can absorb the horizon-sweeping beauty of the tundra and majesty of vast mountain ranges.

ℹ Information

There are excellent visitor information centers (VICs) covering every entry point in the Yukon: Beaver Creek, Carcross, Dawson City, Haines Junction, Watson Lake and Whitehorse.

Thanks to its generous support by the Canadian taxpayer, the Yukon government produces enough literature and information to supply a holiday's worth of reading. Among the highlights are *Camping on Yukon Time, Art Adventures on Yukon Time* and lavish walking guides to pretty much every town with a population greater than 50. Start your collection at the various visitor centers online (www.travelyukon.com). Another good internet resource is www.yukoninfo.com.

A great way to get a feel for the Yukon and its larger-than-life stories is to read some of the vast body of Yukon novels. Start with Jack London, *Call of the Wild* is free online at www.online-literature.com.

ℹ Getting There & Around

Whitehorse is linked by **air** to Vancouver, Calgary, Edmonton and Alaska. There are even flights direct to Germany during summer. Dawson City has flights to Inuvik in the NWT and to Alaska.

There are three major ways to reach the Yukon by road: first by **ferry** to the entry points of Skagway and Haines, Alaska, by the Alaska Hwy from Dawson Creek, BC, and by the Stewart-Cassiar Hwy from northwest BC that joins the Alaska Hwy near Watson Lake.

You can reach Whitehorse from BC by bus. From there a patchwork of companies provides links to Skagway and Alaska (but nothing to Dawson!). Rental cars (and RVs) are expensive and only available in Whitehorse. The Alaska Hwy and Klondike Hwy are paved and have services every 100km to 200km.

Check road conditions in the Yukon (☑511; www.511yukon.ca).

WHITEHORSE

POP 23,800

The leading city and capital of the Yukon, Whitehorse will likely have a prominent role in your journey. The territory's two great highways, the Alaska and the Klondike, cross here; it's a hub for transport. You'll find all manner of outfitters and services for explorations across the territory. Most of its residents have government-related jobs, but they flee for the outdoors no matter what the season.

Utility aside, Whitehorse can delight. It has a well-funded arts community, good restaurants and a range of motels. Exploring the sights within earshot of the rushing Yukon River can easily take a day or more. Look past bland commercial buildings and you'll see a fair number of heritage ones awaiting your discovery.

Whitehorse has always been a transportation hub, first as a terminus for the White Pass & Yukon Route railway from Skagway in the early 1900s. During WWII it was a major center for work on the Alaska Hwy. In 1953, Whitehorse was made the capital of the territory, to the continuing regret of much smaller and isolated Dawson City.

◉ Sights

Museums

SS Klondike   HISTORICAL SITE
(☎867-667-4511; South Access Rd & 2nd Ave; adult/child $6/2; ☺9am-5pm mid-May–mid-Sep) Carefully restored, this was one of the largest sternwheelers used on the Yukon River. Built in 1937, it made its final run upriver to Dawson in 1955 and is now a national historic site. Try not to wish it was making the run now.

MacBride Museum   MUSEUM
(☎867-667-2709; www.mcbridemuseum.com; cnr 1st Ave & Wood St; adult/child $8/4.50; ☺9am-6pm mid-May–Sep, noon-4pm Tue-Sat Oct–mid-May) The Yukon's attic covers the gold rush, First Nations, intrepid Mounties and more. Old photos vie with old stuffed critters, all under a sod roof.

Old Log Church   HISTORICAL BUILDING
(☎867-668-2555; www.oldlogchurchmuseum.ca; 303 Elliott St; adult/child $6/5; ☺10am-6pm mid-May–Aug) The only log-cabin-style cathedral in the world is a 1900 downtown gem. Displays include the compelling story of Rev Isaac Stringer, who boiled and ate his boots while lost in the wilderness for 51 days. Fittingly, all that's left is his sole.

Yukon Beringia Interpretive Centre
                                   MUSEUM
(☎867-667-8855; www.beringia.com; Km1473 Alaska Hwy; adult/child $6/4; ☺9am-6pm) This place focuses on Beringia, a mostly ice-free area that encompassed the Yukon, Alaska and eastern Siberia during the last ice age. Engaging exhibits re-create the time, right down to the giant beaver by the door. It's just south of the airport.

Yukon Transportation Museum   MUSEUM
(☎867-668-4792; www.goytm.ca; 30 Electra Circle; adult/child $6/3; ☺10am-6pm mid-May–Aug)

Find out what the Alaska Hwy was really like back in the day and let's just say mud was a dirty word. Exhibits cover planes, trains and dog-sleds. The museum adjoins the Beringia Centre.

Waterfront
One look at the majestic Yukon River and you'll understand why the waterfront is being reborn. The beautiful **White Pass & Yukon Route Station** (Front St) has been restored and anchors the area.

At the north end of the waterfront, **Shipyards Park** has a growing collection of historic structures gathered territory-wide and a skateboard track and toboggan hill. Linking it all is a cute little **waterfront trolley** (adult/child $2/free; ☺9am-9pm Jun-Aug).

Whitehorse Fishway
Stare down a salmon at the **Whitehorse Fishway** (☎867-633-5965; admission by donation; ☺9am-9pm Jun-Aug), a 366m wooden fish ladder (the world's longest) past the hydroelectric plant south of town. Large viewing windows let you see chinook salmon swim past starting in late July (before that it's grayling). Outside, amidst the thunderous roar of the river's spillway, there's usually a tent where you can learn about the ingenious aboriginal fishing methods. Note that salmon counts and average sizes are decreasing, a feared result of climate change.

The fishway is easily reached on foot from town; see p249.

Art Galleries
Whitehorse is at the center of the Yukon's robust arts community.

Arts Underground   GALLERY
(☎867-667-4080; Hougen Centre lower level, 305 Main St; ☺9am-5:30pm Mon-Sat) Operated by the Yukon Arts Society. There are carefully selected and well-mounted rotating exhibits.

Yukon Artists@Work   GALLERY
(☎867-393-4848; 120 Industrial Rd; ☺noon-5pm daily Jun-Aug, Fri-Sun Sep-May) Operated by 35 local artists, some of whom may be busily creating when you visit. It's just situated north of the big box shopping area.

Midnight Sun Gallery & Gifts
                                 GALLERY, SHOP
(☎867-668-4350; 205C Main St; ☺9am-8pm) Has good selections of Yukon arts, crafts and products.

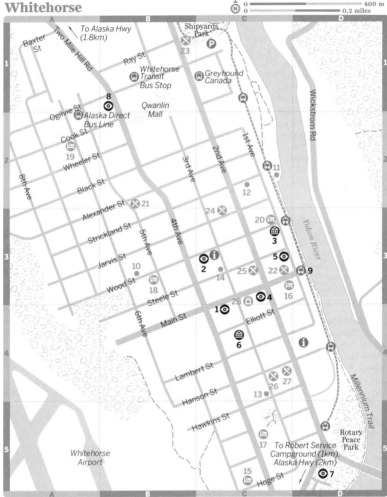

North End Gallery
GALLERY
(☏867-393-3590; 1116 1st Ave; ☉10am-6pm Mon-Sat) High-end Canadian art.

Sundog Carving Studio & Gallery
GALLERY
(☏867-633-4186; 4194 4th Ave; ☉9am-4:30pm Mon-Fri) First Nations artists sell their own works at this cooperative store.

🏃 Activities
The VIC can guide you to numerous local hikes and activities year-round. Otherwise, Whitehorse is a major outfitting center for adventures on Yukon waterways.

Canoeing & Kayaking
Whitehorse is the starting place for popular canoeing and kayaking trips to Carmacks or on to Dawson City. It's an average of eight days to the former and 16 days to the latter. Outfitters offer rentals that include transport back to Whitehorse. Canoe/kayak to Carmacks is about $210/300, to Whitehorse $350/500. Most paddlers use the map *The Yukon River: Marsh Lake to Dawson City* available at www.yukonbooks.com.

Whitehorse

Kanoe People ADVENTURE TOURS
(☏867-668-4899; www.kanoepeople.com; cnr 1st Ave & Strickland St) At the river's edge. Can arrange any type of trip including paddles down Teslin and Big Salmon Rivers. Gear, maps and guides for sale, bikes for rent.

Up North Adventures ADVENTURE TOURS
(☏867-667-7035; www.upnorthadventures.com; 103 Strickland St) Offers rentals and transport on the major rivers. Also paddling lessons, guided mountain-bike trips and winter sports.

Cycling
Whitehorse has scores of bike trails along the Yukon River and into the surrounding hills. The VIC has maps. For bike rentals, try Cadence Cycle (☏867-633-5600; 508 Wood St) which has good used mountain bikes from $20 per day. It also does repairs.

Walking & Hiking
You can walk a scenic 5km loop around Whitehorse's waters that includes a stop at the fishway. From the SS *Klondike* go south on the Millennium Trail until you reach the Robert Service Campground and the Rotary Centennial Footbridge over the river. The fishway is just south. Head north along the water and cross the Robert Campbell Bridge and you are back in the town center.

Tours

**Yukon Historical & Museums
Association** WALKING TOURS
(☏867-667-4704; 3126 3rd Ave; admission $4; ☺9am-3pm Mon-Sat Jun-Aug) Offers quirky and interesting downtown walking tours four times daily. Meet at its office in the 1904 Donneworth House. Ask your guide to show you the WWII-era American latrine that's still not winning any hearts and minds.

FREE **Yukon Conservation Society**
HIKING TOURS
(☏867-668-5678; www.yukonconservation.org; 302 Hawkins St; ☺Jul & Aug) Discover the natural beauty all around Whitehorse with a free Yukon Conservation Society nature hike. There are 10 itineraries ranging from easy to hard.

✷ Festivals & Events
See p245 for some legendary Yukon events that include Whitehorse.

🛏 Sleeping
Whitehorse can get almost full during the peak of summer, so book ahead. The VIC has lists of B&Bs. Whitehorse has a lot of midrange motels that earn the sobriquet 'veteran.' Check a room first before you commit.

High Country Inn
HOTEL **$$**

(☎867-667-4471, 800-554-4471; www.highcountryinn.ca; 4051 4th Ave; r $90-220; ❄@☎) Towering over Whitehorse (four stories!), the High Country is popular with business travelers and high-end groups. The 84 rooms are large – some have huge whirlpools right in the room. A deranged-looking 40ft Mountie stands guard in the parking lot.

Edgewater Hotel
HOTEL **$$**

(☎867-667-2572, 877-484-3334; www.edgewaterhotelwhitehorse.com; 101 Main St; r $90-190; ❄@☎) Much updated, the Edgewater has a dash of style. The 30 rooms are smallish (some lack air-con) but have flat-screen TVs. Better rooms have river views, some have kitchens.

Robert Service Campground
CAMPGROUND **$**

(☎867-668-3721; www.robertservicecampground.com; Robert Service Way; sites $18; ☉mid-May-Sep; @☎) It's a pretty 15-minute walk from town on the Millennium Trail to the 70 sites at this tents-only campground on the river 1km south of town. Excellent coffee, baked goods and ice cream in the cafe.

Historical House B&B
B&B **$$**

(☎867-668-2526; www.yukongold.com; cnr 5th Ave & Wood St; r $85-110; ❄@) A classic wooden home from 1907, there are three rooms here. Top-floor ones have individual bathrooms down the hall and angled ceilings. A larger unit has a huge kitchen. The common area has a wood stove. There's high-speed internet and a nice garden.

Midnight Sun Inn
B&B **$$**

(☎867-667-2255, 800-284-4448; www.midnightsunbb.com; 6188 6th Ave; r $100-135; ❄@) A modern B&B in a sort of overgrown suburban-style house with four themed rooms. The Sun is downtown, has high-speed internet and serves big breakfasts.

Beez Kneez Bakpakers
HOSTEL **$**

(☎867-456-2333; www.bzkneez.com; 408 Hoge St; dm/r $30/65; @☎) Like the home you've left behind, this cheery hostel has a garden, deck, grill and free bikes. Two cabins ($65) are much in demand.

River View Hotel
MOTEL **$$**

(Canada's Best Value Inn; ☎867-667-7801, 888-315-2378; www.riverviewhotel.ca; 102 Wood St; r $90-150; @☎) The floors sound hollow here but many of the 53 rooms have the views implied by the name and all are very large. It's close to everything, yet on a quiet street.

Hi Country RV Park
CAMPGROUND **$**

(☎867-667-7445; www.hicountryrvyukon.com; 91734 Alaska Hwy; tent/RV $18/36; @☎) At the top of Robert Service Way, this woodsy campground offers hookups, showers, laundry and a playground.

✖ Eating

Ignore the influx of chains and enjoy one of Whitehorse's excellent downtown restaurants. There's a great range; look for fresh Yukon salmon in season. The **Fireweed Community Market** (Shipyards Park; ☉3-8pm Thu mid-May–mid-Sep) draws vendors from the region; the berries are fabulous.

⬟ TOP CHOICE ⬟ Klondike Rib & Salmon Bake
CANADIAN **$$**

(☎867-667-7554; 2116 2nd Ave; mains $12-25; ☉4-9pm) It looks touristy and it seems touristy and it *is* touristy, but the food is excellent at this sprawling casual place with two decks. Besides the namesakes, fresh halibut also wins raves.

Giorgio's Cucina
ITALIAN **$$**

(☎867-668-4050; 206 Jarvis St; mains $12-30; ☉11:30am-2pm & 5-10pm) The best place in town for Italian has creative specials. The semi-open kitchen flames things up and the steaks are prime. Portions are mother lode size – make certain your room has a fridge.

Yukon Meat & Sausage
DELI **$**

(☎867-667-6077; 203 Hanson St; sandwiches $6; ☉9am-5:30pm Mon-Sat) The smell of smoked meat wafts out to the street and you walk right in; there's a huge selection of prepared items and custom-made sandwiches. Great for picnics, or eat in.

Sanchez Cantina
MEXICAN **$$**

(☎867-668-5858; 211 Hanson St; mains $10-20; ☉11:30am-3pm & 5-9:30pm) You have to head south across two borders to find Mexican this authentic. Burritos are the thing – get them with the spicy mix of red and green sauces. Settle in for what may be a wait on the broad patio.

Baked Café
CAFE **$**

(☎867-633-6291; 100 Main St; snacks $4; ☉7am-7pm; ☎) In summer, the outdoor tables at this stylish cafe attract swells in shades who you'd think would be reading *Daily Variety*. Smoothies, soups, daily lunch specials, baked goods and more.

⬟ Alpine Bakery
BAKERY **$**

(☎867-668-6871; 411 Alexander St; snacks from $6; ☉8am-6pm Mon-Sat) Everything is organic at this serious bakery where there are daily whole-grain and lunch specials. Fresh juices are just the thing to cool down on that one hot summer day.

Drinking

Whitehorse has a fair number of grotty old boozers. But you can find enjoyable and atmospheric bars in the Edgewater Hotel and High Country Inn . Look for the tasty brews of the local Yukon Brewing Co.

All summer, there are free lunchtime concerts by Yukon musicians and artists at LePage Park (cnr Wood St & 3rd Ave; ⊘noon, Mon-Fri May-Sep).

Coasters (☑867-633-2788; 206 Jarvis St; ⊘3pm-late) has deejays and bands playing rockabilly, hip-hop or something trendy from Vancouver. Sunday is open mike.

Shopping

Many of the galleries listed in Sights are excellent sources of local items.

TOP CHOICE Mac's Fireweed Books BOOKSTORE (☑867-668-2434;www.yukonbooks.com; 203 Main St; ⊘8am-midnight May-Sep, to 9pm Oct-Apr) Mac's has an unrivaled selection of Yukon titles. It also stocks topographical maps, road maps, magazines and newspapers.

ℹ Information

Among local newspapers, the *Yukon News* is feisty, while *What's Up Yukon* (www. whatsupyukon.com) is the source for entertainment listings.

Tourism Whitehorse (☑867-668-8629; www. visitwhitehorse.com; 3128 3rd Ave; ⊘9am-4:30pm Mon-Fri) Located next to the Yukon Historical & Museums Association in a 1905 house. Strictly for the city; good website.

VIC (☑867-667-3084; 100 Hanson St; ⊘8am-8pm May–mid-Sep, 9am-4:30pm Mon-Fri mid-Sep–May) Essential; has territory-wide information.

Whitehorse General Hospital (☑867-393-8700; 5 Hospital Rd; ⊘24hr)

ℹ Getting There & Away

Whitehorse is the transportation hub of the Yukon.

Air

Whitehorse airport (YXY; ☑867-667-8440; www.gov.yk.ca/yxy/) Five minutes west of downtown off the Alaska Hwy.

Air Canada (☑888-247-2262; www.aircanada. com) Serves Vancouver.

Air North (☑800-661-0407; www.flyairnorth. com) Locally owned, serves Dawson City, Old Crow, Inuvik in the NWT, Fairbanks in Alaska, and Vancouver, Edmonton and Calgary.

Condor (☑800-364-1667, in Germany 01805 707 202; www.condor.com) Has twice-weekly flights to/from Frankfurt in summer.

Bus

Bus services, er, come and go; check the latest with the VIC.

Alaska Direct Bus Line (☑867-668-4833; www.alaskadirectbusline.com; 501 Ogilvie St) Service (two/three times weekly winter/summer) to Fairbanks and Anchorage, Alaska via the Alaska Hwy including Haines Junction (US$75, two hours) and Tok, Alaska (US$135, 9½ hours).

Greyhound Canada (☑867-667-2223, 800-661-8747; www.greyhound.ca; 2191 2nd Ave) Service south along the Alaska Hwy to Dawson Creek ($240, 20 hours, three times per week); connects with buses for the rest of BC and Canada.

White Pass & Yukon Route (☑867-633-5710; www.wpyr.com; Whitehorse ticket office, 1109 Front St; ⊘9am-5pm Mon-Sat mid-May–mid-Sep) Offers an enjoyable and scenic rail and bus connection to/from Skagway (adult/child from US$116/58, 4½ hours) via Fraser, BC. There is an option for a longer train ride with the bus transfer at Carcross.

ℹ Getting Around

To/From the Airport

Yellow Cab (☑867-668-4811) About $18 from the center for the 10-minute ride.

Bus

Whitehorse Transit System (☑867-668-7433; ⊘Mon-Sat) Main transfer point at the Qwanlin Mall. Route 2 (ticket $2.50, every 30 to 70 minutes) serves the airport, the center and the Robert Service Campground.

Car & RV

Check your rate very carefully as it's common for a mileage charge to be added after the first 100km, which will not get you far in the Yukon. Also understand your insurance coverage and whether damage from Yukon's rugged roads is covered. There's a reason you see all those ads for windshield replacement.

Budget (☑867-667-6200; www.budget.com), **Hertz** (☑867-668-4224; www.hertz.com) and **National/NorCan** (☑867-456-2277; www. national.com) are at the airport.

Whitehorse Subaru (☑867-393-6550; www. whitehorsesubaru.com; 17 Chilkoot Way) Can usually beat the biggies on price.

Fraserway RV Rentals (☑867-668-3438; www.fraserwayrvrentals.com; 9039 Quartz Rd) Rents all shapes and sizes of RV from $80 to $300 per day depending on size (it matters) and season. Mileage extra.

ALASKA HIGHWAY

It may be called the Alaska Hwy but given that its longest stretch is in the Yukon (958km) perhaps another name is in order...

Roughly 2450km in length from Dawson Creek, BC, to Delta Junction, far inside Alaska, the Alaska Hwy has a meaning well beyond just a road. Sure it's a way to get from point A to point B, but it's also a badge, an honor, an accomplishment. Even though today it's a modern road, the very name still evokes images of big adventure and getting away from it all.

As you drive the Alaska Hwy in the Yukon, know that you're on the most scenic and varied part of the road. From little villages to the city of Whitehorse, from meandering rivers to the upthrust drama of the St Elias Mountains, the scenery will overwhelm you.

BC to Whitehorse

You'll never be far from an excuse to stop on this stretch of the Alcan. Towns, small parks and various roadside attractions appear at regular intervals. None are massively compelling but overall it's a pleasant drive. See p175 for details of the Alaska Hwy in BC.

WORTH A TRIP

LET THERE BE HIGHWAY

Nowadays the aura of the Alaska Hwy is psychological rather than physical. In every way it's a modern two-lane road, with smooth curves, broad sight lines and paving from one end to another, but that has not always been the case. A famous 1943 photo shows a jeep seemingly being sucked down to China through a morass of mud while soldiers look on helplessly.

With the outbreak of WWII, Canada and the US decided that years of debate should end and that a proper road was needed to link Alaska and the Yukon to the rest of Canada and the US.

That a road – any road – could be carved out of the raw tundra and wilderness of the north in a little over a year was a miracle, although unlimited money and manpower (US soldiers and Canadian civilians, including Aboriginal people) helped. The 2450km gravel highway ran between Dawson Creek in BC and Fairbanks in Alaska. The route chosen for the highway followed a series of existing airfields – Fort St John, Fort Nelson, Watson Lake and Whitehorse – known as the Northwest Staging Route.

In April 1946 the Canadian section of the road (1965km) was officially handed over to Canada. In the meantime, private contractors were busy widening, graveling and straightening the highway, leveling its steep grades and replacing temporary bridges with permanent steel ones – a process that has continued since, creating the modern road you drive today.

Known variously as the Alaskan International Hwy, the Alaska Military Hwy and the Alcan (short for Alaska-Canada) Hwy, it's now called the Alaska Hwy. It has transformed both the Yukon and Alaska, opening up the north to year-round travel and forever changing the way of life of the First Nations along the route.

The Alaska Hwy begins at 'Mile 0' in Dawson Creek in northeastern BC and goes to Fairbanks, Alaska, although the official end is at Delta Junction, about 155km southeast of Fairbanks.

Mileposts long served as reference points, but improvements shortening the road and Canada's adoption of the metric system have made mileage references archaic. Historic numbers persist in the names of some businesses and attractions.

For more on the Alaska Hwy and its harrowing past, check out the **Watson Lake VIC** (p253), the **Yukon Transportation Museum** (p247) in Whitehorse and the **Alaska Highway House** in Dawson Creek, BC (p176). For a minutely detailed guide to every feature, including seemingly every pothole and moose turd, look for the *Milepost*, a legendary annual publication.

WATSON LAKE

Originally named after Frank Watson, a British trapper, Watson Lake is the first town in the Yukon on the Alaska Hwy and is just over the border from BC. It's mostly a good rest stop except for the superb VIC (☑867-536-7469; www.watsonlake.ca; ☉8am-8pm summer), which has a good museum about the highway and a passel of territory-wide info. The town offers campgrounds, motels, full services and a Greyhound Canada stop.

The town is famous for its Sign Post Forest just outside the VIC. The first signpost, 'Danville, Illinois,' was nailed up in 1942. Others were added and now there are 68,000 signs, many purloined late at night from municipalities worldwide.

Twenty-six kilometers west of Watson Lake is the junction with the Stewart-Cassiar Hwy (Hwy 37), which heads south into BC (p175). For a discussion of the various routes into the Yukon, see p174.

Just west of the junction, family-run Nugget City (☑867-536-2307, 888-536-2307; www.nuggetcity.com; campsites from $20, cabins from $80; ☎) has accommodations and food that's three cuts above the Alaska Hwy norm. Stop just for the baked goods, especially the berry pie.

Another 110km west, past the 1112km marker, look for the Rancheria Falls Recreation Site. A boardwalk leads to powerful twin waterfalls. It's an excellent stop.

TESLIN

Teslin, on the long, narrow lake of the same name, is 272km west of Watson Lake. Long a home to the Tlingits (lin-*kits*), the Alaska Hwy brought both prosperity and rapid change to this aboriginal population. The engrossing George Johnston Museum (☑867-390-2550; www.gjmuseum.yk.net; Km 1294 Alaska Hwy; adult/child $6/3; ☉9am-5pm mid-May–early Sep) details the life and culture of a 20th-century Tlingits leader through photographs, displays and artifacts.

JOHNSON'S CROSSING

Some 53km north of Teslin is Johnson's Crossing, at the junction of the Alaska Hwy and Canol Rd (Hwy 6). During WWII the US army built the Canol pipeline at tremendous human and financial expense to pump oil from Norman Wells in the NWT to Whitehorse. Like any good military boondoggle, it was abandoned after countless hundreds of millions of dollars (in 1943 money, no less) were spent.

ROBERT CAMPBELL HWY

To get right off the beaten path, consider this lonely gravel road (Hwy 4) which runs 588km from Watson Lake north and west to Carmacks (p260), where you can join the Klondike Hwy for Dawson City. Along its length, the highway parallels various rivers and lakes. Wilderness campers will be thrilled.

Ross River, 373km from Watson Lake at the junction with the Canol Rd (Hwy 6), is home to the Kaska First Nation and a supply center for the local mining industry. There are campgrounds and motels in town.

Whitehorse to Alaska

For long segments west of Whitehorse, the Alaska Hwy has been modernized to the point of blandness. Fortunately, this ends abruptly in Haines Junction. From here the road parallels legendary Kluane National Forest and the St Elias Mountains. The 300km to Beaver Creek is the most scenic part of the entire highway.

HAINES JUNCTION

It's goodbye flatlands when you reach Haines Junction and see the sweep of imposing peaks looming over town. You've reached the stunning Kluane National Park and this is the gateway. The town makes an excellent base for exploring the park or staging a serious four-star mountaineering, backcountry or river adventure. German travelers will hear their language spoken all over town.

The magnificent Haines Hwy heads south from here to Alaska (p256).

Yukon Tourism (☑867-634-2345; www.hainesjunctionyukon.com; ☉10am-6pm May & Sep, 8am-8pm Jun-Aug) and Parks Canada (☑867-634-7250; www.parkscanada.gc.ca/kluane; ☉10am-6pm mid-May–Aug, to 4pm Sep–mid-May) share the VIC (Logan St) in the Kluane National Park headquarters building. There's lots of info from the two agencies and a good model of the local terrain. In summer, rangers give regular nature talks.

All shops, lodging and services are clustered around the Alaska and Haines Hwys junction. And that thing that looks like an acid-trip cupcake? It's a **sculpture** meant to be a winsome tableau of local characters and critters.

🏃 Activities

Even the spectacular ridges surrounding Haines Junction don't begin to hint at the beauty of Kluane National Park. Although the park should be your focus, there are some good activities locally.

For a hike after hours of driving, there's a pretty 5.5km **nature walk** along Dezadeash River where Hwy 3 crosses it at the south end of town.

Paddlewheel Adventures (☑867-634-2683; www.paddlewheeladventures.com; 116 Kathleen St), opposite the VIC, arranges Tatshenshini rafting trips ($125 per person, includes lunch), scenic white-water trips and guided interpretive hikes ($55 to $125). It rents mountain bikes or canoes ($30 per day) and provides local transportation.

Owned by a longtime park warden and guide, **Kruda Ché Boat Tours** (☑867-634-2378; www.krudache.com) will arrange any number of custom tours by boat and on foot within Kluane National Park. Wildlife, history and aboriginal culture are among the themes.

🛏 Sleeping & Eating

There's a cluster of motels and RV parks in Haines Junction. There's a beach and shade at **Pine Lake**, a territorial campground 6km east of town on the Alaska Hwy. Cerulean waters highlight **Kathleen Lake** (sites $15), a Parks Canada campground 24km south of Haines Junction off the Haines Hwy.

Raven Motel   INN **$$**
(☑867-634-2500; www.ravenhotelyukon.com; 181 Alaska Hwy; r $130-160; ❄🐾) There are 12 comfortable motel-style rooms here and guests can partake of a vast German-style break buffet. But the real star is the restaurant, which has the best food between Whitehorse and Alaska. Menus are complex and continental (meals $35 to $50).

Alcan Motor Inn   MOTEL **$$**
(☑867-634-2371, 888-265-1018; www.alcanmotorinn.com; s & d $90-150; ❄🐾) The modern two-story Alcan has 23 large rooms with great views of the jagged Auriol Range. Some have full kitchens and there's a cafe.

Village Bakery & Deli   BAKERY/CAFE **$**
(☑867-634-2867; Logan St; mains $6-10; ⊙7am-9pm May-Aug; 🐾) Across from the VIC, the bakery here turns out excellent goods all day, while the deli counter has tasty sandwiches you can enjoy on the huge deck. On Friday night there's a popular barbecue with live folk music.

Frosty Freeze   BURGERS **$**
(☑867-634-7070; Alaska Hwy; mains $6; ⊙11am-10pm May-Sep) What looks like a humdrum fast-food joint is several orders of magnitude better. The shakes are made with real ice cream, the sundaes feature fresh berries and the burgers (try the mushroom-Swiss number) are huge and juicy.

ℹ Information

Parks Canada has two information centers. One is in Haines Junction and the other at **Tachal Dhal** (Sheep Mountain; Alaska Hwy; ⊙9am-3:30pm late May-early Sep), 130km west of Haines Junction. Get a copy of the *Recreation Guide,* which shows the scope of the park (and how little is actually easily accessible). The map shows hikes ranging from 10 minutes to 10 days.

ℹ Getting There & Away

Alaska Direct Bus Line (☑867-668-4833; www.alaskadirectbusline.com; 501 Ogilvie St) Service (two/three times weekly winter/summer) to Fairbanks and Anchorage in Alaska via the Alaska Hwy through Tok (US$125, 7½ hours); east to Whitehorse (US$75, two hours).

KLUANE NATIONAL PARK & RESERVE

Unesco-recognized as an 'empire of mountains and ice,' Kluane National Park & Reserve looms south of the Alaska Hwy much of the way to the Alaska border. This rugged and magnificent wilderness covers 22,015 sq km of the southwest corner of the territory. Kluane (kloo-wah-neee) gets its far-too-modest name from the Southern Tutchone word for 'lake with many fish.'

With British Columbia's Tatshenshini-Alsek Provincial Park to the south and Alaska's Wrangell-St Elias National Park to the west, this is one of the largest protected wilderness areas in the world. Deep beyond the mountains you see from the Alaska Hwy are over 100 named glaciers and as many unnamed ones.

Winters are long and harsh. Summers are short, making mid-June to early September the best time to visit. Note that winter conditions can occur at any time, especially in the backcountry. See Haines Junction for the park's campground.

👁 Sights

The park consists primarily of the **St Elias Mountains** and the world's largest nonpolar ice fields. Two-thirds of the park is glacier interspersed with valleys, glacial lakes, alpine forest, meadows and tundra. The Kluane Ranges (averaging a height of 2500m) are seen along the western edge of the Alaska Hwy. A greenbelt wraps around the base where most of the animals and vegetation live. Turquoise Kluane Lake is the Yukon's largest. Hidden are the immense ice fields and towering peaks, including Mt Logan (5959m), Canada's highest mountain, and Mt St Elias (5488m), the second highest. Partial glimpses of the interior peaks can be found at the Km 1622 viewpoint on the Alaska Hwy and also around the Donjek River Bridge, but the best views are from the air. You can arrange charters of planes or helicopters in Haines Junction.

🏃 Activities

There's excellent hiking in the forested lands at the base of the mountains, along either marked trails or less-defined routes. There are about a dozen in each category, some following old mining roads, others traditional aboriginal paths. Detailed trail guides and topographical maps are available at the information centers. Talk to the rangers before setting out. They will help select a hike and can provide updates on areas that may be closed due to bear activity. Overnight hikes require backcountry permits ($10 per person per night).

The Tachal Dhal information center is the starting point for Slims West, a popular 60km round-trip trek to Kaskawulsh Glacier – one of the few that can be reached on foot. This is a difficult route that takes from three to five days to complete and includes sweeping views from Observation Mountain (2114m). An easy overnight trip is the 15km Auriol loop, which goes from spruce forest to subalpine barrens and includes a wilderness campground. It's 7km south of Haines Junction.

Fishing is good and wildlife-watching plentiful. Most noteworthy are the thousands of Dall sheep that can be seen on Sheep Mountain in April, May and September. There's a large and diverse population of grizzly bear, as well as black bear, moose, caribou, goats and 150 varieties of birds, among them eagles and the rare peregrine falcon.

Many enjoy skiing or snowshoeing, beginning in February.

DESTRUCTION BAY

This small village on the shore of huge Kluane Lake is 107km north of Haines Junction. It was given its evocative name after a storm tore through the area during construction of the highway. Most of the residents are First Nations, who live off the land through the year. Congdon Creek is 17km east of town on the Alaska Hwy and has an 81-site territorial campground and a fine lakeside setting.

BURWASH LANDING

Commune with an enormous, albeit stuffed, moose at the excellent Kluane Museum (☎867-841-5561; adult/child $4/2; ◷9am-8pm mid-May–early Sep). Enjoy intriguing wildlife exhibits and displays on natural and aboriginal history. There's boating on Kluane Lake, including a good 10km paddle to the wildlife-filled mouth of the Kluane River.

BEAVER CREEK

Wide-spot-in-the-road Beaver Creek is a beacon for sleepy travelers or those who want to get gas – certainly its lackluster

BEETLES RIP?

Even as beetles wreak havoc on forests across BC and the Rockies, the forests of the Yukon may be recovering. Certainly you can't miss the vast swaths of brown as you drive the Alaska Hwy past Kluane National Park: millions upon millions of dead trees killed by the spruce beetle, starting in 1994.

Many reasons for this disaster center on climate change, including warmer winters allowing far more beetles than usual to survive from one year to the next.

In recent years, however, several factors are now working against the beetles: dead trees mean less food, a very cold winter killed many beetles and there is now a population explosion of beetle-eaters. New attacks on trees have plummeted toward historic levels. Meanwhile, nature has opened the door to other trees; birch and alder, which grow fast and are favored by a burgeoning population of moose and other critters.

To get a sense of the devastation caused by beetles in the last decade stop at the short Spruce Beetle Loop, 17km northwest of Haines Junction, just off the highway.

eateries will ensure the latter. The Canadian border checkpoint is just north of town; the US border checkpoint is 27km further west. Both are open 24 hours.

The **VIC** (☎867-862-7321; Km 1202 Alaska Hwy; ⊗8am-8pm May-Sep) has information on all of the Yukon. A strange **sculpture garden** just north tempts the silly (or intoxicated) into unnatural acts.

Of the four motels in town, the **1202 Motor Inn** (☎867-862-7600, 800-661-0540; 1202 Alaska Hwy; r from $60) is the least offensive. The 30 rooms are basic and functional. Get one away from the idling trucks.

ALASKA

Note that the incredible scenery of the Alaska Hwy dims a bit once you cross into its namesake state. The Alaska Hwy department leaves the road much more despoiled than the pristine conditions in the Yukon.

From the US border, it's 63km (39 miles) to **Tetlin National Wildlife Refuge** (tetlin. fws.gov) on the Alaska Hwy. About 117km past Tetlin, you'll reach the junction with the Taylor Hwy (Hwy 5) which connects north with the Top of the World Hwy (p266) to Dawson City.

HAINES HIGHWAY

If you're doing only a short loop between Haines and Skagway via Whitehorse, this 259km road might be the highlight of your trip. In fact, no matter what length your Yukon adventure, the Haines Hwy (Hwy 3) might be the high point. In a relatively short distance you see glaciers, looming snow-clad peaks, lush and wild river valleys, windswept Alpine meadows and a bald-eagle-laced river delta.

Heading south of Haines Junction, look west for a close-up of the St Elias Mountains, those glaciers glimpsed at the top stretch all the way to the Pacific Ocean. About 80km south, look for the **Tatshenshini River viewpoint**. This white-water river flows through protected bear country and a valley that seems timeless.

About 10km further, look for **Million Dollar Falls**. For once the sight lives up to the billing, as water thunders through a narrow chasm. Let the roar lull you to sleep at the nearby territorial **campground**.

The highway crosses into BC for a mere 70km but you'll hope for more as you traverse high and barren alpine wilderness,

where sudden snow squalls happen year-round. At the 1070m Chilkat Pass, an ancient aboriginal route into the Yukon, the road suddenly plunges down for a steep descent into Alaska. The US border is 72km north of Haines, along the wide **Chilkat River Delta**.

Home to scores of **bald eagles** year-round, the handsome birds flock like pigeons each fall when they mass in the trees overlooking the rivers drawn by the comparatively mild weather and steady supply of fish.

Pullouts line the Haines Hwy (Hwy 7 in Alaska), especially between mileposts 19 and 26. Take your time driving and find a place to park. Just a few feet from the road it's quiet, and when you see a small tree covered with 20 pensive – and sizable – bald eagles, you can enjoy your own raptor version of *The Birds*.

Haines (Alaska)

Unlike Skagway just across the Lynn Canal, Haines has escaped the cruise-ship mobs and it's all the better for it. It's a real community with a real downtown close to the working waterfront. There are good shops, a couple of small museums and a historic fort. You can easily walk around much of the town in a few scenic hours. As you gaze out over the beautiful mountain-backed waters – possibly with a relaxing beverage in hand – you're unlikely to be jealous of those aboard the conga line of cruise ships puffing (and we mean puffing, the pollution is deplorable) their way to the next port.

Coming from the south on the Alaska Marine Highway ferries, Haines is definitely the port of choice for accessing the Yukon. For more coverage of Haines and southeast Alaska, see Lonely Planet's *Alaska*.

◉ Sights & Activities

Walk the center and waterfront and then amble over to **Fort Seward**, an old army post dating back 100 years. Now a national historic site, the many mannered buildings have been given a range of new uses, from art galleries to funky stores to B&Bs.

Haines makes the most of its feathered residents and has an **eagle festival** (http://baldeaglefest.org) in their honor every November. Numerous local guides will take you to see the birds in ways you can't do from the side of the Haines Hwy.

📛 Sleeping & Eating

The Haines CVB has oodles of choices at all price ranges.

Captain's Choice Motel　　　MOTEL $$
(📞907-766-3111, 800-478-2345; www.capchoice.com; 108 2nd Ave N; r US$100-180; 🖬🛜) An admiral might even choose this place, as many of the 37 rooms have sweeping water views and all are large. It's right in the center.

Portage Cove State Recreation Site
CAMPGROUND $
(Beach Rd; tent sites US$5; ⊘15 May-Aug) It's worth losing your car so you can stay at this cyclist- and backpacker-friendly campground on the water 1.6km south of town. Light a campfire and let the mist roll in.

Fireweed　　　FUSION $$
(📞907-766-3838; Bldg 37 Blacksmith Rd; mains US$10-20; ⊘11am-10pm; 🛜) In Fort Seward, Fireweed is an oasis of organic and creative cuisine. Enjoy the excellent pizzas, salads, chowders and seafood out on the deck overlooking the Lynn Canal. We swoon over the Haines Brewing Spruce Tip Ale.

Mountain Market & Spirits　　　MARKET $
(📞907-766-3340; 151 3rd Ave; meals US$4-10; ⊘7am-7pm; 🛜) Get your Haines Hwy or Alaska ferry picnic here. Treats include excellent coffee, baked goods, big sandwiches and lots of organic prepared foods.

ℹ️ Information

Prices for Haines are in US$. Haines is on Alaska time, one hour earlier than Yukon time.

Haines Convention & Visitors Bureau (📞907-766-2234, 800-458-3579; www.haines.ak.us; 122 2nd Ave; ⊘9am-5pm May-Sep) Publishes a hugely useful vacation planner and has trail maps plus Yukon info.

ℹ️ Getting There & Away

There's no public transportation from Haines into the Yukon.

Alaska Maritime Highway System (📞800-642-0066; www.ferryalaska.com) Superb service links Haines and the Yukon to BC and the US. Car ferries serve Skagway, the Inside Passage and importantly, Prince Rupert in BC; also Bellingham, Washington in the US. The ferry terminal is situated 6.5km south of town.

Haines-Skagway Fast Ferry (📞907-766-2100, 888-766-2103; www.hainesskagwayfastferry.com) Carries passengers only (adult/child US$35/18, 45 minutes, three or more per day, June to September) and docks near the center.

KLONDIKE HIGHWAY

Beginning seaside in Skagway, Alaska, the 716km Klondike Hwy climbs high to the forbidding Chilkoot Pass before crossing into stunning alpine scenery on the way to Carcross. For much of its length, the road generally follows the Gold Rush Trail, the route of the Klondike prospectors. You'll have a much easier time of it than they did (p259).

North of Whitehorse, the road passes through often-gentle terrain that has been scorched by wildfires through the years. Signs showing the dates let you chart nature's recovery.

Skagway (Alaska)

Skagway has been both delighting and horrifying travelers for over 100 years. In 1898 rogues of all kinds preyed upon arriving miners bound for Dawson. Today it's T-shirt vendors preying on tourists. When several huge cruise ships show up at once, the streets swarm with day-trippers.

However, behind the tat there's a real town that has many preserved attractions. At night, after the cruise ships have sailed, Skagway has its own quiet charm. Still, there's no need to linger, as the Yukon beckons. Although it's in the US, it can only be reached by car on the Klondike Hwy from the Yukon (with a short stretch in BC). It's the starting point for the famed Chilkoot Trail and the White Pass & Yukon Route.

Skagway is the last stop on the Alaska Marine Highway System's inland passage service from the south and as such is an important entry point for the Yukon. Lonely Planet's *Alaska* has extensive coverage of Skagway and the rest of Southeast Alaska.

Prices below are in US$. Skagway is on Alaska time, one hour earlier than the Yukon. Most places close outside of summer.

⊙ Sights

A seven-block corridor along Broadway, part of the Klondike Gold Rush National Historic Park, is home to restored buildings, false fronts and wooden sidewalks from Skagway's gold rush era. The Park Service has tours, a museum and info.

The White Pass & Yukon Route (WP&YR; 📞907-983-2217, 800-343-7373; www.wpyr.com; cnr 2nd Ave & Spring St; adult/child US$110/55; ⊘early May-late Sep) is the stunning reason most people visit Skagway (other than T-shirts). The line twists up the tortuous route to the namesake White Pass, tracing the notorious White Pass trail used during the Klondike Gold Rush.

🛏 Sleeping

Reservations are strongly recommended during July and August. The CVB has comprehensive accommodations lists.

Sergeant Preston's Lodge MOTEL **$$** (☑907-983-2521; www.sgtprestonslodge.com; 370 6th Ave; r US$80-120; 🐾) The 40 bright and clean rooms are right in the historic center. Call for ferry pick-up.

Pullen Creek RV Park CAMPGROUND **$** (☑907-983-2768, 800-936-3731; www.pullen creekrv.com; 501 Congress St; tent/RV US$22/36) This park is right next to the ferry terminal.

North Eden CAFE **$** (☑907-983-2784; 21st Ave at State St; meals $4-8; ⊙7am-2pm) Located inside the You Say Tomato Natural Foods store, stop here for a hearty coffee before you head up the Klondike Hwy or lay in some healthy eats before the ferry south.

ℹ Information

Chilkoot Trail Centre (cnr Broadway & 2nd Ave; ⊙8am-5pm Jun-Aug) Run by Parks Canada (☑800-661-0486; www.pc.gc.ca/chilkoot) and the US National Park Service (☑907-983-3655; www.nps.gov/klgo), this place provides advice, permits, maps and a list of transportation options to/from the Chilkoot Trail.

Skagway Convention & Visitors Bureau (☑907-983-2854, 888-762-1898; www.skag way.com; 245 Broadway; ⊙8am-6pm) Complete area details inside a landmark building.

US National Park Service (☑907-983-2921; cnr Broadway & 2nd Ave; ⊙8am-6pm) Pick up the *Skagway Trail Map* for area hikes; has full details on the Klondike Gold Rush National Historic Park.

ℹ Getting There & Away

From Skagway to Whitehorse on the Klondike Hwy (Hwy 2) is 177km. Customs at the border usually moves fairly quickly.

Boat

Alaska Maritime Highway System (☑800-642-0066; www.ferryalaska.com) Superb service links Haines and the Yukon to BC and the US. Car ferries serve Haines, the Inside Passage and importantly, Prince Rupert in BC;

also Bellingham, Washington in the US. The ferry terminal is right in the center.

Haines-Skagway Fast Ferry (☑907-766-2100, 888-766-2103; www.hainesskagwayfastferry. com) Carries passengers only (adult/child US$35/18, 45 minutes, three or more per day, June to September) and docks near the center.

Bus & Train

White Pass & Yukon Route (☑907-983-2217, 800-343-7373; www.wpyr.com; cnr 2nd Ave & Spring St; adult/child from US$116/58, 4½ hours; ⊙Mon-Sat mid-May–mid-Sep) Offers an enjoyable and scenic rail and bus connection to/from Whitehorse via Fraser, BC. There is an option for a longer train ride with the bus transfer at Carcross.

Chilkoot Trail

Arduous at best and deadly at worst in 1898, the Chilkoot Trail was the route most prospectors took to get over the 1110m Chilkoot Pass from Skagway and into the Yukon. Today, it's not unusual for hikers to reserve spots months in advance to travel the same route.

The well-marked 53km trail begins near **Dyea**, 14km northwest of Skagway, and heads northeast over the pass. It then follows the Taiya River to Lake Bennett in BC, and takes three to five days to hike. It's quite a difficult route in good weather and often treacherous in bad. You must be in good physical condition and come fully equipped. Layers of warm clothes and rain gear are essential.

Hardware, tools and supplies dumped by the prospectors still litter the trail. At several places there are wooden shacks where you can put up for the night, but these are usually full, so a tent and sleeping bag are required. There are 10 designated campgrounds along the route, each with bear caches.

At the Canadian end you can either take the White Pass & Yukon Route train from Bennett back to Skagway or further up the line to Fraser in BC, where you can connect with a bus for Whitehorse.

The Chilkoot Trail is a primary feature of the **Klondike Gold Rush International Historic Park**, a series of sites managed by both Parks Canada and the US National Park Service that stretches from Seattle, Washington, to Dawson City. Each Chilkoot hiker must obtain one of the 50 permits available for each day in summer; reserve well in advance. Parks Canada/US National Park Service charge $53 for a permit plus $12 for a reservation. Each day eight permits are issued on a first-come, first-served basis. For information, contact the Chilkoot Trail Centre in Skagway (p258) or go online. Necessary pre-planning includes determining which campsites you'll use each night.

Carcross

Long a forgotten gold-rush town, cute little Carcross, 74km southeast of Whitehorse, is on a roll. There are daily trains in summer from Skagway on the White Pass & Yukon Route (p258; one-way adult/child $170/85). Some old buildings are being restored and the site on Lake Bennett is superb. (Although Klondike prospectors who had to build boats here to cross the lake didn't think so.)

The VIC (☎867-821-4431; ☉8am-8pm May-Sep) is in the old train station and has an excellent walking tour booklet of the town. The station also has good displays on local history and directly behind is a hall where local artists show their wares.

Carcross Desert, the world's smallest, is the exposed sandy bed of a glacial lake. It's 2km north of town.

Whitehorse to Carmacks

Leaving Whitehorse by the Klondike Hwy is none too exciting. There's land with low trees and a few cattle ranches. After about 40km, however, look for serene Lake Laberge, which has a beach, followed by Fox Lake, 24km further north, and Twin Lakes, 23km south of Carmacks. Each has a government campground with shelters and pump water.

FOOLHARDY & FUTILE

The Klondike Gold Rush continues to be the defining moment for the Yukon. Certainly it was the population high point. Some 40,000 gold seekers washed ashore (some literally) in Skagway, hoping to strike it rich in the gold fields of Dawson City, some 700km north.

To say that most were ill-prepared for the adventure is an understatement. Although some were veterans of other gold rushes, a high percentage were American men looking for adventure. Clerks, lawyers and waiters were just some of those who thought they'd just pop up North and get rich. The reality was different. Landing in Skagway, they were set upon by all manner of flimflam artists, most working for the incorrigible Soapy Smith. Next came dozens of trips hefting their 1000lb of required supplies over the frozen Chilkoot Pass. Then they had to build boats from scratch and make their way across lakes and the Yukon River to Dawson. Scores died trying.

Besides more scamsters, there was another harsh reality awaiting in Dawson: by the summer of 1897 when the first ships reached the west coast of the US with news of the discoveries on Dawson's Bonanza Creek, the best sites had all been claimed. The Klondike Gold Rush mobs were mostly too late to the action by at least a year. Sick and broke, the survivors glumly made their way back to the US. Few found any gold and most sold their gear for pennies to merchants who in turn resold it to incoming gold seekers for top dollar. Several family fortunes in the Yukon today can be traced to this trade.

Today, even the hardiest folk seem like couch potatoes when compared to these harrowing stories. The depravation, disease and heartbreak of these 'dudes' of the day make for fascinating reading. Among the many books about the Klondike Gold Rush, the following are recommended (and easily found in the Yukon):

» The Klondike Fever by Pierre Berton is the classic on the gold rush.

» Sailor on Snowshoes by Dick North traces Jack London's time in the Yukon and the hunt for his cabin. London's stories of the gold rush made his name as a writer.

» Soapy Smith by Stan Sauerwein is a delightful tale about the Skagway scalawag for whom the word incorrigible was invented.

The Klondike Hwy from Skagway via Whitehorse and as far as Minto follows what Parks Canada calls the Gold Rush Trail. To stay on the course of the gold seekers from there you'll need to paddle the Yukon River.

Carmacks

This village of 400 sits right on the Yukon River and is named for one of the discoverers of gold in 1896, George Washington Carmacks. A rogue seaman wandering the Yukon, it was almost by luck that Carmacks (with Robert Henderson, Tagish Charlie and Keish – aka Skookum Jim Mason) made their claim on Bonanza Creek. Soon he was living the high life and it wasn't long before he abandoned his First Nations family and headed south to the US.

Given his record as a husband and father, it's fitting that Carmacks be honored by this uninspired collection of gas stations and places to stay. The main reason to stop is the excellent Tage Cho Hudan Interpretive Centre (☑867-863-5830; admission by donation; ☺9am-4pm May-Sep). Volunteers explain aboriginal life past and present. Like elsewhere in the territory, residents here are keenly attuned to the land, which supplies them with game and fish throughout the year. A pretty 15-minute interpretive walk by the river provides a glimmer of insight into this life.

This is also the junction with the Robert Campbell Hwy (p253).

About 25km north of Carmacks, the Five Finger Recreation Site has excellent views of the treacherous stretch of the rapids that tested the wits of riverboat captains traveling between Whitehorse and Dawson. There's a steep 1.5km walk down to the rapids.

Minto

Easily missed – unless you're toting a canoe or kayak – Minto is where the Klondike Hwy leaves the route of the Gold Rush Trail. This is a popular place to put in for the four- to five-day trip down the Yukon River to Dawson City. It's about 72km north of Carmacks.

Stewart Crossing

Another popular place to get your canoe wet, Stewart Crossing is on the Stewart River, which affords a narrow and somewhat more rugged experience before it joins the Yukon to the west for the trip to Dawson.

Otherwise unexceptional, the village is the junction of the Klondike Hwy (Hwy 2) and the Silver Trail (Hwy 11).

North of Stewart Crossing the Klondike Hwy continues for 139 bland kilometers to the junction with the Dempster Hwy. From here it's only 40km to Dawson City.

DAWSON CITY

If you didn't know its history, Dawson would be a delightful place to pause for a while, plunging into its quirky culture and falling for its seductive, funky vibe. That it's one of the most historic and beautiful towns in Canada is like gold dust on a cake: unnecessary but damn nice.

Set on a narrow shelf at the confluence of the Yukon and Klondike Rivers, a mere 240km south of the Arctic Circle, Dawson City was the center of the Klondike Gold Rush.

Today, you can wander the dirt streets of Dawson, passing old buildings with dubious permafrost foundations leaning on each other for support (that's in comparison to the real drunks you'll see leaning on each other for support outside the local saloons). There's a rich cultural life, with many people finding Dawson the perfect place for free expression (that person doing a shot on the next bar stool may be a dancer, filmmaker, painter or a miner).

Dawson can be busy in the summer, especially during its festivals. But by September the days are getting short, the seasonal workers have fled south and the 2000 year-round residents (professionals, miners, First Nations, dreamers, artists and those who aren't sure where they fit) are settling in for another long and quiet winter.

History

In 1898 more than 30,000 prospectors milled the streets of Dawson – a few newly rich, but most without prospects and at odds with themselves and the world. Shops, bars and prostitutes relieved these hordes of what money they had, but Dawson's fortunes were tied to the gold miners and, as the boom ended, the town began a decades-long slow fade.

The territorial capital was moved to Whitehorse in 1952 and the town lingered on, surviving on the low-key but ongoing gold-mining industry. By 1970 the population was under 900. But then a funny thing happened on the way to Dawson's demise: it was rediscovered. Improvements to the Klondike Hwy and links to Alaska allowed the first major influx of summertime tourists, who found a charmingly moldering time capsule from the gold rush. Parks Canada designated much of the town as historic and began restorations.

◎ Sights

Dawson is small enough to walk around in a few hours, but you can easily fill three or more days with the many local things to see and do. If the summertime hordes get you down, head uphill for a few blocks where you'll find timeless old houses and streets.

Like a gold nugget on a tapped-out creek, street numbers are a rarity in Dawson. Unless noted otherwise, opening hours and times given here cover the period from mid-May to early September. For the rest of the year, most sights, attractions and many businesses are closed.

In a real boon to families, almost all attractions are free for kids 12 and under.

Klondike National Historic Sites
HISTORIC PARK

It's easy to relive the gold rush at myriad preserved and restored places. **Parks Canada** (www.pc.gc.ca/dawson) does an excellent job of providing information and tours. In addition to the individual sight and tour fees listed here, there are various good-value Parks Canada **passes** (adult $14-32); buy tickets and passes at the beautiful **Palace Grand Theatre** (King St; ⊙9:30am-5:30pm), between 2nd and 3rd Aves.

For information, go to the Parks Canada desk in the VIC. See p262 for details on Dredge No 4.

Robert Service Cabin

(cnr 8th Ave & Hanson St; admission free; ⊙2:30-4:30pm) Called the 'Bard of the Yukon,' poet and writer Robert W Service lived in this typical gold-rush cabin from 1909 to 1912. Don't miss the **dramatic readings** (adult $7; ⊙1:30pm & 7pm).

Commissioner's Residence

(Font St; adult $7; ⊙10am-5pm, tour times vary) Built in 1901 to house the territorial commissioner, this proud building was designed to give potential civic investors confidence in the city. The building was the longtime home of Martha Black, who came to the Yukon in 1898, owned a lumberyard and was elected to the Canadian Parliament at age 70. (*Martha Black* by Flo Whyard is a great book about this amazing woman.)

SS KenoYukon

(adult $7; ⊙10am-6pm) The SS *Keno* was one of a fleet of paddle wheelers that worked Yukon's rivers for more than half a century. Grounded along the waterfront, the boat re-creates a time before any highways.

Harrington's Store

(cnr 3rd Ave & Princess St; admission free; ⊙9am-4:30pm) This old shop has historic photos from Dawson's heyday.

TOP CHOICE Jack London Interpretive Centre
MUSEUM

(Firth St; admission $5; ⊙11am-6pm) In 1898 Jack London lived in the Yukon, the setting for his most popular stories, including *Call of the Wild* and *White Fang*. At the writer's cabin there are daily interpretive talks. A labor of love by historian Dick North, Dawne Mitchell and others, this place is a treasure trove of stories – including the search for the original cabin.

Dänojà Zho Cultural Centre
CULTURAL CENTER

(☏867-993-6768; www.trondek.com; Front St; adult $5; ⊙10am-6pm Mon-Sat) Inside this beautiful riverfront wood building there are displays and interpretative talks on the *Hän Hwëch'in* (River People) First Nations. The collection includes traditional artifacts and a re-creation of a 19th-century fishing camp. Check on the schedule for cultural tours and performances of authentic dances.

Dawson City Museum
MUSEUM

(☏867-993-5291; 5th Ave; adult $9; ⊙10am-6pm) Make your own discoveries among the 25,000 gold rush artifacts at this museum. Engaging exhibits walk you through the grim lives of the miners. The museum is housed in the landmark 1901 Old Territorial Administration building.

Midnight Dome
PARK

The slide-scarred face of this hill overlooks the town to the north, but to reach the top you must travel south of town about 1km, turn left off the Klondike Hwy onto New Dome Rd, and continue for about 7km. The Midnight Dome, at 880m above sea level, offers great views of the Klondike Valley, Yukon River and Dawson City. There's also a steep **trail** that takes 90 minutes from Judge St in town; maps are available at the VIC.

Crocus Bluff & Cemeteries
MONUMENTS

A 15-minute walk up King St and Mary McCloud Rd near town leads to 10 **cemeteries**

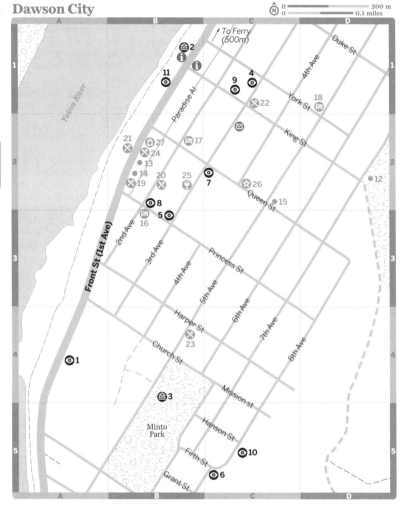

YUKON TERRITORY DAWSON CITY

that are literally filled with characters. Among them: Joe Vogler, who fought to have Alaska secede from the US. He was buried here in 1993, having vowed not to be buried in an Alaska that wasn't free. Todd Palin (husband of Sarah) is among his acolytes.

Near the cemeteries, a short path out to pretty **Crocus Bluff** has excellent views of Dawson and the Klondike and Yukon Rivers. It is a short walk up King St from town. If driving, take New Dome Rd and turn at Mary McLeod Rd (ignoring the 'No Exit' signs).

Mines

The deeply scarred valleys around Dawson speak of the vast amounts of toil that went into the gold hunt. **Dredge No 4** (Bonanza Creek Rd; adult $7; ☉10am-4pm, tour times vary), 13km off the Klondike Hwy, is a massive dredging machine that tore up the Klondike Valley and left the tailings, which remain as a vast, rippled blight on the landscape. The Parks Canada tours are absorbing.

Just 1.5km further up the valley, the Bonanza Creek **Discovery Site** is roughly where gold was first found in 1897. It's a quiet site today with a little water burbling through the rubble.

Galleries

Dawson has a thriving arts community. The **Klondike Institute for Art & Culture** (KIAC; ☑867-993-5005; www.kiac.org; cnr 3rd Ave & Queen St) has an impressive studio building, galleries and educational programs.

KIAC's exhibition space, the **ODD Gallery** (☑867-993-5005; cnr 2nd Ave & Princess St; ⊙hrs vary), shows local works.

Fortymile Gold Workshop/Studio (☑867-993-5690; 3rd Ave btwn York & King Sts) has gold creations from 30 local artists. Watch as jewelry is made from local refined gold, which is silky and has a rich yellow color, as opposed to the bling you see peddled on late-night TV.

🏃 Activities

Besides arriving by **canoe** or **kayak**, many people also exit Dawson via the Yukon River. A popular trip good for novices goes from Dawson for three days and 168km downstream to Eagle City, Alaska.

Dawson Trading Post (☑867-993-5316; Front St; canoe per day $30) rents out canoes and arranges longer trips. Dawson City River Hostel (p264), across the river, is the local agent for **Eagle Canoe Rentals** (www.eaglecanoerentals.com), with canoe rental for the three- to four-day trip to Eagle, plus return transport from US$125.

Besides the walks above town listed under Sights, a three-hour **hike to Moosehead**, an old First Nations village, is popular. The trail follows hillsides above the river north of town. Be sure to get a map at the VIC.

You can explore much of the Dawson area by bike, including the **Ridge Road Heritage Trail**, which winds through the gold fields south of town. Rent bikes at **Circle Cycle** (☑867-993-6270; cnr King St & 7th Ave; bikes per day $30) or the Dawson City River Hostel.

👉 Tours

Parks Canada docents, often in period garb, lead excellent **walking tours** (adult $7; ⊙daily) of Dawson. Learn about individual buildings and the many characters that walked the streets (many of whom could be called 'street-walkers'). You can also take a self-guided **audio tour** (adult $7; ⊘9:30am-4:30pm).

TOP CHOICE **Goldbottom Tours** (☑867-993-5750; www.goldbottom.com; ticket office Front St; ⊘daily) is run by the legendary Millar mining family. Tour their mine 15km up Hunker Creek Rd, which meets Hwy 2 just north of the airport. The 3½-hour tours cost $30 (children free) or you can include transport to/from Dawson for $40. You get to keep what you find. They also provide a shuttle to sites outside Dawson (Midnight Dome, Dredge No 4 etc) for $40.

Sail the Yukon on the **Klondike Spirit** (☑867-993-5323; www.klondikespirit.com; tickets Triple J Hotel, cnr 5th Ave & Queen St; tours from $50), a modern re-created paddle wheeler that offers day and dinner cruises.

★ᲟᲢ Festivals & Events

See p245 for Yukon events that include Dawson.

Dawson City Music Festival (☑867-993-5384; www.dcmf.com) Popular – tickets sell out two months in advance and the city fills up; reservations are essential (late July).

Discovery Days Celebrates the you-know-what of 1896. On the third Monday in August there are parades and picnics. Events, including an excellent art show, begin days before.

🛏 Sleeping

Reservations are a good idea in July and August, although the VIC can help. Many places will pick you up at the airport; ask in advance. Unless otherwise stated, the following are open all year.

TOP CHOICE **Bombay Peggy's** INN $$
(☑867-993-6969; www.bombaypeggys.com; cnr 2nd Ave & Princess St; r $90-200; ⊘Mar-Dec; ❋♠) A renovated brothel, Peggy's allure is its period furnishings and spunky attitude. Budget 'snug' rooms share bathrooms. Rooms are plush in a way that will make you want to wear a garter. The bar is a classy oasis.

Klondike Kate's INN $$
(☑867-993-6527; www.klondikekates.ca; cnr King St & 3rd Ave; cabins $120-140; ⊘Apr-Sep; ♠) The 15 cabins behind the excellent restaurant of the same name are rustic without the rusticisms. High-speed internet, microwaves and fridges ensure comfort.

The porches are perfect for decompressing. Green practices are many.

Dawson City River Hostel HOTEL $
(summer ☑867-993-6823; www.yukonhostels.com; dm $18-22, r from $46; ⊘mid-May–Sep) This delightfully eccentric hostel is across the river from town and five minutes up the hill from the ferry landing. It has good views, cabins, platforms for tents and a communal bathhouse. Tent sites are $14. Owner Dieter Reinmuth is a noted Yukon author.

Aurora Inn INN $
(☑867-993-6860; www.aurorainn.ca; 5th Ave; r $120-170; ❀) All 20 rooms in this European-style inn are large and comfortable. And if there's such a thing as Old World cleanliness, it's here: the admonishments to remove your (invariably) muddy shoes start at the entrance.

Downtown Hotel HOTEL $$
(☑867-993-5346, 800-661-0514; www.downtownhotel.ca; cnr Queen St & 2nd Ave; r $95-150; ❋♠♥) A landmark hotel on a prominent corner, the fittingly named Downtown has 34 rooms in the main heritage building and 25 more in a modern annex. Not all have air-con; ask to see a couple as some are small and/or frumpy.

Yukon River Campground CAMPGROUND $
(sites $12) On the western side of the river about 250m up the road to the right after you get off the ferry, this territorial campground has 98 shady sites.

Gold Rush Campground RV Park CAMPGROUND $
(☑867-993-5247; 866-330-5006; www.goldrushcampground.com; cnr 5th Ave & York St; sites $20-40; ⊘mid-May–mid-Sep; ♠) Convenience trumps atmosphere at this 83-site gravel parking lot for RVs.

✕ Eating

Picnickers, hikers and backcountry campers will find two good grocery stores in town. A **farmers market** (⊘11am-5pm Sat mid-May–mid-Sep) thrives by the iconic waterfront gazebo. The sweet-as-candy carrots are the product of very cold nights. Try some birch syrup.

With exceptions noted below, most places close outside of summer.

TOP CHOICE **Drunken Goat Taverna** GREEK $$
(☑867-993-5800; 2nd Ave; mains $12-25; ⊘noon-9pm) Follow your eyes to the flowers, your ears to the Aegean music and your nose

to the excellent Greek food, run 12-months-a-year by Tony Dovas. Out back there's a simple take-out with beer-absorbing pizzas ($10) in the evening.

Klondike Kate's
FUSION $$
(☎867-993-6527; cnr King St & 3rd Ave; mains $8-25; ☺8am-9pm Apr-Sep) Two ways to know spring has arrived: the river cracks up and Kate's reopens. Locals in the know prefer the latter. The long and inventive menu has fine sandwiches, pastas and fresh Yukon fish. Look for great specials. This is *the* place for breakfast.

La Table on 5th
FUSION $$
(☎867-993-6860; Aurora Inn, 5th Ave; mains $15-35; ☺5-9pm) Ponder a passel of schnitzels or a bevy of steaks at this slightly formal continental restaurant. Make arrangements in advance and a local storyteller will join you at your table.

Cheechako's Bake Shop
BAKERY $
(☎867-993-6590; cnr Front & Princess Sts; meals $4-8; ☺7am-7pm) A real bakery and a good one, on the main strip. Muffins, cookies and treats vie with sandwiches made on home-made bread for your attention.

River West
CAFE $
(☎867-993-6339; near cnr Front & Queen Sts; meals $4-7; ☺7am-7pm Mar-Oct) Busy throughout the day, this excellent coffeehouse, bakery and cafe looks out on the Front St action. Grab an outside table.

Drinking
The spirit of the prospectors lives on in several saloons in Dawson City. On summer nights the action goes on until dawn, which would mean something if it weren't light all night.

TOP CHOICE Bombay Peggy's
PUB
(☎867-993-6969; cnr 2nd Ave & Princess St; ☺11am-11pm) There's always a hint of pleasures to come swirling around the tables of Dawson's most inviting bar. Enjoy good beers, wines and mixed drinks inside or out.

Bars at Westminster Hotel
BARS
(3rd Ave; ☺noon-late) These two bars carry the mostly affectionate monikers 'Snakepit,' 'Armpit' or simply 'Pit.' The places for serious drinkers, with live music many nights.

Billy Goat
PUB
(☎867-993-5800; 2nd Ave; ☺5pm-1am) Not a branch of the famed Chicago original

but a nice, mannered lounge from Tony of Drunken Goat fame.

Downtown Hotel
PUB
(☎867-993-5346; cnr Queen St & 2nd Ave; ☺11am-late) This unremarkable bar comes to life at 9pm in summer for what can best be called the 'Sourtoe Schtick.' Tourists line up to drink a shot of booze ($10) that has a pickled human toe floating in it. It's a long-running gag that's delightfully chronicled in Dieter Reinmuth's *The Saga of the Sourtoe*. (That the toe – it *is* real – looks much like a bit of beef jerky should give pause to anyone used to late-night Slim Jim jonesing…)

☆ Entertainment

TOP CHOICE Diamond Tooth Gertie's Gambling Hall
CASINO
(☎867-993-5575; cnr Queen St & 4th Ave; $6; ☺7pm-2am mid-May–mid-Sep) This popular re-creation of an 1898 saloon is complete with small-time gambling, a honky-tonk piano and dancing girls. The casino helps promote the town and fund culture. Each night there are three floor shows heavy on corn and kicking legs.

🔒 Shopping

Maximilian's
BOOKSTORE
(☎867-993-6537; Front St; ☺8am-8pm) Has an excellent selection of regional books, magazines, out-of-town newspapers and topographical and river maps.

Dawson Trading Post
CURIOS/OUTDOOR GEAR
(☎867-993-5316; Front St; ☺9am-7pm) Sells interesting old mining gadgets, bear traps ($500) and old mammoth tusks so you can take up carving. It has a good bulletin board.

ℹ Information

Much of Dawson is closed October to May. The biweekly, volunteer-run *Klondike Sun* covers special events and activities.

CIBC ATM (2nd Ave) Near Queen St.

Dawson City Community Library (☎867-993-5571; cnr 5th Ave & Queen St; ☺11am-8pm Tue-Sat but can vary) Has internet access.

Dawson Medical Clinic (☎867-993-5744; Church St; ☺9am-noon & 1-5pm Mon-Fri) A private clinic near 6th Ave; nurses are always on call at the adjoining government clinic (☎867-993-4444).

Post office (☎867-993-5342; 3rd Ave; ☺8:30am-5:30pm Mon-Fri, 11:30am-2:30pm Sat) Between King and Queen Sts.

TastyByte Internet Cafe (☑867-993-6105; Front St; per hr $12; ☺8am-4pm) Good coffee and wi-fi access.

VIC (☑867-993-5566; cnr Front & King Sts; ☺8am-8pm May-Sep) Parks Canada information is split between here and the Palace Grand Theatre on King St between 2nd and 3rd Aves.

Western Arctic Information Centre (☑867-993-6167; Front St; ☺8am-8pm mid-May–mid-Sep) Maps and information on the NWT and the Dempster Hwy.

❶ Getting There & Away

Dawson City is 527km from Whitehorse. Public transport to/from Whitehorse is an ongoing problem – there usually is none as you can see by the pleas for rides on the bulletin board by River West. Should you fly in, note there are no rental cars either.

Dawson City airport (YDA) About 19km east of town off the Klondike Hwy.

Air North (☑800-661-0407; www.flyairnorth.com) Serves Whitehorse, Old Crow, Inuvik in the NWT and Fairbanks in Alaska.

Alaska/Yukon Trails (☑800-770-7275; www.alaskashuttle.com) Runs shuttles between Dawson and Tok, Alaska via the Top of the World Hwy and Chicken, Alaska, but confirm all details in advance.

Dawson City to Alaska

From Dawson City, the free ferry crosses the Yukon River to the scenic **Top of the World Hwy** (Hwy 9). Only open in summer, the mostly paved 106km-long ridge-top road to the US border has superb vistas across the region.

You'll continue to feel on top of the world as you cross the border. The land is barren alpine meadows with jutting rocks and often grazing caribou. The **border crossing** (☺9am-9pm Yukon time/8am-8pm Alaska time 15 May–15 Sep) has strict hours – if you're late you'll have to wait until the next day.

On the US side, Alaska shows its xenophobic side, as the 19km connection to the Taylor Hwy (Hwy 5) is mostly dirt and often impassable after storms (expect to get dirt in parts of your vehicle and person you didn't think possible). The old gold-mining town of **Eagle** on the Yukon River is 105km north. Some 47km south over somewhat better roads, you encounter **Chicken**, a delightful place of free-thinkers happy to sell you a stupid T-shirt at one of the gas station-cafes or offer their views regarding government bureaucrats. Another 124km

south and you reach the Alaska Hwy, where a turn east takes you to the Yukon. Just a tick west, **Tok** has services and motels. Alaska time is one hour earlier than the Yukon.

DEMPSTER HIGHWAY

Rather than name this road for an obscure Mountie (William Dempster), this road should be named the Firestone Hwy or the Goodyear Hwy, for the number of tires it's sent to an explosive demise. This 736km thrill ride is one of North America's great adventure roads, winding through stark mountains and emerald valleys, across huge tracts of tundra and passing Tombstone Territorial Park.

The Dempster (Hwy 5 in the Yukon, Hwy 8 in the NWT) starts 40km southeast of Dawson City off the Klondike Hwy and heads north over the Ogilvie and Richardson mountains beyond the Arctic Circle and on to Inuvik in the NWT, near the shores of the Beaufort Sea.

Road Conditions

Built on a thick base of gravel to insulate the permafrost underneath (which would otherwise melt, causing the road to sink without a trace), the Dempster is open most of the year, but the best time to travel is between June and early September, when the ferries over the Peel and Mackenzie Rivers operate. In winter, ice forms a natural bridge over the rivers, which become ice roads. The Dempster is closed during the spring thaw and the winter freeze-up; the timing of these vary by the year and can occur from mid-April to June and mid-October to December, respectively.

Graveled almost its entire length, the highway has a well-deserved reputation for being rough on vehicles. Travel with extra gas and tires and expect to use them. Check road conditions in the Yukon (☑511; www.511yukon.ca) and the NWT (☑800-661-0750; www.dot.gov.nt.ca); the Western Arctic Information Centre in Dawson City is a good resource. It takes 10 to 12 hours to drive to Inuvik without stopping for a break. (Given that William Dempster regularly made 700km dog-sled journeys in sub-zero weather, this rugged and challenging road is properly named after all.)

TOMBSTONE TERRITORIAL PARK

Shades of green and charcoal color the wide valleys here and steep ridges are dotted with small glaciers and alpine lakes. Summer feels tentative but makes its statement with a burst of purple wildflowers in July. Clouds sweep across the tundra, bringing squalls punctuated by brilliant sun. Stand amid this and you'll know the meaning of the sound of silence.

Tombstone Territorial Park (www.yukonparks.ca) lies along Dempster Hwy for about 50km. The park's only formal **campground** (sites $12) has a new and excellent **Interpretive Centre** (☼9am-5pm late May–mid-Sep), which offers walks and talks. It's 71km from the start of the highway and is set in along the headwaters of the Yukon River just before **Tombstone Mountain**, the point where the trees run out and the truly wild northern scenery begins.

There are good **day hikes** near the campground, as well as longer, more rigorous **treks** for experienced wilderness hikers. Permits are required for backcountry camping, especially at several lakes popular in summer. (The park's backcountry camping guide shows refreshing honesty in its answer to this frequently asked question: 'Will you come looking for me if I don't return?' 'No.')

Tombstone is an easy day trip from Dawson City (112km each way). With preparations, however, a multiday park adventure could be the highlight of your trip. The 2011 movie *The Big Year* with Steve Martin, Owen Wilson and Jack Black was partly shot in the park.

🛏 Sleeping & Eating

Accommodations and vehicle services along the route are few. The **Klondike River Lodge** (☎867-993-6892) at the south junction rents jerry cans for gas that you can take north and return on the way back.

The next available services are 369km north in Eagle Plains. The **Eagle Plains Hotel** (☎867-993-2453; eagleplains@northwestel.net; r $100-130) is open year-round and offers 32 rooms. The next service station is 180km further at **Fort McPherson** in the NWT. From there it's 216km to Inuvik.

The Yukon government has three campgrounds – at **Tombstone Mountain** (72km from the start of the highway), **Engineer Creek** (194km) and **Rock River** (447km). There's also a NWT government campground at **Nitainlaii Territorial Park**, 9km south of Fort McPherson. Sites at these campgrounds are $12.

ARCTIC PARKS

North of the Arctic Circle, the Yukon's population numbers a few hundred. It's a lonely land with little evidence of humans and only the hardiest venture here during the short summers.

The 280-person village of **Old Crow** (www.oldcrow.ca) is home to the Vuntut Gwitch'in First Nations and is unreachable by vehicle. Residents subsist on caribou from the legendary 130,000-strong Porcupine herd, which migrates each year between the Arctic National Wildlife Refuge (ANWR) in Alaska and the Yukon. Not surprisingly, the locals are against the perennial threat of oil drilling on the US side of the border in the ANWR.

On the Yukon side of this vast flat arctic tundra, a large swath of land is now protected in two adjoining national parks, Vuntut and Ivvavik. Information on both can be obtained from the Parks Canada office in Inuvik, NWT, where you can get information on the very limited options for organizing visits to the parks (think chartered planes, long treks over land and water, and total self-sufficiency). There are no facilities of any kind in the parks.

Vuntut National Park

Vuntut, a Gwitch'in word meaning 'among the lakes,' is about 100km north of Old Crow, where there is a one-person **park office** (☎867-667-3910; www.pc.gc.ca/vuntut). The 4345-sq-km park was declared a national park in 1993. It lives up to its name with scores of lakes and ponds and is home to 500,000 waterbirds in late summer.

The Yukon could serve as exhibit one in the case for climate change. Every corner of the territory is experiencing rapid changes in the environment because it's getting warmer a lot quicker than anybody ever imagined. In the far north, Herschel Island is literally dissolving as the permafrost thaws. One gruesome sign: long-buried coffins floating to the surface of the melting earth. Unesco has listed it as one of the world's most threatened historic sites.

In Dawson City locals have for decades bet on the day each spring when the Yukon River suddenly breaks up and begins flowing. Detailed records show that the mean date for this has moved one week earlier in the last century to May 5, with the pace accelerating.

Perhaps the most easily seen is the beetle devastation in Kluane National Park (p254). Preparing the Yukon for a radically different and warmer future is now a major political topic, even if nobody has the answers.

Archaeological sites contain fossils of ancient animals such as mammoths, plus evidence of early humans.

Ivvavik National Park

Ivvavik, meaning 'a place for giving birth to and raising the young,' is situated along the Beaufort Sea adjoining Alaska and covers 10,170 sq km. The park (www.pc.gc.ca/ivvavik) is one of the calving grounds for the Porcupine caribou herd; thousands are born over a three-week period beginning in late May.

The park holds one of the world's great white-water rivers, the Firth River, which can be navigated for 130km from Margaret Lake near the Alaskan border north to the Beaufort Sea. When the river meets Joe Creek, the valley narrows to a canyon and there are numerous areas of white water rated Class II and III+.

Herschel Island (Qiqiktaruk) Territorial Park

Its aboriginal name means 'it is island' and indeed it is. Barely rising above the waters of Mackenzie Bay on the Beaufort Sea, Herschel Island (867-667-5648; www.yukonparks.ca) has a long tradition of human habitation. The Inuvialuit lived here for thousands of years, making the most of the prime position on the seal-rich waters. In the late 1800s American whalers set up shop at Pauline Cove, a natural port deep enough for ocean vessels and protected from northerly winds and drifting pack ice.

Abandoned in 1907, the whalers left behind several wooden buildings which survive today, often appearing ghost-like out of the gloom. Evidence can also be found of missionaries, whose position as redeemers of souls was never embraced locally. Today Inuvialuit families use the island for traditional hunting.

There are no permanent residents, although in summer a growing number of scientists set up shop, monitoring the island's steady disintegration as it melts away.

Summer visits to the island are possible via daytime tours from Inuvik. The flight across the Mackenzie Delta to reach the island is spectacular and park rangers often give tours. Backcountry camping during the short summer season (from late June to August) is possible. There are fire rings, wind shelters, pit toilets and limited water. Others visit the island at the end of a kayak trip in Ivvavik National Park.

Understand BC & the Canadian Rockies

population per sq km

BC   USA   FRANCE

👤 ≈ 4 people

BC & the Canadian Rockies Today

Olympic Legacies

When Vancouver hosted the Olympic and Paralympic Winter Games in 2010, the eyes of the world feasted on British Columbia's snowcapped peaks, endless blue skies and street-partying locals. The province used the event to showcase its billion-dollar looks, aiming to encourage tourism and investment. But since the flame went out, the benefits of the Games have been harder to grasp. In its aftermath, government-funded programs were radically cut, while locals – most of whom enjoyed the world's biggest party at the time – now frequently state that it cost too much.

It's an indication, perhaps, that economies need more than mega-sized events to generate development. Alberta proved this after hosting the Winter Olympics in 1988: the province strutted through the recent global recession better than any region in Canada, due to its reputation as a low taxation–big business capital with an economy centered on its booming oil industry. While BC wrings its hands over exploiting gas reserves in its pristine, coastal wilderness, the environmentally controversial northern Alberta oil sands continue to pump out money-spinning black gold.

»» Estimated number of grizzly bears in BC: 13,000

»» Estimated number of wolves in Alberta: 4000

»» Estimated number of caribou in the Yukon: 150,000

Leaping Loonie

Constantly hovering around parity with the US dollar like a persistent housefly, the rising Canadian dollar, known as the 'Loonie' because of the loon bird depicted on $1 coins, is a challenge for the regional economy. While the country was not subjected to the bankruptcy-threatening damage that recently afflicted other nations, the fact that the US is by far Canada's main trading partner has serious consequences here. Dollar parity means that fewer American tourists are traveling north. And while visitors from China, Australia and the UK are rising, they can't fill the massive deficit from what has always been the region's biggest tourist market.

Newspapers

Vancouver Sun The west coast's leading daily broadsheet; entertainment pull-out on Thursdays. **Georgia Straight** Vancouver's free alternative weekly. **Calgary Herald** Alberta's main newspaper, along with its *Edmonton Journal* sister.

Top Blogs

The Tyee (www.thetyee.com) Alternative news source. **Miss 604** (www.miss604.com) Vancouver's leading blog, with a lifestyle and local history focus. **Urban Yukon** (www.urbanyukon. com) Dozens of local bloggers come together on one handy site.

Top Music

Letter from an Occupant New Pornographers
I Love Myself Today Bif Naked
In My Fingertips The Buttless Chaps
Smash the State DOA
Everything is Automatic Matthew Good Band

belief systems
(% of population)

45 British

16 Catholic, Christian and others

6 Aboriginal

if British Columbia were 100 people

74 would be white
20 would be Asian
2 would be Latino

3 would be Aboriginal
1 would be black

It's not all Green

The 2011 federal election encapsulated the differences between the regions of western Canada. BC's bucolic Salt Spring Island elected Canada's first Green Party MP – party leader, Elizabeth May – while the rest of the province gave one of the highest votes in the country to the left-wing New Democratic Party (NDP), helping it to become the official opposition in Ottawa for the first time. On the other side of the Rockies, Alberta gave the NDP its second-lowest proportion of the votes in Canada and gave by far the highest vote across the country to the Conservative Party. Not surprisingly, Conservative Prime Minister Stephen Harper was hanging out in Calgary on election day.

Meanwhile in the Yukon

Although BC and the Yukon share a border, they share little else. The history of the Yukon has always been more closely linked to that of neighboring Alaska. The Yukon remains in many ways as it was 200 years ago: a forbidding wilderness bursting into life during a brief summer. Its politics lean towards the conservative, an outgrowth of the area's popular image of self-reliance. But while the Yukon (which changed its only MP from Liberal to Conservative in the 2011 election) has for years kept itself quietly under the radar, things may soon change dramatically.

Few doubt that enormous energy and mineral riches lie under the Yukon. The territory's remoteness currently limits efforts to explore further, but that will eventually change. Will the region adopt Alberta's oil sands approach or struggle with environmental considerations as BC has?

Adbusters magazine, published in Vancouver, promotes an anti-corporate, anti-consumerism lifestyle even as it uses a slick design to do so. It's one of North America's most popular alternative magazines and has legions of starry-eyed students lining up to become interns.

Fun Facts

» Canadians eat three times as many doughnuts as people in the US.

» Duncan BC is home to the world's largest hockey stick.

» Drumheller in Alberta houses the world's largest dinosaur (model).

Dos & Dont's

» Smoking is banned in most of the region's public places.

» French is rarely spoken in this region, even though this is officially a bilingual country.

» Don't mistake Canadians for Americans: they won't be amused.

History

Western Canada's intriguing human history began around 15,000 years ago when Aboriginal locals began establishing thriving communities along the salmon-rich coastline as well as in the forested foothills and wide plains of the Rockies region. Everything changed rapidly, though, when the first Europeans turned up from the mid-18th century onwards. Finding an irresistible combination of untold abundance and locals that had yet to discover guns, the Europeans quickly transformed the area with trade, industry and pioneer settlements. Much of this colorful heritage is accessible to visitors, with 163 national historic sites – from forts to famous homes – studding British Columbia, Alberta and the Yukon.

First Peoples Kick Things Off

The ancestors of western Canada's Aboriginal peoples were settlers who showed up in North America at least 15,000 years ago. The most prominent theory is that, after the last Ice Age, they crossed to Alaska on a land bridge over what is now the Bering Strait. Some settled along the Pacific coast, while others found their way to the interior – Alberta, the Yukon and beyond – ultimately populating the rest of North America. This theory is not without its detractors: in recent years archaeologists have discovered the remnants of communities that appear to predate the arrival of the Bering Strait settlers.

Whatever the true story, there is little dispute over who was here first. The Aboriginal peoples of this region, thriving on abundant food and untold resources, developed sophisticated cultures and intricate trade networks over many thousands of years. Coastal peoples dwelled as extended families in large, single-roofed cedar lodges, while inland and mountain communities generally had a tougher time, facing extremes of weather and leading nomadic subsistence lives: in the north they hungrily pursued migratory herds of animals such as moose and caribou, while in the south they chased down bison.

TIMELINE

800	1754	1778
An ash-spewing eruption of the Yukon volcano now known as Mt Churchill causes many to flee to southwest USA, where they may have evolved into the Navajo and Apaches.	The first European, fur trader Anthony Henday, reaches Alberta from eastern Canada. He spends the winter with Aboriginal locals, hunting buffalo with them.	Captain James Cook spreads word of BC's riches to England. He had been looking for a route across North America from the Pacific to the Atlantic – the Northwest Passage.

Despite now being called Vancouver, the city's early monikers included Gastown (from a bar owner called 'Gassy Jack' who triggered the first significant settlement) and Granville (from an English earl in the Victorian era). But it's worth remembering that the Spanish arrived before the English, and there are several reminders of this fact around the region. Spanish Banks – a beach near the city's University of British Columbia campus – is where Captain Vancouver and the Spaniards Valdez and Galiano met in 1792. In addition, there are Galiano, Texada and Saturna islands between the mainland and Vancouver Island that can trace their names directly to the early Spanish explorers.

Europeans Poke Around

During the 18th century, European explorers hungry for new sources of wealth appeared off the west coast as well as in the Rockies region after traveling through the wilderness from eastern Canada. On the coast, Russian Alexsey Chirikov is thought to have been first in 1741, followed by the Spaniards: they sent three expeditions between 1774 and 1779 in search of the fabled Northwest Passage. They ended up by the entrance to Nootka Sound on Vancouver Island but didn't initially venture into the Strait of Georgia.

British explorer Captain James Cook also elbowed in from the South Pacific in 1778. He had a similar Northwest Passage motive, and a similar result: he hit the west coast of Vancouver Island and believed it to be the mainland. It wasn't until 1791 that the mainland-lined Strait of Georgia was properly explored. Spanish navigator José María Narváez did the honors, sailing all the way into Burrard Inlet. He named part of this area Islas de Langara.

Next up was Captain George Vancouver, a British navigator who had previously sailed with Cook. In 1792 he glided into the inner harbor and spent one day there, meeting briefly with Spanish captains Valdez and Galiano who had already claimed the area. Then he sailed away, not thinking twice about a place that would eventually carry his name.

Despite Captain Van's seeming indifference, the Brits' interest in the area grew as its abundant resources became obvious. Finally, a 1794 treaty signed with the Spanish saw war averted and the British assuming control.

Fur: the New Gold

The fur trade was the main lure for the pioneers who followed on the heels of these first European forays, and trade grew rapidly as western Canada's easy prey became clear. Fur trader Anthony Henday was reputedly the first European to arrive in Alberta, exploring the outback areas

Southern Alberta's ancient Siksika Nation is still renowned for its dancing prowess, especially its celebrated Chicken Dance. Inspired by the courtship moves of a chicken, it's performed by young males. Check out June's World Chicken Dance Championship at the Blackfoot Crossing National Historical Park (www.blackfootcrossing.ca).

1793	1805	1842	1846
Crossing the continent, Alexander Mackenzie almost reaches the Pacific Ocean near Bella Coola. Blocked by the Nuxalk people, he writes his name on a rock then heads back east.	The Northwest Trading Company establishes a fur-trading post at Hudson's Hope in northeast BC. It is later taken over by the Hudson's Bay Company (HBC).	Alberta receives its first Catholic missionary, Jean-Baptiste Thibault. Some of the region's future towns are initially built at mission sites, including what later becomes the city of St Albert.	The US and Britain agree to the Oregon Treaty, meant to settle the border between the US and BC. However, the devil is in the details, and years of debate ensue.

now known as Edmonton and Red Deer in 1754. The region's Aboriginals – inland and on the coast – soon came into contact with the Europeans.

Legendary trappers like Alexander Mackenzie, Simon Fraser and David Thompson also explored overland routes from the east during this period. At the same time, the Hudson's Bay Company (HBC) rapidly became the catalyst for settler development, building fort communities and fostering trade routes throughout the region.

Of these early explorers, Mackenzie is probably the most interesting. Often compared to the Lewis and Clark expedition in the US, he traversed Canada in 1793, more than 10 years before the Americans crossed their country to the south. Exploring the Rockies, the continental divide and the Fraser River, he later produced a book on his exploits titled *Voyages...to the Frozen and Pacific Oceans*.

By the 1840s the US was making its own claims on the area and the HBC dispatched James Douglas to Vancouver Island, where he established Fort Victoria. A few years later the British and Americans settled their claims and the border was solidified, ensuring that tourists to Victoria would enjoy high tea as opposed to the mocha-decaf-soy-milk-half-shot lattes found south of the crossing.

Despite it's relative remoteness, the Yukon was also becoming part of the action. The HBC's Robert Campbell became the first European to travel extensively in the region, followed by a ragtag wave of fur traders, prospectors, whalers and – as always – missionaries. Campbell established Fort Selkirk on the Yukon River as a trading post.

Gold: the New Fur

The discovery of gold along BC's Fraser River in 1858 brought a tidal wave of avaricious visitors to the region. A second wave arrived when the yellow stuff was discovered further north in the Cariboo area. Although the gold rush only lasted a few years, many of those who came stayed behind. You can experience a sanitized version of a gold rush town – ie without the effluent, drunkenness and prostitution – at the restored Barkerville Historic Town.

By this stage, desperate travelers were panning and scraping for gold across the region, with large imaginary nuggets forming like misshapen pupils in their eyes. But for every prospector who made his fortune, there were hundreds who failed to find more than a whiff of the elusive treasure.

Of course, that didn't stop people trying. For years, the Yukon became a byword for broken dreams and shattered fortune hunters...right up until 1896, when a discovery on a tributary of the Klondike River near what became Dawson City changed everything. The region's ensuing gold rush attracted hopefuls from around the world – over 99% of whom found no fortune while losing their own

Alberta: A History in Photographs (2009), by Faye Reineberg Holt, is packed with grainy, highly evocative images of the region's pioneer and cowboy era, including some spectacular photos of the region's 19th-century Aboriginal residents.

1866	1874	1876	1887
Mainland BC and Vancouver Island unite, not out of any love but because mainland BC has nowhere to turn after it overspends on infrastructure.	The Mounties establish their first Alberta post at Fort Macleod. One of their first missions is to take control of the chaotic local whisky trade.	American cowboy John Ware brings the first cattle into Alberta from the US, triggering a ranch-based economy that drives the province for decades. Many early ranchers are from England.	The Canadian Pacific Railway arrives in Vancouver, linking Canada's west with the east and conquering untold mountains arrayed across BC like swells at sea. It is an engineering marvel.

Rail Link Opens the West

After mainland BC and Vancouver Island were united, Victoria was named BC's new provincial capital in 1868. Meanwhile, in 1867, the UK government had passed the British North American Act, creating the Dominion of Canada. The eastern provinces of Canada united under this confederation, while BC joined in 1871 and Alberta joined in 1905.

But rather than duty to the Crown, it was the train that made them sign on the dotted line. Western Canada remained a distant and forbidding frontier but the fledgling Canadian government promised to build a railway link to the rest of the country within a decade. The Canadian Pacific Railway rolled into Alberta in 1883, nosing into BC four years later.

The construction of the transcontinental railway is one of the most impressive and important chapters in the region's history. The railroad was crucial in unifying the distant east and west wings of the vast country in order to encourage immigration and develop business opportunities. But it came with a large price: the much-quoted statistic that a Chinese laborer died for every mile of track built is almost certainly true.

With the train link came a modicum of law and order for the region. Aiming to tame the 'wild west', or at least make it less trigger-happy, the government created the North-West Mounted Police (NWMP) in 1873, which later became the Royal Canadian Mounted Police (RCMP). Nicknamed 'Mounties', they still serve as the country's national police force.

Also during this period, wealth from gold and revenue from the people looking for it helped the Yukon become a separate territory in 1898, with Dawson City the capital. But the northern party was short-lived: by 1920 economic decline had set in and the population dropped to just 5000, a fraction of its gold-rush heyday. And although the construction of the Alaska Hwy in 1942 opened up the territory to development and provided it with its first tangible link to BC, the glory days were over.

Inspector Constantine of the North-West Mounted Police arrived in the Yukon with a team of 20 hardy men in 1895. Their mission was to maintain law and order and uphold Canadian sovereignty, which included acting as magistrates, customs collectors and Dominion of Canada land agents.

Big Cities Emerge...Then Burn Down

While all this thrusting nation-building was going on, the region's first cities were quietly laying their foundations. And while some – Prince Rupert and New Westminster, for example – were considered as potential regional capitals (New West actually held the position in BC until Victoria took over), it was eventually Vancouver that became western Canada's biggest metropolis. But although it celebrated its 125th anniversary with a big party in 2011, it's worth remembering that the City of Glass almost didn't make it. In fact, its start could hardly have been less auspicious.

In 1867, near the middle of what's now called Maple Tree Sq, John 'Gassy Jack' Deighton opened a waterfront saloon for thirsty sawmill

1896

Sparkly stuff found in Bonanza Creek near today's Dawson City sets off the legendary Klondike gold rush. After three frantic years, the madness subsides.

1905

Alberta becomes a province, although it is another 25 years before the federal government allows it to control its own resources. Which prove useful a few years later.

MICHAEL GEBICKI/LONELY PLANET IMAGES ©

» Dredge No 4 (p262), Bonanza Creek, Dawson City

The transcontinental train line reached Alberta in 1883, triggering a wave of new settlement. In 1881 there were an estimated 1000 settlers in Alberta, but within 10 years this had risen to almost 18,000. Ranchers, attracted by the area's bucolic foothills and wide plains, were the most successful early arrivals, and many of them were Brits – combined with a contingent of American cowboys who had brought the first cattle to Alberta in 1876. There was still plenty of room for development by the end of the century, though, and in the late 1890s a large campaign was launched to encourage more Europeans to start a new life in western Canada. Along with those from the UK, many Germans and Ukrainians answered the call: their cultural influences can still be seen today in the small towns and communities of the region. The campaign to bolster the local population worked: between 1901 and 1921, Alberta's population grew from 73,000 to 584,000.

workers. Attracting an attendant ring of squalid shacks, the ramshackle area around the bar soon became known as Gastown. As the ad hoc settlement grew, the colonial administration decided to formalize it, creating the new town of Granville in 1870. Most people still called it Gastown, especially when Deighton opened a larger saloon nearby a few years later.

In 1886, though, the town's name was officially changed to Vancouver and plans were laid for a much larger city, encompassing the old Gastown /Granville area. But within a few weeks, a giant fire swept rapidly through the fledgling city, destroying around 1000 mostly wooden buildings in less than an hour.

When reconstruction began, stone replaced wood – which explains why this area of Vancouver is now packed with old brick and rock buildings that look like they were constructed to last forever. It's now home to many of Vancouver's best bars, restaurants and boutique stores. Gassy Jack, now standing atop a whisky barrel in statue form near the site of his first bar, would be proud

Aboriginal Turmoil

Despite the successes of colonization, the Aboriginals, who had thrived here for centuries, were almost decimated by the arrival of the Europeans. Imported diseases – especially smallpox – wiped out huge numbers of people who had no natural immunity or medicines for dealing with them. At the same time, highly dubious land treaties were 'negotiated' which gave the Europeans title to land which had been traditional Aboriginal territory. In exchange, the locals were often reduced to living on small reserves.

1914	1915	1920	1921
The opening of the Panama Canal considerably shortens ocean journeys between BC and Europe. This is particularly good for Vancouver and adds to the port's growth in grain exports.	The Vancouver Millionaires win hockey's Stanley Cup, the last local team to strike it rich on the ice. (In 2011, the Vancouver Canucks make the finals for the first time since 1994, but lose to Boston.)	Having dropped significantly since the turn of the century, the population of the Yukon falls below 5000. It doesn't increase greatly until after the Alaska Hwy is built in 1942–43.	Kwakwaka'wakw chief Dan Cranmer defies the ban on potlatches, staging a giant gathering to celebrate and exchange gifts. Scores are arrested at the Alert Bay event.

Among the most intriguing buildings you'll come across as you stroll the boardwalk through the Britannia Shipyard in Steveston – a historic waterfront fishing village in BC's Lower Mainland – is the Murakami House. Originally built over marshland in 1885, it was home to a large Japanese family between 1929 and 1942. Asayo Murakami was brought over from Japan in 1924 to marry a Canadian, but after meeting him for the first time and deciding she didn't like him, she worked independently at the cannery to pay off the amount spent on her passage and free herself from the match.

She later met and married a boat builder and they started a small workshop operation next door. Raising 10 children in the house – the rooms have been re-created and are full of everyday items like toys and books – the entire family was suddenly and unceremoniously moved to Manitoba in 1942 as part of Canada's controversial wartime Japanese internment program.

Many Japanese families in BC and Alberta met a similar fate and after the war only a few returned to their original homes. In 2001, on her 100th birthday, several of Murakami's children came back to the former family residence to plant a garden in her honor. She died soon after in her Alberta home aged 104.

But the treatment of the Aboriginals went further than a mere land grab. In what is now regarded as one of the darkest chapters in Canada's history, a process of cultural strangulation took place that ranged from attempting to indoctrinate Aboriginals (especially children) with Christianity and preventing them from practicing certain age-old rites, including the potlatch (gift-giving ceremonial feast). Only in the past 50 years have governments attempted to make amends, launching new treaty negotiations and finally (in 1951) repealing the anti-potlatch laws.

Protests, Prejudice & Prohibition

The Panama Canal, completed in 1914, made it easier for western Canada to peddle its lumber to the US east coast and Europe. As big business grew, so did big unions. Workers in great numbers organized into labor unions in the 1910s, protesting about working conditions and pay rates. A number of strikes targeted key industries like lumber mills and shipping; in several instances the government sided with its business-owning patrons and sent armed thugs after workers.

But the unions, the government and businesses found common ground in racial prejudice: all felt that the growing Chinese and Japanese population should be harassed, banned and beaten. During WWII, Japanese Canadians were removed from their land and their fishing boats, and were interned in camps.

Best Museums

» Glenbow Museum, Calgary

» Whyte Museum of the Canadian Rockies, Banff

» Royal British Columbia Museum, Victoria

» Museum of Vancouver

» West Coast Railway Heritage Park, Squamish

1941	**1947**	**1953**	**1960**
The Pearl Harbor attack spurs the US into working with Canada to open up the north for their common defense. One of the enduring legacies is the Alaska Hwy.	Alberta makes a major oil discovery at Leduc, not far from Edmonton. As more oil and gas is discovered, the province changes forever, bringing vast wealth into the region.	Whitehorse becomes the Yukon's capital, replacing Dawson City. It is a transport hub (mostly American-funded), having the Alaska Hwy, a good airport and the railway to Skagway.	Aboriginals get the right to vote in BC, a key advance in a decades-long initiative to restore the rights of the province's original residents and agree to compensation.

When not abusing foreigners, BC's elite showed a remarkable ability to get rich. Canada controversially tried prohibiting alcohol from 1917 to 1921. Besides enraging hockey fans, it predictably triggered a vast black market that enriched the criminal classes. When the Americans ignored Canada's lesson and instituted their own prohibition later in the 1920s, the old bootleg network was able to spring back to life and vast wealth flowed north of the border. Many see parallels in BC's thriving, albeit slightly underground, latter-day pot-exporting business.

Moving On & Making Amends

After WWII, the region couldn't mine its minerals and chop its trees down fast enough, and a lot of money flowed in. Road and rail links were pushed into all manner of formerly remote places, such as those along the Stewart-Cassiar Hwy. The 1961 Columbia River Treaty with the US resulted in massive dam-building projects that flooded pristine valleys and displaced people. The Americans paid BC to hold back huge amounts of

Best Historical Sites

» Klondike National Historic Sites, Yukon

» Fort Langley, BC

» Barkerville, BC

» Head-Smashed-In Buffalo Jump, Alberta

» Gulf of Georgia Cannery, BC

THAT OTHER ROYAL COUPLE

Members of the British royal family have a historic affinity for western Canada and have visited dozens of times over the years: Charles and Diana opened Vancouver's Expo '86; Prince Edward joined his mother for Victoria's 1994 Commonwealth Games; and the Queen partied in Alberta to celebrate its 2005 centenary.

At the time of research for this book, the newly married Duke and Duchess of Cambridge (otherwise known as Kate and Wills) were planning to head to Canada for their first overseas engagement in summer 2011 – a schedule that included Alberta but not BC. But the photogenic couple will be lucky to match the fervor triggered by one cross-country royal tour that happened more than 60 years ago.

The royals were a distant and mysterious presence for subjects of the empire in the 1930s. So when King George VI and consort Queen Elizabeth – recently portrayed in the movie *The King's Speech* – traversed Canada by train in 1939, the locals were in almost uncontrollable awe. *The Vancouver Sun* noted that when the train made an unscheduled stop in the BC Kootenay town of Revelstoke, it was instantly surrounded by thousands of cheering, hat-waving well-wishers.

Trundling into the Lower Mainland, even larger crowds greeted them. Fervent royalists lined every sidewalk as the couple was driven around in an open-topped car to inaugurate the new Lions Gate Bridge and take in Surrey, Chilliwack and New Westminster.

If you're craving a taste of the royal high life, nip into downtown's Fairmont Hotel Vancouver. On the lobby wall you'll find photos of the visit – the couple officially opened the swanky property – plus a menu showing that they lunched on 'stuffed eggs and chicken supreme,' which was presumably the height of decadence at the time.

1964	1971	1988	1998
Implementation of the Columbia River Treaty starts the construction of huge dams that forever change the Kootenays. One creates Arrow Lakes, causing Nakusp to be moved, while obliterating other towns.	Greenpeace is founded in Vancouver. A small group of activists sets sail in a fishing boat to 'bear witness' to US underground nuclear tests on an island off Alaska.	Calgary hosts the Olympic Winter Games, introducing Eddie 'The Eagle' Edwards to an amused world. Twenty-two years later, he shows up as a commentator at the Vancouver Olympics.	BC, the federal government and the Nisga'a peoples agree on the first modern-day treaty, a huge settlement for the impoverished people living at Nass Camp near the Nisga'a Lava Bed.

water that could be released to hydroelectric plants south of the border whenever power use demanded.

More recently, scores of family-run logging mills have been replaced by vast paper, pulp and plywood operations run by a just a few huge conglomerates. The world can thank BC for an endless supply of cheap particle board, the bowed backbone of budget bookcases everywhere.

In another switch from the recent past, Vancouver hung out the welcome sign to Asians in a big way starting in the 1980s, when Expo '86 showcased the city to the world. Calgary had its own moment in the spotlight two years later when the city became the first in Canada to host the Olympic Winter Games – Vancouver joined the party in 2010 by hosting it, too.

BC has made progress in making amends for past Aboriginal injustices. The first modern-day treaty – signed with the Nisga'a peoples in 1998 – provided about $200 million and allowed some self-governance. But this new process is highly controversial and not everyone is on board: many non-Aboriginal locals do not want the claims to go too far and only 20% of Aboriginal groups have even begun negotiations.

Making Money & Hosting a Party

Alberta has always been better at making money than BC and the region is currently enjoying a wave of economic success based on the exploitation of its oil sands. Located in northern Alberta, this is a controversial enterprise involving the labor-intensive extraction of bitumen. It has attracted the ire of environmentalists who believe it's one of the dirtiest and most ecologically damaging methods for producing oil. The companies involved – some of the world's biggest petroleum corporations – state that they operate to the highest standards and follow all government guidelines.

Healthy profits of a different kind were enjoyed by suppliers and developers involved with the biggest party to hit Canada in decades. The 2010 Olympic and Paralympic Winter Games, staged in Vancouver and Whistler, initially divided the locals neatly into two camps.

Many were deliriously happy to be staging the planet's biggest event while at least as many others felt the vast budget could be spent on far more important region-wide improvements. But while the day-one death of Georgian luge athlete Nodar Kumaritashvili and the massive challenges of staging alpine events in what came to be the city's hottest winter for a century threatened to turn the Games into a huge Canadian embarrassment, a sudden transformation happened a couple of days after the flame was lit that changed the event dramatically.

Often regarded as a city that doesn't really know how to party, the first two nights of the Olympics in Vancouver were tame affairs, but on day

In *Greetings from British Columbia,* Fred Thirkell and Bob Scullion present a collection of old postcard views of BC communities. Many have changed beyond recognition: the cannery town of Port Essington is long gone while Kelowna today is unrecognizable.

2003
Vancouver is named the site for the 2010 Winter Olympics, after a 10-year bidding process. It beats Quebec City and Calgary to be the Canadian candidate.

2003
BC and Ontario lead the way in North America by making same-sex marriage legal. Many gay and lesbian couples travel to Vancouver to be married.

JIM WEST/ALAMY

» A lesbian couple legally wed in Ontario.

HISTORY OF TOTEMS

The artistry of northwest coast native groups – Tsimshian, Haida, Tlingit, Kwakwaka'wakw and Nuxalk – is as intricate as it is simple. One of the most spectacular examples of this is the totem pole, which has become such a symbolic icon that it's part of popular culture, not least because of the entire concept of the low man.

The carving of totem poles was largely quashed after the Canadian government outlawed the potlatch ceremony in 1884. Most totems only last 60 to 80 years, though some on Haida Gwaii are more than 100 years old. When a totem falls, tradition says that it should be left there until another is erected in its place.

Today, totem carving is again widespread, though the poles are often constructed for non-traditional uses, such as public art. Modern totems commissioned for college campuses, museums and public buildings no longer recount the lineage of any one household but instead stand to honor the Aboriginals, their outstanding artistry and their beliefs.

Totem poles abound in northern BC. Elsewhere, you can see a clutch of exceptional poles in Thunderbird Park at the Royal British Columbia Museum in Victoria. There are a lot of other amazing aboriginal works there as well – the museum's mask gallery is highly recommended. If you're in Vancouver, head to the Museum of Anthropology at the University of British Columbia as well as Stanley Park: while many of the totems there are reproductions of earlier poles, some impressive new Coast Salish gateway carvings were added to the collection in 2010.

three – perhaps spurred by negative media coverage around the world – the locals took to the downtown streets en masse...and never really left.

Maple leaf flags and face tattoos became the norm as Vancouverites transformed Robson and Granville Sts into a wandering carnival of family-friendly bonhomie. And while national pride is something few Canadians are used to exhibiting in public, the nighttime shenanigans changed all that with rampant flag-waving and regular, heartfelt sing-a-longs of *O Canada*. As a record haul of Canadian medals fueled the crowds, the streets soon became the best place to hang out and catch the Olympic spirit – along with 200,000 of your closest new friends.

When the flame was extinguished at the closing ceremony, the locals wiped off the red face paint and trudged back to their regular lives. But there was a widely held feeling that the province had grown up a little, coupled with talk of reigniting the mass community spirit with more giant events like this one.

Western Canada has thousands of years of Aboriginal history but BC, Alberta and the Yukon are still relatively young enterprises at the start of their development. Hopefully, the best is yet to come.

2010

Vancouver hosts the Olympic and Paralymic Winter Games, in front of a global TV audience estimated to be more than two billion. There's plenty of flag-waving.

2011

Vancouver commemorates its 125th anniversary with a year of celebrations. Ranging from street parties to art festivals, 'Vancouver 125' also marks the city's year as Cultural Capital of Canada.

» The Olympic Cauldron (p43), Vancouver.

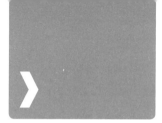

Outdoor Activities

Even if you're a city visitor here, you'll feel the region's wilderness – especially its gigantic forests, wild coastline and huge sawtooth mountains – impressing itself on your consciousness. Rather than shy away, jump right in. There's no shortage of world-class hiking, biking, skiing, kayaking, rafting or climbing in British Columbia and beyond – and the experience will likely be one you'll brag about for years to come. Alternatively, rub shoulders with the friendly locals and watch someone else do all the work by taking in some of the area's popular spectator sports.

Cycling & Mountain Biking

Mountain biking is as huge as the mountains in BC and the Rockies. This is the birthplace of 'freeride', which combines downhill and dirt-jumping.

Home to some of BC's best technical trails, Rossland is the mountain-biking capital of BC (and possibly Canada). You can get a ride to the top of a different trail each day and be picked up (hopefully in one piece) at the bottom.

Whistler has the province's best-organized mountain-bike park with jumps, beams and bridges winding through 200km of maintained downhill trails. In summer, the resort hosts the giant Kokanee Crankworx festival (www.crankworx.com), a pedal-packed nirvana of contests, demos and live music.

In nearby Squamish, you'll find 100 or so forested off-road trails twisting around the region. These are a visiting freeriders' fantasy, with narrow boards and logs spanning lush, wet ferns. You'll find a similar set-up – and a burgeoning local scene – in north Vancouver: see www.nsmba.ca for more information.

Back in the urban sprawl, Victoria is one of Canada's best cycling cities, closely trailed by Vancouver, which has been carving out new citywide routes for cyclists in recent years.

In the Rockies region, Canmore and Banff are the biking hot spots, with the latter offering a good combination of road and off-road options and plenty of wildlife-spotting opportunities.

Hiking

Hiking in this region ranges from a leisurely wander around Vancouver's salt-sprayed Stanley Park seawall to tramping across glaciers under a cathedral-like blue sky at the Columbia Icefield between Banff and Jasper. Whatever your level, a walk through nature is a must-do highlight here.

On Vancouver Island, the spectacular Pacific Rim National Park Reserve offers some of Mother Nature's most dramatic vistas: swaying old-growth rainforest fringing white-sand beaches. The park's signature

Vancouver-based *Momentum Magazine* is the publication of choice for visiting bike enthusiasts. Issues are archived and available for free download at www.momentumplanet.com.

» **Discovery Trail, Jasper** Easy 8km circle around the townsite with a high possibility of elk and deer sightings.

» **Lake Louise, Banff** Stroll around the shoreline or hit the 1.6km uphill trail to the Big Beehive lookout for a grand panorama.

» **Stanley Park, Vancouver** Spectacular tree-lined seawall trail with ocean and mountain vistas.

» **Athabasca Glacier, Columbia Icefields** Uphill tramping on a crunchy glacier, complete with breathtaking views.

North Vancouver's Grouse Grind is the Lower Mainland's favorite outdoor workout. It's an ultra-steep, 2.9km trek up the side of Grouse Mountain and usually takes one or two hours, depending on just how steely your calves are.

West Coast Trail is a challenge but it's one you'll never forget: rock-face ladders, stream crossings and wandering wildlife, plus the occasional passing whale, make it a rite of passage for serious hikers. It links to the lesser-known Juan de Fuca Marine Trail if you still need more. Atop Vancouver Island, the remote and much newer North Coast Trail is equally dramatic but far less busy: ideal if you like hiking without other people around.

In contrast, the Okanagan's Kettle Valley Rail Trail meanders over towering wooden trestle bridges in Myra Canyon. It offers hikers the perfect chance to explore this beautiful valley without having to worry about traffic or steep hills. It's also a popular bike route.

In the Rockies you'll find a hikers' paradise. There are plenty of easy short walks at popular attractions like the impossibly azure Lake Louise. But once you turn your back on the tour bus crowds, you'll suddenly feel at one with the vastness of nature. Banff is the hot spot for Rockies hikers and its top routes include the Sawback Trail and the Hoodoos Trail.

In the northern Yukon region, those who like a challenge should check out the steep and difficult Chilkoot Trail, still lined with the detritus of those who desperately tried to seek their fortune in the gold rush. Elsewhere in the territory, Kluane National Park and Reserve and Tombstone Territorial Park offer world-class challenges and spectacles such as thousands of migrating caribou.

Rock Climbing & Mountaineering

All those inviting crags you've spotted on your trip are an indication that western Canada is a major climbing capital, ideal for short scales or multiday crampon-picking jaunts.

Near Banff, the Rocky Mountain resort town of Canmore is an ideal first stop, no matter what your skill level. Climbing stores, a climbing school (www.yamnuska.com) and thousands of limestone sport climbs within a 30-minute radius make this a one-stop shop for rock fans.

Further west, BC's Squamish 'Chief' is the highlight – and one of the most challenging climbs – of a burgeoning local scene that includes dozens of area peaks. Tap the local scene via Squamish Rock Guides (www.squamishrockguides.com).

If mountaineering is more your thing, the Rockies are, not surprisingly, a hot spot. On the border with BC, the Matterhorn of Canada is Mt Assiniboine. Other western classics include Alberta's Mt Edith Cavell, in Jasper; BC's Mt Robson; and Sir Donald in the Rockies. Closer to Vancouver, Garibaldi Peak, in Garibaldi Provincial Park, lures many city-based climbers for weekend jaunts.

If you need a guide, check in with the excellent Alpine Club of Canada (www.alpineclubofcanada.ca).

Skiing & Snowboarding

Vancouver and Whistler are still basking in the glow of hosting the 2010 Winter Olympics. If you're staying in Vancouver, you can be on the slopes within a 20-minute drive from downtown, while Whistler is one of North America's most popular resort towns.

But many would argue that even better skiing in BC is found in the east of the province, where vast swaths of mountains – especially in the

SKIING HOT SPOTS

Some of the region's best ski resorts:

» **Apex Mountain Resort** Known for its plethora of double-black-diamond and technical runs (the drop is over 600m), as well as gladed chutes and vast powdery bowls. Near Penticton.

» **Banff National Park ski resorts** Three excellent mountain resorts, Ski Banff@ Norquay, Sunshine Village and Lake Louise Ski Area, offer 250 runs of every description. Sunshine Village is the most popular.

» **Big White Ski Resort** BC's highest ski resort features 118 runs, and is excellent for downhill and backcountry skiing. The drop is 777m and you can night ski. Near Kelowna.

» **Cypress Mountain** 2010's Winter Olympic snowboarding and freestyle skiing venue, with 52 runs, 19km of cross-country runs and a snowboard park. Near Vancouver.

» **Fernie Alpine Resort** With 114 runs across five large bowls, there's plenty of virgin powder where you can leave your mark. Near Fernie.

» **Grouse Mountain Resort** A 20-minute drive from Vancouver, Grouse is a favorite for its night skiing and snowmaking capabilities.

» **Kicking Horse Mountain Resort** A challenging 60% of the 106 runs here are rated advanced or expert. A gondola gives you a great vantage over the 1260 vertical meters of this relatively snow-heavy location. Near Golden.

» **Kimberley Alpine Resort** With over 7 sq km of skiable terrain and 80 runs, this is a good all-round resort – if you like smaller ones with comparatively minimal nightlife. Near Kimberley.

» **Mt Seymour** Some 1000m up, this North Shore provincial resort offers 23 runs including Brockton, Mystery Peak and Mushroom Junior Park. Also family-friendly tobogganing and inner tube runs. Near North Vancouver.

» **Mt Washington Alpine Resort** Vancouver Island's main ski resort; there are 60 runs, a snowshoe park and 55km of cross-country trails. Near Comox.

» **Red Mountain Ski Resort** Comprising two mountains – Red and Granite – and offering some of the province's best black-diamond runs. There are six lifts and a drop of 890m. Near Rossland.

» **Revelstoke Mountain Resort** BC's newest major resort has 52 runs with a focus on intermediate and advanced runs. Heli-skiing operators can take you out to track-free bowls across the ranges. Near Revelstoke.

» **Silver Star Mountain Resort** With 115 runs and a pioneer town aesthetic, there are 12 lifts and a 760m vertical drop. Near Vernon.

» **Sun Peaks Resort** BC's second-largest resort with three mountains, 122 runs, 11 lifts and a 881m drop. Snow-shoeing, dog sledding and Nordic skiing also available. Near Kamloops.

» **Whistler-Blackcomb** Host resort for the 2010 Olympic Winter Games, this world-famous, dual-mountain paradise has 38 lifts, which include a new 4.4km-long gondola linking Mts Whistler and Blackcomb. More than 200 runs and 29 sq km of bowls, glades and slopes keep the international crowds happy. Near Whistler.

» **Whitewater Winter Resort** Small, charming resort that's popular with backcountry skiers and snowboarders. Near Nelson.

Fishing – saltwater and freshwater – draws anglers from around the world to this region. Saltwater aficionados particularly like to cast their lines in the waters around Vancouver Island, where several places (particularly Campbell River) claim the title 'salmon capital of the world.' Also consider Prince Rupert and Queen Charlotte Islands, known for their halibut fishing. You'll find good river and lake fishing in every region.

Ask at visitor centers and sporting goods stores for information on the profusion of fishing licenses. The BC Ministry of Environment (www.env.gov.bc.ca/fw) controls freshwater licenses. The federal Department of Fisheries & Oceans (www.pac.dfo-mpo.gc.ca) issues licenses for saltwater/tidal fishing.

Kootenays – are annually covered by 10 or more meters of snow. In fact this region now boasts the 'Powder Hwy,' a marketing moniker for a series of roads linking the major ski resorts. Major players are investing billions in resorts here, so the area will only grow in stature.

Elsewhere in the province, the Okanagan has resorts like Sun Peaks, Apex and Big White boasting good snow year after year. Snowpack here ranges from 2m to 6m-plus, depending on how close the resort is to the Pacific Ocean.

> For a handy introduction to skiing in the Canadian Rockies, check out the information at www.canadianrockies.net.

You'll slide through stunning postcard landscapes in the Rockies, especially at Sunshine in Banff National Park. But for amazing cross-country skiing, head to Canmore: its popular trails were part of that other Canadian Winter Olympics, Calgary in 1988.

For insights and resources covering the region and beyond, check the website of the Canadian Ski Council (www.skicanada.org).

Diving

Justly famous for its superb, albeit chilly conditions, BC features two of the top-ranked ocean dive spots in the world: Vancouver Island and the Gulf Islands. It's best to go in winter, when the plankton has decreased and visibility often exceeds 20m.

The water temperature drops to between 7°C and 10°C in winter; in summer, it may reach 15°C. At depths of more than 15m, visibility remains good throughout the year and temperatures rarely rise above 10°C. Expect to see a full range of marine life, including oodles of crabs, from tiny hermits to intimidating kings. If you're lucky you may also encounter seals and sea lions or bizarre creatures such as wolf eels and giant octopuses.

Popular dive areas include Bamfield, Comox and Campbell River but Nanaimo on Vancouver Island lures many with its aquatic wildlife and its sunk-to-order navy vessels. See www.divenanaimo.travel for more information.

Paddlesports

BC and beyond offers hundreds of opportunities for those who like messing about on the water. Lakes, rivers and coastline abound, just waiting for the dip of an oar. Major paddling spots usually have stations where you can rent canoes, kayaks and gear. See local listings in this book for details.

Inland

The 116km Bowron Lake canoe circuit in Bowron Lake Provincial Park is one of the world's great canoe trips, covering 10 lakes with easy portages between each. Slightly less fabled – and less crowded – is the 116km-long circuit in Wells Gray Provincial Park.

During the short Yukon summer, scores of paddlers from around the world paddle the famed Yukon River and its tributaries, the route of the Klondike gold rush. You can still experience the stunning raw wilderness that the prospectors encountered, but from a modern canoe or kayak rather than a raft of lashed-together logs. Whitehorse is the center for guides and gear.

For the ultimate adrenaline rush, try white-water rafting. Rugged canyons and seasonal melting snow make BC's rivers great for white-water action. You don't need to be experienced to have a go, as licensed commercial rafting operators offer guided tours for all abilities. Trips can last from three hours (average cost $100) up to a couple of weeks. Popular areas include the Thompson River near Lytton and the Kootenays – many consider the Kicking Horse River near Golden as one of province's best raft trips. In the Yukon, Haines Junction is also a good base, while in the Rockies the Jasper region has several popular operators.

Coast

Although some people swear by their ocean-going canoes, the BC coast is truly the domain of kayaks. Since humans first stretched skin over a frame and deployed a double paddle some 4000 years ago, the little craft have been an excellent marriage of man and mode.

Options are as numerous as BC's endlessly crenulated coast and islands. The greatest concentration of outfitters is on Vancouver Island, which is one big paddling playground. The Broken Group Islands offer BC's best wilderness kayaking, revered for remoteness, rugged natural beauty and the opportunity to kayak to the little islands and camp overnight.

It's always safest to kayak with other people. Someone in the group should know how to plot a course by navigational chart and compass, pilot in fog, read weather patterns, assess water hazards, interpret tide tables, handle boats in adverse conditions and perform group- and self-rescues. Always check weather forecasts before setting out and don't expect your cell phone (mobile) to work.

If you have less time, you can rent a kayak for a few hours or take an introductory lesson in pretty much any of the island's coastal towns – check the activities listings for Victoria, Tofino and beyond in this book.

Urban paddlers can also take in Vancouver's cityscape from the waters of False Creek (rentals available on Granville Island) while in the Rockies, Banff has several operators if you'd like to paddle the region's glassy, mountain-backed lakes.

The official Tourism BC visitor website (www.hellobc.com) is packed with suggestions for outdoor activities throughout the region. For the Rockies, Travel Alberta (www.travelalberta.com) also has plenty of tempting ideas.

Surfing

If you're aiming to become a temporary beach bum on your Canada trip, head to the wild west coast of BC's Vancouver Island and hang out around Tofino. Surfing schools and gear rentals stud the area: you'll have an awesome time riding the swells or just watching everyone else as you stretch out on the idyllic sand. Backed by verdant rainforest, this is a perfect spot to spend your time whether or not you plan to surf. June to September is the height of the season here but serious surfer dudes also

WINDSURFING & KITEBOARDING

The breeze-licked tidal flats around Vancouver are popular with windsurfers. On many a day you'll see scores of colorful sails darting around the shallows like flocks of birds – it's a signature photo from the Kitsilano coastline. But further north, Squamish is the real center of the region's kiteboarding and windsurfing frenzy: an hour from Vancouver, its wind-whipped Squamish Spit area is often studded with adrenaline-fueled locals.

OLYMPICS

like to drop by in winter to face down the lashing waves. Check Surfing Vancouver Island (www.surfingvancouverisland.com) for a taste of what to expect.

Horseback Riding

Surveying the region's spectacular scenery from between the perky ears of a trusty steed is historically blessed, ecologically sound and just plain fun. Plus you get to release your inner Mountie – feel free to bring your own costume. BC's Cariboo and Chilcotin regions have long been horse-riding areas: you can stay on a ranch here or climb into the saddle for a tour, moseying past serene lakes and craggy peaks. Alternatively, in the midst of the Great Bear Rainforest, there are plenty of trails to explore in the Bella Coola Valley. And saddling up in Banff or Jasper is one of the best ways to feel at one with the region.

Spectator Sports

For the inside track on Vancouver's 2010 Olympic Winter Games, pick-up a copy of *Patriot Hearts: Inside the Olympics that Changed a Country* (2011) by John Furlong and Gary Mason.

Sport is the lifeblood of many communities in western Canada with hockey leading the way: mild-mannered locals can transform into fevered, face-painted nutbars on game night, especially if there's a chance of winning the Stanley Cup. But there's more to watching a game here than shelling out big bucks for NHL hockey: Canadian football and soccer are the region's other top professionals sports, while a host of smaller grass-roots options ensure there are plenty of opportunities for visitors to hangout with sports-mad locals. See individual sections throughout this book for recommendations.

Hockey

While Canada is a multifaith country, there's one religion that rises above all others. Hockey – don't even bother calling it *ice* hockey here – rouses rabid emotions in die-hard fans and can trigger group hugging or uncontrollable sobbing at the drop of a puck, especially when the local team has just lost in the annual Stanley Cup play-offs.

BC and Alberta has three teams in the elite, US-dominated National Hockey League (NHL): the Vancouver Canucks, Calgary Flames and Edmonton Oilers.

While tickets can be hard to come by – Vancouver Canucks games routinely sell out, for example, and booking as far ahead as possible for the September to June season is essential – you don't have to hit a stadium to catch a game: head to a local pub on game night and you'll be swept up in the passion.

But it's not all about the pros: catching a game with lower league teams like the Kamloops Blazers, Prince George Cougars, Kelowna Rockets and Vancouver Giants is much cheaper and it's an entertaining glimpse at the sport's less-glamorous level.

For an introduction to hockey in this region and across Canada, visit CBC Television's dedicated website at www.cbc.ca/sports/hockey.

HOT WHEELS

Catch a gladiatorial sporting contest with a difference via Vancouver's Terminal City Rollergirls league (www.terminalcityrollergirls.com). Surging in popularity in recent years, the league's all-female amateur flat-track roller-derby teams – with names like Riot Girls, Bad Reputations and Faster Pussycats – whistle around the track at break-neck speeds, triggering waves of hollers and a party atmosphere among crowds of up to 2000. League nights are staged at arenas across the city, and with 2011's promotion to the Women's Flat Track Derby Association, visiting teams from Seattle, Portland, Los Angeles and beyond will add to the fun. Tickets usually run from $17 to $24.

Football

It's not soccer and it's not American Football, but with eight pro teams across the country, the Canadian Football League (CFL) is second only to hockey in the hearts and minds of many. And while it's similar to American Football – think hefty padding and the kind of crunching tackles that would stop a grizzly bear – the Canadian version involves teams of 12 players and is fought on a larger pitch. And the trophy they all pursue? It's called the Grey Cup.

The region's teams are the BC Lions (www.bclions.com), Edmonton Eskimos (www.esks.com) and the Calgary Stampeders (www.stampeders.com). Tickets are usually easy to come by, except during Grey Cup time. Check their websites for schedules and ticket prices.

Regular season games run from June to November: expect a family atmosphere and a party-like vibe with cheerleaders and noisy crowd interaction. For more information on the league, peruse its official website at www.cfl.ca.

Soccer

Canada's most popular participation sport, soccer – you won't get far calling it football here – has traditionally mirrored the US experience by never quite reaching the heights of the continent's more established professional sports. But you can't keep a good pastime down and the game is currently on a serious spectator upswing in Vancouver and beyond.

Arguably Canada's biggest pro soccer team, the Vancouver Whitecaps (www.whitecapsfc.com) was promoted to the top-level Major League Soccer (MLS) league in 2011. It now plays games against leading sides across North America and regularly attracts crowds of over 15,000 cheering fans.

People, Arts & Culture

Western Canada has a surprisingly diverse culture, from its founding aboriginal traditions to the contemporary Asian presence that colors Vancouver and beyond. And that's before we even mention Alberta's rich cowboy heritage and the entire region's undercurrent of historic European immigrant influences. The area is a microcosm of the Canadian approach: widely differing ethnic groups, cultures and interests combining to create a dynamic multilayered society. One result is a cosmopolitan, often challenging arts scene that's uniquely shaped by this blending of ideas and influences.

People

Regional Identities

British Columbia, Alberta and the Yukon cover such a vast area and have such a diverse population that it's hard to sum up the locals with a single characteristic. In particular, the Rocky Mountains seem to divide Alberta and BC into two very distinct provinces that have little in common: BC often claims a closer affinity with the US Pacific Northwest states of Washington and Oregon – a cross-border area known as Cascadia – while Alberta feels more of a pull to the Canadian prairie provinces of Saskatchewan and Manitoba.

This apparent absence of affinity manifests in a number of ways: Alberta, with its cowboy culture and oil sands, is often seen as 'right wing' by those in BC. In contrast, if you ask an Albertan what BC is like, the words 'hippies,' 'tree-huggers,' 'dope-heads' and possibly 'communists' soon emerge. The reality, of course, is far more complex than these widely held stereotypes.

But there is one thing that unites the country's two westernmost provinces: both frequently feel marginalized by the distant national power base in Ottawa. Rather than combining to bargain for shared federal leverage, though, the two provinces continue eyeing each other warily, like a yoga-loving Lululemon shopper having a cordial but arms-length conversation with a no-nonsense, Stetson-wearing cowboy.

Local Rivalries

On a local level, BC's Vancouver is the region's biggest city and its immigrant-fueled cosmopolitanism shapes everything from dining to cultural events. In contrast, Calgary is a business center focused primarily on making money, leaving Edmonton – its smaller Alberta sibling – to develop a more substantial arts and cultural scene. Victoria, the BC capital on Vancouver Island, has worked hard to shake off its colonial yoke in recent years, becoming much more vibrant in the process.

But this region mostly exists outside its cities, with vast tracts of spectacular terrain dominating the geography. The smaller communities from Haida Gwaii to the Okanagan Valley and across into the Rockies often exhibit the kind of independent, self-sufficient approach to life that can be traced directly back to pioneer days.

But even here there are small, usually good-natured rivalries: Banff and Jasper will try to convince you of their superiority over the other; BC's Sunshine Coast communities – including Sechelt and Powell River – frequently gossip about the perceived deficiencies of their neighbors; and while southern Vancouver Islanders will tell you there's nothing worth seeing past Campbell River, the northerners will happily inform you they don't bother heading down south anyway because there's nothing they need there.

Multiculturalism & Religion

Canada west of the Rocky Mountains is the quintessential melting pot of cultures, beliefs and ethnicities, making the region as varied culturally as it is ecologically. Canada aims to promote cultural diversity and the west coast – and Vancouver in particular – has been a portal for immigrants from Asia, India and Europe. Still, as multicultural as Vancouver seems, you won't travel far before the stark whiteness of the wider population in this region is apparent.

BC, Alberta and the Yukon are predominantly Christian, with the major denominations being Catholic and Protestant, and no real territorial claim by either. Most Jewish people arriving in BC move to the Vancouver region, which is now the third-largest Jewish community in Canada. Alongside the influx of various cultures over the years, so too their beliefs – Buddhist, Sikh and Hindu temples are found all over the Lower Mainland.

Aboriginal Communities

The lush coast of BC supported a rich variety of communities for thousands of years. Because food such as salmon was relatively plentiful, people like the Haida, Nuxalk and Tsimshian thrived and had time to develop complex and sophisticated cultures. Inland BC didn't enjoy the same bounty and the Aboriginal Salish people in places like the Okanagan Valley had to devote much more of their time to subsistence living and surviving the long winters. In the far north, the Tagish, Gwich'in and others depended on migrating moose and caribou.

The Golden Spruce (2005), by John Vaillant, is one of the best books ever written in BC. It tells the true story of a former logger who felled a protected 300-year-old Sitka spruce tree that was sacred to the Aboriginal people of Haida Gwaii.

PEOPLE, ARTS & CULTURE PEOPLE

HOW THE LOCALS LIVE

Just as regional identities vary, so do lifestyles. BC's Lower Mainland, comprising the metro Vancouver area, is solidly first world and mostly suburban in lifestyle. The average household income is $80,000 for two-income households where both partners work (75% of women do). However, not every household in BC, Alberta or the Yukon is composed of a man and a woman. Gays and lesbians enjoy a tolerant culture and same-sex marriage has been legal in Canada since 2005.

In rural and mountain areas, suburban conveniences fade in importance and the emphasis is much more on day-to-day living and just getting by. Incomes are more variable, with many subject to the whims of the markets. In small communities the price of lumber and/or minerals decide if people have money for a new pick-up or for new clothes for kids to wear to school.

Social problems such as alcohol and drug use are thorny issues in some parts of this region – drugs are generally a bigger issue in big cities but alcoholism in some remote rural communities is at dangerously high levels.

Disease imported by early European visitors such as Captain Cook started the long slide for these peoples. Outright racism was rampant as well as official discrimination. In 1859 the governor of BC, James Douglas, declared that all the land and any wealth underneath belonged to the Crown.

Laws enacted during much of the 20th century brutalized Aboriginal culture. A notorious one banned the potlatch, a vital ceremony held over many days by communities to mark special occasions, and establish ranks and privileges. Dancing, feasting and elaborate gift-giving from the chief to his people are features.

In the Rockies region of Alberta, similar devastating challenges were faced by the Sioux, Cree and Blackfoot Aboriginals. This region is also the traditional home of the Métis, which translates from the French word for mixed blood and historically refers to the children born from Cree and French fur traders. It now refers to anyone born of mixed Cree and Aboriginal ancestry. Métis account for one-third of Canada's Aboriginal population and Edmonton is home to one of the country's largest populations.

The last 40 years have seen both an effort by governments to reverse the grim course of previous decades and a resurgence of Aboriginal culture. A long and difficult process has begun to settle claims from the 1859 proclamation through negotiations with the various bands. So far, the one treaty signed – with the Nisga'a peoples – provides about $200 million and allows some self-governance. Given the money involved, it's easy to see why the treaty process is one big vat of contention in BC (eg much of the land under downtown Vancouver is subject to Aboriginal claims). Only 20% of Aboriginal groups have even begun negotiations.

The *Recognition and Reconciliation Act* is BC's effort to literally rewrite all of its laws regarding the Aboriginals. It includes schemes to organize the province's 203 bands into 30 indigenous governments. That, plus provisions that would carve out a big piece of the mineral wealth pie for Aboriginal people, sparked enormous debate through 2009.

Relations in the Yukon have been less contentious as the size of the land has overwhelmed the conflicts among the tiny population.

Arts & Culture

Literature

Perhaps due to the long winters in Alberta and the week-long rainfests on the BC coast, western Canadians are big readers. And they don't go short of local tomes to dip into: BC has an estimated 1500 professional

Top Aboriginal Cultural Attractions

» Museum of Anthropology, Vancouver

» Royal British Columbia Museum, Victoria

» Haida Heritage Centre at Qay'llnagaay, Haida Gwaii

» Museum of Northern British Columbia, Prince Rupert

» Head-Smashed-in Buffalo Jump, Fort Macleod

RIOTOUS ARTWORK

Look for the large London Drugs shop in the Woodwards building on W Hastings St in Vancouver and enter the building's new courtyard, carved from what was originally the interior of one of the city's largest department stores. The space is now dominated by the city's most evocative – and perhaps provocative – public artwork.

Measuring 15m by 9m and created by Stan Douglas, *Abbott & Cordova, 7 August 1971* is a mammoth double-sided black-and-white photo montage depicting a key moment in the history of local social protest: the night when police in full riot gear broke up a pro-marijuana smoke-in being staged in the downtown Eastside.

The action (the image shows mounted police pushing against unarmed locals and miscreants being stuffed into police wagons) soon spiraled out of control, with pitched battles and general chaos triggering a siege-like atmosphere on the areas streets. Later, the event became known as the 'Gastown Riot' and 'The Battle of Maple Tree Sq.'

» *Runaway: Diary of a Street Kid,* by Evelyn Lau, tells the true story of the author's dangerous life on the streets of downtown Vancouver.

» *Red Dog, Red Dog,* by Patrick Lane, follows two brothers trying to navigate tough times in the 1950s Okanagan Valley. It's a gripping look at heartbreak, corruption and the tough lives of those who settled Canada.

» *Stanley Park,* by Timothy Taylor, stirs together a haute-cuisine chef with a park's dark secrets. The result is a story capturing Vancouver's quirky modern ambience.

» *The Cremation of Sam McGee,* by Robert W Service, the renowned Bard of the Yukon, is a classic of regional prose about two gold miners, the cold and what men will sometimes do. It's Service at his peak.

» *Klondike Tales,* by Jack London, draws on his first-hand experiences for these 23 stories showing the hardships, triumphs and betrayals of the Yukon gold rush. 'Call of the Wild' wins new fans every year. Learn more about London and his books at the Jack London Interpretive Centre in Dawson City.

authors and dozens of publishers to provide material for the region's insatiable bookworms.

This bulging bookshelf of authors includes WP Kinsella (author of *Shoeless Joe,* the story that became the *Field of Dreams* movie); William Gibson (sci-fi creator of cyberpunk); and Malcolm Lowry, who wrote his *Under the Volcano* masterpiece here.

But there's a rich vein of contemporary work, too. One of Canada's most celebrated authors, Douglas Coupland, lives in West Vancouver and has produced genre-defining titles such as *Generation X, Girlfriend in a Coma* and the excellent 'alternative guidebook' *City of Glass,* which showcases his love for Vancouver with quirky mini-essays and evocative photography. Coupland is joined by Timothy Taylor, Evelyn Lau and Laurence Gough, some other exciting BC modern authors.

A revered nonfiction scene has also developed in this region in recent years, with books from local lads James Mackinnon and Charles Montgomery winning prestigious national awards.

Sage Birchwater's book *Chiwid* tells the fantastic and true story of a Chilcotin (Tsilhqot'in) woman who suffered abuse and chose to live as a hermit in the wilderness. *Wisdom of the Elders: Sacred Native Stories of Nature,* by legendary David Suzuki and Peter Knudtson, provides a thought-provoking and insightful view of the relationship Aboriginal groups have with nature, and the Western world's need to learn the same.

While Alberta doesn't reach the heady heights of BC when it comes to literary output, it's nevertheless a great idea to dip into a couple of books before you arrive for a richer understanding of the area. Consider *The Wild Rose Anthology of Alberta Prose,* edited by George Melnyk and Tamara Seiler, or *Writing the Terrain: Travelling Through Alberta with the Poets,* edited by Robert Stamp. And for the Yukon, dip into almost anything by the legendary Robert W Service and you'll increase your understanding of this rugged region exponentially.

Cinema & Television

Western Canada is a hot spot for TV producers and moviemakers looking for a handy stand-in for American locations, hence the name 'Hollywood North' used to describe the film sector up here. You probably didn't know it, but blockbusters like *X-Men* and *I, Robot* were filmed around Vancouver – the center of the region's production – while the bucolic ranchlands of Alberta served as the backdrop for *Brokeback Mountain.*

FILM WEBSITE

The website of the National Film Board of Canada (www.nfb.ca) is a treasure trove of north-of-the-border films available for free online viewing. Recommended is *Carts of Darkness,* a riveting 2008 exploration of shopping cart races among the homeless in North Vancouver.

Vancouver's Bard on the Beach (www.bardonthebeach.org) is a quintessentially west coast way to catch a show. The June-to-September event includes a roster of three or four Shakespeare or Shakespeare-related plays performed in tents on the Kitsilano waterfront, with the North Shore mountains peeking through the back of the stage. It sells almost to capacity every year, making it one of North America's most successful and enduring Shakespeare festivals.

But it's not all about making US-set flicks. Canada has a thriving independent filmmaking sector and catching a couple of locally made movies before you arrive can provide some handy insights into the differences between the US and Canada. Look out for locally shot indie flicks including *Mount Pleasant* and *Double Happiness.*

It's not unusual to spot movie trucks and trailers on your travels here – especially in downtown Vancouver – and you might like to try your hand at becoming an extra on your visit. The website of the BC Film Commission (www.bcfilmcommission.com) gives the lowdown on what's filming and provides contact information for potential 'background performers.'

If you prefer to watch, there are some popular movie, TV and media festivals throughout the year in this region, including the Banff World Media Festival (www.banffmediafestival.com), Calgary International Film Festival (www.calgaryfilm.com), Edmonton International Film Festival (www.edmontonfilmfest.com), Vancouver International Film Festival (www.viff.org) and Whistler Film Festival (www.whistlerfilmfestival.com).

Music

Ask visitors to name Canadian musicians and they'll stutter to a halt after Celine Dion and Justin Beiber. But ask the locals in BC, Alberta and the Yukon, and they'll hit you with a roster of local performers you've probably never heard of, plus some that you probably thought were American.

Superstars Michael Buble, Sarah McLachlan, Bryan Adams and Diana Krall are all from BC and their slightly less stratospheric colleagues include Nelly Furtado and Spirit of the West. For those who like their music with an indie hue, Black Mountain, Dan Mangan and CR Avery are among the area's most popular grassroots performers.

Alberta has also spawned several big names: Joni Mitchell was born there for starters! Fans of indie rock would be familiar with Feist, as well as Tegan and Sarah. Pop and country music singer/songwriter, k.d. lang also hails from Edmonton, Alberta.

Bars are a great place to start if you want to take the pulse of the local music scene: expect to pay anything from zero to $10 for cover. Larger cities like Vancouver, Calgary and Edmonton offer a wide range of dedicated venues for shows, including stadiums.

Perhaps even better, the region is bristling with great music festivals. Look out for toe-tapping options like the Vancouver International Jazz Festival (www.coastaljazz.ca), Mertitt Mountain Music Festival (www.mountainfest.com), Live at Squamish (www.liveatsquamish.com), MusicFest Vancouver (www.musicfestvancouver.ca), Jazz on the Mountain at Whistler (www.whistlerjazzfest.com) and the Calgary Folk Music Festival (www.calgaryfolkfest.com).

Vancouver's free *Georgia Straight* weekly newspaper also has a great website listing local happenings in the music scene and beyond. Check it out at www.straight.com.

Visual Arts

When JB Harkin, first commissioner of the National Parks Board of Canada, stated that the Rocky Mountains were like priceless works of art, he had a valid point. The challenge for artists in this spectacular region is that whatever they produce, nature will always be ahead of the game. Despite that, some regional artists have risen to the challenge splendidly.

Emily Carr made her name by painting Aboriginal villages and swirling forest landscapes on Vancouver Island. She is often referred to as an honorary member of Canada's famous Group of Seven. Painting a few decades later, the rich, stylized canvases of EJ Hughes vividly depict coastal life in the region.

In recent years, Vancouver has become Western Canada's contemporary art capital with photoconceptualism especially revered. Locals Stan Douglas and Rodney Graham (who also works in multimedia) are celebrated but it's Jeff Wall, a photorealist whose large works have the quality of cinematic production, that has attained global recognition.

Theater & Dance

Local theaters can be found throughout BC and beyond, with even the smallest communities providing a venue for grassroots performing troupes and visiting shows. Bigger cities like Vancouver, Victoria, Edmonton and Calgary often have several large auditoria with their own repertory theater companies – Vancouver's Playhouse Theatre Company (www.vancouverplayhouse.com) is the region's biggest. The performance season usually runs from October to April, but there are frequently shows treading the boards outside this period.

Vancouver is one of Canada's dance capitals, second only to Montreal, and it's two main annual events are popular with visiting fans: Vancouver International Dance Festival (www.vidf.ca) and Dancing on the Edge (www.dancingontheedge.org).

Aboriginal Arts

There was formerly little outside recognition of the art produced by Canada's Aboriginal communities. But over the last 40 years or so, there's been a strong and growing appreciation of this unique creative force. For most visitors, totem poles are their entry point, but this region's cultural treasures go way beyond totems. Artworks such as masks, drums and paintings feature the distinctive black and red sweeping brush strokes depicting wolves, ravens and other animals from the spirit world.

Though most Aboriginal groups lack formal written history as we know it, centuries of cultural traditions live on. Art has long been a method of expression, intimately linked with historical and cultural preservation, religion and social ceremony.

Top Art Galleries

» Vancouver Art Gallery

» Art Gallery of Alberta, Edmonton

» Art Gallery of Calgary

» Art Gallery of Greater Victoria

» Emily Carr House, Victoria

PEOPLE, ARTS & CULTURE ARTS & CULTURE

YUKON SHOOTING STAR

Only one Yukoner has a star on the Hollywood Walk of Fame and that's Victor Jory. Like any good northerner, his story is better than the plots of the 200 or so movies and TV shows that have his name in the credits. He was born in 1902 to a single mother who ran a rooming house near Dawson City. Hanging around Hollywood got him his first role in 1930 and over the next 50 years he had parts in big pictures (quarrelsome field boss in Gone with the Wind) and small ones (the lead in Cat-Women of the Moon). Reflecting the ethos of the Yukon, he never said no to anything that might put food on his plate.

Today, Lawrence Paul Yuxweluptun explores politics, the environment and Aboriginal issues with his paintings that take inspiration from Coast Salish mythology. Shuswap actor and writer Darrell Dennis tackles Aboriginal stereotypes head-on in his thrilling one-man show *Tales of an Urban Indian*. Among the memorable lines: 'I can't even make it rain for God sakes.'

Tofino-based Roy Henry Vickers fuses mystical and traditional themes with contemporary approaches, while Lawrence Paul Yuxweluptun and Brian Jungen have gained national and international recognition for their challenging abstract approaches.

The free Van Dop Arts and Cultural Guide to BC lists galleries, studios and festivals across the province. It's online at www. art-bc.com.

Regional Cuisine

While dining out in British Columbia, Alberta and the Yukon used to involve a tricky choice between doughnut varieties at the local Tim Hortons outlet (the Canadian Maple always wins), western Canada is now sitting at the grownups table when it comes to great grub.

And after years of favoring imported food for that generic North American supermarket taste, the region has also discovered and fully embraced the unique larder of ingredients grown, raised and foraged on its own doorstep. It's important not to underestimate this seismic sea change: 25 years ago, only the poor and eco-crazed ate local food; now it's the first consideration for almost every diner when perusing a menu here.

For culinary adventurers, this means that BC and beyond provide a lip-smacking taste trip. Seafood fans on the west coast will soon be stuffed to the gills with Fanny Bay oysters and the kind of velvet-soft scallops that you could happily eat until you explode (don't try this, since it creates quite a mess).

In contrast, hungry carnivores visiting the Rockies region will find themselves in the Canadian capital of steak. But while this used to mean nothing more than a giant slab of blood-oozing T-bone hanging over the sides of your plate, Alberta has also raised its game, adding subtleties to its meat-friendly menu such as organic, locally raised and gourmet charcuterie approaches.

Throughout the region, locally grown produce has entered a golden age. Hugely popular farmers markets are popping up faster than mushrooms after a storm and if you don't arrive in the morning, you'll find all the good eats are gone. Ubiquitous in spring and summer, you'll spot a cornucopia of treats, from heirloom tomatoes and sweet carrots to the kind of seasonal, flavor-packed fruit – especially peaches, apricots, blueberries, apples and cherries – that will make you swear off supermarket chains forever.

Whatever you decide to sink your teeth into, you'll find dine-out scenes in many towns and cities that have developed exponentially in recent years. But while fine-dining restaurants often make the most noise about their slow-food credentials, you don't have to pay top-dollar for great regional meals. Western Canada offers plenty of midrange, home-style eateries where the menus are sometimes just as impressive as top city spots. And remember: there's a huge list of increasingly excellent regional beer and wine to add to the bacchanalian fun.

Now, loosen that belt, act like an esurient local and get scoffing.

Farmers markets are exploding across the region, bringing home-grown produce to the tables of locals and epicurious visitors. For BC locations, see www.bcfarmers market.org; for Alberta, check www.alberta markets.com.

Seafood

Don't tell Atlantic Canada, but the west coast is the country's seafood capital. In fact, a trip here that doesn't include a full-on face plant into BC's brimming marine larder is like visiting London without having a cup of tea: you can do it, but it's not advisable.

Tasty food blogs

» Calgary is Awesome (www. calgaryis awesome.com)

» Chow Times (www.chowtimes. com)

» Only Here for the Food (www. onlyherefor the food.ca)

» Urban Diner (www.urbandiner. ca)

» Vancouver Foodster (www. vancouver foodster.com)

If you're starting in Vancouver, you'll find an astonishing array of innovative seafood dishes. This is arguably the world's best sushi city outside Japan and there are hundreds of spots to choose from. Leading local chef Hidekazu Tojo is said to have invented the California roll, but these days the menu at his eponymous restaurant is the height of sophistication: this is a must-do pilgrimage destination for fans of the best in Japanese seafood preparation.

You'll also find a full table of traditional and innovative dishes in the area's Chinese restaurants, from the chatty dim-sum dining rooms of old Chinatown to the contemporary fusion joints in Richmond, a bustling, Hong Kong–like foodie heaven. If you're feeling adventurous, look out for *geoduck* (pronounced 'gooey duck'), a giant saltwater clam. It's a delicacy in Chinese dining and is even shipped from here to chefs across the world.

But it's not just ethnic approaches that bring BC's seafood to local diners. Vancouver's Pacific Northwest eateries almost always feature seasonal fresh catches. And as you travel around the region, you'll find the same amazing seafood – at non-city prices – almost everywhere you go. Juicy wild salmon is a signature here and in the autumn it dominates menus – do not miss it. Almost as popular is the early-spring spot prawn season when the sweet, crunchy little creatures turn up on tables throughout BC.

If you fancy meeting the fishers and choosing some grub straight off the back of their boats, you can also do that. The boats bobbling around the government wharf near Vancouver's Granville Island are a good spot to try, as well as the evocative boardwalk area in Steveston. This south Richmond heritage fishing village is an ideal destination for seafood fans: there are two excellent museums recalling the area's days as the center of the once-mighty regional fishing fleet and there are several finger-licking restaurants offering perhaps the best fish and chips in BC.

If you're lucky enough to make it to Haida Gwaii, you'll encounter some of the best seafood you've ever had in your life, typically caught that day and prepared in a simple manner that reveals the rich flavors of the sea. Especially keep your appetite primed here for halibut, scallops and crab, often plucked from the shallow waters just off the beach by net-wielding locals walking along the sand.

Local Flavors

While Vancouver now rivals – and arguably surpasses – Montréal and Toronto as Canada's fine-dining capital, it wins over both those cities with its surfeit of excellent ethnic dining options. You'll be hard-pressed to find a bad Chinese or Japanese restaurant here, while its Pacific Northwest dining choices (usually fused with intriguing international influences) bring the best of the region to tables across the city.

BC FOR FARM-HOPPERS

Ask Vancouverites where the food on their tables comes from and most will point vacantly at a nearby supermarket, while others will confidently tell you about the Fraser Valley. This lush interior region starts about 50km from the city and has been studded with busy farms for decades. In recent years, farmers and the people they feed have started to get to know one another on a series of five Circle Farm Tours. These self-guided driving tours take you around the communities of Langley, Abbotsford, Chilliwack, Agassiz and Harrison Mills, and Maple Ridge and Pitt Meadows, pointing out recommended pit-stops – farms, markets, wineries and dining suggestions – along the way and adding a cool foodie adventure to your BC trip. The tour maps can be downloaded free at www.circlefarmtour.ca.

Writers are increasingly inspired to wax lyrical over the region's foodie fashions. Check out these local magazines for the inside track on local scenes:

» **Avenue Magazine** (www.avenuecalgary.com) Lifestyle publication illuminating the Calgary restaurant scene for hungry locals, with a separate Edmonton edition (www.avenueedmonton.com) also available.

» **City Food** (www.cityfood.com) Freebie quarterly covering Vancouver's food and dine-out scene.

» **City Palate** (www.citypalate.ca) Covering Calgary's food and dining scene.

» **Eat Magazine** (www.eatmagazine.ca) Free mag covering BC food and wine happenings.

» **Edible Vancouver** (www.ediblecommunities.com/vancouver) Free quarterly with an organic and slow-food bent, available at choice local food shops.

» **Vancouver Magazine** (www.vanmag.com) City lifestyle glossy with good coverage of local dining.

In recent years, some of the country's most innovative chefs have set up shop, inspired by the twin influences of an abundant local larder of unique flavors and the most cosmopolitan – especially Asian – population in Canada. Fusion is the starting point here, but there's also a high-level of authenticity in traditional ethnic dining: amazing sushi bars and Japanese izakayas jostle for attention with superb Vietnamese and Korean eateries that feel like they've been transported from halfway around the world.

Outside Vancouver, the urban areas of Vancouver Island – especially in downtown Victoria – plus the Okanagan Valley offer additional top-notch eateries. And if you're heading up to Whistler, you can expect plenty of surprisingly gourmet restaurants to restore your energy after an exhilarating day on the slopes.

But eating well is not just about fine dining, and you'll find many welcoming places to nosh in more rustic areas of BC, Alberta and the Yukon, many of them delivering some tastebud-popping surprises. Follow the locals to waterfront seafood diners in coastal communities like Gibsons, Salt Spring Island and Prince Rupert for the kind of freshly caught aquatic treats that would often cost several times as much in the big city.

Even the smallest towns can usually rustle up a decent meal – including those ubiquitous 'Chinese and Canadian' eateries where the menu usually combines deep-fried cheeseburgers with gelatinous sweet-and-sour pork dishes. There are also many family-oriented, midpriced eateries and chatty diners for those traveling with kids. And unlike pubs in the UK and other countries, bars here are usually just as interested in serving food as they are beer.

This foodie nirvana stretches across the Rockies into Alberta, Canada's cowboy country. It's the nation's beef capital – you'll find top-notch Alberta steak on menus at leading restaurants across the country. But it's not all about steak here: look out for caribou and venison, both rising in popularity in recent years. If you're offered 'prairie oysters,' though, you might want to know (or maybe you'd prefer not to) that they're bull's testicles prepared in a variety of intriguing ways designed to take your mind off their origin.

Wherever your traveling taste buds take you, try to score some unique local flavors with a sampling of aboriginal food. Canada's Aboriginal people have many fascinating and accessible culinary traditions. Reliant on meat and seafood (try a juicy halibut stew on BC's Haida Gwaii) there's also an aboriginal tradition of bannock bread, imported by the

Scots and appropriated by Canada's original locals. And if you think you're an expert on desserts, try some 'Indian ice cream.' Made from whipped soapberries, it's sweetened with sugar to assuage its bitter edge.

Festivals & Events

Food and drink is the foundation of having a good time in BC, Alberta and the Yukon. Languid summer barbecues, fall's feast-like Thanksgiving Day and winter family get-togethers at Christmas traditionally center on tables groaning with meat and seafood dishes, diet-eschewing fruit desserts and plentiful wine and beer.

In addition, there's a full menu of annual festivals where you can dive into the flavors of the region and bond with the locals over tasty treats.

Recommended events in the region include:

Dine Out Vancouver (www.tourismvancouver.com/visitors/dineout.php) A three-week-long January event where local restaurants offer great-value two- or three-course tasting menus.

Feast! (www.feastbc.com) A month-long menu of Tofino and Ucluelet events in May and June focused on local seafood.

Taste of Edmonton (www.eventsedmonton.ca) A 10-day outdoor event in July showcasing local eateries and producers. There's also a similar, smaller event in Calgary (www.tasteofcalgary.com) in August.

Feast of Fields (www.feastoffields.com) Local produce and top chefs at alfresco party days in Metro Vancouver, the Okanagan and on Vancouver Island throughout August and September.

Cowichan Wine & Culinary Festival (www.wines.cowichan.net) A September celebration of local treats on Vancouver Island.

Cornucopia (www.whistlercornucopia.com) A bacchanalian November food and wine fest in Whistler.

Vegetarians & Vegans

In urban BC there's a full roster of vegetarian and vegan options for traveling herbivores, with many places also boasting their organic creden-

Elizabeth Levinson's *An Edible Journey: Exploring the Islands' Fine Food, Farms and Vineyards* is a lip-smacking taste trip around the foodie destinations of Vancouver Island and the Southern Gulf Islands.

EAT STREETS

Some thoroughfares in this region seem permanently suffused with the aroma of great cooking, as well as an attendant chorus of satisfied-looking diners rubbing their bellies and surreptitiously loosening their straining belts. If you're hungry, heading to these areas is the way to go – you'll meet the locals and have a great taste-of-the-region meal into the bargain.

If you're in Vancouver, there are several tasty options to choose from. Near Stanley Park, the West End's Denman St is teeming with good-value midrange restaurants. There's a huge variety here, from Vietnamese to Ukrainian and from pizza to Pacific Northwest. The menu is similarly diverse on adjoining Davie St and on Kitsilano's West 4th Ave. But if fine dining floats your boat, check out Hamilton St and Mainland St in Yaletown: both are lined with fancy joints for that romantic, special-occasion meal.

Across the region, Richmond's 'Golden Village' area is packed with superb Asian dining, while the streets radiating from Chinatown in Victoria house some treats. The city's Johnson St is also studded with tempting joints. And if you're up north in Prince Rupert, you won't have to go hungry: head to Cow Bay Rd for fish and chips and some great bistro options.

Over in Alberta, the Whyte Ave stretch of Edmonton's Old Strathcona neighborhood offers some excellent independent dining options, including plenty of taste-tripping ethnic eateries. In Calgary – where the dining scene has leapt in quality in recent years – the top dining thoroughfares are downtown's Stephen St as well as in the neighborhoods of Kensington, Mission and Ingelwood.

Aiming to emulate Portland's legendary street-food scene, Vancouver's sidewalk-dining revolution started in mid-2010 with the introduction of 17 diverse food carts across the city. Suddenly, barbecued pulled pork, organic tacos and gourmet Korean-fusion take-out were available to hungry locals. Despite a few teething troubles, the network was expanded with 19 more carts the following year.

It remains to be seen whether Vancouver will eventually emulate Portland's 500 plus vendors, but for visitors it's a great alfresco dining option: grab a pulled-pork-filled bun from Re-Up BBQ and sit on the sunny steps of the Vancouver Art Gallery to watch the world go by. Or pick-up some spicy duck sliders from Roaming Dragon and decamp to Stanley Park for a picnic. Carts are spread across the city, but you'll usually find several radiating from the Granville and W Georgia Sts intersection. Tried and tested favorites include Cartel, Coma, Kaboom Box, Off the Wagon and JapaDog.

For more information on the growing scene, visit www.vancouverstreeteats.ca.

tials. Eat heartily before you leave the city, though, since your options will diminish as the towns shrink in size. In the smaller settlements of BC and the Yukon, vegetarian options can be limited to salads, sandwiches or portobello mushroom burgers, with the occasional veggie-only joint standing out like a beacon – not a bacon – in the carnivorous darkness.

Crossing into the meat-loving Rockies, your choices will diminish faster than an ice cube on a sunny sidewalk. But it's not all doom and gloom: Calgary and Edmonton have their own dedicated veggie eateries, and you can usually find some meat-free pasta options available in Banff and Jasper restaurants.

Eating With Kids

Children are generally welcome at most dining establishments in BC and beyond, although fine-dining restaurants may sometimes be a little snotty about accommodating junior, especially if he/she noisily wrecks the romantic atmosphere of the joint by eating the candles and peeling off the wallpaper.

Avoid any possible embarrassments – apparently tantrums and food fights are not acceptable everywhere – by hitting midrange eateries with your sprogs. While some restaurants have kids menus, others will happily prepare a half-order of a regular dish if you ask nicely. Many chain restaurants will also provide highchairs.

White Spot, BC's very own restaurant chain, is a great place to dine with kids. Its main menu ranges from burgers (with secret 'Triple-O' sauce) to seafood pastas and Asian stir-frys, while its kids meals are served in cardboard pirate ships that are often eyed enviously by adults at other tables (the chain produced a one-time-only adult version of the 'pirate pack' in 2010 that reduced many locals to teary-eyed nostalgia).

Dining Time?

You can get virtually anything your belly craves at almost any time of the day in Vancouver, but outside the region's main metropolis restaurants may shut early, even in seemingly hip places like Victoria, Edmonton and Whistler. Be at the restaurant by 8pm outside peak summer weekends or you may be out of luck.

Breakfast is usually eaten between 6am and 10am. Many hotels offer at least a continental breakfast (a hot drink, juice, toast, muffins and maybe cereal) during these hours. Most local residents eat breakfast at home on weekdays or grab a quick bite on the run with their morning coffee. But on weekends, a much more leisurely breakfast or brunch at a

If you're inspired by the region's local food credentials, pick-up a copy of *The Zero-Mile Diet: A Year-Round Guide to Growing Organic Food* (2010) by BC's Carolyn Herriot. It's packed with ideas for sparking your own foodie revolution.

cafe or restaurant is a favorite pastime – in fact, weekend brunch service often stretches well into the afternoon at restaurants in this region.

The midday meal is typically taken between 11am and 1pm. It can be as simple as a snack bought from a farmers market or hot dog stand, or a picnic taken on your hike. Dinner is served anytime from about 5pm to 8pm, often later on weekends and in large cities as well as resort areas such as Whistler and Banff.

Dress is casual almost everywhere. In most restaurants, you'll be fine no matter what you're wearing (although nudity tends to put others off their food). For more formal places, the clichéd 'smart casual' is perfectly acceptable.

Cooking Courses

If you're inspired by the bounty on offer in this region, consider adding an educational side dish to your trip. Check out the following culinary courses or contact your destination's tourism organization to see what's on offer.

Amateurs and pros alike will find a course to suit their level at Vancouver's popular Dirty Apron Cooking School (www.dirtyapron.com). An ever-changing smorgasbord of regional cuisines is the approach and the classes – mostly taught by French-influenced chef David Robertson – aim to make students feel comfortable about mastering the required skills for a wide array of approaches.

Vancouver's popular cooking-themed bookstore, Barbara-Jo's Books to Cooks (www.bookstocooks.com), also stages regular demonstrations and classes in its swanky on-site kitchen. Check the website to see what's coming up and book ahead before you leave home.

There's a similar operation in Calgary, where the Cookbook Co Cooks (www.cookbookcooks.com) offers tomes for sale as well as a diverse menu of workshops and classes for locals and visitors.

Culinary Tours

If following your nose is an unreliable method for tapping into the region's culinary scene, consider an escort: BC is especially well served by operators who can guide you through the area's flavors on a tasty tour.

REGIONAL COOKBOOKS

Western Canada's top chefs, food experts and finest restaurants have been sharing their tips and recipes with the locals in book form for years. Pick up one of these unique souvenirs of your visit at bookstores and giftshops across the region:

» *Fresh: Seasonal Recipes Made with Local Foods*, John Bishop (2007) – A celebration of BC produce and its dedicated growers, this sumptuous 100-recipe book underlines Bishop's credentials as the city's leading sustainable restaurateur.

» *High Plains: The Joy of Alberta Cuisine,* Cinda Chavich (2008) – Local food journo Chavich explores the region's local bounty beyond beef.

» *Ocean Wise Cookbook,* Jane Mundy (2010) – Created by the Vancouver Aquarium, Ocean Wise encourages restaurants and seafood purveyors across Canada to employ sustainable fishing practices. This book showcases great seafood recipes from chefs and eateries in Vancouver and beyond.

» *Simple Treasures,* Alistair Barnes (2008) – Local ingredients are prepared to an elevated gourmet high in this popular Rockies-region recipe book.

» *Vancouver Cooks 2,* Chefs' Table Society (2009) – Seventy Vancouver-area chefs come together to offer more than 100 great recipes that give a true taste of the region and its cosmopolitan, sometimes eclectic, dining approach. Look out for treats from Rob Feenie, Vikram Vij and Tojo Hidekazu, among others.

Slip into your pants with the elasticized waist and hit the road for what may well be the highlight of your visit.

If you're attracted to Vancouver Island's produce cornucopia, consider an educational tour of the verdant Cowichan Valley farm region, offered by Travel with Taste (www.travelwithtaste.com). You'll meet and sample from artisan cheese makers and boutique vintners before tucking into a gourmet lunch of wild BC salmon. The company also offers lip-smacking guided tours around Victoria and Salt Spring Island.

Alternatively, if you don't plan to stray far from big city Vancouver, consider a Granville Island Market tour with Edible BC (www.edible britishcolumbia.com). You'll be guided around the colorful market and shown how to pick ingredients for that perfect meal – there are also samples aplenty.

Or consider a wander with Vancouver Food Tour (www.vancouver foodtour.com). Among its offerings is the popular four-hour Gastown Tasting Tour, which includes samples, dinner and a beer in arguably the city's best dining district. There's also a Chinatown tour, enabling visitors to check out one of North America's best Asian culinary scenes.

Wine & Beer

A few years back, the locals used to be happy downing generic fizzy beers from Labatt and Molson or sipping glasses of lip-puckering fruit wine made with foraged blackberries. But mirroring the rise in gourmet regional cuisine in recent years, Albertans and British Columbians have developed one of Canada's tastiest homegrown tipple scenes – and visitors should dive right in.

The wine sector led the way, pioneered by BC's Okanagan Valley, where dozens of nationally (and sometimes internationally) recognized operations stripe the verdant hills tumbling down to the lakes. Soon, smaller satellite winery regions popped up around BC and even in Alberta. Tours and tastings are recommended wherever you base yourself – complete with a designated driver, of course.

The Okanagan's great wine rival in Canada is Ontario's Niagara region. But when it comes to North American–style beer – the country's other favorite tipple – this region leads the nation. Quebec has been making its super-strong European-style brews for decades, but BC's burgeoning craft beer scene has entered a golden age in recent years. Finally joining the Pacific Northwest's celebrated beer scene south of the border, there are dozens of good local brews made here. And while there are far fewer to choose from in Alberta, the Rockies region has some equally tasty beers on hand.

Wherever you end up on your regional beer and wine crawl, it's a great way to break the ice with the locals: ask them for tips on what to try – from merlot to ice wine to frothy Indian Pale Ale – and you'll have a new friend and a tasty insight into what makes the area tick. And if you're not asking your wait staff at every restaurant for some local recommendations, you might as well stay home.

The website of the BC Wine Institute (www.winebc.com) is an invaluable resource for planning a vintage trawl around the region. It has route maps for several wine tours around the area.

WINE WEBSITE

Wine Regions

Overseas visitors are often surprised to learn that wine is produced here, but their skepticism is usually tempered after a choice drink or two. BC's wines have gained ever-greater kudos in recent years and while smaller-scale production and the industry dominance of wine regions like Napa means they'll never be a global market leader, there are some surprisingly tasty treats awaiting.

Since the best way to sample any wine is to head straight to the source – where you can taste the region in the glass – consider doing some homework and locating the nearest vineyards on your visit: they'll likely be a lot closer than you think. The following are the region's main wine areas, but there are also wineries – alone or in mini-clusters – in BC's Fraser Valley and Southern Gulf Islands. And while Alberta has far fewer wineries, keep your eyes peeled while you're on the road: there are a handful of friendly fruit wine joints worth stopping at.

Wherever your tipple-craving takes you, drink widely and deeply. And make sure you have plenty of room in your suitcase – packing materials are always available, but you may drink everything before you make it to the airport anyway.

For background and further information before you arrive, pour a large glass and peruse the handy regional pages on the Wines of Canada website (www.winesofcanada.com) and the BC Wine Lover blog (www.bcwinelover.com).

Okanagan Valley

The rolling hills of this lakeside BC region are well worth the five-hour drive from Vancouver. Studded among the vine-striped slopes are around 100 wineries enjoying a diverse climate that fosters both crisp whites and bold reds. With varietals including pinot noir, pinot gris, pinto blanc, merlot and chardonnay, there's a wine here to suit almost every palate. Most visitors base themselves in Kelowna, the Okanagan's wine capital, before fanning out to well-known blockbuster wineries like Mission Hill, Quail's Gate, Cedar Creek and Summerhill Pyramid Winery (yes, it has a pyramid). Many of them have excellent vista-hugging restaurants. See also p140.

The first Okanagan vineyards were planted in the mid-1800s when catholic priests began producing sacramental wine for local services.

Golden Mile

Some of BC's best Okanagan wineries are centered south of the valley around the historic town of Oliver, where the Golden Mile's hot climate fosters a long, warm, growing season. Combined with gravel, clay and sandy soils, this area is ideally suited to varietals like merlot, chardonnay, gewürztraminer and cabernet sauvignon. While the 20 or so wineries here are not actually crammed into 1 mile – it's more like 20km – the proximity of celebrated producers like Burrowing Owl, Tinhorn Creek and Road 13 Vineyards makes this an ideal touring area. If you're still thirsty, continue south to Osoyoos and check out Nk'Mip Cellars, a First Nations winery on the edge of a desert.

Vancouver Island

Long-established as a farming area, Vancouver Island's verdant Cowichan Valley is also home to some great little wineries. A short drive from Victoria, you'll find Averill Creek, Blue Grouse, Cherry Point Vineyards and Venturie-Schulze. Also consider Merridale Estate Cidery, which produces six celebrated ciders on its gently sloped orchard grounds. For more information on Vancouver Island's wineries, visit www.wineislands.ca.

DOWNING ICE WINE IN THE SNOW

There are many good reasons to visit the Okanagan's Winter Festival of Wine – accessible educational seminars, dinner events, cozy alpine-lodge ambience and some of BC's best outdoor winter activities – but the evening Progressive Tasting is the best. Twenty wineries set up their stalls and offer more than 100 wines at locations throughout the Christmas-card village, while increasingly tipsy visitors slip, slide and tumble their way between them in an attempt to keep their glasses as full as possible.

Staged in the third week of January, the annual festival is particularly renowned for celebrating a distinctive tipple that's become a signature of Canadian wineries. Made from grapes frozen on the vine at −8°C (there are plenty of fakes on the market that don't meet this simple criterion), Canadian ice wine is a premium, uber-sweet dessert drink sold in distinctive slender bottles at upwards of $50 a pop. While Austria, Germany and other countries produce their own ice wines, it's a product that reflects Canada's enduring international image as a snowy winter wonderland.

Here for the Beer?

Western Canadians don't only drink wine, of course – beer is arguably an even more important beverage here. And while the usual round of bland factory suds and those international usual suspects (you know the ones we mean) are available, a little digging – actually hardly any digging at all – uncovers a thriving regional microbrewing scene that's dripping with distinctive craft beers.

John Schreiner's Okanagan Wine Tour Guide, by John Schreiner (2010), is an in-depth tome covering the region for visiting oenophiles. It's packed with great suggestions for how to make the most of a wine-based trawl around the region.

BC in particular is packed like a clamorous Friday-night pub with almost 40 microbreweries, many of them only established in the past 15 years. On your thirst-slaking travels, look out for taps from celebrated producers like Tree Brewing (Kelowna), Central City Brewing (Surrey), Phillips Brewing (Victoria), Howe Sound Brewing (Squamish), Storm Brewing (Vancouver) and the near-legendary Crannóg Ales (Sorrento), which crafts a rich, velvety Back Hand of God stout that few can resist.

You don't have to go thirsty in the Rockies region either: travelers in Alberta should hunt down local beverages from Calgary's Wild Rose Brewery, Edmonton's Alley Kat Brewing and Yellowhead Brewery, and the popular Jasper Brewing Company brewpub, evocatively located in the heart of the national park.

The smaller the brewery, the more likely it is to produce tipples that make generic fizzy beers taste like something you'd rather wash your car with. Ales, bitters, lagers, pilsners, bocks, porters, stouts and even hemp beers are often available at pubs, bars and restaurants throughout the region. Some bars (notably a handful in downtown Vancouver) host weekly cask nights when they crack open a guest keg of something special: check ahead and find out what's available during your visit.

If you want to see how it's all done – and stoke your thirst in the process – Granville Island Brewing in Vancouver and Big Rock Brewery in Calgary are among those offering short tours coupled with satisfyingly leisurely sample tastings. Cheers!

Festivals

Time your visit well and you'll be sipping glasses of wine or downing pints of beer (or perhaps the other way around) at a series of regional events. Large or small, they're a great way to hang out with the locals.

Wine lovers are well served in the Okanagan, where there's an event for each of the four seasons. The biggest is the 10-day Fall Wine Festival, while January's Winter Okanagan Wine Festival is evocatively hosted in an icicle-draped ski resort: there's usually plenty of ice wine to go around. For information on the four events, see www.thewinefestivals.com.

If you're in Vancouver in March, connect with the Vancouver Playhouse International Wine Festival (www.playhousewinefest.com). It's the city's largest and oldest wine-based celebration and it focuses on one wine region every year.

A SIX-PACK OF TOP BEERS

On your travels around the region, look out for these great taste-tested brews:

» **Central City Brewing's Red Racer ESB** (www.centralcitybrewing.com)
» **Crannóg Ales' Back Hand of God Stout** (www.crannogales.com)
» **Howe Sound Brewing's Father John's Winter Ale** (www.howesound.com)
» **Russell Brewing's Wee Angry Scotch Ale** (www.russellbeer.com)
» **Saltspring Island Ale's Whaletail Ale** (www.gulfislandsbrewery.com)
» **Tree Brewing's Hop Head IPA** (treebeer.com)

If you've explored BC's wine and beer scene a little too enthusiastically, you may need a strong, java-based pick-me-up. Luckily, Vancouver is the country's leading coffee city. On many street corners you'll spot ubiquitous Tim Hortons and Starbucks outlets – Vancouver was the location for the first non-US Starbucks in 1987 – but follow the locals and you'll uncover a rich, aromatic venti-sized cup of great independent coffee shops. The Kitsilano, Commercial Drive and South Main (SoMa) neighborhoods are your best bets for a twitchy afternoon with the locals, and you'll find everything from old-school Italian haunts to slick hipster hangouts.

Combining drinks and grub, Alberta's Rocky Mountain Wine and Food Festival (www.rockymountainwine.com) takes place on three different dates in Calgary, Edmonton and Banff.

If beer floats your boat, you can sample all those BC microbrews you've been craving at the ever-popular Vancouver Craft Beer Week (www.vancouvercraftbeerweek.com) in May. It's the province's biggest beer event but it's not the only one: check out Victoria's Great Canadian Beer Festival (www.gcbf.com) and the Calgary International Beerfest (www.calgarybeerfest.com). Don't miss Vancouver's annual Hopscotch Festival (www.hopscotchfestival.com), which focuses on whisky as well as beer.

Where to Drink

You don't have to visit wineries or breweries if you want to find a good drink in this region: BC, Alberta and the Yukon are well stocked with watering holes, from traditional pubs to slick wine bars and sparkling cocktail joints, although finding a perfect Moscow Mule in smaller towns may be harder than locating a local grooming service for your traveling Chihuahua. Keep in mind that most bars follow the North American table service approach: unlike other countries, servers come to the table for your order rather than expecting you to hang around trying to get your own drink at the bar.

While craft beer is taking off across the region, brewpubs are still underrepresented in some areas: you'll find a handful in Vancouver and Victoria, plus single beacons of beery delight in towns like Banff, Jasper, Kelowna and Nanaimo.

If you're looking for some takeout, you'll find two different systems operating in BC and Alberta: while partially deregulated, most booze in BC is sold through government-run liquor stores (see www.bcliquorstores.com for locations), although private beer and wine shops have begin emerging in recent years. Alberta fully privatized its liquor store sector in 1993. For a handy search engine showing where you can buy your favorite tipples, see www.alberta-liquor-guide.com.

The legal drinking age in BC and the Yukon is 19, while it's 18 in Alberta. If you 'look young' you should expect to be asked for identification. Canada is very serious about curbing drink-driving, and you may encounter mandatory roadside checkpoints, especially on summer evenings or around winter holidays.

Classes & Tours

If you're jealous of those people who confidently swirl their glasses before airily proclaiming their wine is oaky with a hint of pineapple and Old Spice, get your own back by learning some wine-snob tricks of your own. If you have the time and money, you could consider a full-on sommelier course. But if you're looking for something a little less grueling (and expensive), check out some of the short courses staged across the region.

Past Whistler on the Sea to Sky Hwy, the small town of Pemberton has been a potato-growing center for generations. But it's also the home of Pemberton Distillery (www.pembertondistillery.com), which uses the region's spuds to make its celebrated, multi-award-winning Shramm Vodka.

TEA

Vancouver Island's Victoria is the tea capital of North America with tasty traditional offerings as well as Asian-fusion teashops for those who like to push the teabag envelope beyond Earl Grey.

Among the best are those available in Vancouver. The East Vancouver Wine Academy (www.waldorfhotel.com/east-van-wine-academy) is a great-value, snob-free series of evenings where a different wine region is explored and tasted in a chatty atmosphere. One of the city's best liquor stores, Firefly Fine Wines & Ales (www.fireflyfinewinesandales.com), offers regular evening events where you'll learn about and taste a few wines based around a theme – often a country like Spain or Chile – in a convivial setting with a dozen or so others.

If you'd rather hit the road and visit the wineries but need a little help finding them, head to Kelowna in the heart of the Okanagan Valley. The downtown visitor center stocks a great wine trails brochure (free) with directions and information on five distinctive grape-based trails around the region.

If you'd rather have company, Top Cat Tours (www.topcattours.com) has a tempting menu of fully guided options around the Okanagan. These include a Great Estates tour that drives you to the region's biggest wineries as well as a South Okanagan Tour that includes the Golden Mile.

Wildlife

British Columbia, Alberta and the Yukon provides a diverse safari of often jaw-dropping wildlife sightings. And while the locals tend to be a little blasé about the creatures they share their home with, visitors frequently rave about the impressive animals they've spotted on their travels here – this is arguably Canada's best critter-watching region. Expect a spine-tingling frisson when you see your first black bear nonchalantly scoffing berries by the roadside or watch a bald eagle dive-bombing a salmon-stuffed river. Then there are the whales: boat tours are extremely popular on the west coast but sometimes you'll simply catch sight of an orca pod from a ferry deck or see a grey whale sliding silently past the remote beach you're standing on. The word 'magical' doesn't even come close.

Bears

The number one viewing target for many western Canada visitors, grizzly bears – *ursus arctos horribilis* to all you Latin scholars – are most commonly viewed in the Rockies. Identifiable by their distinctive shoulder hump, they stand up to 3m tall and are solitary mammals with no natural enemies (except humans). While they enjoy fresh-catch meals of elk, moose and caribou, most of their noshing centers on salmon and wild berries.

Confusingly, grizzlies are almost black, while their smaller and much more numerous relation, the black bear, is sometimes brown. More commonly spotted in the wild than grizzlies, black bears reside in large numbers in northern BC and in the Banff and Jasper areas, where 'wildlife jams' are a frequent issue among rubber-necking motorists. You may also see these bears as far south as Whistler and in the foothills of North Vancouver.

In 1994, coastal BC's Khutzeymateen Grizzly Bear Sanctuary (near the northern town of Prince Rupert) was officially designated for protected status. Over 50 grizzlies currently live on this 45,000-hectare refuge. A few ecotour operators have permits for viewing these animals if you want to check them out face-to-face. There are also tiny bear sanctuaries in Banff and on Grouse Mountain in North Vancouver.

Kermode bears, sometimes called spirit bears, are a subspecies of the black bear but are whitish in color. They're unique to BC, and are found in the north, from Bella Coola through the Great Bear Rainforest to Stewart, mostly along the lower Skeena River Valley.

The Biodiversity Centre for Wildlife Studies (www.wildlifebc.org) has the world's largest wildlife database, with seven million records for BC dating back 120 years. Sources include trappers, bird-watchers, government agencies and loggers.

BY THE NUMBERS

This region is home to more than 160 mammal species, 500 bird species, 500 fish species, 20 reptile species and 20 types of amphibians. About 100 species (including most of the whales, the burrowing owl and Vancouver Island marmot) are on the province's endangered species list; another 100 or so are at risk. Ecosystems are at their most diverse in southern BC, but that's also where threats from human pressures are at their greatest.

BEAR AWARE

Bears are rarely in the business of attacking humans but, if provoked, they'll certainly have a go. And it won't be pretty. Most bear attacks on tourists result from ignorance on the part of the visitor, so keep the following points in mind when you're on the road in bear country:

» On foot, travel in groups. Consider wearing bear bells as a way to make some noise – bears will generally steer clear of you if they know where you are.

» Follow any notices you see about bears in the area and ask park staff about recent sightings.

» Keep pets on a leash and do not linger near any dead animals.

» Never approach a bear, and keep all food and food smells away from bears; always use bear-resistant food containers.

If the above fails and a bear attacks, do the following:

» Don't drop your pack – it can provide protection.

» Try to walk backwards slowly.

» Don't run – a bear will always outrun you.

» Try to get somewhere safe, like a car.

» If attacked, use bear spray. If this fails, deploy one of the following approaches, depending on the type of bear: for black bears, try to appear larger, shout a lot and fight back; for grizzlies, playing dead, curling into a ball and protecting your head is recommended.

The best time to spot grizzlies and black bears in the wild is from mid-April to mid-June, when they've emerged from hibernation and are busy feeding. Kermode's are best spotted from September to mid-October.

Whales

Whale-watching is a must-do activity on the west coast and tours (typically up to three hours for around $100 per person) are justly popular. The waters around Vancouver Island, particularly in Johnstone Strait, teem with orcas every summer and tours frequently depart from Tofino, Telegraph Cove, Victoria, Richmond and beyond. The Inside Passage cruise ship and ferry route between Port Hardy and Prince Rupert is also a popular long-haul viewing spot.

Other Local Critters

» Raccoon
» Skunk
» Marmot
» Cougar
» Porcupine
» Beaver
» Wolverine

While orcas – also known as killer whales – dominate the region's viewing, you might also sight some of the 20,000 Pacific gray whales that migrate along the coastline here twice a year. If you're lucky, you'll also see majestic humpbacks, which average 15m in length.

Orcas get their 'killer' moniker from the fast-paced way they pursue and attack the area's marine life and not from attacks on humans, which are more rare than whale sightings in the Rockies. On your tour you'll likely spot the orcas' preferred nosh languishing on rocks or nosing around your boat – keep your camera primed for porpoises, dolphins, seals, Steller sea lions and sea otters.

Prime orca-viewing season is May to mid-July; for gray whales, it's mid-August to October; and for humpbacks, it's August to October.

Wolves

Wolves, perhaps the most intriguing and mysterious of all Canada's wild animals, hunt cleverly and tenaciously in packs and have no qualms about taking on prey much larger than themselves. Human attacks are extremely rare but you'll nevertheless feel nervous excitement if you're lucky enough to spot one in the wild – typically in the distance, across the other side of a wide river.

The Rockies are your most likely spot for seeing a wolf. You may also hear them howling at the moon at night if you're camping in the bush.

It's extremely unlikely that you'll be approached by a wolf but they sometimes become habituated to human contact, typically through access to uncovered food on campsites. If a wolf approaches you and seems aggressive or unafraid:

» Wave your arms in the air to make yourself appear larger.

» Reverse slowly and do not turn your back.

» Make noise and throw sticks and/or stones.

Elk, Caribou & Deer

Although they're usually placid, male elk have sometimes charged into vehicles in the Jasper area after spotting their reflection in the shiny paintwork and believing they've met a rival for their harem of eligible females. They're mostly docile, though, and it's common to see this large deer species wandering around the edges of the townsite for much of the year. November's rut is the best time to visit, though: you'll see the bugling males at their finest, strutting around and taking on their rivals with head-smashing displays of strength.

More common in northern Québec and Labrador, woodland caribou – which have an unfortunate reputation for being far from smart – show up in small groups in BC and the Rockies, although the Jasper population almost wiped itself out a couple of years ago by triggering an avalanche that buried nearly all of them.

Deer are common sights away from the cities in much of BC and beyond. Expect to spot jumpy white-tailed deer and mule deer flitting among the trees and alongside the roads in the Rockies. You might also spot the Columbia black-tailed deer, a small subspecies native to Vancouver Island and BC's west coast.

Moose

Western Canada's postcard-hogging shrub-nibbler is the largest member of the deer family and owes its popularity to a distinctively odd appearance: skinny legs supporting a humungous body and a cartoonish head that looks inquisitive and clueless at the same time. And then there are the antlers: males grow a spectacular rack every summer, only to discard them in November.

You'll spot moose foraging for twigs and leaves – their main diet – near lakes, muskegs and streams, as well as in the mountain forests of the Rockies and the Yukon.

Moose are generally not aggressive, and will often stand stock still for photographs. They can be unpredictable, though, so don't startle them. During mating season (September), the giant males can become belligerent, so keep your distance: great photos are not worth a sharply pronged antler charge from a massive, angry moose.

GREY WOLF

This region is home to the grey wolf, also known as the timber wolf. They hunt in packs of up to a dozen strong and mate for life. The females give birth to as many as 11 pups each spring.

TOP WILDLIFE-WATCHING SPOTS

» Maligne Lake Rd – eagles, deer, elk, bighorn sheep and maybe a moose are likely spottings in this Jasper National Park area.

» Icefields Parkway – the 230km drive between Banff and Jasper is lined with monumental mountain peaks and a regular chorus of deer, bighorns and black bears.

» Khutzeymateen Grizzly Bear Sanctuary – over 50 grizzlies live in this refuge and ecotour operators have permits for viewing.

» Bella Coola Valley – boat tours along rivers are thick with sightings of grizzly bears wandering the banks.

SALMON RUNS WILD

After years of depressingly declining returns, the 2010 wild Pacific sockeye salmon run on BC's Fraser River surprised and delighted scientists and local fishing operators by being the largest for almost 100 years. More than 34 million gasping salmon reportedly pushed themselves up the river to lay their eggs and die, a spectacle that turned regional rivers red with the sight of millions of crimson sockeye. The previous year had seen less than two million fish return to the area in what was regarded as a catastrophic low. However, while restaurants fell over themselves to offer wild salmon dishes for several months, scientists were already predicting that the record run was a flash-in-the-pan and not an indication of long-term recovery in the salmon sector.

Bighorn Sheep

Often spotted clinging tenaciously to the almost-sheer cliff faces overlooking the roads around Banff and Jasper, bighorn sheep are a signature Rockies sight. They're also here in large numbers, so are one of the easiest animals to spot. On the drive between Banff and Jasper via the Icefields Parkway, you'll likely see them: they look like stock-still sculptures standing sentinel on the rocks. The best viewing season is September and October when the rut is on and the males are smashing their heads together to prove their mate-worthy credentials.

Birdlife

BULL
MOOSE

The bull moose can grow to almost 3m and weigh as much as 600kg. His spectacular flat antlers, which are shed every year, can be as much as 2m wide with 30 tines (or spikes).

Of the region's 500-plus bird species, the black-and-blue Steller's jay is among the most famous; it was named BC's official bird after a government-sponsored contest. Other prominent feathered locals include ravens, great horned owls and peregrine falcons. You don't have to trek into the wilderness for an up-close glimpse: head to Lost Lagoon on the edge of Vancouver's Stanley Park and you'll discover an oasis just a few steps from the city. Look out here for beady-eyed great blue herons.

The most visually arresting birds in western Canada are eagles, especially of the bald variety. Its wingspan can reach up to 2m and, like wolves, they are a spine-tingling sight for anyone lucky enough to see one in the wild. Good viewing sites include Brackendale, near Squamish in BC, where up to 4000 eagles nest in winter and an annual bird count lures visitors. Also train your camera lens on Vancouver Island's southern and western shorelines: it won't be long before something awesome sweeps into view.

Sealife

Divers off the BC coastline can encounter a startling and often bizarre range of aquatic life. The swimming scallop looks like the fake teeth your Uncle Ed leaves in a glass by the side of the bed; in fact, it's a fascinating symbiotic creature able to move under its own power, nabbing floating nutrients while a sponge attached to its shell provides protection. Giant Pacific octopuses with tentacles of up to 2m in length are found on shallow rocky ocean bottoms. The record weight of one of these creatures is 272kg. Wolf eels are known for darting out of crevices to inspect wetsuit-clad visitors and often snuggling in the crooks of their arms.

Salmon are possibly the most important fish in BC. They're sacred to many Aboriginal bands and a mainstay of the province's fishing industry. Salmon come in five species: Chinook (also called king), Coho, chum, sockeye and pink.

Survival Guide

Directory A-Z

Accommodations

British Columbia and Alberta offer a good range of hotels, B&Bs and hostels. There's plenty of both accessible and far-flung campsites. Options are dramatically reduced in northern BC and the Yukon: budget options are often replaced by modest but pricey motels.

Booking Ahead

» In Rockies hotspots Banff and Jasper, accommodation is severely limited in summer so advance booking is critical. Reserving ahead in summer is also a good idea throughout BC and Alberta, especially in July and August and around holidays. Winter (particularly December to February) is a peak season in ski areas like BC's Whistler and Alberta's Sunshine Meadows, so booking is vital.

» *British Columbia Approved Accommodation Guide*, an extensive annual directory published by **Tourism BC** (www.hellobc.com), is a detailed guide with options in all classes of lodgings. It's free and is available at visitor information centers, from Tourism BC or online.

» **Travel Alberta** (www.travelalberta.com) also offers an accommodation service via its website.

Prices

» Prices listed in this book are for peak-season travel and do not include taxes. Off-season rates can be considerably lower, so consider traveling in spring or fall.

» Hotels and resorts in popular areas frequently charge for parking – check at time of booking.

» The following accommodation types and rate categories are used in this book:

TYPE	RATES
budget (campsites, hostels and basic hotels and motels, often with shared bathroom)	up to $80 for a double
midrange(B&Bs, motels and hotels, usually with private bathrooms)	$80-180 for a double
top end (quality hotels and resorts and luxury B&Bs; extras may include spa and business center)	from $180 for a double

Discounts

» To look for deals, check out an establishment's website first and then cross-reference it with one of the large internet booking services (although these services often do not list interesting, independent places). Some internet booking services:

Expedia (www.expedia.com)
Hotwire (www.hotwire.com)
Priceline (www.priceline.com)
Travelocity (www.travelocity.com)

B&Bs

» North American B&Bs are typically more upscale than the casual, family-style pensions found in Europe. There are thousands to choose from – with many unique or romantic options – across the region.

» Booking ahead is essential since B&Bs often have only one to three rooms.

» Check the rules: many are adult-only and do not accept pets. Others only open seasonally and/or require a two-night minimum stay.

» Parking is usually free at B&Bs.

» Local visitor centers usually have good B&B listings for their areas. Also see **Bed and Breakfast Online** (www.bbcanada.com) for listings across the region.

Camping

» This region is a campers' paradise with thousands of government-run and private options.

» Options range from basic pitches nestled in the remote wilderness to highly accessible, amenity-packed campgrounds popular with families.

» Campgrounds are typically open from May to September but dates vary by location.

» Some popular sites are sold out months in advance: booking ahead is recommended, especially for holiday weekends and the summer peak season.

» Facilities vary widely. Expect little more than pit toilets and a fire ring at backcountry sites, while larger campgrounds may have shower blocks and guided interpretive programs.

» Camping in national or provincial parks can cost up to $39 per night, although many are around the $20 mark. Private sites may offer more facilities and charge a little more.

» For information, listings and bookings for government-run sites in national and local parks, see **Parks Canada** (www.pccamping.ca), **BC Parks** (www.discovercamping. ca) and **Alberta Parks** (www.albertaparks.ca).

» The annual Tourism BC *Super Camping Guide* (www.camping.bc.ca) is also a good source for private, RV-oriented campgrounds in this province.

Guest Ranches

BC and Alberta have dozens of enticing guest ranches, the euphemism for dude ranches of *City Slickers* fame, where you can join a trail ride or sit by a mountain lake. The Cariboo-Chilcotin region is a guest ranch hotbed.

Hostels

» Independent and Hostelling International (HI) hostels are easy to find in popular visitor destinations, with some areas enjoying healthy competition between several establishments.

» Dorms (typically $25 to $40) may be small or sleep up to 20 people and facilities usually include shared bathrooms, kitchen and common areas. Laundry facilities, bike storage and wi-fi (or computer terminals) are also common.

» Private rooms in hostels are increasingly popular: they are also the most sought after, so book far ahead.

» Many outdoorsy hostels offer extras like bike or kayak rentals while city-based hostels often have free/low-cost

social programs that include guided tours or pub nights.

» While city hostels are often open 24 hours, those in other areas may be closed during the day – check ahead.

» Booking ahead for hostels in popular destinations like Tofino, Whistler and Banff is essential in summer.

» For locations, listings and bookings across the region, see **Hostelling International** (www.hihostels.ca), **SameSun** (www.samesun. com) and **Backpackers Hostels Canada** (www.backpackers.ca).

Motels & Hotels

» Rates vary tremendously around the province. Plan to spend at least $100 for a basic double room with a private bathroom during summer in Vancouver and Victoria. In less-visited areas, $80 is closer to the norm.

» Boutique properties and high-end hotels are readily available in Vancouver and Victoria, with chateaux-like resorts common in Whistler and the Rockies.

» Wilderness retreats are dotted around the BC coastline and in some parts of the Rockies, offering spas and top-notch dining packages.

» Midrange hotel and motel rooms typically include a private bathroom, one or two large beds, a tea and coffee maker, and a TV with dozens of channels.

» Your hotel may not include air-conditioning. If this is a deal-breaker, check before you book.

» In distant areas such as northern BC, the Alberta outback and remote Yukon

spots, you'll find hotels folksy at best.

» Many motels (and an increasing number of suite-style hotels) offer handy kitchenettes.

» Children can often stay free in the same room as their parents – check to see if there's a charge for roll-away beds.

Business Hours

Following are the standard opening hours for businesses across this region. Reviews throughout the book show specific hours only where they deviate from these norms.

BUSINESS	STANDARD HOURS
banks	9am or 10am-5pm Mon-Fri; some open 9am-noon Sat
bars	11am-midnight or later; some only open from 5pm
post offices	9am-5pm Mon-Fri
restaurants	breakfast 7-11am, lunch 11:30am-2pm, dinner 5-9:30pm (8pm in rural areas)
shops	10am-5pm or 6pm Mon-Sat; noon-5pm Sunday; some (especially in malls) open to 8pm or 9pm Thu and/or Fri
supermarkets	9am-8pm; some open 24hr

BOOK YOUR STAY ONLINE

For more accommodations reviews by Lonely Planet authors, check out hotels.lonelyplanet.com/Canada. You'll find independent reviews, as well as recommendations on the best places to stay. Best of all, you can book online.

Children

Family-friendly western Canada is stuffed with things to do with vacationing kids, from child-oriented museums and science centers in the big cities to outdoor activities in the regions. And then there's the promise of seeing a bear or two in the wild.

» Most attractions offer discounted child rates, although there may also be a slightly higher 'youth rate' that kicks in for teens. Family tickets are also widely offered.

» Most restaurants here are welcoming to adults with children, although some top-end joints are not quite so amenable. If there's no kids menu available, ask for a half-order from the main menu.

Practicalities

» Children can usually stay with their parents at motels and hotels for no extra charge. Some B&Bs may refuse to accept pint-sized patrons, often preferring to keep themselves adult-oriented, while others charge full price for tots. Some hostels have family rooms.

» Car-hire companies rent car seats, which are legally required for young children, for a few dollars per day, but you'll need to reserve them in advance.

» Make sure children coming to Canada from other countries (including the US) have a passport or birth certificate with them. Divorced parents with a child should also carry a copy of their custody agreement. Children traveling with a nonparent should have a letter of permission from the parent or legal guardian.

» For more on holidaying with children, check out Lonely Planet's *Travel With Children*.

Customs Regulations

» Check in with the **Canada Border Services Agency** (www.cbsa.gc.ca) for the latest customs lowdown.

» The duty-free allowance coming into Canada is 1.14L (40oz) of liquor, 1.5L (or two 750mL bottles) of wine or 24 cans or bottles of beer, as well as up to 200 cigarettes, 50 cigars or 200g of tobacco.

» You are allowed to bring in gifts up to a total value of $60. Gifts above $60 are subject to duty and taxes on the over-limit value.

» Fresh and prepared foods are the subject of myriad rules and regulations here. Just buy what you need in Canada.

» You can bring in or take out up to $10,000 in cash – report larger amounts at the border.

» Register excessive or expensive sporting goods and cameras with customs, as this will save you time and trouble when leaving, especially if you plan on crossing the Canada-US border.

» If you are bringing a dog or cat into the country you will need proof that it has had a rabies shot in the past 36 months.

» Pistols, fully automatic weapons, any firearms less than 66cm (26in) in length and self-defense sprays (like pepper or mace) are not permitted into Canada.

Discount Cards

» Discounts for seniors, students and families are commonly offered at attractions throughout this region. Students from overseas will usually need a valid International **Student Identity Card** (www.isiccard.com).

» A **Parks Canada Discovery Pass** (www.pc.gc.ca; adult/child/family $67.70/33.30/136.40) is good value if you're planning to visit national parks and historic sites across the region.

» The **See Vancouver Card** (www.seevancouvercard.com; 2/3/5 days adult $125/155/229 child $85/105/155) is useful if you plan to visit as many city-wide attractions as possible in a limited time.

Electricity

120v/60hz

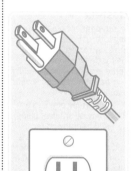

120v/60hz

Embassies & Consulates

Consulates in the region include the following:

Australia (☎604-684-1177; Suite 2050, 1075 W Georgia St, Vancouver)

France (☎604-681-4345; Suite 1100, 1130 W Pender St, Vancouver)

Germany Calgary (☎403-247-3357; Suite 600, 550 11th Ave SW, Calgary); Vancouver (☎604-684-8377; Suite 704, 999 Canada Pl, Vancouver)

Ireland (☎604-683-9233; 100 W Pender St, Vancouver)

Netherlands Calgary (☎403-266-2710; 304 8th Ave, Calgary); Vancouver (☎604-684-6448; 595 Burrard St, Vancouver)

New Zealand (☎604-684-7388; Suite 1200, 888 Dunsmuir St, Vancouver)

UK (☎604-683-4421; Suite 800, 1111 Melville St, Vancouver)

USA Macleod Trail SE (☎403-266-8962; Suite 1000, 615 Macleod Trail SE, Vancouver); W Pender St (☎604-685-4311; 1095 W Pender St, Vancouver)

Gay & Lesbian Travelers

In BC and Alberta, attitudes toward gays and lesbians are relaxed, especially in urban areas like Vancouver and Calgary where there are dedicated rainbow-hued nightlife scenes.

While you won't find as open a gay and lesbian culture in other parts of the region, throughout the provinces and in the Yukon attitudes are generally tolerant. That said, the lack of prominent gay and lesbian communities outside urban centers tends to mean that most people keep their orientation to themselves.

The following are useful resources for gay travelers:

Gay & Lesbian Business Association of BC (www.glba.org) Queer-friendly business listings throughout BC.

Gay Canada (www.gaycanada.com) Queer-friendly forums and resources across the region.

Xtra (www.xtra.ca) Gay and lesbian newspaper with large online presence.

Insurance

Make sure you have adequate travel insurance to cover your trip in this region. Luggage theft or loss insurance is handy but health coverage for medical emergencies and treatment is vital: medical treatment for non-Canadians is expensive.

Worldwide travel insurance is available at www.lonelyplanet.com/travel_services. You can buy, extend and claim online anytime – even if you're already on the road.

Internet Access

» Wi-fi or wired internet connections are increasingly standard in accommodations across BC, Alberta and the Yukon.

» You'll also find wi-fi and internet-access computers in libraries, some cafes and internet cafes in larger towns. Paid access usually costs about $1 per 10 minutes.

» In this book, the internet icon (@) is used for places with public internet computers. The wi-fi icon (🛜) is used for any place with wi-fi access. In accommodations listings, it also means that at least some rooms have wi-fi.

Legal Matters

» The Canadian federal government permits the use of marijuana for medicinal purposes, but official prescription cannabis is strictly regulated.

» It's illegal to consume alcohol anywhere other than a residence or licensed premises, which puts parks, beaches and other public spaces off limits.

» You can incur stiff fines, jail time and penalties if caught driving under the influence of alcohol or any illegal substance. The blood-alcohol limit is 0.08%, which is reached after just two beers. Penalties include being thrown in jail overnight, followed by a court appearance, heavy fine and/or further incarceration.

» Canada has strict regulations banning smoking in all public places. This can

PRACTICALITIES

» The power supply is 120 volts, 60Hz AC; plugs have two flat parallel pins with an optional round grounding pin, the same as the US.

» The metric system is used throughout Canada, although popular references to the imperial system (as used in the US) still survive.

» Canada is in DVD region 1. Buy or watch videos on the NTSC system.

» Most towns have a daily or weekly newspaper. *The Vancouver Sun* and *Calgary Herald* provide reasonable regional coverage.

» Signs at the entrances to towns provide local frequencies for CBC Radio One (www.cbc.ca/radio).

» Smoking is banned inside public buildings across the region.

HEALTH

There's a high level of hygiene in this region, so most common infectious diseases will not be a major concern for travelers. No special vaccinations are required, but all travelers should be up-to-date on standard immunizations, such as tetanus and measles.

Insurance

The Canadian healthcare system is one of the best in the world and excellent care is widely available. Benefits are generous for Canadian citizens, but foreigners aren't covered, which can make treatment prohibitively expensive.

Make sure you have travel-health insurance if your regular policy doesn't apply when you're abroad. Find out in advance if your insurance plan will make payments directly to providers or reimburse you later for overseas health expenditures.

Availability & Cost of Health Care

For immediate medical assistance anywhere in BC and Alberta, call ☎911; in the Yukon, call ☎867-667-5555, except for Whitehorse, which has 911 service. In general, if you have a medical emergency, it's best to find the nearest hospital emergency room.

If you have a choice, a university hospital can be preferable to a community hospital, although you can often find superb medical care in small local hospitals, and the waiting time is usually shorter. If the problem isn't urgent, you can call a nearby hospital and ask for a referral to a local physician – less expensive than a trip to the emergency room.

Pharmacies are abundantly supplied; however, you may find that some medications that are available over the counter in your home country require a prescription in Canada. In the largest cities you'll be able to find 24-hour pharmacies, although most drugstores typically keep regular store hours.

Importing Medications

Bring medications in their original containers, clearly labeled. A signed, dated letter from your physician describing all medical conditions and medications, including generic names, is also a good idea. If carrying syringes or needles be sure to have a physician's letter documenting their medical necessity.

Infectious Diseases

You need to be aware of the following, particularly if you're traveling in wilderness areas:

» **Giardiasis** A parasitic infection of the small intestine. Its symptoms may include nausea, bloating, cramps and diarrhea, and may last for weeks. Avoid drinking directly from lakes, ponds, streams and rivers, which may be contaminated by animal or human feces.

» **Lyme Disease** Transmitted by tiny deer ticks and mostly occurring in late spring and summer in southern areas. The first symptom is usually an expanding red rash. Flu-like symptoms, including fever, headache, joint pains and body aches, are also common.

» **West Nile Virus** Recently observed in provinces including Alberta, the virus is transmitted by Culex mosquitoes, which are active in late summer and early fall, and generally bite after dusk. Most infections are mild, but the virus may infect the central nervous system, leading to fever, headache, confusion, coma and sometimes death.

Websites

» **Public Health Agency of Canada** (www.publichealth.gc.ca) General Canadian government health resource.

» **MD Travel Health** (www.mdtravelhealth.com) Travel-related health information for countries around the world.

» **World Health Organization** (www.who.int) General health information covering all countries.

» **Australia** (www.smartraveller.gov.au) Health advice for Australians traveling abroad.

» **United Kingdom** (www.nhs.uk/livewell/travelhealth) Travel resources for UK citizens traveling overseas.

» **United States** (www.cdc.gov/travel) Health advice for traveling Americans.

include patios and other outdoor spaces. Your best bet is to light up in the middle of a big empty parking lot.

» The legal driving age throughout the region is 16 and the voting age is 18. However, the drinking age is 19 in BC and the Yukon and 18 in Alberta.

Maps

» Members of the Canadian Automobile Association (CAA), American Automobile Association (AAA) or affiliated clubs can get free road maps before leaving home or from offices throughout BC and Alberta.

» Bookstores, gas stations and convenience stores usually sell a wide variety of maps ranging from regional overviews to detailed street atlases.

» For extended hikes or multiday backcountry treks, it's a good idea to carry a topographic map. The best are the series of 1:50,000 scale maps published by the government's **Centre for Topographic Information** (www.maps.nrcan.gc.ca). These are sold by approximately 900 map dealers around the country; check the website for vendors. You can also download and print maps from www.geobase.ca.

» **Gem Trek Publishing** (www.gemtrek.com) offers some of the best Rocky Mountains maps in scales from 1:35,000 to 1:100,000.

Money

» All prices in this book are in Canadian dollars, unless stated.

» The Canadian dollar ($) is divided into 100 cents (¢). Coins come in 1¢ (penny), 5¢ (nickel), 10¢ (dime), 25¢ (quarter), $1 (Loonie) and $2 (tipi toonie) pieces.

» Notes come in $5, $10, $20, $50 and $100 denominations; $50 and $100 bills

can prove difficult to cash. Canadian bills are all the same size but vary in their colors and images.

ATMs

ATMs are common throughout BC, Alberta and the larger towns of the Yukon. Canadian ATM fees are generally low but your bank at home may charge another fee on top of that.

Changing Money

If you're not going to withdraw cash as needed from ATMs, exchange your dosh when you arrive in Canada. There are currency exchange counters at international airports such as Vancouver and Calgary. Currency exchange offices are also common in the area's bigger towns and cities as well as in tourist destinations like Whistler and Banff. Keep in mind that larger banks may also exchange currency and their rates are usually better. US dollars are often accepted by businesses at larger tourist towns like Victoria and Whistler – especially in gift shops – but keep in mind that the exchange rates they use are typically not favorable.

Credit Cards

Credit and debit cards are almost universally accepted and, in fact, you'll find it hard or impossible to rent a car, book a room or order tickets online or over the phone without one.

Taxes & Refunds

BC and Alberta have different consumer tax rates. The federal Goods and Services Tax (GST) adds 5% to nearly every product, service or transaction in Alberta. This is also the case in the Yukon.

In BC, there is instead a 12% Harmonized Sales Tax (HST) levied on most transactions. Controversially introduced in 2010, the HST has proved unpopular and may be rescinded or reduced in future.

Almost all tax rebate schemes have been killed, but if you booked your trip as part of a package, you may be able to get a refund on tax paid on accommodations. Check in with the **Canada Revenue Agency** (www.craarc.gc.ca/E/pbg/gf/gst115) for the latest information.

Tipping

Gratuities are part of the price you'll pay for visiting this part of the world. The following are typical rates:

SERVICE	USUAL TIP
restaurant wait staff	15%
bar servers	$1 per drink
hotel bellhops	$1 to $2 per bag
hotel room cleaners	$2 per day
taxi drivers	10-15%

Traveler's Checks

The days of traveler's checks are waning and they're becoming increasingly obsolete as ATMs spread and become more convenient for vacationers. Traveler's checks issued in Canadian dollars are generally treated like cash by most businesses, especially in larger, heavily visited areas like Banff, Jasper, Vancouver, Victoria and Whistler.

Traveler's checks issued in most other currencies must be exchanged for Canadian dollars at a bank or foreign-currency office.

Post

» **Canada Post** (www.canadapost.ca) is reliable and easy to use. Look for the red storefronts around towns and cities denoting main branches.

» Even more ubiquitous are the full-service Canada Post counters tucked into the back of convenience stores, drug stores and supermarkets. Look for the signs in their windows. They often have extended opening hours.

» Your hotel may also sell individual stamps, while books of stamps are available in many convenience stores.

» Rates for postcards and letters to the US are $1.03, to the rest of the world $1.75.

Public Holidays

National public holidays are celebrated throughout Canada with BC, Alberta and the Yukon each observing an additional statutory holiday – often called a 'stat' – at separate times of the year. Banks, schools and government offices (including post offices) are closed, and transportation, museums and other services may operate on a Sunday schedule. Holidays falling on a weekend are usually observed the following Monday and long weekends are among the busiest on the region's roads and ferry routes.

New Year's Day January 1

Family Day third Monday in February; Alberta only

Easter (Good Friday & Easter Monday) March/April

Victoria Day Monday preceding May 25

Canada Day July 1

BC Day first Monday in August; BC only

Discovery Day third Monday in August; Yukon only

Labour Day first Monday in September

Thanksgiving second Monday in October

Remembrance Day November 11

Christmas Day December 25

Boxing Day December 26; many stores open, other businesses closed

Telephone

» If you are calling a number within the same area code, you still need to dial all 10 digits. If you are dialing any other region in North America, you need to dial ☏1, then the 10 digits.

» For calling outside of North America, dial ☏011 followed by the country code and the number. When calling North America from abroad the country code is ☏1.

» Pay phones are increasingly disappearing from sidewalks across the region. If you do find one, you'll need coins or a long-distance phonecard to work them. Phonecards are available from myriad companies and are sold in myriad places (convenience stores, post offices, gas stations etc). Shop around for the best card deals.

» Cell (mobile) phones use the GSM and CDMA systems, depending on the carrier. If you have an unlocked GSM phone, you should be able to buy a SIM card for under $50, which will include a bit of talk time. Using your home-country cell-phone service in Canada will be subject to rates much like those of hotel phones: extortionate. And note that much of the backcountry has no cell-phone signal.

» Toll-free numbers begin with ☏800, ☏877 or ☏866. However, these numbers do not typically work when calling from overseas.

Time

» Most of BC and the Yukon operate on Pacific Time, which is eight hours behind Greenwich Mean Time.

» Alberta is on Mountain Time, which is one hour later than Pacific Time.

» Clocks are turned forward one hour on the second Sunday in March and are turned back one hour on the first Sunday in November.

» Canada's time zones mirror those across the border in the US.

LOCAL HOLIDAYS: WHAT THEY MEAN

Aside from the public holidays enjoyed by everyone across the region, BC, Alberta and the Yukon have their own distinctive extra days off when they spend at least a couple of hours phoning their neighbors across the country to brag about not having to go into work. On these days you can expect shops and businesses to be operating on reduced hours (or to be closed), so plan ahead. The region's three separate public holidays:

» **BC Day** Officially called British Columbia Day, this welcome August holiday (a trigger for many locals to take a summertime long-weekend) was introduced in 1974 and was intended to recognize the pioneers that kick-started the region.

» **Discovery Day** The Yukon's mid-August holiday marks the 1896 gold discovery in Bonanza Creek that triggered the Klondike Gold Rush. It kicks off a week-long Dawson City festival that includes historic re-creations.

» **Family Day** Shared with the provinces of Ontario and Saskatchewan, this February statutory holiday was instituted in Alberta in 1990.

Tourist Information

With tourism such a major part of this region's economy, resources for travelers are excellent: official websites are useful for trip planning and there are hundreds of visitor centers dotted across the area.

Many smaller regions have their own organizations (see individual chapters for information) but they usually operate under the umbrella of these larger bodies:

Tourism BC (☑800-435-5622; www.hellobc.com)

Travel Alberta (☑800-252-3782; www.travelalberta.com)

Tourism Yukon (☑800-661-0494; www.travelyukon.com)

Travelers with Disabilities

» Guide dogs may legally be brought into restaurants, hotels and other businesses.

» Many public service phone numbers and some payphones are adapted for the hearing impaired.

» Most public buildings are wheelchair accessible and many parks feature trails that are likewise accessible.

» Many newer or renovated hotels also have dedicated accessible rooms.

» Public transport is increasingly accessible with all buses in Vancouver, for example, now fully wheelchair accessible.

» Start your trip planning at **Access to Travel** (www.accesstotravel.gc.ca), the federal government's dedicated website. It has information on air, bus, rail and ferry transportation.

» Other helpful resources:

BC Coalition of People with Disabilities (www.bccpd.bc.ca)

Canadian National Institute for the Blind (www.cnib.ca)

BORDER CROSSING

Many points of entry on the US-Canada border are open 24 hours. The exceptions are some minor ones and those in the Yukon that have limited hours and/or close for the season. Entering Canada by land from the US usually goes smoothly at the dozens of border crossings from the continental US and Alaska. But there may be a wait on weekends – especially holiday weekends – particularly at the I-5/Hwy 99 crossing south of Vancouver, where you may have to wait several hours. Either avoid crossing at these times, or drive to one of the other Lower Mainland crossings such as Aldergrove.

The website www.borderlineups.com has live cameras showing the situation at major crossings as well stats on wait times.

US citizens flying home should note that you must clear US Immigration and Customs at Vancouver and Calgary airports *before* you fly to the US. This means two things: get to those two airports at least an hour earlier than normal as the US lines can be long; and when your plane arrives in the US, you are treated as a domestic passenger, so you're on your way.

Canadian Paraplegic Association (www.canparaplegic.org)

Mobility International (www.miusa.org)

Society for Accessible Travel & Hospitality (www.sath.org)

Visas

Visitors from most of the US, Western Europe and many Commonwealth countries normally don't require a visa for a tourist stay of less than 180 days. But citizens of another 130 countries do. **Citizenship & Immigration Canada** (www.cic.gc.ca) has the latest visa details on its website and it has links to Canadian embassies and consulates worldwide so you can check requirements locally.

Women Travelers

» BC, Alberta and the Yukon are generally safe places for women traveling alone, although the usual precautions apply: just use the same commonsense you would at home.

» In Vancouver, the Main and Hastings Sts area is best avoided and it's not a good idea to go for a walk in Stanley Park on your own after dark. In more remote parts of the province, particularly in Northern BC, women traveling alone will find themselves a distinct minority, although there's no shortage of feisty locals ready to assist a sister in need, especially in the Yukon.

» In bars and nightclubs, solo women will likely attract a lot of male attention. If you don't want company, a firm 'No thank you' typically does the trick. If you feel threatened in an area where there are other people, protesting loudly will usually bring others to your defense.

» Note that carrying mace or pepper spray is illegal throughout Canada.

» Attacks are unlikely but if you are assaulted, call the police immediately. Rape crisis hotlines include **Cal-gary** (☎403-237-5888) and **Vancouver** (☎877-392-7583).

Work

» In almost all cases, non-Canadians need a valid work permit to get a job in Canada. Obtaining one may be difficult, as employment opportunities go to Canadians first. Some jobs are exempt from the permit requirement.

» For full details on temporary work, check with **Citizenship & Immigration Canada** (www.cic.gc.ca/english/work/index.asp).

» Those aged 18 to 30 may be able to get work permits as students or as part of a working holiday program. See the CIC website for details.

» Don't try to work without a permit: if you're caught, that will be the end of your Canadian dream.

» Short-term jobs, such as restaurant and bar work, are generally plentiful in popular tourist spots like Whistler and Banff, where the turnover is predictably high. Often there will be postings on the resort website.

» Resources for potential job-seekers:

International Experience Canada (www.international.gc.ca/iyp-pij/intro_incoming-intro_entrant.aspx)

Student Work Abroad Program (www.swap.ca)

Transportation

GETTING THERE & AWAY

British Colombia and Alberta are directly accessible from international and US destinations, while the Yukon usually requires a plane connection. Flights, tours and rail tickets can be booked online at www.lonelyplanet.com/bookings.

Entering the Region

When flying into Canada, you will be expected to show your passport (plus visa, if required – see p319) to an immigration officer and answer a few questions about the duration and purpose of your visit. After clearing customs, you'll be on your way.

Driving across the border from the US can be a little more complex. Questioning is sometimes more intense and, in some cases, your car may be searched.

See **Citizenship and Immigration Canada** (www.cic.gc.ca) for the latest information on entry requirements.

Air

BC-bound travelers typically fly into Vancouver. But if the Rockies is your main attraction, Calgary or Edmonton will be more convenient. Many visitors fly into one of these Alberta airports, then travel to BC via the Rockies before departing from Vancouver.

Airports

Calgary International Airport (YYC; www.calgaryairport.com)
Edmonton International Airport (YEG; www.flyeia.com)
Kelowna International Airport (YLW; www.kelownaairport.com)
Vancouver International Airport (YVR; www.yvr.ca)
Victoria International Airport (YYJ; www.victoriaairport.com)
Whitehorse Airport (YXY)

Airlines

International airlines:
Air Canada (www.aircanada.com)
Air New Zealand (www.airnewzealand.com)
Air Transat (www.airtransat.com)
Alaska Airlines (www.alaskaair.com)
American Airlines (www.aa.com)
British Airways (www.ba.com)
Cathay Pacific (www.cathaypacific.com)
China Airlines (www.chinaairlines.com)
Continental Airlines (www.continental.com)
Delta (www.delta.com)
Eva Air (www.evaair.com)
Japan Airlines (www.jal.com)
KLM (www.klm.com)
Lufthansa (www.lufthansa.com)
United Airlines (www.united.com)

Airlines flying in from other parts of Canada:
Air Canada Express (www.aircanada.com) (formerly Air Canada Jazz)
WestJet (www.westjet.com)

Land

From the USA
BUS

You can travel from the US to many places in BC and Alberta (plus, non-directly, Whitehorse in the Yukon) with **Greyhound** (☑800-231-2222; www.greyhound.com). You will have to stop at the border to clear Canadian customs and immigration and you may be transferred to a different bus. Order tickets online in advance for the best prices – see the table on p323 for sample fares to and around the region.

Quick Coach Lines (☑800-665-2122; www.quickcoach.com) also runs daily express buses between Seattle, Seattle's Sea-Tac International Airport and downtown Vancouver.

CAR & MOTORCYCLE

The US highway system connects directly with Canadian roads at numerous points along the BC and Alberta borders. Gas is generally cheaper in the US, so fill up before you head north.

Cars rented in the US can generally be driven over the Canadian border and back, but double-check this on your rental agreement.

The Blaine Peace Arch and Pacific Hwy border crossings near Vancouver are the region's busiest, especially on holiday weekends: consider the quieter Lynden or Sumas crossings instead.

TRAIN

Amtrak (☏800-872-7245; www.amtrak.com) trundles into Vancouver from south-of-the-border Bellingham, Seattle and Portland. Be aware that buses are used instead of trains on some runs – check at time of booking. In the US, you can also connect from San Francisco, Los Angeles, Chicago and beyond. Book ahead for the best fares.

From Canada

BUS

Greyhound Canada (☏800-661-8747; www.greyhound.ca) has services into Alberta, BC and the Yukon from points east across the country. See the table on p323 for sample standard fares. Booking ahead and/or online delivers better prices but the best fares are also non-refund-able. Photo ID is required for will-call ticket pick-up.

TRAIN

The **VIA Rail** (☏888-842-7245; www.viarail.ca) *Canadian* service trundles into Vancouver from Toronto three times a week, with stops in Edmonton and Jasper. It's a slow but highly picturesque trip and there is a wide range of tickets available, from sleeper cabins to regular seats. Book in advance for the best prices.

Sea

Most ferry services into BC from the US terminate in Victoria's Inner Harbour, where you'll be expected to clear Canadian customs and immigration. **Alaska Marine Highway System** (www.ferryalaska.com) ferries roll into northern Prince Rupert from Alaska.

The following operators service US routes into Victoria:

Black Ball Ferry Line (☏360-457-4491; www.cohoferry.com)

Victoria Clipper (☏800-888-2535; www.clippervacations.com)

GETTING AROUND

See the Information sections of specific destinations throughout this book for detailed listings and resources on local transportation options.

Air

WestJet and Air Canada Express (formerly Air Canada Jazz) are the dominant airlines servicing the larger towns and cities in this region. But there's also an extensive network of smaller operators – often using propeller planes or floatplanes – that provide excellent, although not often cheap, quick-hop services. See table on p324 for sample routes and keep in mind that reduced fares are offered for advance booking.

Airlines providing regional services in BC, Alberta and the Yukon:

Air Canada Express (www.aircanada.ca)

Air North (www.flyairnorth.com)

Central Mountain Air (www.flycma.com)

Harbour Air (www.harbourair.com)

Orca Airways (www.flyorcaair.com)

Pacific Coastal Airlines (www.pacific-coastal.com)

Salt Spring Air (www.saltspringair.com)

West Coast Air (www.westcoastair.com)

WestJet (www.westjet.com)

Bicycle

If you have the time, cycling is one of the best ways to get around and immerse yourself in this region – so long as you

---

CLIMATE CHANGE & TRAVEL

Every form of transport that relies on carbon-based fuel generates CO_2, the main cause of human-induced climate change. Modern travel is dependent on aeroplanes, which might use less fuel per kilometer per person than most cars but travel much greater distances. The altitude at which aircraft emit gases (including CO_2) and particles also contributes to their climate change impact. Many websites offer 'carbon calculators' that allow people to estimate the carbon emissions generated by their journey and, for those who wish to do so, to offset the impact of the greenhouse gases emitted with contributions to portfolios of climate-friendly initiatives throughout the world. Lonely Planet offsets the carbon footprint of all staff and author travel.

GREYHOUND BUS ROUTES & FARES

ROUTE	DURATION	FREQUENCY	FULL FARE (ONE WAY)
Seattle-Vancouver	4hr	5 daily	US$37.50
Portland-Vancouver	9hr	4 daily	US$71
Toronto-Calgary	2 days	3 daily	$189
Calgary-Edmonton	5hr	7 daily	$54.40
Kamloops-Vancouver	5hr	7 daily	$66.70
Vancouver-Whistler	2.5hr	7 daily	$29.80
Edmonton-Jasper	5hr	4 daily	$64.70
Vancouver-Calgary	15hr	7 daily	$93

also have the stamina. Cities such as Vancouver and Victoria are especially welcoming, with their ever-increasing bike route networks.

Helmets are mandatory in BC (and in Alberta for under-18s). Many forms of public transportation – the BC Ferries system and Vancouver's TransLink buses, for example – enable you to take your bike with you.

Off-road mountain biking is also highly popular here, with some ski resorts transforming into bike parks in summer. Bike-rental operators are common, especially in larger towns. You'll likely need a credit card for the deposit, and rental rates are typically around $40 per day.

Area resources:

Alberta Bicycle Association (www.albertabicycle.ab.ca)

British Columbia Cycling Coalition (www.bccc.bc.ca)

Vancouver Area Cycling Coalition (www.vacc.bc.ca)

Boat

BC Ferries (☎888-223-3779; www.bcferries.com) services 36 routes in the province's coastal waters. Its extensive network includes frequent busy runs – with giant 'superferries' – between the mainland and Vancouver Island. There are also dozens of community routes, with much smaller vessels, linking shoreline communities and the Gulf Islands. The signature long-haul route is from Port Hardy to Prince Rupert, a day-long glide along the spectacular Inside Passage.

It's one of the world's biggest ferry networks, and well worth scheduling a trip as part of your visit. Many of the routes are vehicle-accessible but walk-on passengers pay much lower fares. Off-season fares are usually cheaper, while the BC Ferries SailPass includes four ($210) or seven ($250) days of consecutive travel for a car and two people across much of the network.

Popular routes:

» Lower Mainland to Vancouver Island The two busiest routes are from Tsawwassen (an hour's drive south of Vancouver) to Swartz Bay (30 minutes north of Victoria), and from Horseshoe Bay (30 minutes north of downtown Vancouver) to Departure Bay near Nanaimo on central Vancouver Island. Vehicle reservations are recommended for summer and weekend travel.

» Inside Passage Among one of the most scenic boat trips in the world. In summer the service is scheduled for 15-hour daylight runs between Port Hardy and Prince Rupert, in different directions on alternate days. Sailings between October and May typically include stops in tiny Aboriginal villages and can take up to two days. Reserve ahead, especially in the summer peak, and consider an additional ferry trip to Haida Gwaii when you reach Prince Rupert.

» Discovery Coast Passage This additional long-haul journey covers the dramatic route between Port Hardy and Bella Coola on the central BC coast. It's shorter than the Inside Passage route, but equally scenic. Runs from mid-June to mid-September. Reservations necessary.

Bus

Greyhound Canada (☎800-661-8747; www.greyhound.ca) covers much of BC and Alberta and also offers services into the Yukon's Whitehorse via the Alaska Hwy. The fares listed throughout this book are full price, but booking as far ahead as possible and/or online usually delivers lower rates. See the table for sample routes and standard fares.

Additional regional bus operators:

REGIONAL AIRLINE ROUTES & FARES

ROUTE	AIRLINE	DURATION	FREQUENCY	FULL FARE (ONE WAY; EXCLUDING TAXES)
Vancouver-Masset (Haida Gwaii)	Pacific Coastal Airlines	2½hr	1 daily	$279
Vancouver-Whitehorse	Air North	2½hr	2 daily	$399
Vancouver-Dawson Creek	Central Mountain Air	2hr	1 daily	$340
Victoria-Vancouver	Harbour Air	30min	multiple daily services	$140
Vancouver-Tofino	Orca Airways	1hr	1 daily	$159
Edmonton-Vancouver	WestJet	1½hr	10 daily	$149
Prince Rupert-Vancouver	Air Canada Express	2hr	2 daily	$304

Brewster Transportation (☑866-606-6700; www.brewster.ca) Runs regular services between Jasper, Banff and Lake Louise.

Malaspina Coach Lines (☑877-227-8287; www.malaspinacoach.com) Runs a twice-daily service between Vancouver and BC's Sunshine Coast communities.

Pacific Coach Lines (☑800-661-1725; www.pacificcoach.com) For services between Whistler, Vancouver and Victoria.

SnowBus (☑888-794-5511; www.snowbus.com) Winter-only services between Vancouver and Whistler.

Tofino Bus (☑866-986-3466; www.tofinobus.com) Operates Vancouver Island services between Tofino, Ucluelet, Nanaimo and Victoria.

Car & Motorcycle

Although BC, Alberta and the Yukon cover a huge area, driving is the best way to travel here. Generally the highways are excellent.

Automobile Associations

British Columbia Automobile Association (www.bcaa.com) provides its members, and the members of other auto clubs (such as the AAA in the US), with travel information, maps, travel insurance and hotel reservations. It also provides a service in the Yukon. **Alberta Motor Association** (www.ama.ab.ca) operates a similar service in the east.

Bring Your Own Vehicle

Cars licensed to drive in North America may be driven across the border and into Canada. Make sure you have all your vehicle registration papers, driver's license and proof of insurance.

Car Hire

Major car-rental firms have offices at airports in BC, Alberta and Whitehorse, as well as in larger city centers. In smaller towns there may be independent firms. Clarify your insurance coverage for things like gravel damage if you're going to be driving off major paved roads.

Shop around for deals but watch out for offers that don't include unlimited kilometers of driving. Never buy the rental-car company's gas if offered when you pick up your car – it's a bad deal. Buy your own and return it full. If you are considering a one-way rental, be aware of high fees.

You generally have to be over 25 to rent a car, although some companies will rent to those between 21 and 24 for an additional premium. Regular rates for an economy-sized vehicle are between $35 and $65 per day.

All the usual rental companies operate here, including the following:

Avis (☑800-437-0358; www.avis.com)

Budget (☑800-268-8900; www.budget.com)

Enterprise (☑800-736-8222; www.enterprise.com)

Hertz (☑800-263-0600; www.hertz.com)

National (☑800-227-7368; www.nationalcar.com)

Thrifty (✆800-847-4389; www.thrifty.com)

RECREATIONAL VEHICLES

Recreational vehicles (RVs) are hugely popular in western Canada, and rentals must be booked well in advance of the summer season. In high season, RVs typically cost $165 to $265 or more a day. One-way rentals are possible, but you'll pay a surcharge. Also budget plenty for fuel as RVs typically get miserable mileage.

Large rental companies have offices in Vancouver, Calgary, Whitehorse and bigger BC towns. Operators include the following:

Canadream Campers (✆800-461-7368; www.canadream.com)

Go West Campers (✆800-661-8813; www.go-west.com)

West Coast Mountain Campers (✆888-878-3200; www.wcmcampers.com)

Driver's License

Your home driver's license is valid for up to six months in BC. If you plan to drive here for longer, you'll also need an International Drivers Permit.

Fuel

Gasoline is sold in liters in Canada, where it's typically more expensive than in the US. In Calgary – headquarters of the region's oil sands petroleum business – prices are often among the best in the country. Gas prices are usually much higher in remote areas than in the cities.

Road Hazards

It's best to avoid driving in areas with heavy snow, but if you do, be sure your vehicle has snow tires or tire chains as well as an emergency kit of blankets etc. If you get stuck, don't stay in the car with the engine going: every year people die of carbon monoxide poisoning. A single candle burning in the car will keep it reasonably warm.

Make sure the vehicle you're driving is in good condition and take along some tools, flares, water, food and a spare tire. Rural areas usually do not have cell phone service.

SAMPLE DRIVING DISTANCES

ROUTE	DISTANCE	DURATION
Banff-Fernie	360km	4hr
Calgary-Edmonton	300km	3½hr
Edmonton-Jasper	365km	4hr
Jasper-Banff	290km	4hr
Kelowna-Banff	480km	6hr
Prince George-Prince Rupert	705km	8½hr
Prince Rupert-Whitehorse (via Stewart-Cassiar Hwy)	1375km	19hr
Vancouver-Kelowna	390km	4hr
Vancouver-Prince George	790km	9hr
Whitehorse-Dawson City	530km	7hr

Be careful on logging roads as logging trucks always have the right of way and often pay little heed to other vehicles. It's best not to drive on logging roads at all during weekday working hours.

Gravel roads of all kinds – such as those in the Yukon – can take a toll on windshields and tires. Keep a good distance from the vehicle in front, and when you see an oncoming vehicle (or a vehicle overtaking you), slow down and keep well to the right.

Wild animals are another potential hazard. Most run-ins with deer, moose and other critters occur at night when wildlife is active and visibility is poor. Many areas have roadside signs alerting drivers to possible animal crossings. Keep scanning both sides of the road and be prepared to stop or swerve. A vehicle's headlights will often mesmerize an animal, leaving it frozen in the middle of the road.

For handy updates on driving conditions around the region, peruse these online resources:

» Rocky Mountains: www.pc.gc.ca/banff
» BC: www.drivebc.ca
» Alberta: www.ama.ab.ca/road-reports
» Yukon: www.511yukon.ca

Road Rules

North Americans drive on the right side of the road. Speed limits, which are posted in kilometers, are generally 50km/h in built-up areas and 90km/h on highways. A right turn is permitted at a red light after you have come to a complete stop, as is a left turn from a one-way street onto another one-way street. U-turns are not allowed. Traffic in both directions must stop when stationary school buses have their red lights flashing – this means that children are getting off and on. In cities with pedestrian

SAILING THE INSIDE PASSAGE

Taking a BC Ferries cruise along the stunning Inside Passage is likely to be the transportation highlight of your trip. Expect to see marine life ranging from whales to dolphins to lazy-looking seals. Look for eagles overhead and bears on the shore as you spend hours passing deserted islands and rocky coasts accented by waterfalls. On these runs the crew is friendly and the captain will slow the ship when, say, a pod of orcas swims past. You'll spend most of your time basking on deck, but consider paying extra for a cabin so you can really chill out.

crosswalks, cars must stop to allow pedestrians to cross.

Seat belt use is compulsory in Canada. Children under the age of five must be in a restraining seat. Motorcyclists must use lights and wear helmets. The blood-alcohol limit when driving is 0.08% (about two drinks) and is strictly enforced with heavy fines, bans and jail terms.

Hitchhiking

Hitchhiking is not common in BC, Alberta and the Yukon. It's never entirely safe in any country in the world, and is not recommended. Travelers who decide to hitchhike (or pick up hitchhikers) should understand that they are taking a risk. If you do choose to hitchhike, do it only in pairs. Hitching on the Trans-Canada Hwy is illegal until 40km past the Vancouver city limits.

Local Transportation

BC has excellent, widespread local public transportation in the areas around Vancouver and Victoria. Similarly, Calgary and Edmonton have good transit systems. Outside of these areas, service can be sparse, erratic or infrequent. Check the regional

chapters for details on each town's offerings.

Most places have taxi companies, but some can be extortionately expensive, so check the rates before you hop in.

In the Yukon, public transit in Whitehorse will suffice for getting around town but you'll have a hard time getting around this area without a car.

Tours

There are lots of options for traveling with company around this region, and tours range from backpacker level to high-end luxe. Browse the options here and also check the Information sections of destinations in this book for more options. In addition, see p30 for tour operators with a particular focus on Banff, Jasper et al.

Backroads (☏800-462-2848; www.backroads.com) Guided cycling, walking and kayaking tours in the Rockies.

Hammerhead Scenic Tours (☏403-590-6930; www.hammerheadtours.com) Calgary-based bus tour company offering excursions to Banff, Drumheller, Head-Smashed-In Buffalo Jump and beyond.

Harbour Air (☏800-665-0212; www.harbour-air.com) Spectacular floatplane tours

over BC's Lower Mainland coast and mountain region.

Just Dive In Adventures (☏250-816-2241; www.just diveinadventures.com) Guided underwater excursions on the east coast of Vancouver Island, including a popular scuba-with-the-seals package.

Moose Travel Network (☏888-244-6673; www.moosenetwork.com) Runs small backpacker tour buses throughout BC and the Rockies. You can get on and off anywhere along the route. Each day's run ends at a hostel.

Mountain High River Adventures (☏877-423-4555; www.raftfernie.com) Fernie-based operator offering adrenalin-pumping rafting trips in the region.

Nahanni River Adventures (☏800-297-6927; www.nahanni.com) Rafting and kayaking expeditions in BC, the Yukon and Alaska.

Prince Rupert Adventure Tours (☏800-201-8377; www.adventuretours.net) Grizzly-bear-watching boat tours are the highlight, as well as its whale-watching excursions.

Up North Adventures (☏867-667-7035; www.up northadventures.com) Whitehorse-based company offers a plethora of services including guided kayak, fishing and snowmobile tours.

Train

Passenger train services are limited in BC and virtually nonexistent in Alberta. The national carrier, **VIA Rail** (☏888-842-7245; www.viarail. ca), has only one route from Vancouver. The *Canadian* departs a paltry three times a week and makes a few stops in BC before reaching Jasper. The 18½-hour trip takes in some beautiful scenery.

Fares from Vancouver to Jasper start at $179 and rise exponentially if you'd like a private sleeping cabin with gourmet meals and access to the dome car.

VIA also runs a lovely route between Jasper and Prince Rupert thrice weekly. It's a daytime-only trip with an overnight stay in Prince George, plus stops in Terrace, New Hazelton, Smithers, Houston and Burns Lake. You have to find your own lodgings in Prince George. Fares from Jasper to Prince Rupert start at $196, and there's a deluxe service with observation car available in the summer.

On Vancouver Island, VIA's *Malahat* service trundles from Victoria to Courtenay up the coast of Vancouver Island, with one train daily in each direction. Fares are up to $37 one way, depending on where you want to alight.

Book ahead for all VIA services: advance tickets offer the best deals.

In addition to the older trains of the government-run VIA system, this region is also home to two major players in the luxury train travel market.

Rocky Mountaineer (✆877-460-3200; www.rocky mountaineer.com) runs lovely, half-day trips between North Vancouver and Whistler as well as even more luxurious multiday services from Vancouver through the Rocky Mountains into Alberta. The trains travel at 'Polaroid speed' so you can be sure to get all the photos you need.

Even higher-end is the exclusive **Royal Canadian Pacific** (✆877-665-3044; www.royalcanadianpacific. com), an uber-luxe trip of a lifetime which loops through the mountains of Alberta via Calgary and includes posh dining along with wildlife-watching and golf packages. It markets itself as the world's finest luxury train.

behind the scenes

SEND US YOUR FEEDBACK

We love to hear from travelers – your comments keep us on our toes and help make our books better. Our well-traveled team reads every word on what you loved or loathed about this book. Although we cannot reply individually to postal submissions, we always guarantee that your feedback goes straight to the appropriate authors, in time for the next edition. Each person who sends us information is thanked in the next edition – and the most useful submissions are rewarded with a free book.

Visit **lonelyplanet.com/contact** to submit your updates and suggestions or to ask for help. Our award-winning website also features inspirational travel stories, news and discussions.

Note: We may edit, reproduce and incorporate your comments in Lonely Planet products such as guidebooks, websites and digital products, so let us know if you don't want your comments reproduced or your name acknowledged. For a copy of our privacy policy visit lonelyplanet.com/privacy.

OUR READERS

Many thanks to the travelers who used the last edition and wrote to us with helpful hints, useful advice and interesting anecdotes:
Marla Cohen, Elizabeth Gunston, Cody Hawver, Chloe Jacobs, Gillian Jeens, Brian Miller, Kirsty-leigh Mulley, Raphael Richards, Carla Schellart, Kevin Segrave, Rowena Volkers, Fran Waes, Darryl Wilson.

AUTHOR THANKS

John Lee

Hearty thanks to Jennye and Sasha at Lonely Planet for...well you know what for. Thanks also to my usual writing partner on this title, Ryan Ver Berkmoes: here's to working together again in the future. I'd also like to thank my friends and family for keeping me relatively sane throughout this assignment, especially during the straggly-beard-growing, pajama-wearing write-up phase. Which reminds me: thanks to the local pub for serving a beer that tasted like nectar at the end of it all.

THIS BOOK

This fifth edition of Lonely Planet's British Columbia & the Canadian Rockies was researched and written by John Lee, Ryan Ver Berkmoes and Brendan Sainsbury. The fourth edition was also written by John Lee and Ryan Ver Berkmoes. This guidebook was commissioned in Lonely Planet's Oakland office, and produced by the following:

Commissioning Editor Jennye Garibaldi
Coordinating Editor Karyn Noble
Coordinating Cartographer Brendan Streager
Coordinating Layout Designer Kerrianne Southway
Managing Editors Sasha Baskett, Anna Metcalfe, Kirsten Rawlings
Managing Cartographer Alison Lyall

Managing Layout Designer Chris Girdler
Assisting Editors Andrea Dobbin, Dianne Schallmeiner
Cover Research Rebecca Skinner
Internal Image Research Sabrina Dalbesio
Thanks to Adrian Blackburn, Ryan Evans, Justin Flynn, Corey Hutchison, Gerard Walker, Lisa Knights.

Brendan Sainsbury

Thanks to all the untold bus drivers, tourist info volunteers, restaurateurs, dinosaur experts and innocent bystanders who helped me during research, particularly to Jennye Garibaldi for offering me the gig in the first place and to Karla Zimmerman. Special thanks to Ann Morrow in Banff for granting me a spontaneous interview and opening my eyes to the beauty of the park. Thanks also to my wife Liz and Kieran for their company on the road.

Ryan Ver Berkmoes

The number of folks to thank outnumber Kermode bears but here's a few: Jim 'kootchie-kootchie' Kemshead never fails to deliver both beer and drama. In BC, Prince Rupert's Bruce Wishart is good for both info and drinks of all kinds. Karla Zimmerman was simply ace. It's always good to share a title page with John Lee and folks at Lonely Planet like Jennye, Alison and Bruce are pure delight. Of course, Erin put the Sweety in the pie.

ACKNOWLEDGMENTS

Climate map data adapted from Peel MC, Finlayson BL & McMahon TA (2007) 'Updated World Map of the Köppen-Geiger Climate Classification', *Hydrology and Earth System Sciences*, 11, 163344.

Cover photograph: Garibaldi Provincial Park near Whistler, BC. Josh McCulloch

Many of the images in this guide are available for licensing from Lonely Planet Images: www.lonelyplanetimages.com.

Sun	– drive to Louise	L
Mon	– day in Banff	L
Tues	– day in Louise	L
Wed	– Icefields etc	J
Thurs	– around Jasper	J
Fri	– train 2pm	T
Sat		V
Sun		V
Mon		V
Tues		6pm flight

index

000 Map pages
000 Photo pages

how to use this book

These symbols will help you find the listings you want:

- ⊙ Sights
- 🏃 Activities
- 🗢 Courses
- 👉 Tours
- 🎊 Festivals & Events
- 🛌 Sleeping
- ✗ Eating
- 🍷 Drinking
- ☆ Entertainment
- 🛍 Shopping
- ℹ Information/Transport

These symbols give you the vital information for each listing:

- ☎ Telephone Numbers
- ⊙ Opening Hours
- P Parking
- ⊜ Nonsmoking
- ✳ Air-Conditioning
- @ Internet Access
- 🛜 Wi-Fi Access
- 🏊 Swimming Pool
- 🌱 Vegetarian Selection
- 📖 English-Language Menu
- 👪 Family-Friendly
- 🐾 Pet-Friendly
- 🚌 Bus
- ⛴ Ferry
- Ⓜ Metro
- Ⓢ Subway
- ⊖ London Tube
- 🚊 Tram
- 🚃 Train

Reviews are organised by author preference.

Map Legend

Sights
- ⊙ Beach
- ⊙ Buddhist
- ⊗ Castle
- ⊙ Christian
- ⊙ Hindu
- ⊙ Islamic
- ⊕ Jewish
- ⊙ Monument
- ⊕ Museum/Gallery
- ⊙ Ruin
- ⊕ Winery/Vineyard
- ⊛ Zoo
- ⊙ Other Sight

Activities, Courses & Tours
- ⊝ Diving/Snorkelling
- ⊛ Canoeing/Kayaking
- ⊙ Skiing
- ⊙ Surfing
- ⊙ Swimming/Pool
- ⊙ Walking
- ⊙ Windsurfing
- ⊙ Other Activity/Course/Tour

Sleeping
- ⊙ Sleeping
- ⊘ Camping

Eating
- ⊗ Eating

Drinking
- ⊙ Drinking
- ⊖ Cafe

Entertainment
- ⊙ Entertainment

Shopping
- ⊕ Shopping

Information
- ⊗ Post Office
- ⊙ Tourist Information

Transport
- ⊙ Airport
- ⊗ Border Crossing
- ⊚ Bus
- ⊕ Cable Car/Funicular
- ⊙ Cycling
- ⊙ Ferry
- Ⓜ Metro
- ⊙ Monorail
- P Parking
- Ⓢ S-Bahn
- ⊙ Taxi
- ⊕ Train/Railway
- ⊙ Tram
- ⊙ Tube Station
- Ⓤ U-Bahn
- • Other Transport

Routes
- Tollway
- Freeway
- Primary
- Secondary
- Tertiary
- Lane
- Unsealed Road
- Plaza/Mall
- Steps
- Tunnel
- Pedestrian Overpass
- Walking Tour
- Walking Tour Detour
- Path

Boundaries
- International
- State/Province
- Disputed
- Regional/Suburb
- Marine Park
- Cliff
- Wall

Population
- ⊙ Capital (National)
- ⊙ Capital (State/Province)
- ⊙ City/Large Town
- ⊙ Town/Village

Geographic
- ⊙ Hut/Shelter
- ⊙ Lighthouse
- ⊙ Lookout
- ▲ Mountain/Volcano
- ⊙ Oasis
- ⊙ Park
-)(Pass
- ⊙ Picnic Area
- ⊙ Waterfall

Hydrography
- River/Creek
- Intermittent River
- Swamp/Mangrove
- Reef
- Canal
- Water
- Dry/Salt/Intermittent Lake
- Glacier

Areas
- Beach/Desert
- + + + Cemetery (Christian)
- × × × Cemetery (Other)
- Park/Forest
- Sportsground
- Sight (Building)
- Top Sight (Building)

OUR STORY

A beat-up old car, a few dollars in the pocket and a sense of adventure. In 1972 that's all Tony and Maureen Wheeler needed for the trip of a lifetime – across Europe and Asia overland to Australia. It took several months, and at the end – broke but inspired – they sat at their kitchen table writing and stapling together their first travel guide, *Across Asia on the Cheap*. Within a week they'd sold 1500 copies. Lonely Planet was born.

Today, Lonely Planet has offices in Melbourne, London and Oakland, with more than 600 staff and writers. We share Tony's belief that 'a great guidebook should do three things: inform, educate and amuse'.

OUR WRITERS

John Lee

National & Regional Parks; BC & the Canadian Rockies Today; History; Outdoor Activities; People, Arts & Culture; Regional Cuisine; Wine & Beer; Wildlife Born in southeast England, John moved to British Columbia to study at the University of Victoria in the 1990s, relocating to Vancouver and launching a full-time freelance travel writing career in 1999. Since then, he's been covering the region (and beyond) for major newspapers and magazines throughout the world. Becoming a Lonely Planet author in 2005, he has contributed to 20 titles, including writing the most recent edition of the *Vancouver* City Guide. To read his latest stories and see what he's up to next, visit www.johnleewriter.com.

Brendan Sainsbury

Alberta An expat Brit from Hampshire, England, Brendan is a former fitness instructor, volunteer teacher, wannabe musician and travel guide who now writes about travel full-time. In 2003 he met a Canadian girl from Saskatoon in Spain. After romancing in Cuba and getting married in Mexico, they now live (with their son, Kieran) in White Rock, BC. Brendan is a long time lover of Alberta's national parks and is the co-author of Lonely Planet's current *Banff, Jasper & Glacier National Parks* guide.

Ryan Ver Berkmoes

British Columbia, Yukon Territory Ryan's been bouncing around BC and the Yukon for more than two decades and doing more critter-spotting than he'd ever imagined possible. But it's fitting given Ryan's background with moose. At his first newspaper job he was tasked with placing random moose jokes in the classifieds to pique reader interest (eg What's a moose's favorite philosopher? Cammoose). For better jokes than that, surf over to ryanverberkmoes.com.

Published by Lonely Planet Publications Pty Ltd
ABN 36 005 607 983
5th edition – Oct 2011
ISBN 978 1 74179 804 3
© Lonely Planet 2011   Photographs © as indicated 2011
10 9 8 7 6 5 4 3 2
Printed in China